Inflation Rate
(GDP Deflator)

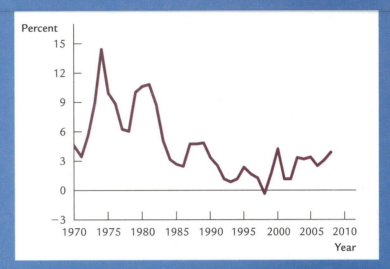

Nominal Interest
Rate
(Three-Month
Treasury Bills)

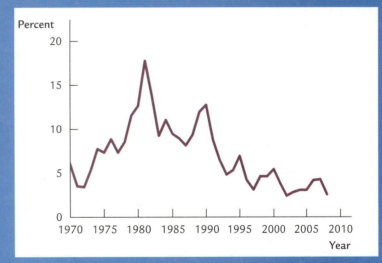

MACROECONOMICS

CANADIAN EDITION

FOURTH EDITION

MACROECONOMICS

N. GREGORY MANKIW ■ WILLIAM SCARTH

Harvard University McMaster University

Worth Publishers

Senior Publishers: Catherine Woods and Craig Bleyer
Senior Acquisitions Editor: Sarah Dorger
Senior Development Editor: Marie McHale
Senior Marketing Manager: Scott Guile
Associate Managing Editor: Tracey Kuehn
Production Manager: Barbara Seixas
Art Director: Babs Reingold
Cover and Text Designer: Kevin Kall
Photo Editor: Cecilia Varas
Project Editor: Kerry O'Shaughnessy
Project Manager: Susan Bothwell, TSI Graphics
Composition: TSI Graphics
Printing and Binding: RR Donnelley
Cover Art: Stefan Fiedorowicz, *Land of a Thousand Words*

ISBN-13: 978-1-4292-3490-0
ISBN-10: 1-4292-3490-3

© 2011, 2008, 2004, 2001 by Worth Publishers

Printed in the United States of America

First printing

Worth Publishers
41 Madison Avenue
New York, NY 10010
www.worthpublishers.com

To Deborah and Kathy

about the authors

Photo by Deborah Mankiw

N. Gregory Mankiw is Professor of Economics at Harvard University. He began his study of economics at Princeton University, where he received an A.B. in 1980. After earning a Ph.D. in economics from MIT, he began teaching at Harvard in 1985 and was promoted to full professor in 1987. Today, he regularly teaches both undergraduate and graduate courses in macroeconomics. He is also author of the popular introductory textbook, *Principles of Economics* (Cengage Learning).

Professor Mankiw is a regular participant in academic and policy debates. His research ranges across macroeconomics and includes work on price adjustment, consumer behavior, financial markets, monetary and fiscal policy, and economic growth. In addition to his duties at Harvard, he has been a research associate of the National Bureau of Economic Research, a member of the Brookings Panel on Economic Activity, and an adviser to the Federal Reserve Bank of Boston and the Congressional Budget Office. From 2003 to 2005 he was chairman of the President's Council of Economic Advisers.

Professor Mankiw lives in Wellesley, Massachusetts, with his wife Deborah; children Catherine, Nicholas, and Peter; and their border terrier Tobin.

Photo by Kathy Scarth

William M. Scarth is Professor of Economics and Chair of the Department at McMaster University. His introduction to the subject came at Queen's University, where he obtained the Gold Medal in economics upon graduating with his B.A. After receiving M.A. and Ph.D. degrees at the universities of Essex and Toronto, he began teaching at McMaster where he has received both the President's Best Teacher Award and the McMaster Student Union Lifetime Achievement Award. He has held a number of visiting positions at other universities in Canada, Australia, and England.

Professor Scarth has published many articles in academic journals, often writing on such topics as the stabilization policy problems faced by small open economies and the challenges posed by the desire to generate—and share fairly—rising living standards. He is also the author of other textbooks—one that introduces graduate students to advanced methods in macroeconomics, and two introductory books. In addition to research and teaching at McMaster, he is a Research Fellow at the C. D. Howe Institute, Canada's leading nonprofit policy institute.

Professor Scarth lives in Dundas, Ontario, with his wife, Kathy. They enjoy the visits of their grown sons, Brian and David, their partners, Renee and Anna, and their grandson, Cameron.

Those branches of politics, or of the laws of social life, on which there exists a collection of facts sufficiently sifted and methodized to form the beginning of a science should be taught *ex professo*. Among the chief of these is Political Economy, the sources and conditions of wealth and material prosperity for aggregate bodies of human beings. . . .

The same persons who cry down Logic will generally warn you against Political Economy. It is unfeeling, they will tell you. It recognises unpleasant facts. For my part, the most unfeeling thing I know of is the law of gravitation: it breaks the neck of the best and most amiable person without scruple, if he forgets for a single moment to give heed to it. The winds and waves too are very unfeeling. Would you advise those who go to sea to deny the winds and waves—or to make use of them, and find the means of guarding against their dangers? My advice to you is to study the great writers on Political Economy, and hold firmly by whatever in them you find true; and depend upon it that if you are not selfish or hardhearted already, Political Economy will not make you so.

— John Stuart Mill, 1867

brief contents

contents

part IV Business Cycle Theory: The Economy in the Short Run   289

part VI More on the Microeconomics Behind Macroeconomics

Chapter 17 Consumption   573

preface

An economist must be "mathematician, historian, statesman, philosopher, in some degree. . . as aloof and incorruptible as an artist, yet sometimes as near the earth as a politician." So remarked John Maynard Keynes, the great British economist who, as much as anyone, could be called the father of macroeconomics. No single statement summarizes better what it means to be an economist.

As Keynes's assessment suggests, students who aim to learn economics need to draw on many disparate talents. The job of helping students find and develop these talents falls to instructors and textbook authors. When writing this textbook for intermediate-level courses in macroeconomics, our goal was to make macroeconomics understandable, relevant, and (believe it or not) fun. Those of us who have chosen to be professional macroeconomists have done so because we are fascinated by the field. More important, we believe that the study of macroeconomics can illuminate much about the world and that the lessons learned, if properly applied, can make the world a better place. We hope this book conveys not only our profession's accumulated wisdom but also its enthusiasm and sense of purpose.

This Book's Approach

Although macroeconomists share a common body of knowledge, they do not all have the same perspective on how that knowledge is best taught. Let us begin this new edition by recapping four of our objectives, which together define this book's approach to the field.

First, we try to offer a balance between short-run and long-run issues in macroeconomics. All economists agree that public policies and other events influence the economy over different time horizons. We live in our own short run, but we also live in the long run that our parents bequeathed us. As a result, courses in macroeconomics need to cover both short-run topics, such as the business cycle and stabilization policy, and long-run topics, such as economic growth, the natural rate of unemployment, persistent inflation, and the effects of government debt. Neither time horizon trumps the other.

Second, we integrate the insights of Keynesian and classical theories. Although Keynes's *General Theory* provides the foundation for much of our current understanding of economic fluctuations, it is important to remember that classical economics provides the right answers to many fundamental questions. In this book we incorporate many of the contributions of the classical economists before Keynes and the new classical economists of the past three decades. Substantial coverage is given, for example, to the loanable-funds theory of the interest rate, the quantity theory of money, and the problem of time inconsistency. At the same time, we recognize that many of the ideas of Keynes and the new Keynesians are necessary for understanding economic fluctuations. Substantial coverage is given also to the *IS–LM* model of aggregate demand, the short-run tradeoff between inflation and unemployment, and modern models of business-cycle fluctuations.

Third, we present macroeconomics using a variety of simple models. Instead of pretending that there is one model that is complete enough to explain all facets of the economy, we encourage students to learn how to use and compare a set of prominent models. This approach has the pedagogical value that each model can be kept relatively simple and presented within one or two chapters. More important, this approach asks students to think like economists, who always keep various models in mind when analyzing economic events or public policies.

Fourth, we emphasize that macroeconomics is an empirical discipline, motivated and guided by a wide array of experience. This book contains numerous case studies that use macroeconomic theory to shed light on real-world data or events. To highlight the broad applicability of the basic theory, we have drawn the case studies both from current issues facing the world's economies and from dramatic historical episodes. The case studies analyze the policies of Mark Carney (Governor of the Bank of Canada), our current Finance Minister, many former Canadian politicians and central bankers, government initiatives in other countries, and even the policies of Henry Ford. They teach the reader how to apply economic principles to issues from fourteenth-century Europe, the island of Yap, the land of Oz, and today's newspaper.

What's New in the Fourth Edition?

This edition includes some of the most significant changes since the book was first published. The revision reflects new events in the economy as well as new research about the best way to understand macroeconomic developments.

By far the biggest change is the addition of Chapter 14, "A Dynamic Model of Aggregate Demand and Aggregate Supply." In recent years, academic research and policy analyses of short-run economic fluctuations have increasingly centered on dynamic, stochastic, general equilibrium models with nominal rigidities. These models are too complex to present in full detail to most undergraduate students, but the essential insights of these models can be taught with both simplicity and rigour. That is the purpose of this new chapter. It builds on ideas the students have seen before, both in previous chapters and in previous courses, and it exposes students to ideas that are prominent at the research and policy frontier. Since this new chapter introduces students to what is known as the New NeoClassical Synthesis, we include material from the old Chapter 19—on aspects of New Classical and New Keynesian economics—in the appendix to this new-synthesis chapter.

The other chapters in the book have been updated to incorporate the latest data and recent events, including recent turmoil in financial markets and the economy more broadly. In making the changes we have consistently focused on our primary objective—to have theory and policy analysis truly integrated.

Here is a list of some of the notable features of this new edition, in the order that they appear:

- Chapter 3 includes a new box called "The Financial System: Markets, Intermediaries, and the Crisis of 2008 and 2009."

- Chapter 4 has a new Case Study about the recent hyperinflation in Zimbabwe.

- Chapter 9 includes a new Case Study called "A Monetary Lesson from French History."

- Chapter 9 includes a new FYI box on the monetary theory of David Hume.

- Chapter 10 has a new Case Study on the recession of 2008–2009 and the economic stimulus response of the government.

- Chapter 11 includes a new Case Study called "The Financial Crisis and Economic Downturn of 2008 and 2009," as well as an up-to-date discussion of quantitative easing and the associated challenge facing the Bank of Canada—the zero lower bound on nominal interest rates. The latter is highlighted within Chapter 12 as well.

- Chapter 16 has a new Case Study on the U.S. Troubled Asset Relief Program (TARP).

- Chapter 17 has a discussion of our government's GST policy—refusing to adjust it temporarily for stabilization purposes while choosing to cut it permanently—thereby limiting the success of the government's overall economic growth initiatives.

- Chapter 18 includes a new discussion of the recent boom and bust in the housing market.

- Chapter 19 has a new section on bank capital, leverage, and capital requirements.

As always, all the changes that we made, and the many others that we considered, were evaluated keeping in mind the benefits of brevity. From our own experience as students, we know that long books are less likely to be read. Our goal in this book has been to offer the clearest, most up-to-date, most accessible course in macroeconomics in the fewest words possible.

The Canadian Perspective

Maintaining brevity was not our only concern as we wrote this book. We were determined to strengthen the other feature of the earlier editions that have been most appreciated by users—that the book truly integrates theory and policy. All important policy issues are covered in this way. To mention just a few:

- the role of tax incentives and disinflation in stimulating saving and investment, the importance of credibility and time-consistency,

➤ how the Bank of Canada pursues price stability and thereby affect the economy's built-in stability properties,

➤ the reasons for the large changes in the value of the Canadian dollar,

➤ how the benefits of lower interest rates and lower debt can be measured,

➤ the spillover effects of provincial fiscal policies,

➤ the implications of the aging baby-boom generation,

➤ calculation of the "sacrifice ratio,"

➤ challenges to the natural-rate hypothesis,

➤ the different implications of unanticipated and anticipated fiscal policies,

➤ how fiscal policy can be used to simultaneously lower unemployment and raise productivity growth—despite the constraint imposed by globalization.

Systematically relating macro theory to the "big" issues in Canadian policy debates is one of the ways we hope to transfer our excitement about our discipline to as many readers as possible.

Finally, there are two important things concerning the new Canadian edition that are not in the book itself. With this edition, two of the many supplements are available in Canadian editions. Students will value the *Student Guide and Workbook*, and instructors will be grateful for the Test Bank.

The Arrangement of Topics

This fourth edition maintains the strategy of first examining the long run when prices are flexible and then examining the short run when prices are sticky. That is, it begins with classical models of the economy and explains fully the long-run equilibrium before discussing deviations from that equilibrium. Our text was the first to adopt this now-standard practice. This strategy has several advantages. First, because the classical dichotomy permits the separation of real and monetary issues, the long-run material is easier for students to understand. Second, when students begin studying short-run fluctuations, they understand fully the long-run equilibrium around which the economy is fluctuating. Third, beginning with market-clearing models makes clearer the link between macroeconomics and microeconomics. Fourth, students learn first the material that is less controversial among macroeconomists. For all these reasons, the strategy of beginning with long-run classical models simplifies the teaching of macroeconomics.

Let's now move from strategy to tactics. What follows is a whirlwind tour of the book.

Part One: Introduction

The introductory material in Part One is brief so that students can get to the core topics quickly. Chapter 1 discusses the broad questions that macroeconomists address and the economist's approach of building models to explain the world.

Chapter 2 introduces the key data of macroeconomics, emphasizing gross domestic product, the consumer price index, and the unemployment rate.

Part Two: Classical Theory: The Economy in the Long Run

Part Two examines the long run over which prices are flexible. Chapter 3 presents the basic classical model of national income. In this model, the factors of production and the production technology determine the level of income, and the marginal products of the factors determine its distribution to households. In addition, the model shows how fiscal policy influences the allocation of the economy's resources among consumption, investment, and government purchases, and it highlights how the real interest rate equilibrates the supply and demand for goods and services.

Money and the price level are introduced in Chapter 4. Because prices are assumed to be fully flexible, the chapter presents the prominent ideas of classical monetary theory: the quantity theory of money, the inflation tax, the Fisher effect, the social costs of inflation, and the causes and costs of hyperinflation.

The study of open-economy macroeconomics begins in Chapter 5. Maintaining the assumption of full employment, this chapter presents models to explain the trade balance and the exchange rate. Various policy issues are addressed: the relationship between the budget deficit and the trade deficit, the macroeconomic impact of protectionist trade policies, the effect of monetary policy on the value of a currency in the market for foreign exchange, and the effects of government debt reduction and tax reform on standards of living.

Chapter 6 relaxes the assumption of full employment by discussing the dynamics of the labour market and the natural rate of unemployment. It examines various causes of unemployment, including job search, minimum-wage laws, union power, and efficiency wages. It also presents some important facts about patterns of unemployment and policy options concerning less-skilled workers.

Part Three: Growth Theory: The Economy in the Very Long Run

Part Three makes the classical analysis of the economy dynamic by developing the tools of modern growth theory. Chapter 7 introduces the Solow growth model as a description of how the economy evolves over time. This chapter emphasizes the roles of capital accumulation and population growth. Chapter 8 then adds technological progress to the Solow model. It uses the model to discuss growth experiences around the world as well as public policies that influence the level and growth of the standard of living. Finally, Chapter 8 introduces students to the modern theories of endogenous growth.

Part Four: Business Cycle Theory: The Economy in the Short Run

Part Four examines the short run when prices are sticky. It begins in Chapter 9 by introducing the model of aggregate supply and aggregate demand as well as the role of stabilization policy. Subsequent chapters refine the ideas introduced here.

Chapters 10 and 11 look more closely at aggregate demand. Chapter 10 presents the Keynesian cross and the theory of liquidity preference and uses these models as building blocks for developing the *IS–LM* model. Chapter 11 uses the *IS–LM* model to explain economic fluctuations and the aggregate demand curve. It concludes with an extended case study of the Great Depression.

The study of short-run fluctuations continues in Chapter 12, which focuses on aggregate demand in an open economy. This chapter presents the Mundell–Fleming model and shows how monetary and fiscal policies affect the economy under floating and fixed exchange-rate systems. It also discusses the debate over whether exchange rates should be floating or fixed. Several extensions to the basic model are covered in the appendix, where the zero lower bound on nominal interest rates problem is further discussed.

Chapter 13 looks more closely at aggregate supply. It examines various approaches to explaining the short-run aggregate supply curve and discusses the short-run tradeoff between inflation and unemployment and challenges to the natural-rate hypothesis.

Chapter 14 develops a dynamic model of aggregate demand and aggregate supply. It builds on ideas that students have already encountered and uses those ideas as stepping-stones to take the student close to the frontier of knowledge concerning short-run economic fluctuations. The appendix provides more discussion of recent research within the two schools of thought that lie behind this dynamic synthesis—New Classical and New Keynesian theory.

Part Five: Macroeconomic Policy Debates

Once the student has command of standard long-run and short-run models of the economy, the book uses these models as the foundation for discussing some of the key debates over economic policy. Chapter 15 considers the debate over how policymakers should respond to short-run economic fluctuations. It emphasizes two broad questions. Should monetary and fiscal policy be active or passive? Should policy be conducted by rule or by discretion? The chapter presents arguments on both sides of these questions.

Chapter 16 focuses on the various debates over government debt and budget deficits. It gives some sense of the magnitude of government indebtedness, discusses why measuring budget deficits is not always straightforward, recaps the traditional view of the effects of government debt, presents Ricardian equivalence as an alternative view, and discusses various other perspectives on government debt. As in the previous chapter, students are not handed conclusions but are given the tools to evaluate the alternative viewpoints on their own, and to evaluate the debate on the "fiscal dividend."

Part Six: More on the Microeconomics behind Macroeconomics

After developing theories to explain the economy in the long run and in the short run and then applying those theories to macroeconomic policy debates, the book turns to several topics that refine our understanding of the economy. The last four chapters analyze more fully the microeconomics behind macroeconomics. These chapters can be presented at the end of a course, or they can be covered earlier, depending on an instructor's preferences.

Chapter 17 presents the various theories of consumer behaviour, including the Keynesian consumption function, Fisher's model of intertemporal choice, Modigliani's life-cycle hypothesis, Friedman's permanent-income hypothesis, Hall's random-walk hypothesis, and Laibson's model of instant gratification. Chapter 18 examines the theory behind the investment function. Chapter 19 provides additional material on the money market, including the role of the banking system in determining the money supply, monetary policy indicators, and the Baumol-Tobin model of money demand.

Epilogue

The book ends with a brief epilogue that reviews the broad lessons about which most macroeconomists agree and discusses some of the most important open questions. Regardless of which chapters an instructor chooses to cover, this capstone chapter can be used to remind students how the many models and themes of macroeconomics relate to one another. Here and throughout the book we emphasize that, despite the disagreements among macroeconomists, there is much that we know about how the economy works.

Alternative Routes through the Text

Although we have organized the material in the way that we prefer to teach intermediate-level macroeconomics, we understand that other instructors have different preferences. We tried to keep this in mind as we wrote the book, so that it would offer a degree of flexibility. Here are a few ways that instructors might consider rearranging the material:

➤ Some instructors are eager to cover short-run economic fluctuations. For such a course, we recommend covering Chapters 1 through 4 so students are grounded in the basics of classical theory and then jumping to Chapters 9 through 14 to cover the model of aggregate demand and aggregate supply.

➤ Some instructors are eager to cover long-run economic growth. These instructors can cover Chapters 7 and 8 immediately after Chapter 3.

➤ An instructor who wants to defer open-economy macroeconomics can put off Chapters 5 and 12 without loss of continuity.

➤ An instructor who wants to emphasize the microeconomic foundations of macroeconomics can teach chapters 17, 18, and 19 early in the course, such as immediately after chapter 6 (or even earlier).

Experience with previous editions suggests this text complements well a variety of approaches to the field.

Learning Tools

We are pleased that students have found the previous edition of this book user friendly. We have tried to make this fourth edition even more so.

Case Studies

Economics comes to life when it is applied to understanding actual events. There-fore, the numerous case studies (many new or revised in this edition) are important learning tools that are integrated closely with the theoretical material presented in each chapter. The frequency with which these case studies occur ensures that a student does not have to grapple with an overdose of theory before seeing the theory applied. Students report that the case studies are their favourite part of the book.

FYI Boxes

These boxes present ancillary material "for your information." We use these boxes to clarify difficult concepts, to provide additional information about the tools of economics, and to show how economics relates to our daily lives. Several are new or revised in this edition. A particularly useful FYI box appears below.

Macroeconomic Data for Canada

While the text contains many graphs and tables containing data pertaining to the Canadian economy (see, in particular, the convenient graphs on the inside front and back covers of the book), readers of both the text and the study guide will want to have convenient access to the latest observations that emerge after these books have been published. We indicate the most straightforward options here.

The most recent observations on many major series are available on Statistics Canada's website at

http://www.statcan.gc.ca.

You have two options: (i) click on *Find Statistics,* then *Subjects* and then the category you want (such as labour, prices, national accounts); (ii) click on *Find Statistics,* then on *Summary Tables,* and then enter the keyword you want (such as unemployment rate). While convenient, this free-access site provides only the most recent observations.

Entire historical times series can be had as follows. On your own university website, you can go to the library page and click on *e-resources.* Then, retrieve—under *journal title*—the *Canadian Economic Observer*—a summary publication produced by Statistics Canada. Once at this page, click on *Canadian Economic Observer Historical Supplement* (choosing the HTML view option). You can then choose from the various tables that are available.

The series reference numbers in these tables are the ones that are given in the source entries for each table in this text.

Other useful websites are:

http://www.fin.gc.ca

The Federal Department of Finance site has a *Frequently Asked Questions* section (under the *About Us* heading), as well as the annual *Budget* documents (each Spring) and the annual *Fiscal Update* (each fall).

http://bankofcanada.ca

The Bank of Canada site has very useful *Frequently Asked Questions* as well (under the *Monetary Policy* heading).

http://www.cabe.ca

The Canadian Association of Business Economists site gives links to a number of interesting downloads.

Finally, you can read recent reports on numerous macroeconomic topics by checking the recent releases tab on several economic policy think tanks. For example, Google the C.D. Howe Institute, the Institute for Research on Public Policy, the Canadian Centre for Policy Alternatives, and the Fraser Institute. Finally, the economics departments of the major chartered banks have excellent macroeconomic reports. See, for example, http://www.td.com/economics.

Graphs

Understanding graphical analysis is a key part of learning macroeconomics, and we have worked hard to make the figures easy to follow. We use four colours and comment boxes within figures that describe briefly and draw attention to the important points that the figures illustrate. Both innovations should help students both learn and review the material.

Mathematical Notes

We use occasional mathematical footnotes to keep more difficult material out of the body of the text. These notes make an argument more rigourous or present a proof of a mathematical result. They can easily be skipped by those students who have not been introduced to the necessary mathematical tools.

Chapter Summaries

Every chapter ends with a brief, nontechnical summary of its major lessons. Students can use the summaries to place the material in perspective and to review for exams.

Key Concepts

Learning the language of a field is a major part of any course. Within the chapter, each key concept is in **boldface** when it is introduced. At the end of the chapter, the key concepts are listed for review.

Questions for Review

After studying a chapter, students can immediately test their understanding of its basic lessons by answering the Questions for Review.

Problems and Applications

Every chapter includes Problems and Applications designed for homework assignments. Some of these are numerical applications of the theory in the chapter. Others encourage the student to go beyond the material in the chapter by addressing new issues that are closely related to the chapter topics.

Chapter Appendixes

Several chapters include appendixes that offer additional material, sometimes at a higher level of mathematical sophistication. These are designed so that professors can cover certain topics in greater depth if they wish. The appendixes can be skipped altogether without loss of continuity.

Glossary

To help students become familiar with the language of macroeconomics, a glossary of more than 250 terms is provided at the back of the book.

Supplements for Students

Student Guide and Workbook

The study guide, by Roger Kaufman (Boston College) and William Scarth, offers various ways for students to learn the material in the text and assess their understanding.

➤ *Fill-In Questions* give students the opportunity to review and check their knowledge of the key terms and concepts in the chapter.

➤ *Multiple-Choice Questions* allow students to test themselves on the chapter material.

➤ *Exercises* guide students step by step through the various models using graphs and numerical examples.

➤ *Problems* ask students to apply the models on their own.

➤ *Questions to Think About* require critical thinking as well as economic analysis.

➤ *Data Questions* ask students to obtain and learn about readily available economic data.

Companion Website (www.worthpublishers.com/mankiw)

Students may find the following features of the site produced for the associated U.S. edition of the text useful:

➤ *Self-Tests.* Students can test their knowledge of the material by taking multiple-choice tests on any chapter.

➤ *Sample Essays.* Students can view chapter-specific essay questions followed by sample essay answers.

➤ *Student Tutorials.* Mannig Simidian has developed *Mankiw's Macroeconomics Modules: A PowerPoint Tutorial,* an animated set of tutorial slides for students. For each chapter, key points are highlighted, and students are offered another way to learn the material. Dynamic macroeconomic models come alive with shifting curves, colorful equations, graphics, and humor.

➤ *Web Links.* Students can access real-world information via specifically chosen hyperlinks relating to chapter content.

➤ *Flashcards.* Students can test their knowledge of the definitions in the glossary with these virtual flashcards.

The following items on the website pertain to the U.S. economy. Nevertheless, since much of the book covers items which are not specific to the small open economy case, Canadian students may find these items instructive:

➤ *Data Plotter.* Students can explore macroeconomic data with time-series graphs and scatterplots.

➤ *2012: A Game for Macroeconomists.* The game allows students to become President of the United States in the year 2012 and to make macroeconomic policy decisions based on news events, economic statistics, and approval ratings. It gives students a sense of the complex interconnections that influence the economy. It is also fun to play.

Supplements for Instructors

Additional supplements are available from Worth Publishers to help instructors enhance their courses.

Test Bank

Nancy Jianakopolos (Colorado State University) and William Scarth have produced a *Test Bank* that includes nearly 2,000 multiple-choice questions, numerical problems, and short-answer graphical questions to accompany each chapter of the text. The *Test Bank* is available on a CD-ROM that also includes our flexible test-generating software. Using the Diploma software, instructors can easily write and edit questions as well as create and print tests.

The following other instructor resources (produced for the associated U.S. edition of the text) may also be useful for Canadian instructors:

Instructor's Resources

Robert G. Murphy (Boston College) has revised the impressive resource manual for instructors that appears on the instructor's portion of the website. For each chapter, the manual contains notes to the instructor, a detailed lecture outline, additional case studies, and coverage of advanced topics.

Solutions Manual

Nora Underwood (University of Central Florida) has updated the *Solutions Manual* for all of the Questions for Review and Problems and Applications in the text. The manual also contains the answers to selected questions from the *Student Guide and Workbook*.

PowerPoint Slides

Ron Cronovich (Carthage College) has prepared PowerPoint presentations of the material in each chapter. They feature graphs with effective animation, careful explanations of the core material, additional case studies and data, helpful notes to the instructor, and innovative pedagogical features. Designed to be customized or used "as is," they include easy instructions for professors who have little experience with PowerPoint. They are available on the website.

Acknowledgments

We benefited from the input of many reviewers, colleagues, and government agencies. Several Canadian economists were particularly helpful in the preparation of several Canadian editions. Norm Cameron (University of Manitoba), Bryan Campbell (Concordia University), Vincenzo Caponi (Ryerson University), Miquel Faig (University of Toronto), George Georgopoulos (York University), Brian Glabb (Carleton University), Ron Kneebone (University of Calgary), Dan Otchere (Concordia University), Tony Myatt (University of New Brunswick), Leon Sydor (University of Windsor), and Mary Ann Vaughan (University of Waterloo) all made many useful suggestions. In addition, we wish to acknowledge the discussions we have had with colleagues at our own universities and the input given by a number of economists teaching in the United States (whose helpful comments found their way into this Canadian edition). This latter group is listed in the seventh U.S. edition of the book.

The people at Worth Publishers have continued to be congenial, dedicated and effective. We are grateful to Marie McHale, Norma Beasley, and Chris Spavins in particular. The hard working team at Worth Publishers made this book possible. Thanks are due to Senior Publisher Craig Bleyer, Senior Acquisitions Editor Sarah Dorger, Associate Managing Editor Tracey Kuehn, Executive Marketing Manager Scott Guile, Production Manager Barbara Seixas, Art Director Babs Reingold, and designer Kevin Kall.

Finally, we would like to thank our families for being so understanding, supportive, and inspirational.

N. Gregory Mankiw

Cambridge, Massachusetts
January 2010

William Scarth

Hamilton, Ontario
January 2010

MACROECONOMICS

PART I

Introduction

CHAPTER 1

The Science of Macroeconomics

The whole of science is nothing more than the refinement of everyday thinking.

— *Albert Einstein*

1-1 What Macroeconomists Study

Why have some countries experienced rapid growth in incomes over the past century while others stay mired in poverty? Why do some countries have high rates of inflation while others maintain stable prices? Why do all countries experience recessions and depressions—recurrent periods of falling incomes and rising unemployment—and how can government policy reduce the frequency and severity of these episodes? **Macroeconomics**, the study of the economy as a whole, attempts to answer these and many related questions.

To appreciate the importance of macroeconomics, you need only read the newspaper or listen to the news. Every day you can see headlines such as GDP GROWTH SLOWS, THE BANK OF CANADA MOVES TO COMBAT INFLATION, GOVERNMENT BUDGET INVOLVES RECORD DEFICIT, or STOCKS FALL AMID RECESSION FEARS. These macroeconomic events may seem abstract, but they touch all of our lives. Business executives forecasting the demand for their products must guess how fast consumers' incomes will grow. Senior citizens living on fixed incomes wonder how fast prices will rise. Recent graduates looking for jobs hope that the economy will boom and that firms will be hiring.

Because the state of the economy affects everyone, macroeconomic issues play a central role in national political debates. Voters are keenly aware of how the economy is doing, and they know that government policy can affect the economy in powerful ways. As a result, the popularity of the government often rises when the economy is doing well and falls when it is doing poorly. During the federal election of 1993, for example, Liberal strategists kept the former government on the defensive by keeping the campaign focused on the economy. Every speech included the refrain "jobs, jobs, jobs."

Macroeconomic issues are also at the center of world politics, and if you read the international news, you will quickly start thinking about a variety of macroeconomic questions. Was it a good move for much of Europe to adopt a common currency? Why did the Canadian dollar rise in recent months?

Should China maintain a fixed exchange rate against the U.S. dollar? Why is the United States running large trade deficits? How can poor nations raise their standard of living? When world leaders meet, these topics are often high on their agenda.

Although the job of making economic policy belongs to world leaders, the job of explaining how the economy as a whole works falls to macroeconomists. Toward this end, macroeconomists collect data on incomes, prices, unemployment, and many other variables from different time periods and different countries. They then attempt to formulate general theories that help to explain these data. Like astronomers studying the evolution of stars or biologists studying the evolution of species, macroeconomists cannot conduct controlled experiments in a laboratory. Instead, they must make use of the data that history gives them. Macroeconomists observe that economies differ from one another and that they change over time. These observations provide both the motivation for developing macroeconomic theories and the data for testing them.

To be sure, macroeconomics is a young and imperfect science. The macroeconomist's ability to predict the future course of economic events is no better than the meteorologist's ability to predict next month's weather. But, as you will see, macroeconomists know quite a lot about how economies work. Since the Canadian economy is a mixture of markets and government policy involvement, this knowledge is useful both for explaining economic events and for formulating economic policy.

Every era has its own economic problems. In the 1970s, the Liberal government of Pierre Trudeau wrestled in vain with a rising rate of inflation. In the 1980s, inflation subsided, but the Conservative government of Brian Mulroney continued to struggle with large federal budget deficits. In the 1990s, as the Liberals formed the government once again, the budget deficit shrank and even turned into a small budget surplus, but federal taxes as a share of national income reached a historic high. In the early years of the new century, the federal government became increasingly focused on how productivity growth might be stimulated, and on how the challenges of increased globalization and an aging population are to be met in the coming years. Then a major recession hit—a dramatic upheaval started by mortgage defaults and the bankruptcies of several major financial institutions in the United States. The final magnitude of the downturn was uncertain as this book was going to press, but some observers feared the recession might be deep. In some minds, the financial crisis raised the spectre of the Great Depression of the 1930s; in its worst year, one out of four Canadians who wanted to work could not find a job. In 2009, officials in the Bank of Canada lowered its trend-setting overnight interest rate essentially to zero, and the federal budget set a record deficit of $50 billion. Both of these actions were designed to prevent a recurrence of the 1930s outcome.

Macroeconomic history is not a simple story, but it provides a rich motivation for macroeconomic theory. Although the basic principles of macroeconomics do not change from decade to decade, the macroeconomist must apply these principles with flexibility and creativity to meet changing circumstances.

CASE STUDY

The Historical Performance of the Canadian Economy

Economists use many types of data to measure the performance of an economy. Three macroeconomic variables are particularly important: real gross domestic product (GDP), the inflation rate, and the unemployment rate. **Real GDP** measures the total income of everyone in the economy (adjusted for the level of prices). The **inflation rate** measures how quickly prices are rising. The **unemployment rate** measures the fraction of the labour force that is out of work. Macroeconomists study how these variables are determined, why they change over time, and how they interact with one another.

Figure 1-1 shows real GDP per person for the Canadian economy—widely regarded as a measure of our standard of living. Two aspects of this figure are

FIGURE 1-1

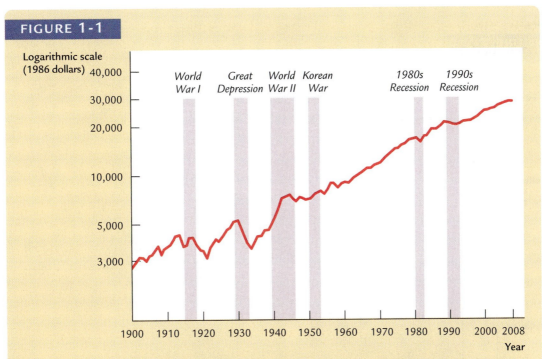

Real GDP per Person in the Canadian Economy Real GDP measures the total output of the economy. Real GDP per person measures the income of the average person in the economy.

Note: Real GDP is plotted here on a logarithmic scale. On such a scale, equal distances on the vertical axis represent equal *percentage* changes. Thus, the distance between $5,000 and $10,000 is the same as the distance between $10,000 and $20,000.

Source: Reproduced and adapted by authority of the Minister of Industry, 2006. Statistics Canada CANSIM Series 1992044, 1992067 and 1; also *Canadian Economic Observer Catalogue* 11-210, (Historical Statistical Supplement 1991/92): 7, 98 and *Catalogue* 11-010 (Statistical Summary, March 1994): 4, 12; Morris Altman, "Revised Real GNP Estimates and Canadian Economic Growth, 1870-1926," *Review of Income and Wealth*, Series 38, No. 4 (December 1992): 458-59; and *Canada 1930: A Handbook of Present Conditions and Recent Progress in the Dominion Bureau of Statistics* (Ottawa: Dominion Bureau of Statistics): 40.

noteworthy. First, real GDP grows over time. Measured in terms of 2008 market prices, real GDP per person today is about 42.2 thousand dollars—about eleven times its level in 1900. This growth in average income allows us to enjoy a *much* higher standard of living than our great-grandparents did. Second, although real GDP rises in most years, this growth is not steady. There are repeated periods during which real GDP is falling, a dramatic example being the 1930s. Such periods are called **recessions** if they are mild and **depressions** if they are more severe. Not surprisingly, periods of declining income are associated with substantial economic hardship.

Figure 1-2 shows the Canadian inflation rate. You can see that inflation varies substantially. Before 1945, the inflation rate averaged about zero. Periods of falling prices, called **deflation,** were almost as common as periods of rising prices. In more recent history, inflation has been the norm. The inflation problem became most severe during the mid-1970s, when prices rose persistently at a rate of almost 10 percent per year. Inflation returned to near zero in the 1990s, but it has crept back up somewhat during the early years of this century.

FIGURE 1-2

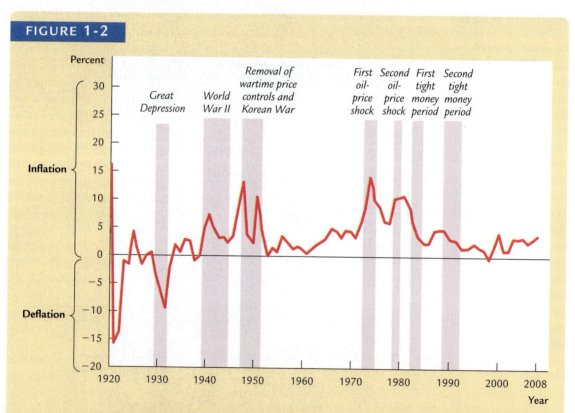

The Inflation Rate in the Canadian Economy The inflation rate measures the percentage change in the average level of prices from the year before. A negative inflation rate indicates that prices are falling.

Note: The inflation rate is measured here using the GDP deflator.
Source: Reproduced and adapted by authority of the Minister of Industry, 2006, Statistics Canada CANSIM Series 1997756; 22; Morris Altman, "Revised Real GNP Estimates and Canadian Economic Growth, 1870–1926," *Review of Income and Wealth,* Series 38, No. 4.

FIGURE 1-3

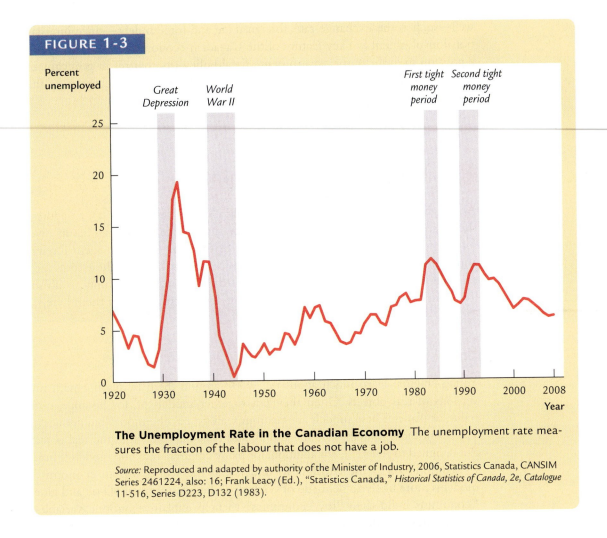

The Unemployment Rate in the Canadian Economy The unemployment rate measures the fraction of the labour that does not have a job.

Source: Reproduced and adapted by authority of the Minister of Industry, 2006, Statistics Canada, CANSIM Series 2461224, also: 16; Frank Leacy (Ed.), "Statistics Canada," *Historical Statistics of Canada, 2e, Catalogue* 11-516, Series D223, D132 (1983).

Figure 1-3 shows the Canadian unemployment rate since 1921, the first year for which data exist. This figure shows that there is always some unemployment and that the amount varies from year to year. Recessions and depressions are associated with unusually high unemployment. The highest rates of unemployment were reached during the Great Depression of the 1930s. As the figure shows, since World War II, there has been a gradual upward trend in unemployment. We will discuss the likely causes of this troubling fact in Chapter 6. Evidence for the last 15 years suggests that this disturbing trend may be starting to reverse itself.

These three figures offer a glimpse at the history of the Canadian economy. They show that unemployment falls and inflation rises when total spending is high (such as during World War II and the early 1960s), and that unemployment rises when inflation is reduced by government policy that decreases total spending (such as during the early 1980s and 1990s).

In the chapters that follow, we first discuss how these variables are measured and then explain how they behave—of course, we will look at other data as well—such as the exchange rate, foreign trade and foreign debt—since international involvement is a key feature of the Canadian economy. We will then be in a position to evaluate the government's fiscal policy (its changes in government spending and taxing) and its monetary policy (changes in the growth of the nation's money supply).

1-2 How Economists Think

Although economists often study politically charged issues, they try to address these issues with a scientist's objectivity. Like any science, economics has its own set of tools—terminology, data, and a way of thinking—that can seem foreign and arcane to the layman. The best way to become familiar with these tools is to practice using them, and this book will afford you ample opportunity to do so. To make these tools less forbidding, however, let's discuss a few of them here.

Theory as Model Building

Young children learn much about the world around them by playing with toy versions of real objects. Often they put together models of, for instance, cars, trains, or planes. These models are far from realistic, but the model-builder learns a lot from them nonetheless. The model illustrates the essence of the real object it is designed to resemble. (In addition, for many children, building models is fun.)

Economists also use **models** to understand the world, but an economist's model is more likely to be made of symbols and equations than plastic and glue. Economists build their "toy economies" to help explain economic variables, such as GDP, inflation, and unemployment. Economic models illustrate, often in mathematical terms, the relationships among the variables. Models are useful because they help us to dispense with irrelevant details and to focus on underlying connections more clearly. (In addition, for many economists, building models is fun.)

Models have two kinds of variables: endogenous variables and exogenous variables. **Endogenous variables** are those variables that a model tries to explain. **Exogenous variables** are those variables that a model takes as given. The purpose of a model is to show how the exogenous variables affect the endogenous variables. In other words, as Figure 1-4 illustrates, exogenous variables come from outside the model and serve as the model's input, whereas endogenous variables are determined inside the model and are the model's output.

To make these ideas more concrete, let's review the most celebrated of all economic models—the model of supply and demand. Imagine that an economist wanted to figure out what influences the price of pizza and the quantity of pizza sold. He or she would proceed by developing a model that described the behaviour of pizza buyers, the behaviour of pizza sellers, and their interaction in the market for pizza. For example, the economist supposes that the quantity of pizza

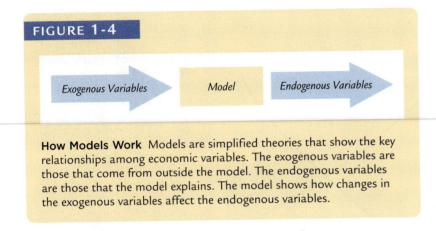

FIGURE 1-4

Exogenous Variables → Model → Endogenous Variables

How Models Work Models are simplified theories that show the key relationships among economic variables. The exogenous variables are those that come from outside the model. The endogenous variables are those that the model explains. The model shows how changes in the exogenous variables affect the endogenous variables.

demanded by consumers Q^d depends on the price of pizza P and on aggregate income Y. This relationship is expressed in the equation

$$Q^d = D(P, Y),$$

where $D(\ )$ represents the demand function. Similarly, the economist supposes that the quantity of pizza supplied by pizzerias Q^s depends on the price of pizza P and on the price of materials P_m, such as cheese, tomatoes, flour, and anchovies. This relationship is expressed as

$$Q^s = S(P, P_m),$$

where $S(\ )$ represents the supply function. Finally, the economist assumes that the price of pizza adjusts to bring the quantity supplied and quantity demanded into balance:

$$Q^s = Q^d.$$

These three equations compose a model of the market for pizza.

The economist illustrates the model with a supply-and-demand diagram, as in Figure 1-5. The demand curve shows the relationship between the quantity of pizza demanded and the price of pizza, holding aggregate income constant. The demand curve slopes downward because a higher price of pizza encourages consumers to switch to other foods and buy less pizza. The supply curve shows the relationship between the quantity of pizza supplied and the price of pizza, holding the price of materials constant. The supply curve slopes upward because a higher price of pizza makes selling pizza more profitable, which encourages pizzerias to incur the opportunity costs and produce more. The equilibrium for the market is the price and quantity at which the supply and demand curves intersect. At the equilibrium price, consumers choose to buy exactly the amount of pizza that pizzerias choose to produce.

This model of the pizza market has two exogenous variables and two endogenous variables. The exogenous variables are aggregate income and the price of

FIGURE 1-5

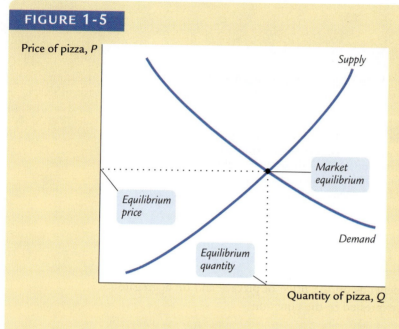

Price of pizza, P

Supply

Market equilibrium

Equilibrium price

Demand

Equilibrium quantity

Quantity of pizza, Q

The Model of Supply and Demand The most famous economic model is that of supply and demand for a good or service—in this case, pizza. The demand curve is a downward-sloping curve relating the price of pizza to the quantity of pizza that consumers demand. The supply curve is an upward-sloping curve relating the price of pizza to the quantity of pizza that pizzerias supply. The price of pizza adjusts until the quantity supplied equals the quantity demanded. The point where the two curves cross is the market equilibrium, which shows the equilibrium price of pizza and the equilibrium quantity of pizza.

materials. The model does not attempt to explain them but instead takes them as given (perhaps to be explained by another model). The endogenous variables are the price of pizza and the quantity of pizza exchanged. These are the variables that the model attempts to explain.

The model shows how a change in one of the exogenous variables affects both endogenous variables. For example, if aggregate income increases, then the demand for pizza increases, as in panel (a) of Figure 1-6. The model shows that both the equilibrium price and the equilibrium quantity of pizza rise. Similarly, if the price of materials increases, then the supply of pizza decreases, as in panel (b) of Figure 1-6. The model shows that in this case the equilibrium price of pizza rises and the equilibrium quantity of pizza falls. Thus, the model shows how changes either in aggregate income or in the price of materials affect price and quantity in the market for pizza.

Like all models, this model of the pizza market makes many simplifying assumptions. The model does not take into account, for example, that every pizzeria is in a different location. For each customer, one pizzeria is more convenient than the others, and thus pizzerias have some ability to set their own prices. Although the model assumes that there is a single price for pizza, in fact there could be a different price at every pizzeria.

How should we react to the model's lack of realism? Should we discard the simple model of pizza supply and demand? Should we attempt to build a more complex model that allows for diverse pizza prices? The answers to these

FIGURE 1-6

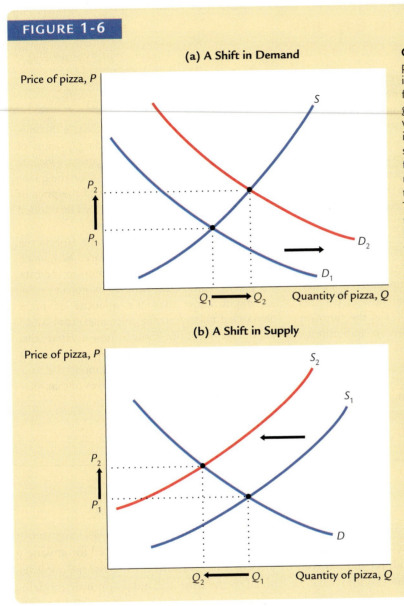

(a) A Shift in Demand

Price of pizza, P

S

P_2

P_1

D_2

D_1

$Q_1 \longrightarrow Q_2$ Quantity of pizza, Q

(b) A Shift in Supply

Price of pizza, P

S_2

S_1

P_2

P_1

D

$Q_2 \longleftarrow Q_1$ Quantity of pizza, Q

Changes in Equilibrium In panel (a), a rise in aggregate income causes the demand for pizza to increase: at any given price, consumers now want to buy more pizza. This is represented by a rightward shift in the demand curve from D_1 to D_2. The market moves to the new intersection of supply and demand. The equilibrium price rises from P_1 to P_2, and the equilibrium quantity of pizza rises from Q_1 to Q_2. In panel (b), a rise in the price of materials decreases the supply of pizza: at any given price, pizzerias find that the sale of pizza is less profitable and therefore choose to produce less pizza. This is represented by a leftward shift in the supply curve from S_1 to S_2. The market moves to the new intersection of supply and demand. The equilibrium price rises from P_1 to P_2, and the equilibrium quantity falls from Q_1 to Q_2.

questions depend on our purpose. If our goal is to explain how the price of cheese affects the average price of pizza and the amount of pizza sold, then the diversity of pizza prices is probably not important. The simple model of the pizza market does a good job of addressing that issue. Yet if our goal is to explain why towns with three pizzerias have lower pizza prices than towns with one pizzeria, the simple model is less useful.

The art in economics is in judging when a simplifying assumption (such as assuming a single price of pizza) clarifies our thinking and when it misleads us.

FYI

Using Functions to Express Relationships Among Variables

All economic models express relationships among economic variables. Often, these relationships are expressed as functions. A *function* is a mathematical concept that shows how one variable depends on a set of other variables. For example, in the model of the pizza market, we said that the quantity of pizza demanded depends on the price of pizza and on aggregate income. To express this, we use functional notation to write

$$Q^d = D(P, Y).$$

This equation says that the quantity of pizza demanded Q^d is a function of the price of pizza P and aggregate income Y. In functional notation, the variable preceding the parentheses denotes the function. In this case, $D(\ )$ is the function expressing how the variables in parentheses determine the quantity of pizza demanded.

If we knew more about the pizza market, we could give a numerical formula for the quantity of pizza demanded. For example, we might be able to write

$$Q^d = 60 - 10P + 2Y.$$

In this case, the demand function is

$$D(P, Y) = 60 - 10P + 2Y.$$

For any price of pizza and aggregate income, this function gives the corresponding quantity of pizza demanded. For example, if aggregate income is $10 and the price of pizza is $2, then the quantity of pizza demanded is 60 pies; if the price of pizza rises to $3, the quantity of pizza demanded falls to 50 pies.

Functional notation allows us to express the general idea that variables are related even when we do not have enough information to indicate the precise numerical relationship. For example, we might know that the quantity of pizza demanded falls when the price rises from $2 to $3, but we might not know by how much it falls. In this case, functional notation is useful: as long as we know that a relationship among the variables exists, we can remind ourselves of that relationship using functional notation.

Simplification is a necessary part of building a useful model: any model constructed to be completely realistic would be too complicated for anyone to understand. Yet models lead to incorrect conclusions if they assume away features of the economy that are crucial to the issue at hand. Economic modeling therefore requires care and common sense.

The Use of Multiple Models

Macroeconomists study many facets of the economy. For example, they examine the influence of fiscal policy on economic growth, the impact of employment insurance on the unemployment rate, the effect of inflation on interest rates, and the influence of trade policy on the exchange rate.

Although economists use models to address all these issues, no single model can answer all questions. Just as carpenters use different tools for different tasks, economists uses different models to explain different economic phenomena.

Students of macroeconomics, therefore, must keep in mind that there is no single "correct" model that is universally applicable. Instead, there are many models, each of which is useful for shedding light on a different facet of the economy. The field of macroeconomics is like a Swiss army knife—a set of complementary but distinct tools that can be applied in different ways in different circumstances.

This book therefore presents many different models that address different questions and that make different assumptions. Remember that a model is only as good as its assumptions and that an assumption that is useful for some purposes may be misleading for others. When using a model to address a question, the economist must keep in mind the underlying assumptions and judge whether these are reasonable for studying the matter at hand.

Prices: Flexible Versus Sticky

Throughout this book, one group of assumptions will prove especially important—those concerning the speed with which wages and prices adjust to changing economic conditions. Economists normally presume that the price of a good or a service moves quickly to bring quantity supplied and quantity demanded into balance. In other words, they assume that markets are normally in equilibrium, so the price of any good or service is found where the supply and demand curves intersect. This assumption is called **market clearing** and is central to the model of the pizza market discussed earlier. For answering most questions, economists use market-clearing models.

Yet the assumption of *continuous* market clearing is not entirely realistic. For markets to clear continuously, prices must adjust instantly to changes in supply and demand. In fact, many wages and prices adjust slowly. Labour contracts often set wages for up to three years. Many firms leave their product prices the same for long periods of time—for example, magazine publishers typically change their newsstand prices only every three or four years. Although market-clearing models assume that all wages and prices are **flexible,** in the real world some wages and prices are **sticky.**

The apparent stickiness of prices does not necessarily make market-clearing models useless. After all, prices are not stuck forever; eventually, they do adjust to changes in supply and demand. Market-clearing models might not describe the economy at every instant, but they do describe the equilibrium toward which the economy slowly gravitates. Therefore, most macroeconomists believe that price flexibility is a good assumption for studying long-run issues, such as the growth in real GDP that we observe from decade to decade.

For studying short-run issues, such as year-to-year fluctuations in real GDP and unemployment, the assumption of price flexibility is less plausible. Over short periods, many prices are fixed at predetermined levels. Therefore, most macroeconomists believe that price stickiness is a better assumption for studying the short-run behaviour of the economy.

Nobel Macroeconomists

The Nobel Prize in economics is announced every October. Many winners have been macroeconomists whose work we study in this book. Here are a few of them, along with some of their own words about how they chose their field of study:

Milton Friedman (Nobel 1976): "I graduated from college in 1932, when the United States was at the bottom of the deepest depression in its history before or since. The dominant problem of the time was economics. How to get out of the depression? How to reduce unemployment? What explained the paradox of great need on the one hand and unused resources on the other? Under the circumstances, becoming an economist seemed more relevant to the burning issues of the day than becoming an applied mathematician or an actuary."

James Tobin (Nobel 1981): "I was attracted to the field for two reasons. One was that economic theory is a fascinating intellectual challenge, on the order of mathematics or chess. I liked analytics and logical argument. . . . The other reason was the obvious relevance of economics to understanding and perhaps overcoming the Great Depression."

Franco Modigliani (Nobel 1985): "For awhile it was thought that I should study medicine because my father was a physician. . . . I went to the registration window to sign up for medicine, but then I closed my eyes and thought of blood! I got pale just thinking about blood and decided under those conditions I had better keep away from medicine. . . . Casting about for something to do, I happened to get into some economics activities. I knew some German and was asked to translate from German into Italian some articles for one of the trade associations. Thus I began to be exposed to the economic problems that were in the German literature."

Robert Solow (Nobel 1987): "I came back [to college after being in the army] and, almost without thinking about it, signed up to finish my undergraduate degree as an economics major. The time was such that I had to make a

decision in a hurry. No doubt I acted as if I were maximizing an infinite discounted sum of one-period utilities, but you couldn't prove it by me. To me it felt as if I were saying to myself: 'What the hell.'"

Robert Lucas (Nobel 1995): "In public school science was an unending and not very well organized list of things other people had discovered long ago. In college, I learned something about the process of scientific discovery, but what I learned did not attract me as a career possibility. . . . What I liked thinking about were politics and social issues."

George Akerlof (Nobel 2001): "When I went to Yale, I was convinced that I wanted to be either an economist or an historian. Really, for me it was a distinction without a difference. If I was going to be an historian, then I would be an economic historian. And if I was to be an economist I would consider history as the basis for my economics."

Edward Prescott (Nobel 2004): "Through discussion with [my father], I learned a lot about the way businesses operated. This was one reason why I liked my microeconomics course so much in my first year at Swarthmore College. The price theory that I learned in that course rationalized what I had learned from him about the way businesses operate. The other reason was the textbook used in that course, Paul A. Samuelson's *Principles of Economics.* I loved the way Samuelson laid out the theory in his textbook, so simply and clearly."

Robert Mundell (Nobel 1999), who was an undergraduate at the University of British Columbia, is one of the two Canadians to win the prize in economics. (The other was Myron Scholes, an undergraduate at McMaster, who won for his work on finance in 1997.) In his Nobel-prize interview, Mundell noted the importance of his Canadian background for his career. Canada was the first country to drop controls that limit the flow of capital across borders, and to have a flexible exchange rate – during the 1950s. These developments motivated Mundell to construct macroeconomic models based on the assumption of international capital mobility. This work was recognized as the important analytical base for the development of more recent work on the implications of "globalization".

Edmund Phelps (Nobel 2006): "Like most Americans entering college, I started at Amherst College without a predetermined course of study or without even a career goal. My tacit assumption was that I would drift into the world of business—of money, doing some-

thing terribly smart. In the first year, though, I was awestruck by Plato, Hume and James. I would probably have gone into philosophy were it not that my father cajoled and pleaded with me to try a course in economics, which I did the second year. . . . I was hugely impressed to see that it was possible to subject the events in those newspapers I had read about to a formal sort of analysis."

If you want to learn more about the Nobel Prize and its winners, go to www.nobelprize.org.[1]

Microeconomic Thinking and Macroeconomic Models

Microeconomics is the study of how households and firms make decisions and how these decisionmakers interact in the marketplace. A central principle of microeconomics is that households and firms *optimize*—they do the best they can for themselves given their objectives and the constraints they face. In microeconomic models, households choose their purchases to maximize their level of satisfaction, which economists call *utility,* and firms make production decisions to maximize their profits.

Because economy-wide events arise from the interaction of many households and firms, macroeconomics and microeconomics are inextricably linked. When we study the economy as a whole, we must consider the decisions of individual economic actors. For example, to understand what determines total consumer spending, we must think about a family deciding how much to spend today and how much to save for the future. To understand what determines total investment spending, we must think about a firm deciding whether to build a new factory. Because aggregate variables are simply the sum of the variables describing many individual decisions, macroeconomic theory inevitably rests on a microeconomic foundation.

Although microeconomic decisions underlie all economic models, in many models the optimizing behaviour of households and firms is implicit rather than explicit. The model of the pizza market we discussed earlier is an example. Households' decisions about how much pizza to buy underlie the demand for pizza, and pizzerias' decisions about how much pizza to produce underlie the supply of pizza. Presumably, households make their decisions to maximize

---

[1] The first five quotations are from William Breit and Barry T. Hirsch, eds., *Lives of the Laureates,* 4th ed. (Cambridge: MIT Press, 2004). The next three are from the Nobel website, where the interview with Robert Mundell can be accessed. The last one is from Arnold Heertje, ed., *The Makers of Modern Economics,* vol. II (Aldershot: Edward Elgar Publishing, 1995).

utility, and pizzerias make their decisions to maximize profit. Yet the model does not focus on how these microeconomic decisions are made; instead, it leaves these decisions in the background. Similarly, although microeconomic decisions lie behind all macroeconomic phenomena, macroeconomic models do not necessarily focus on the optimizing behaviour of households and firms but, instead, sometimes leave that behaviour in the background.

1-3 How This Book Proceeds

This book has six parts. This chapter and the next make up Part One, the Introduction. Chapter 2 discusses how economists measure economic variables, such as aggregate income, the inflation rate, and the unemployment rate.

Part Two, Classical Theory: The Economy in the Long Run, presents the classical model of how the economy works. The key assumption of the classical model is that prices are flexible. That is, with rare exceptions, the classical model assumes that markets clear. Because the assumption of price flexibility describes the economy only in the long run, classical theory is best suited for analyzing a time horizon of at least several years.

Part Three, Growth Theory: The Economy in the Very Long Run, builds on the classical model. It maintains the assumptions of price flexibility and market clearing but adds a new emphasis on growth in the capital stock, the labour force, and technological knowledge. Growth theory is designed to explain how the economy evolves over a period of several decades.

Part Four, Business Cycles Theory: The Economy in the Short Run, examines the behaviour of the economy when prices are sticky. The non-market-clearing model developed here is often referred to as the Keynesian model since this approach was pioneered by British economist John Maynard Keynes in the 1930's. It is designed to analyze short-run issues, such as the reasons for economic fluctuations and the influence of government policy on those fluctuations. It is best suited for analyzing the changes in the economy we observe from month to month or from year to year.

Part Five, Macroeconomic Policy Debates, builds on the previous analysis to consider what role the government should have in the economy. It considers how, if at all, the government should respond to short-run fluctuations in real GDP and unemployment. It also examines the various views of how government debt affects the economy.

Part Six, More on the Microeconomics Behind Macroeconomics, presents some of the microeconomic models that are useful for analyzing macroeconomic issues. For example, it examines the household's decisions regarding how much to consume and how much money to hold and the firm's decision regarding how much to invest. These individual decisions together form the larger macroeconomic picture. The goal of studying these microeconomic decisions in detail is to refine our understanding of the aggregate economy.

Summary

1. Macroeconomics is the study of the economy as a whole—including growth in incomes, changes in prices, and the rate of unemployment. Macroeconomists attempt both to explain economic events and to devise policies to improve economic performance.

2. To understand the economy, economists use models—theories that simplify reality in order to reveal how exogenous variables influence endogenous variables. The art in the science of economics is in judging whether a model usefully captures the important economic relationships for the matter at hand. Because no single model can answer all questions, macroeconomists use different models to look at different issues.

3. A key feature of a macroeconomic model is whether it assumes that prices are flexible or sticky. According to most macroeconomists, models with flexible prices describe the economy in the long run, whereas models with sticky prices offer a better description of the economy in the short run.

4. Microeconomics is the study of how firms and individuals make decisions and how these decisionmakers interact. Because macroeconomic events arise from many microeconomic interactions, all macroeconomic models must be consistent with microeconomic foundations, even if those foundations are only implicit.

KEY CONCEPTS

Macroeconomics	Depression	Market clearing
Real GDP	Deflation	Flexible and sticky prices
Inflation rate	Models	Microeconomics
Unemployment rate	Endogenous variables	
Recession	Exogenous variables	

QUESTIONS FOR REVIEW

1. Explain the difference between macroeconomics and microeconomics. How are these two fields related?

2. Why do economists build models?

3. What is a market-clearing model? When is it appropriate to assume that markets clear?

PROBLEMS AND APPLICATIONS

1. What macroeconomic issues have been in the news lately?

2. What do you think are the defining characteristics of a science? Does the study of the economy have these characteristics? Do you think macroeconomics should be called a science? Why or why not?

3. Use the model of supply and demand to explain how a fall in the price of frozen yogurt would affect the price of ice cream and the quantity of ice cream sold. In your explanation, identify the exogenous and endogenous variables.

4. How often does the price you pay for a haircut change? What does your answer imply about the usefulness of market-clearing models for analyzing the market for haircuts?

CHAPTER 2

The Data of Macroeconomics

It is a capital mistake to theorize before one has data. Insensibly one begins to twist facts to suit theories, instead of theories to fit facts.

— *Sherlock Holmes*

Scientists, economists, and detectives have much in common: they all want to figure out what's going on in the world around them. To do this, they rely on a combination of theory and observation. They build theories in an attempt to make sense of what they see happening. Having developed these theories, they turn to more systematic observation to evaluate the theories' validity. Only when theory and data come into line do they feel they understand the situation. This chapter discusses the types of data used to create and test macroeconomic theories. Casual observation is one source of information about what's happening in the economy. When you go shopping, you see how fast prices are rising. When you look for a job, you learn whether firms are hiring. Because we are all participants in the economy, we get some sense of economic conditions as we go about our lives.

A century ago, economists monitoring the economy had little more to go on than these casual observations. Such fragmentary information made economic policymaking all the more difficult. One person's anecdote would suggest the economy was moving in one direction, while a different person's anecdote would suggest it was moving in another. Economists needed some way to combine many individual experiences into a coherent whole. There was an obvious solution: as the old quip goes, the plural of "anecdote" is "data."

Today, economic data offer a systematic and objective source of information, and almost every day the newspaper has a story about some newly released statistic. Most of these statistics are produced by the government. Various government agencies survey households and firms to learn about their economic activity—how much they are earning, what they are buying, what prices they are charging, and so on. From these surveys, various statistics are computed that summarize the state of the economy. These statistics are used by economists to study the economy and by policymakers to monitor economic developments and formulate appropriate policies.

This chapter focuses on the three economic statistics that economists and policymakers use most often. **Gross domestic product,** or **GDP,** tells us the nation's total income and the total expenditure on its output of goods and services.

The **consumer price index,** or **CPI,** measures the level of prices. The **unemployment rate** tells us the fraction of workers who are unemployed. In the following pages, we see how these statistics are computed and what they tell us about the economy. In later chapters, we focus on additional statistics that are also very important—statistics such as interest rates, the exchange rate and the money supply.

2-1 Measuring the Value of Economic Activity: Gross Domestic Product

Gross domestic product is often considered the best measure of how well the economy is performing. This measure, which Statistics Canada computes every three months, is computed from a large number of primary data sources that include both administrative and statistical data. Administrative data are byproducts of government functions such as tax collection, education programs, and regulation. Statistical data come from government surveys of, for example, retail establishments, manufacturing firms, and farm activity. The purpose of GDP is to summarize all these data in a single number that represents the total dollar value of economic activity in a given time period. More precisely, GDP equals the total value of all final goods and services produced within Canada during a particular year or quarter. *If* it were the case that (1) no Canadian worker had a job in another country, (2) no foreigner had a job in Canada, and (3) all machines and factories used both here and elsewhere were owned by domestic residents, then this total value of goods produced would also measure the total value of Canadians' incomes. But, since some income *is* received from individuals owning capital equipment in other countries, GDP is not a perfect measure of total Canadian income. *GDP is total income earned* domestically. It includes income earned domestically by foreigners, but it does not include income earned by domestic residents on foreign ground. The total income earned by Canadians includes the income that we earn abroad, but it does not include the income earned within our country by foreigners.

For the purpose of stabilizing employment, we are interested in a broad measure of job-creating activity within Canada. GDP is that measure. For evaluating trends in the standard of living of Canadians, it is appropriate to subtract that part of our GDP that represents income to foreigners. This figure is reported by Statistics Canada in the Balance of International Payments accounts. To have some idea of the magnitude of this difference between our GDP and what part of it represents Canadian incomes, we consider two years. First, in 1993, 3.7 percent of Canadian GDP represented income for foreigners. Starting in that year, the federal government embarked on a concerted effort to eliminate its budget deficit. That policy has resulted in a decrease in the government's debt and—indirectly—to a decrease in the indebtedness of all Canadians with the rest of the world. This lower indebtedness means that Canadians now own a bigger fraction of the machines and factories that operate within the country than we did back in 1993. As a result, by 2008, just under 1 percent of Canadian GDP represented income to foreigners. The higher income for Canadians is one of the benefits that has followed from the government's drive to reduce its deficit and debt.

Luckily, when we subtract off the foreign incomes part of the GDP, we see that the timing and size of the cyclical swings in the resulting series and in the GDP itself are almost identical. As a result, for discussing business cycles and stabilization policy, nothing is lost by focusing on the overall GDP. Thus, throughout much but not all of this book, we abstract from the phenomenon of foreign-owned factors of production, and we assume that GDP simultaneously measures all three of the following concepts:

- The total output of goods and services
- The total income of all individuals
- The total expenditure of all individuals.

How can GDP measure both the economy's income and its expenditure on output? The reason is that these two quantities are really the same: for the economy as a whole, income must equal expenditure. That fact, in turn, follows from an even more fundamental one: because every transaction has a buyer and a seller, every dollar of expenditure by a buyer must become a dollar of income to a seller. When Joe paints Jane's house for $1,000, that $1,000 is income to Joe and expenditure by Jane. The transaction contributes $1,000 to GDP, regardless of whether we are adding up all income or adding up all expenditure.

To understand the meaning of GDP more fully, we turn to **national accounting,** the accounting system used to measure GDP and many related statistics.

Income, Expenditure, and the Circular Flow

Imagine an economy that produces a single good, bread, from a single input, labour. Figure 2-1 illustrates all the economic transactions that occur between households and firms in this economy.

The inner loop in Figure 2-1 represents the flows of bread and labour. The households sell their labour to the firms. The firms use the labour of their workers to produce bread, which the firms in turn sell to the households. Hence, labour flows from households to firms, and bread flows from firms to households.

The outer loop in Figure 2-1 represents the corresponding flow of dollars. The households buy bread from the firms. The firms use some of the revenue from these sales to pay the wages of their workers, and the remainder is the profit belonging to the owners of the firms (who themselves are part of the household sector). Hence, expenditure on bread flows from households to firms, and income in the form of wages and profit flows from firms to households.

GDP measures the flow of dollars in this economy. We can compute it in two ways. GDP is the total income from the production of bread, which equals the sum of wages and profit—the top half of the circular flow of dollars. GDP is also the total expenditure on purchases of bread—the bottom half of the circular flow of dollars. To compute GDP, we can look at either the flow of dollars from firms to households or the flow of dollars from households to firms.

FIGURE 2-1

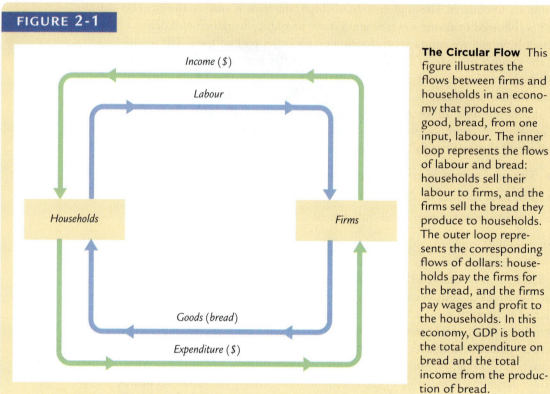

Income ($)

Labour

Households

Firms

Goods (bread)

Expenditure ($)

The Circular Flow This figure illustrates the flows between firms and households in an economy that produces one good, bread, from one input, labour. The inner loop represents the flows of labour and bread: households sell their labour to firms, and the firms sell the bread they produce to households. The outer loop represents the corresponding flows of dollars: households pay the firms for the bread, and the firms pay wages and profit to the households. In this economy, GDP is both the total expenditure on bread and the total income from the production of bread.

These two ways of computing GDP must be equal because the expenditure of buyers on products is, by the rules of accounting, income to the sellers of those products. Every transaction that affects expenditure must affect income, and every transaction that affects income must affect expenditure. For example, suppose that a firm produces and sells one more loaf of bread to a household. Clearly this transaction raises total expenditure on bread, but it also has an equal effect on total income. If the firm produces the extra loaf without hiring any more labour (such as by making the production process more efficient), then profit increases. If the firm produces the extra loaf by hiring more labour, then wages increase. In both cases, expenditure and income increase equally.

Some Rules for Computing GDP

In an economy that produces only bread, we can compute GDP by adding up the total expenditure on bread. Real economies, however, include the production and sale of a vast number of goods and services. To compute GDP for such a complex economy, it will be helpful to rely on the more precise definition given above: *Gross domestic product (GDP) is the market value of all final goods and services produced within an economy in a given period of time.* To see how this definition is applied, let's discuss some of the rules that economists follow in constructing this statistic.

Adding Apples and Oranges The Canadian economy produces many different goods and services—hamburgers, haircuts, cars, computers, and so on. GDP combines the value of these goods and services into a single measure. The diversity of products in the economy complicates the calculation of GDP because different products have different values.

Suppose, for example, that the economy produces four apples and three oranges. How do we compute GDP? We could simply add apples and oranges and conclude that GDP equals seven pieces of fruit. But this makes sense only if we thought apples and oranges had equal value, which is generally not true. (This would be even clearer if the economy had produced four watermelons and three grapes.)

To compute the total value of different goods and services, the national accounts use market prices because these prices reflect how much people are

---

Stocks and Flows

Many economic variables measure a quantity of something—a quantity of money, a quantity of goods, and so on. Economists distinguish between two types of quantity variables: stocks and flows. A **stock** is a quantity measured at a given point in time, whereas a **flow** is a quantity measured per unit of time.

A bathtub, as shown in Figure 2-2, is the classic example used to illustrate stocks and flows. The amount of water in the tub is a stock: it is the quantity of water in the tub at a given point in time. The amount of water coming out of the faucet is a flow: it is the quantity of water being added to the tub per unit of time. Note that we measure stocks and flows in different units. We say that the bathtub contains 50 *litres* of water,

but that water is coming out of the faucet at 5 *litres per minute*.

GDP is probably the most important flow variable in economics: it tells us how many dollars are flowing around the economy's circular flow per unit of time. When you hear someone say that the Canadian GDP is $1.6 trillion, you should understand that this means that it is $1.6 trillion *per year*. (Equivalently, we could say that Canadian GDP is $4.38 billion per day.)

Stocks and flows are often related. In the bathtub example, these relationships are clear. The stock of water in the tub represents the accumulation of the flow out of the faucet, and the flow of water represents the change in the stock. When building theories to explain economic variables, it is often useful to determine whether the variables are stocks or flows and whether any relationships link them.

Here are some examples of related stocks and flows that we study in future chapters:

➤ A person's wealth is a stock; his income and expenditure are flows.

➤ The number of unemployed people is a stock; the number of people losing their jobs is a flow.

➤ The amount of capital in the economy is a stock; the amount of investment is a flow.

➤ The government debt is a stock; the government budget deficit is a flow.

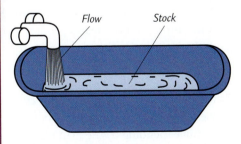

Figure 2-2 Stocks and Flows The amount of water in a bathtub is a stock: it is a quantity measured at a given moment in time. The amount of water coming out of the faucet is a flow: it is a quantity measured per unit of time.

willing to pay for a good or service. Thus, if apples cost $0.50 each and oranges cost $1.00 each, GDP would be

$$\text{GDP} = (\text{Price of Apples} \times \text{Quantity of Apples})$$
$$+ (\text{Price of Oranges} \times \text{Quantity of Oranges})$$
$$= (\$0.50 \times 4) + (\$1.00 \times 3)$$
$$= \$5.00.$$

GDP equals $5.00—the value of all the apples, $2.00, plus the value of all the oranges, $3.00.

Used Goods When a sporting goods company makes a package of hockey cards and sells it for 50 cents, that 50 cents is added to the nation's GDP. But what about when a collector sells a rare Rocket Richard card to another collector for $500? That $500 is not part of GDP. GDP measures the value of currently produced goods and services. The sale of the Rocket Richard card reflects the transfer of an asset, not an addition to the economy's income. Thus, the sale of used goods is not included as part of GDP. Similarly, when an individual buys a financial asset, this transaction is not counted as part of the GDP. This is because a swap of one pre-existing asset (money) for another (the stock or bond) does not involve any productive activity. For this same reason, however, the financial services provider's wages are counted in the GDP.

The Treatment of Inventories Imagine that a bakery hires workers to produce more bread, pays their wages, and then fails to sell the additional bread. How does this transaction affect GDP?

The answer depends on what happens to the unsold bread. Let's first suppose that the bread spoils. In this case, the firm has paid more in wages but has not received any additional revenue, so the firm's profit is reduced by the amount that wages have increased. Total expenditure in the economy hasn't changed because no one buys the bread. Total income hasn't changed either—although more is distributed as wages and less as profit. Because the transaction affects neither expenditure nor income, it does not alter GDP.

Now suppose, instead, that the bread is put into inventory to be sold later. In this case, the transaction is treated differently. The owners of the firm are assumed to have "purchased" the bread for the firm's inventory, and the firm's profit is not reduced by the additional wages it has paid. Because the higher wages raise total income, and greater spending on inventory raises total expenditure, the economy's GDP rises.

What happens later when the firm sells the bread out of inventory? This case is much like the sale of a used good. There is spending by bread consumers, but there is inventory disinvestment by the firm. This negative spending by the firm offsets the positive spending by consumers, so the sale out of inventory does not affect GDP.

The general rule is that when a firm increases its inventory of goods, this investment in inventory is counted as expenditure by the firm owners. Thus, production for inventory increases GDP just as much as production for final sale. A sale out of inventory, however, is a combination of positive spending (the purchase) and negative spending (inventory disinvestment), so it does not influence

GDP. This treatment of inventories ensures that GDP reflects the economy's current production of goods and services.

Intermediate Goods and Value Added Many goods are produced in stages: raw materials are processed into intermediate goods by one firm and then sold to another firm for final processing. How should we treat such products when computing GDP? For example, suppose a cattle rancher sells one-quarter pound of meat to McDonald's for $0.50, and then McDonald's sells you a hamburger for $1.50. Should GDP include both the meat and the hamburger (a total of $2.00), or just the hamburger ($1.50)?

The answer is that GDP includes only the value of final goods. Thus, the hamburger is included in GDP but the meat is not: GDP increases by $1.50, not by $2.00. The reason is that the value of intermediate goods is already included as part of the market price of the final goods in which they are used. To add the intermediate goods to the final goods would be double counting—that is, the meat would be counted twice. Hence, GDP is the total value of final goods and services produced.

One way to compute the value of all final goods and services is to sum the value added at each stage of production. The **value added** of a firm equals the value of the firm's output less the value of the intermediate goods that the firm purchases. In the case of the hamburger, the value added of the rancher is $0.50 (assuming that the rancher bought no intermediate goods), and the value added of McDonald's is $1.50 − $0.50, or $1.00. Total value added is $0.50 + $1.00, which equals $1.50. For the economy as a whole, the sum of all value added must equal the value of all final goods and services. Hence, GDP is also the total value added of all firms in the economy.

Housing Services and Other Imputations Although most goods and services are valued at their market prices when computing GDP, some are not sold in the marketplace and therefore do not have market prices. If GDP is to include the value of these goods and services, we must use an estimate of their value. Such an estimate is called an **imputed value.**

Imputations are especially important for determining the value of housing. A person who rents a house is buying housing services and providing income for the landlord; the rent is part of GDP, both as expenditure by the renter and as income for the landlord. Many people, however, live in their own homes. Although they do not pay rent to a landlord, they are enjoying housing services similar to those that renters purchase. To take account of the housing services enjoyed by homeowners, GDP includes the "rent" that these homeowners "pay" to themselves. Of course, homeowners do not in fact pay themselves this rent. Statistics Canada estimates what the market rent for a house would be if it were rented and includes that imputed rent as part of GDP. This imputed rent is included both in the homeowner's expenditure and in the homeowner's income.

Imputations also arise in valuing government services. For example, police officers, fire fighters, and legislators provide services to the public. Giving a value to these services is difficult because they are not sold in a marketplace and therefore do not have a market price. The national accounts include these services in GDP by valuing them at their cost. That is, the wages of these public servants are used as a measure of the value of their output.

In many cases, an imputation is called for in principle but, to keep things simple, is not made in practice. Because GDP includes the imputed rent on owner-occupied houses, one might expect it also to include the imputed rent on cars, lawn mowers, jewelry, and other durable goods owned by households. Yet the value of these rental services is left out of GDP. In addition, some of the output of the economy is produced and consumed at home and never enters the marketplace. For example, meals cooked at home are similar to meals cooked at a restaurant, yet the value added in meals at home is left out of GDP. Statistics Canada does not try to estimate the value of "household production" like this on any regular basis. Just to give some idea of the magnitude involved, however, the agency published an estimate for 1991. According to this study, household production in Canada is equal to about one-third of the measured GDP.

Finally, no imputation is made for the value of goods and services sold in the *underground economy*. The underground economy is the part of the economy that people hide from the government either because they wish to evade taxation or because the activity is illegal. Home construction, repairs, and cleaning services paid "under the table" are examples of the underground economy. The illegal drug trade is another.

Because the imputations necessary for computing GDP are only approximate, and because the value of many goods and services is left out altogether, GDP is an imperfect measure of total economic activity. These imperfections are most problematic when comparing standards of living across countries. The size of the underground economy, for instance, varies from country to country. Yet as long as the magnitude of these imperfections remains fairly constant over time, GDP is useful for comparing economic activity from year to year.

Real GDP versus Nominal GDP

Economists use the rules just described to compute GDP, which values the economy's total output of goods and services. But is GDP a good measure of economic well-being? Consider once again the economy that produces only apples and oranges. In this economy GDP is the sum of the value of all the apples produced and the value of all the oranges produced. That is,

$$GDP = (\text{Price of Apples} \times \text{Quantity of Apples})$$
$$+ (\text{Price of Oranges} \times \text{Quantity of Oranges}).$$

Economists call the value of goods and services measured at current prices **nominal GDP.** Notice that nominal GDP can increase either because prices rise or because quantities rise.

It is easy to see that GDP computed this way is not a good gauge of economic well-being. That is, this measure does not accurately reflect how well the economy can satisfy the demands of households, firms, and the government. If all prices doubled without any change in quantities, GDP would double. Yet it would be misleading to say that the economy's ability to satisfy demands has doubled, because the quantity of every good produced remains the same.

A better measure of economic well-being would tally the economy's output of goods and services without being influenced by changes in prices. For this purpose, economists use **real GDP,** which is the value of goods and services measured using a constant set of prices. That is, real GDP shows what would have happened to expenditure on output if quantities had changed but prices had not.

To see how real GDP is computed, imagine we wanted to compare output in 2009, 2010, and 2011 in our apple-and-orange economy. We could begin by choosing a set of prices, called *base-year prices,* such as the prices that prevailed in 2009. Goods and services are then added up using these base-year prices to value the different goods in both years. Real GDP for 2009 would be

$$\text{Real GDP} = (2009 \text{ Price of Apples} \times 2009 \text{ Quantity of Apples})$$
$$+ (2009 \text{ Price of Oranges} \times 2009 \text{ Quantity of Oranges}).$$

Similarly, real GDP in 2010 would be

$$\text{Real GDP} = (2009 \text{ Price of Apples} \times 2010 \text{ Quantity of Apples})$$
$$+ (2009 \text{ Price of Oranges} \times 2010 \text{ Quantity of Oranges}).$$

And real GDP in 2011 would be

$$\text{Real GDP} = (2009 \text{ Price of Apples} \times 2011 \text{ Quantity of Apples})$$
$$+ (2009 \text{ Price of Oranges} \times 2011 \text{ Quantity of Oranges}).$$

Notice that 2009 prices are used to compute real GDP for all three years. Because the prices are held constant, real GDP varies from year to year only if the quantities produced vary. Because a society's ability to provide economic satisfaction for its members ultimately depends on the quantities of goods and services produced, real GDP provides a better measure of economic well-being than nominal GDP.

The GDP Deflator

From nominal GDP and real GDP we can compute a third statistic: the GDP deflator. The **GDP deflator,** also called the implicit price deflator for GDP, is defined as the ratio of nominal GDP to real GDP:

$$\text{GDP Deflator} = \frac{\text{Nominal GDP}}{\text{Real GDP}}.$$

The GDP deflator reflects what's happening to the overall level of prices in the economy.

To understand this better, consider again an economy with only one good, bread. If P is the price of bread and Q is the quantity sold, then nominal GDP is the total number of dollars spent on bread in that year, $P \times Q$. Real GDP is the number of loaves of bread produced in that year times the price of bread in some base year, $P_{\text{base}} \times Q$. The GDP deflator is the price of bread in that year relative to the price of bread in the base year, P/P_{base}.

The definition of the GDP deflator allows us to separate nominal GDP into two parts: one part measures quantities (real GDP) and the other measures prices (the GDP deflator). That is,

$$\text{Nominal GDP} = \text{Real GDP} \times \text{GDP Deflator}.$$

Nominal GDP measures the current dollar value of the output of the economy. Real GDP measures output valued at constant prices. The GDP deflator measures the price of output relative to its price in the base year.

We can also write this equation as

$$\text{Real GDP} = \frac{\text{Nominal GDP}}{\text{GDP Deflator}}.$$

In this form, you can see how the deflator earns its name: it is used to deflate (that is, take inflation out of) nominal GDP to yield real GDP.

Chain-Weighted Measures of Real GDP

We have been discussing real GDP as if the prices used to compute this measure never change from their base-year values. If this were truly the case, over time the prices would become more and more dated. For instance, the price of computers has fallen substantially in recent years, while the price of a year at university has risen. When valuing the production of computers and education, it would be misleading to use the prices that prevailed ten or twenty years ago.

To solve this problem, the traditional approach involved Statistics Canada updating periodically the prices used to compute real GDP. About every five years, a new base year was chosen. The prices were then held fixed and used to measure year-to-year changes in the production of goods and services until the base year is updated once again.

Since 2001 Statistics Canada has been using a new policy for dealing with changes in the base year. In particular, it now calculates *chain-weighted* measures of real GDP. With these new measures, the base year changes continuously over time. In essence, average prices in 2008 and 2009 are used to measure real growth from 2008 to 2009; average prices in 2009 and 2010 are used to measure real growth from 2009 to 2010; and so on. These various year-to-year growth rates are then put together to form a "chain" that can be used to compare the output of goods and services between any two dates.

This new chain-weighted measure of real GDP is better than the more traditional measure because it ensures that the prices used to compute real GDP are never far out of date. For most purposes, however, the differences are not significant. It turns out that the two measures of real GDP are highly correlated with each other. As a practical matter, then, both the old and new measures of real GDP reflect the same thing: economy-wide changes in the production of goods and services.

The Components of Expenditure

Economists and policymakers care not only about the economy's total output of goods and services but also about the allocation of this output among alternative uses. The national accounts divide GDP into four broad categories of spending:

■ Consumption (*C*)
■ Investment (*I*)

- Government purchases (G)
- Net exports (NX).

Thus, letting Y stand for GDP,

$$Y = C + I + G + NX.$$

GDP is the sum of consumption, investment, government purchases, and net exports. Each dollar of GDP falls into one of these categories. This equation is an *identity*—an equation that must hold because of the way the variables are defined. It is called the **national accounts identity.**

Consumption consists of the goods and services bought by households. It is divided into three subcategories: durable goods, nondurable goods, and services.

FYI

Two Arithmetic Tricks for Working With Percentage Changes

For manipulating many relationships in economics, there is an arithmetic trick that is useful to know: *The percentage change of a product of two variables is approximately the sum of the percentage changes in each of the variables.*

To see how this trick works, consider an example. Let P denote the GDP deflator and Y denote real GDP. Nominal GDP is $P \times Y$. The trick states that

Percentage Change in $(P \times Y)$
≈ (Percentage Change in P)
+ (Percentage Change in Y).

For instance, suppose that in one year, real GDP is 100 and the GDP deflator is 2; the next year, real GDP is 103 and the GDP deflator is 2.1. We can calculate that real GDP rose by 3 percent and that the GDP deflator rose by 5 percent. Nominal GDP rose from 200 the first year to 216.3 the second year, an increase of 8.15 percent. Notice that the growth in nominal GDP (8.15 percent) is

approximately the sum of the growth in the GDP deflator (5 percent) and the growth in real GDP (3 percent).[1]

A second arithmetic trick follows as a corollary to the first: *The percentage change of a ratio is approximately the percentage change in the numerator minus the percentage change in the denominator.* Again, consider an example. Let Y denote GDP and L denote the population, so that Y/L is GDP per person. The second trick states

Percentage Change in (Y/L)
≈ (Percentage Change in Y)
− (Percentage Change in L).

For instance, suppose that in the first year, Y is 100,000 and L is 100, so Y/L is 1,000; in the second year, Y is 110,000 and L is 103, so Y/L is 1,068. Notice that the growth in GDP per person (6.8 percent) is approximately the growth in income (10 percent) minus the growth in population (3 percent).

---

[1] *Mathematical note:* The proof that this trick works begins with the chain rule from calculus:

$$d(PY) = Y \, dP + P \, dY.$$

Now divide both sides of this equation by PY to obtain:

$$d(PY)/(PY) = dP/P + dY/Y.$$

Notice that all three terms in this equation are percentage changes.

What Is Investment?

Newcomers to macroeconomics are sometimes confused by how macroeconomists use familiar words in new and specific ways. One example is the term "investment." The confusion arises because what looks like investment for an individual may not be investment for the economy as a whole. The general rule is that the economy's investment does not include purchases that merely reallocate existing assets among different individuals. Investment, as macroeconomists use the term, creates new capital.

Let's consider some examples. Suppose we observe these two events:

➤ Smith buys for himself a 100-year-old Victorian house.

➤ Jones builds for herself a brand-new contemporary house.

What is total investment here? Two houses, one house, or zero?

A macroeconomist seeing these two transactions counts only the Jones house as investment. Smith's transaction has not created new housing for the economy; it has merely reallocated existing housing. Smith's purchase is investment for Smith, but it is disinvestment for the person selling the house. By contrast, Jones has added new housing to the economy; her new house is counted as investment.

Similarly, consider these two events:

➤ Clarke buys $5 million in Air Canada stock from White on the Toronto Stock Exchange.

➤ Toyota sells $10 million in stock to the public and uses the proceeds to build a new car factory.

Here, investment is $10 million. In the first transaction, Clarke is investing in Air Canada stock, and White is disinvesting; there is no investment for the economy. By contrast, Toyota is using some of the economy's output of goods and services to add to its stock of capital; hence, its new factory is counted as investment.

Finally, consider this event:

➤ Black buys $2 million of Toyota stock.

This transaction simply involves Black swapping one financial asset for another. While such transactions are referred to as investments in the financial press, this transaction is not an investment in terms of how economists use this term.

Durable goods are goods that last a long time, such as cars and TVs. Nondurable goods are goods that last only a short time, such as food and clothing. Services include the work done for consumers by individuals and firms, such as haircuts and doctor visits.

Investment consists of goods bought for future use. Investment is also divided into three subcategories: business fixed investment, residential construction, and inventory investment. Business fixed investment is the purchase of new plant and equipment by firms. Residential construction is the purchase of new housing by households and landlords. Inventory investment is the increase in firms' inventories of goods (if inventories are falling, inventory investment is negative).

Government purchases are the goods and services bought by federal, provincial, and municipal governments. This category includes such items as military equipment, highways, and the services that government workers provide. It does not include transfer payments to individuals, such as the Canada Pension, employment insurance benefits, and welfare. Because transfer payments reallocate existing income and are not made in exchange for currently produced goods and services, they are not part of GDP.

The last category, **net exports,** accounts for trade with other countries. Net exports are the value of goods and services sold to other countries (our exports) minus the value of goods and services that foreigners sell us (our imports). Net exports are positive when the value of our exports is greater than the value of our imports and negative when the value of our imports is greater than the value of our exports. Net exports represent the net expenditure from abroad on our goods and services, which provides income for domestic producers.

CASE STUDY

GDP and Its Components

In 2008 the GDP of Canada totaled 1600.1 billion. This number is so large that it is almost impossible to comprehend. We can make it easier to understand by dividing it by the 2008 Canadian population of 33.21 million. In this way, we obtain GDP per person—the amount of expenditure for the average Canadian—which equaled $48,178 in 2008.

How did we use this GDP? Table 2-1 shows that just under 56 percent of it, or $26,834 per person, was spent on consumption. Investment was $9,572 per

TABLE 2-1

GDP and the Components of Expenditure: 2008

	Total (billions of dollars)	Per Person (dollars)
Gross Domestic Product	$1,600.1	$48,178
Consumption	891.2	26,834
Durables and nondurables	399.4	12,025
Services	491.8	14,808
Investment	317.9	9,572
Business fixed investment (factories, machinery)	201.0	6,052
Residential construction	108.2	3,258
Inventory investment	8.7	262
Government Purchases	367.0	11,050
Net Exports	25.4	765
Exports	562.2	16,928
Imports	536.8	16,163

Source: Statistics Canada, *National Income and Expenditure Accounts,*
http://www.statcan.gc.ca/pub/13-010-x/2009001/t/tab03-eng.htm

person, and government purchases were $11,050 per person (so government programs represented about 23 percent of the economy).

The average person bought $16,163 of goods imported from abroad and produced $16,928 of goods that were exported to other countries. Thus, net exports were a small positive amount. Since we earned more from selling to foreigners than we spent on foreign goods, we used up the difference by paying a small part of the annual interest obligation that the average Canadian owed on the country's foreign debt.

It is interesting to compare how Canadians use their GDP to the spending patterns in other countries. Even when compared to Americans, there are significant differences. While Canadians spend 33.5 percent of per-capita GDP on imports, Americans limit spending on imports to 17 percent. Canadians leave almost 23 percent of per-capita GDP to be spent by various levels of government, while Americans limit this proportion to 19 percent. ■

Several Measures of Income

The national accounts include other measures of income that differ slightly in definition from GDP. It is important to be aware of the various measures, because economists and the press often refer to them.

We can see how the alternative measures of income relate to one another, by starting with GDP and subtracting various quantities. As explained above, to obtain the gross total of Canadian income that flows from GDP, the GNP, we subtract the net income of foreigners who own factors of production employed in Canada:

$$\text{Gross National Income} = \text{GDP} - \text{Net Income of Foreigners.}$$

To obtain *net national income,* we subtract the depreciation of capital—the amount of the economy's stock of plants, equipment, and residential structures that wears out during the year:

$$\text{Net National Income} = \text{Gross National Income} - \text{Depreciation.}$$

In the national accounts, depreciation is called the *capital consumption allowances.* In 2008, it equaled about 13.1 percent of gross national income. Since the depreciation of capital is a cost of producing the output of the economy, subtracting depreciation shows the net result of economic activity. For this reason, some economists believe that net national income is a better measure of economic well-being.

The next adjustment in the national accounts is for indirect business taxes, such as sales taxes. These taxes, which make up 12 percent of net national income, place a wedge between the price that consumers pay for a good and the price that firms receive. Because firms never receive this tax wedge, it is not part of their income. Once we subtract indirect business taxes, we obtain a measure called simply *national income.* National income is a measure of how much everyone in the economy has earned.

The national accounts divide national income into four components, depending on the way the income is earned. The four categories, and the percentage of national income that each comprises, in 2008, are:

- *Compensation of employees (67.7 percent).* The wages and fringe benefits earned by workers
- *Corporate profits (17.7 percent).* The income of corporations after payments to their workers and creditors
- *Nonincorporated business income (7.9 percent).* The income of noncorporate businesses, such as small farms and law partnerships, and the income that landlords receive, including the imputed rent that homeowners "pay" to themselves, less expenses, such as depreciation
- *Net interest (6.7 percent).* The interest domestic businesses pay minus the interest they receive, plus interest earned from foreigners.

A series of adjustments takes us from national income to *personal income,* the amount of income that households and noncorporate businesses receive. Three of these adjustments are most important. First, we reduce national income by the amount that corporations earn but do not pay out, either because the corporations are retaining earnings or because they are paying taxes to the government. This adjustment is made by subtracting corporate profits (which equals the sum of corporate taxes, dividends, and retained earnings) and adding back dividends. Second, we increase national income by the net amount the government pays out in transfer payments. This adjustment equals government transfers to individuals minus social insurance contributions paid to the government. Third, we adjust national income to include the interest that households earn rather than the interest that businesses pay. This adjustment is made by adding personal interest income and subtracting net interest. (The difference between personal interest and net interest arises in part from the interest on the government debt.) Thus, personal income is

Personal Income = National Income
− Corporate Profits
− Social Insurance Contributions
− Net Interest
+ Dividends
+ Government Transfers to Individuals
+ Personal Interest Income.

Next, if we subtract personal tax payments, we obtain *personal disposable income:*

Personal Disposable Income = Personal Income
− Personal Tax Payments.

We are interested in personal disposable income because it is the amount households and noncorporate businesses have available to spend after satisfying their tax obligations to the government.

CASE STUDY

Seasonal Adjustment

Because real GDP and the other measures of income reflect how well the economy is performing, economists are interested in studying the quarter-to-quarter fluctuations in these variables. Yet when we start to do so, one fact leaps out: all these measures of income exhibit a regular seasonal pattern. The output of the economy rises during the year, reaching a peak in the fourth quarter (October, November, and December), and then falling in the first quarter (January, February, and March) of the next year. These regular seasonal changes are substantial. From the fourth quarter to the first quarter, real GDP falls on average about 5 percent.[2]

It is not surprising that real GDP follows a seasonal cycle. Some of these changes are attributable to changes in our ability to produce: for example, building homes is more difficult during the cold weather of winter than during other seasons. In addition, people have seasonal tastes: they have preferred times for such activities as vacations and Christmas shopping.

When economists study fluctuations in real GDP and other economic variables, they often want to eliminate the portion of fluctuations due to predictable seasonal changes. You will find that most of the economic statistics reported in the newspaper are *seasonally adjusted*. This means that the data have been adjusted to remove the regular seasonal fluctuations. Therefore, when you observe a rise or fall in real GDP or any other data series, you must look beyond the seasonal cycle for the explanation. ■

2-2 Measuring the Cost of Living: The Consumer Price Index

A dollar today doesn't buy as much as it did twenty years ago. The cost of almost everything has gone up. This increase in the overall level of prices is called *inflation,* and it is one of the primary concerns of economists and policymakers. In later chapters we examine in detail the causes and effects of inflation. Here we discuss how economists measure changes in the cost of living.

The Price of a Basket of Goods

The most commonly used measure of the level of prices is the **consumer price index (CPI).** Statistics Canada has the job of computing the CPI. It begins by collecting the prices of thousands of goods and services. Just as GDP turns the

---

[2] Robert B. Barsky and Jeffrey A. Miron, "The Seasonal Cycle and the Business Cycle," *Journal of Political* Economy 97 (June 1989): 503–534.

quantities of many goods and services into a single number measuring the value of production, the CPI turns the prices of many goods and services into a single index measuring the overall level of prices.

How should economists aggregate the many prices in the economy into a single index that reliably measures the price level? They could simply compute an average of all prices. Yet this approach would treat all goods and services equally. Because people buy more chicken than caviar, the price of chicken should have a greater weight in the CPI than the price of caviar. Statistics Canada weights different items by computing the price of a basket of goods and services purchased by a typical consumer. The CPI is the price of this basket of goods and services relative to the price of the same basket in some base year.

For example, suppose that the typical consumer buys 5 apples and 2 oranges every month. Then the basket of goods consists of 5 apples and 2 oranges, and the CPI is

$$CPI = \frac{(5 \times \text{Current Price of Apples}) + (2 \times \text{Current Price of Oranges})}{(5 \times 2002 \text{ Price of Apples}) + (2 \times 2002 \text{ Price of Oranges})}.$$

In this CPI, as in Canada at the time this book went to press, 2002 is the base year. The index tells us how much it costs now to buy 5 apples and 2 oranges relative to how much it cost to buy the same basket of fruit in 2002.

The consumer price index is the most closely watched index of prices, but it is not the only such index. Another is the producer price index, which measures the price of a typical basket of goods bought by firms rather than consumers. In addition to these overall price indices, Statistics Canada computes price indices for specific types of goods, such as food, housing, and energy, and for different cities in Canada. Another statistic, sometimes called *core inflation* and often a focus of the Bank of Canada in its Monetary Policy Reports, measures the increase in price of a consumer basket that excludes food and energy products. Because food and energy prices exhibit substantial short-run volatility, core inflation is sometimes viewed as a better gauge of ongoing inflation trends.

The CPI versus the GDP Deflator

Earlier in this chapter we saw another measure of prices—the implicit price deflator for GDP, which is the ratio of nominal GDP to real GDP. The GDP deflator and the CPI give somewhat different information about what's happening to the overall level of prices in the economy. There are three key differences between the two measures.

The first difference is that the GDP deflator measures the prices of all goods and services produced, whereas the CPI measures the prices of only the goods and services bought by consumers. Thus, an increase in the price of goods bought by firms or the government will show up in the GDP deflator but not in the CPI.

The second difference is that the GDP deflator includes only those goods produced domestically. Imported goods are not part of GDP and do not show up in the GDP deflator. Hence, an increase in the price of a Volkswagen made in Germany and sold in this country affects the CPI, because the Volkswagen is bought by consumers, but it does not affect the GDP deflator.

The third and most subtle difference results from the way the two measures aggregate the many prices in the economy. The CPI assigns fixed weights to the prices of different goods, whereas the GDP deflator assigns changing weights. In other words, the CPI is computed using a fixed basket of goods, whereas the GDP deflator allows the basket of goods to change over time as the composition of GDP changes. The following example shows how these approaches differ. Suppose that major frosts arrive early and destroy the nation's crop of apples. The quantity of apples produced falls to zero, and the price of the few apples that remain on grocers' shelves is driven sky-high. Because apples are no longer part of GDP, the increase in the price of apples does not show up in the GDP deflator. But because the CPI is computed with a fixed basket of goods that includes apples, the increase in the price of apples causes a substantial rise in the CPI.

Economists call a price index with a fixed basket of goods a *Laspeyres index* and a price index with a changing basket a *Paasche index*. Economic theorists have studied the properties of these different types of price indices to determine which is a better measure of the cost of living. The answer, it turns out, is that neither is clearly superior. When prices of different goods are changing by different amounts, a Laspeyres (fixed basket) index tends to overstate the increase in the cost of living because it does not take into account that consumers have the opportunity to substitute less expensive goods for more expensive ones. By contrast, a Paasche (changing basket) index tends to understate the increase in the cost of living. While it accounts for the substitution of alternative goods, it does not reflect the reduction in consumers' welfare that may result from such substitutions.

The example of the destroyed apple crop shows the problems with Laspeyres and Paasche price indices. Because the CPI is a Laspeyres index, it overstates the impact of the increase in apple prices on consumers: by using a fixed basket of goods, it ignores consumers' ability to substitute other foods for apples. By contrast, because the GDP deflator is a Paasche index, it understates the impact on consumers: the GDP deflator shows no rise in prices, yet surely the higher price of apples makes consumers worse off.[3] .

Luckily, the difference between the GDP deflator and the CPI is usually not large in practice. Figure 2-3 shows the percentage change in the GDP deflator and the percentage change in the CPI for each year since 1948. Both measures usually tell the same story about how quickly prices are rising.

---

[3] Because a Laspeyres index overstates inflation and a Paasche index understates inflation, one might strike a compromise by taking an average of the two measured rates of inflation. This is the approach taken by another type of index, called a *Fisher index*. In this case, the average is the square root of the product of the two measured rates.

FIGURE 2-3

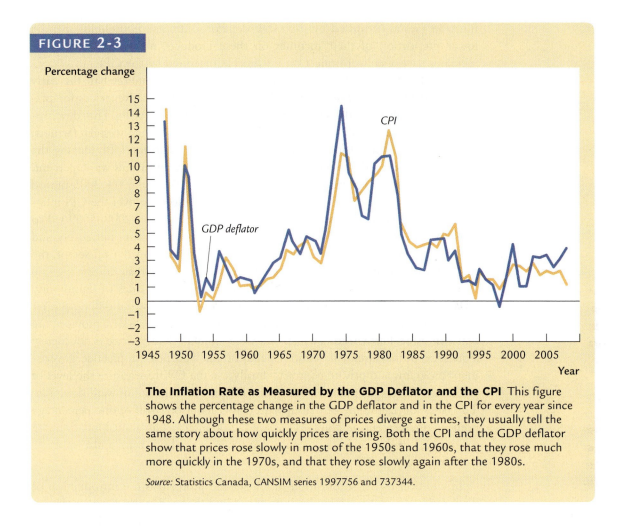

The Inflation Rate as Measured by the GDP Deflator and the CPI This figure shows the percentage change in the GDP deflator and in the CPI for every year since 1948. Although these two measures of prices diverge at times, they usually tell the same story about how quickly prices are rising. Both the CPI and the GDP deflator show that prices rose slowly in most of the 1950s and 1960s, that they rose much more quickly in the 1970s, and that they rose slowly again after the 1980s.

Source: Statistics Canada, CANSIM series 1997756 and 737344.

CASE STUDY

Difficulties in Measuring Inflation

From 1973 to 1976 prices in Canada rose at a very rapid pace. But exactly how much did they rise? This question was asked by public policymakers who had to judge the seriousness of the inflation problem. It was also asked by private decisionmakers: many private contracts, such as wage agreements and pensions, are indexed to correct for the effects of rising prices.

The magnitude of the price rise depends on which measure of prices one uses. According to the GDP deflator, prices rose an average of 10.5 percent per year during these four years. According to the CPI, prices rose 9.2 percent per year. Over the four-year period, the accumulated difference is over 5 percent.

This discrepancy is partly attributable to the large increase in the price of natural resources that occurred in the mid-1970s. A significant part of the Canadian economy involves primary commodity industries. As a result, big price increases in these commodities make a significant contribution to the overall

inflation rate as measured by the GDP deflator. But since households spend a lower proportion of their incomes on these products, natural resource price increases have a smaller impact on inflation as measured by the CPI.

A similar discrepancy between the two price indices emerged in the early 1990s and in the 2002–2005 periods. In the 1990s, the relative prices for primary commodities had fallen to their lowest levels in 60 years. This development, which was particularly hard on many individuals, such as western farmers, caused the GDP deflator to increase at a slower rate than the CPI. During the 1990–1994 period, the cumulative difference in the two measures was 6 percent. The cummulative difference (in the other direction) in the 2003–2005 period was 2.5 percent. This excess of the GDP deflator inflation rate over the CPI inflation rate has widened again in recent years. The recession in 2008–2009 led to even lower CPI inflation, but since world oil prices were rising noticeably, and since a significant fraction of Canada's GDP is derived from the oil sector, the GDP inflation rate was 2.7 percentage points higher in 2008 alone.

When price indices differ, as they did during these episodes of commodity price volatility, it is usually possible to identify the sources of the differences. Yet accounting for the differences is easier than deciding which index provides the better measure. Furthermore, which index one should use in practice is not merely a question of measurement; it also depends on one's purpose. In practice, government programs and private contracts usually use the CPI to measure the level of prices, despite the fact that we know the CPI is biased in the upward direction. The range of magnitude of that upward bias is about one-half of one percentage point to one percentage point.[4] Thus, we should interpret an annual inflation rate for the CPI in this range as evidence that we have reached "zero" inflation. ■

In addition to the substitution bias, a second problem is the introduction of new goods. When a new good is introduced into the marketplace, consumers are better off, because they have more products from which to choose. In effect, the introduction of new goods increases the real value of the dollar. Yet this increase in the purchasing power of the dollar is not reflected in a lower CPI.

A third problem is unmeasured changes in quality. When a firm changes the quality of a good it sells, not all of the good's price change reflects a change in the cost of living. Statistics Canada does its best to account for changes in the quality of goods over time. For example, with computers, it is possible to make some adjustment for the increase in speed and memory over time. But for other products this is less easy to do. For instance, if Ford increases the horsepower of a particular car model from one year to the next, the CPI will reflect the change: the quality-adjusted price of the car will not rise as fast as the unadjusted price. Yet many changes in quality, such as comfort or safety, are hard to measure. If unmeasured quality improvement (rather than unmeasured quality deterioration) is typical, then the measured CPI rises faster than it should.

---

[4] Allan Crawford, "Measuring Biases in the Canadian CPI," in *Bank of Canada Technical Report* No. 64(1993), and Pierre Fortin, "Do We Measure Inflation Correctly?" in *Zero Inflation: The Goal of Price Stability*, R.G. Lipsey, ed. (Toronto: C.D. Howe Institute, 1990).

2-3 Measuring Joblessness: The Unemployment Rate

One aspect of economic performance is how well an economy uses its resources. Because an economy's workers are its chief resource, keeping workers employed is a paramount concern of economic policymakers. The unemployment rate is the statistic that measures the percentage of those people wanting to work who do not have jobs. Some employment occurs because of friction in labour markets. For example, there are job vacancies in Alberta, but the unemployed in Newfoundland cannot take advantage of this fact. This sort of unemployment is often called structural. But some unemployment is cyclical; it occurs when the overall level of economic activity is insufficient to employ all those wanting work. The measured unemployment rate includes both structural and cyclical components.

Every month Statistics Canada computes the unemployment rate and many other statistics with which economists and policymakers monitor developments in the labour market. These statistics come from the Labour Force Survey of about 56,000 households. Based on the responses to survey questions, each adult (15 years and older) in each household is placed into one of three categories: employed, unemployed, or not in the labour force. A person is employed if he or she spent most of the previous week working at a paid job, as opposed to keeping house, going to school, or doing something else. A person is unemployed if he or she is not employed and is waiting

"Well, so long Eddie, the recession's over."

for the start date of a new job, is on temporary layoff, or has been looking for a job. A person who fits into neither of the first two categories, such as a full-time student or retiree, is not in the labour force. A person who wants a job but has given up looking—a *discouraged worker*—is counted as not being in the labour force.

The **labour force** is defined as the sum of the employed and unemployed, and the **unemployment rate** is defined as the percentage of the labour force that is unemployed. That is,

Labour Force = Number of Employed + Number of Unemployed,

and

$$\text{Unemployment Rate} = \frac{\text{Number of Unemployed}}{\text{Labour Force}} \times 100.$$

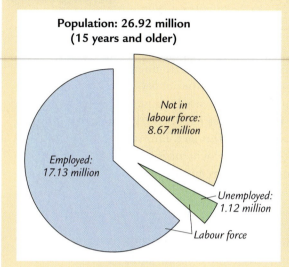

**Population: 26.92 million
(15 years and older)**

Employed:
17.13 million

Not in
labour force:
8.67 million

Unemployed:
1.12 million

Labour force

The Three Groups of the Population When Statistics Canada surveys the population, it places people in one of three categories: employed, unemployed, or not in the labour force. This figure shows the number of people in each category in 2008. The Canadian population was 33.2 million in 2008, while the sum of the three categories in this figure is only 26.92 million. The difference is explained by the fact that the Labour Force Survey deliberately excludes individuals in all of the following categories: (1) persons younger than 15 years old; (2) persons residing in the Yukon, the Northwest Territories, and on Native reserves; (3) full-time members of the armed forces; and inmates in institutions.

Source: Statistics Canada, http://www40.statcan.ca/01/cst01/econ10-eng.htm

A related statistic is the **labour-force participation rate,** the percentage of the adult population that is in the labour force:

$$\text{Labour-Force Participation Rate} = \frac{\text{Labour Force}}{\text{Adult Population}} \times 100.$$

Statistics Canada computes these statistics for the overall population and for groups within the population: men and women, teenagers and prime-age workers.

Figure 2-4 shows the breakdown of the population into the three categories for 2008. The statistics broke down as follows:

$$\text{Labour Force} = 17.13 + 1.12 = 18.25 \text{ million.}$$

$$\text{Unemployment Rate} = (1.12/18.25) \times 100 = 6.1\%.$$

$$\text{Labour-Force Participation Rate} = (18.25/26.92) \times 100 = 67.8\%.$$

Hence, about two-thirds of the adult population was in the labour force, and 6.1 percent of those in the labour force did not have a job.

CASE STUDY

Trends in Labour-Force Participation

The data on the labour market collected by Statistics Canada reflect not only economic developments, such as the booms and busts of the business cycle, but also a variety of social changes. Longer-term social changes in the roles of men and women in society, for example, are evident in the data on labour-force participation.

Just after World War II, men and women had very different economic roles. Only about one third of women were working or looking for work, in contrast to a seven-eights ratio for men. Since then, the difference between the participation rates of men and women has gradually diminished, as growing numbers of women have entered the labour force and some men have left it. Data for 2008 show that 63 percent of women were in the labour force, in contrast to 73 percent of men. As measured by labour-force participation, men and women are now playing a more equal role in the economy.

There are many reasons for this change. In part, it is due to new technologies, such as the washing machine, clothes dryer, refrigerator, freezer, and dishwasher, which have reduced the amount of time required to complete routine household tasks. In part, it is due to improved birth control, which has reduced the number of children born to the typical family. And in part, this change in women's role is due to changing political and social attitudes. Together these developments have had a profound impact, as demonstrated by these data.

Although the increase in women's labour-force participation is easily explained, the fall in men's participation may seem puzzling. There are several developments at work. First, young men now stay in school longer than their fathers and grandfathers did. Second, older men now retire earlier and live longer. Third, with more women employed, more fathers now stay at home to raise their children. Full-time students, retirees, and stay-at-home fathers are all counted as out of the labour force.

Looking ahead, many economists believe that labour-force participation for both men and women may gradually decline over the next several decades. The reason is demographic. People today are living longer and having fewer children today than did their counterparts in previous generations. As a result, the elderly are representing an increasing share of the population. Because the elderly are more often retired and less often members of the labour force, the rising elderly share of the population will tend to reduce the economy's labour-force participation rate.

Unemployment, GDP, and Okun's Law

What relationship should we expect to find between unemployment and real GDP? Because employed workers help to produce goods and services and unemployed workers do not, increases in the unemployment rate should be associated with decreases in real GDP. This negative relationship between cyclical unemployment and GDP is called **Okun's law,** after Arthur Okun, the economist who first studied it.[5]

---

[5] Arthur M. Okun, "Potential GNP: Its Measurement and Significance," in *Proceedings of the Business and Economics Statistics Section, American Statistical Association* (Washington, DC: American Statistical Association, 1962), 98–103; reprinted in Arthur M. Okun, *Economics for Policymaking* (Cambridge, MA: MIT Press, 1983), 145–158.

FIGURE 2-5

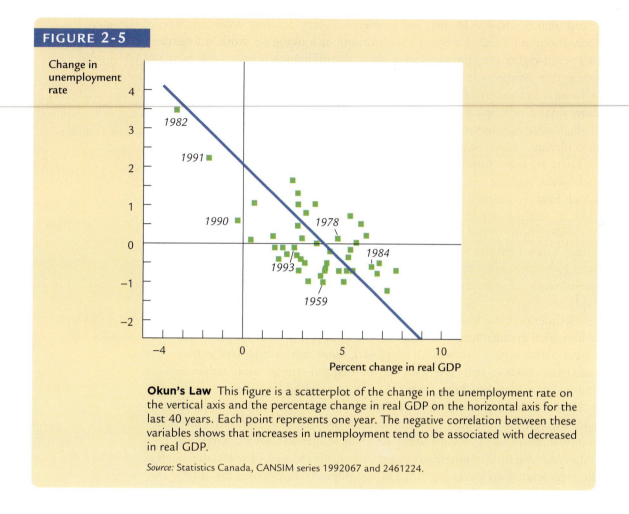

Okun's Law This figure is a scatterplot of the change in the unemployment rate on the vertical axis and the percentage change in real GDP on the horizontal axis for the last 40 years. Each point represents one year. The negative correlation between these variables shows that increases in unemployment tend to be associated with decreased in real GDP.

Source: Statistics Canada, CANSIM series 1992067 and 2461224.

Figure 2-5 uses annual data for Canada to illustrate Okun's law. This figure is a scatterplot—a scatter of points where each point represents one observation (in this case, the data for a particular year). The vertical axis represents the change in the unemployment rate from the previous year, and the horizontal axis represents the percentage change in GDP. This figure shows clearly that year-to-year changes in the unemployment rate are associated with year-to-year changes in real GDP.

We can be more precise about the magnitude of the Okun's law relationship. The summary line drawn through the scatter of points tells us that

$$\text{Change in the Unemployment Rate} = -0.5 \left[\left(\begin{array}{c} \text{Percent Change} \\ \text{in Real GDP} \end{array} \right) - 4 \right]$$

On average, real GDP has grown by about 4 percent each year since 1950; this normal growth is due to population growth, capital accumulation, and technological progress. Okun's law indicates that this is roughly the amount of growth that is necessary to keep the growth in the number of jobs in pace with the

growing size of the labour force—so that the unemployment rate can stay constant. If, however, real GDP growth is only 3 percent, this relationship tells us that the unemployment rate will rise by about one-half of one percentage point.

The implications for unemployment are more dramatic in a recession (when real GDP growth is negative). For example, when real growth is −1 percent, unemployment rises by 0.5 (1 + 4) = 2.5 percentage points. Policymakers often try to stabilize GDP growth around its long-run average value, with a view toward minimizing these disruptive swings in the unemployment rate. ∎

2-4 Conclusion: From Economic Statistics to Economic Models

The three statistics discussed in this chapter—gross domestic product, the consumer price index, and the unemployment rate—quantify the performance of the economy. Public and private decisionmakers use these statistics to monitor changes in the economy and to formulate appropriate policies. Economists use these statistics to develop and test theories about how the economy works.

In the chapters that follow, we examine some of these theories. That is, we build models that explain how these variables are determined and how economic policy affects them. Having learned how to measure economic performance, we now learn how to explain it.

Summary

1. Gross domestic product (GDP) measures both the total output of the economy and the total expenditure on the economy's output of goods and services. Ignoring the net income earned by foreigners operating in Canada, GDP also measures the total income of all Canadians.

2. Nominal GDP values goods and services at current prices. Real GDP values goods and services at constant prices. Real GDP rises only when the amount of goods and services has increased, whereas nominal GDP can rise either because output has increased or because prices have increased.

3. GDP is the sum of four categories of expenditure: consumption, investment, government purchases, and net exports.

4. The consumer price index (CPI) measures the price of a fixed basket of goods and services purchased by a typical consumer. Like the GDP deflator, which is the ratio of nominal GDP to real GDP, the CPI measures the overall level of prices.

5. The unemployment rate shows what fraction of those who would like to work do not have a job. When real GDP grows more slowly than its normal rate, unemployment rises.

KEY CONCEPTS

Gross domestic product (GDP)

Consumer price index (CPI)

Unemployment rate

National accounting

Stocks and flows

Value added

Imputed value

Nominal versus real GDP

GDP deflator

National accounts identity

Consumption

Investment

Government purchases

Net exports

Labour force

Labour-force participation rate

Okun's law

QUESTIONS FOR REVIEW

1. List the two things that GDP measures. How can GDP measure two things at once?

2. What does the consumer price index measure?

3. List the three categories used by Statistics Canada to classify everyone in the economy. How is the unemployment rate calculated?

4. Explain Okun's law.

PROBLEMS AND APPLICATIONS

1. Look at the newspapers for the past few days. What new economic statistics have been released? How do you interpret these statistics?

2. A farmer grows some wheat and sells it to a miller for $1.00. The miller turns the wheat into flour and then sells the flour to a baker for $3.00. The baker uses the flour to make bread and sells the bread to an engineer for $6.00. The engineer eats the bread. What is the value added by each person? What is GDP?

3. Suppose that a woman marries her butler. After they are married, her husband continues to wait on her as before, and she continues to support him as before (but as a husband rather than as an employee). How does the marriage affect GDP? How should it affect GDP?

4. Place each of the following transactions in one of the four components of expenditure: consumption, investment, government purchases, and net exports.

 a. A domestic airline manufacturer sells an airplane to the government.

 b. A domestic airline manufacturer sells an airplane to a domestic airline operator.

 c. A domestic airline manufacturer sells an airplane to Air France.

 d. A domestic airline manufacturer sells an airplane to a Canadian golf professional.

 e. A domestic airline manufacturer builds an airplane to be sold next year.

5. Find data on GDP and its components, and compute the percentage of GDP for the following components for 1950, 1970, and 1990.

 a. Personal consumption expenditures

 b. Gross private domestic investment

 c. Government purchases

 d. Net exports

 e. Federal government purchases

 f. Provincial and municipal government purchases

 g. Imports

Do you see any stable relationships in the data? Do you see any trends? (*Hint:* A good place to look for data is the Historical Statistical Supplement of the *Canadian Economic Observer*—an annual summary publication of Statistics Canada. Alternatively, you can access Statistics Canada over the internet. Follow the suggestions described in the preface to this book.

	Year 2000	Year 2000
Price of an automobile	$50,000	$60,000
Price of a loaf of bread	$10	$20
Number of auto-mobiles produced	100	120
Number of loaves of bread produced	500,000	400,000

6. Consider an economy that produces and consumes bread and automobiles. In the table below are data for two different years.

   a. Using the year 2000 as the base year, compute the following statistics for each year: nominal GDP, real GDP, the implicit price deflator for GDP, and a fixed-weight price index such as the CPI.

   b. How much have prices risen between year 2000 and year 2010? Compare the answers given by the Laspeyres and Paasche price indices. Explain the difference.

   c. Suppose you are a member of Parliament writing a bill to update the indexing provisions for the Canada Pension Plan. Would you use the GDP deflator or the CPI? Why?

7. Abby consumes only apples. In year 1, red apples cost $1 each, green apples cost $2 each, and Abby buys 10 red apples. In year 2, red apples cost $2, green apples cost $1, and Abby buys 10 green apples.

   a. Compute a consumer price index for apples for each year. Assume that year 1 is the base year in which the consumer basket is fixed. How does your index change from year 1 to year 2?

   b. Compute Abby's nominal spending on apples in each year. How does it change from year 1 to year 2?

   c. Using year 1 as the base year, compute Abby's real spending on apples in each year. How does it change from year 1 to year 2?

   d. Defining the implicit price deflator as nominal spending divided by real spending, compute the deflator for each year. How does the deflator change from year 1 to year 2?

   e. Suppose that Abby is equally happy eating red or green apples. How much has the true cost of living increased for Abby? Compare this answer to your answers to parts (a) and (d). What does this example tell you about Laspeyres and Paasche price indices?

8. Consider how each of the following events is likely to affect real GDP. Do you think the change in real GDP reflects a similar change in economic well-being?

   a. A hurricane in Ontario forces Canada's Wonderland to shut down for a month.

   b. The discovery of a new, easy-to-grow strain of wheat increases farm harvests.

   c. Increased hostility between unions and management sparks a rash of strikes.

   d. Firms throughout the economy experience falling demand, causing them to lay off workers.

   e. The government passes new environmental laws that prohibit firms from using production methods that emit large quantities of pollution.

   f. More high-school students drop out of school to take jobs mowing lawns.

   g. Fathers around the country reduce their workweeks to spend more time with their children.

9. In a speech that Senator Robert Kennedy gave when he was running for president of the United States in 1968, he said the following about GDP:

> [It] does not allow for the health of our children, the quality of their education, or the joy of their play. It does not include the beauty of our poetry or the strength of our marriages, the intelligence of our public debate or the integrity of our public officials. It measures neither our courage, nor our wisdom, nor our devotion to our country. It measures everything, in short, except that which makes life worthwhile, and it can tell us everything about America except why we are proud that we are Americans.

Was Robert Kennedy right? If so, why do we care about GDP?

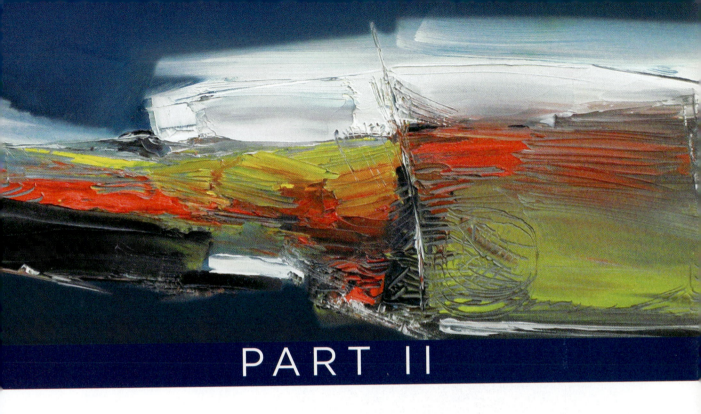

PART II

Classical Theory:
The Economy
in the Long Run

CHAPTER 3

National Income: Where It Comes From and Where It Goes

A large income is the best recipe for happiness I ever heard of.

— *Jane Austen*

T he most important macroeconomic variable is gross domestic product (GDP). As we have seen, GDP measures both a nation's total output of goods and services and its total income. To appreciate the significance of GDP, one needs only to take a quick look at international data: compared with their poorer counterparts, nations with a high level of GDP per person have everything from better childhood nutrition to more televisions per household. A large GDP does not ensure that all of a nation's citizens are happy, but it is surely the best recipe for happiness that macroeconomists have to offer.

This chapter addresses four groups of questions about the sources and uses of a nation's GDP:

- How much do the firms in the economy produce? What determines a nation's total income?

- Who gets the income from production? How much goes to compensate workers and how much goes to compensate owners of capital?

- Who buys the output of the economy? How much do households purchase for consumption, how much do households and firms purchase for investment, and how much does the government buy for public purposes?

- What equilibrates the demand for and supply of goods and services? What ensures that desired spending on consumption, investment, and government purchases equals the level of production?

To answer these questions, we must examine how the various parts of the economy interact.

A good place to start is the circular flow diagram. In Chapter 2 we traced the circular flow of dollars in a hypothetical economy that used one input (labour services) to produce one output. Figure 3-1 more accurately reflects how real economies function. It shows the linkages among the economic actors—

FIGURE 3-1

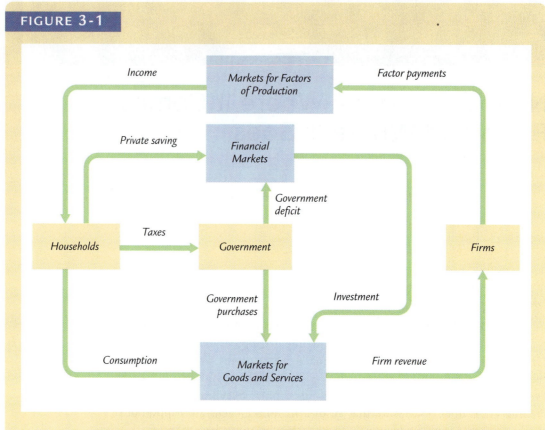

The Circular Flow of Dollars Through the Economy This figure is a more realistic version of the circular flow diagram found in Chapter 2. Each red box represents an economic actor—households, firms, and the government. Each blue box represents a type of market—the markets for goods and services, the markets for the factors of production, and financial markets. The green arrows show the flow of dollars among the economic actors through the three types of markets.

households, firms, and the government—and how dollars flow among them through the various markets in the economy.

Let's look at the flow of dollars from the viewpoints of these economic actors. Households receive income and use it to pay taxes to the government, to consume goods and services, and to save through the financial markets. Firms receive revenue from the sale of goods and services and use it to pay for the factors of production. Both households and firms borrow in financial markets to buy investment goods, such as housing, and factories. The government receives revenue from taxes, uses it to pay for government purchases. Any excess of tax revenue over government spending is called *public saving,* which can be either positive (a *budget surplus*) or negative (a *budget deficit*).

In this chapter we develop a basic classical model to explain the economic interactions depicted in Figure 3-1. We begin with firms and look at what determines their level of production (and, thus, the level of national income). Then we examine how the markets for the factors of production distribute this income to households. Next, we consider how much of this income households consume and how much they save. In addition to discussing the demand for goods and services arising from the consumption of households, we discuss the demand arising from investment and government purchases. Finally, we come full circle and examine how the demand for goods and services (the sum of consumption, investment, and government purchases) and the supply of goods and services (the level of production) are brought into balance.

3-1 What Determines the Total Production of Goods and Services?

An economy's output of goods and services—its GDP—depends on (1) its quantity of inputs, called the factors of production, and (2) its ability to turn inputs into output, as represented by the production function. We discuss each of these in turn.

The Factors of Production

Factors of production are the inputs used to produce goods and services. The two most important factors of production are capital and labour. Capital is the set of tools that workers use: the construction worker's crane, the accountant's calculator, and this book's authors' personal computers. Labour is the time people spend working. We use the symbol K to denote the amount of capital and the symbol L to denote the amount of labour. In later analyses, we will consider three inputs, by dividing capital into two components—physical capital (such as machines) and knowledge (sometimes referred to as human capital). But for now we simply assume a given state of knowledge and focus only on physical capital.

In this chapter we take the economy's factors of production as given. In other words, we assume that the economy has a fixed amount of capital and a fixed amount of labour. We write

$$K = \bar{K}.$$

$$L = \bar{L}.$$

The overbar means that each variable is fixed at some level. In Chapter 7 we examine what happens when the factors of production change over time, as they do in the real world. For now, to keep our analysis simple, we assume fixed amounts of capital and labour.

We also assume here that the factors of production are fully utilized—that is, that no resources are wasted. Again, in the real world, part of the labour force is unemployed, and some capital lies idle. In Chapter 6 we examine the reasons for unemployment, but for now we assume that capital and labour are fully employed.

The Production Function

The available production technology determines how much output is produced from given amounts of capital and labour. Economists express this relationship using a **production function.** Letting Y denote the amount of output, we write the production function as

$$Y = F(K, L).$$

This equation states that output is a function of the amount of capital and the amount of labour.

The production function reflects the available technology for turning capital and labour into output. If someone invents a better way to produce a good, the result is more output from the same amounts of capital and labour. Thus, technological change alters the production function.

Many production functions have a property called **constant returns to scale.** A production function has constant returns to scale if an increase of an equal percentage in all factors of production causes an increase in output of the same percentage. If the production function has constant returns to scale, then we get 10 percent more output when we increase both capital and labour by 10 percent. Mathematically, a production function has constant returns to scale if

$$zY = F(zK, zL)$$

for any positive number z. This equation says that if we multiply both the amount of capital and the amount of labour by some number z, output is also multiplied by z. In the next section we see that the assumption of constant returns to scale has an important implication for how the income from production is distributed.

As an example of a production function, consider production at a bakery. The kitchen and its equipment are the bakery's capital, the workers hired to make the bread are its labour, and the loaves of bread are its output. The bakery's production function shows that the number of loaves produced depends on the amount of equipment and the number of workers. If the production function has constant returns to scale, then doubling the amount of equipment and the number of workers doubles the amount of bread produced.

The Supply of Goods and Services

We can now see that the factors of production and the production function together determine the quantity of goods and services supplied, which in turn equals the economy's output. To express this mathematically, we write

$$Y = F(\bar{K}, \bar{L})$$

$$= \bar{Y}.$$

In this chapter, because we assume that the supplies of capital and labour and the technology are fixed, output is also fixed (at a level denoted here as $\bar{Y}$). When we discuss economic growth in Chapters 7 and 8, we will examine how increases in capital and labour and advances in technology lead to growth in the economy's output.

3-2 How Is National Income Distributed to the Factors of Production?

As we discussed in Chapter 2, the total output of an economy equals its total income. Because the factors of production and the production function together determine the total output of goods and services, they also determine national income. The circular flow diagram in Figure 3-1 shows that this national income flows from firms to households through the markets for the factors of production.

In this section we continue to develop our model of the economy by discussing how these factor markets work. Economists have long studied factor markets to understand the distribution of income. (For example, Karl Marx, the noted nineteenth-century economist, spent much time trying to explain the incomes of capital and labour. The political philosophy of communism was in part based on Marx's now-discredited theory.)

Here we examine the modern theory of how national income is divided among the factors of production. It is based on the classical (18th century) idea that prices adjust to balance supply and demand (applied here to the markets for the factors of production) together with the more recent (19th century) idea that the demand for each factor of production depends on the marginal productivity of that factor. This theory, called the *neoclassical theory of distribution,* is accepted by most economists today as the best place to start in understanding how the economy's income is distributed from firms to households.

Factor Prices

The distribution of national income is determined by factor prices. **Factor prices** are the amounts paid to the factors of production—the wage workers earn and the rent the owners of capital collect. As Figure 3-2 illustrates, the rental

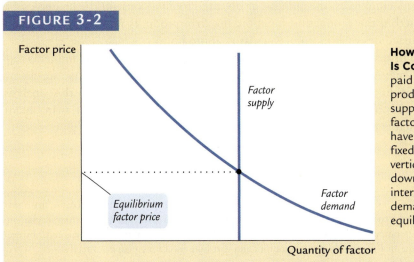

FIGURE 3-2

Factor price

Factor supply

Equilibrium factor price

Factor demand

Quantity of factor

How a Factor of Production Is Compensated The price paid to any factor of production depends on the supply and demand for that factor's services. Because we have assumed that supply is fixed, the supply curve is vertical. The demand curve is downward sloping. The intersection of supply and demand determines the equilibrium factor price.

price each factor of production receives for its services is in turn determined by the supply and demand for that factor. Because we have assumed that the economy's factors of production are fixed, the factor supply curve in Figure 3-2 is vertical. Regardless of the factor price, the quantity of the factor supplied to the market is the same. The intersection of the downward-sloping factor demand curve and the vertical supply curve determines the equilibrium factor price.

To understand factor prices and the distribution of income, we must examine the demand for the factors of production. Because factor demand arises from the thousands of firms that use capital and labour, we start by examining the decisions a typical firm makes about how much of these factors to employ.

The Decisions Facing the Competitive Firm

The simplest assumption to make about a typical firm is that it is competitive. A **competitive firm** is small relative to the markets in which it trades, so it has little influence on market prices. For example, our firm produces a good and sells it at the market price. Because many firms produce this good, our firm can sell as much as it wants without causing the price of the good to fall, or it can stop selling altogether without causing the price of the good to rise. Similarly, our firm cannot influence the wages of the workers it employs because many other local firms also employ workers. The firm has no reason to pay more than the market wage, and if it tried to pay less, its workers would take jobs elsewhere. Therefore, the competitive firm takes the prices of its output and its inputs as given *by market conditions*.

To make its product, the firm needs two factors of production, capital and labour. As we did for the aggregate economy, we represent the firm's production technology by the production function

$$Y = F(K, L),$$

where Y is the number of units produced (the firm's output), K the number of machines used (the amount of capital), and L the number of hours worked by the firm's employees (the amount of labour). Holding constant the technology as expressed in the production function, the firm produces more output if it uses more machines or if its employees work more hours.

The firm sells its output at a price P, hires workers at a wage W, and rents capital at a rate R. Notice that when we speak of firms renting capital, we are assuming that households own the economy's stock of capital. In this analysis, households rent out their capital, just as they sell their labour. The firm obtains both factors of production from the households that own them.[1]

---

[1] This is a simplification. In the real world, the ownership of capital is indirect because firms own capital and households own the firms. That is, real firms have two functions: owning capital and producing output. To help us understand how the factors of production are compensated, however, we assume that firms only produce output and that households own capital directly.

The goal of the firm is to maximize profit. *Profit* is revenue minus costs—it is what the owners of the firm keep after paying for the costs of production. Revenue equals $P \times Y$, the selling price of the good P multiplied by the amount of the good the firm produces Y. Costs include both labour costs and capital costs. Labour costs equal $W \times L$, the wage W times the amount of labour L. Capital costs equal $R \times K$, the rental price of capital R times the amount of capital K. We can write

$$\text{Profit} = \text{Revenue} - \text{Labour Costs} - \text{Capital Costs}$$

$$= PY - WL - RK.$$

To see how profit depends on the factors of production, we use the production function $Y = F(K, L)$ to substitute for Y to obtain

$$\text{Profit} = PF(K, L) - WL - RK.$$

This equation shows that profit depends on the product price P, the factor prices W and R, and the factor quantities L and K. The competitive firm takes the product price and the factor prices as given and chooses the amounts of labour and capital that maximize profit.

The Firm's Demand for Factors

We now know that our firm will hire labour and rent capital in the quantities that maximize profit. But how does it figure out what those profit-maximizing quantities are? To answer this question, we first consider the quantity of labour and then the quantity of capital.

The Marginal Product of Labour The more labour the firm employs, the more output it produces. The **marginal product of labour (*MPL*)** is the extra amount of output the firm gets from one extra unit of labour, holding the amount of capital fixed. We can express this using the production function:

$$MPL = F(K, L + 1) - F(K, L).$$

The first term on the right-hand side is the amount of output produced with K units of capital and $L + 1$ units of labour; the second term is the amount of output produced with K units of capital and L units of labour. This equation states that the marginal product of labour is the difference between the amount of output produced with $L + 1$ units of labour and the amount produced with only L units of labour.

Most production functions have the property of **diminishing marginal product:** holding the amount of capital fixed, the marginal product of labour decreases as the amount of labour increases. To see why, consider again the production of bread at a bakery. As a bakery hires more labour, it produces more bread. The *MPL* is the amount of extra bread produced when an extra unit of labour is hired. As more labour is added to a fixed amount of capital, however, the *MPL* falls. Fewer additional loaves are produced because workers are less productive when the

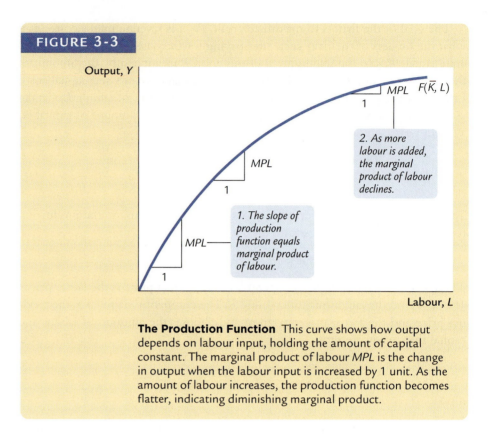

FIGURE 3-3

Output, Y

2. As more labour is added, the marginal product of labour declines.

MPL

1

$F(\bar{K}, L)$

MPL

1

MPL

1. The slope of production function equals marginal product of labour.

MPL

1

Labour, L

The Production Function This curve shows how output depends on labour input, holding the amount of capital constant. The marginal product of labour *MPL* is the change in output when the labour input is increased by 1 unit. As the amount of labour increases, the production function becomes flatter, indicating diminishing marginal product.

kitchen is more crowded. In other words, holding the size of the kitchen fixed, each additional worker adds fewer loaves of bread to the bakery's output.

Figure 3-3 graphs the production function. It illustrates what happens to the amount of output when we hold the amount of capital constant and vary the amount of labour. This figure shows that the marginal product of labour is the slope of the production function. As the amount of labour increases, the production function becomes flatter, indicating diminishing marginal product.

From the Marginal Product of Labour to Labour Demand When the competitive, profit-maximizing firm is deciding whether to hire an additional unit of labour, it considers how that decision would affect profits. It therefore compares the extra revenue from the increased production that results from the added labour to the extra cost of higher spending on wages. The increase in revenue from an additional unit of labour depends on two variables: the marginal product of labour and the price of the output. Because an extra unit of labour produces MPL units of output and each unit of output sells for P dollars, the extra revenue is $P \times MPL$. The extra cost of hiring one more unit of labour is the wage W. Thus, the change in profit from hiring an additional unit of labour is

$$\Delta\text{Profit} = \Delta\text{Revenue} - \Delta\text{Cost}$$

$$= (P \times MPL) - W.$$

The symbol Δ (called *delta*) denotes the change in a variable.

We can now answer the question we asked at the beginning of this section: How much labour does the firm hire? The firm's manager knows that if the extra revenue $P \times MPL$ exceeds the wage W, an extra unit of labour increases profit. Therefore, the manager continues to hire labour until the next unit would no longer be profitable—that is, until the MPL falls to the point where the extra revenue equals the wage. The competitive firm's demand for labour is determined by

$$P \times MPL = W.$$

We can also write this as

$$MPL = W/P.$$

W/P is the **real wage**—the payment to labour measured in units of output rather than in dollars. To maximize profit, the firm hires up to the point at which the marginal product of labour equals the real wage.

For example, again consider a bakery. Suppose the price of bread P is $2 per loaf, and a worker earns a wage W of $20 per hour. The real wage W/P is 10 loaves per hour. In this example, the firm keeps hiring workers as long as the additional worker would produce at least 10 loaves per hour. When the MPL falls to 10 loaves per hour or less, hiring additional workers is no longer profitable.

Figure 3-4 shows how the marginal product of labour depends on the amount of labour employed (holding the firm's capital stock constant). That is, this figure graphs the MPL schedule. Because the MPL diminishes as the amount of labour increases, this curve slopes downward. For any given real wage, the firm hires up to the point at which the MPL equals the real wage. Hence, the MPL schedule is also the firm's labour demand curve.

FIGURE 3-4

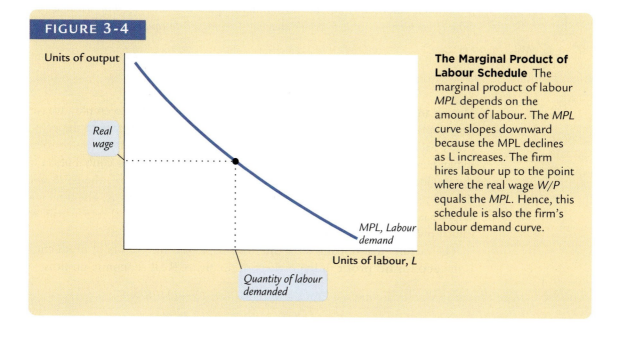

The Marginal Product of Labour Schedule The marginal product of labour MPL depends on the amount of labour. The MPL curve slopes downward because the MPL declines as L increases. The firm hires labour up to the point where the real wage W/P equals the MPL. Hence, this schedule is also the firm's labour demand curve.

The Marginal Product of Capital and Capital Demand The firm decides how much capital to rent in the same way it decides how much labour to hire. The **marginal product of capital (MPK)** is the amount of extra output the firm gets from an extra unit of capital, holding the amount of labour constant:

$$MPK = F(K + 1, L) - F(K, L).$$

Thus, the marginal product of capital is the difference between the amount of output produced with $K + 1$ units of capital and that produced with only K units of capital.

Like labour, capital is subject to diminishing marginal product. Once again consider the production of bread at a bakery. The first several ovens installed in the kitchen will be very productive. However, if the bakery installs more and more ovens, while holding its labour force constant, it will eventually contain more ovens than its employees can effectively operate. Hence, the marginal product of the last few ovens is lower than that of the first few.

The increase in profit from renting an additional machine is the extra revenue from selling the output of that machine minus the machine's rental price:

$$\Delta\text{Profit} = \Delta\text{Revenue} - \Delta\text{Cost}$$

$$= (P \times MPK) - R.$$

To maximize profit, the firm continues to rent more capital until the MPK falls to equal the real rental price:

$$MPK = R/P.$$

The **real rental price of capital** is the rental price measured in units of goods rather than in dollars.

To sum up, the competitive, profit-maximizing firm follows a simple rule about how much labour to hire and how much capital to rent. *The firm demands each factor of production until that factor's marginal product falls to equal its real factor price.*

The Division of National Income

Having analyzed how a firm decides how much of each factor to employ, we can now explain how the markets for the factors of production distribute the economy's total income. If all firms in the economy are competitive and profit-maximizing, then each factor of production is paid its marginal contribution to the production process. The real wage paid to each worker equals the MPL, and the real rental price paid to each owner of capital equals the MPK. The total real wages paid to labour are therefore $MPL \times L$, and the total real return paid to capital owners is $MPK \times K$.

The income that remains after the firms have paid the factors of production is the **economic profit** of the owners of the firms. Real economic profit is

$$\text{Economic Profit} = Y - (MPL \times L) - (MPK \times K).$$

Because we want to examine the distribution of national income, we rearrange the terms as follows:

$$Y = (MPL \times L) + (MPK \times K) + \text{Economic Profit}.$$

Total income is divided among the return to labour, the return to capital, and economic profit.

How large is economic profit? The answer is surprising: if the production function has the property of constant returns to scale, as is often thought to be the case, then economic profit must be zero. That is, nothing is left after the factors of production are paid. This conclusion follows from a famous mathematical result called *Euler's theorem*,[2] which states that if the production function has constant returns to scale, then

$$F(K, L) = (MPK \times K) + (MPL \times L).$$

If each factor of production is paid its marginal product, then the sum of these factor payments equals total output. In other words, constant returns to scale, profit maximization, and competition together imply that economic profit is zero.

If economic profit is zero, how can we explain the existence of "profit" in the economy? The answer is that the term "profit" as normally used is different from economic profit. We have been assuming that there are three types of agents: workers, owners of capital, and owners of firms. Total income is divided among wages, return to capital, and economic profit. In the real world, however, most firms own rather than rent the capital they use. Because firm owners and capital owners are the same people, economic profit and the return to capital are often lumped together. If we call this alternative definition **accounting profit,** we can say that

$$\text{Accounting Profit} = \text{Economic Profit} + (MPK \times K).$$

Under our assumptions—constant returns to scale, profit maximization, and competition—economic profit is zero. If these assumptions approximately describe the world, then the "profit" in the national income accounts must be mostly the return to capital.

We can now answer the question posed at the beginning of this chapter about how the income of the economy is distributed from firms to households. Each factor of production is paid its marginal product, and these factor payments exhaust total output. *Total output is divided between the payments to capital and the payments to labour, depending on their marginal productivities.*

---

[2] *Mathematical note:* To prove Euler's theorem, begin with the definition of constant returns to scale: $zY = F(zK, zL)$. Now differentiate with respect to z to obtain

$$Y = F_1(zK, zL)\ K + F_2(zK, zL)\ L,$$

where F_1 and F_2 denote partial derivatives with respect to the first and second arguments of the function. Evaluating this expression at $z = 1$, and noting that the partial derivatives equal the marginal products, yields Euler's theorem.

The Black Death and Factor Prices

According to the neoclassical theory of distribution, factor prices equal the marginal products of the factors of production. Because the marginal products depend on the quantities of the factors, a change in the quantity of any one factor alters the marginal products of all the factors. Therefore, a change in the supply of a factor alters equilibrium factor prices.

Fourteenth-century Europe provides a vivid example of how factor quantities affect factor prices. The outbreak of the bubonic plague—the Black Death—in 1348 reduced the population of Europe by about one-third within a few years. Because the marginal product of labour increases as the amount of labour falls, this massive reduction in the labour force raised the marginal product of labour. (The economy moved to the left along the curves in Figures 3-3 and 3-4.) Real wages did increase substantially during the plague years—doubling, by some estimates. The peasants who were fortunate enough to survive the plague enjoyed economic prosperity.

The reduction in the labour force caused by the plague also affected the return to land, the other major factor of production in medieval Europe. With fewer workers available to farm the land, an additional unit of land produced less additional output. This fall in the marginal product of land led to a decline in real rents of 50 percent or more. Thus, while the peasant classes prospered, the landed classes suffered reduced incomes.[3] ∎

The Cobb-Douglas Production Function

What production function describes how actual economies turn capital and labour into GDP? The answer to this question came from a historic collaboration between a U.S. senator and a mathematician.

Paul Douglas was a U.S. senator from Illinois from 1949 to 1966. In 1927, however, when he was still a professor of economics, he noticed a surprising fact: the division of national income between capital and labour had been roughly constant over a long period. In other words, as the economy grew more prosperous over time, the total income of workers and the total income of capital owners grew at almost exactly the same rate. This observation caused Douglas to wonder what conditions lead to constant factor shares.

Douglas asked Charles Cobb, a mathematician, what production function, if any, would produce constant factor shares if factors always earned their marginal products. The production function would need to have the property that

$$\text{Capital Income} = MPK \times K = \alpha Y,$$

and

$$\text{Labour Income} = MPL \times L = (1 - \alpha) \, Y,$$

---

[3] Carlo M. Cipolla, *Before the Industrial Revolution: European Society and Economy, 1000–1700,* 2d ed. (New York: Norton, 1980), 200-202.

where α is a constant between zero and one that measures capital's share of income. That is, α determines what share of income goes to capital and what share goes to labour. Cobb showed that the function with this property is

$$Y = F(K,L) = A\,K^{\alpha}L^{1-\alpha},$$

where A is a parameter greater than zero that measures the productivity of the available technology. This function became known as the *Cobb–Douglas production function.*

Let's take a closer look at some of the properties of this production function. First, the Cobb–Douglas production function has constant returns to scale. That is, if capital and labour are increased by the same proportion, then output increases by that proportion as well.[4]

Next, consider the marginal products for the Cobb–Douglas production function. The marginal product of labour is[5]

$$MPL = (1 - \alpha)\,AK^{\alpha}L^{-\alpha},$$

and the marginal product of capital is

$$MPK = \alpha AK^{\alpha-1}L^{1-\alpha}.$$

From these equations, recalling that α is between zero and one, we can see what causes the marginal products of the two factors to change. An increase in the amount of capital raises the *MPL* and reduces the *MPK*. Similarly, an increase in the amount of labour reduces the *MPL* and raises the *MPK*. A technological advance that increases the parameter A raises the marginal product of both factors proportionately.

---

[4] *Mathematical note:* To prove that the Cobb-Douglas production function has constant returns to scale, examine what happens when we multiply capital and labor by a constant z:

$$F(zK, zL) = A(zK)^{\alpha}(zL)^{1-\alpha}.$$

Expanding terms on the right,

$$F(zK, zL) = Az^{\alpha}\,K^{\alpha}z^{1-\alpha}L^{1-\alpha}.$$

Rearranging to bring like terms together, we get

$$F(zK, zL) = z^{\alpha}\,z^{1-\alpha}AK^{\alpha}L^{1-\alpha}.$$

Since $z^{\alpha}\,z^{1-\alpha} = z$, our function becomes

$$F(zK, zL) = zAK^{\alpha}L^{1-\alpha}.$$

But $AK^{\alpha}L^{1-\alpha} = F(K, L)$. Thus,

$$F(zK, zL) = zF(K, L) = zY.$$

Hence, the amount of output Y increases by the same factor z, which implies that this production function has constant returns to scale.

[5] *Mathematical note:* Obtaining the formulas for the marginal products from the production function requires a bit of calculus. To find the *MPL*, differentiate the production function with respect to L. This is done by multiplying by the exponent $(1 - \alpha)$, and then subtracting 1 from the old exponent to obtain the new exponent, $-\alpha$. Similarly, to obtain the *MPK*, differentiate the production function with respect to K.

The marginal products for the Cobb–Douglas production function can also be written as[6]

$$MPL = (1 - \alpha)Y/L.$$

$$MPK = \alpha Y/K.$$

The *MPL* is proportional to output per worker, and the *MPK* is proportional to output per unit of capital. Y/L is called *average labour productivity,* and Y/K is called *average capital productivity.* If the production function is Cobb–Douglas, then the marginal productivity of a factor is proportional to its average productivity.

We can now verify that if factors earn their marginal products, then the parameter α indeed tells us how much income goes to labour and how much goes to capital. The total wage bill, which we have seen is $MPL \times L$, equals $(1 - \alpha)Y$. Therefore, $(1 - \alpha)$ is labour's share of output. Similarly, the total return to capital, $MPK \times K$, is αY, and α is capital's share of output. The ratio of labour income to capital income is a constant, $(1 - \alpha)/\alpha$, just as Douglas observed. The factor shares depend only on the parameter α, not on the amounts of capital or labour or on the state of technology as measured by the parameter A.

More recent data are also consistent with the Cobb–Douglas production function. Figure 3-5 shows the ratio of labour income to total income in Canada from 1945 to 2005. Despite the many changes in the economy over more than 60 years, this ratio has remained about 0.67. This division of income is easily explained by a Cobb–Douglas production function in which the parameter α is about 0.33. According to this parameter, capital receives one-third of income, and labour receives two-thirds.

The Cobb-Douglas production function is not the last word in explaining the economy's production of goods and services or the distribution of national income between capital and labor. It is, however, a good place to start.

CASE STUDY

Labour Productivity as the Key Determinant of Real Wages

The neoclassical theory of distribution tells us that the real wage W/P equals the marginal product of labour. The Cobb-Douglas production function tells us that the marginal product of labour is proportional to average labour productivity Y/L. If this theory is right, then workers should enjoy rapidly rising living standards when labour productivity is growing robustly. Is this true?

Table 3-1 presents some data on growth in productivity and real wages for the Canadian economy, over a 46-year period. From 1961 to 2007, productivity as measured by output per unit of labour input grew at 1.7 percent per year. Real wages grew at the same rate of 1.7 percent. With a growth rate such as this, productivity and real wages double about every 42 years.

---

[6] *Mathematical note:* To check these expressions for the marginal products, substitute in the production function for Y to show that these expressions are equivalent to the earlier formulas for the marginal products.

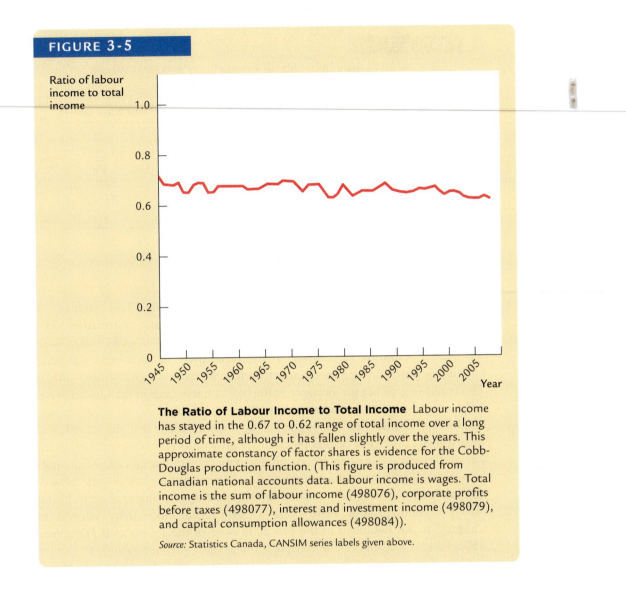

FIGURE 3-5

The Ratio of Labour Income to Total Income Labour income has stayed in the 0.67 to 0.62 range of total income over a long period of time, although it has fallen slightly over the years. This approximate constancy of factor shares is evidence for the Cobb-Douglas production function. (This figure is produced from Canadian national accounts data. Labour income is wages. Total income is the sum of labour income (498076), corporate profits before taxes (498077), interest and investment income (498079), and capital consumption allowances (498084)).

Source: Statistics Canada, CANSIM series labels given above.

Productivity growth varies over time. The table shows the data for four shorter periods that economists have identified as having different productivity experiences. (Case Studies in Chapter 8 examine some of the reasons for these changes in productivity growth.) Around 1973, both the Canadian and U.S. economies experienced a significant slowdown in productivity growth. The cause of the productivity slowdown is not well understood, but the link between productivity and real wages is exactly as standard theory predicts. The slowdown in productivity growth from 3.0% in the earlier period (1961–1973) to 1.3% in the 1973–1981 period coincided with a slowdown in real wage growth from 3.9 to 1.4 percent per year. A similar correspondence between productivity growth and real wage growth is evident in the more recent sub-periods in Table 3-1.

There are two disturbing features about recent developments in Canada. The first involves comparing our productivity performance with that in the United States. In the United States, productivity growth picked up again around 1995,

TABLE 3-1		
Annual Growth in Labour Productivity and Real Wages: The Canadian Experience		
Time Period	**Labour Productivity Growth**	**Real Wage Growth**
1961–2007	1.7%	1.7%
1961–1973	3.0%	3.9%
1973–1981	1.3%	1.4%
1981–1989	1.2%	0.3%
1989–2000	1.5%	0.8%
2000–2007	1.0%	1.2%

Source: www.csls.ca/ipm/17/IPM-17-sharpe.pdf

and many observers hailed the arrival of the "new economy." This productivity acceleration is often attributed to the spread of computers and information technology. As theory predicts, growth in real wages picked up as well—but only in the United States. As we can see in the table, there has not been the same rebound in productivity growth (and, therefore, in real wage growth) in Canada. The resulting growing gap between material living standards in the United States and Canada has many Canadian policymakers concerned.

The second issue that has puzzled analysts somewhat is that since 1981, real wage growth has lagged behind productivity growth to some extent. Contrary to Canada's earlier experience, labour productivity growth has exceeded real wage growth by an accumulated amount equal to 37 percent over this 26-year period. You can learn the reasons by reading an article written by Sharpe, Arsenault, and Harrison entitled "Why Have Real Wages Lagged Productivity Growth in Canada?" It was published in the Fall 2008 issue of the *International Productivity Monitor* and is available on the Website given as the source for Table 3-1.

Overall, the moral of the story is that productivity growth is important. When Canadians have done poorly achieving productivity increases, we have paid the price in terms of having to endure quite meager increases in our material standard of living. We conclude that both theory and history confirm the close link between labour productivity and real wages. This lesson is the key to understanding why workers today are better off than workers in previous generations. ∎

3-3 What Determines the Demand for Goods and Services?

We have seen what determines the level of production and how the income from production is distributed to workers and owners of capital. We now continue our tour of the circular flow diagram, Figure 3-1, and examine how the output from production is used.

In Chapter 2 we identified the four components of GDP:

- Consumption (C)
- Investment (I)
- Government purchases (G)
- Net exports (NX).

The circular flow diagram contains only the first three components. For now, to simplify the analysis, we assume a *closed economy*—a country that does not trade with other countries. Thus, net exports are always zero. (We examine the macroeconomics of *open economies* in Chapter 5.)

A closed economy has three uses for the goods and services it produces. These three components of GDP are expressed in the national accounts identity:

$$Y = C + I + G.$$

Households consume some of the economy's output; firms and households use some of the output for investment; and the government buys some of the output for public purposes. We want to see how GDP is allocated among these three uses.

Consumption

When we eat food, wear clothing, or go to a movie, we are consuming some of the output of the economy. All forms of consumption together make up almost 56 percent of GDP. Because consumption is so large, macroeconomists have devoted much energy to studying how households decide how much to consume. Chapter 17 examines this work in detail. Here we consider the simplest description of the aggregate consumption behaviour of all households.

Households receive income from their labour and their ownership of capital, pay taxes to the government, and then decide how much of their after-tax income to consume and how much to save. As we discussed in Section 3-2, the income that households receive equals the output of the economy Y. The government then taxes households an amount T. (Although the government imposes many kinds of taxes, such as personal and corporate income taxes and sales taxes, for our purposes in this introductory analysis we can lump all these taxes together.) We define income after the payment of all taxes, $Y - T$, as **disposable income.** Households divide their disposable income between consumption and saving.

We assume that the level of consumption depends directly on the level of disposable income. The higher is disposable income, the greater is consumption. Thus,

$$C = C(Y - T).$$

This equation states that consumption is a function of disposable income. The relationship between consumption and disposable income is called the **consumption function.**

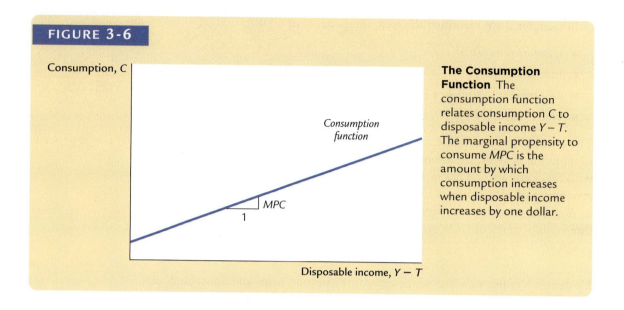

FIGURE 3-6

Consumption, C

Consumption function

MPC
1

Disposable income, Y − T

The Consumption Function The consumption function relates consumption C to disposable income Y − T. The marginal propensity to consume MPC is the amount by which consumption increases when disposable income increases by one dollar.

The **marginal propensity to consume (MPC)** is the amount by which consumption changes when disposable income increases by one dollar. The MPC is between zero and one: an extra dollar of income increases consumption, but by less than one dollar. Thus, if households obtain an extra dollar of income, they save a portion of it. For example, if the MPC is 0.7, then households spend 70 cents of each additional dollar of disposable income on consumer goods and services and save 30 cents.

Figure 3-6 illustrates the consumption function. The slope of the consumption function tells us how much consumption increases when disposable income increases by one dollar. That is, the slope of the consumption function is the MPC.

Investment

Both firms and households purchase investment goods. Firms buy investment goods to add to their stock of capital and to replace existing capital as it wears out. Households buy new houses, which are also part of investment. Total investment in Canada averages about 18 percent of GDP.

The quantity of investment goods demanded depends on many things such as the rate of increase in new knowledge, the expectations firms have about the likelihood that households are ready to spend, the level of taxes and the **interest rate.** The interest rate matters since it measures the cost of the funds used to finance investment. For an investment project to be profitable, its return (the revenue from increased future production of goods and services) must exceed its cost (the payments for borrowed funds). If the interest rate rises, fewer investment projects are profitable, and the quantity of investment goods demanded falls.

For example, suppose that a firm is considering whether it should build a $1 million factory that would yield a return of $100,000 per year, or 10 percent. The firm compares this return to the cost of borrowing the $1 million. If the

The Many Different Interest Rates

If you look in the business section of a newspaper, you will find many different interest rates reported. By contrast, throughout this book, we will talk about "the" interest rate, as if there were only one interest rate in the economy. The only distinction we will make is between the nominal interest rate (which is not corrected for inflation) and the real interest rate (which is corrected for inflation). Almost all of the interest rates reported in the newspaper are nominal.

Why does the newspaper report so many interest rates? The various interest rates differ in three ways:

➤ *Term*. Some loans in the economy are for short periods of time, even as short as overnight. Other loans are for thirty years or even longer. The interest rate on a loan depends on its term. Long-term interest rates are usually, but not always, higher than short-term interest rates.

➤ *Credit risk*. In deciding whether to make a loan, a lender must take into account the probability that the borrower will repay. The law allows borrowers to default on their loans by declaring bankruptcy. The higher the perceived probability of default, the higher the interest rate. The safest credit risk is the government, and so government bonds tend to pay a low interest rate. At the other extreme, financially shaky corporations can raise funds only by issuing *junk bonds,* which pay a high interest rate to compensate for the high risk of default.

➤ *Currency denomination.* A lender must be concerned about possible changes in international exchange rates. For example, an American who lends money to a provincial government by buying a bond denominated in Canadian dollars will form expectations concerning the likely change in the value of the Canadian dollar over the period she is making this loan. If the Canadian dollar is expected to fall in value, perhaps due to uncertainty concerning Quebec separation, Canadian borrowers have to pay a higher interest rate than do borrowers in the United States. Thus, the spread between Canadian and American interest rates widens whenever the Canadian dollar is perceived as "weak."

When you see two different interest rates in the newspaper, you can almost always explain the difference by considering the term, credit risk, and currency denomination of the loan.

Although there are many different domestic interest rates, macroeconomists can usually ignore these distinctions. The various interest rates tend to move up and down together. For many purposes, it is acceptable to assume that there is only one interest rate.

interest rate is below 10 percent, the firm borrows the money in financial markets and makes the investment. If the interest rate is above 10 percent, the firm forgoes the investment opportunity and does not build the factory.

The firm makes the same investment decision even if it does not have to borrow the $1 million but rather uses its own funds. The firm can always deposit this money in a bank or a money market fund and earn interest on it. Building the factory is more profitable than the deposit if and only if the interest rate is less than the 10 percent return on the factory.

A person wanting to buy a new house faces a similar decision. The higher the interest rate, the greater the cost of carrying a mortgage. A $100,000 mortgage costs $8,000 per year if the interest rate is 8 percent and $10,000 per year if the interest rate is 10 percent. As the interest rate rises, the cost of owning a home rises, and the demand for new homes falls.

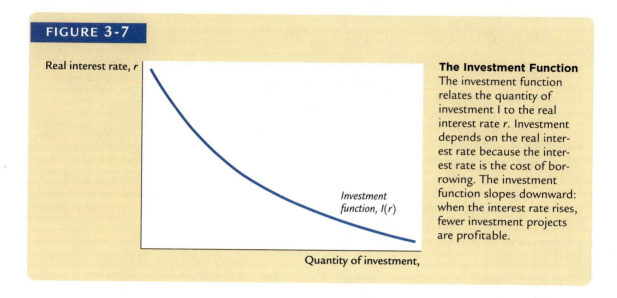

FIGURE 3-7

Real interest rate, r

Investment function, $I(r)$

Quantity of investment,

The Investment Function
The investment function relates the quantity of investment I to the real interest rate r. Investment depends on the real interest rate because the interest rate is the cost of borrowing. The investment function slopes downward: when the interest rate rises, fewer investment projects are profitable.

When studying the role of interest rates in the economy, economists distinguish between the nominal interest rate and the real interest rate. This distinction is relevant when the overall level of prices is changing. The **nominal interest rate** is the interest rate as usually reported: it is the rate of interest that investors pay to borrow money. The **real interest rate** is the nominal interest rate corrected for the effects of inflation. If the nominal interest rate is 8 percent and the inflation rate is 3 percent, then the real interest rate is 5 percent. In Chapter 4 we discuss the relation between nominal and real interest rates in detail. Here it is sufficient to note that the real interest rate measures the true cost of borrowing and, thus, determines the quantity of investment.

We can summarize this discussion with an equation relating investment I to the real interest rate r:

$$I = I(r).$$

Figure 3-7 shows this investment function. It slopes downward, because as the interest rate rises, the quantity of investment demanded falls. The position of this investment function shifts if there is any significant change in the other determinants of investment spending (which we have assumed to be constant when drawing Figure 3-7).

Government Purchases

Government purchases are the third component of the demand for goods and services. The federal government buys helicopters, computers, and the services of government employees. Provincial and municipal governments buy library books, build schools and hospitals, and hire teachers and doctors. Governments at all levels build roads and other public works. All these transactions make up government purchases of goods and services, which account for about 22 percent of GDP in Canada.

These purchases are only one type of government spending. The other type is transfer payments to households, such as welfare for the poor and Canada Pension payments for the elderly. Unlike government purchases, transfer payments are not made in exchange for some of the economy's output of goods and services. Therefore, they are not included in the variable G.

Transfer payments do affect the demand for goods and services indirectly. Transfer payments are the opposite of taxes: they increase households' disposable income, just as taxes reduce disposable income. Thus, an increase in transfer payments financed by an increase in taxes leaves disposable income unchanged. We can now revise our definition of T to equal taxes minus transfer payments. Disposable income, $Y - T$, includes both the negative impact of taxes and the positive impact of transfer payments.

If government purchases equal taxes minus transfers, then $G = T$, and the government has a *balanced budget*. If G exceeds T, the government runs a *budget deficit*, which it funds by issuing government debt—that is, by borrowing in the financial markets. If G is less than T, the government runs a *budget surplus*, which it can use to repay some of its outstanding debt.

Here we do not try to explain the political process that leads to a particular fiscal policy—that is, to the level of government purchases and taxes. Instead, we take government purchases and taxes as exogenous variables. To denote that these variables are fixed outside of our model of national income, (that is, determined by events that we are not trying to explain in this model—such as a natural disaster that would prompt government to take action) we write

$$G = \bar{G}.$$

$$T = \bar{T}.$$

We do, however, want to examine the impact of fiscal policy on the variables determined within the model, the endogenous variables. The endogenous variables here are consumption, investment, and the interest rate.

To see how the exogenous variables affect the endogenous variables, we must complete the model. This is the subject of the next section.

3-4 What Brings the Supply and Demand for Goods and Services Into Equilibrium?

We have now come full circle in the circular flow diagram, Figure 3-1. We began by examining the supply of goods and services, and we have just discussed the demand for them. How can we be certain that all these flows balance? In other words, what ensures that the sum of consumption, investment, and government purchases equals the amount of output produced? We will see that in this classical model, the interest rate is the price that has the crucial role of equilibrating supply and demand.

There are two ways to think about the role of the interest rate in the economy. We can consider how the interest rate affects the supply and demand for goods and services. Or we can consider how the interest rate affects the supply and demand for loanable funds. As we will see, these two approaches are two sides of the same coin.

Equilibrium in the Market for Goods and Services: The Supply and Demand for the Economy's Output

The following equations summarize the discussion of the demand for goods and services in Section 3-3:

$$Y = C + I + G.$$

$$C = C(Y - T).$$

$$I = I(r).$$

$$G = \overline{G}.$$

$$T = \overline{T}.$$

The demand for the economy's output comes from consumption, investment, and government purchases. Consumption depends on disposable income; investment depends on the real interest rate; and government purchases and taxes are the exogenous variables set by fiscal policymakers.

To this analysis, let's add what we learned about the supply of goods and services in Section 3-1. There we saw that the factors of production and the production function determine the quantity of output supplied to the economy:

$$Y = F(\overline{K}, \overline{L})$$

$$= \overline{Y}.$$

Now let's combine these equations describing the supply and demand for output. If we substitute the consumption function and the investment function into the national accounts identity, we obtain

$$Y = C(Y - T) + I(r) + G.$$

Because the variables G and T are fixed by policy, and the level of output Y is fixed by the factors of production and the production function, we can write

$$\overline{Y} = C(\overline{Y} - \overline{T}) + I(r) + \overline{G}.$$

This equation states that the supply of output equals its demand, which is the sum of consumption, investment, and government purchases.

Notice that the interest rate r is the only variable not already determined in the last equation. This is because the interest rate still has a key role to play: it must adjust to ensure that the demand for goods equals the supply. The greater the interest rate, the lower the level of investment, and thus the lower the demand for goods and services, $C + I + G$. If the interest rate is too high, investment is too low, and the demand for output falls short of the supply. If the interest rate is too low, investment is too high, and the demand exceeds the supply. *At the equilibrium interest rate, the demand for goods and services equals the supply.*

This conclusion may seem somewhat mysterious: How does the interest rate gets to the level that balances the supply and demand for goods and services? The best way to answer this question is to consider how financial markets fit into the story.

Equilibrium in the Financial Markets: The Supply and Demand for Loanable Funds

Because the interest rate is the cost of borrowing and the return to lending in financial markets, we can better understand the role of the interest rate in the economy by thinking about the financial markets. To do this, rewrite the national accounts identity as

$$Y - C - G = I.$$

The term $Y - C - G$ is the output that remains after the demands of consumers and the government have been satisfied; it is called **national saving** or simply **saving (S).** In this form, the national accounts identity shows that saving equals investment.

To understand this identity more fully, we can split national saving into two parts—one part representing the saving of the private sector and the other representing the saving of the government:

$$(Y - T - C) + (T - G) = I.$$

The term $(Y - T - C)$ is disposable income minus consumption, which is **private saving.** The term $(T - G)$ is government revenue minus government spending, which is **public saving.** (If government spending exceeds government revenue, the government runs a budget deficit, and public saving is negative.) National saving is the sum of private and public saving. The circular flow diagram in Figure 3-1 reveals an interpretation of this equation: this equation states that the flows into the financial markets (private and public saving) must balance the flows out of the financial markets (investment).

To see how the interest rate brings financial markets into equilibrium, substitute the consumption function and the investment function into the national accounts identity:

$$Y - C(Y - T) - G = I(r).$$

Next, note that G and T are fixed by policy and Y is fixed by the factors of production and the production function:

$$\bar{Y} - C(\bar{Y} - \bar{T}) - \bar{G} = I(r).$$
$$\bar{S} = I(r).$$

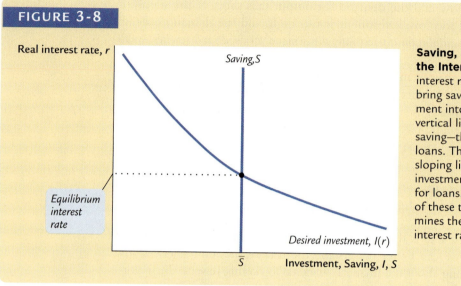

FIGURE 3-8

Real interest rate, r

Saving, S

Equilibrium interest rate

Desired investment, $I(r)$

$\overline{S}$ Investment, Saving, I, S

Saving, Investment, and the Interest Rate The interest rate adjusts to bring saving and investment into balance. The vertical line represents saving—the supply of loans. The downward-sloping line represents investment—the demand for loans. The intersection of these two curves determines the equilibrium interest rate.

The left-hand side of this equation shows that national saving depends on income Y and the fiscal policy variables G and T. For fixed values of Y, G, and T, national saving S is also fixed. The right-hand side of the equation shows that investment depends on the interest rate.

Figure 3–8 graphs saving and investment as a function of the interest rate. The saving function is a vertical line because in this model saving does not depend on the interest rate (we relax this assumption later). The investment function slopes downward: the higher the interest rate, the fewer investment projects are profitable.

From a quick glance at Figure 3–8, one might think it was a supply and demand diagram for a particular good. In fact, saving and investment can be interpreted in terms of supply and demand. In this case, the "good" is **loanable funds,** and its "price" is the interest rate. Saving is the supply of loanable funds—households lend their saving to investors or deposit their saving in a bank that then loans the funds out. Investment is the demand for loanable funds—investors borrow from the public directly by selling bonds or indirectly by borrowing from banks. Because investment depends on the interest rate, the quantity of loanable funds demanded also depends on the interest rate.

The interest rate adjusts until the amount that firms want to invest equals the amount that households want to save. If the interest rate is too low, investors want more of the economy's output than households want to save. Equivalently, the quantity of loans demanded exceeds the quantity supplied. When this happens, the interest rate rises. Conversely, if the interest rate is too high, households want to save more than firms want to invest; because the quantity of loans supplied is greater than the quantity demanded, the interest rate falls. The equilibrium interest rate is found where the two curves cross. *At the equilibrium interest rate, households' desire to save balances firms' desire to invest, and the quantity of loans supplied equals the quantity demanded.*

The Financial System: Markets, Intermediaries, and the Crisis of 2008

The model presented in this chapter represents the economy's financial system with a single market—the market for loanable funds. Those who have some income that they don't want to consume immediately bring their saving to this market. Those who want to undertake investment projects finance them by borrowing in this market. The interest rate adjusts to bring saving and investment into balance.

The actual financial system is a bit more complicated. As in this model, the goal of the system is to channel resources from savers into various forms of investment. But the system includes a variety of mechanisms to facilitate this transfer of resources.

One part of the financial system is the group of *financial markets* through which households can directly provide resources for investment. Two important financial markets are the market for *bonds* and the market for *stocks*. A person who buys a bond from Apple Corporation becomes a creditor of the company, while a person who buys newly issued stock from Apple becomes a part owner of the company. (A purchase of stock on a stock exchange, however, represents a transfer of ownership shares from one person to another and does not provide new funds for investment projects.) Raising investment funds by issuing bonds is called *debt finance,* and raising funds by issuing stock is called *equity finance*.

Another part of the financial system is the group of *financial intermediaries* through which households can indirectly provide resources for investment. As the term suggests, a financial intermediary stands between the two sides of the market and helps direct financial resources toward their best use. Banks are the best-known type of financial intermediary. They take deposits from savers and use these deposits to make loans to those who have investments to make. Other examples of financial intermediaries include mutual funds, pension funds, and insurance companies. When a financial intermediary is involved, the saver is often unaware of the investments that are financed by his saving.

In 2008, the world financial system experienced a historic crisis. Many banks and other financial intermediaries had previously made loans, called *mortgages,* to homeowners and had purchased many mortgage-backed securities (financial instruments whose value derives from a pool of mortgages). A large decline in housing prices throughout the United States, however, caused many homeowners to default on their mortgages, which in turn led to large losses at these financial institutions. Many banks and other financial intermediaries found themselves nearly bankrupt, and the financial system started having difficulty in performing its key functions. To address the problem, the U.S. Congress authorized the U.S. Treasury to spend $700 billion, which was largely used to put further resources into the banking system.

In Chapter 11, we will examine more fully the financial crisis of 2008. But for our purposes in this chapter, and as a building block for further analysis, representing the entire financial system by a single market for loanable funds is a useful simplification.

Changes in Saving: The Effects of Fiscal Policy

We can use our model to show how fiscal policy affects the economy. When the government changes its spending or the level of taxes, it affects the demand for the economy's output of goods and services and alters national saving, investment, and the equilibrium interest rate.

An Increase in Government Purchases Consider first the effects of an increase in government purchases by an amount ΔG. The immediate impact is to

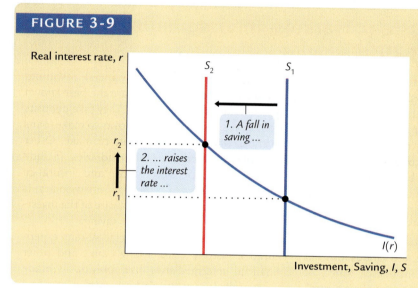

FIGURE 3-9

Real interest rate, r

S_2 S_1

r_2

1. A fall in saving...

2. ... raises the interest rate ...

r_1

$I(r)$

Investment, Saving, I, S

A Reduction in Saving A reduction in saving, possibly the result of a change in fiscal policy, shifts the saving schedule to the left. The new equilibrium is the point at which the new saving schedule crosses the investment schedule. A reduction in saving lowers the amount of investment and raises the interest rate. Fiscal-policy actions that reduce saving are said to crowd out investment.

increase the demand for goods and services by ΔG. But since total output is fixed by the factors of production, the increase in government purchases must be met by a decrease in some other category of demand. Since disposable income $Y - T$ is unchanged, consumption C is unchanged as well. The increase in government purchases must be met by an equal decrease in investment.

To induce investment to fall, the interest rate must rise. Hence, the increase in government purchases causes the interest rate to increase and investment to decrease. Government purchases are said to **crowd out** investment.

To grasp the effects of an increase in government purchases, consider the impact on the market for loanable funds. Since the increase in government purchases is not accompanied by an increase in taxes, the government finances the additional spending by borrowing—that is, by reducing public saving. Since private saving is unchanged, this government borrowing reduces national saving. As Figure 3-9 shows, a reduction in national saving is represented by a leftward shift in the supply of loanable funds available for investment. At the initial interest rate, the demand for loans exceeds the supply. The equilibrium interest rate rises to the point where the investment schedule crosses the new saving schedule. Thus, an increase in government purchases causes the interest rate to rise from r_1 to r_2.

CASE STUDY

Wars and Interest Rates in the United Kingdom, 1730–1920

Wars are traumatic—both for those who fight them and for a nation's economy. Because the economic changes accompanying them are often large, wars provide a natural experiment with which economists can test their theories. We can learn

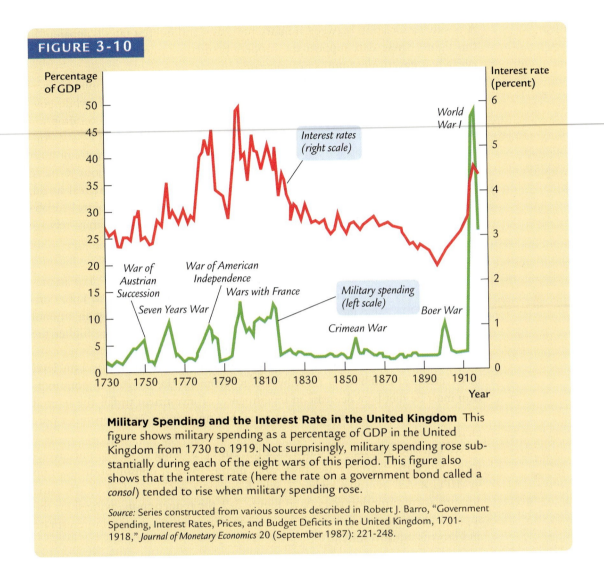

FIGURE 3-10

Military Spending and the Interest Rate in the United Kingdom This figure shows military spending as a percentage of GDP in the United Kingdom from 1730 to 1919. Not surprisingly, military spending rose substantially during each of the eight wars of this period. This figure also shows that the interest rate (here the rate on a government bond called a *consol*) tended to rise when military spending rose.

Source: Series constructed from various sources described in Robert J. Barro, "Government Spending, Interest Rates, Prices, and Budget Deficits in the United Kingdom, 1701-1918," *Journal of Monetary Economics* 20 (September 1987): 221-248.

about the economy by seeing how in wartime the endogenous variables respond to the major changes in the exogenous variables.

One exogenous variable that changes substantially in wartime is the level of government purchases. Figure 3-10 shows military spending as a percentage of GDP for the United Kingdom from 1730 to 1919. This graph shows, as one would expect, that government purchases rose suddenly and dramatically during the eight wars of this period.

Our model predicts that this wartime increase in government purchases—and the increase in government borrowing to finance the wars—should have raised the demand for goods and services, reduced the supply of loanable funds, and raised the interest rate. To test this prediction, Figure 3-10 also shows the interest rate on long-term government bonds, called *consols* in the United Kingdom.

A positive association between military purchases and interest rates is apparent in this figure. These data support the model's prediction: interest rates do tend to rise when government purchases increase.[7]

One problem with using wars to test theories is that many economic changes may be occurring at the same time. For example, in World War II, while government purchases increased dramatically, rationing also restricted consumption of many goods. In addition, the risk of defeat in the war and default by the government on its debt presumably increases the interest rate the government must pay. Economic models predict what happens when one exogenous variable changes and all the other exogenous variables remain constant. In the real world, however, many exogenous variables may change at once. Unlike controlled laboratory experiments, the natural experiments on which economists must rely are not always easy to interpret. ■

A Decrease in Taxes Now consider a reduction in taxes of ΔT. The immediate impact of the tax cut is to raise disposable income and thus to raise consumption. Disposable income rises by ΔT, and consumption rises by an amount equal to ΔT times the marginal propensity to consume *MPC*. The higher the *MPC*, the greater the impact of the tax cut on consumption.

Since the economy's output is fixed by the factors of production and the level of government purchases is fixed by the government, the increase in consumption must be met by a decrease in investment. For investment to fall, the interest rate must rise. Hence, a reduction in taxes, like an increase in government purchases, crowds out investment and raises the interest rate.

We can also analyze the effect of a tax cut by looking at saving and investment. Since the tax cut raises disposable income by ΔT, consumption goes up by $MPC \times \Delta T$. National saving S, which equals $Y - C - G$, falls by the same amount as consumption rises. As in Figure 3-9, the reduction in saving shifts the supply of loanable funds to the left, which increases the equilibrium interest rate and crowds out investment.

CASE STUDY

Fiscal Policy in the 1980s and 1990s

One of the most dramatic economic events in recent history was the large change in fiscal policies of most Western countries in the latter three decades of the twentieth century. Before this period, all governments had run deficits during numerous short intervals of time. But governments had often run surpluses

---

[7] Daniel K. Benjamin and Levis A. Kochin, "War, Prices, and Interest Rates: A Martial Solution to Gibson's Paradox," in M. D. Bordo and A. J. Schwartz, eds., *A Retrospective on the Classical Gold Standard, 1821–1931* (Chicago: University of Chicago Press, 1984), 587–612; Robert J. Barro, "Government Spending, Interest Rates, Prices, and Budget Deficits in the United Kingdom, 1701-1918," *Journal of Monetary Economics* 20 (September 1987): 221–248.

as well, so that, over the longer run, there was not a large increase in their national debts. Starting in the mid-1970s, however, the excess of government spending over tax revenues increased by a wide margin, and this gap became a permanent fixture of fiscal policy. It was not until the mid-1990s that deficits were worked down.

As our model predicts, this change in fiscal policy led to higher world interest rates and lower levels of saving. In Canada's case, the real interest rate (the difference between the yield on government bonds and the inflation rate) rose from 0.8 percent in the 1960–1975 period to 3.9 percent in the 1976–1993 period. Total saving in Canada averaged 10 percent of national income in the 1960–1975 period, and only 2 percent in the early 1990s.[8] The change in fiscal policy in the 1980s certainly had the effects that our simple model of the economy predicts. ■

Changes in Investment Demand

So far, we have discussed how fiscal policy can change national saving. We can also use our model to examine the other side of the market—the demand for investment. In this section we look at the causes and effects of changes in investment demand.

One reason investment demand might increase is technological innovation. Suppose, for example, that someone invents a new technology, such as the railroad or the computer. Before a firm or household can take advantage of the innovation, it must buy investment goods. The invention of the railroad had no value until railroad cars were produced and tracks were laid. The idea of the computer was not productive until computers were manufactured. Thus, technological innovation leads to an increase in investment demand.

Investment demand may also change because the government encourages or discourages investment through the tax laws. For example, suppose that the government increases personal income taxes and uses the extra revenue to provide tax cuts for those who invest in new capital. Such a change in the tax laws makes more investment projects profitable and, like a technological innovation, increases the demand for investment goods.

Figure 3-11 shows the effects of an increase in investment demand. At any given interest rate, the demand for investment goods (and also for loans) is higher. This increase in demand is represented by a shift in the investment schedule to the right. The economy moves from the old equilibrium, point A, to the new equilibrium, point B.

The surprising implication of Figure 3-11 is that the equilibrium amount of investment is unchanged. Under our assumptions, the fixed level of saving determines the amount of investment; in other words, there is a fixed supply of loans. An increase in investment demand merely raises the equilibrium interest rate.

---

[8] See William B.P. Robson, "Digging Holes and Hitting Walls: Canada's Fiscal Prospects in the Mid-1990s," *Commentary* No. 56 (Toronto: C.D. Howe Institute, 1994).

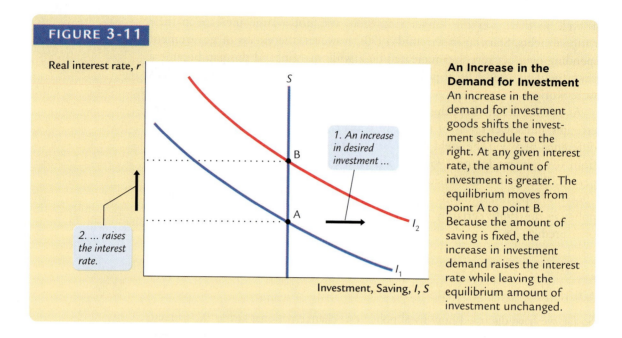

FIGURE 3-11

Real interest rate, r

1. An increase in desired investment ...

2. ... raises the interest rate.

Investment, Saving, I, S

An Increase in the Demand for Investment An increase in the demand for investment goods shifts the investment schedule to the right. At any given interest rate, the amount of investment is greater. The equilibrium moves from point A to point B. Because the amount of saving is fixed, the increase in investment demand raises the interest rate while leaving the equilibrium amount of investment unchanged.

We would reach a different conclusion, however, if we modified our simple consumption function and allowed consumption (and its flip side, saving) to depend on the interest rate. Because the interest rate is the return to saving (as well as the cost of borrowing), a higher interest rate might reduce consumption and increase saving. If so, the saving schedule would be upward sloping, as it is in Figure 3-12, rather than vertical.

With an upward-sloping saving schedule, an increase in investment demand would raise both the equilibrium interest rate and the equilibrium quantity of investment. Figure 3-13 shows such a change. The increase in the interest rate causes households to consume less and save more. The decrease in consumption frees resources for investment.

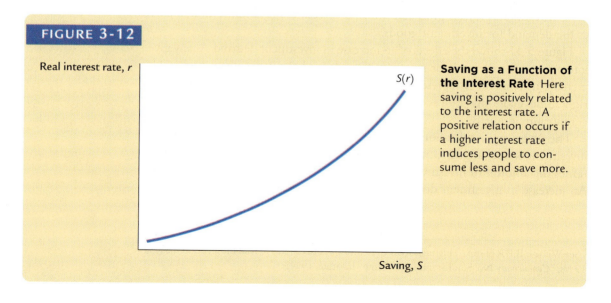

FIGURE 3-12

Real interest rate, r

$S(r)$

Saving, S

Saving as a Function of the Interest Rate Here saving is positively related to the interest rate. A positive relation occurs if a higher interest rate induces people to consume less and save more.

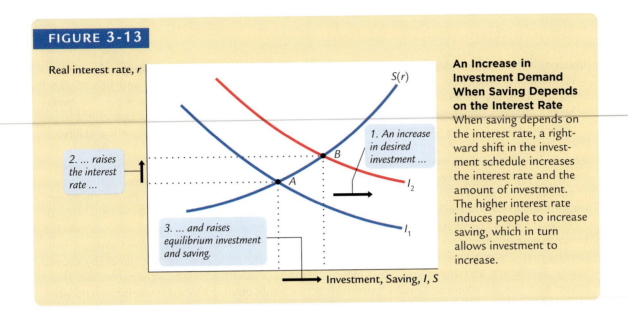

FIGURE 3-13

Real interest rate, r

2. ... raises the interest rate ...

1. An increase in desired investment ...

3. ... and raises equilibrium investment and saving.

$S(r)$

B

A

I_2

I_1

Investment, Saving, I, S

An Increase in Investment Demand When Saving Depends on the Interest Rate When saving depends on the interest rate, a rightward shift in the investment schedule increases the interest rate and the amount of investment. The higher interest rate induces people to increase saving, which in turn allows investment to increase.

3-5 Conclusion

In this chapter we have developed a model that explains the production, distribution, and allocation of the economy's output of goods and services. Because the model incorporates all the interactions illustrated in the circular flow diagram in Figure 3-1, it is sometimes called a *general equilibrium model*. The model emphasizes how prices adjust to equilibrate supply and demand. Factor prices equilibrate factor markets. The interest rate equilibrates the supply and demand for goods and services (or, equivalently, the supply and demand for loanable funds).

Throughout the chapter, we have discussed various applications of the model. The model can explain how income is divided among the factors of production and how factor prices depend on factor supplies. We have also used the model to discuss how fiscal policy alters the allocation of output among its alternative uses—consumption, investment, and government purchases—and how it affects the equilibrium interest rate.

At this point it is useful to review some of the simplifying assumptions we have made in this chapter. In the following chapters we relax some of these assumptions to address a greater range of questions.

- We have ignored the role of money, the asset with which goods and services are bought and sold. In Chapter 4 we discuss how money affects the economy and the influence of monetary policy.

- We have assumed that there is no trade with other countries. In Chapter 5 we consider how international interactions affect our conclusions.

- We have assumed that the labour force is fully employed. In Chapter 6 we examine the reasons for unemployment and see how public policy influences the level of unemployment.

The Identification Problem

In our model, investment depends on the interest rate. The higher the interest rate, the fewer investment projects are profitable. The investment schedule therefore slopes downward.

Economists who look at macroeconomic data, however, usually fail to find an obvious association between investment and interest rates. In years when interest rates are high, investment is not always low. In years when interest rates are low, investment is not always high.

How do we interpret this finding? Does it mean that investment does not depend on the interest rate? Does it suggest that our model of saving, investment, and the interest rate is inconsistent with how the economy actually functions?

Luckily, we do not have to discard our model. The inability to find an empirical relationship between investment and interest rates is an example of the *identification problem*. The identification problem arises when variables are related in more than one way. When we look at data, we are observing a combination of these different relationships, and it is difficult to "identify" any one of them.

To understand this problem more concretely, consider the relationships among saving, investment, and the interest rate. Suppose, on the one hand, that all changes in the interest rate resulted from changes in saving—that is, from shifts in the saving schedule. Then, as shown in the left-hand side of panel (a) in Figure 3-14, all changes would represent movement along a fixed investment schedule. As the right-hand side of panel (a) shows, the data would trace out this investment schedule. Thus, we would observe a negative relationship between investment and interest rates.

Suppose, on the other hand, that all changes in the interest rate resulted from technological innovations—that is, from shifts in the investment schedule. Then, as shown in panel (b), all changes would represent movements in the investment schedule along a fixed saving schedule. As the right-hand side of panel (b) shows, the data would reflect this saving schedule. Thus, we would observe a positive relationship between investment and interest rates.

In the real world, interest rates change sometimes because of shifts in the saving schedule and sometimes because of shifts in the investment schedule. In this mixed case, as shown in panel (c), a plot of the data would reveal no recognizable relation between interest rates and the quantity of investment, just as economists observe in actual data. The moral of the story is simple and is applicable to many other situations: the empirical relationship we expect to observe depends crucially on which exogenous variables we think are changing. Students who major in economics will learn how applied economists solve the identification problem in their statistics courses.

- We have assumed that the capital stock, the labour force, and the production technology (knowledge) are fixed. In Chapters 7 and 8 we see how changes over time in each of these lead to growth in the economy's output of goods and services.

- We have ignored the role of short-run sticky prices. In Chapters 9 through 14, we develop a model of short-run fluctuations that includes sticky prices. We then discuss how the model of short-run fluctuations relates to the model of national income developed in this chapter.

Before going on to these chapters, go back to the beginning of this one and make sure you can answer the four groups of questions about national income that begin the chapter.

FIGURE 3-14

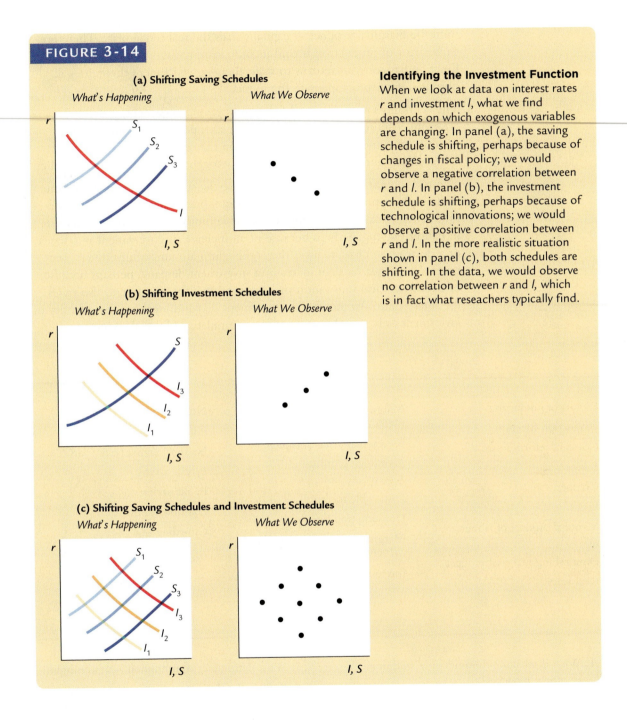

(a) Shifting Saving Schedules

What's Happening   *What We Observe*

I, S I, S

(b) Shifting Investment Schedules

What's Happening   *What We Observe*

I, S I, S

(c) Shifting Saving Schedules and Investment Schedules

What's Happening   *What We Observe*

I, S I, S

Identifying the Investment Function
When we look at data on interest rates *r* and investment *I*, what we find depends on which exogenous variables are changing. In panel (a), the saving schedule is shifting, perhaps because of changes in fiscal policy; we would observe a negative correlation between *r* and *I*. In panel (b), the investment schedule is shifting, perhaps because of technological innovations; we would observe a positive correlation between *r* and *I*. In the more realistic situation shown in panel (c), both schedules are shifting. In the data, we would observe no correlation between *r* and *I*, which is in fact what researchers typically find.

Summary

1. The factors of production and the production technology determine the economy's output of goods and services. An increase in one of the factors of production or a technological advance raises output.

2. Competitive, profit-maximizing firms hire labour until the marginal product of labour equals the real wage. Similarly, these firms rent capital

until the marginal product of capital equals the real rental price. Therefore, each factor of production is paid its marginal product. If the production function has constant returns to scale, then—given Euler's theorem—all output is used to compensate the inputs.

3. The economy's output is used for consumption, investment, and government purchases. Consumption depends positively on disposable income. Investment depends negatively on the real interest rate. Government purchases and taxes are the exogenous variables of fiscal policy.

4. The real interest rate adjusts to equilibrate the supply and demand for the economy's output—or, equivalently, to equilibrate the supply of loanable funds (saving) and the demand for loanable funds (investment). A decrease in national saving, perhaps because of an increase in government purchases or a decrease in taxes, reduces the equilibrium amount of investment and raises the interest rate. An increase in investment demand, perhaps because of a technological innovation or a tax incentive for investment, also raises the interest rate. An increase in investment demand increases the quantity of investment only if higher interest rates stimulate additional saving.

KEY CONCEPTS

Factors of production

Production function

Constant returns to scale

Factor prices

Competition

Profit

Marginal product of labour (*MPL*)

Diminishing marginal product

Real wage

Marginal product of capital (*MPK*)

Real rental price of capital

Economic profit versus accounting profit

Disposable income

Consumption function

Marginal propensity to consume (*MPC*)

Interest rate

Nominal interest rate

Real interest rate

National saving (saving) (*S*)

Private saving

Public saving

Loanable funds

Crowding out

QUESTIONS FOR REVIEW

1. What determines the amount of output an economy produces?

2. Explain how a competitive, profit-maximizing firm decides how much of each factor of production to demand.

3. What is the role of constant returns to scale in the distribution of income?

4. Write down a Cobb-Douglas production function for which capital earns one-fourth of total income.

5. What determines consumption and investment?

6. Explain the difference between government purchases and transfer payments. Give two examples of each.

7. What makes the demand for the economy's output of goods and services equal the supply?

8. Explain what happens to consumption, investment, and the interest rate when the government increases taxes

PROBLEMS AND APPLICATIONS

1. Use the neoclassical theory of distribution to predict the impact on the real wage and the real rental price of capital of each of the following events:

   a. A wave of immigration increases the labour force.

   b. An earthquake destroys some of the capital stock.

   c. A technological advance improves the production function.

2. If a 10-percent increase in both capital and labour causes output to increase by less than 10 percent, the production function is said to exhibit *decreasing returns to scale*. If it causes output to increase by more than 10 percent, the production function is said to exhibit *increasing returns to scale*. Why might a production function exhibit decreasing or increasing returns to scale?

3. Suppose that the production function is Cobb–Douglas with parameter $\alpha = 0.3$.

   a. What fractions of income do capital and labour receive?

   b. Suppose that immigration raises the labour force by 10 percent. What happens to total output (in percent)? The rental price of capital? The real wage?

   c. Suppose that a gift of capital from abroad raises the capital stock by 10 percent. What happens to total output (in percent)? The rental price of capital? The real wage?

   d. Suppose that a technological advance raises the value of the parameter A by 10 percent. What happens to total output (in percent)? The rental price of capital? The real wage?

4. Figure 3-5 shows that in Canadian data, labour's share of total income is approximately a constant over time. Table 3-1 shows that the trend in the real wage closely tracks the trend in labour productivity. How are these facts related? Could the first fact be true without the second also being true?

5. According to the neoclassical theory of distribution, the real wage earned by any worker equals that worker's marginal productivity. Let's use this insight to examine the incomes of two groups of workers: farmers and barbers.

   a. Over the past century, the productivity of farmers has risen substantially because of technological progress. According to the neoclassical theory, what should have happened to their real wage?

   b. In what units is the real wage discussed in part (a) measured?

   c. Over the same period, the productivity of barbers has remained constant. What should have happened to their real wage?

   d. In what units is the real wage in part (c) measured?

   e. Suppose workers can move freely between being farmers and being barbers. What does this mobility imply for the wages of farmers and barbers?

   f. What do your previous answers imply for the price of haircuts relative to the price of food?

   g. Who benefits from technological progress in farming—farmers or barbers?

6. (This problem requires the use of calculus.) Consider a Cobb–Douglas production function with three inputs. K is capital (the number of machines), L is labour (the number of workers), and H is human capital (the number of college degrees among the workers). The production function is
   $$Y = K^{1/3}L^{1/3}H^{1/3}.$$

   a. Derive an expression for the marginal product of labour. How does an increase in the amount of human capital affect the marginal product of labour?

   b. Derive an expression for the marginal product of human capital. How does an increase in the amount of human capital affect the marginal product of human capital?

   c. What is the income share paid to labour? What is the income share paid to human capital? In the national income accounts of this economy, what share of total income do you think workers would appear to receive? (*Hint:* Consider where the return to human capital shows up.)

   d. An unskilled worker earns the marginal product of labour, whereas a skilled worker earns the marginal product of labour plus the marginal product of human capital. Using your answers to (a) and (b), find the ratio of the skilled wage to the unskilled wage. How does an increase in the amount of human capital affect this ratio? Explain.

e. Some people advocate government funding of college scholarships as a way of creating a more egalitarian society. Others argue that scholarships help only those who are able to go to college. Do your answers to the preceding questions shed light on this debate?

7. The government raises taxes by $100 billion. If the marginal propensity to consume is 0.6, what happens to the following? Do they rise or fall? By what amounts?

   a. Public saving.

   b. Private saving.

   c. National saving.

   d. Investment.

8. Suppose that an increase in consumer confidence raises consumers' expectations of future income and thus the amount they want to consume today. This might be interpreted as an upward shift in the consumption function. How does this shift affect investment and the interest rate?

9. Consider an economy described by the following equations:

$$Y = C + I + G,$$
$$Y = 5,000,$$
$$G = 1,000,$$
$$T = 1,000,$$
$$C = 250 + 0.75(Y - T),$$
$$I = 1,000 - 50\ r.$$

   a. In this economy, compute private saving, public saving, and national saving.

   b. Find the equilibrium interest rate (measured in percentage points).

   c. Now suppose that G rises to 1,250. Compute private saving, public saving, and national saving.

   d. Find the new equilibrium interest rate.

10. Suppose that the government increases taxes and government purchases by equal amounts. What happens to the interest rate and investment in response to this balanced budget change? Does your answer depend on the marginal propensity to consume?

11. When the government subsidizes investment, such as with an investment tax credit, the subsidy often applies to only some types of investment. This question asks you to consider the effect of such a change. Suppose there are two types of investment in the economy: business investment and residential investment. And suppose that the government institutes an investment tax credit only for business investment.

   a. How does this policy affect the demand curve for business investment? The demand curve for residential investment?

   b. Draw the economy's supply and demand for loanable funds. How does this policy affect the supply and demand for loans? What happens to the equilibrium interest rate?

   c. Compare the old and the new equilibrium. How does this policy affect the total quantity of investment? The quantity of business investment? The quantity of residential investment?

12. If consumption depended on the interest rate, how would that affect the conclusions reached in this chapter about the effects of fiscal policy?

13. Macroeconomic data do not show a strong correlation between investment and interest rates. Use our model in which the interest rate adjusts to equilibrate the supply of loanable funds (which is upward sloping) and the demand for loanable funds (which is downward sloping) to explain why this might be the case.

   a. Suppose the demand for loanable funds were stable but the supply fluctuated from year to year. What might cause these fluctuations in supply? In this case, what correlation between investment and interest rates would you find?

   b. Suppose the supply of loanable funds were stable but the demand fluctuated from year to year. What might cause these fluctuations in demand? In this case, what correlation between investment and interest rates would you find now?

   c. Suppose that both supply and demand in this market fluctuated over time. If you were to construct a scatterplot of investment and the interest rate, what would you find?

   d. Which of the above three cases seems most empirically realistic to you?

Money and Inflation

Lenin is said to have declared that the best way to destroy the Capitalist System was to debauch the currency. . . . Lenin was certainly right.

There is no subtler, no surer means of overturning the existing basis of society than to debauch the currency. The process engages all the hidden forces of economic law on the side of destruction, and does it in a manner which not one man in a million is able to diagnose.

— *John Maynard Keynes*

I n 1950, a shopping cart of groceries could be purchased for \$25. In 2005, that same cart of groceries cost \$228. Other prices—such as the average wage rate—increased even more over this 55-year period, so—in real terms—the material living standard for the average Canadian has increased. Recall from Chapter 1 that real GDP per capita has risen by more than a factor of 4 since 1950. The overall increase in prices is called **inflation,** and it is the subject of this chapter.

The rate of inflation—the percentage change in the overall level of prices— varies substantially over time and across countries. Indeed a *one-time* increase in the cost of living is not considered inflation; the term is reserved for situations in which there is an *ongoing* increase in prices. In Canada, prices rose an average of 2.9 percent per year in the 1960s, 7.8 percent per year in the 1970s, 5.8 percent per year in the 1980s, 1.5 percent per year in the 1990s, and 2.2 percent per year in the present century. Inflation in Canada has, by international standards, been moderate. In Russia in 1998, for instance, inflation was running about 50 percent per year. In Germany in 1923 and in Zimbabwe in 2008, prices rose an average of 500 percent *per month*. Such an episode of extraordinarily high inflation is called a **hyperinflation.**

In this chapter we examine the classical theory of the causes, effects, and social costs of inflation. The theory is "classical" in the sense that it assumes that prices are fully flexible. As we first discussed in Chapter 1, most economists believe this assumption accurately describes the behaviour of the economy in the long run. By contrast, many prices are thought to be sticky in the short run, and beginning in Chapter 9, we incorporate this fact into our analysis. Yet, for now, we ignore short-run price stickiness. As we will see, the classical theory of inflation not only provides a good description of the long run, it also provides a useful foundation for the short-run analysis we develop later.

The "hidden forces of economic law" that lead to inflation are not as mysterious as Keynes claims in the quotation that opens this chapter. Inflation is simply an increase in the average level of prices, and a price is the rate at which money is exchanged for a good or a service. To understand inflation, therefore, we must understand money—what it is, what affects its supply and demand, and what influence it has on the economy. Thus, Section 4-1 begins our analysis of inflation by discussing the economist's concept of "money" and how, in most modern economies, the government plays a big part in determining the quantity of money in the hands of the public. Section 4-2 shows that the quantity of money determines the price level and that the rate of growth in the quantity of money determines the rate of inflation.

Inflation in turn has numerous effects of its own on the economy. Section 4-3 discusses the revenue that governments can raise by printing money, sometimes called the *inflation tax*. Section 4-4 examines how inflation affects the nominal interest rate. Section 4-5 discusses how the nominal interest rate in turn affects the quantity of money people wish to hold and, thereby, the price level.

After completing our analysis of the causes and effects of inflation, in Section 4-6 we address what is perhaps the most important question about inflation: Is it a major social problem? Does inflation really amount to "overturning the existing basis of society," as the chapter's opening quotation suggests?

Finally, in Section 4-7, we discuss the extreme case of hyperinflation. Hyperinflations are interesting to examine because they show clearly the causes, effects, and costs of inflation. Just as seismologists learn much by studying earthquakes, economists learn much by studying how hyperinflations begin and end.

4-1 What Is Money?

When we say that a person has a lot of money, we usually mean that he or she is wealthy. By contrast, economists use the term *money* in a more specialized way. To an economist, money does not refer to all wealth but only to one type of it: **money** is the stock of liquid financial assets that can be readily used to make transactions. Roughly speaking, the dollars in the hands of the public make up the nation's stock of money.

The Functions of Money

Money has three purposes. It is a store of value, a unit of account, and a medium of exchange.

As a **store of value,** money is a way to transfer purchasing power from the present to the future. If I work today and earn $100, I can hold the money and spend it tomorrow, next week, or next month. Of course, money is an imperfect store of value: if prices are rising, the amount you can buy with any given quantity of money is falling. Even so, people hold money because they can trade it for goods and services at some time in the future.

As a **unit of account,** money provides the terms in which prices are quoted and debts are recorded. Microeconomics teaches us that resources are allocated according to relative prices—the prices of goods relative to other goods—yet stores post their prices in dollars and cents. A car dealer tells you that a car costs $15,000, not 400 shirts (even though it may amount to the same thing). Similarly, most debts require the debtor to deliver a specified number of dollars in the future, not a specified amount of some commodity. Money is the unit in which we measure economic transactions.

As a **medium of exchange,** money is what we use to buy goods and services. "This note is legal tender" is printed on all Canadian bills. When we walk into stores, we are confident that the shopkeepers will accept our money in exchange for the items they are selling. The ease with which an asset can be converted into the medium of exchange and used to buy other things—goods and services—is sometimes called the asset's *liquidity*. Because money is the medium of exchange, it is the economy's most liquid asset.

To understand better the functions of money, try to imagine an economy without it: a barter economy. In such a world, trade requires the *double coincidence of wants*—the unlikely happenstance of two people each having a good that the other wants at the right time and place to make an exchange. A barter economy permits only simple transactions.

Money makes more indirect transactions possible. A professor uses her salary to buy books; the book publisher uses its revenue from the sale of books to buy paper; the paper company uses its revenue from the sale of paper to pay the lumberjack; the lumberjack uses his income to send his child to university; and the university uses its tuition receipts to pay the salary of the professor. In a complex, modern economy, trade is usually indirect and requires the use of money.

The Types of Money

Money takes many forms. In the Canadian economy we make transactions with an item whose sole function is to act as money: dollars. These coins and pieces of paper would have little value if they were not widely accepted as money. Money that has no intrinsic value is called **fiat money** because it is established as money by government decree, or fiat.

Although fiat money is the norm in most economies today, historically most societies have used a commodity with some intrinsic value for money. This type of money is called **commodity money.** The most widespread example of commodity

"And how would you like your funny money?"

money is gold. When people use gold as money (or use paper money that is redeemable for gold), the economy is said to be on a **gold standard.** Gold is a form of commodity money because it can be used for various purposes—jewelry, dental fillings, and so on—as well as for transactions. The gold standard was common throughout the world during the late nineteenth century.

CASE STUDY

Money in a POW Camp

An unusual form of commodity money developed in some Nazi prisoner of war (POW) camps during World War II. The Red Cross supplied the prisoners with various goods—food, clothing, cigarettes, and so on. Yet these rations were allocated without close attention to personal preferences, so naturally the allocations were often inefficient. One prisoner may have preferred chocolate, while another may have preferred cheese, and a third may have wanted a new shirt. The differing tastes and endowments of the prisoners led them to trade with one another.

Barter proved to be an inconvenient way to allocate these resources, however, because it required the double coincidence of wants. In other words, a barter system was not the easiest way to ensure that each prisoner received the goods he valued most. Even the limited economy of the POW camp needed some form of money to facilitate transactions.

Eventually, cigarettes became the established "currency" in which prices were quoted and with which trades were made. A shirt, for example, cost about 80 cigarettes. Services were also quoted in cigarettes: some prisoners offered to do other prisoners' laundry for 2 cigarettes per garment. Even nonsmokers were happy to accept cigarettes in exchange, knowing they could trade the cigarettes in the future for some good they did enjoy. Within the POW camp the cigarette became the store of value, the unit of account, and the medium of exchange.[1] ∎

The Development of Fiat Money

It is not surprising that in any society, regardless of its stage of development, some form of commodity money arises to facilitate exchange: people are willing to accept a commodity currency such as gold because it has intrinsic value. The development of fiat money, however, is more perplexing. What would make people begin to value something that is intrinsically useless?

---

[1] R.A. Radford, "The Economic Organisation of a P.O.W. Camp," *Economica* (November 1945): 189–201. The use of cigarettes as money is not limited to this example. In the Soviet Union in the late 1980s, packs of Marlboros were preferred to the ruble in the large underground economy.

To understand how the evolution from commodity money to fiat money takes place, imagine an economy in which people carry around bags of gold. When a purchase is made, the buyer measures out the appropriate amount of gold. If the seller is convinced that the weight and purity of the gold are right, the buyer and seller make the exchange.

The government might first get involved in the monetary system to help people reduce transaction costs. Using raw gold as money is costly because it takes time to verify the purity of the gold and to measure the correct quantity. To reduce these costs, the government can mint gold coins of known purity and weight. The coins are easier to use than gold bullion because their values are widely recognized.

The next step is for the government to accept gold from the public in exchange for gold certificates—pieces of paper that can be redeemed for a certain quantity of gold. If people believe the government's promise to redeem the paper bills for gold, the bills are just as valuable as the gold itself. In addition, because the bills are lighter than gold (and gold coins), they are easier to use in transactions. Eventually, no one carries gold around at all, and these gold-backed government bills become the monetary standard.

Finally, the gold backing becomes irrelevant. If no one ever bothers to redeem the bills for gold, no one cares if the option is abandoned. As long as everyone continues to accept the paper bills in exchange, they will have value and serve as money. Thus, the system of commodity money evolves into a system of fiat money. Notice that in the end, the use of money in exchange is largely a social convention, in the sense that everyone values fiat money simply because they expect everyone else to value it. (The role of private banks in this historical evolution, the drift from 100 percent reserves to fractional reserves, and now our system of zero required reserves are discussed in Chapter 18.)

CASE STUDY

Money and Social Conventions on the Island of Yap

The economy of Yap, a small island in the Pacific, once had a type of money that was something between commodity and fiat money. The traditional medium of exchange in Yap was *fei,* stone wheels up to 12 feet in diameter. These stones had holes in the center so that they could be carried on poles and used for exchange.

Large stone wheels are not a convenient form of money. The stones were heavy, so it took substantial effort for a new owner to take his *fei* home after completing a transaction. Although the monetary system facilitated exchange, it did so at great cost.

Eventually, it became common practice for the new owner of the *fei* not to bother to take physical possession of the stone. Instead, the new owner merely accepted a claim to the *fei* without moving it. In future bargains, he traded this claim for goods that he wanted. Having physical possession of the stone became less important than having legal claim to it.

This practice was put to a test when an extremely valuable stone was lost at sea during a storm. Because the owner lost his money by accident rather than through negligence, it was universally agreed that his claim to the *fei* remained valid. Even generations later, when no one alive had ever seen this stone, the claim to this *fei* was still valued in exchange.[2] ∎

How the Quantity of Money Is Controlled

The quantity of money available in an economy is called the **money supply.** In a system of commodity money, the money supply is the quantity of that commodity. In an economy that uses fiat money, such as most economies today, the government controls the supply of money: legal restrictions give the government a monopoly on the printing of money. Just as the level of taxation and the level of government purchases are policy instruments of the government, so is the quantity of money. The government's control over the money supply is called **monetary policy.**

In Canada and many other countries, monetary policy is delegated to a partially independent institution called the **central bank.** The central bank of Canada is the **Bank of Canada.** If you look at Canadian paper currency, you will see that each bill is signed by the Governor of the Bank of Canada, who is appointed by the federal cabinet for a term of seven years. The Governor and the Minister of Finance together decide on monetary policy.

Ultimately, the power to make monetary policy decisions rests with the federal cabinet. The Minister of Finance communicates the overall desires of the government to the Governor of the Bank, and the Governor is left to implement those broad instructions on a day-to-day basis. For 15 years now, the mandate for monetary policy has been that the Governor of the Bank of Canada should issue as much money as is appropriate to ensure that the Canadian annual inflation rate stays within a target range of 1–3 percent. While no dispute has emerged during this period, if the government were to lose confidence in the Governor, it cannot simply fire him or her. First, it must issue detailed written instructions concerning the changes it wants. If the Governor feels that the government's instructions represent an inappropriate policy, the Governor must resign. But the Governor has significant power, since the resignation must be preceded by a formal directive—a written document in which the government makes quite explicit what it wants done. Thus, both the resignation and the details of the disagreement between the government and a respected banker become very public. Governments do not want to force a Governor's resignation unless they are sure that they can defend their views on monetary policy under heavy scrutiny. The Governor of the Bank can use this power to influence policy.

---

[2] Norman Angell, *The Story of Money* (New York: Frederick A. Stokes Company, 1929), pp. 88–89.

The primary way in which the Bank of Canada attempts to control the supply of money is through **open-market operations**—the purchase and sale of government bonds (mostly short-term bonds called treasury bills). To increase the supply of money, the Bank of Canada uses dollars to buy government bonds from the public. This purchase increases the quantity of dollars in circulation. To decrease the supply of money, the Bank of Canada sells some of its government bonds. This open-market sale of bonds takes some dollars out of the hands of the public, decreasing the quantity of money in circulation.

In Chapter 19 we discuss in detail how the Bank of Canada attempts to control the supply of money by influencing the chartered banking system. In addition to buying and selling bonds, the Bank of Canada adjusts the size of the government's deposits at chartered banks. Also in Chapter 19, we explain how the money supply is the product of the monetary base (what the Bank of Canada controls) and the money multiplier (which depends on the behaviour of chartered banks and their customers). Because the central bank cannot directly control the size of the money multiplier, monetary policy is imprecise. In Chapter 19, we discuss the money multiplier and we study the indicator used by the Bank of Canada to summarize the stance of monetary policy—the overnight lending rate—as officials attempt to keep the inflation rate on target. But, for our current discussion, these details are not crucial. It is sufficient simply to assume that the Bank of Canada directly controls the supply of money.

How the Quantity of Money Is Measured

One of the goals of this chapter is to determine how the money supply affects the economy; we turn to that topic in the next section. As a background for that analysis, let's first discuss how economists measure the quantity of money.

Because money is the stock of assets used for transactions, the quantity of money is the quantity of those assets. In simple economies, this quantity is easily measured. In the POW camp, the quantity of money was the number of cigarettes in the camp. But how can we measure the quantity of money in more complex economies such as ours? The answer is not obvious, because no single asset is used for all transactions. People can use various assets to make transactions, such as cash or cheques, although some assets are more convenient than others. This ambiguity leads to numerous measures of the quantity of money.

The most obvious asset to include in the quantity of money is **currency,** the sum of outstanding paper money and coins. Many day-to-day transactions use currency as the medium of exchange.

A second type of asset used for transactions is **demand deposits,** the funds people hold in their chequing accounts. If most sellers accept personal cheques, assets in a chequing account are almost as convenient as currency. In both cases, the assets are in a form ready to facilitate a transaction. Demand deposits are therefore added to currency when measuring the quantity of money.

FYI

How Do Credit Cards and Debit Cards Fit into the Monetary System?

Many people use credit or debit cards to make purchases. Because money is the medium of exchange, one might naturally wonder how these cards fit into the measurement and analysis of money.

Let's start with credit cards. Although one might guess that credit cards are part of the economy's stock of money, in fact measures of the quantity of money do not take credit cards into account. Credit cards are not really a method of payment but a method of *deferring* payment. When you buy an item with a credit card, the bank that issued the card pays the store what it is due. Later, you have to repay the bank. When the time comes to pay your credit card bill, you will likely do so by writing a cheque against your chequing account. The balance in this chequing account is part of the economy's stock of money.

The story is different with debit cards, which automatically withdraw funds from a bank account to pay for items bought. Rather than allowing users to postpone payment for their purchases, a debit card allows users immediate access to deposits in their bank accounts. Using a debit card is similar to writing a cheque. The account balances that lie behind debit cards are included in the measures of the quantity of money.

Even though credit cards are not a form of money, they are still important for analyzing the monetary system. Because people with credit cards can pay many of their bills all at once at the end of the month, rather than sporadically as they make purchases, they may hold less money on average than people without credit cards. Thus, the increased popularity of credit cards may reduce the amount of money that people choose to hold. In other words, credit cards are not part of the supply of money, but they have likely reduced the demand for money.

Once we admit the logic of including demand deposits in the measured money stock, many other assets become candidates for inclusion. Funds in savings accounts, for example, can be easily transferred into chequing accounts; these assets are almost as convenient for transactions. Further, funds in similar accounts in trust companies and the Caisses Populaires in Quebec can be easily used for transactions. Thus, they could be included in the quantity of money.

Because it is hard to judge exactly which assets should be included in the money stock, various measures are available. Table 4-1 presents five measures of the money stock that the Bank of Canada calculates for the Canadian economy, together with a list of which assets are included in each measure. From the smallest to the largest, they are designated B, $M1$, $M2$, $M2+$, and $M3$. The most commonly used measures for studying the effects of money on the economy are $M1$ and $M2+$. There is no consensus, however, about which measure of the money stock is best, and other aggregates (than the several catalogued in Table 4-1) are in use. Disagreements about monetary policy sometimes arise because different measures of money are moving in different directions.

Luckily, the different measures normally move together and so tell the same story about whether the quantity of money is growing quickly or slowly.

TABLE 4-1

The Measures of Money

Symbol	Assets Included	Amount in December 2008 (billions of dollars)
B	Currency plus chartered bank deposits at the Bank of Canada	$51.1
M1	Sum of currency in circulation, demand deposits, and other chequing deposits at chartered banks	211.7
M2	Sum of *M1* plus personal savings deposits and nonpersonal notice deposits at chartered banks	891.1
M2+	Sum of *M2* plus all deposits and shares at trust companies, mortgage loan companies, credit unions, and Caisses Populaires	1,228.2
M3	Sum of *M2* plus fixed-term deposits of firms at chartered banks	1,317.1

Source: *Weekly Financial Statistics* (Ottawa: Bank of Canada), Tables B2 and E1.

4-2 The Quantity Theory of Money

Having defined what money is and described how it is controlled and measured, we need a theory of how the quantity of money is related to other economic variables, such as prices and incomes. The theory we will now develop, called the *quantity theory of money,* has its roots in the work of the early monetary theorists, including the philosopher and economist David Hume (1711–1776). It remains the leading explanation for how money affects the economy in the long run.

Transactions and the Quantity Equation

People hold money to buy goods and services. The more money they need for such transactions, the more money they hold. Thus, the quantity of money in the economy is closely related to the number of dollars exchanged in transactions.

The link between transactions and money is expressed in the following equation, called the **quantity equation:**

$$\text{Money} \times \text{Velocity} = \text{Price} \times \text{Transactions}$$
$$M \times V = P \times T.$$

Let's examine each of the four variables in this equation.

The right-hand side of the quantity equation tells us about transactions. T represents the total number of transactions during some period of time, say, a year. In other words, T is the number of times in a year that goods or services are exchanged for money. P is the price of a typical transaction—the number of dollars exchanged. The product of the price of a transaction and the number of transactions, PT, equals the number of dollars exchanged in a year.

The left-hand side of the quantity equation tells us about the money used to make the transactions. M is the quantity of money. V is called the **transactions velocity of money** and measures the rate at which money circulates in the economy. In other words, velocity tells us the number of times a dollar bill changes hands in a given period of time.

For example, suppose that 60 loaves of bread are sold in a given year at $0.50 per loaf. Then T equals 60 loaves per year, and P equals $0.50 per loaf. The total number of dollars exchanged is

$$PT = \$0.50/\text{loaf} \times 60 \text{ loaves/year} = \$30/\text{year}.$$

The right-hand side of the quantity equation equals $30 per year, which is the dollar value of all transactions.

Suppose further that the quantity of money in the economy is $10. By rearranging the quantity equation, we can compute velocity as

$$V = PT/M$$

$$= (\$30/\text{year})/(\$10)$$

$$= 3 \text{ times per year.}$$

That is, for $30 of transactions per year to take place with $10 of money, each dollar must change hands 3 times per year.

The quantity equation is an *identity:* the definitions of the four variables make it true. This type of equation is useful because it shows that if one of the variables changes, one or more of the others must also change to maintain the equality. For example, if the quantity of money increases and the velocity of money stays unchanged, then either the price or the number of transactions must rise.

From Transactions to Income

When studying the role of money in the economy, economists usually use a slightly different version of the quantity equation than the one just introduced. The problem with the first equation is that the number of transactions is difficult to measure. To solve this problem, the number of transactions T is replaced by the total output of the economy Y.

Transactions and output are closely related, because the more the economy produces, the more goods are bought and sold. They are not the same, however. When one person sells a used car to another person, for example, they make a transaction using money, even though the used car is not part of current output. Nonetheless, the dollar value of transactions is roughly proportional to the dollar value of output.

If Y denotes the amount of output and P denotes the price of one unit of output, then the dollar value of output is PY. We encountered measures for these variables when we discussed the national accounts in Chapter 2: Y is real GDP, P the GDP deflator, and PY nominal GDP. The quantity equation becomes

$$\text{Money} \times \text{Velocity} = \text{Price} \times \text{Output}$$
$$M \times V = P \times Y.$$

Because Y is also total income, V in this version of the quantity equation is called the **income velocity of money.** The income velocity of money tells us the number of times a dollar bill enters someone's income in a given period of time. This version of the quantity equation is the most common, and it is the one we use from now on.

The Money Demand Function and the Quantity Equation

When we analyze how money affects the economy, it is often useful to express the quantity of money in terms of the quantity of goods and services it can buy. This amount, M/P, is called **real money balances.**

Real money balances measure the purchasing power of the stock of money. For example, consider an economy that produces only bread. If the quantity of money is $10, and the price of a loaf is $0.50, then real money balances are 20 loaves of bread. That is, at current prices, the stock of money in the economy is able to buy 20 loaves.

A **money demand function** is an equation that shows the determinants of the quantity of real money balances people wish to hold. A simple money demand function is

$$(M/P)^d = kY,$$

where k is a constant that tells us how much money people want to hold for every dollar of income. This equation states that the quantity of real money balances demanded is proportional to real income.

The money demand function is like the demand function for a particular good. Here the "good" is the convenience of holding real money balances. Just as owning an automobile makes it easier for a person to travel, holding money makes it easier to make transactions. Therefore, just as higher income leads to a greater demand for automobiles, higher income also leads to a greater demand for real money balances.

This money demand function offers another way to view the quantity equation. To see this, add to the money demand function the condition that the demand for real money balances $(M/P)^d$ must equal the supply M/P. Therefore,

$$M/P = kY.$$

A simple rearrangement of terms changes this equation into

$$M(1/k) = PY,$$

which can be written as

$$MV = PY,$$

where $V = 1/k$. These few steps of simple mathematics show the link between the demand for money and the velocity of money. When people want to hold a lot of money for each dollar of income (k is large), money changes hands infrequently (V is small). Conversely, when people want to hold only a little money (k is small), money changes hands frequently (V is large). In other words, the money demand parameter k and the velocity of money V are opposite sides of the same coin.

The Assumption of Constant Velocity

The quantity equation can be viewed as merely a definition: it defines velocity V as the ratio of nominal GDP, PY, to the quantity of money M. Yet if we make the additional assumption that the velocity of money is constant, then the quantity equation becomes a useful theory about the effects of money, called the **quantity theory of money.**

As with many of the assumptions in economics, the assumption of constant velocity is only a simplification of reality. Velocity does change if the money demand function changes. For example, when automatic teller machines were introduced, people could reduce their average money holdings, which meant a fall in the money demand parameter k and an increase in velocity V. Nonetheless, experience shows that the assumption of constant velocity provides a useful approximation to the truth in many situations. Let's therefore assume that velocity is constant and see what this assumption implies about the effects of the money supply on the economy.

With this assumption included, the quantity equation can be seen as a theory of what determines nominal GDP. The quantity equation says

$$M\bar{V} = PY,$$

where the bar over V means that velocity is fixed. Therefore, a change in the quantity of money (M) must cause a proportionate change in nominal GDP (PY). That is, if velocity is fixed, the quantity of money determines the dollar value of the economy's output.

Money, Prices, and Inflation

We now have a theory to explain what determines the economy's overall level of prices. The theory has three building blocks:

1. The factors of production and the production function determine the level of output Y. We borrow this conclusion from Chapter 3.

2. The money supply determines the nominal value of output, PY. This conclusion follows from the quantity equation and the assumption that the velocity of money is fixed.

3. The price level P is then the ratio of the nominal value of output, PY, to the level of output Y.

In other words, the productive capability of the economy determines real GDP, the quantity of money determines nominal GDP, and the GDP deflator is the ratio of nominal GDP to real GDP.

This theory explains what happens when the central bank changes the supply of money. Because velocity is fixed, any change in the supply of money leads to a proportionate change in nominal GDP. Because the factors of production and the production function have already determined real GDP, nominal GDP can adjust only if the price level changes. Hence, the quantity theory implies that the price level is proportional to the money supply.

Because the inflation rate is the percentage change in the price level, this theory of the price level is also a theory of the inflation rate. The quantity equation, written in percentage-change form, is

$$\% \text{ Change in } M + \% \text{ Change in } V = \% \text{ Change in } P + \% \text{ Change in } Y.$$

Consider each of these four terms. First, the percentage change in the quantity of money M is under the control of the central bank. Second, the percentage change in velocity V reflects shifts in money demand; we have assumed that velocity is constant, so the percentage change in velocity is zero. Third, the percentage change in the price level P is the rate of inflation; this is the variable in the equation that we would like to explain. Fourth, the percentage change in output Y depends on growth in the factors of production and on technological progress, which for our present purposes we can take as given. This analysis tells us that (except for a constant that depends on exogenous growth in output) the growth in the money supply determines the rate of inflation.

Thus, the quantity theory of money states that the central bank, which controls the money supply, has ultimate control over the rate of inflation. If the central bank keeps the money supply stable, the price level will be stable. If the central bank increases the money supply rapidly, the price level will rise rapidly.

CASE STUDY

Inflation and Money Growth

"Inflation is always and everywhere a monetary phenomenon." So wrote Milton Friedman, the great economist who won the Nobel Prize in economics in 1976. The quantity theory of money leads us to agree that the growth in the quantity of money is the primary determinant of the inflation rate. Yet Friedman's claim is empirical, not theoretical. To evaluate his claim, and to judge the usefulness of our theory, we need to look at data on money and prices.

Friedman, together with fellow economist Anna Schwartz, wrote two treatises on monetary history that documented the sources and effects of changes in the quantity of money over the past century.[3] Figure 4-1 uses some of their data

---

[3] Milton Friedman and Anna J. Schwartz, *A Monetary History of the United States, 1867–1960* (Princeton, NJ: Princeton University Press, 1963); Milton Friedman and Anna J. Schwartz, *Monetary Trends in the United States and the United Kingdom: Their Relation to Income, Prices, and Interest Rates, 1867–1975* (Chicago: University of Chicago Press, 1982).

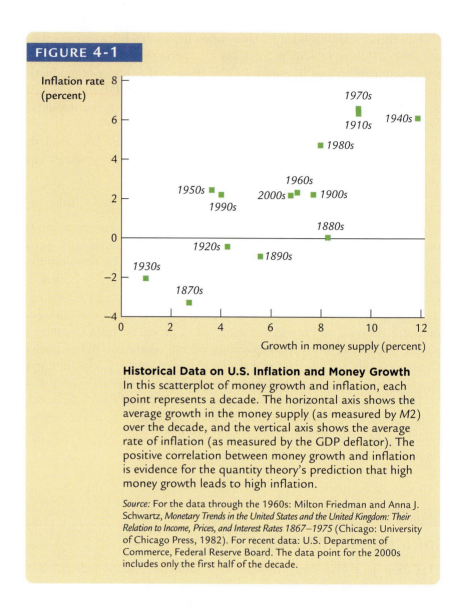

FIGURE 4-1

Historical Data on U.S. Inflation and Money Growth
In this scatterplot of money growth and inflation, each point represents a decade. The horizontal axis shows the average growth in the money supply (as measured by *M2*) over the decade, and the vertical axis shows the average rate of inflation (as measured by the GDP deflator). The positive correlation between money growth and inflation is evidence for the quantity theory's prediction that high money growth leads to high inflation.

Source: For the data through the 1960s: Milton Friedman and Anna J. Schwartz, *Monetary Trends in the United States and the United Kingdom: Their Relation to Income, Prices, and Interest Rates 1867–1975* (Chicago: University of Chicago Press, 1982). For recent data: U.S. Department of Commerce, Federal Reserve Board. The data point for the 2000s includes only the first half of the decade.

and plots the average rate of money growth and the average rate of inflation in the United States over each decade since the 1870s. The data verify the link between inflation and growth in the quantity of money. Decades with high money growth (such as the 1970s) tend to have high inflation, and decades with low money growth (such as the 1930s) tend to have low inflation.

Figure 4-2 examines the same question with international data. It shows the average rate of inflation and the average rate of money growth in 165 countries plus the Euro Area during the period from 1999 to 2007. Again, the link between money growth and inflation is clear. Countries with high money growth (such as Turkey) tend to have high inflation, and countries with low money growth (such as Singapore) tend to have low inflation.

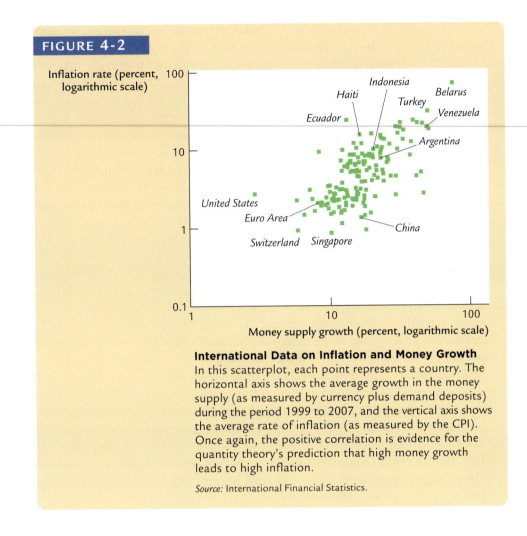

FIGURE 4-2

International Data on Inflation and Money Growth
In this scatterplot, each point represents a country. The horizontal axis shows the average growth in the money supply (as measured by currency plus demand deposits) during the period 1999 to 2007, and the vertical axis shows the average rate of inflation (as measured by the CPI). Once again, the positive correlation is evidence for the quantity theory's prediction that high money growth leads to high inflation.

Source: International Financial Statistics.

If we looked at monthly data on money growth and inflation, rather than data for 10-year periods, we would not see as close a connection between these two variables. This is because real GDP is not independent of the money supply in the short run. Thus, the quantity theory of inflation works best in the long run, not in the short run. We examine the short-run impact of changes in the quantity of money when we turn to economic fluctuations in Part Four of this book.

4-3 Seigniorage: The Revenue from Printing Money

So far, we have seen how growth in the money supply causes inflation. With inflation as a consequence, what would ever induce a central bank to increase the money supply so much? Here we examine one answer to this question.

Let's start with an indisputable fact: all governments spend money. Some of this spending is to buy goods and services (such as roads and police), and some is to provide transfer payments (for the poor and elderly, for example). A government can finance its spending in three ways. First, it can raise revenue through taxes, such as personal and corporate income taxes. Second, it can borrow from the public by selling government bonds. Third, it can simply print money. It does this indirectly—by selling bonds to the central bank and having the central bank issue new money to pay for the bonds.

The revenue raised by the printing of money is called **seigniorage.** The term comes from *seigneur,* the French word for "feudal lord." In the Middle Ages, the lord had the exclusive right on his manor to coin money. Today this right belongs to the central government, and it is one source of revenue.

When the government prints money to finance expenditure, it increases the money supply. The increase in the money supply, in turn, causes inflation. Printing money to raise revenue is like imposing an *inflation tax.*

At first it may not be obvious that inflation can be viewed as a tax. After all, no one receives a bill for this tax—the government merely prints the money it needs. Who then pays the inflation tax? The answer is the holders of money. As prices rise, the real value of the money in your wallet falls. When the government prints new money for its use, it makes the old money in the hands of the public less valuable. Thus, inflation is like a tax on holding money.

The amount of revenue raised by printing money varies substantially from country to country. In North America, the amount has been small: seigniorage has usually accounted for only about 1 percent of government revenue. In Italy and Greece, seigniorage has often been over 10 percent of government revenue.[4] In countries experiencing hyperinflation, seigniorage is often the government's chief source of revenue—indeed, the need to print money to finance expenditure is a primary cause of hyperinflation.

CASE STUDY

American and Russian Inflations

Although seigniorage has not been a major source of revenue for either the Canadian or the American government in recent history, the situation was very different two centuries ago in the United States, and it has been very different in Russia recently. We consider first the American history.

---

[4] William Scarth, "A Note on the Desirability of a Separate Quebec Currency," in David Laidler and William Robson, *Two Nations, One Money?* (Toronto: C.D. Howe Institute, 1991): 76; Stanley Fischer, "Seigniorage and the Case for a National Money," *Journal of Political Economy* 90 (April 1982): 295–313.

Beginning in 1775 the Continental Congress needed to find a way to finance the Revolution, but it had limited ability to raise revenue through taxation. It therefore relied heavily on the printing of fiat money to help pay for the war. The Continental Congress's reliance on seigniorage increased over time. In 1775 new issues of continental currency were approximately $6 million. This amount increased to $19 million in 1776, $13 million in 1777, $63 million in 1778, and $125 million in 1779.

Not surprisingly, this rapid growth in the money supply led to massive inflation. At the end of the war, the price of gold measured in continental dollars was more than 100 times its level of only a few years earlier. The large quantity of the continental currency made the continental dollar nearly worthless. This experience also gave birth to a once popular expression: people used to say something was "not worth a continental" to mean that the item had little real value.

When the new nation won its independence, there was a natural skepticism about fiat money. Upon the recommendation of the first Secretary of Treasury, Alexander Hamilton, the Congress passed the Mint Act of 1792, which established gold and silver as the basis for a new system of commodity money.

The Russian ruble is another currency that has fallen precipitously in value. During the early 1990s, the former system of central planning was abandoned. But without a well-developed market system and without the trade that had taken place earlier with the other former Soviet republics, many factories found that there was no demand for their output. To avoid massive layoffs, the government simply printed up vast quantities of money to subsidize the operation of the factories. As the quantity theory predicts, prices began to soar. In the final months of 1992, for example, inflation was running at a rate of 1,300 percent per year. ■

4-4 Inflation and Interest Rates

As we first discussed in Chapter 3, interest rates are among the most important macroeconomic variables. In essence, they are the prices that link the present and the future. Here we discuss the relationship between inflation and interest rates.

Two Interest Rates: Real and Nominal

Suppose you deposit your savings in a bank account that pays 8 percent interest annually. Next year, you withdraw your savings and the accumulated interest. Are you 8 percent richer than you were when you made the deposit a year earlier?

The answer depends on what "richer" means. Certainly, you have 8 percent more dollars than you had before. But if prices have risen, so that each dollar buys less, then your purchasing power has not risen by 8 percent. If the inflation rate was 5 percent, then the amount of goods you can buy has increased by only 3 percent. And if the inflation rate was 10 percent, then your purchasing power actually fell by 2 percent.

The interest rate that the bank pays is called the **nominal interest rate** and the increase in your purchasing power is called the **real interest rate.** If i denotes the nominal interest rate, r the real interest rate, and p the rate of inflation, then the relationship among these three variables can be written as

$$r = i - \pi.$$

The real interest rate is the difference between the nominal interest rate and the rate of inflation.[5]

The Fisher Effect

Rearranging terms in our equation for the real interest rate, we can show that the nominal interest rate is the sum of the real interest rate and the inflation rate:

$$i = r + \pi.$$

The equation written in this way is called the **Fisher equation,** after economist Irving Fisher (1867–1947). It shows that the nominal interest rate can change for two reasons: because the real interest rate changes or because the inflation rate changes.

Once we separate the nominal interest rate into these two parts, we can use this equation to develop a theory that explains the nominal interest rate. Chapter 3 showed that the real interest rate adjusts to equilibrate saving and investment. The quantity theory of money shows that the rate of money growth determines the rate of inflation. The Fisher equation then tells us to add the real interest rate and the inflation rate together to determine the nominal interest rate.

The quantity theory and the Fisher equation together tell us how money growth affects the nominal interest rate. *According to the quantity theory, an increase in the rate of money growth of 1 percent causes a 1 percent increase in the rate of inflation. According to the Fisher equation, a 1 percent increase in the rate of inflation in turn causes a 1 percent increase in the nominal interest rate.* The one-for-one relation between the inflation rate and the nominal interest rate is called the **Fisher effect.**

---

[5] *Mathematical note:* This equation relating the real interest rate, nominal interest rate, and inflation rate is only an approximation. The exact formula is $(1 + r) = (1 + i)/(1 + \pi)$. The approximation in the text is reasonably accurate as long as r, i, and π are relatively small (say, less than 20 percent per year).

Inflation and Nominal Interest Rates

How useful is the Fisher effect in explaining interest rates? To answer this question we look at two types of data on inflation and nominal interest rates.

Figure 4-3 shows the variation over time in the nominal interest rate and the inflation rate in Canada. You can see that the Fisher effect has done a good job of explaining fluctuations in the nominal interest rate over the past fifty years. When inflation is high, nominal interest rates are typically high, and when inflation is low, nominal interest rates are typically low as well.

Similar support for the Fisher effect comes from examining the variation across countries at a single point in time. As Figure 4-4 shows, a nation's inflation rate and its nominal interest rate are closely related. Countries with high inflation tend to have high nominal interest rates as well, and countries with low inflation tend to have low nominal interest rates.

The link between inflation and interest rates is well known to investment firms. Because bond prices move inversely with interest rates, one can get rich by predicting correctly the direction in which interest rates will move. Many investment firms hire *central bank watchers* to monitor monetary policy and news about inflation in order to anticipate changes in interest rates.

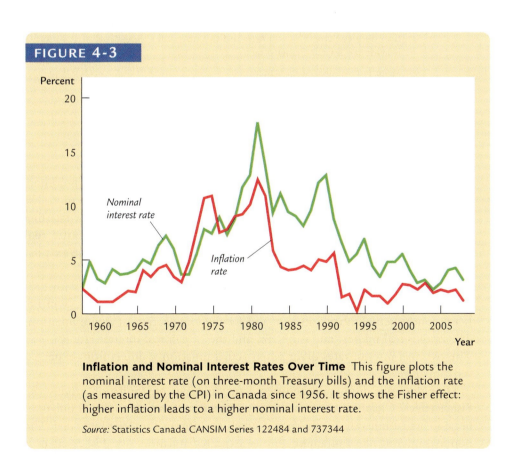

FIGURE 4-3

Inflation and Nominal Interest Rates Over Time This figure plots the nominal interest rate (on three-month Treasury bills) and the inflation rate (as measured by the CPI) in Canada since 1956. It shows the Fisher effect: higher inflation leads to a higher nominal interest rate.

Source: Statistics Canada CANSIM Series 122484 and 737344

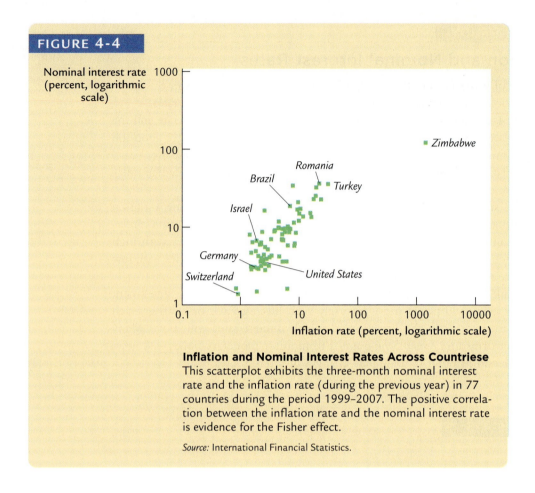

FIGURE 4-4

Nominal interest rate (percent, logarithmic scale)

Inflation rate (percent, logarithmic scale)

Inflation and Nominal Interest Rates Across Countriese
This scatterplot exhibits the three-month nominal interest rate and the inflation rate (during the previous year) in 77 countries during the period 1999–2007. The positive correlation between the inflation rate and the nominal interest rate is evidence for the Fisher effect.

Source: International Financial Statistics.

Two Real Interest Rates: *Ex Ante* and *Ex Post*

When a borrower and lender agree on a nominal interest rate, they do not know what the inflation rate over the term of the loan will be. Therefore, we must distinguish between two concepts of the real interest rate: the real interest rate that the borrower and lender expect when the loan is made, called the **ex ante real interest rate,** and the real interest rate that is actually realized, called the **ex post real interest rate.**

Although borrowers and lenders cannot predict future inflation with certainty, they do have some expectation about what the inflation rate will be. Let π denote actual future inflation and $E\pi$ the expectation of future inflation. The *ex ante* real interest rate is $i - E\pi,$ and the *ex post* real interest rate is $i - \pi$. The two real interest rates differ when actual inflation π differs from expected inflation $E\pi$.

How does this distinction between actual and expected inflation modify the Fisher effect? Clearly, the nominal interest rate cannot adjust to actual inflation, because actual inflation is not known when the nominal interest rate is set. The nominal interest rate can adjust only to expected inflation. The Fisher effect is more precisely written as

$$i = r + E\pi.$$

The *ex ante* real interest rate *r* is determined by equilibrium in the market for goods and services, as described by the model in Chapter 3. The nominal interest rate *i* moves one-for-one with changes in expected inflation $E\pi$.

CASE STUDY

Nominal Interest Rates in the Nineteenth Century

Although recent data show a positive relationship between nominal interest rates and inflation rates, this finding is not universal. In data from the late nineteenth and early twentieth centuries, high nominal interest rates did not accompany high inflation. The apparent absence of any Fisher effect during this time puzzled Irving Fisher. He suggested that inflation "caught merchants napping."

How should we interpret the absence of an apparent Fisher effect in nineteenth-century data? Does this period of history provide evidence against the adjustment of nominal interest rates to inflation? Recent research suggests that this period has little to tell us about the validity of the Fisher effect. The reason is that the Fisher effect relates the nominal interest rate to expected inflation and, according to this research, inflation at this time was largely unexpected.

Although expectations are not directly observable, we can draw inferences about them by examining the persistence of inflation. In recent experience, inflation has been highly persistent: when it is high one year, it tends to be high the next year as well. Therefore, when people have observed high inflation, it has been rational for them to expect high inflation in the future. By contrast, during the nineteenth century, when the gold standard was in effect, inflation had little persistence. High inflation in one year was just as likely to be followed the next year by low inflation as by high inflation. Therefore, high inflation did not imply high expected inflation and did not lead to high nominal interest rates. So, in a sense, Fisher was right to say that inflation "caught merchants napping."[6] ■

4-5 The Nominal Interest Rate and the Demand for Money

The quantity theory is based on a simple money demand function: it assumes that the demand for real money balances is proportional to income. Although the quantity theory is a good place to start when analyzing the effects of money on the economy, it is not the whole story. Here we add another determinant of the quantity of money demanded—the nominal interest rate.

---

[6] Robert B. Barsky, "The Fisher Effect and the Forecastability and Persistence of Inflation," *Journal of Monetary Economics* 19 (January 1987): 3–24.

The Cost of Holding Money

The money you hold in your wallet does not earn interest. If instead of holding that money you used it to buy government bonds or deposited it in a savings account, you would earn the nominal interest rate. Therefore, the nominal interest rate is the opportunity cost of holding money: it is what you give up by holding money rather than bonds.

Another way to see that the cost of holding money equals the nominal interest rate is by comparing the real returns on alternative assets. Assets other than money, such as government bonds, earn the real return r. Money earns an expected real return of $-E\pi$, because its real value declines at the rate of inflation. When you hold money, you give up the difference between these two returns. Thus, the cost of holding money is $r - (-E\pi)$, which the Fisher equation tells us is the nominal interest rate i.

Just as the quantity of bread demanded depends on the price of bread, the quantity of money demanded depends on the price of holding money. Hence, the demand for real money balances depends both on the level of income and on the nominal interest rate. We write the general money demand function as

$$(M/P)^d = L(i, Y).$$

The letter L is used to denote money demand because money is the economy's most liquid asset (the asset most easily used to make transactions). This equation states that the demand for the liquidity of real money balances is a function of income and the nominal interest rate. The higher the level of income Y, the greater the demand for real money balances. The higher the nominal interest rate i, the lower the demand for real money balances. This dependence of money demand on the interest rate is central to our discussion of short-run stabilization policy in Chapters 11 and 12.

Of course, money demand depends on other things as well—such as innovations in the financial sector (for example, the development of money substitutes). Our discussion abstracts from such other long-run trends.

Future Money and Current Prices

Money, prices, and interest rates are now related in several ways. Figure 4-5 illustrates the linkages we have discussed. As the quantity theory of money explains, money supply and money demand together determine the equilibrium price level. Changes in the price level are, by definition, the rate of inflation. Inflation, in turn, affects the nominal interest rate through the Fisher effect. But now, because the nominal interest rate is the cost of holding money, the nominal interest rate feeds back to affect the demand for money.

Consider how introduction of this last link affects our theory of the price level. First, equate the supply of real money balances M/P to the demand $L(i, Y)$:

$$M/P = L(i, Y).$$

FIGURE 4-5

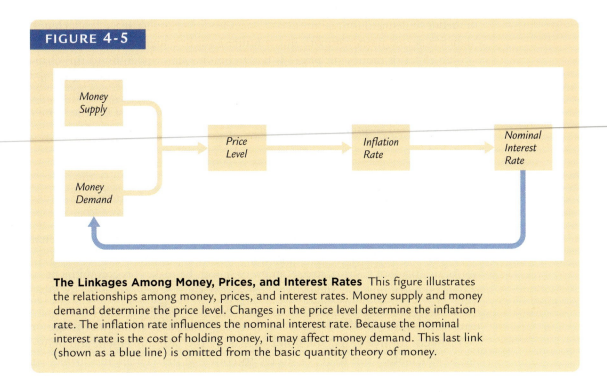

The Linkages Among Money, Prices, and Interest Rates This figure illustrates the relationships among money, prices, and interest rates. Money supply and money demand determine the price level. Changes in the price level determine the inflation rate. The inflation rate influences the nominal interest rate. Because the nominal interest rate is the cost of holding money, it may affect money demand. This last link (shown as a blue line) is omitted from the basic quantity theory of money.

Next, use the Fisher equation to write the nominal interest rate as the sum of the real interest rate and expected inflation:

$$M/P = L(r + E\pi, Y).$$

This equation states that the level of real money balances depends on the expected rate of inflation.

The last equation tells a more sophisticated story about the determination of the price level than does the quantity theory. The quantity theory of money says that today's money supply determines today's price level. This conclusion remains partly true: if the nominal interest rate and the level of output are held constant, the price level moves proportionately with the money supply. Yet the nominal interest rate is not constant; it depends on expected inflation, which in turn depends on growth in the money supply. The presence of the nominal interest rate in the money demand function yields an additional channel through which money supply affects the price level.

This general money demand equation implies that the price level depends not just on today's money supply but also on the money supply expected in the future. To see why, suppose the Bank of Canada announces that it will increase the money supply in the future, but it does not change the money supply today. This announcement causes people to expect higher money growth and higher inflation. Through the Fisher effect, this increase in expected inflation raises the nominal interest rate. The higher nominal interest rate immediately increases the cost of holding money and therefore reduces the demand for real money balances. Because the central bank has not changed the quantity of money available today, the reduced demand for real money balances leads to a higher price level. Hence, higher expected money growth in the future leads to a higher price level today.

The effect of money on prices is fairly complex. The appendix to this chapter presents the *Cagan model,* which shows how the price level is related to current and expected future money. The conclusion of the analysis is that the price level depends on a weighted average of the current money supply and the money supply expected to prevail in the future.

Canadian Monetary Policy

Given the fact that the price level depends on the money supply that is expected to prevail in the future, it is not surprising that Mark Carney, the current Governor of the Bank of Canada, stresses in every speech he makes his commitment to maintaining low inflation. Indeed, well before Mr. Carney was appointed in 2008, the government had opted for a series of five-year inflation targets—a commitment that the Bank of Canada would keep inflation within the range of 1–3 percent for five years. The point of making this announcement and drawing so much attention to it was to try to convince individuals and firms that the Bank of Canada really would keep money growth limited for the foreseeable future. Clearly, the officials in both the Department of Finance and the Bank of Canada believe that inflation *now* depends very much on the rate at which private agents *expect* the Bank will issue money in the *future.* Policy is based on the view that the Bank of Canada's "credibility" must be maintained, and that this stance involves convincing private individuals that money growth will not be excessive.

In the debates on constitutional change in 1992, one of the federal government's proposals was that the Bank of Canada Act be changed to make the maintenance of price stability the *sole* objective of monetary policy. The government wanted to dispell any notions people might have that the Bank would give up its commitment to price stability, even if some other crisis, such as a deep recession, emerged. Clearly, officials believe that the analysis we have just summarized is directly relevant to the Canadian policy challenge. ■

4-6 The Social Costs of Inflation

Our discussion of the causes and effects of inflation does not tell us much about the social problems that result from inflation. We turn to those problems now.

The Layman's View and the Classical Response

If you ask the average person why inflation is a social problem, he will probably answer that inflation makes him poorer. "Each year my boss gives me a raise, but prices go up and that takes some of my raise away from me." The implicit assumption in this statement is that if there were no inflation, he would get the same raise and be able to buy more goods.

This complaint about inflation is a common fallacy. From Chapters 3, 7, and 8, we know that increases in the purchasing power of labour come from capital accumulation and technological progress. In particular, the real wage does not depend on how much money the government chooses to print. If the central bank reduces inflation by slowing the rate of money growth, workers will not see their real wage increasing more rapidly. Instead, when inflation slows, firms will increase the prices of their products less each year and, as a result, will give their workers smaller raises.

According to the classical theory of money, a change in the overall price level is like a change in the units of measurement. It is as if we switched from measuring distances in metres to measuring them in centimetres: numbers get larger, but nothing really changes. Imagine that tomorrow morning you wake up and find that, for some reason, all dollar figures in the economy have been multiplied by ten. The price of everything you buy has increased tenfold, but so has your wage and the value of your savings. What difference would such a price increase make in your life? All numbers would have an extra zero at the end, but nothing else would change. Your economic well-being depends on relative prices, not the overall price level.

Why, then, is a persistent increase in the price level a social problem? It turns out that the costs of inflation are subtle. Indeed, economists disagree about the size of the social costs. To the surprise of many laymen, some economists argue that the costs of inflation are small—at least for the moderate rates of inflation that most countries have experienced in recent years.[7]

CASE STUDY

What Economists and the Public Say About Inflation

As we have been discussing, laymen and economists hold very different views about the costs of inflation. In 1996, economist Robert Shiller documented this difference of opinion in a survey of the two groups. The survey results are striking, for they show how radically the study of economics changes a person's attitudes.

In one question, Shiller asked people whether their "biggest gripe about inflation" was that "inflation hurts my real buying power, it makes me poorer." Of the general public, 77 percent agreed with this statement, compared to only 12 percent of economists. Shiller also asked people whether they agreed with the following statement: "When I see projections about how many times more a college education will cost, or how many times more the cost of living will be in coming decades, I feel a sense of uneasiness; these inflation projections really make me worry that my own income will not rise as much as such costs

---

[7] See, for example, Chapter 2 of Alan Blinder, *Hard Heads, Soft Hearts: Tough-Minded Economics for a Just Society* (Reading, MA: Addison Wesley, 1987).

will." Among the general public, 66 percent said they fully agreed with this statement, while only 5 percent of economists agreed with it.

Survey respondents were asked to judge the seriousness of inflation as a policy problem: "Do you agree that preventing high inflation is an important national priority, as important as preventing drug abuse or preventing deterioration in the quality of our schools?" Shiller found that 52 percent of laymen, but only 18 percent of economists, fully agreed with this view. Apparently, inflation worries the public much more than it does the economics profession.

The public's distaste for inflation may be partly psychological. Shiller asked those surveyed if they agreed with the following statement: "I think that if my pay went up I would feel more satisfaction in my job, more sense of fulfillment, even if prices went up just as much." Of the public, 49 percent fully or partly agreed with this statement, compared to 8 percent of economists.

Do these survey results mean that laymen are wrong and economists are right about the costs of inflation? Not necessarily. But economists do have the advantage of having given the issue more thought. So let's now consider what some of the costs of inflation might be.[8] ■

The Costs of Expected Inflation

Consider first the case of expected inflation. Suppose that every month the price level rose by 1 percent. What would be the social costs of such a steady and predictable 12 percent annual inflation?

One cost is the distortion of the inflation tax on the amount of money people hold. As we have already discussed, a higher inflation rate leads to a higher nominal interest rate, which in turn leads to lower real money balances. If people are to hold lower money balances on average, they must make more frequent trips to the bank to withdraw money—for example, they might withdraw $50 twice a week rather than $100 once a week. The inconvenience of reducing money holding is metaphorically called the **shoeleather cost** of inflation, because walking to the bank more often causes one's shoes to wear out more quickly.

A second cost of inflation arises because high inflation induces firms to change their posted prices more often. Changing prices is sometimes costly: for example, it may require printing and distributing a new catalogue. These costs are called **menu costs,** because the higher the rate of inflation, the more often restaurants have to print new menus.

A third cost of inflation arises because firms facing menu costs change prices infrequently; therefore, the higher the rate of inflation, the greater the variability in relative prices. For example, suppose a firm issues a new catalogue every January. If there is no inflation, then the firm's prices relative to the overall price level are constant over the year. Yet if inflation is 1 percent per month, then from the beginning to the end of the year the firm's relative prices fall by 12 percent.

---

[8] Robert J. Shiller, "Why Do People Dislike Inflation?" in Christina D. Romer and David H. Romer, eds., *Reducing Inflation: Motivation and Strategy* (Chicago: University of Chicago Press, 1997).

Sales from this catalogue will tend to be low early in the year (when its prices are relatively high) and high later in the year (when its prices are relatively low). Hence, when inflation induces variability in relative prices, it leads to microeconomic inefficiencies in the allocation of resources.

A fourth cost of inflation results from the tax laws. Many provisions of the tax system do not take into account the effects of inflation. Inflation can alter an individual's tax liability, often in ways that lawmakers did not intend.

One example of the failure of the tax system to deal with inflation is the tax treatment of capital gains. Suppose you buy some stock today and sell it a year from now at the same real price. It would seem reasonable for the government not to levy a tax, since you have earned no real income from this investment. Indeed, if there is no inflation, a zero tax liability would be the outcome. But suppose the rate of inflation is 12 percent and you initially paid $100 per share for the stock; for the real price to be the same a year later, you must sell the stock for $112 per share. In this case the personal income tax system, which ignores the effects of inflation, says that you have earned $12 per share in income, and the government taxes you on this capital gain. The problem, of course, is that the tax system measures income as the nominal rather than the real capital gain. In this example, and in many others, inflation distorts how taxes are levied.

A similar problem occurs with interest-income taxes. Because the Canadian tax system was designed for a zero-inflation environment, it does not work well when inflation occurs. It turns out that when inflation and the tax system interact, the result is a powerful disincentive to save and invest. And worse still, this problem occurs even for mild inflations and even when all individuals anticipate inflation perfectly. Let us see how this problem develops, by adding interest-income taxes to our discussion of the Fisher equation.

If t stands for the tax rate that an individual must pay on her interest income, the *after-tax* real yield is

$$\text{After–tax } r = i(1 - t) - \pi.$$

Consider what happens to this effective yield on savings if inflation rises from 0 percent to 10 percent. Assume that the nominal interest rate rises by the same 10 percentage points—enough to compensate lenders fully for the inflation, if it were not for the tax system. The revised Fisher equation makes clear that the after-tax real yield must fall by t times 10 percent in this case. If the individual's marginal tax rate is 50 percent, the reduction in the real return to saving is a full $t\pi = 5$ percentage points. Most economists believe that this represents a significant disincentive to save, and so inflation reduces capital accumulation and future living standards.

The problem is that the tax system taxes nominal interest income instead of real interest income. During an inflationary time, much of an individual's nominal interest receipts are just a compensation for the fact that the loan's principal value is shrinking. Since that "inflation premium" part of interest is not income at all, it should not be taxed. If the tax system were fully indexed, it would not be taxed. In that case, the after-tax real yield would be given by

$$\text{After–tax } r = (i - \pi)(1 - t).$$

In this case, as long as the nominal interest rate rises one-for-one with inflation (as we discussed in the nonindexed tax case), the after-tax real yield is *not* reduced at all by inflation. The disincentive for saving and investment is removed.

Nevertheless, because our tax system does not limit taxes on interest earnings to just real returns, one of the central costs of inflation is that it lowers the economy's accumulation of capital, and so it reduces the standard of living for all members of future generations.

A fifth cost of inflation is the inconvenience of living in a world with a changing price level. Money is the ruler with which we measure economic transactions. When there is inflation, that ruler is changing in length. To continue the analogy, suppose that Parliament passed a law specifying that a metre would equal 100 centimetres in 2010, 95 centimetres in 2011, 90 centimetres in 2012, and so on. Although the law would result in no ambiguity, it would be highly inconvenient. When someone measured a distance in metres, it would be necessary to specify whether the measurement was in 2010 metres or 2011 metres; to compare distances measured in different years, one would need to make an "inflation" correction. Similarly, the changing value of the dollar requires that we correct for inflation when comparing dollar figures from different times.

For example, a changing price level complicates personal financial planning. One important decision that all households face is how much of their income to consume today and how much to save for retirement. A dollar saved today and invested at a fixed nominal interest rate will yield a fixed dollar amount in the future. Yet the real value of that dollar amount—which will determine the retiree's living standard—depends on the future price level. Deciding how much to save would be much simpler if people could count on the price level in 30 years being similar to its level today.

The Costs of Unexpected Inflation

Unexpected inflation has an effect that is more pernicious than any of the costs of steady, anticipated inflation: it arbitrarily redistributes wealth among individuals. You can see how this works by examining long-term loans. Loan agreements typically specify a nominal interest rate, which is based on the rate of inflation expected at the time of the agreement. If inflation turns out differently from what was expected, the *ex post* real return that the debtor pays to the creditor differs from what both parties anticipated. On the one hand, if inflation turns out to be higher than expected, the debtor wins and the creditor loses because the debtor repays the loan with less valuable dollars. On the other hand, if inflation turns out to be lower than expected, the creditor wins and the debtor loses because the repayment is worth more than the two parties anticipated.

Consider, for example, a person taking out a mortgage in 1960. At the time, a 30-year mortgage had an interest rate of about 6 percent per year. This rate was based on a low rate of expected inflation—inflation over the previous decade had averaged only 2.5 percent. The creditor probably expected to receive a real return of about 3.5 percent, and the debtor expected to pay this real return. In fact, over the life of the mortgage, the inflation rate averaged 5.5 percent, so the *ex post* real return was only 0.5 percent. This unanticipated inflation benefited the debtor at the expense of the creditor.

Unanticipated inflation also hurts individuals on fixed pensions. Workers and firms often agree on a fixed nominal pension when the worker retires (or even earlier). Since the pension is deferred earnings, the worker is essentially providing the firm a loan: the worker provides labour services to the firm while young but does not get fully paid until old age. Like any creditor, the worker is hurt when inflation is higher than anticipated. Like any debtor, the firm is hurt when inflation is lower than anticipated. The magnitudes involved in these arbitrary redistributions of income can be very large. For example, with inflation of just 5 percent per year, the purchasing power of money *halves* in value in fewer than 15 years. So in a period when inflation is underpredicted by 5 percent, pensioners' real income is cut in half well before they are expected to die. This reduction in real income can be devastating.

These situations provide a clear argument against highly variable inflation. The more variable the rate of inflation, the greater the uncertainty that both debtors and creditors face. Since most people are *risk averse*—they dislike uncertainty—the unpredictability caused by highly variable inflation hurts almost everyone.

Given these effects of uncertain inflation, it is puzzling that nominal contracts are so prevalent. One might expect debtors and creditors to protect themselves from this uncertainty by writing contracts in real terms—that is, by indexing to some measure of the price level. In economies with extremely high and variable inflation, indexation is often widespread; sometimes this indexation takes the form of writing contracts using a more stable foreign currency. In economies with moderate inflation, such as Canada, indexation is less common. Yet even in Canada, some long-term obligations are indexed. For example, Canada Pension benefits for the elderly are adjusted annually in response to changes in the consumer price index, as is the basic personal exemption in the income tax system.

Finally, in thinking about the costs of inflation, it is important to note a widely documented but little understood fact: high inflation is variable inflation. That is, countries with high average inflation also tend to have inflation rates that change greatly from year to year. The implication is that if a country decides to pursue a high-inflation monetary policy, it will likely have to accept highly variable inflation as well. As we have just discussed, highly variable inflation increases uncertainty for both creditors and debtors by subjecting them to arbitrary and potentially large redistributions of wealth.

CASE STUDY

The Wizard of Oz

The redistributions of wealth caused by unexpected changes in the price level are often a source of political turmoil, as evidenced by the Free Silver movement in the late nineteenth century in the United States. From 1880 to 1896 the price level in the United States fell 23 percent. This deflation was good for creditors, primarily the bankers of the Northeast, but it was bad for debtors, primarily the farmers of the South and West. One proposed solution to this problem was to replace the gold standard with a bimetallic standard, under which both gold and silver could be minted into coin. The move to a bimetallic standard would increase the money supply and stop the deflation.

The silver issue dominated the presidential election of 1896. William McKinley, the Republican nominee, campaigned on a platform of preserving the gold standard. William Jennings Bryan, the Democratic nominee, supported the bimetallic standard. In a famous speech, Bryan proclaimed, "You shall not press down upon the brow of labor this crown of thorns, you shall not crucify mankind upon a cross of gold." Not surprisingly, McKinley was the candidate of the conservative eastern establishment, while Bryan was the candidate of the southern and western populists.

This debate over silver found its most memorable expression in a children's book, *The Wizard of Oz*. Written by a midwestern journalist, L. Frank Baum, just after the 1896 election, it tells the story of Dorothy, a girl lost in a strange land far from her home in Kansas. Dorothy (representing traditional American values) makes three friends: a scarecrow (the farmer), a tin woodman (the industrial worker), and a lion whose roar exceeds his might (William Jennings Bryan). Together, the four of them make their way along a perilous yellow brick road (the gold standard), hoping to find the Wizard who will help Dorothy return home. Eventually they arrive in Oz (Washington), where everyone sees the world through green glasses (money). The Wizard (William McKinley) tries to be all things to all people but turns out to be a fraud. Dorothy's problem is solved only when she learns about the magical power of her silver slippers.[9]

Although the Republicans won the election of 1896 and the United States stayed on a gold standard, the Free Silver advocates got what they ultimately wanted: inflation. Around the time of the election, gold was discovered in Alaska, Australia, and South Africa. In addition, gold refiners devised the cyanide process, which facilitated the extraction of gold from ore. These developments led to increases in the money supply and in prices. From 1896 to 1910 the price level rose 35 percent. ∎

One Possible Benefit of Inflation

So far we have discussed the many costs of inflation. These costs lead many economists to conclude that monetary policymakers should aim for zero inflation. Yet there is another side to the story. Some economists believe that a little bit of inflation—say, 2 percent per year—can be a good thing.

The argument for moderate inflation starts with the observation that cuts in nominal wages are rare: firms are reluctant to cut their workers' nominal wages, and workers are reluctant to accept such cuts. A 2 percent wage cut in a zero inflation world is, in real terms, the same as a 3 percent raise with 5 percent inflation, but workers do not always see it that way. The 2 percent wage cut may seem like an insult, whereas the 3 percent raise is, after all, still a raise. Empirical studies confirm that nominal wages rarely fall.

This finding suggests that some inflation may make labour markets work better. The supply and demand for different kinds of labour are always changing.

---

[9] The movie made forty years later hid much of the allegory by changing Dorothy's slippers from silver to ruby. For more on this topic, see Henry M. Littlefield, "The Wizard of Oz: Parable on Populism," *American Quarterly* 16 (Spring 1964): 47–58; and Hugh Rockoff, "The Wizard of Oz as a Monetary Allegory," *Journal of Political Economy* 98 (August 1990): 739–760.

Sometimes an increase in supply or decrease in demand leads to a fall in the equilibrium real wage for a group of workers. If nominal wages can't be cut, then the only way to cut real wages is to allow inflation to do the job. Without inflation, the real wage will be stuck above the equilibrium level, resulting in higher unemployment.

For this reason, some economists argue that inflation "greases the wheels" of labour markets. Only a little inflation is needed: an inflation rate of 2 percent lets real wages fall by 2 percent per year, or 20 percent per decade, without cuts in nominal wages. Such automatic reductions in real wages are impossible with zero inflation.[10]

4-7 Hyperinflation

Hyperinflation is often defined as inflation that exceeds 50 percent per month, which is just over 1 percent per day. Compounded over many months, this rate of inflation leads to very large increases in the price level. An inflation rate of

---

Keynes (and Lenin) on the Cost of Inflation

The great economist John Maynard Keynes was no friend of inflation, as this chapter's opening quotation indicates. Here is the more complete passage from his famous book, *The Economic Consequences of the Peace,* in which Keynes predicted (correctly) that the treaty imposed on Germany after World War I would lead to economic hardship and renewed international tensions:

> Lenin is said to have declared that the best way to destroy the Capitalist System was to debauch the currency. By a continuing process of inflation, governments can confiscate, secretly and unobserved, an important part of the wealth of their citizens. By this method they not only confiscate, but they confiscate *arbitrarily;* and, while the process impoverishes many, it actually enriches some. The sight of this arbitrary rearrangement of riches strikes not only at security, but at confidence in the equity of the existing distribution of wealth. Those to whom the system brings windfalls, beyond their deserts and even beyond their expectations or desires, become "profiteers," who are the object of the hatred of the bourgeoisie, whom the inflationism has impoverished, not less than of the proletariat. As the inflation proceeds and the real value of the currency fluctuates wildly from month to month, all permanent relations between debtors and creditors, which form the ultimate foundation of capitalism, become so utterly disordered as to be almost meaningless; and the process of wealth-getting degenerates into a gamble and a lottery.
>
> Lenin was certainly right. There is no subtler, no surer means of overturning the existing basis of society than to debauch the currency. The process engages all the hidden forces of economic law on the side of destruction, and does it in a manner which not one man in a million is able to diagnose.[11]

History has given ample support to this assessment. A recent example occurred in Russia in 1998, where many citizens saw high rates of inflation wipe out their ruble-denominated savings. And, as Lenin would have predicted, this inflation put the country's burgeoning capitalist system in serious jeopardy.

---

[10] For a paper examining this benefit of inflation, see George A. Akerlof, William T. Dickens, and George L. Perry, "The Macroeconomics of Low Inflation," *Brookings Papers on Economic Activity* 1 (1996): pp. 1–76. There is another way to defend the proposition that a small positive inflation rate may be desirable—one that is a little more difficult to explain but one that is more appealing since it does not rely on the idea that workers can be fooled by a little inflation. We focus on this alternative rationale in Chapter 13.

[11] John Maynard Keynes, *The Economic Consequences of the Peace* (London: Macmillan, 1920): 219–220

50 percent per month implies a more than 100-fold increase in the price level over a year, and a more than 2-million-fold increase over three years. Here we consider the costs and causes of such extreme inflation.

The Costs of Hyperinflation

Although economists debate whether the costs of moderate inflation are large or small, no one doubts that hyperinflation extracts a high toll on society. The costs are qualitatively the same as those we discussed earlier. When inflation reaches extreme levels, however, these costs are more apparent because they are so severe.

The shoeleather costs associated with reduced money holding, for instance, are serious under hyperinflation. Business executives devote much time and energy to cash management when cash loses its value quickly. By diverting this time and energy from more socially valuable activities, such as production and investment decisions, hyperinflation makes the economy run less efficiently.

Menu costs also become larger under hyperinflation. Firms have to change prices so often that normal business practices, such as printing and distributing catalogues with fixed prices, become impossible. In one restaurant during the German hyperinflation of the 1920s, a waiter would stand up on a table every 30 minutes to call out the new prices.

Similarly, relative prices do not do a good job of reflecting true scarcity during hyperinflations. When prices change frequently by large amounts, it is hard for customers to shop around for the best price. Highly volatile and rapidly rising prices can alter behaviour in many ways. According to one report, when patrons entered a pub during the German hyperinflation, they would often buy two pitchers of beer. Although the second pitcher would lose value by getting warm over time, it would lose value less rapidly than the money left sitting in the patron's wallet.

Tax systems are also distorted by hyperinflation—but in ways that are different from the distortions of moderate inflation. In most tax systems there is a delay between the time when a tax is levied and the time when the tax is paid to the government. In Canada, for example, taxpayers are required to make estimated income tax payments every three months. This short delay does not matter much under low inflation. By contrast, during hyperinflation, even a short delay greatly reduces real tax revenue. By the time the government gets the money it is due, the money has fallen in value. As a result, once hyperinflations start, the real tax revenue of the government often falls substantially.

Finally, no one should underestimate the sheer inconvenience of living with hyperinflation. When carrying money to the grocery store is as burdensome as carrying the groceries back home, the monetary system is not doing its best to facilitate exchange. The government tries to overcome this problem by adding more and more zeros to the paper currency, but often it cannot keep up with the exploding price level.

Eventually, these costs of hyperinflation become intolerable. Over time, money loses its role as a store of value, unit of account, and medium of exchange. Barter becomes more common. And more stable unofficial monies—cigarettes or the U.S. dollar—naturally start to replace the official money.

Life During the Bolivian Hyperinflation

The following article from the *Wall Street Journal* shows what life was like during the Bolivian hyperinflation of 1985.[12] What costs of inflation does this article emphasize?

Precarious Peso—Amid Wild Inflation, Bolivians Concentrate on Swapping Currency

LA PAZ, Bolivia When Edgar Miranda gets his monthly teacher's pay of 25 million pesos, he hasn't a moment to lose. Every hour, pesos drop in value. So, while his wife rushes to market to lay in a month's supply of rice and noodles, he is off with the rest of the pesos to change them into black-market dollars.

Mr. Miranda is practicing the First Rule of Survival amid the most out-of-control inflation in the world today. Bolivia is a case study of how runaway inflation undermines a society. Price increases are so huge that the figures build up almost beyond comprehension. In one six-month period, for example, prices soared at an annual rate of 38,000%. By official count, however, last year's inflation reached 2,000%, and this year's is expected to hit 8,000%—though other estimates range many times higher. In any event, Bolivia's rate dwarfs Israel's 370% and Argentina's 1,100%—two other cases of severe inflation.

It is easier to comprehend what happens to the 38-year-old Mr. Miranda's pay if he doesn't quickly change it into dollars. The day he was paid 25 million pesos, a dollar cost 500,000 pesos. So he received $50. Just days later, with the rate at 900,000 pesos, he would have received $27.

"We think only about today and converting every peso into dollars," says Ronald MacLean, the manager of a gold-mining firm. "We have become myopic."

And intent on survival. Civil servants won't hand out a form without a bribe. Lawyers, accountants, hairdressers, even prostitutes have almost given up working to become money-changers in the streets. Workers stage repeated strikes and steal from their bosses. The bosses smuggle production abroad, take out phony loans, duck taxes—anything to get dollars for speculation.

The production at the state mines, for example, dropped to 12,000 tons last year from 18,000. The miners pad their wages by smuggling out the richest ore in their lunch pails, and the ore goes by a contraband network into neighboring Peru. Without a major tin mine, Peru now exports some 4,000 metric tons of tin a year.

"We don't produce anything. We are all currency speculators," a heavy-equipment dealer in La Paz says. "People don't know what's good and bad anymore. We have become an amoral society. . . ."

It is an open secret that practically all of the black-market dollars come from the illegal cocaine trade with the U.S. Cocaine traffickers earn an estimated $1 billion a year. . . .

But meanwhile the country is suffering from inflation largely because the government's revenues cover a mere 15% of its expenditures and its deficit has widened to nearly 25% of the country's total annual output. The revenues are hurt by a lag in tax payments, and taxes aren't being collected largely because of widespread theft and bribery. ■

---

[12] Reprinted by permission of the *Wall Street Journal,* © August 13, 1985, page 1, Dow Jones & Company, Inc. All Rights Reserved Worldwide.

The Causes of Hyperinflation

Why do hyperinflations start, and how do they end? This question can be answered at different levels.

The most obvious answer is that hyperinflations are due to excessive growth in the supply of money. When the central bank prints money, the price level rises. When it prints money rapidly enough, the result is hyperinflation. To stop the hyperinflation, the central bank must simply reduce the rate of money growth.

This answer is incomplete, however, for it leaves open the question of why central banks in hyperinflating economies choose to print so much money. To address this deeper question, we must turn our attention from monetary to fiscal policy. Most hyperinflations begin when the government has inadequate tax revenue to pay for its spending. Although the government might prefer to finance this budget deficit by issuing debt, it may find itself unable to borrow, perhaps because

"I told you the Fed should have tightened."

lenders view the government as a bad credit risk. To cover the deficit, the government sells the bonds to the central bank, thereby turning to the only mechanism at its disposal—the printing press. The result is rapid money growth and hyperinflation.

Once the hyperinflation is under way, the fiscal problems become even more severe. Because of the delay in collecting tax payments, real tax revenue falls as inflation rises. Thus, the government's need to rely on seigniorage is self-reinforcing. Rapid money creation leads to hyperinflation, which leads to a larger budget deficit, which leads to even more rapid money creation.

The ends of hyperinflations almost always coincide with fiscal reforms. Once the magnitude of the problem becomes apparent, the government finally musters the political will to reduce government spending and increase taxes. These fiscal reforms reduce the need for seigniorage, which allows a reduction in money growth. Hence, even if inflation is always and everywhere a monetary phenomenon, the end of hyperinflation is usually a fiscal phenomenon as well.[13]

Hyperinflation in Interwar Germany

After World War I, Germany experienced one of history's most spectacular examples of hyperinflation. At the war's end, the Allies demanded that Germany pay substantial reparations. These payments led to fiscal deficits in

[13] For more on these issues, see Thomas J. Sargent, "The End of Four Big Inflations," in Robert Hall, ed., *Inflation* (Chicago: University of Chicago Press, 1983), 41–98; and Rudiger Dornbusch and Stanley Fischer, "Stopping Hyperinflations: Past and Present," *Weltwirtschaftliches Archiv* 122 (April 1986): 1–47.

Germany, which the German government eventually financed by printing large quantities of money.

Panel (a) of Figure 4-6 shows the quantity of money and the general price level in Germany from January 1922 to December 1924. During this period both money

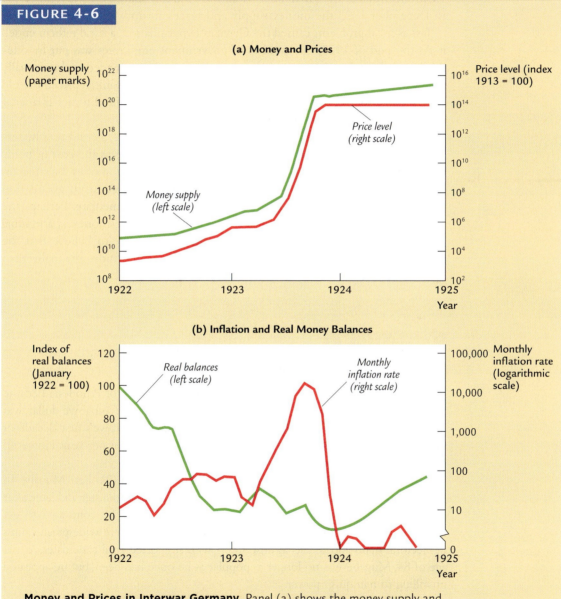

FIGURE 4-6

(a) Money and Prices

(b) Inflation and Real Money Balances

Money and Prices in Interwar Germany Panel (a) shows the money supply and the price level in Germany from January 1922 to December 1924. The immense increases in the money supply and the price level provide a dramatic illustration of the effects of printing large amounts of money. Panel (b) shows inflation and real money balances. As inflation rose, real money balances fell. When the inflation ended at the end of 1923, real money balances rose.

Source: Adapted from Thomas J. Sargent, "The End of Four Big Inflations," in Robert Hall, ed., *Inflation* (Chicago: University of Chicago Press, 1983): 41–98.

and prices rose at an amazing rate. For example, the price of a daily newspaper rose from 0.30 mark in January 1921 to 1 mark in May 1922, to 8 marks in October 1922, to 100 marks in February 1923, and to 1,000 marks in September 1923. Then, in the fall of 1923, prices really took off: the newspaper sold for 2,000 marks on October 1, 20,000 marks on October 15, 1 million marks on October 29, 15 million marks on November 9, and 70 million marks on November 17. In December 1923 the money supply and prices abruptly stabilized.[14]

Just as fiscal problems caused the German hyperinflation, a fiscal reform ended it. At the end of 1923, the number of government employees was cut by one-third, and the reparations payments were temporarily suspended and eventually reduced. At the same time, a new central bank, the Rentenbank, replaced the old central bank, the Reichsbank. The Rentenbank was committed to not financing the government by printing money.

According to our theoretical analysis of money demand, an end to a hyperinflation should lead to an increase in real money balances as the cost of holding money falls. Panel (b) of Figure 4-6 shows that real money balances in Germany did fall as inflation increased, and then increased again as inflation fell. Yet the increase in real money balances was not immediate. Perhaps the adjustment of real money balances to the cost of holding money is a gradual process. Or perhaps it took time for people in Germany to believe that the inflation had really ended, so that expected inflation fell more gradually than actual inflation. ■

CASE STUDY

Hyperinflation in Zimbabwe

In 1980, after years of colonial rule, the old British colony of Rhodesia became the new African nation of Zimbabwe. A new currency, the Zimbabwe dollar, was introduced to replace the Rhodesian dollar. During Zimbabwe's first decade of independence, inflation was modest—about 10 to 20 percent per year. However, this rate would soon change.

The hero of the Zimbabwe independence movement was Robert Mugabe. In general elections in 1980, he became the nation's first prime minister and later, after a government reorganization, its president. Over the years, he continued to get reelected, most recently in 2008. That year, however, there were widespread claims of electoral fraud and threats against voters who supported rival candidates. At the age of 84, Mugabe was no longer as popular as he once had been, but he appeared unwilling to relinquish power.

Throughout his tenure, Mugabe's economic philosophy was Marxist, and one of his goals was to redistribute wealth. In the 1990s, his government instituted a series

---

[14] The data on newspaper prices are from Michael Mussa, "Sticky Individual Prices and the Dynamics of the General Price Level," *Carnegie-Rochester Conference on Public Policy* 15 (Autumn 1981): 261–296.

of land reforms with the ostensible purpose of redistributing land from the white minority, who had ruled Zimbabwe during the colonial era, to the historically disenfranchised black population. One result of these reforms was widespread corruption. Many abandoned and expropriated white farms ended up in the hands of cabinet ministers and senior government officials. Another result was a substantial decline in farm output. Productivity fell as many of the experienced white farmers fled the country.

The decline in the economy's output led to a drop in the government's tax revenue. The government responded to this revenue shortfall by printing money to pay the salaries of government employees. As textbook economic theory predicts, the monetary expansion led to higher inflation.

Mugabe tried to deal with inflation by imposing price controls. Once again, the results were predictable: a shortage of many goods and the growth of an underground economy in which price controls and tax collection were evaded. The government's tax revenue declined further, inducing even more monetary expansion and yet higher inflation. In July 2008, the officially reported annual inflation rate was 231 million percent. Other observers put the inflation rate even higher.

The hyperinflation had widespread repercussions. In an article in the *Washington Post,* one Zimbabwean citizen described the situation: "If you don't get a bill collected in 48 hours, it isn't worth collecting, because it is worthless. Whenever we get money, we must immediately spend it, just go and buy what we can. Our pension was destroyed ages ago. None of us have any savings left."

The end of this story is still to be told. As this book was going to press, Robert Mugabe was continuing to run the country, but violence was increasing, and there was no end in sight to Zimbabwe's hyperinflation. ∎

4-8 Conclusion: The Classical Dichotomy

We have finished our discussion of money and inflation. Let's now step back and examine a key assumption that has been implicit in our discussion.

In Chapter 3, we explained many macroeconomic variables. Some of these variables were *quantities,* such as real GDP and the capital stock; others were *relative prices,* such as the real wage and the real interest rate. But all of these variables had one thing in common—they measured a physical (rather than a monetary) quantity. Real GDP is the quantity of goods and services produced in a given year, and the capital stock is the quantity of machines and structures available at a given time. The real wage is the quantity of output a worker earns for each hour of work, and the real interest rate is the quantity of output a person earns in the future by lending one unit of output today. All variables measured in physical units, such as quantities and relative prices, are called **real variables.**

In this chapter we examined **nominal variables**—variables expressed in terms of money. The economy has many nominal variables, such as the price level, the inflation rate, and the dollar wage a person earns.

At first it may seem surprising that we were able to explain real variables without introducing nominal variables or the existence of money. In Chapter 3, we studied the level and allocation of the economy's output without mentioning the price level or the rate of inflation. Our theory of the labour market explained the real wage without explaining the nominal wage.

Economists call this theoretical separation of real and nominal variables the **classical dichotomy.** It is the hallmark of classical macroeconomic theory. The classical dichotomy is an important insight because it greatly simplifies economic theory. In particular, it allows us to examine real variables, as we have done, while ignoring nominal variables. The classical dichotomy arises because, in classical economic theory, changes in the money supply do not influence real variables. This irrelevance of money for real variables is called **monetary neutrality.** For many purposes—in particular for studying long-run issues—monetary neutrality is approximately correct.

Yet monetary neutrality does not fully describe the world in which we live. Beginning in Chapter 9, we discuss departures from the classical model and monetary neutrality. These departures are crucial for understanding many macroeconomic phenomena, such as short-run economic fluctuations.

Summary

1. Money is the stock of assets used for transactions. It serves as a store of value, a unit of account, and a medium of exchange. Different sorts of assets are used as money: commodity money systems use an asset with intrinsic value, whereas fiat money systems use an asset whose sole function is to serve as money. In modern economies, a central bank such as the Bank of Canada is responsible for controlling the supply of money.

2. The quantity theory of money assumes that the velocity of money is stable and concludes that nominal GDP is proportional to the stock of money. Because the factors of production and the production function determine real GDP, the quantity theory implies that the price level is proportional to the quantity of money. Therefore, the rate of growth in the quantity of money determines the inflation rate.

3. Seigniorage is the revenue that the government raises by printing money. It is a tax on money holding. Although seigniorage is quantitatively small in most economies, it is often a major source of government revenue in economies experiencing hyperinflation.

4. The nominal interest rate is the sum of the real interest rate and the inflation rate. The Fisher effect says that the nominal interest rate moves one-for-one with expected inflation.

5. The nominal interest rate is the opportunity cost of holding money. Thus, one might expect the demand for money to depend on the nominal interest rate. If it does, then the price level depends on both the current quantity of money and the quantities of money expected in the future.

6. The costs of expected inflation include shoeleather costs, menu costs, the cost of relative price variability, tax distortions (such as the disincentive to save and invest), and the inconvenience of making inflation corrections. In addition, unexpected inflation causes arbitrary redistributions of wealth between debtors and creditors.

7. During hyperinflations, most of the costs of inflation become severe. Hyperinflations typically begin when governments finance large budget deficits by printing money. They end when fiscal reforms eliminate the need for seigniorage.

8. According to classical economic theory, money is neutral: the money supply does not affect real variables. Therefore, classical theory allows us to study how real variables are determined without any reference to the money supply. The equilibrium in the money market then determines the price level and, as a result, all other nominal variables. This theoretical separation of real and nominal variables is called the classical dichotomy.

KEY CONCEPTS

Inflation

Hyperinflation

Money

Store of value

Unit of account

Medium of exchange

Fiat money

Commodity money

Gold standard

Money supply

Monetary policy

Central bank

Bank of Canada

Open-market operations

Currency

Demand deposits

Quantity equation

Transactions velocity of money

Income velocity of money

Real money balances

Money demand function

Quantity theory of money

Seigniorage

Nominal and real interest rates

Fisher equation and Fisher effect

Ex ante and *ex post* real interest

rates

Shoeleather costs

Menu costs

Real and nominal variables

Classical dichotomy

Monetary neutrality

QUESTIONS FOR REVIEW

1. Describe the functions of money.

2. What is fiat money? What is commodity money?

3. Who controls the money supply and how?

4. Write the quantity equation and explain it.

5. What does the assumption of constant velocity imply?

6. Who pays the inflation tax?

7. If inflation rises from 6 to 8 percent, what happens to real and nominal interest rates according to the Fisher effect?

8. List all the costs of inflation you can think of, and rank them according to how important you think they are.

9. Explain the roles of monetary and fiscal policy in causing and ending hyperinflations.

10. Define the terms *real variable* and *nominal variable,* and give an example of each.

PROBLEMS AND APPLICATIONS

1. What are the three functions of money? Which of the functions do the following items satisfy? Which do they not satisfy?

   a. A credit card

   b. A painting by Rembrandt

   c. A subway token

2. In the country of Wiknam, the velocity of money is constant. Real GDP grows by 5 percent per year, the money stock grows by 14 percent per year, and the nominal interest rate is 11 percent. What is the real interest rate?

3. A newspaper article once reported that the U.S. economy was experiencing a low rate of inflation. It said that "low inflation has a downside: 45 million recipients of Social Security and other benefits will see their checks go up by just 2.8 percent next year."

   a. Why does inflation affect the increase in Social Security and other benefits?

   b. Is this effect a cost of inflation, as the article suggests? Why or why not?

4. Suppose a country has a money demand function $(M/P)^d = kY$, where k is a constant parameter. The money supply grows by 12 percent per year, and real income grows by 4 percent per year.

   a. What is the average inflation rate?

   b. How would inflation be different if real income growth were higher? Explain.

   c. Suppose that instead of a constant money demand function, the velocity of money in this economy was growing steadily because of financial innovation. How would this situation affect the inflation rate? Explain.

5. Suppose you are advising a small country (such as Bermuda) on whether to print its own money or to use the money of its larger neighbour (such as the United States). What are the costs and benefits of a national money? You could also think of advising a sovereign Quebec, after separation from the rest of Canada. Should a separate Quebec use the Canadian dollar? Should the rest of Canada permit Quebec to use its currency? Does the relative political stability of the two countries have any role in this decision?

6. During World War II, both Germany and England had plans for a paper weapon: they each printed the other's currency, with the intention of dropping large quantities by airplane. Why might this have been an effective weapon?

7. Suppose that the money demand function takes the form

$$(M/P)^d = L(i, Y) = Y/(5i)$$

   a. If output grows at rate g, at what rate will the demand for real balances grow (assuming constant nominal interest rates)?

   b. What is the velocity of money in this economy?

c. If inflation and nominal interest rates are constant, at what rate, if any, will velocity grow?

d. How will a permanent (once-and-for-all) increase in the level of interest rates affect the level of velocity? How will it affect the subsequent growth rate of velocity?

8. Calvin Coolidge (U.S. president in the 1920s) once said that "inflation is repudiation." What might he have meant by this? Do you agree? Why or why not? Does it matter whether the inflation is expected or unexpected?

9. Some economic historians have noted that during the period of the gold standard, gold discoveries were most likely to occur after a long deflation. (The discoveries of 1896 are an example.) Why might this be true?

10. Suppose that consumption depends on the level of real money balances (on the grounds that real money balances are part of wealth). Show that if real money balances depend on the nominal interest rate, then an increase in the rate of money growth affects consumption, investment, and the real interest rate. Does the nominal interest rate adjust more than one-for-one or less than one-for-one to expected inflation?

This deviation from the classical dichotomy and the Fisher effect is called the *Mundell–Tobin effect*. How might you decide whether the Mundell–Tobin effect is important in practice?

11. Use the Internet to identify a country with high inflation over the past year and another country that has had low inflation. (*Hint:* One useful Website is http://www.economist.com/markets/indicators/.) For the two countries, find the rate of money growth and the current level of the nominal interest rate. Relate your findings to the theories presented in this chapter.

APPENDIX

The Cagan Model: How Current and Future Money Affect the Price Level

In this chapter we showed that if the quantity of real money balances demanded depends on the cost of holding money, the price level depends on both the current money supply and the future money supply. This appendix develops the *Cagan model* to show more explicitly how this relationship works.[15]

To keep the math as simple as possible, we posit a money demand function that is linear in the natural logarithms of all the variables. The money demand function is

$$m_t - p_t = -\gamma(p_{t+1} - p_t), \tag{A1}$$

where m_t is the log of the quantity of money at time t, p_t is the log of the price level at time t, and γ is a parameter that tells us the sensitivity of money demand to the rate of inflation. By the property of logarithms, $m_t - p_t$ is the log of real money balances, and $p_{t+1} - p_t$ is the inflation rate between period t and period $t + 1$. This equation states that if inflation goes up by 1 percentage point, real money balances fall by γ percent.

We have made a number of assumptions in writing the money demand function in this way. First, by excluding the level of output as a determinant of money demand, we are implicitly assuming that it is constant. Second, by including the rate of inflation rather than the nominal interest rate, we are assuming that the real interest rate is constant. Third, by including actual inflation rather than expected inflation, we are assuming perfect foresight. All of these assumptions are to keep the analysis as simple as possible.

We want to solve Equation A1 to express the price level as a function of current and future money. To do this, note that Equation A1 can be rewritten as

$$p_t = \left(\frac{1}{1 + \gamma}\right) m_t + \left(\frac{\gamma}{1 + \gamma}\right) p_{t+1}. \tag{A2}$$

This equation states that the current price level is a weighted average of the current money supply and the next period's price level. The next period's price level will be determined the same way as this period's price level:

$$p_{t+1} = \left(\frac{1}{1 + \gamma}\right) m_{t+1} + \left(\frac{\gamma}{1 + \gamma}\right) p_{t+2}. \tag{A3}$$

Use Equation A3 to substitute for p_{t+1} in Equation A2 to obtain

$$p_t = \frac{1}{1 + \gamma} m_t + \frac{\gamma}{(1 + \gamma)^2} m_{t+1} + \frac{\gamma^2}{(1 + \gamma)^2} p_{t+2}. \tag{A4}$$

---

[15] This model is derived from Phillip Cagan, "The Monetary Dynamics of Hyperinflation," in Milton Friedman, ed., *Studies in the Quantity Theory of Money* (Chicago: University of Chicago Press, 1956).

Equation A4 states that the current price level is a weighted average of the current money supply, the next period's money supply, and the following period's price level. Once again, the price level in $t+2$ is determined as in Equation A2:

$$p_{t+2} = \left(\frac{1}{1+\gamma}\right) m_{t+2} + \left(\frac{\gamma}{1+\gamma}\right) p_{t+3}. \tag{A5}$$

Now use Equation A5 to substitute into Equation A4 to obtain

$$p_t = \frac{1}{1+\gamma} m_t + \frac{\gamma}{(1+\gamma)^2} m_{t+1} + \frac{\gamma^2}{(1+\gamma)^3} m_{t+2} + \frac{\gamma^3}{(1+\gamma)^3} p_{t+3}. \tag{A6}$$

By now you see the pattern. We can continue to use Equation A2 to substitute for the future price level. If we do this an infinite number of times, we find

$$p_t = \left(\frac{1}{1+\gamma}\right) \left[m_t + \left(\frac{\gamma}{1+\gamma}\right) m_{t+1} \right.$$
$$\left. + \left(\frac{\gamma}{1+\gamma}\right)^2 m_{t+2} + \left(\frac{\gamma}{1+\gamma}\right)^3 m_{t+3} + \cdots \right], \tag{A7}$$

where ". . ." indicates an infinite number of analogous terms. According to Equation A7, the current price level is a weighted average of the current money supply and all future money supplies.

Note the importance of γ, the parameter governing the sensitivity of real money balances to inflation. The weights on the future money supplies decline geometrically at rate $\gamma/(1+\gamma)$. If γ is small, then $\gamma/(1+\gamma)$ is small, and the weights decline quickly. In this case, the current money supply is the primary determinant of the price level. (Indeed, if γ equals zero, then we obtain the quantity theory of money: the price level is proportional to the current money supply, and the future money supplies do not matter at all.) If γ is large, then $\gamma/(1+\gamma)$ is close to 1, and the weights decline slowly. In this case, the future money supplies play a key role in determining today's price level.

Finally, let's relax the assumption of perfect foresight. If the future is not known with certainty, then we should write the money demand function as

$$m_t - p_t = -\gamma(Ep_{t+1} - p_t), \tag{A8}$$

where Ep_{t+1} is the expected price level. Equation A8 states that real money balances depend on expected inflation. By following steps similar to those above, we can show that

$$p_t = \left(\frac{1}{1+\gamma}\right) \left[m_t + \left(\frac{\gamma}{1+\gamma}\right) Em_{t+1} \right.$$
$$\left. + \left(\frac{\gamma}{1+\gamma}\right)^2 Em_{t+2} + \left(\frac{\gamma}{1+\gamma}\right)^3 Em_{t+3} + \cdots \right]. \tag{A9}$$

Equation A9 states that the price level depends on the current money supply and expected future money supplies.

Some economists use this model to argue that *credibility* is important for ending hyperinflation. Because the price level depends on both current and expected future money, inflation depends on both current and expected future money growth. Therefore, to end high inflation, both money growth and expected money growth must fall. Expectations, in turn, depend on credibility—the perception that the central bank is truly committed to a new, more stable policy.

How can a central bank achieve credibility in the midst of hyperinflation? Credibility is often achieved by removing the underlying cause of the hyperinflation—the need for seigniorage. Thus, a credible fiscal reform is often necessary for a credible change in monetary policy. This fiscal reform might take the form of reducing government spending and making the central bank more independent from the government. Reduced spending decreases the need for seigniorage in the present. Increased independence allows the central bank to resist government demands for seigniorage in the future.

MORE PROBLEMS AND APPLICATIONS

1. In the Cagan model, if the money supply is expected to grow at some constant rate μ (so that $Em_{t+s} = m_t + s\mu$), then Equation A9 can be shown to imply that $p_t = m_t + \gamma\mu$.

   a. Intepret this result.

   b. What happens to the price level p_t when the money supply m_t changes, holding the money growth rate μ constant?

   c. What happens to the price level p_t when the money growth rate μ changes, holding the current money supply m_t constant?

   d. If a central bank is about to reduce the rate of money growth μ but wants to hold the price level p_t constant, what should it do with m_t? Can you see any practical problems that might arise in following such a policy?

   e. How do your previous answers change in the special case where money demand does not depend on the expected rate of inflation (so that $\gamma = 0$)?

CHAPTER 5

The Open Economy

No nation was ever ruined by trade.

— *Benjamin Franklin*

Even if you never leave your home town, you are an active participant in a global economy. When you go to the grocery store, for instance, you might choose between apples grown in British Columbia and oranges grown in Florida. When you make a deposit into your local bank, the bank might lend those funds to your next-door neighbour or to a Japanese company building a factory outside Tokyo. Because our economy is integrated with many others around the world, consumers have more goods and services from which to choose, and savers have more opportunities to invest their wealth.

In previous chapters we simplified our analysis by assuming a closed economy. In actuality, however, most economies are open: they export goods and services abroad, they import goods and services from abroad, and they borrow and lend in world financial markets. Figure 5-1 gives some sense of the importance of these international interactions by showing imports and exports as a percentage of GDP for seven major industrial countries. As the figure shows, receipts from Canadian exports of goods and services were about 30 percent of GDP in 2007. This proportion has been rising—from 22 percent in 1950, to today's much higher level of economic integration. In countries such as Canada, international trade is central to analyzing economic developments and formulating economic policies.

This chapter begins our study of open-economy macroeconomics. We begin in Section 5-1 with questions of measurement. To understand how an open economy works, we must understand the key macroeconomic variables that measure the interactions among countries. Accounting identities reveal a key insight: the flow of goods and services across national borders is always matched by an equivalent flow of funds to finance capital accumulation.

In Section 5-2 we examine the determinants of these international flows. We develop a model of the small open economy that corresponds to our model of the closed economy in Chapter 3. The model shows the factors that determine whether a country is a borrower or a lender in world markets, and how policies at home and abroad affect the flows of capital and goods.

In Section 5-3 we extend the model to discuss the prices at which a country makes exchanges in world markets. We examine what determines the price of

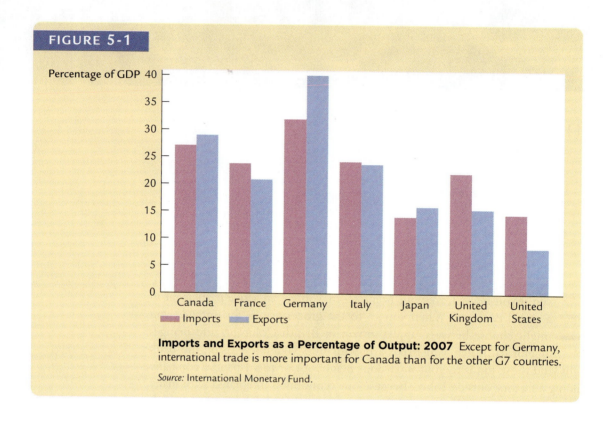

FIGURE 5-1

Imports and Exports as a Percentage of Output: 2007 Except for Germany, international trade is more important for Canada than for the other G7 countries.

Source: International Monetary Fund.

domestic goods relative to foreign goods. We also examine what determines the rate at which the domestic currency trades for foreign currencies. Our model shows how protectionist trade policies—policies designed to protect domestic industries from foreign competition—influence the amount of international trade and the exchange rate.

5-1 The International Flows of Capital and Goods

The key macroeconomic difference between open and closed economies is that, in an open economy, a country's spending in any given year need not equal its output of goods and services. A country can spend more than it produces by borrowing from abroad, or it can spend less than it produces and lend the difference to foreigners. To understand this more fully, let's take another look at national accounting, which we first discussed in Chapter 2.

The Role of Net Exports

Consider the expenditure on an economy's output of goods and services. In a closed economy, all output is sold domestically, and expenditure is divided into three components: consumption, investment, and government purchases. In an open economy, some output is sold domestically and some is exported to be sold abroad. We can divide expenditure on an open economy's output Y into four components:

1. C^d, consumption of domestic goods and services,
2. I^d, investment in domestic goods and services,
3. G^d, government purchases of domestic goods and services,
4. X, exports of domestic goods and services.

The division of expenditure into these components is expressed in the identity

$$Y = C^d + I^d + G^d + X.$$

The sum of the first three terms, $C^d + I^d + G^d$, is domestic spending on domestic goods and services. The fourth term, X, is foreign spending on domestic goods and services.

A bit of manipulation can make this identity more useful. Note that domestic spending on all goods and services is the sum of domestic spending on domestic goods and services and on foreign goods and services. Hence, total consumption C equals consumption of domestic goods and services C^d plus consumption of foreign goods and services C^f; total investment I equals investment in domestic goods and services I^d plus investment in foreign goods and services I^f; and total government purchases G equals government purchases of domestic goods and services G^d plus government purchases of foreign goods and services G^f. Thus,

$$C = C^d + C^f,$$
$$I = I^d + I^f,$$
$$G = G^d + G^f.$$

We substitute these three equations into the identity above:

$$Y = (C - C^f) + (I - I^f) + (G - G^f) + X.$$

We can rearrange to obtain

$$Y = C + I + G + X - (C^f + I^f + G^f).$$

The sum of domestic spending on foreign goods and services $(C^f + I^f + G^f)$ is expenditure on imports (IM). We can thus write the national accounts identity as

$$Y = C + I + G + X - IM.$$

Because spending on imports is included in domestic spending $(C + I + G)$, and because goods and services imported from abroad are not part of a country's output, this equation subtracts spending on imports. Defining **net exports** to be exports minus imports $(NX = X - IM)$, the identity becomes

$$Y = C + I + G + NX.$$

This equation states that expenditure on domestic output is the sum of consumption, investment, government purchases, and net exports. This is the most common form of the national accounts identity; it should be familiar from Chapter 2.

The national accounts identity shows how domestic output, domestic spending, and net exports are related. In particular,

$$NX = \quad Y \quad - (C + I + G)$$
$$\text{Net Exports} = \text{Output} - \text{Domestic Spending.}$$

This equation shows that in an open economy, domestic spending need not equal the output of goods and services. *If output exceeds domestic spending, we export the difference: net exports are positive. If output falls short of domestic spending, we import the difference: net exports are negative.*

Net Foreign Investment and the Trade Balance

In an open economy, as in the closed economy we discussed in Chapter 3, financial markets and goods markets are closely related. To see the relationship, we must rewrite the national accounts identity in terms of saving and investment. Begin with the identity

$$Y = C + I + G + NX.$$

Subtract C and G from both sides to obtain

$$Y - C - G = I + NX.$$

Recall from Chapter 3 that $Y - C - G$ is national saving S, which equals the sum of private saving, $Y - T - C$, and public saving, $T - G$, where T stands for taxes. Therefore,

$$S = I + NX.$$

Subtracting I from both sides of the equation, we can write the national accounts identity as

$$S - I = NX.$$

This form of the national accounts identity shows that an economy's net exports must always equal the difference between its saving and its investment.

Let's look more closely at each part of this identity. The easy part is the right-hand side, NX, the net export of goods and services. Another name for net exports is the **trade balance,** because it tells us how our trade in goods and services departs from the benchmark of equal imports and exports.

The left-hand side of the identity is the difference between domestic saving and domestic investment, $S - I$, which we'll call **net capital outflow.** (It's sometimes called *net foreign investment*.) Net capital outflow equals the amount that domestic residents are lending abroad minus the amount that foreigners are lending to us. If net capital outflow is positive, the economy's saving exceeds its investment, and it is lending the excess to foreigners. If the net capital outflow is negative, the economy is experiencing a capital inflow: investment exceeds saving, and the economy is financing this extra investment by borrowing from abroad. Thus, net capital outflow reflects the international flow of funds to finance capital accumulation.

The national accounts identity shows that net captial outflow always equals the trade balance. That is,

$$\text{Net Capital Outflow} = \text{Trade Balance}$$
$$S - I \quad = \quad NX.$$

If $S - I$ and NX are positive, we have a **trade surplus.** In this case, we are net lenders in world financial markets, and we are exporting more goods than we are importing. If $S - I$ and NX are negative, we have a **trade deficit.** In this case, we are net borrowers in world financial markets, and we are importing more goods than we are exporting. If $S - I$ and NX are exactly zero, we are said to have **balanced trade** because the value of imports equals the value of exports.

The national accounts identity shows that the international flow of funds to finance capital accumulation and the international flow of goods and services are two sides of the same coin. If domestic saving exceeds domestic investment, the surplus saving is used to make loans to foreigners. Foreigners require these loans because we are providing them with more goods and services than they are providing us. That is, we are running a trade surplus. If investment exceeds saving, the extra investment must be financed by borrowing from abroad. These foreign loans enable us to import more goods and services than we export. That is, we are running a trade deficit. Table 5-1 summarizes these lessons.

Note that the international flow of capital can take many forms. It is easiest to assume—as we have done so far—that when we run a trade deficit, foreigners make loans to us. This happens, for example, when Americans buy the debt issued by Canadian corporations or by provincial governments. But, equivalently, the flow of capital can take the form of foreigners buying domestic assets. For example, if a Japanese investor buys an apartment building in Vancouver, that transaction reduces the net capital outflow, and so it reduces

TABLE 5-1		
International Flows of Goods and Capital: Summary of the Three Outcomes an Open Economy Can Experience		
Trade Surplus	**Balanced Trade**	**Trade Deficit**
Exports > Imports	Exports = Imports	Exports < Imports
Net Exports > 0	Net Exports = 0	Net Exports < 0
$Y > C + I + G$	$Y = C + I + G$	$Y < C + I + G$
Saving > Investment	Saving = Investment	Saving < Investment

net foreign investment by Canadians. In both the case of foreigners buying domestically issued debt and the case of foreigners buying domestically owned assets, foreigners are obtaining a claim to the future returns to domestic capital. In other words, in both cases, foreigners end up owning some of the domestic capital stock.

International Flows of Goods and Capital: An Example

The equality of net exports and net capital outflow is an identity: it must hold because of the way the variables are defined and the numbers are added up. But it is easy to miss the intuition behind this important relationship. The best way to understand it is to consider an example.

Imagine that Bill Gates sells a copy of the Windows operating system to a Japanese consumer for 5,000 yen. Because Mr. Gates is a U.S. resident, the sale represents an export of the United States. Other things equal, U.S. net exports rise. What else happens to make the identity hold? It depends on what Mr. Gates does with the 5,000 yen.

Suppose Mr. Gates decides to stuff the 5,000 yen in his mattress. In this case, Mr. Gates has allocated some of his saving to an investment in the Japanese economy (in the form of the Japanese currency) rather than to an investment in the U.S. economy. Thus, U.S. saving exceeds U.S. investment. The rise in U.S. net exports is matched by a rise in the U.S. net capital outflow.

If Mr. Gates wants to invest in Japan, however, he is unlikely to make currency his asset of choice. He might use the 5,000 yen to buy some stock in, say, the Sony Corporation, or he might buy a bond issued by the Japanese government. In either case, some of U.S. saving is flowing abroad. Once again, the U.S. net capital outflow exactly balances U.S. net exports.

The opposite situation occurs in Japan. When the Japanese consumer buys a copy of the Windows operating system, Japan's purchases of goods and services $(C + I + G)$ rise, but there is no change in what Japan has produced (Y). The transaction reduces Japan's saving $(S = Y - C - G)$ for a given level of investment (I). While the U.S. experiences a net capital outflow, Japan experiences a net capital inflow.

Now let's change the example. Suppose that, instead of investing his 5,000 yen in a Japanese asset, Mr. Gates uses it to buy something made in Japan, such as a Sony Walkman. In this case, imports into the United States rise. Together, the Windows export and the Walkman import represent balanced trade between Japan and the United States. Because exports and imports rise equally, net exports and net capital outflow are both unchanged.

A final possibility is that Mr. Gates exchanges his 5,000 yen for U.S. dollars at a local bank. But this doesn't change the situation: the bank now has to do something with the 5,000 yen. It can buy Japanese assets (a U.S. net capital outflow); it can buy a Japanese good (a U.S. import); or it can sell the yen to another American who wants to make such a transaction. If you follow the money, you can see that, in the end, U.S. net exports must equal U.S. net capital outflow.

FYI

The Irrelevance of Bilateral Trade Balances

The trade balance we have been discussing measures the difference between a nation's exports and its imports with the rest of the world. Sometimes you might hear in the media a report on a nation's trade balance with one other nation. This is called a *bilateral* trade balance. For example, the U.S. bilateral trade balance with China equals exports that the United States sells to China minus imports that the United States buys from China.

The overall trade balance is, as we have seen, inextricably linked to a nation's saving and investment. That is not true of a bilateral trade balance. Indeed, a nation can have large trade deficits and surpluses with specific trading partners, while having balanced trade overall.

For example, suppose the world has three countries: the United States, China, and Canada. The United States sells $10 billion in machine tools to Canada, Canada sells $10 billion in wheat to China, and China sells $10 billion in toys to the United States. In this case, the United States has a bilateral trade deficit with China, China has a bilateral trade deficit with Canada, and Canada has a bilateral trade deficit with the United States. But each of the three nations has balanced trade overall, exporting and importing $10 billion in goods.

Bilateral trade deficits receive more attention in the political arena than they deserve. This is in part because international relations are conducted country to country, so politicians and diplomats are naturally drawn to statistics measuring county-to-country economic transactions. Most economists, however, believe that bilateral trade balances are not very meaningful. From a macroeconomic standpoint, what matters is a nation's trade balance with all foreign nations put together.

The same lesson applies to individuals as it does to nations. Your own personal trade balance is the difference between your income and your spending, and you may be concerned if these two variables are out of line. But you should not be concerned with the difference between your income and spending with a particular person or firm. Economist Robert Solow once explained the irrelevance of bilateral trade balances as follows: "I have a chronic deficit with my barber, who doesn't buy a darned thing from me." But that doesn't stop Mr. Solow from living within his means or getting a haircut when he needs it.

5-2 Saving and Investment in a Small Open Economy

So far in our discussion of the international flows of goods and capital, we have rearranged accounting identities. That is, we have defined some of the variables that measure transactions in an open economy, and we have shown the links among these variables that follow from their definitions. Our next step is to develop a model that explains the behaviour of these variables. We can then use the model to answer questions such as how the trade balance responds to changes in policy.

Capital Mobility and the World Interest Rate

In a moment we present a model of the international flows of capital and goods. Because the trade balance equals the net capital outflow, which in turn equals saving minus investment, our model focuses on saving and investment.

To develop this model, we use some elements that should be familiar from Chapter 3, but in contrast to the Chapter 3 model, we do not assume that the real interest rate equilibrates saving and investment. Instead, we allow the economy to run a trade deficit and borrow from other countries, or to run a trade surplus and lend to other countries.

If the real interest rate does not adjust to equilibrate saving and investment in this model, what *does* determine the real interest rate? We answer this question here by considering the simple case of a **small open economy** with perfect capital mobility. By "small" we mean that this economy is a small part of the world market and thus, by itself, can have only a negligible effect on the world interest rate. By "perfect capital mobility" we mean that residents of the country have full access to world financial markets. In particular, the government does not impede international borrowing or lending.

Because of this assumption of perfect capital mobility, the interest rate in our small open economy, r, must equal the **world interest rate** r^*, the real interest rate prevailing in world financial markets, plus the risk premium θ associated with that particular economy. We write

$$r = r^* + \theta.$$

The small open economy takes the world real rate of interest as given, but its policies can have some effect on the risk premium.

Foreign lenders demand a risk premium when lending funds to Canadian firms and governments if they anticipate that the Canadian dollar may fall in value while the loan is outstanding. If that happens, foreign lenders will suffer a capital loss when they turn their earnings back into their own currency after the loan is repaid. To be compensated for that expected capital loss, lenders demand a yield that exceeds the world interest rate.

Figure 5-2 shows data for Canadian and American interest rates since 1962. Because we can interpret the U.S. interest rate as the "world" interest rate in our theoretical analysis, we see that the Canadian risk premium was quite small (and sometimes even negative) before 1975. Then, the risk premium widened somewhat, and many analysts attribute this to the fact that foreign lenders had become uneasy about both the size of Canadian government budget deficits and the prospect of prolonged political uncertainty surrounding the question of Quebec separation. Both these problems were expected to decrease the government's resolve in maintaining zero inflation. If Canada inflates at a more rapid rate than other countries, the Canadian dollar has to fall in value to keep Canada's exports from being priced out of foreign markets. With the federal and most provincial budget deficits eliminated by the end of the 1990s, with the perception that Quebec separation had become less likely, and with increased certainty concerning the Bank of Canada's commitment to low inflation, the risk premium has been virtually eliminated in recent years.

The interest rate differential shown in Figure 5-2 involves many short-run variations. These variations cannot be explained by longer-run issues, such as trends in political uncertainty. Instead, they are a result of the fact that it takes some time for international lenders to react to yield differentials. For example, if

FIGURE 5-2

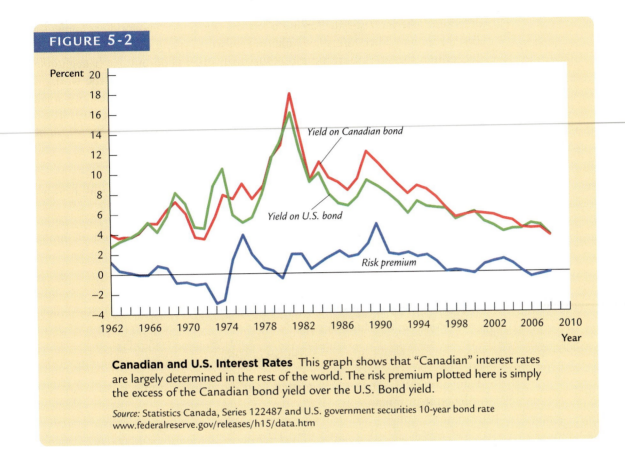

Canadian and U.S. Interest Rates This graph shows that "Canadian" interest rates are largely determined in the rest of the world. The risk premium plotted here is simply the excess of the Canadian bond yield over the U.S. Bond yield.

Source: Statistics Canada, Series 122487 and U.S. government securities 10-year bond rate www.federalreserve.gov/releases/h15/data.htm

the Canadian interest rate rises above the American yield, it takes some time for lenders to notice that there is a substantial payoff to rearranging their bond holdings. Then, they must sell bonds in the rest of the world to obtain the funds necessary to buy Canadian bonds. Only after enough lenders have made this switch will the price paid for Canadian bonds be bid up sufficiently to force the effective yield earned by new buyers back down to equality with opportunities elsewhere. It is not surprising, therefore, that there are short-run departures from the equilibrium relationship.

For much of our discussion, we abstract from issues of longer term political uncertainty, and shorter term lags, and so we set the risk premium, θ, equal to 0. In other words, given the longer-run focus on economic issues in this chapter, we give little emphasis to the temporary departures from the equal yield relationship, and we assume

$$r = r^*.$$

The small open economy takes its interest rate as given by the world real interest rate.

Let us discuss for a moment what determines the world real interest rate. In a closed economy, the equilibrium of domestic saving and domestic investment determines the interest rate. Barring interplanetary trade, the world economy is a closed economy. Therefore, the equilibrium of world saving and world investment determines the world interest rate. Our small open economy has a negligible effect on the world real interest rate because, being a small part of the world, it has a negligible effect on world saving and world investment. Hence, our small open economy takes the world interest rate as an exogenously given variable.

The Model

To build the model of the small open economy, we take three assumptions from Chapter 3:

1. The economy's output Y is fixed by the factors of production and the production function. We write this as

$$Y = \bar{Y} = F(\bar{K}, \bar{L}).$$

2. Consumption C is positively related to disposable income $Y - T$. We write the consumption function as

$$C = C(Y - T).$$

3. Investment I is negatively related to the real interest rate r. We write the investment function as

$$I = I(r).$$

These are the three key parts of our model. If you do not understand these relationships, review Chapter 3 before continuing.

We can now return to the accounting identity and write it as

$$NX = (Y - C - G) - I$$
$$= S - I.$$

Substituting the previous assumptions and the assumption that the interest rate equals the world interest rate, we obtain

$$NX = [\bar{Y} - C(\bar{Y} - T) - G] - I(r^*)$$
$$= \qquad \bar{S} \qquad - I(r^*).$$

This equation shows that the trade balance NX depends on variables that determine saving S and investment I. Because saving depends on fiscal policy (lower government purchases G or higher taxes T raise national saving) and investment depends on the world real interest rate r^* (high interest rates make some investment projects unprofitable), the trade balance depends on these variables as well.

In Chapter 3 we graphed saving and investment as in Figure 5-3. In the closed economy studied in that chapter, the real interest rate adjusts to equilibrate saving and investment—that is, the real interest rate is found where the saving and investment curves cross. In the small open economy, however, the real interest

FIGURE 5-3

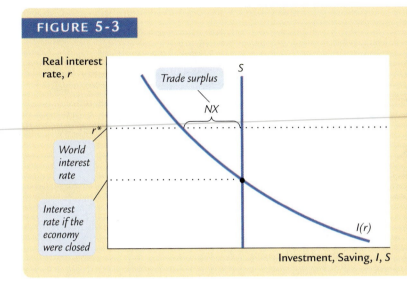

Real interest rate, r

Trade surplus

S

NX

$r*$

World interest rate

Interest rate if the economy were closed

$I(r)$

Investment, Saving, I, S

Saving and Investment in a Small Open Economy In a closed economy, the real interest rate adjusts to equilibrate saving and investment. In a small open economy, the interest rate is determined in world financial markets. The difference between saving and investment determines the trade balance. Here there is a trade surplus, because at the world interest rate, saving exceeds investment.

rate equals the world real interest rate. *The trade balance is determined by the difference between saving and investment at the world interest rate.*

At this point, you might wonder about the mechanism that causes the trade balance to equal net foreign investment. The determinants of net foreign investment are easy to understand. When domestic saving falls short of domestic investment, domestic investors borrow from abroad; when saving exceeds investment, the excess is lent to other countries. But what causes those who import and export to behave in a way that ensures that the international flow of goods exactly balances this international flow of capital? For now we leave this question unanswered, but we return to it in Section 5-3 when we discuss the determination of exchange rates.

How Policies Influence the Trade Balance

Suppose that the economy begins in a position of balanced trade. That is, at the world interest rate, investment I equals saving S, and net exports NX equal zero. Let's use our model to predict the effects of government policies at home and abroad.

Fiscal Policy at Home Consider first what happens to the small open economy if the government expands domestic spending by increasing government purchases. The increase in G reduces national saving, because $S = Y - C - G$. With an unchanged world real interest rate, investment remains the same. Therefore, saving falls below investment, and some investment must now be financed by borrowing from abroad. Since $NX = S - I$, the fall in S implies a fall in NX. The economy now runs a trade deficit.

The same logic applies to a decrease in taxes. A tax cut lowers T, raises disposable income $Y - T$, stimulates consumption, and reduces national saving. (Even though some of the tax cut finds its way into private saving, public saving

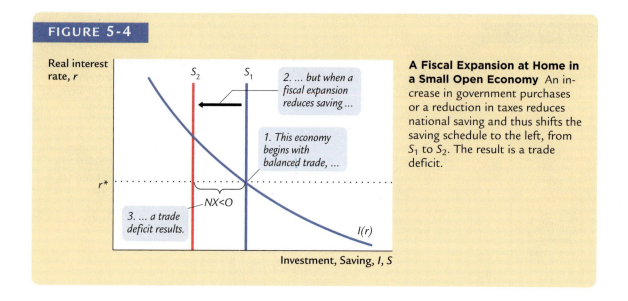

FIGURE 5-4

A Fiscal Expansion at Home in a Small Open Economy An increase in government purchases or a reduction in taxes reduces national saving and thus shifts the saving schedule to the left, from S_1 to S_2. The result is a trade deficit.

In figure: Real interest rate, r — S_2 — S_1 — *2. ... but when a fiscal expansion reduces saving ...* — *1. This economy begins with balanced trade, ...* — r^* — $NX<O$ — *3. ... a trade deficit results.* — $I(r)$ — Investment, Saving, I, S

falls by the full amount of the tax cut; in total, saving falls.) Since $NX = S - I$, the reduction in national saving in turn lowers NX.

Figure 5-4 illustrates these effects. A fiscal policy change that increases private consumption C or public consumption G reduces national saving $(Y - C - G)$ and, therefore, shifts the vertical line that represents saving from S_1 to S_2. Because NX is the distance between the saving schedule and the investment schedule at the world interest rate, this shift reduces NX. Hence, *starting from balanced trade, a change in fiscal policy that reduces national saving leads to a trade deficit.* A change in fiscal policy that stimulates domestic investment spending has the same effect.

Fiscal Policy Abroad Consider now what happens to a small open economy when foreign governments increase their government purchases. If these foreign countries are a small part of the world economy, then their fiscal change has a negligible impact on other countries. But if these foreign countries are a large part of the world economy, their increase in government purchases reduces world saving and causes the world interest rate to rise, just as we saw in our closed economy model (remember, Earth is a closed economy).

The increase in the world interest rate raises the cost of borrowing and, thus, reduces investment in our small open economy. Because there has been no change in domestic saving, saving S now exceeds investment I, and some of our saving begins to flow abroad. Since $NX = S - I$, the reduction in I must also increase NX. Hence, reduced saving abroad leads to a trade surplus at home.

Figure 5-5 illustrates how a small open economy starting from balanced trade responds to a foreign fiscal expansion. Because the policy change is occurring abroad, the domestic saving and investment schedules remain the same. The only change is an increase in the world interest rate from r_1^* to r_2^*. The trade balance is the difference between the saving and investment schedules; because saving exceeds investment at r_2^*, there is a trade surplus. *Hence, starting from balanced trade, an increase in the world interest rate due to a fiscal expansion abroad leads to a trade surplus.*

FIGURE 5-5

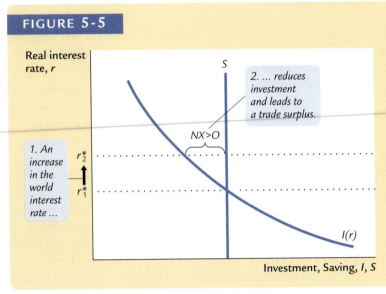

Real interest rate, r

2. ... reduces investment and leads to a trade surplus.

$NX > 0$

1. An increase in the world interest rate ...

r_2^*

r_1^*

S

$I(r)$

Investment, Saving, I, S

A Fiscal Expansion Abroad in a Small Open Economy A fiscal expansion in a foreign economy large enough to influence world saving and investment raises the world interest rate from r_1^* to r_2^*. The higher world interest rate reduces investment in this small open economy, causing a trade surplus.

Shifts in Investment Demand Consider what happens to our small open economy if its investment schedule shifts outward—that is, if the demand for investment goods at every interest rate increases. This shift would occur if, for example, the government changed the tax laws to encourage investment by providing an investment tax credit. Figure 5-6 illustrates the impact of a shift in the investment schedule. At a given world interest rate, investment is now higher. Because saving is unchanged, some investment must now be financed by borrowing from abroad, which means net foreign investment is negative. Put differently, because $NX = S - I$, the increase in I implies a decrease in NX. Hence, *an outward shift in the investment schedule causes a trade deficit.*

FIGURE 5-6

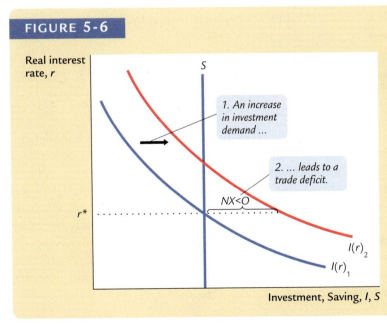

Real interest rate, r

1. An increase in investment demand ...

2. ... leads to a trade deficit.

$NX < 0$

r^*

S

$I(r)_2$

$I(r)_1$

Investment, Saving, I, S

A Shift in the Investment Schedule in a Small Open Economy An outward shift in the investment schedule from $I(r)1$ to $I(r)2$ increases the amount of investment at the world interest rate r^*. As a result, investment now exceeds saving, which means the economy is borrowing from abroad and running a trade deficit.

Evaluating Economic Policy

Our model of the open economy shows that the flow of goods and services measured by the trade balance is inextricably connected to the flow of funds for capital accumulation. The net capital outflow is the difference between domestic saving and domestic investment. Thus, the impact of economic policies on the trade balance can always be found by examining their impact on domestic saving and domestic investment. Policies that increase investment or decrease saving tend to cause a trade deficit, and policies that decrease investment or increase saving tend to cause a trade surplus.

Our analysis of the open economy has been positive, not normative. That is, our analysis of how economic policies influence the international flows of capital and goods has not told us whether these policies are desirable. Evaluating economic policies and their impact on the open economy is a frequent topic of debate among economists and policymakers.

When a country runs a trade deficit, policymakers must confront the question of whether the trade deficit represents a national problem. Most economists view a trade deficit not as a problem in itself, but perhaps as a symptom of a problem. Trade deficits typically reflect a low saving rate. A low saving rate means that we are putting away less for the future. In a closed economy, low saving leads to low investment and a smaller future capital stock. In an open economy, low saving leads to a trade deficit and a growing foreign debt, which eventually must be repaid. In both cases, high current consumption leads to lower future consumption, implying that future generations bear the burden of low national saving.

Yet trade deficits are not always a reflection of economic malady. When poor rural economies develop into modern industrial economies, they sometimes finance their high levels of investment with foreign borrowing. In these cases, trade deficits are a sign of economic development. For example, South Korea ran large trade deficits throughout the 1970s, and it became one of the success stories of economic growth. The lesson is that one cannot judge economic performance from the trade balance alone. Instead, one must look at the underlying causes of the international flows.

CASE STUDY

The U.S. Trade Deficit

During the 1980s, 1990s, and early 2000s, the United States ran large trade deficits. Panel (a) of Figure 5-7 documents this experience by showing net exports as a percentage of GDP. The exact size of the trade deficit fluctuated over time, but it was large throughout these two and a half decades. In 2007, the trade deficit was $708 billion, or 5.1 percent of GDP. As accounting identities require, this trade deficit had to be financed by borrowing from abroad (or equivalently by selling U.S. assets abroad). During this period, the United States went from being the world's largest creditor to the world's largest debtor.

What caused the U.S. trade deficit? There is no single explanation. But to understand some of the forces at work, it helps to look at American national saving

FIGURE 5-7

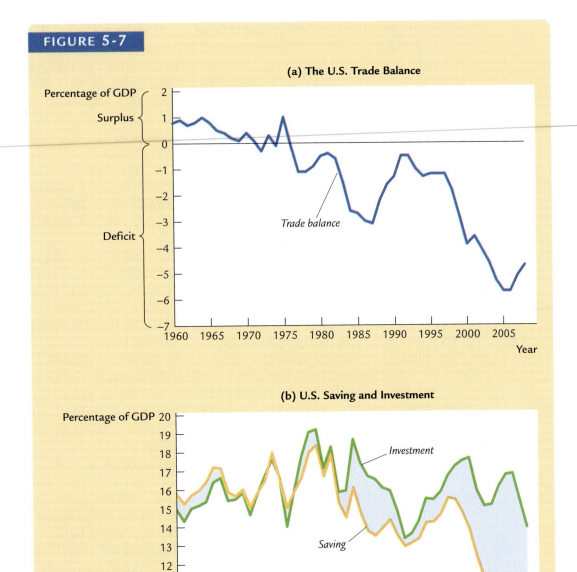

(a) The U.S. Trade Balance

Percentage of GDP

Surplus

Deficit

Year

(b) U.S. Saving and Investment

Percentage of GDP

Investment

Saving

Year

The Trade Balance, Saving, and Investment: The U.S. Experience
Panel (a) shows the trade balance as a percentage of GDP. Positive numbers represent a surplus, and negative numbers represent a deficit. Panel (b) shows national saving and investment as a percentage of GDP since 1960. The trade balance equals saving minus investment.

Source: U.S. Department of Commerce.

and domestic investment, as shown in panel (b) of the figure. Keep in mind that the trade deficit is the difference between saving and investment.

The start of the trade deficit coincided with a fall in national saving. This development can be explained by the expansionary fiscal policy in the 1980s. With the support of President Reagan, the U.S. Congress passed legislation in 1981 that substantially cut personal income taxes over the next three years. Because these tax cuts were not met with equal cuts in government spending, the federal budget went into deficit. These budget deficits were among the largest ever experienced in a period of peace and prosperity, and they continued long after Reagan left office. According to our model, such a policy should reduce national saving, thereby causing a U.S. trade deficit. In fact, that is exactly what happened. Because the government budget and trade balance went into deficit at roughly the same time, these shortfalls were called the *twin deficits.*

Things started to change in the 1990s, when the U.S. federal government got its fiscal house in order. The first President Bush and President Clinton both signed tax increases, while Congress kept a lid on spending. In addition to these policy changes, rapid productivity growth in the late 1990s raised incomes and thus further increased tax revenue. These developments moved the U.S. federal budget from deficit to surplus, which in turn caused national saving to rise.

Why didn't the increase in national saving generate a shrinking trade deficit? The reason is that domestic investment spending rose at the same time. The likely explanation for this development is that the boom in information technology caused an expansionary shift in the U.S. investment function. Even though fiscal policy was pushing the trade deficit toward surplus, the investment boom was an even stronger force pushing the trade balance toward deficit.

In the early 2000s, fiscal policy once again put downward pressure on national saving. With the second President Bush in the White House, tax cuts were signed into law in 2001 and 2003, while the war on terror and in Iraq led to substantial increases in government spending. The federal government was again running budget deficits. National saving fell to historic lows, and the trade deficit reached historic highs.

A few years later, the trade deficit started to shrink somewhat as the economy experienced a substantial decline in housing prices (a phenomenon examined in case studies in Chapters 11 and 18). Lower housing prices reduced residential investment and made households poorer, inducing them to reduce consumption and increase saving. As a result, the trade deficit fell from 6.1 percent of GDP at its peak in the fourth quarter of 2005 to 4.9 percent in the third quarter of 2007.

The history of the U.S. trade deficit shows that this statistic, by itself, does not tell us much about what is happening in the economy. We have to look deeper at saving, investment, and the policies and events that cause them to change over time.[1] No country can "solve" its trade deficit "problem" without achieving some combination of reducing its government budget deficit, increasing its rate of private saving, and decreasing its rate of investment spending.

---

[1] For more on this topic, see Catherine L. Mann, *Is the U.S. Trade Deficit Sustainable?* (Washington, DC: Institute for International Economics, 1999).

It is interesting to interpret the rhetoric on both sides concerning the massive trade imbalance. One such imbalance that has been in the news recently concerns China and the United States. The United States is concerned about the large magnitude of the net surplus China has in the trade between the two nations. American politicians argue that the Chinese should raise the value of their currency to stimulate Chinese imports from the United States. This would help reduce the U.S. trade deficit, without the Americans' having to make painful choices themselves. Like everyone else, the Americans find it difficult to make large cuts in their own government budget deficit or to make cuts in domestic investment (since these cuts lower capital accumulation and future living standards within the country). Knowledge of the twin deficits relationship allows us to understand the logic behind these trade disputes. ■

CASE STUDY

Why Doesn't Capital Flow to Poor Countries?

The U.S. trade deficit discussed in the previous case study represents a flow of capital into the United States from the rest of the world. What countries were the source of the capital flows? Because the world is a closed economy, the capital must be coming from countries that were running trade surpluses. In 2008, this group included many nations that were far poorer than the United States, such as Russia, Malaysia, Venezuela, and China. In these nations, saving exceeded investment in domestic capital. These countries were sending funds abroad to countries like the United States, where investment in domestic capital exceeded saving.

From one perspective, the direction of international capital flows is a paradox. Recall our discussion of production functions in Chapter 3. There, we established that an empirically realistic production function is the Cobb–Douglas form:

$$F(K,L) = A \, K^{\alpha} L^{1-\alpha},$$

where K is capital, L is labour, A is a variable representing the state of technology, and α is a parameter that determines capital's share of total income. For this production function, the marginal product of capital is

$$MPK = \alpha \, A \, (K/L)^{\alpha-1}.$$

The marginal product of capital tells us how much more output an extra unit of capital would produce. Because α is capital's share, it must be less than 1, so $\alpha - 1 < 0$. This means that an increase in K/L decreases MPK. In other words, holding other variables constant, the more capital a nation has, the less valuable an extra unit of capital is. This phenomenon of diminishing marginal product says that capital should be more valuable when capital is scarce.

This prediction, however, seems at odds with the international flow of capital represented by trade imbalances. Capital does not seem to flow to nations where it should be most valuable. Instead of capital-rich countries like the United States lending to capital-poor countries, we often observe the opposite. Why is that?

One reason is that there are important differences among nations other than their accumulation of capital. Poor nations have not only lower levels of capital accumulation (represented by K/L) but also inferior production capabilities (represented by the variable A). For example, compared to rich nations, poor nations may have less access to advanced technologies, lower levels of education (or *human capital*), or less efficient economic policies. Such differences could mean less output for given inputs of capital and labour; in the Cobb–Douglas production function, this is translated into a lower value of the parameter A. If so, then capital need not be more valuable in poor nations, even though capital is scarce.

A second reason why capital might not flow to poor nations is that property rights are often not enforced. Corruption is typically extensive; revolutions, coups, and expropriation of wealth are common; and governments often default on their debts. So, even if capital is more valuable in poor nations, foreigners may avoid investing their wealth there simply because they are afraid of losing it. Moreover, local investors face similar incentives. Imagine that you lived in a poor nation and you happened to be lucky enough to have wealth to invest; you might well decide that putting it in a safe country like the United States is your best option, even if the marginal product of capital is less there than in your home country.

Whichever of the two reasons is correct, the challenge for poor nations is to find ways to reverse the situation. If these nations offered the same production efficiency and legal protections as the U.S. economy, the direction of international capital flows would likely reverse. The U.S. trade deficit would become a trade surplus, and capital would flow to these emerging nations. Such a change would help the poor of the world escape poverty.[2] ■

5-3 Exchange Rates

Having examined the international flows of capital and of goods and services, we now extend the analysis by considering the prices that apply to these transactions. The *exchange rate* between two countries is the price at which residents of those countries trade with each other. In this section we first examine precisely what the exchange rate measures, and we then discuss how exchange rates are determined.

Nominal and Real Exchange Rates

Economists distinguish between two exchange rates: the nominal exchange rate and the real exchange rate. Let's discuss each in turn and see how they are related.

The Nominal Exchange Rate The **nominal exchange rate** is the relative price of the currency of two countries. For example, if the exchange rate between the Canadian dollar and the Japanese yen is 100 yen per dollar, then you

---

[2] For more on this topic, see Robert E. Lucas, "Why Doesn't Capital Flow from Rich to Poor Countries?" *American Economic Review* 80 (May 1990): 92–96.

How Newspapers Report the Exchange Rate

You can find exchange rates reported daily in many newspapers, although, increasingly, newspapers expect readers to look up exchange rates on the Internet. Alternatively, newspapers transfer users of their own Web-based editions to the Bank of Canada exchange-rate Website. To view that Website, visit http://www.bank-banque-canada.ca/, then click on "English," then "Rates and Statistics," and then "Exchange Rates." You then have many options, such as a currency converter for 56 currencies. The material reproduced in this box represents what was available on July 7, 2009, when the US$/CAN$ closing rate summary" was chosen.

Notice that on that date, one U.S. dollar bought 1.1661 Canadian dollars. Often you will read or hear the exchange rate reported as the value of the Canadian dollar, not the value of the U.S. dollar—as it is here. This alternative measure is simply the inverse. On July 7, 2009, the value of the Canadian dollar in terms of U.S. dollars was

(1/1.1661) = 0.8576, so the news media reported that the Canadian dollar was worth about 86 U.S. cents. As you can see, these two ways of reporting the exchange rate are equivalent ways of expressing the relative price of the two currencies. This book always expresses the exchange rate in units of foreign currency per Canadian dollar—the inverse of the practice followed on the Bank of Canada exchange-rate Website.

You can see that the value of the Canadian dollar varies quite a lot. For example, at the beginning of 2009, the U.S. dollar was higher (at $1.2265 Canadian), while six months earlier, the U.S. dollar was lower (at $1.0240 Canadian). Since we are defining the value of the Canadian dollar as our exchange rate, we say that there was a *depreciation* in the value of our currency and exchange rate between July 2008 and January 2009 and that there was an *appreciation* in our currency and exchange rate between January 2009 and July 2009.

Bank of Canada

Rates and Statistics
Exchange rates
US$/CAN$ closing rate summary

US$/CAN$ Summary of Closing Rates	
Latest closing:	(07/07/2009) – $1.1661
Past 12 months	
High	(09/03/2009) – $1.2991
Low	(21/07/2008) – $1.0014
From 1949 to present	
High	(18/01/2002) – $1.6125
Low	(06/11/2007) – $0.9215

Monthly closing, past 12 months			
June	2009	1.1630	
May	2009	1.0917	
April	2009	1.1930	
March	2009	1.2613	
February	2009	1.2723	
January	2009	1.2265	
December	2008	1.2180	
November	2008	1.2370	
October	2008	1.2045	
September	2008	1.0642	
August	2008	1.0620	
July	2008	1.0240	
June	2008	1.0197	

Rates equal the price of 1 U.S. dollar, in Canadian dollars.
Latest closing rate is updated at about 16:30 ET the same business day.
Source: Copyright © 1995–2009, Bank of Canada.

can exchange 1 dollar for 100 yen in world markets for foreign currency. A Japanese who wants to obtain dollars would pay 100 yen for each dollar she bought. A Canadian who wants to obtain yen would get 100 yen for each dollar he paid. When people refer to "the exchange rate" between two countries, they usually mean the nominal exchange rate.

The Real Exchange Rate The **real exchange rate** is the relative price of the goods of two countries. That is, the real exchange rate tells us the rate at which we can trade the goods of one country for the goods of another. The real exchange rate is sometimes called the *terms of trade*.

To see the relation between the real and nominal exchange rates, consider a single good produced in many countries: cars. Suppose a Canadian car costs $20,000 and a similar Japanese car costs 2,400,000 yen. To compare the prices of the two cars, we must convert them into a common currency. If a dollar is worth 100 yen, then the Canadian car costs 2,000,000 yen. Comparing the price of the Canadian car (2,000,000 yen) and the price of the Japanese car (2,400,000 yen), we conclude that the Canadian car costs five-sixths of what the Japanese car costs. In other words, at current prices, we can exchange 6 Canadian cars for 5 Japanese cars.

We can summarize our calculation above as follows:

$$\text{Real Exchange Rate} = \frac{(100 \text{ yen/dollar}) \times (20,000 \text{ dollars/Canadian Car})}{(2,400,000 \text{ yen/Japanese Car})}$$

$$= 0.83 \, \frac{\text{Japanese Car}}{\text{Canadian Car}}.$$

At these prices and this exchange rate, we obtain five-sixths of a Japanese car per Canadian car. More generally, we can write this calculation as

$$\frac{\text{Real Exchange}}{\text{Rate}} = \frac{\text{Nominal Exchange Rate} \times \text{Price of Domestic Good}}{\text{Price of Foreign Good}}.$$

The rate at which we exchange foreign and domestic goods depends on the prices of the goods in the local currencies and on the rate at which the currencies are exchanged.

This calculation of the real exchange rate for a single good suggests how we should define the real exchange rate for a broader basket of goods. Let e be the nominal exchange rate (the number of yen per dollar), P be the price level in Canada (measured in dollars), and P^* be the price level in Japan (measured in yen). Then the real exchange rate ϵ is

$$
\begin{array}{ccc}
\text{Real} & \text{Nominal} & \text{Ratio of} \\
\text{Exchange} = \text{Exchange} \times & \text{Price} \\
\text{Rate} & \text{Rate} & \text{Levels} \\
\epsilon \quad = & e \quad \times & (P/P^*).
\end{array}
$$

The real exchange rate between two countries is computed from the nominal exchange rate and the price levels in the two countries. *If the real exchange rate is high, foreign goods are relatively cheap, and domestic goods are relatively expensive. If the real exchange rate is low, foreign goods are relatively expensive, and domestic goods are relatively cheap.*

The Real Exchange Rate and the Trade Balance

What macroeconomic influence does the real exchange rate exert? To answer this question, remember that the real exchange rate is nothing more than a relative price. Just as the relative price of hamburgers and pizza determines which you choose for lunch, the relative price of domestic and foreign goods affects the demand for these goods.

Suppose first that the real exchange rate is low. In this case, because domestic goods are relatively cheap, domestic residents will want to purchase fewer imported goods: they will buy Fords rather than Volkswagens, drink Coors rather than Heineken, and vacation in the Rockies rather than Europe. For the same reason, foreigners will want to buy many of our goods. As a result of both of these actions, the quantity of our net exports demanded will be high.

The opposite occurs if the real exchange rate is high. Because domestic goods are expensive relative to foreign goods, domestic residents will want to buy many imported goods, and foreigners will want to buy few of our goods. Therefore, the quantity of our net exports demanded will be low.

We write this relationship between the real exchange rate and net exports as

$$NX = NX(\epsilon).$$

This equation states that net exports are a function of the real exchange rate. Figure 5-8 illustrates this negative relationship between the trade balance and the real exchange rate.

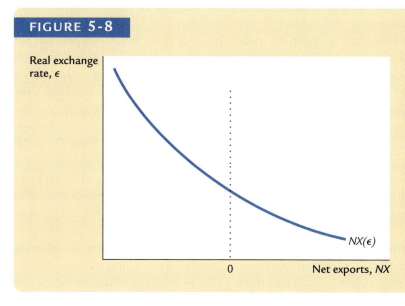

FIGURE 5-8

Net Exports and the Real Exchange Rate The figure shows the relationship between the real exchange rate and net exports: the lower the real exchange rate, the less expensive are domestic goods relative to foreign goods, and thus the greater are our net exports. Note that a portion of the horizontal axis measures negative values of *NX*: because imports can exceed exports, net exports can be less than zero.

Traders Respond to the Exchange Rate

The value of the Canadian dollar has fluctuated rather dramatically over the years. Back in 1986, the Canadian dollar bought only $0.72 U.S. By 1991, Canadian currency had so increased in value that it bought $0.87 U.S. Then, by the end of the century, the Canadian dollar had dropped again, and it could only bring $0.69 U.S. in trades on the foreign exchange market. In 2006, the value of the Canadian dollar was back up to $0.90 U.S., and it peaked at $1.09 U.S. in November 2007. As this book was going to press, the Canadian dollar was back at $0.87 U.S. Given this pattern, it is not surprising that trade across the Canada–United States border has been affected.

The phenomenon of "cross-border shopping" has been widely discussed in the media. While the Canadian dollar was high in value, many Canadians made one-day trips to border towns in the United States to capitalize on the bargains that could be had in the "warehouse malls" there. On weekend days, there were tremendous traffic jams at the border, as cross-border shoppers swamped the facilities at the customs points. Canadian retailers pleaded with governments to "do something" to help keep their businesses from failing (and many did fail). By the mid-1990s, the cross-border shopping "problem" had all but disappeared. Indeed, the media carried stories about how the traffic had started to go the other way. Americans had started to realize how much their currency then could buy in Canada. These developments are perfectly predictable, given the large changes in the exchange rate. Cross-border shopping is just one more instance of households and firms choosing to consume more of the items that are available at lower relative prices.

The variation in the Canada–United States exchange rate during this period also caused controversy regarding the Canada–U.S. Free Trade Agreement, which came into effect in January 1989. From Canada's point of view, one of the purposes of the deal was to allow Canadian firms to gain better access to the large U.S. market (for selling Canadian goods). But there were competing effects on the competitiveness of Canadian firms. The removal of U.S. tariffs that formed part of the Free Trade Agreement made Canadian firms more competitive, but the fact that the Canadian dollar was so much more expensive to buy in 1989 (than it was in 1986) made Canadian firms less competitive. Many analysts argue that the high value of the Canadian exchange rate at that time delayed the benefits that Canada should have obtained from signing the trade deal.

It is not just trade with the United States that is affected by exchange-rate changes. In 1990, 1 Canadian dollar bought 123 Japanese yen. By 1994, the Canadian dollar had fallen to the point where it could only buy 75 yen. Consumers responded in the obvious way. Back in 1990, North American car manufacturers were suffering losses in sales and were offering large "cashbacks" to attract customers. North American sales of Japanese cars, on the other hand, were booming. Then, by 1994, the Japanese manufacturers were suffering large drops in car sales, and the North American car sales had recovered. The fortunes of these domestic car manufacturers subsequently reversed again, as the Canadian dollar rose in the early years of the present century.

The point of these stories is that the negative slope we have shown for the net export schedule in Figure 5-8 should not be controversial. ■

The Determinants of the Real Exchange Rate

We now have all the pieces needed to construct a model that explains what factors determine the real exchange rate. In particular, we combine the relationship between net exports and the real exchange rate we just discussed with the model of the trade balance we developed earlier in the chapter. We can summarize the analysis as follows:

■ The real exchange rate is related to net exports. When the real exchange rate is lower, domestic goods are less expensive relative to foreign goods, and net exports are greater.

■ The trade balance (net exports) must equal net foreign investment, which in turn equals saving minus investment. Saving is fixed by the consumption function and fiscal policy; investment is fixed by the investment function and the world interest rate.

Figure 5-9 illustrates these two conditions. The line showing the relationship between net exports and the real exchange rate slopes downward because a low real exchange rate—a "competitive" domestic economy—makes domestic goods relatively inexpensive. The line representing the excess of saving over investment, $S - I$, is vertical because neither saving nor investment depends on the real exchange rate. The crossing of these two lines determines the equilibrium exchange rate.

Figure 5-9 looks like an ordinary supply-and-demand diagram. In fact, you can think of this diagram as representing the supply and demand for foreign-currency exchange. The vertical line, $S - I$, represents the excess of domestic saving over domestic investment, and thus the supply of Canadian dollars to be exchanged into foreign currency and invested abroad. The downward-sloping line, NX, represents the net demand for Canadian dollars coming from foreigners who want Canadian dollars to buy our goods. *At the equilibrium real exchange rate, the supply of Canadian dollars available for net foreign investment balances the demand for dollars by foreigners buying our net exports.*

FIGURE 5-9

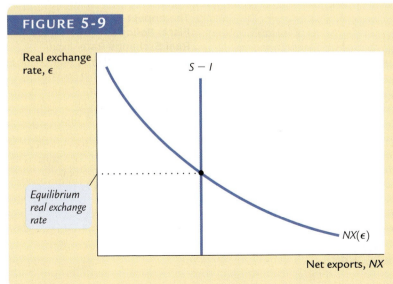

How the Real Exchange Rate is Determined The real exchange rate is determined by the intersection of the vertical line representing saving minus investment and the downward-sloping net-exports schedule. At this intersection, the quantity of Canadian dollars supplied for net foreign investment equals the quantity of dollars demanded for the net export of goods and services.

How Policies Influence the Real Exchange Rate

We can use this model to show how the changes in economic policy we discussed earlier affect the real exchange rate.

Fiscal Policy at Home What happens to the real exchange rate if the government reduces national saving by increasing government purchases or cutting taxes? As we discussed earlier, this reduction in saving lowers $S - I$ and thus NX. That is, the reduction in saving causes a trade deficit.

Figure 5-10 shows how the equilibrium real exchange rate adjusts to ensure that NX falls. The change in policy shifts the vertical $S - I$ line to the left, lowering the supply of Canadian dollars to be invested abroad. The lower supply causes the equilibrium real exchange rate to rise from ϵ_1 to ϵ_2—that is, the dollar becomes more valuable. Because of the rise in the value of the dollar, domestic goods become more expensive relative to foreign goods, which causes exports to fall and imports to rise. The change in exports and the change in imports both act to reduce net exports.

Fiscal Policy Abroad What happens to the real exchange rate if foreign governments increase government purchases or cut taxes? This change in fiscal policy reduces world saving and raises the world interest rate. The increase in the world interest rate reduces domestic investment I, which raises $S - I$ and thus NX. That is, the increase in the world interest rate causes a trade surplus.

Figure 5-11 shows that this change in policy shifts the vertical $S - I$ line to the right, raising the supply of Canadian dollars to be invested abroad. The equilibrium real exchange rate falls. That is, the dollar becomes less valuable, and domestic goods become less expensive relative to foreign goods.

Shifts in Investment Demand What happens to the real exchange rate if investment demand at home increases, perhaps because the Canadian government

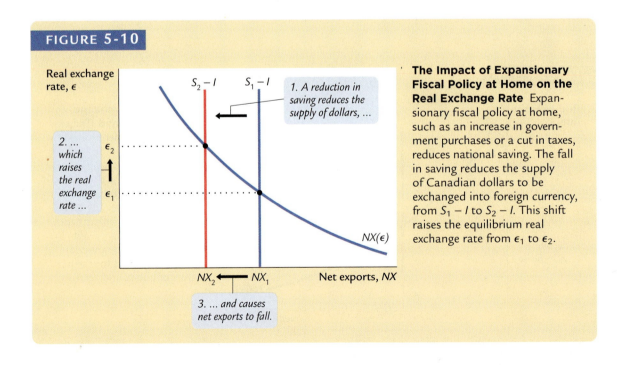

FIGURE 5-10

1. A reduction in saving reduces the supply of dollars, ...

2. ... which raises the real exchange rate ...

3. ... and causes net exports to fall.

The Impact of Expansionary Fiscal Policy at Home on the Real Exchange Rate Expansionary fiscal policy at home, such as an increase in government purchases or a cut in taxes, reduces national saving. The fall in saving reduces the supply of Canadian dollars to be exchanged into foreign currency, from $S_1 - I$ to $S_2 - I$. This shift raises the equilibrium real exchange rate from ϵ_1 to ϵ_2.

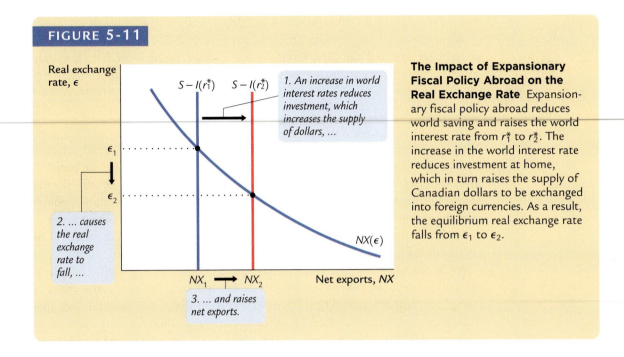

FIGURE 5-11

1. An increase in world interest rates reduces investment, which increases the supply of dollars, ...

2. ... causes the real exchange rate to fall, ...

3. ... and raises net exports.

The Impact of Expansionary Fiscal Policy Abroad on the Real Exchange Rate Expansionary fiscal policy abroad reduces world saving and raises the world interest rate from r_1^* to r_2^*. The increase in the world interest rate reduces investment at home, which in turn raises the supply of Canadian dollars to be exchanged into foreign currencies. As a result, the equilibrium real exchange rate falls from ϵ_1 to ϵ_2.

introduces an investment tax credit? At the given world interest rate, the increase in investment demand leads to higher investment. A higher value of I means lower values of $S - I$ and NX. That is, the increase in investment demand causes a trade deficit.

Figure 5-12 shows that the increase in investment demand shifts the vertical $S - I$ line to the left, reducing the supply of Canadian dollars to be invested abroad.

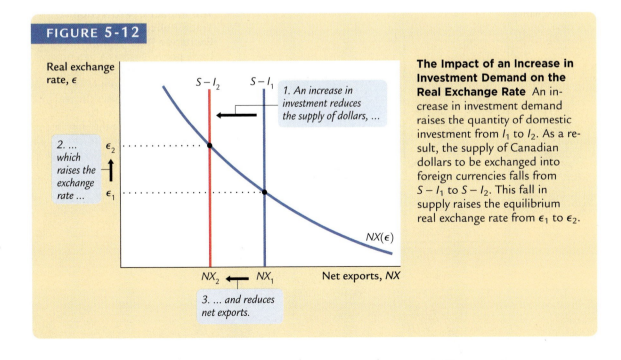

FIGURE 5-12

1. An increase in investment reduces the supply of dollars, ...

2. ... which raises the exchange rate ...

3. ... and reduces net exports.

The Impact of an Increase in Investment Demand on the Real Exchange Rate An increase in investment demand raises the quantity of domestic investment from I_1 to I_2. As a result, the supply of Canadian dollars to be exchanged into foreign currencies falls from $S - I_1$ to $S - I_2$. This fall in supply raises the equilibrium real exchange rate from ϵ_1 to ϵ_2.

The equilibrium real exchange rate rises. Hence, when the investment tax credit makes investing in Canada more attractive, it also increases the value of the Canadian dollars necessary to make these investments. When the dollar appreciates, domestic goods become more expensive relative to foreign goods, and net exports fall.

The Effects of Trade Policies

Now that we have a model that explains the trade balance and the real exchange rate, we have the tools to examine the macroeconomic effects of trade policies. Trade policies, broadly defined, are policies designed to influence directly the amount of goods and services exported or imported. Most often, trade policies take the form of protecting domestic industries from foreign competition—either by placing a tax on foreign imports (a tariff) or restricting the amount of goods and services that can be imported (a quota).

As an example of a protectionist trade policy, consider what would happen if the government prohibited the import of foreign cars. For any given real exchange rate, imports would now be lower, implying that net exports (exports minus imports) would be higher. Thus, the net-exports schedule shifts outward, as in Figure 5-13. To see the effects of the policy, we compare the old equilibrium and the new equilibrium. In the new equilibrium, the real exchange rate is higher, and net exports are unchanged. Despite the shift in the net-exports schedule, the equilibrium level of net exports remains the same, assuming the protectionist policy does not alter either saving or investment.

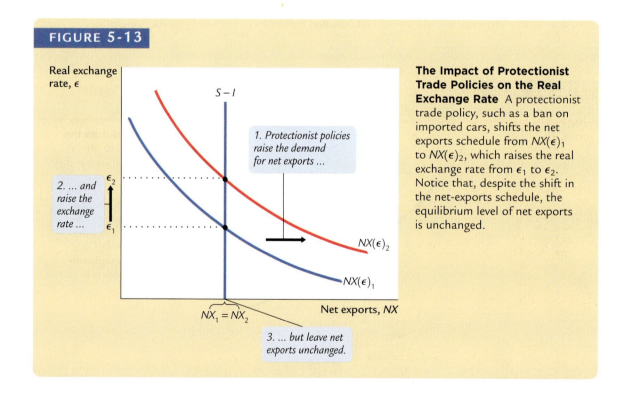

FIGURE 5-13

The Impact of Protectionist Trade Policies on the Real Exchange Rate A protectionist trade policy, such as a ban on imported cars, shifts the net exports schedule from $NX(\epsilon)_1$ to $NX(\epsilon)_2$, which raises the real exchange rate from ϵ_1 to ϵ_2. Notice that, despite the shift in the net-exports schedule, the equilibrium level of net exports is unchanged.

1. Protectionist policies raise the demand for net exports ...

2. ... and raise the exchange rate ...

3. ... but leave net exports unchanged.

This analysis shows that protectionist trade policies do not affect the trade balance. This surprising conclusion is often overlooked in the popular debate over trade policies. Because a trade deficit reflects an excess of imports over exports, one might guess that reducing imports—such as by prohibiting the import of foreign cars—would reduce a trade deficit. Yet our model shows that protectionist policies lead only to an appreciation of the real exchange rate. The increase in the price of domestic goods relative to foreign goods tends to lower net exports by stimulating imports and depressing exports. Thus, the appreciation offsets the increase in net exports that is directly attributable to the trade restriction.

Although protectionist trade policies do not alter the trade balance, they do affect the amount of trade. As we have seen, because the real exchange rate appreciates, the goods and services we produce become more expensive relative to foreign goods and services. We therefore export less in the new equilibrium. Since net exports are unchanged, we must import less as well. (The appreciation of the exchange rate does stimulate imports to some extent, but this only partly offsets the decrease in imports due to the trade restriction.) Thus, protectionist policies reduce both the quantity of imports and the quantity of exports.

This fall in the total amount of trade is the reason economists almost always oppose protectionist policies. International trade benefits all countries by allowing each country to specialize in what it produces best and by providing each country with a greater variety of goods and services. Protectionist policies diminish these gains from trade. Although these policies benefit certain groups within society—for example, a ban on imported cars helps domestic car producers—society on average is worse off when policies reduce the amount of international trade.

CASE STUDY

The "Neo-Conservative" Policy Agenda in the 1980s and 1990s

During the 1984–1993 period, Canada's Conservative government had an economic plan that involved four key elements:

- Tax reform
- Deficit reduction
- Disinflation
- Free trade

It is instructive to evaluate this package of initiatives using the analysis of this chapter.

The broad principle underlying tax reform was a move toward sales taxes and away from income taxes. This general move took several forms: (1) the introduction of the goods and services tax (GST), (2) the introduction of the capital gains tax exemption, and (3) the increase in the allowed contributions to registered retirement savings plans. All these initiatives were intended to stimulate private saving. Deficit reduction by the government itself is also a direct move toward higher national saving (since overall saving in the country is the excess of private saving over the government budget deficit). The reduction of inflation was also geared to stimulating saving, since (as we noted in Chapter 4) with nominal (not real) interest income subject to tax in Canada, lower inflation is equivalent to a cut in interest-income taxes.

Thus, the first three government initiatives were intended to shift the $S - I$ line to the right, and so to lower the real exchange rate and increase the trade surplus. By increasing the rate at which Canadians become less indebted to foreigners, this policy package was intended to increase the standard of living for future generations.

The fourth policy initiative—free trade—has a less obvious effect on the trade balance. The Free Trade Agreement with the United States involved both countries dropping their tariffs by essentially the same amount. Thus, it involved at most a small net shift in the position of the net-exports schedule. But one of the expected outcomes was an increased level of investment spending in Canada. With access to the large U.S. market guaranteed (for firms located in Canada), it was expected that plants in Canada would expand. They no longer had to limit their operations to serve the small Canadian market. Such an increase in investment spending in Canada shifts the $S - I$ line to the left. Thus, free trade involves competing effects on welfare: individuals can consume more goods at lower prices, but the investment effect that may accompany the removal of trade restrictions *in the rest of the world* leads to a larger trade deficit, and so (other things equal) to an increased level of foreign indebtedness in the future. The government was confident that the benefits would exceed the costs in this tradeoff for two reasons. First, the return on the extra capital employed in Canada should generate enough extra Canadian income for Canadians to be able to afford higher interest payments to foreigners. Second, the other three initiatives in the policy package were intended to increase domestic saving more than free trade increased investment. Thus, the net effect of the package was expected to be an increase in the trade surplus.

While this policy package can be rationalized easily within our analytical framework, it turned out that there were several slips between the design and the execution of these measures. First, the attempt to reduce the government's budget failed; indeed, government deficits increased during this period. Second, changes to the tax system were only partial. The GST turned out to be an administrative headache, and it raised less revenue than was expected. Also, the capital gains exemption was reduced and then was eliminated in 1994. As a result, disinflation was the only policy (of the first three listed above) that was fully and successfully implemented while the Conservatives were in power. Thus, much of what was to shift the $S - I$ line to the right did not materialize. As a result, the current account surplus did not rise appreciably. Unfortunately, for future generations of Canadians, the rate of foreign debt accumulation was not decreased appreciably.

This fact was not only a concern for future generations. Without the intended increase in national saving, the exchange rate remained higher in the late 1980s and early 1990s than had been the government's intention. The high value of the Canadian dollar removed the competitive advantage that Canadian firms were getting through the reduction of U.S. tariffs. In the end, the fact that the government succeeded with respect to its monetary policy objective (disinflation) but failed with respect to its fiscal policy objective (deficit reduction) meant that the overall outcome for both current and future generations was far less than was possible given the basic consistency of the overall package of intended policies.

When the Liberals took power in the 1990s, they maintained the Conservative policy agenda. They made no further changes to the taxation of interest income and capital gains; they extended the Free Trade Agreement to include Mexico; and they maintained the low inflation policy. Since they contracted fiscal policy sufficiently to eliminate the budget deficit, national saving was increased and the current account surplus rose as a result. In the years that followed, Canadians enjoyed a lower level of indebtedness to foreigners. ■

The Determinants of the Nominal Exchange Rate

Having seen what determines the real exchange rate, we now turn our attention to the nominal exchange rate—the rate at which the currencies of two countries trade. Recall the relationship between the real and the nominal exchange rate:

$$\text{Real Exchange Rate} = \text{Nominal Exchange Rate} \times \text{Ratio of Price Levels}$$

$$\epsilon = e \times (P/P^*).$$

We can write the nominal exchange rate as

$$e = \epsilon \times (P^*/P).$$

This equation shows that the nominal exchange rate depends on the real exchange rate and the price levels in the two countries. Given the value of the real exchange rate, if the domestic price level P rises, then the nominal exchange rate e will fall: because a dollar is worth less, a dollar will buy fewer yen. On the other hand, if the Japanese price level P^* rises, then the nominal exchange rate will increase: because the yen is worth less, a dollar will buy more yen.

It is instructive to consider changes in exchange rates over time. The exchange rate equation can be written

$$\% \text{ Change in } e = \% \text{ Change in } \epsilon + \% \text{ Change in } P^* - \% \text{ Change in } P.$$

The percentage change in ϵ is the change in the real exchange rate. The percentage change in P is the domestic inflation rate π, and the percentage change in P^* is the foreign country's inflation rate π^*. Thus, the percentage change in the nominal exchange rate is

$$\% \text{ Change in } e = \% \text{ Change in } \epsilon + (\pi^* - \pi)$$

$$\underset{\text{Nominal Exchange Rate}}{\text{Percentage Change in}} = \underset{\text{Real Exchange Rate}}{\text{Percentage Change in}} + \underset{\text{Inflation Rates.}}{\text{Difference in}}$$

This equation states that the percentage change in the nominal exchange rate between the currencies of two countries equals the percentage change in the real exchange rate plus the difference in their inflation rates. *If a country has a high rate of inflation relative to Canada, a Canadian dollar will buy an increasing amount of the foreign currency over time. If a country has a low rate of inflation relative to Canada, a Canadian dollar will buy a decreasing amount of the foreign currency over time.*

This analysis shows how monetary policy affects the nominal exchange rate. We know from Chapter 4 that high growth in the money supply leads to high inflation. Here, we have just seen that one consequence of high inflation is a depreciating currency: high π implies falling e. In other words, just as growth in the amount of money raises the price of goods measured in terms of money, it also tends to raise the price of foreign currencies measured in terms of the domestic currency.

CASE STUDY

Inflation and Nominal Exchange Rates

If we look at data on exchange rates and price levels of different countries, we quickly see the importance of inflation for explaining changes in the nominal exchange rate. The most dramatic examples come from periods of very high inflation. For example, the price level in Mexico rose by 2,300 percent from 1983 to 1988. Because of this inflation, the number of pesos a person could buy with a U.S. dollar rose from 144 in 1983 to 2,281 in 1988.

The same relationship holds true for countries with more moderate inflation. Figure 5-14 is a scatterplot showing the relationship between inflation and the exchange rate for 15 countries. On the horizontal axis is the difference between each country's average inflation rate and the average inflation rate of the United States, our base for comparison. This is our measure of $(\pi^* - \pi)$. On the vertical axis is the average percentage change in the exchange rate between each country's currency and the U.S. dollar (% Change in e). The positive relationship between these two variables is clear in this figure. Countries with relatively high inflation tend to have depreciating currencies, and countries with relatively low inflation tend to have appreciating currencies.

As an example, consider the exchange rate between Swiss francs and U.S. dollars. Both Switzerland and the United States have experienced inflation over the past twenty years, so both the franc and the dollar buy fewer goods than they once did. But, as Figure 5-14 shows, inflation in Switzerland has been lower than

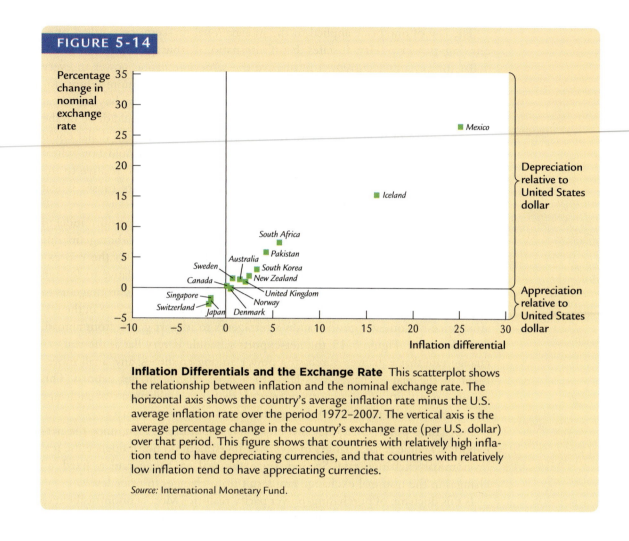

FIGURE 5-14

Inflation Differentials and the Exchange Rate This scatterplot shows the relationship between inflation and the nominal exchange rate. The horizontal axis shows the country's average inflation rate minus the U.S. average inflation rate over the period 1972–2007. The vertical axis is the average percentage change in the country's exchange rate (per U.S. dollar) over that period. This figure shows that countries with relatively high inflation tend to have depreciating currencies, and that countries with relatively low inflation tend to have appreciating currencies.

Source: International Monetary Fund.

inflation in the United States. This means that the value of the franc has fallen less than the value of the dollar. Therefore, the number of Swiss francs one can buy with a U.S. dollar has been falling over time. ■

The Special Case of Purchasing-Power Parity

A famous hypothesis in economics, called the *law of one price,* states that the same good cannot sell for different prices in different locations at the same time. If a tonne of wheat sold for less in Calgary than in Winnipeg, it would be profitable to buy wheat in Calgary and then sell it in Winnipeg. This profit opportunity would become quickly apparent to astute arbitrageurs—people who specialize in "buying low" in one market and "selling high" in another. As the arbitrageurs took advantage of this opportunity, they would increase the demand for wheat in Calgary and increase the supply in Winnipeg. This would drive the price up in Calgary and down in Winnipeg—thereby ensuring that prices are equalized in the two markets.

The law of one price applied to the international marketplace is called **purchasing-power parity.** It states that if international arbitrage is possible, then a dollar (or any other currency) must have the same purchasing power in every country. The argument goes as follows. If a dollar could buy more wheat domestically than abroad, there would be opportunities to profit by buying wheat domestically and selling it abroad. Profit-seeking arbitrageurs would drive up the domestic price of wheat relative to the foreign price. Similarly, if a dollar could buy more wheat abroad than domestically, the arbitrageurs would buy wheat abroad and sell it domestically, driving down the domestic price relative to the foreign price. Thus, profit-seeking by international arbitrageurs causes wheat prices to be the same in all countries.

We can interpret the doctrine of purchasing-power parity using our model of the real exchange rate. The quick action of these international arbitrageurs implies that net exports are highly sensitive to small movements in the real exchange rate. A small decrease in the price of domestic goods relative to foreign goods—that is, a small decrease in the real exchange rate—causes arbitrageurs to buy goods domestically and sell them abroad. Similarly, a small increase in the relative price of domestic goods causes arbitrageurs to import goods from abroad. Therefore, as in Figure 5-15, the net-exports schedule is very flat at the real exchange rate that equalizes purchasing power among countries: any small movement in the real exchange rate leads to a large change in net exports. This extreme sensitivity of net exports guarantees that the equilibrium real exchange rate is always close to the level that ensures purchasing-power parity.

Purchasing-power parity has two important implications. First, since the net-exports schedule is flat, changes in saving or investment do not influence the real or nominal exchange rate. Second, since the real exchange rate is fixed, all changes in the nominal exchange rate result from changes in price levels.

Is this doctrine of purchasing-power parity realistic? Most economists believe that, despite its appealing logic, purchasing-power parity does not provide a

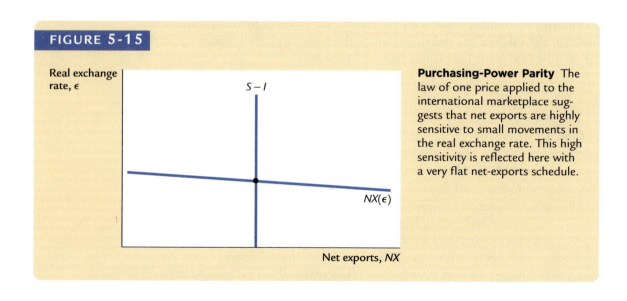

FIGURE 5-15

Real exchange rate, ϵ

$S - I$

$NX(\epsilon)$

Net exports, NX

Purchasing-Power Parity The law of one price applied to the international marketplace suggests that net exports are highly sensitive to small movements in the real exchange rate. This high sensitivity is reflected here with a very flat net-exports schedule.

completely accurate description of the world. First, many goods are not easily traded. A haircut can be more expensive in Tokyo than in Toronto, yet there is no room for international arbitrage since it is impossible to transport haircuts. Second, even tradeable goods are not always perfect substitutes. Some consumers prefer Toyotas, and others prefer Fords. Thus, the relative price of Toyotas and Fords can vary to some extent without leaving any profit opportunities. For these reasons, real exchange rates do in fact vary over time.

Although the doctrine of purchasing-power parity does not describe the world perfectly, it does provide a reason why movement in the real exchange rate will be limited. There is much validity to its underlying logic: the farther the real exchange rate drifts from the level predicted by purchasing-power parity, the greater the incentive for individuals to engage in international arbitrage in goods. Although we cannot rely on purchasing-power parity to eliminate all changes in the real exchange rate, this doctrine does provide a reason to expect that a significant number of the changes in the real exchange rate may be temporary.[3]

CASE STUDY

The Big Mac Around the World

The doctrine of purchasing-power parity says that after we adjust for exchange rates, we should find that goods sell for the same price everywhere. Conversely, it says that the exchange rate between two currencies should depend on the price levels in the two countries.

To see how well this doctrine works, *The Economist*, an international newsmagazine, regularly collects data on the price of a good sold in many countries: the McDonald's Big Mac hamburger. According to purchasing-power parity, the price of a Big Mac should be closely related to the country's nominal exchange rate. The higher the price of a Big Mac in the local currency, the higher the exchange rate (measured in units of local currency per U.S. dollar) should be.

Table 5-2 presents the international prices in 2008, when a Big Mac sold for $3.57 in the United States (this was the average price in New York, San Francisco, Chicago, and Atlanta). With these data we can use the doctrine of purchasing-power parity to predict nominal exchange rates. For example, because a Big Mac cost 32 pesos in Mexico, we would predict that the exchange rate between the dollar and the peso was 32/3.57, or around 8.96, pesos per dollar. At this exchange rate, a Big Mac would have cost the same in Mexico and the United States.

Table 5-2 shows the predicted and actual exchange rates for 32 countries, ranked by the predicted exchange rate. You can see that the evidence on purchasing-power parity is mixed. As the last two columns show, the actual and predicted exchange

---

[3] To learn more about purchasing-power parity, see Kenneth A. Froot and Kenneth Rogoff, "Perspectives on PPP and Long-Run Real Exchange Rates," in Gene M. Grossman and Kenneth Rogoff, eds., *Handbook of International Economics,* vol. 3 (Amsterdam: North-Holland, 1995).

TABLE 5-2				

Big Mac Prices and the Exchange Rate: An Application of Purchasing-Power Parity

Country	Currency	Price of a Big Mac	Exchange Rate (per U.S. dollar)	
			Predicted	Actual
Indonesia	Rupiah	18700.00	5238	9152
South Korea	Won	3200.00	896	1018
Chile	Peso	1550.00	434	494
Hungary	Forint	670.00	188	144
Japan	Yen	280.00	78.4	106.8
Taiwan	Dollar	75.00	21.0	30.4
Czech Republic	Koruna	66.10	18.5	14.5
Thailand	Baht	62.00	17.4	33.4
Russia	Ruble	59.00	16.5	23.2
Norway	Kroner	40.00	11.2	5.08
Sweden	Krona	38.00	10.6	5.96
Mexico	Peso	32.00	8.96	10.20
Denmark	Krone	28.00	7.84	4.70
South Africa	Rand	16.90	4.75	7.56
Hong Kong	Dollar	13.30	3.73	7.80
Egypt	Pound	13.00	3.64	5.31
China	Yuan	12.50	3.50	6.83
Argentina	Peso	11.00	3.08	3.02
Saudi Arabia	Riyal	10.00	2.80	3.75
UAE	Dirhams	10.00	2.80	3.67
Brazil	Real	7.50	2.10	1.58
Poland	Zloty	7.00	1.96	2.03
Switzerland	Franc	6.50	1.82	1.02
Malaysia	Ringgit	5.50	1.54	3.20
Turkey	Lire	5.15	1.44	1.19
New Zealand	Dollar	4.90	1.37	1.32
Canada	Dollar	4.09	1.15	1.00
Singapore	Dollar	3.95	1.11	1.35
United States	Dollar	3.57	1.00	1.00
Australia	Dollar	3.45	0.97	1.03
Euro Area	Euro	3.37	0.94	0.63
United Kingdom	Pound	2.29	0.64	0.50

Note: The predicted exchange rate is the exchange rate that would make the price of a Big Mac in that country equal to its price in the United States.
Source: *The Economist*, July 24, 2008.

rates are usually in the same ballpark. Our theory predicts, for instance, that a U.S. dollar should buy the greatest number of Indonesian rupiahs and fewest British pounds, and this turns out to be true. In the case of Mexico, the predicted exchange rate of 8.96 pesos per dollar is close to the actual exchange rate of 10.2. Yet the theory's predictions are far from exact and in many cases are off by 30 percent or more. Hence, although the theory of purchasing-power parity provides a rough guide to the level of exchange rates, it does not explain exchange rates completely. Part of the explanation for this incomplete matching between theory and evidence is surely related to the fact that arbitrage is difficult with a perishable commodity such as a hamburger. ■

5-4 Large Versus Small Open Economies

In this chapter we have seen how a small open economy works. We have examined the determinants of the international flow of funds for capital accumulation and the international flow of goods and services. We have also examined the determinants of a country's real and nominal exchange rates. Our analysis shows how various policies—monetary policies, fiscal policies, and trade policies—affect the trade balance and the exchange rate.

The economy we have studied is "small" in the sense that its interest rate is fixed by world financial markets. That is, we have assumed that this economy does not affect the world interest rate, and that the economy can borrow and lend at the world interest rate in unlimited amounts. This assumption contrasts with the assumption we made when we studied the closed economy in Chapter 3. In the closed economy, the domestic interest rate equilibrates domestic saving and domestic investment, implying that policies that influence saving or investment alter the equilibrium interest rate.

The small-open-economy specification is directly applicable to Canada. But which analysis should we apply to an economy like the United States? The answer is a little of both. The United States is neither so large nor so isolated that it is immune to developments occurring abroad. The large U.S. trade deficits since 1980 show the importance of international financial markets for funding U.S. investment. Hence, the closed-economy analysis of Chapter 3 cannot by itself fully explain the impact of policies on the U.S. economy.

Yet the U.S. economy is not so small and so open that the analysis of this chapter applies perfectly either. First, the United States is large enough that it can influence world financial markets. For example, large U.S. budget deficits were often blamed for the high real interest rates that prevailed throughout the world in the 1980s. Second, capital may not be perfectly mobile across countries. If individuals prefer holding their wealth in domestic rather than foreign assets, funds for capital accumulation will not flow freely to equate interest rates in all countries. For these two reasons, we cannot directly apply our model of the small open economy to the United States.

When analyzing policy for a country like the United States, we need to combine the closed-economy logic of Chapter 3 and the small-open-economy logic of this chapter. The results, not surprisingly, are a mixture of the two polar cases we have already examined. Consider, for example, a reduction in national saving due to a fiscal expansion. As in the closed economy, this policy raises the real interest rate and crowds out domestic investment. As in the small open economy, it also reduces net capital outflow, leading to a trade deficit and an appreciation of the exchange rate. Hence, although the model of the small open economy examined here does not precisely describe an economy like the United States, it does provide approximately the right answer to how policies affect the trade balance and the exchange rate.

Summary

1. Net exports are the difference between exports and imports. They are equal to the difference between what we produce and what we demand for consumption, investment, and government purchases.

2. The net capital outflow is the excess of domestic saving over domestic investment. The trade balance is the amount received for our net exports of goods and services. The national income accounts identity shows that net capital outflow always equals the trade balance.

3. The impact of any policy on the trade balance can be determined by examining its impact on saving and investment. Policies that raise saving or lower investment lead to a trade surplus, and policies that lower saving or raise investment lead to a trade deficit.

4. The nominal exchange rate is the rate at which people trade the currency of one country for the currency of another country. The real exchange rate is the rate at which people trade the goods produced by the two countries. The real exchange rate equals the nominal exchange rate multiplied by the ratio of the price levels in the two countries.

5. Because the real exchange rate is the price of domestic goods relative to foreign goods, an appreciation of the real exchange rate tends to reduce net exports. The equilibrium real exchange rate is the rate at which the quantity of net exports demanded equals net foreign investment.

6. The nominal exchange rate is determined by the real exchange rate and the price levels in the two countries. Other things equal, a high rate of inflation leads to a depreciating currency.

KEY CONCEPTS

Net exports	Balanced trade	Nominal exchange rate
Trade balance	Small open economy	Real exchange rate
Net capital outflow	World interest rate	Purchasing-power parity
Trade surplus and trade deficit		

QUESTIONS FOR REVIEW

1. What are net foreign investment and the trade balance? Explain how they are related.

2. Define the nominal exchange rate and the real exchange rate.

3. If a small open economy cuts defense spending, what happens to saving, investment, the trade balance, the interest rate, and the exchange rate?

4. If a small open economy bans the import of Japanese DVD players, what happens to saving, investment, the trade balance, the interest rate, and the exchange rate?

5. If Japan has low inflation and Mexico has high inflation, what will happen to the exchange rate between the Japanese yen and the Mexican peso?

PROBLEMS AND APPLICATIONS

1. Use the model of the small open economy to predict what would happen to the trade balance, the real exchange rate, and the nominal exchange rate in response to each of the following events.

    a. A fall in consumer confidence about the future induces consumers to spend less and save more.

    b. The introduction of a stylish line of Volkswagens makes some consumers prefer foreign cars over domestic cars.

    c. The introduction of automatic teller machines reduces the demand for money.

2. Consider an economy described by the following equations:

$$Y = C + I + G + NX,$$
$$Y = 5,000,$$
$$G = 1,000,$$
$$T = 1,000,$$
$$C = 250 + 0.75(Y - T),$$
$$I = 1,000 - 50r,$$
$$NX = 500 - 500\epsilon,$$
$$r = r^* = 5.$$

    a. In this economy, solve for national saving, investment, the trade balance, and the equilibrium exchange rate.

    b. Suppose now that G rises to 1,250. Solve for national saving, investment, the trade balance, and the equilibrium exchange rate. Explain what you find.

    c. Now suppose that the world interest rate rises from 5 to 10 percent. (G is again 1,000.) Solve for national saving, investment, the trade balance, and the equilibrium exchange rate. Explain what you find.

3. The country of Leverett is a small open economy. Suddenly, a change in world fashions makes the exports of Leverett unpopular.

    a. What happens in Leverett to saving, investment, net exports, the interest rate, and the exchange rate?

    b. The citizens of Leverett like to travel abroad. How will this change in the exchange rate affect them?

    c. The fiscal policymakers of Leverett want to adjust taxes to maintain the exchange rate at its previous level. What should they do? If they do this, what are the overall effects on saving, investment, net exports, and the interest rate?

4. What will happen to the trade balance and the real exchange rate of a small open economy when government purchases increase, such as during a war? Does your answer depend on whether this is a local war or a world war?

5. In 2005, Federal Reserve Governor Ben Bernanke said in a speech: "Over the past decade a combination of diverse forces has created a significant increase in the global supply of saving—a global saving glut—which helps to explain both the increase in the U.S. current account deficit [a broad measure of the trade deficit] and the relatively low level of long-term real interest rates in the world today." Is this statement consistent with the models you have learned? Explain.

6. A case study in this chapter concludes that, if poor nations offered better production efficiency and legal protections, the trade balance in rich nations such as the United States would move toward surplus. Let's consider why this might be the case.

   a. If the world's poor nations offer better production efficiency and legal protection, what would happen to the investment demand function in those countries?

   b. How would the change you describe in part (a) affect the demand for loanable funds in world financial markets?

   c. How would the change you describe in part (b) affect the world interest rate?

   d. How would the change in the world interest rate you describe in part (c) affect the trade balance in rich nations?

7. The president of the United States is considering placing a tariff on the import of Japanese luxury cars. Discuss the economics and politics of such a policy. In particular, how would the policy affect the U.S. trade deficit? How would it affect the exchange rate? Who would be hurt by such a policy? Who would benefit?

8. Suppose China exports television sets and uses the yuan as its currency, whereas Russia exports vodka and uses the ruble. China has a stable money supply and slow, steady technological progress in producing television sets, whereas Russia has very rapid growth in the money supply and no technological progress in vodka production. Based on this information, what would you predict for the real exchange rate (measured as bottles of vodka per television set) and the nominal exchange rate (measured as rubles per yuan)? Explain your reasoning. (*Hint:* For the

real exchange rate, think about the link between scarcity and relative prices.)

9. Suppose that some foreign countries begin to subsidize investment by instituting an investment tax credit.

   a. What happens to world investment demand as a function of the world interest rate?

   b. What happens to the world interest rate?

   c. What happens to investment in our small open economy?

   d. What happens to our trade balance?

   e. What happens to our real exchange rate?

10. "Travelling in Mexico is much cheaper now than it was ten years ago," says a friend. "Ten years ago, a dollar bought 10 pesos; this year, a dollar buys 15 pesos."

    Is your friend right or wrong? Given that total inflation over this period was about 25 percent in Canada and 100 percent in Mexico, has it become more or less expensive to travel in Mexico? Write your answer using a concrete example—such as a Canadian hotdog versus a Mexican taco—that will convince your friend.

11. You read in a newspaper that the nominal interest rate is 12 percent per year in Canada and 8 percent per year in the United States. Suppose that the real interest rates are equalized in the two countries and that purchasing-power parity holds.

    a. Using the Fisher equation (discussed in Chapter 4), what can you infer about expected inflation in Canada and in the United States?

    b. What can you infer about the expected change in the exchange rate between the Canadian dollar and the U.S. dollar?

    c. A friend proposes a get-rich-quick scheme: borrow from a U.S. bank at 8 percent, deposit the money in a Canadian bank at 12 percent, and make a 4 percent profit. What's wrong with this scheme?

The Open Economy in the Very Long Run

The main body of this chapter involves the small-open-economy version of the Chapter 3 material. In this appendix, we consider the small-open-economy version of some of the material that is in Chapters 7 and 8. The closed-economy analysis focuses on how saving leads to capital accumulation and higher living standards in the future. In the open setting, the assumption of perfect capital mobility makes the quantity of capital employed within the domestic economy independent of national saving. Thus, with both the capital stock and the labour force determined exogenously, real GDP can*not* be increased by national saving. But GNP *is* affected. With higher national saving, the level of foreign indebtedness can be reduced. Higher consumption is possible in the long run as a result of the corresponding reduction in interest payment obligations to foreigners. The purpose of this appendix is to explain this process in detail.

Foreign Debt

In the main part of this chapter, we did not need to distinguish between the trade balance and the current account balance. But now it is helpful to do so. To that end, we divide net exports into two components: the net sale of goods and non-financial services to the rest of the world (the trade balance) minus the net interest payments Canadians make each year to foreigners to pay for that year's lending services that were imported. Letting NX stand for the first component, and letting Z and r denote the level of foreign debt and the interest rate involved on that debt, the overall current account balance is $NX - rZ$. As before, the excess of national saving over domestic investment, $S - I$, must equal the current account balance, so in this more detailed specification,

$$S - I = NX - rZ.$$

Another way to appreciate this relationship is to note that, when the distinction between GNP and GDP is not ignored for simplicity, private saving is GNP $- T - C$. Since GNP = GDP $- rZ$, and since GDP $= C + I + G + NX$, these two relationships imply $S - I = NX - rZ$.

National wealth is the excess of our assets over our debt, that is, $K - Z$. Since saving is the increase in national wealth ($S = \Delta K - \Delta Z$), and since investment is the change in the capital stock ($I = \Delta K$), the fundamental equation given above can be re-expressed as foreign debt accumulation identity:

$$\Delta Z = rZ - NX.$$

This equation states that our debt to foreigners increases whenever interest payment obligations on the pre-existing debt for that period, rZ, exceed what we earn from our net-export sales from other items that period, NX.

A long-run equilibrium exists when the foreign debt-to-GDP ratio, Z/Y, is constant. Defining the GDP growth rate as n ($\Delta Y / Y = n$), long-run equilibrium requires $\Delta Z/Z = n$, or $\Delta Z = nZ$. Substituting this balanced growth requirement into the accumulation identity, we have the long-run equilibrium condition

$$(r - n)Z = NX.$$

Before we use these two relationships—the accumulation identity to determine outcomes initially and the equilibrium condition to determine outcomes eventually—we clarify two things. First, this analysis takes both r and n as exogenous variables. The interest rate is determined in the rest of the world via the assumption of perfect capital mobility. The growth rate of the effective labour force is exogenous, as in the Solow model (explained in Chapter 7). The second thing to bear in mind is that the interest rate (the marginal product of capital) exceeds the growth rate, so $(r - n)$ is positive. We will learn why this is the case when we discover that Canada has a smaller capital labour ratio than the Golden Rule value (Chapter 7).

Fiscal Policy

We are now in a position to see how our analysis of fiscal policy can be enriched by considering these longer-term relationships. The main initiative of the Canadian government during the 1990s was deficit reduction—accomplished primarily by cuts in government spending. Thus, in Figure 5-16 we explore the effect of a cut in government spending. Initially, the analysis duplicates what we

FIGURE 5-16

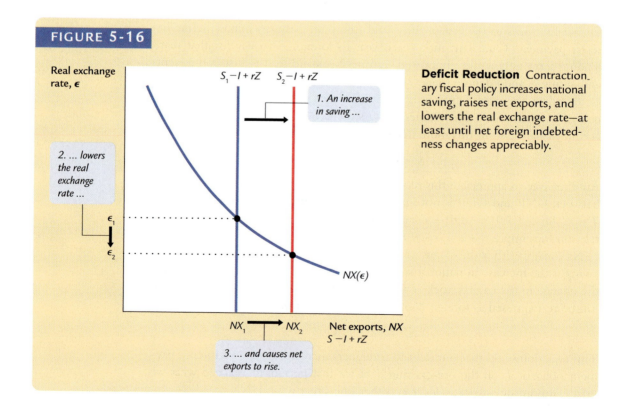

Deficit Reduction Contractionary fiscal policy increases national saving, raises net exports, and lowers the real exchange rate—at least until net foreign indebtedness changes appreciably.

learned when studying Figure 5-10; the only difference here is that spending is decreased, not increased. The graph shows the key implication of fiscal retrenchment—that net exports rise.

We can now appreciate the longer-term implication of this rise in net exports. Consider each term in the foreign debt accumulation identity. Since the preexisting level of Z is determined by whatever history took place *before* this fiscal policy, and since r is exogenous (equal to r^*), higher NX implies lower ΔZ. Thus a higher level of net exports initially makes our foreign debt obligations shrink.

What are the long-term implications of lower debt? This question can be answered by considering the full equilibrium condition. Given that $(r - n)$ is positive and that Z is eventually lower, the left-hand side of the equilibrium condition must be smaller. This means that, eventually, NX must be smaller too. So, as time passes, net exports *must* move in the *opposite* direction from what occurs initially.

To appreciate why this occurs, we must realize that the consumption function requires an amendment to make it applicable in this longer-term setting. In particular, to be both realistic and consistent with the optimization-based theories of consumption, which are introduced in Chapter 17, we must assume that consumption depends on both disposable income and wealth (and therefore foreign indebtedness: $C = C(Y - T, Z)$). Since households cannot afford to consume as much when they are heavily in debt, we know that consumption depends inversely on foreign debt. As a result, since national saving is $(Y - C - G)$, S depends positively on Z. Figure 5-17 shows the result of this dependence. While

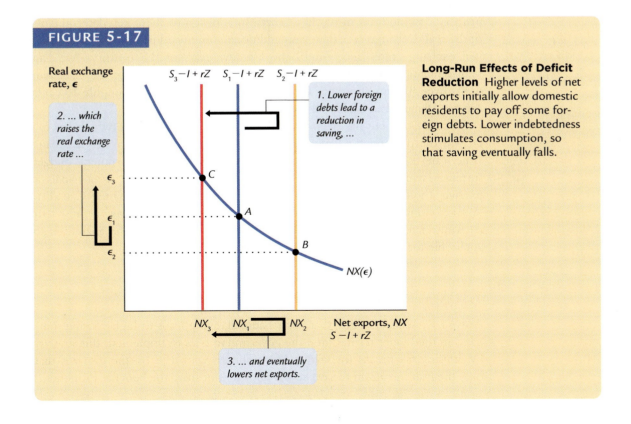

FIGURE 5-17

Long-Run Effects of Deficit Reduction Higher levels of net exports initially allow domestic residents to pay off some foreign debts. Lower indebtedness stimulates consumption, so that saving eventually falls.

Real exchange rate, ϵ

$S_3 - I + rZ$ $S_1 - I + rZ$ $S_2 - I + rZ$

1. Lower foreign debts lead to a reduction in saving, ...

2. ... which raises the real exchange rate ...

ϵ_3

C

ϵ_1

A

ϵ_2

B

$NX(\epsilon)$

NX_3 NX_1 NX_2 Net exports, NX
$S - I + rZ$

3. ... and eventually lowers net exports.

the cut in G increases the public sector component of national savings and so shifts the net savings line to the right initially, the falling level of foreign debt induces a gradual drop in the private sector component of national savings; so the net savings line drifts back to the left. The algebraic version of the long-run equilibrium condition indicates that this process is not complete until a point like C in Figure 5-17 is reached.

It is instructive to summarize the time path of the real exchange rate following fiscal retrenchment. That response is from point A to B initially, and then from B to C later on. Thus, the analysis predicts that the domestic currency falls in value initially, but that this outcome is reversed and that the exchange rate rises eventually. Many commentators on exchange-rate developments appear to reason in a way that does not reflect this "overshoot" in the real exchange rate. For example, it is usually presumed that tight fiscal policy—since it involves "getting our fiscal house in order"—causes a straightforward appreciation of our currency. The limited success of empirical studies on exchange-rate determination may have a lot to do with the fact that the reversal and overshoot features in the theory are often precluded in the way statistical studies are performed.

But we should not be too critical of the empirical work. On balance, our theory suggests that Canada's real exchange rate (vis-à-vis the U.S. dollar) should have fallen during the 1970–2000 time period—both because we had a looser fiscal policy and because we have a more resource-based economy than do the Americans. As a result of our increased dependence on the resource sectors, the demand for our net exports was more affected by the drop in the demand for primary commodities in world markets. In addition to these key determinants of the real exchange rate, there was additional downward pressure on our nominal exchange rate, since—until the last few years of the century—we had higher inflation. It has been estimated that of the 30-cent fall in the Canadian dollar over 30 years (from par with the U.S. currency in 1970), roughly 10 cents can be attributed to each of these three factors.

Since 2000, there has been a world commodity price boom (which has increased the demand for Canadian exports) and a major reversal in Canadian-American fiscal policy. Until 2009, we have had large government budget surpluses, while Americans have recorded record budget deficits. As our analysis predicts, the long-run implications of these developments is a rising Canadian dollar (a rising Canada-U.S. dollar exchange rate). As this book goes to press, that exchange rate was back up to $0.87 U.S. It is reassuring that the analysis is so applicable for interpreting economic history.

Trickle-Down Economics

As we have seen, anything that raises national saving leads to higher living standards in the longer term. Often the government tries to implement this strategy by offering tax breaks for saving. This policy is criticized on the grounds that only the rich can afford to save, so the poor do not share the benefits. Proponents

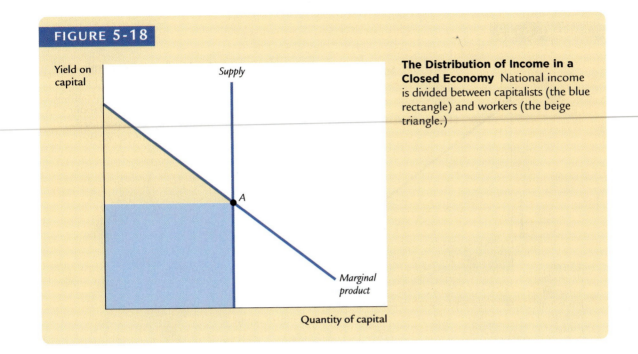

FIGURE 5-18

Yield on capital

Supply

A

Marginal product

Quantity of capital

The Distribution of Income in a Closed Economy National income is divided between capitalists (the blue rectangle) and workers (the beige triangle.)

of this approach answer this criticism by arguing that the benefits "trickle down" indirectly to those on lower incomes, so everyone benefits indirectly after all. Let us assess the validity of this claim—first in a closed-economy setting as a base for comparison, and then in an open setting.

Figure 5-18 shows the diminishing marginal product of capital relationship. Initially, the quantity of capital is given by the position of the supply curve in Figure 5-18. The equilibrium return on capital (the interest rate) is given by the intersection of supply and demand in Figure 5-18: the height of point A. The total earnings of capital (the yield per unit times number of units) is given by the light blue rectangle. Since the area under the marginal product curve is total output, labourers receive the light beige triangle, and total GDP is the sum of capital's rectangle and labour's triangle. To assess the trickle-down theory, let us assume that capital owners are "rich," while labourers are "poor." We now consider whether an increase in national saving helps labour.

In a closed economy, higher saving means more investment, which leads eventually to a larger capital stock. We show that higher capital stock by moving the supply curve to the right in Figure 5-19. GDP has increased by an amount equal to the trapezoid of dark shaded regions on the right (labour gets the beige part, capital gets the blue part). Labour's total income has increased by the trapezoid created by the two horizontal dotted lines (both the light and dark beige regions in Figure 5-19). We can conclude that, even if labour does not benefit in any direct way from the tax cut (or other initiative used to stimulate saving), there appears to be solid support for the trickle-down view. The intuition behind this

FIGURE 5-19

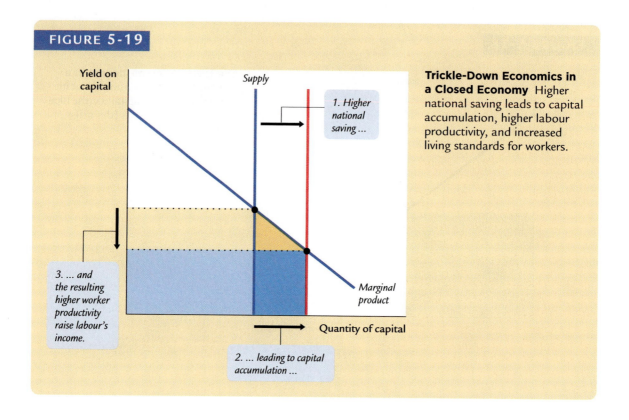

Trickle-Down Economics in a Closed Economy Higher national saving leads to capital accumulation, higher labour productivity, and increased living standards for workers.

conclusion is that each worker has more capital with which to work and so receives higher wages.

Does this conclusion carry over to a small open economy? The initial situation in this case is shown in Figure 5-20. With perfect capital mobility, there is a perfectly elastic supply of capital (from the rest of the world) at the prevailing world yield on capital. Supply and demand for capital intersect at point A, so GDP is determined by the trapazoid formed by the perpendicular dropped from point A. Capital owners receive the lower rectangles, while labour receives the upper, beige triangle. The vertical line in Figure 5-20 indicates what part of the capital is owned by domestic residents. Given the position of this line, we have assumed that domestic residents own the proportion of the capital that is denoted by point B. Thus, domestic capitalists receive the light blue rectangle and foreigners receive the green rectangle. Since GNP is GDP minus income going to foreigners, GNP is the entire coloured area minus this green region.

As in the closed economy, the results of higher saving are shown by shifting the vertical line to the right—as illustrated in Figure 5-21. In this case, the location of point A is unaffected, so GDP is no different. Wealth still increases, because the higher saving allows domestic residents to reduce foreign debt. The smaller interest payment obligation to foreigners is shown by the fact that the green region is smaller in Figure 5-21. Thus GNP increases, even though

FIGURE 5-20

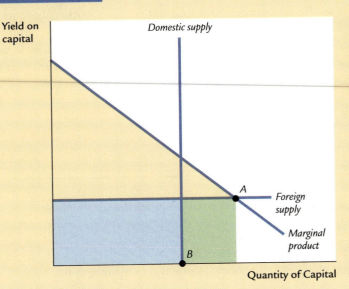

The Distribution of Income in a Small Open Economy National income is divided between capitalists (the shaded rectangles) and labour (the beige triangle.) Foreign capitalists receive the green rectangle; domestic capitalists receive the blue rectangle.

FIGURE 5-21

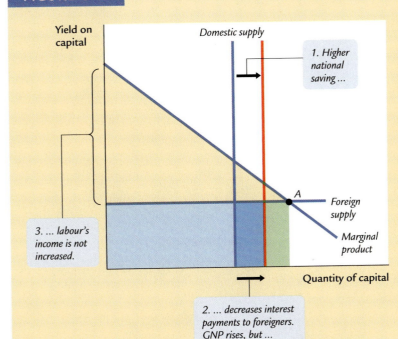

Trickle-Down Economics in a Small Open Economy Higher national saving leads to lower foreign interest payment obligation, so the incomes of domestic capitalists rise.

GDP does not. Since GNP is national income, the aggregate effect is much the same even if the reason for it differs. Domestic residents are better off because they have a smaller mortgage to finance, not because workers have more capital to work with. However, the *distribution* of the benefit is very different. Because workers have no more capital, wages are no higher, and this is why the size of labour's beige triangle is not affected. We conclude that there is *not* strong support for trickle down in a small open economy setting.

MORE PROBLEMS AND APPLICATIONS

1. Explain why empirical studies have had difficulty "explaining" changes in the exchange rate.

2. Spokespersons for the labour movement have been highly critical of the "conservative" agenda that has formed the basis of federal government policy in Canada for the last twenty years. Whether the initiative was tax reform, deficit reduction, or disinflation, these individuals criticized the government. Explain whether macroeconomic theory supports this critique.

Unemployment

A man willing to work, and unable to find work, is perhaps the saddest sight

that fortune's inequality exhibits under the sun.

— *Thomas Carlyle*

Unemployment is the macroeconomic problem that affects people most directly and severely. For most people, the loss of a job means a reduced living standard and psychological distress. It is no surprise that unemployment is a frequent topic of political debate and that politicians often claim that their proposed policies would help create jobs.

Economists study unemployment to identify its causes and to help improve the public policies that affect the unemployed. Some of these policies, such as job-training programs, assist people find employment. Others, such as employment insurance, alleviate some of the hardships that the unemployed face. Still other policies affect the prevalence of unemployment inadvertently. Laws mandating a high minimum wage, for instance, are widely thought to raise unemployment among the least skilled and experienced members of the labour force. By showing the effects of various policies, economists help policymakers evaluate their options.

Our discussions of the labour market so far have ignored unemployment. Our model of national income in Chapter 3 was built with the assumption that the economy was always at full employment. In reality, of course, not everyone in the labour force has a job all the time: all free-market economies experience some unemployment.

Figure 6-1 shows the rate of unemployment—the percentage of the labour force unemployed—in Canada since 1950. The figure shows that there is always some unemployment, although the amount fluctuates from year to year. In recent years in Canada about 1 out of every 15 people wanting a job does not have one.

In this chapter we begin our study of unemployment by discussing why there is always some unemployment and what determines its level. We do not study what determines the year-to-year fluctuations in the rate of unemployment until Part Four of this book, where we examine short-run economic fluctuations. Here we examine the determinants of the **natural rate of unemployment**— the average rate of unemployment around which the economy fluctuates. The natural rate is the rate of unemployment toward which the economy gravitates in the long run, given all the labour-market imperfections that impede workers from instantly finding jobs. Another term that is often used as a synonym for the

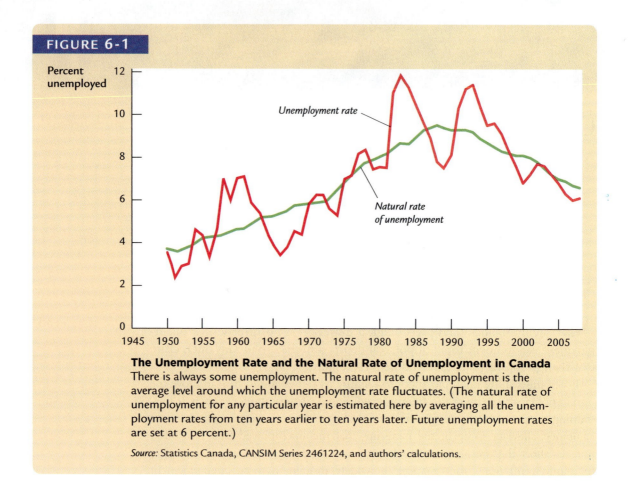

FIGURE 6-1

The Unemployment Rate and the Natural Rate of Unemployment in Canada
There is always some unemployment. The natural rate of unemployment is the average level around which the unemployment rate fluctuates. (The natural rate of unemployment for any particular year is estimated here by averaging all the unemployment rates from ten years earlier to ten years later. Future unemployment rates are set at 6 percent.)

Source: Statistics Canada, CANSIM Series 2461224, and authors' calculations.

natural unemployment rate is the level of "structural" and "frictional" unemployment. Unemployment rises above this long-run average level when the economy is in recession, and it falls below this level when the economy is overheated. These short-run variations in the unemployment rate are referred to as cyclical unemployment. At any point in time, overall, the actual unemployment rate is the sum of the natural rate and that period's level of cyclical unemployment. Since we abstract from short-run cycles until Chapter 9, the present chapter focuses exclusively on structural and frictional unemployment.

6-1 Job Loss, Job Finding, and the Natural Rate of Unemployment

Every day some workers lose or quit their jobs, and some unemployed workers are hired. This perpetual ebb and flow determines the fraction of the labour force that is unemployed. In this section we develop a model of labour-force dynamics that shows what determines the natural rate of unemployment.[1]

We start with some notation. Let L denote the labour force, E the number of employed workers, and U the number of unemployed workers. Because every worker is either employed or unemployed, the labour force is the sum of the employed and the unemployed:

$$L = E + U$$

In this notation, the rate of unemployment is U/L.

To see what factors determine the unemployment rate, we assume that the labour force L is fixed and focus on the transition of individuals in the labour force between employment and unemployment. This is illustrated in Figure 6-2. Let s denote the rate of job separation, the fraction of employed individuals who lose or leave their job each month. Let f denote the rate of job finding, the fraction of unemployed individuals who find a job each month. Together, the rate of job separation s and the rate of job finding f determine the rate of unemployment.

If the unemployment rate is neither rising nor falling—that is, if the labour market is in a steady state—then the number of people finding jobs must equal the number of people losing jobs. The number of people finding jobs is fU and the number of people losing jobs is sE, so we can write the steady-state condition as

$$fU = sE.$$

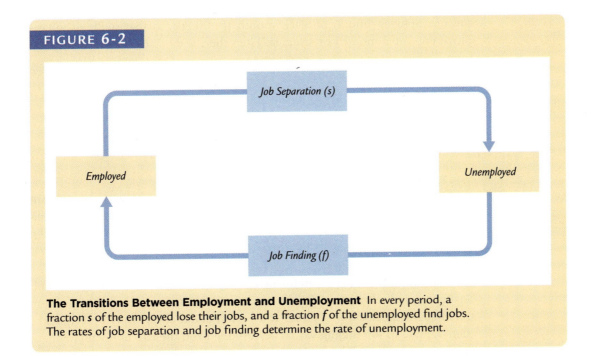

FIGURE 6-2

The Transitions Between Employment and Unemployment In every period, a fraction s of the employed lose their jobs, and a fraction f of the unemployed find jobs. The rates of job separation and job finding determine the rate of unemployment.

---

[1] Robert E. Hall, "A Theory of the Natural Rate of Unemployment and the Duration of Unemployment," *Journal of Monetary Economics* 5 (April 1979): 153–169.

We can use this equation to find the steady-state unemployment rate. From an earlier equation, we know that $E = L - U$; that is, the number of employed equals the labour force minus the number of unemployed. If we substitute $(L - U)$ for E in the steady-state condition, we find

$$f U = s(L - U).$$

Next, we divide both sides of this equation by L to obtain

$$f \frac{U}{L} = s(1 - \frac{U}{L}).$$

Now we can solve for U/L to find

$$\frac{U}{L} = \frac{s}{s + f} = \frac{1}{1 + f/s}.$$

This equation shows that the steady-state rate of unemployment U/L depends on the rates of job separation s and job finding f. The higher the rate of job separation, the higher the unemployment rate. The higher the rate of job finding, the lower the unemployment rate.

Here's a numerical example. Suppose that 1 percent of the employed lose their jobs each month ($s = 0.01$). This means that on average jobs last 100 months, or about 8 years. Suppose further that about 20 percent of the unemployed find a job each month ($f = 0.20$), so that spells of unemployment last 5 months on average. Then the steady-state rate of unemployment is

$$\frac{U}{L} = \frac{0.01}{0.01 + 0.20}$$

$$= 0.0476.$$

The rate of unemployment in this example is about 5 percent.

This simple model of the natural rate of unemployment has an important implication for public policy. *Any policy aimed at lowering the natural rate of unemployment must either reduce the rate of job separation or increase the rate of job finding. Similarly, any policy that affects the rate of job separation or job finding also changes the natural rate of unemployment.*

Although this model is useful in relating the unemployment rate to job separation and job finding, it fails to answer a central question: Why is there unemployment in the first place? If a person could always find a job quickly, then the rate of job finding would be very high and the rate of unemployment would be near zero. This model of the unemployment rate assumes that job finding is not instantaneous, but it fails to explain why. In the next two sections, we examine two underlying reasons for unemployment: job search and wage rigidity.

6-2 Job Search and Frictional Unemployment

One reason for unemployment is that it takes time to match workers and jobs. The equilibrium model of the aggregate labour market discussed in Chapter 3 assumes that all workers and all jobs are identical, and therefore that all workers are equally well suited for all jobs. If this were really true and the labour market were in equilibrium, then a job loss would not cause unemployment: a laid-off worker would immediately find a new job at the market wage.

In fact, workers have different preferences and abilities, and jobs have different attributes. Furthermore, the flow of information about job candidates and job vacancies is imperfect, and the geographic mobility of workers is not instantaneous. For all these reasons, searching for an appropriate job takes time and effort, and this tends to reduce the rate of job finding. Indeed, because different jobs require different skills and pay different wages, unemployed workers may not accept the first job offer they receive. The unemployment caused by the time it takes workers to search for a job is called **frictional unemployment.**

Some frictional unemployment is inevitable in a changing economy. For many reasons, the types of goods that firms and households demand vary over time. As the demand for goods shifts, so does the demand for the labour that produces those goods. The invention of the personal computer, for example, reduced the demand for typewriters and, as a result, the demand for labour by typewriter manufacturers. At the same time, it increased the demand for labour in the electronics industry. Similarly, because different regions produce different goods, the demand for labour may be rising in one part of the country while it is falling in another. An increase in the price of oil may cause the demand for labour to rise in an oil-producing province such as Alberta, but because expensive oil makes driving more expensive, it decreases the demand for labour in an auto-producing province, such as Ontario. Economists call a change in the composition of demand among industries or regions a **sectoral shift.** Because sectoral shifts are always occurring, and because it takes time for workers to change sectors, there is always frictional unemployment.

Sectoral shifts are not the only cause of job separation and frictional unemployment. In addition, workers find themselves unexpectedly out of work when their firm fails, when their job performance is deemed unacceptable, or when their particular skills are no longer needed. Workers also may quit their jobs to change careers or to move to different parts of the country. Regardless of the cause of the job separation, it will take time and effort for the worker to find a new job. As long as the supply and demand for labour among firms is changing, frictional unemployment is unavoidable.

Public Policy and Frictional Unemployment

Many public policies seek to decrease the natural rate of unemployment by reducing frictional unemployment. Government employment agencies disseminate information about job vacancies with a view to matching jobs and workers more efficiently. Publicly funded retraining programs are designed to ease the transition of workers from declining to growing industries. If these programs succeed at increasing the rate of job finding, they decrease the natural rate of unemployment.

Other government programs inadvertently increase the amount of frictional unemployment. One of these is **employment insurance (EI).** Under this program, unemployed workers can collect a fraction of their wages for a certain period after losing their jobs. Although the precise terms of the program differ from year to year and from province to province, a typical worker covered by employment insurance in Canada has received about 50 percent of his or her former wages for about half a year. Before change in the EI program in the mid-1990s, Canada's insurance system was one of the most generous in the world.

By softening the economic hardship of unemployment, employment insurance increases the amount of frictional unemployment and raises the natural rate. The unemployed who receive employment-insurance benefits are less pressed to search for new employment and are more likely to turn down unattractive job offers. Both of these changes in behaviour reduce the rate of job finding. In addition, because workers know that their incomes are partially protected by employment insurance, they are less likely to seek jobs with stable employment prospects and are less likely to bargain for guarantees of job security. These behavioural changes raise the rate of job separation.

That employment insurance raises the natural rate of unemployment does not necessarily imply that the policy is ill advised. The program has the benefit of reducing workers' uncertainty about their incomes. Moreover, inducing workers to reject unattractive job offers may lead to a better matching between workers and jobs. Evaluating the costs and benefits of different systems of employment insurance is a difficult task that continues to be a topic of much research.

Economists often propose reforms to the EI system that would reduce the amount of unemployment. One common proposal is to require a firm that lays off a worker to bear the full cost of that worker's employment benefits. Such a system is called *100 percent experience rated,* because the rate that each firm pays into the employment-insurance system fully reflects the unemployment experience of its own workers. The programs in many countries are *partially experience rated.* Under this system, when a firm lays off a worker, it is charged for only part of the worker's employment benefits; the remainder comes from the program's general revenue. Because a firm pays only a fraction of the cost of the unemployment it causes, it has an incentive to lay off workers when its demand for labour is temporarily low. Canada's system has no experience rating, so this incentive problem is acute. By reducing that incentive, the proposed reform may reduce the prevalence of temporary layoffs.

As this book went to press, Canada's unemployment rate was rising quickly during the 2009 recession, reaching 8.6 percent, up two and a half percentage points over a one-year period. Heated debate centred on the regional disparities and the incomplete coverage features of Canada's EI system. The opposition Liberals made a call for reform on these issues their central attack on the governing Conservatives. An excellent assessment of these controversies is available in a special report published in April 2009 entitled *Is Canada's Employment Insurance Program Adequate?* Andrew Coyne, National Editor of Maclean's, Canada's national news magazine, also wrote a thought-provoking article on EI reform at this time entitled "What Would Real Job Loss Insurance Look Like?"[2]

CASE STUDY

Employment Insurance and the Rate of Job Finding

Between World War I and World War II, Britain experienced persistently high unemployment. From 1920 to 1938 the unemployment rate in Britain averaged 14 percent and never fell below 9 percent.

Economists Daniel Benjamin and Levis Kochin have suggested that Britain's generous unemployment benefits can largely explain this high rate of unemployment. They cite three pieces of evidence to support their view. First, during this period, increases in British unemployment benefits coincided with increases in the economy's unemployment rate. Second, teenagers, who received few or no unemployment benefits, had much lower unemployment rates than adults. Third, when the benefits for married women were reduced in 1932, their unemployment rate dropped significantly relative to that for men. All three pieces of evidence suggest a connection between unemployment benefits and unemployment rates.

This explanation of interwar British unemployment is controversial among economists who study this period. One difficulty in interpreting the evidence is that the data on unemployment benefits and unemployment rates may reflect two different relationships—one economic and one political. On the one hand, the higher the level of benefits, the more likely it is that an unemployed person will turn down an unattractive job offer, and the higher the level of frictional unemployment. On the other hand, the higher the rate of unemployment, the more pressing unemployment becomes as a political issue, and the higher the level of benefits the government chooses to offer. Hence, high unemployment rates may have caused high unemployment benefits, rather than the other way around. When we observe an empirical relationship between unemployment rates and unemployment benefits, we cannot tell whether we have identified an economic connection, a political connection, or some combination of the two.[3] Given this problem, other studies have examined data on uemployed individuals, rather than data on economy-wide rates of unemployment. Individual data sometimes provide evidence that is less open to alternative interpretations.

---

[2] The April 2009 report published by TD Economics of the TD Bank Financial Group is available at http://www.td.com/economics/special/gb0409_EI.pdf. The Maclean's article is available at http://www2.macleans.ca/2009/07/02/what-would-real-job-loss-insurance-look-like/.

[3] Daniel Benjamin and Levis Kochin, "Searching for an Explanation of Unemployment in Interwar Britain," *Journal of Political Economy* 87 (June 1979): 441–478. For critical comments on this article and a reply by the authors, see *Journal of Political Economy* 90 (April 1982): 369–436.

One finding from individual data is that when unemployed workers become ineligible for employment insurance, the probability of their finding a new job rises markedly. Canadian evidence shows that the probability of an unemployed person finding employment varies—depending on how many weeks that person has been unemployed and how many weeks of employment-insurance benefits remain. In the first few weeks after becoming unemployed, the probability of being employed is about 15 percent. Then, if the person remains unemployed, the probability of a job falls to quite a low number—3 percent or 4 percent after 20–25 weeks of unemployment. As the unemployment spell lasts even longer, however, the probability of work rises again—to the 12–13 percent range—as the exhaustion of employment-insurance benefits is approached. Many economists interpret this evidence as verifying that at least some part of recorded unemployment is voluntary.[4]

More evidence in this vein comes from considering the regional dimensions of the Canadian unemployment system. The Canadian employment-insurance program has been substantially more generous in the high-unemployment regions of the country. These differences have been mainly due to differences in what is called the *duration ratio*—the maximum number of weeks one can collect benefits relative to the minimum number of weeks of work that generate the insurable earnings necessary to become elligible for any benefits. This ratio has varied between 26/14 in relatively low-unemployment provinces like Saskatchewan to 42/10 in relatively high-unemployment provinces like New-foundland. Multiplying these duration ratios by the proportion of a worker's wage that could be received through employment insurance (0.57 at the time these particular duration ratios were relevant) generates an estimated wage subsidy that varies between 1.06 and 2.39. These values indicate the number of weeks of insurance benefits and leisure (at full pay) to which Canadians were entitled for each week of work completed up to the minimum qualifying value (of 10 weeks or 14 weeks). Clearly, work disincentives were much greater in high-unemployment provinces. Many economists have concluded that the Canadian employment-insurance system has exacerbated regional unemployment disparities by discouraging the migration of labour from high- to low-unemployment rate regions.

Additional evidence on how economic incentives affect job search comes from an American experiment that the state of Illinois ran in 1985. Randomly selected new claimants for unemployment insurance were each offered a $500 bonus if they found employment within 11 weeks. The subsequent experience of this group was compared to that of a control group not offered the incentive. The average duration of unemployment for the group that was offered the $500 bonus was 17.0 weeks, compared to 18.3 weeks for the control group. Thus, the bonus reduced the average spell of unemployment by 7 percent,

---

[4] Miles Corak, "Unemployment Insurance, Work Disincentives, and the Canadian Labour Market: An Overview," *Unemployment Insurance: How to Make It Work* (Toronto: C.D. Howe Institute, 1994): 117.

suggesting that more effort was devoted to job search. This experiment shows that the incentives provided by the employment-insurance system affect the rate of job finding.[5] ■

6-3 Real-Wage Rigidity and Structural Unemployment

A second reason for unemployment is **wage rigidity**—the failure of wages to adjust to a level at which labour supply equals labour demand. In the equilibrium model of the labour market, as outlined in Chapter 3, the real wage adjusts to equilibrate labour supply and labour demand. Yet wages are not always flexible. Sometimes the real wage is stuck above the market-clearing level.

Figure 6-3 shows why wage rigidity leads to unemployment. When the real wage is above the level that equilibrates supply and demand, the quantity of labour supplied exceeds the quantity demanded. Firms must in some way ration the scarce jobs among workers. Real-wage rigidity reduces the rate of job finding and raises the level of unemployment.

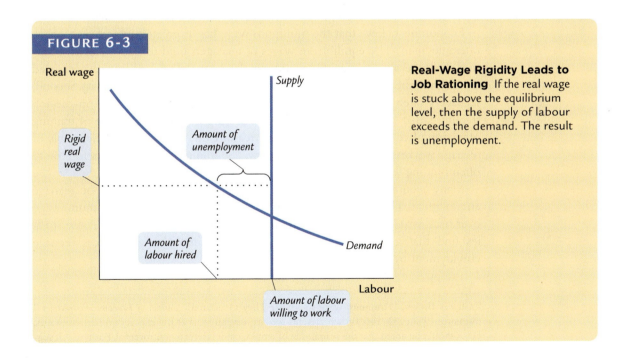

FIGURE 6-3

Real-Wage Rigidity Leads to Job Rationing If the real wage is stuck above the equilibrium level, then the supply of labour exceeds the demand. The result is unemployment.

[5] Stephen A. Woodbury and Robert G. Spiegelman, "Bonuses to Workers and Employers to Reduce Unemployment: Randomized Trials in Illinois," *American Economic Review* 77 (September 1987): 513–530.

The unemployment resulting from wage rigidity and job rationing is often called **structural unemployment.** Workers are unemployed not because they are actively searching for the jobs that best suit their individual skills but because there is a fundamental mismatch between the number of people who want to work and the number of jobs available. At the going wage, the quantity of labour supplied exceeds the quantity of labour demanded, so many workers are simply waiting for jobs to open up.

To understand wage rigidity and structural unemployment, we must examine why the labour market does not clear. When the real wage exceeds the equilibrium level and the supply of workers exceeds the demand, we might expect firms to lower the wages they pay. Structural unemployment arises because firms fail to reduce wages despite an excess supply of labour. We now turn to three causes of this wage rigidity: minimum-wage laws, the monopoly power of unions, and efficiency wages.

Minimum-Wage Laws

The government causes wage rigidity when it prevents wages from falling to equilibrium levels. Minimum-wage laws set a legal minimum on the wages that firms pay their employees. For most workers, this minimum wage is not binding, because they earn well above the minimum. Yet for some workers, especially the unskilled and inexperienced, the minimum wage raises their wage above its equilibrium level and therefore reduces the quantity of their labour that firms demand.

Economists believe that the minimum wage has its greatest impact on teenage unemployment. The equilibrium wages of teenagers tend to be low for two reasons. First, because teenagers are among the least skilled and least experienced members of the labour force, they tend to have low marginal productivity. Second, teenagers often take some of their "compensation" in the form of on-the-job training rather than direct pay. An apprenticeship is a classic example of training offered in place of wages. For both these reasons, the wage at which the supply of teenage workers equals the demand is low. The minimum wage is therefore more often binding for teenagers than for others in the labour force.

Many economists have studied the impact of the minimum wage on teenage employment. These researchers compare the variation in the minimum wage over time with the variation in the number of teenagers with jobs. These studies find that a 10-percent increase in the minimum wage reduces teenage employment by 1 to 3 percent.[6]

---

[6] Charles Brown, "Minimum Wage Laws: Are They Overrated?" *Journal of Economic Perspectives* 2 (Summer 1988): 133–146. Brown presents the mainstream view of the effects of minimum wages, but it should be noted that the magnitude of employment effects is controversial. For research suggesting negligible employment effects, see David Card and Alan Krueger, *Myth and Measurement: The New Economics of the Minimum Wage* (Princeton, NJ: Princeton University Press, 1995), and Lawrence Katz and Alan Krueger, "The Effects of the Minimum Wage on the Fast-Food Industry," *Industrial and Labor Relations Review* 46 (October 1992): 6–21. For research suggesting the opposite conclusion, see David Neumark and William Wascher, "Employment Effects of Minimum and Sub-minimum Wages: Panel Data on State Minimum Wage Laws," *Industrial and Labor Relations Review* 46 (October 1992): 55–81.

Canadian studies have reached similar conclusions. Estimates reported by the Ontario Ministry of Labour in 1989 showed that a 10-percent increase in the minimum wage eliminated 25,000 jobs. Also, economist Walter Block performed a cross-sectional study of provincial minimum-wage laws.[7] Back in 1985 when the study was done, Manitoba and Saskatchewan had the highest minimum-wage laws—some 15 percent above those provinces (British Columbia and Alberta) with the lowest legal minimums. Block compared all provinces according to the ratio of their youth unemployment rate to that of their prime-aged residents (those over 24 years old). By comparing this ratio of unemployment rates, rather than just youth unemployment rates directly, Block was trying to ensure that he was not focusing inadvertently on the differences across provinces that were due to influences other than the minimum wage. Block found that Manitoba and Saskatchewan had the highest youth unemployment ratios (2.9 times and 2.6 times the unemployment rate for prime-aged labour), while British Columbia and Alberta had the lowest youth unemployment ratios (1.9 times and 1.8 times the unemployment rate for prime-aged workers).

The minimum wage is a perennial source of political debate. Advocates of a higher minimum wage view it as a means of raising the income of the working poor. Certainly, the minimum wage provides only a meager standard of living. In most provinces, a full-time worker receiving the minimum wage earns an income that is below the official poverty line. While minimum-wage advocates often admit that the policy causes unemployment for some workers, they argue that this cost is worth bearing to raise others out of poverty.

Opponents of a higher minimum wage claim that it is not the best way to help the working poor. They contend not only that the increased labour costs would raise unemployment, but also that the minimum wage is poorly targeted. Many minimum-wage earners are teenagers from middle-class homes working for discretionary spending money, rather than heads of households working to support their families.

Many economists and policymakers believe that tax credits are a better way to increase the incomes of the working poor. A refundable *income tax credit* is an amount that poor working families are allowed to subtract from the taxes they owe. For a family with very low income, the credit exceeds its taxes, and the family receives a payment from the government. Unlike the minimum wage, the refundable income tax credit does not raise labour costs to firms and, therefore, does not reduce the quantity of labour that firms demand. It has the disadvantage of reducing the government's tax revenue, but in the appendix to this chapter we explore how the government can offer initiatives of this sort as part of a revenue-neutral package. In the final economic document of the Chretien/Martin Liberal government—the *Fiscal Update* (November 2005)—this very policy (called the *Working Income Tax Benefit*) was introduced and promised to start in 2008. The funding for this program was expanded by the Conservatives in the 2009 federal budget. Noting the success of the similar *earned income tax credit* program in the

---

[7] Walter Block, *The Fraser Forum* (Vancouver: The Fraser Institute August 1985): 4–5.

United States, our governments have argued that such a policy is fundamentally needed if the Government is to make progress in reducing—simultaneously—our high unemployment problem and our lagging productivity growth problem. There is growing evidence that such programs can make a significant contribution in promoting the transition from welfare to work.[8]

Unions and Collective Bargaining

A second cause of wage rigidity is the monopoly power of unions. Table 6-1 shows the importance of unions in a number of major countries. In Canada, a little over one-third of workers belong to unions. This rate of union membership is about twice that of the United States, but unions play a greater role in many European countries.

TABLE 6-1

Percent of Workers Covered by Collective Bargaining

United States	18%
Japan	23
Canada	38
United Kingdom	47
Switzerland	53
New Zealand	67
Spain	68
Netherlands	71
Norway	75
Portugal	79
Australia	80
Sweden	83
Belgium	90
Germany	90
France	92
Finland	95
Austria	98

Source: OECD Employment Outlook 2004, as reported in Alberto Alesina, Edward Glaeser, and Bruce Sacerdote, "Work and Leisure in the U.S. and Europe: Why So Different?" *NBER Macroeconomics Annual* 2005.

[8] To learn more about our Working Income Tax Benefit programs, read K. Battle, *Beneath the Budget of 2009: taxes and benefits.* Caledon Institute of Social Policy (February 2009), available at www.caledoninst.org/Publications/PDF/751ENG%2Epdf, and W. Scarth and L. Tang, "An Evaluation of the Working Income Tax Benefit," *Canadian Public Policy/Analyse de Politique* 34, no. 1, (March 2008): 25–36.

The wages of unionized workers are determined not by the equilibrium of supply and demand but by bargaining between union leaders and firm management. Often, the final agreement raises the wage above the equilibrium level and allows the firm to decide how many workers to employ. The result is a reduction in the number of workers hired, a lower rate of job finding, and an increase in structural unemployment.

Unions can also influence the wages paid by firms whose work forces are not unionized because the threat of unionization can keep wages above the equilibrium level. Most firms dislike unions. Unions not only raise wages but also increase the bargaining power of labour on many other issues, such as hours of employment and working conditions. A firm may choose to pay its workers high wages to keep them happy in order to discourage them from forming a union.

The unemployment caused by unions and by the threat of unionization is an instance of conflict between different groups of workers—**insiders** and **outsiders.** Those workers already employed by a firm, the insiders, typically try to keep their firm's wages high. The unemployed, the outsiders, bear part of the cost of higher wages because at a lower wage they might be hired. These two groups inevitably have conflicting interests. The effect of any bargaining process on wages and employment depends crucially on the relative influence of each group.

The conflict between insiders and outsiders is resolved differently in different countries. In some countries, such as those in North America, wage bargaining takes place at the level of the firm or plant. In other countries, such as Sweden, wage bargaining takes place at the national level—with the government often playing a key role. Despite a highly unionized labour force, Sweden has not experienced extraordinarily high unemployment throughout its history. One possible explanation is that the centralization of wage bargaining and the role of the government in the bargaining process give more influence to the outsiders, which keeps wages closer to the equilibrium level.

Efficiency Wages

Efficiency-wage theories propose a third cause of wage rigidity in addition to minimum-wage laws and unionization. These theories hold that high wages make workers more productive. The influence of wages on worker efficiency may explain the failure of firms to cut wages despite an excess supply of labour. Even though a wage reduction would lower a firm's wage bill, it would also— if these theories are correct—lower worker productivity and the firm's profits.

Economists have proposed various theories to explain how wages affect worker productivity. One efficiency-wage theory, which is applied mostly to poorer countries, holds that wages influence nutrition. Better-paid workers can afford a more nutritious diet, and healthier workers are more productive. A firm may decide to pay a wage above the equilibrium level to maintain a healthy work force. Obviously, this consideration is not important for employers in wealthy countries, such as Canada, the United States, and most of Europe, since the equilibrium wage is well above the level necessary to maintain good health.

A second efficiency-wage theory, which is more relevant for developed countries, holds that high wages reduce labour turnover. Workers quit jobs for many reasons—to accept better positions at other firms, to change careers, or to move to other parts of the country. The more a firm pays its workers, the greater their incentive to stay with the firm. By paying a high wage, a firm reduces the frequency at which its workers quit, thereby decreasing the time and money spent hiring and training new workers.

A third efficiency-wage theory holds that the average quality of a firm's work force depends on the wage it pays its employees. If a firm reduces its wage, the best employees may take jobs elsewhere, leaving the firm with inferior employees who have fewer alternative opportunities. Economists recognize this unfavourable sorting as an example of *adverse selection*—the tendency of people with more information (in this case, the workers, who know their own outside opportunities) to self-select in a way that disadvantages people with less information (the firm). By paying a wage above the equilibrium level, the firm may reduce adverse selection, improve the average quality of its work force, and thereby increase productivity.

A fourth efficiency-wage theory holds that a high wage improves worker effort. This theory posits that firms cannot perfectly monitor their employees' work effort, and that employees must themselves decide how hard to work. Workers can choose to work hard, or they can choose to shirk and risk getting caught and fired. Economists recognize this possibility as an example of *moral hazard*—the tendency of people to behave inappropriately when their behaviour is imperfectly monitored. The firm can reduce the problem of moral hazard by paying a high wage. The higher the wage, the greater the cost to the worker of getting fired. By paying a higher wage, a firm induces more of its employees not to shirk and thus increases their productivity.

Although these four efficiency-wage theories differ in detail, they share a common theme: because a firm operates more efficiently if it pays its workers a high wage, the firm may find it profitable to keep wages above the level that balances supply and demand. The result of this higher-than-equilibrium wage is a lower rate of job finding and greater structural unemployment.[9]

CASE STUDY

Henry Ford's $5 Workday

In 1914 the Ford Motor Company started paying its U.S. workers $5 per day. Since the prevailing wage at the time was between $2 and $3 per day, Ford's wage was well above the equilibrium level. Not surprisingly, long lines of job seekers waited outside the Ford plant gates hoping for a chance to earn this high wage.

---

[9] For more extended discussions of efficiency wages, see Janet Yellen, "Efficiency Wage Models of Unemployment," *American Economic Review Papers and Proceedings* (May 1984): 200–205; and Lawrence Katz, "Efficiency Wages: A Partial Evaluation," *NBER Macroeconomics Annual* (1986): 235–276.

What was Ford's motive? Henry Ford later wrote, "We wanted to pay these wages so that the business would be on a lasting foundation. We were building for the future. A low wage business is always insecure . . . . The payment of five dollars a day for an eight hour day was one of the finest cost cutting moves we ever made."

From the standpoint of traditional economic theory, Ford's explanation seems peculiar. He was suggesting that *high* wages imply *low* costs. But perhaps Ford had discovered efficiency-wage theory. Perhaps he was using the high wage to increase worker productivity.

Evidence suggests that paying such a high wage did benefit the company. According to an engineering report written at the time, "The Ford high wage does away with all the inertia and living force resistance. . . . The workingmen are absolutely docile, and it is safe to say that since the last day of 1913, every single day has seen major reductions in Ford shops' labor costs." Absenteeism fell by 75 percent, suggesting a large increase in worker effort. Alan Nevins, a historian who studied the early Ford Motor Company, wrote, "Ford and his associates freely declared on many occasions that the high wage policy had turned out to be good business. By this they meant that it had improved the discipline of the workers, given them a more loyal interest in the institution, and raised their personal efficiency."[10] ■

6-4 Labour Market Experience: Canada

So far we have developed the theory behind the natural rate of unemployment. We began by showing that the economy's steady-state unemployment rate depends on the rates of job separation and job finding. Then we discussed two reasons why job finding is not instantaneous: the process of job search (which leads to frictional unemployment) and wage rigidity (which leads to structural unemployment). Wage rigidity, in turn, arises from minimum-wage laws, unionization, and efficiency wages.

With these theories as background, we now examine some additional facts about unemployment, focusing at first on the case of the Canadian and American Labour markets. These facts will help us to evaluate our theories and assess public policies aimed at reducing unemployment.

The Duration of Unemployment

When a person becomes unemployed, is the spell of unemployment likely to be short or long? The answer to this question is important because it indicates the reasons for the unemployment and what policy response is appropriate.

---

[10] Jeremy I. Bulow and Lawrence H. Summers, "A Theory of Dual Labor Markets With Application to Industrial Policy, Discrimination, and Keynesian Unemployment," *Journal of Labor Economics* 4 (July 1986): 376–414; Daniel M. G. Raff and Lawrence H. Summers, "Did Henry Ford Pay Efficiency Wages?" *Journal of Labor Economics* 5 (October 1987, Part 2): S57–S86.

Economists decompose the unemployment rate into two components: incidence and duration. Incidence is the likelihood that an individual suffers an unemployment spell, and duration is the average length of that spell. If the unemployment rate is 5 percent, it could be that duration is high and incidence is low (say, for example, if 5 percent of the labour force is permanently unemployed), or it could be that incidence is high and duration is low (for example, if everyone is unemployed for 5 percent of the year). In this second case, since unemployment is short-term, one might argue that it is frictional and perhaps unavoidable. Unemployed workers may need some time to search for the job that is best suited to their skills and tastes. On the other hand, long-term unemployment cannot easily be attributed to the time it takes to match jobs and workers: we would not expect this matching process to take many months. Long-term unemployment is more likely to be structural unemployment representing a mismatch between the number of jobs available and the number of people who want work. Thus, data on the duration of unemployment can affect our view about the reasons for unemployment.

Estimates on the duration and incidence of unemployment have changed over the years. In 1993, Statistics Canada estimated that about two-thirds of any increase in the unemployment rate was due to longer duration and one-third to higher incidence. But more recently it has been estimated that most of the variation in structural unemployment can be attributed to changes in the incidence of unemployment over time and that the average duration of an unemployment spell has remained remarkably constant at about 2.3 months.[11]

The confusing evidence on the duration of unemployment has an important implication for public policy. If the goal is to lower substantially the natural rate of unemployment, policies must aim at the long-term unemployed, because these individuals account for a large amount of unemployment. Yet policies must be carefully targeted, because the long-term unemployed still constitute a minority of those who become unemployed at some point during the year. It is still the case that most people who become unemployed find work within a fairly short time.

Variation in the Unemployment Rate Across Age Groups and Regions

The rate of unemployment varies substantially across different groups within the population. Table 6-2 presents the unemployment rates for different age groups in 2007. While the country's overall unemployment rate was 6 percent, this unemployment was not equally distributed by age. The unemployment rate for teenagers was 3 times that of people in the 55-and-over age category. While younger Canadians have always had higher unemployment rates than prime-aged

---

[11] For the earlier evidence, see Miles Corak, "The Duration of Unemployment During Boom and Bust," *Canadian Economic Observer* (September 1993): 4.9. For the more recent evidence, see Michelle Campolieti, "An Analysis of Unemployment Incidence and Duration: Some New Evidence from Canada," CLSRN Working Paper No. 7 (January 2009).

TABLE 6-2	
Unemployment by Age Groups: 2007	
Age	**Unemployment Rate (%)**
15–19	14.8
20–24	8.7
25–54	5.1
55 and over	4.8

Source: Statistics Canada, *The Canadian Labour Market at a Glance* Catalogue No. 71-222-X.

adults, they now account for a smaller proportion of unemployed people than they did three decades ago. The aging of the Canadian population has resulted in a change in the age structure of unemployment. In 1976, almost half of all unemployed people were 15 to 24 years old, compared with one-third in 2007. Not surprisingly, education affects employment prospects as well. Over the last 35 years, the unemployment rate for those with only primary-level education has been 2.75 times that facing those with a university education. Most analysts expect this gap to widen in years to come.

To explain the differences in unemployment across age groups, recall our model of the natural rate of unemployment. The model isolates two possible causes for a high rate of unemployment: a low rate of job finding, or a high rate of job separation. When economists study data on the transition of individuals between employment and unemployment, they find that those groups with high unemployment tend to have high rates of job separation. They find less variation across groups in the rate of job finding.

These findings help explain the higher unemployment rates for younger workers. Younger workers have only recently entered the labour market, and they are often uncertain about their career plans. It may be best for them to try different types of jobs before making a long-term commitment to a specific occupation. If so, we should expect a higher rate of job separation and a higher rate of frictional unemployment for this group.

Finally, unemployment varies significantly across Canadian regions. Again considering 2007, the unemployment rate in Newfoundland and Labrador was 13.6 percent (more than twice the national average), while in Alberta the unemployment rate was 3.5 percent (just over one-half the national average). This regional variation helps explain why it is difficult to reform the employment-insurance system so that it operates as a true insurance policy instead of being a means for performing *ongoing* income redistribution. Without some other policies to support those in the depressed regions, many policymakers oppose changes and cuts in the current employment-insurance system. There is a certain irony in this outcome. It is concern for the welfare of Canadians living in the depressed regions in the *short run* that limits reforms to employment insurance from being implemented. Nevertheless, it can hurt the welfare of those same individuals in the *long run* if employment insurance is not reformed. Without reform, these regions can never escape the long-run dependency trap.

Trends in Unemployment

Over the past 50 years, the natural rate of unemployment in Canada has not been constant. If you look back at Figure 6-1, you will see that unemployment averaged well below 5 percent in the 1950s and 1960s, and above 9 percent in the 1980s and 1990s. The average unemployment rate has drifted back down somewhat in recent years. Although economists do not have a conclusive explanation for these changes, they have proposed various hypotheses.

Demographics One explanation stresses the changing composition of the Canadian labour force. After World War II, birth rates rose dramatically, producing a baby-boom generation that began entering the labour force around 1970. Because younger workers have higher unemployment rates, this influx of baby boomers into the labour force increased the average level of unemployment. At roughly the same time, the participation of women in the labour force also was increasing significantly. Since women historically have had higher unemployment rates than men (a difference that has disappeared since the early 1980s), the increasing proportion of women in the labour force may have raised the average unemployment rate, at least in the 1970s.

These two demographic changes, however, cannot fully explain the upward trend in unemployment because the trend also was apparent for fixed demographic groups. For example, for prime-aged males (men aged between 25 and 54 years), the average unemployment rate rose from below 3 percent in the 1950s and 1960s to 4.2 percent in the 1970s, 7.1 percent in the 1980s, and 9.1 percent in the 1990s.

Another point to bear in mind is that some of the demographic shifts and microeconomic rigidities that can explain rising unemployment in the 1970s have since reversed—without a corresponding decrease in unemployment. For example, as a proportion of the population, the 15–24 age group dropped from 26 percent of the population in the mid-1970s to under 18 percent in 1992. Also the *ratio* of the minimum wage to the average hourly wage available in Canada *fell* by 15 percent over this same period.[12]

Sectoral Shifts A second possible explanation for the upward trend in unemployment is that sectoral shifts have become more prevalent. The greater the amount of sectoral reallocation, the greater the rate of job separation and the higher the level of frictional unemployment.[13] One source of sectoral shifts has

---

[12] Pierre Fortin, "Slow Growth, Unemployment and Debt: What Happened? What Can We Do?" in *The Bell Canada Papers on Economic and Public Policy* (Kingston: John Deutsch Institute for the Study of Economic Policy, 1994).

[13] David M. Lilien, "Sectoral Shifts and Cyclical Unemployment," *Journal of Political Economy* 90 (August 1982): 777–793.

been the increased pace of technological change involving robotics and major breakthroughs in the methods of information storage and transfer. Another series of sectoral shifts has resulted from the major shifts in natural resource prices. The world price of oil has been *far* more volatile since the mid-1970s, and the relative price of most of the natural resources that Canada exports has changed appreciably over the decades.

Productivity A third possible explanation for rising unemployment emphasizes the link between unemployment and productivity. As Chapter 8 discusses more fully, the 1970s experienced a slowdown in productivity growth, and perhaps this raised the natural rate of unemployment. Why such an effect would occur, however, is not obvious. In standard theories of the labour market, lower productivity means reduced labour demand and thus lower real wages, but unemployment is unchanged. This prediction is consistent with the long-term data, which show consistent upward trends in both productivity and real wages, but no trend in unemployment. Yet suppose that workers are slow to catch on to news about productivity. When productivity changes, workers may only gradually alter the real wages they ask from their employers, making real wages sluggish in response to labour demand. Thus, a falloff in productivity growth, such as that experienced during the 1970s, will decrease labour demand and, with workers' real wage claims sluggish—that is, remaining high for a prolonged period—the decrease in labour demand must show up in the form of rising unemployment.[14]

Another consideration is skill-biased technical change. There is no question that the demand for unskilled workers has fallen relative to the demand for skilled workers. This change in demand is probably due to changes in technology: computers, for example, increase the demand for workers who can use them while reducing the demand for those who cannot. In the United States, this change in demand has been reflected in wages rather than unemployment: over the past two decades, the wages of unskilled workers have fallen substantially relative to the wages of skilled workers. In Canada and Europe, however, public programs provide unskilled workers with an alternative to working for low wages. As the wages of unskilled workers fall, more workers may view employment insurance and welfare as their best available options. The result is higher unemployment. We consider policy options to combat skill-biased technical change in the appendix to this chapter.

In the end, the upward drift in the unemployment rate over the second half of the twentieth century is probably the result of all these unrelated developments operating at the same time. Luckily, unemployment started coming down at the turn of the century to 6 percent in 2007. As this book goes to press in 2009, the world-wide recession has caused unemployment rates to rise (to 8.6 percent in Canada in mid-2009). However, most economists believe that this increase was due to a cyclical downturn and was not an increase in structural unemployment.

---

[14] On the role of productivity, see Laurence Ball and Robert Moffitt, "Productivity Growth and the Phillips Curve," in Alan B. Krueger and Robert Solow, eds., *The Roaring Nineties: Can Full Employment Be Sustained?* (New York: The Russell Sage Foundation and the Century Foundation Press, 2001).

It will take the passage of more time to be sure, but if this view proves correct, then perhaps the era of the long-term rise in joblessness is behind us.

Transitions Into and Out of the Labour Force So far we have ignored an important aspect of labour market dynamics: the movement of individuals into and out of the labour force. Our model of the natural rate of unemployment assumes that the labour force is fixed. In this case, the sole reason for unemployment is job separation, and the sole reason for leaving unemployment is job finding.

In fact, movements into and out of the labour force are important. The fact that individuals enter and leave the labour force makes the unemployment statistics more difficult to interpret. On the one hand, some individuals calling themselves unemployed may not be seriously looking for a job and perhaps should best be viewed as out of the labour force. Their "unemployment" may not represent a social problem. On the other hand, some individuals, called **discouraged workers,** may want a job but, after an unsuccessful search, have given up looking. These discouraged workers are counted as being out of the labour-force and do not show up in unemployment statistics. Even though their joblessness is unmeasured, it may nonetheless be a social problem.

It is important to have some idea of the magnitude of these unemployed who do not usually get measured. Periodically, Statistics Canada does a study that is much more extensive than the usual monthly labour-force survey. Through these interviews, they can estimate the number of discouraged workers. Officials find that when these discouraged individuals are transferred from the "not in the labour force" category to the "unemployed" category, the unemployment rate rises by 1 percentage point. A further dimension adds to the "disguised unemployment" problem. All individuals who want to work full-time but who only have part-time jobs are counted as employed. One adjustment of the figures that can be made to accommodate this practice is to count half of these involuntary part-timers as unemployed. When this adjustment to the figures is made, it adds another full percentage point to the unemployment rate.

CASE STUDY

Comparing Unemployment in the United States and Canada

Throughout the 1960s and 1970s, the United States and Canada had similar labour markets. The rates of unemployment in the two countries were about the same on average, and they fluctuated together. By 1980, the experiences of the two countries began to diverge. Unemployment became much more prevalent in Canada than in the United States. In the 1980s and 1990s, the Canadian unemployment rate averaged about 4 percentage points above the U.S. rate. More recently, the excess of the Canadian unemployment rate over its American counterpart has shrunk. Indeed, it vanished in 2008 when the U.S. unemployment rate moved above Canada's by about one percentage point. Why has the historical Canadian record been so disappointing, and why has our relative performance improved in recent years?

Studies[15] have concluded that the earlier 4-percentage-point gap can be decomposed into three components. One percentage point can be explained by the different ways in which unemployment is defined in the two countries. Two percentage points can be rationalized by the fact that the Canadian economy was operating at a lower level of capacity utilization than the United States throughout the 1980s and much of the 1990s. Finally, one percentage point can be attributed to a set of structural factors. We discuss each of these issues in turn.

The primary measurement issue concerns how actively individuals must be looking for work to be counted among the unemployed. In Canada, simply "looking at job advertisements" is sufficient, while a more active search is required in the United States. As a result, a number of individuals who are counted as "unemployed" in Canada are counted as "not in the labour force" in the United States. There are some other differences, but they are less important. For one thing, Canada excludes Aboriginals living on reserves from the monthly labour force survey, while the Americans do not exclude them. Since the incidence of unemployment is higher among this group, the Canadian practice leads to a lower measured unemployment rate. On the other hand, both countries exclude those in prisons from their labour force surveys. Since many of these individuals would be unemployed if they were not in these institutions and since a higher proportion of the population is in prison in the United States, this exclusion leads to Canada's measured unemployment rate being higher. It turns out that, from an overall quantitative point of view, these latter two considerations approximately cancel off, so the one-percentage-point measurement difference is mostly due to the fact that Canada deems a "passive" search strategy to be sufficient to label an individual as unemployed.

Unemployment results from both structural factors (as discussed in this chapter) and cyclical factors (discussed in later sections, starting in Chapter 9). When our economy suffers a recession, unemployment rises temporarily above the natural rate. This is cyclical, not structural, unemployment. Compared to the United States, the Canadian economy was more recessed during the 1980s and early 1990s, and the result was a higher level of cyclical unemployment in Canada. The evidence suggests that this difference averaged about two percentage points. One of the main reasons for our more recessed economic conditions was our contractionary monetary policy. Canada entered this period with higher inflation than the United States, and our central bank attacked the problem vigorously. By raising interest rates to dampen spending, the Bank of Canada lowered the demand for labour in Canada. Since workers resisted wage cuts, this decreased demand took the form of layoffs, and a temporary but prolonged increase in cyclical unemployment was the result. After eliminating this difference in cyclical unemployment from the data, only a two-percentage-point gap between the two countrie's natural unemployment rates remained to be explained.

So, after both capacity-utilization differences and measurement differences are accounted for, we are left with a one-percentage-point gap in the natural

---

[15] See W. Craig Riddell, "Why Is Canada's Unemployment Rate Persistently Higher than in the United States?" *Canadian Public Policy/Analyse de Politiques* 31 (March 2005): 93-100.

unemployment rates of the two countries. Several considerations have been studied, and the changing roles of unions in the two countries is one possible explanation for this divergence. In the 1960s, about 30 percent of the labour force was unionized in each country. But Canadian labour laws did more to foster unionization than U.S. laws did. Unionization rose in Canada while it fell in the United States.

As one might have predicted, changes in real wages accompanied the change in unionization. The real wage in Canada increased by about 30 percent relative to the real wage in the United States. This evidence suggests that unions in Canada pushed the real wage further above the equilibrium level, leading to more structural unemployment.

The divergence in the two unemployment rates may also be attributable to the increase in the availability of employment-insurance benefits in Canada. Not only does employment insurance raise search times and the amount of frictional unemployment, but it also interacts with the effects of unionization in two ways. First, employment insurance makes unemployed workers more willing to wait for a high-wage job in a unionized firm rather than take a lower-wage job in a nonunion firm. Second, because employment insurance partially protects the incomes of unemployed workers, it makes unions more willing to press for high wages at the expense of lower employment.

In the 1980s and early 1990s Canada's employment-insurance program was more than twice as generous as that in the United States. Our program is still about 60 percent more generous. Many economists believe that this difference, along with the fact that our program contains no experience-rating feature, is one of the factors that can explain the one percentage point of Canada's "excess" unemployment rate that can be attributed to structural factors. Canada's unemployment rate has risen less than that of the United States in the 2007–2009 period because short-run cyclical problems have been more pronounced south of the border. The financial crisis was far more severe in the United States, and our larger primary products sector—with its level of activity buoyed up by high commodity prices—kept employment higher here.[16] ■

6-5 Labour Market Experience: Europe

Although our discussion has focused on Canada (and to some extent on the United States), many fascinating and sometimes puzzling phenomena become apparent when economists compare the experiences of North Americans in the labour market with those of Europeans.

---

[16] For more on the recent flip in the relative magnitude of Canadian and American unemployment rates, see Vincent Ferrao, "The Recent Labour Market in Canada and the United States," *Perspectives on Labour and Income* 10, no. 8 (March 2009), Statistics Canada Catalogue no. 75-001-XIE:14–18.

The Rise in European Unemployment

Figure 6-4 shows the rate of unemployment from 1960 to 2007 in the four largest European countries—France, Germany, Italy, and the United Kingdom. As you can see, the rate of unemployment in these countries has risen substantially. For France and Germany, the change is particularly pronounced: unemployment averaged about 2 percent in the 1960s and about 10 percent in recent years.

What is the cause of rising European unemployment? No one knows for sure, but there is a leading theory. Many economists believe that the problem can be traced to the interaction between a long-standing policy and a more recent shock. The long-standing policy is generous benefits for unemployed workers. The recent shock is a technologically driven fall in the demand for unskilled workers relative to skilled workers (the so-called skill-biased technical change phenomenon that we noted earlier in this chapter).

There is no question that most European countries have generous programs for those without jobs. These programs go by various names: social insurance, the welfare state, or simply "the dole." Many countries allow the unemployed to collect benefits for years, rather than for only a short period of time (such as a maximum of 26 weeks). In some sense, those living on the dole are really out of the labour force: given the employment opportunities available, taking a job is less attractive than remaining without work. Yet these people are often counted as unemployed in government statistics.

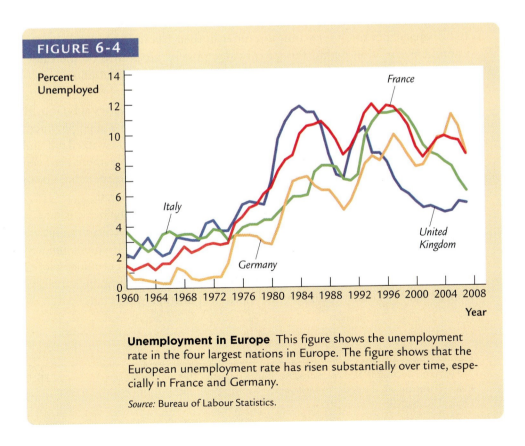

FIGURE 6-4

Unemployment in Europe This figure shows the unemployment rate in the four largest nations in Europe. The figure shows that the European unemployment rate has risen substantially over time, especially in France and Germany.

Source: Bureau of Labour Statistics.

There is also no question that the demand for unskilled workers has fallen relative to the demand for skilled workers. This change in demand is probably due to changes in technology: computers, for example, increase the demand for workers who can use them and reduce the demand for those who cannot. In the United States, this change in demand has been reflected in wages rather than in unemployment: over the past two decades, the wages of unskilled workers have fallen substantially relative to the wages of skilled workers in the United States. In Europe, however, the welfare state provides unskilled workers with an alternative to working for low wages. As the wages of unskilled workers fall, more workers view the dole as their best available option. The result is higher unemployment. Many analysts see Canada as occupying an intermediate position in this regard—with more commitment to a welfare state than the United States, but less compared to some European countries. Perhaps, then, it is not surprising that the Canadian unemployment rate is usually between the U.S. and European levels.

This diagnosis of high European unemployment does not suggest an easy remedy. Reducing the magnitude of government benefits for the unemployed would encourage workers to get off the dole and accept low-wage jobs. But it would also exacerbate economic inequality—the very problem that welfare state policies were designed to address.[17]

Unemployment Variation Within Europe

Europe is not a single labour market but rather a collection of national labour markets, separated not only by national borders but also by differences in culture and language. Because these countries differ in their labour market policies and institutions, variation within Europe provides a useful perspective on the causes of unemployment. Many empirical studies have therefore focused on the international differences,

The first noteworthy fact is that the unemployment rate varies substantially from country to country. For example, in August 2008, when the unemployment rate was 6.1 percent in the United States, it was 2 percent in Switzerland and 11.3 percent in Spain. Although in recent years average unemployment has been higher in Europe than in the United States, about a third of Europeans have been living in nations with unemployment rates lower than the U.S. rate.

A second notable fact is that much of the variation in unemployment rates is attributable to the long-term unemployed. The unemployment rate can be separated into two pieces—the percentage of the labour force that has been unemployed for less than a year and the percentage of the labour force that has been unemployed for more than a year. The long-term unemployment rate exhibits more variability from country to country than does the short-term unemployment rate.

---

[17] For more discussion of these issues, see Paul Krugman, "Past and Prospective Causes of High Unemployment," in *Reducing Unemployment: Current Issues and Policy Options,* Federal Reserve Bank of Kansas City (August 1994).

National unemployment rates are correlated with a variety of labour market policies. Unemployment rates are higher in nations with more generous employment insurance, as measured by the replacement rate—the percentage of previous wages that are replaced when a worker loses a job. In addition, nations tend to have higher unemployment, especially higher long-term unemployment, if benefits can be collected for longer periods of time.

Although government spending on employment insurance seems to raise unemployment, spending on "active" labour market policies appears to decrease it. These active labour market policies include job training, assistance with job search, and subsidized employment. Spain, for instance, has historically had a high rate of unemployment, a fact that can be explained by the combination of generous payments to the unemployed with minimal assistance at helping them find new jobs.

The role of unions also varies from country to country, as we saw in Table 6-1. This fact also helps explain differences in labour-market outcomes. National unemployment rates are positively correlated with the percentage of the labour force whose wages are set by collective bargaining with unions. The adverse impact of unions on unemployment is smaller, however, in nations with substantial coordination among employers in bargaining with unions, perhaps because coordination may moderate the upward pressure on wages.

A word of warning: Correlation does not imply causation, so empirical results such as these should be interpreted with caution. But they do suggest that a nation's unemployment rate, rather than being immutable, is instead a function of the choices a nation makes.[18]

CASE STUDY

The Secrets to Happiness

Why are some people more satisfied with their lives than others? This is a deep and difficult question, most often left to philosophers, psychologists, and self-help gurus. But part of the answer is macroeconomic. Recent research has shown that people are happier when they are living in a country with low inflation and low unemployment.

From 1975 to 1991, a survey called the Euro-Barometer Survey Series asked 264,710 people living in 12 European countries about their happiness and overall satisfaction with life. One question asked, "On the whole, are you very satisfied, fairly satisfied, not very satisfied, or not at all satisfied with the life you lead?" To see what determines happiness, the answers to this question were correlated with individual and macroeconomic variables. Other things equal, people are more satisfied with their lives if they are rich, educated, married, in

---

[18] Stephen Nickell, "Unemployment and Labor Market Rigidities: Europe Versus North America, *Journal of Economic Perspectives* 11 (September 1997): 55–74.

school, self-employed, retired, female, and young or old (as opposed to middle-aged). They are less satisfied if they are unemployed, divorced, or living with adolescent children. (Some of these correlations may reflect the effects, rather than causes, of happiness: for example, a happy person may find it easier than an unhappy one to keep a job and a spouse.)

Beyond these individual characteristics, the economy's overall rates of unemployment and inflation also play a significant role in explaining reported happiness. An increase in the unemployment rate of 4 percentage points is large enough to move 11 percent of the population down from one life satisfaction category to another. The overall unemployment rate reduces satisfaction even after controlling for an individual's employment status. That is, the employed in a high-unemployment nation are less happy than their counterparts in a low-unemployment nation, perhaps because they are more worried about job loss or perhaps out of sympathy with their fellow citizens.

High inflation is also associated with lower life satisfaction, although the effect is not as large. A 1.7 percentage point increase in inflation reduces happiness by about as much as a 1 percentage point increase in unemployment. The commonly cited "misery index," which is the sum of the inflation and unemployment rates, apparently gives too much weight to inflation relative to unemployment.[19] ■

The Rise of European Leisure

Not only are Europeans more likely to be unemployed than Americans, but they also typically work fewer hours than do their American counterparts. Figure 6-5 presents some data on how many hours a typical person works in the United States, France, and Germany. In the 1960s, the number of hours worked was about the same in each of these countries, and it was declining gradually on both sides of the Atlantic. But around 1980, hours worked settled at a plateau in the United States, while it continued to decline in Europe. Today, the typical American works about 20 percent more hours than does the typical resident of western Europe. The difference in hours worked reflects two facts. First, the average employed person in the United States works more hours per year than the average employed person in Europe. Europeans typically enjoy shorter workweeks and more frequent holidays. Second, more potential workers are employed in the United States. That is, the employment-to-population ratio is higher in the United States than it is in Europe. Earlier retirement in Europe is another source of the differing employment rates.

What is the underlying cause of these differences in work patterns? Economists have proposed several hypotheses. Edward Prescott, the 2004 winner of the Nobel

[19] Rafael Di Tella, Robert J. MacCulloch, and Andrew J. Oswald, "Preferences over Inflation and Unemployment: Evidence from Surveys of Happiness," *American Economic Review* 91, (March 2001): 335–341.

FIGURE 6-5

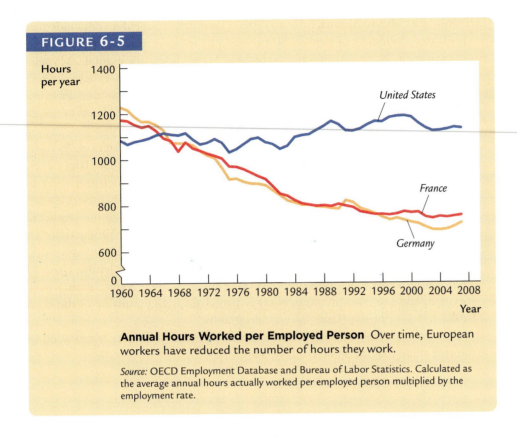

Annual Hours Worked per Employed Person Over time, European workers have reduced the number of hours they work.

Source: OECD Employment Database and Bureau of Labor Statistics. Calculated as the average annual hours actually worked per employed person multiplied by the employment rate.

Prize in economics, has concluded that "virtually all of the large differences between U.S. labour supply and those of Germany and France are due to differences in tax systems." This hypothesis is consistent with two facts: (1) Europeans face higher tax rates than Americans, and (2) European tax rates have risen significantly over the past several decades. Some economists take these facts as powerful evidence for the impact of taxes on work effort. Yet others are skeptical, arguing that to explain the differences in hours worked by tax rates alone requires an implausibly large wage elasticity of labour supply.

A related hypothesis is that the difference in observed work effort may be attributable to the underground economy. When tax rates are high, people have a greater incentive to work "off the books" to evade taxes. For obvious reasons, data on the underground economy are hard to come by. But economists who study the subject believe the underground economy is larger in Europe than it is in the United States. This fact suggests that the difference in actual hours worked, including work in the underground economy, may be smaller than the difference in measured hours worked.

Another hypothesis stresses the role of unions. As we have seen, collective bargaining is more important in European than in U.S. labour markets. Unions often push for shorter workweeks in contract negotiations, and they lobby the government for a variety of labor market regulations, such as official holidays.

Economists Alberto Alesina, Edward Glaeser, and Bruce Sacerdote conclude that "mandated holidays can explain 80 percent of the difference in weeks worked between the U.S. and Europe and 30 percent of the difference in total labor supply between the two regions." They suggest that Prescott may overstate the role of taxes because, looking across countries, tax rates and unionization rates are positively correlated; as a result, the effects of high taxes and the effects of widespread unionization are hard to disentangle.

A final hypothesis emphasizes the possibility of different preferences. As technological advance and economic growth have made all advanced countries richer, people around the world must decide whether to take the greater prosperity in the form of increased consumption of goods and services or increased leisure. According to economist Olivier Blanchard, "the main difference [between the continents] is that Europe has used some of the increase in productivity to increase leisure rather than income, while the U.S. has done the opposite." Blanchard believes that Europeans simply have more taste for leisure than do Americans. (As a French economist working in the United States, he may have special insight into this phenomenon.) If Blanchard is right, this raises the even harder question of why tastes vary by geography.

Economists continue to debate the merits of these alternative hypotheses. In the end, there may be some truth to all of them.[20]

6-5 Conclusion

Unemployment represents wasted resources. Unemployed workers have the potential to contribute to national income but are not doing so. Those searching for jobs to suit their skills are happy when the search is over, and those waiting for jobs in firms that pay above-equilibrium wages are happy when positions open up.

Unfortunately, neither frictional unemployment nor structural unemployment can be easily reduced. The government cannot make job search instantaneous, nor can it easily bring wages closer to equilibrium levels. Zero unemployment is not a plausible goal for free-market economies.

Yet public policy is not powerless in the fight to reduce unemployment. Job-training programs, the employment-insurance system, the minimum wage, and the laws governing collective bargaining are often topics of political debate. The policies we choose are likely to have important effects on the economy's natural rate of unemployment.

---

[20] To read more about this topic, see Prescott Edward C., "Why Do Americans Work So Much More Than Europeans?" *Federal Reserve Bank of Minneapolis Quarterly Review*, 28, no. 1, (July 2004): 2–13; Alberto Alesina, Edward Glaeser, and Bruce Sacerdote, "Work and Leisure in the U.S. and Europe: Why So Different? *NBER Macroeconomics Annual* (2005); Olivier Blanchard, "The Economic Future of Europe," *Journal of Economic Perspectives,* vol. 18, no. 4 (Fall 2004): 3–26.

Summary

1. The natural rate of unemployment is the steady-state rate of unemployment. It depends on the rate of job separation and the rate of job finding.

2. Because it takes time for workers to search for the job that best suits their individual skills and tastes, some frictional unemployment is inevitable. Various government policies, such as employment insurance, alter the amount of frictional unemployment.

3. Structural unemployment results when the real wage remains above the level that equilibrates labour supply and labour demand. Minimum-wage legislation is one cause of wage rigidity. Unions and the threat of unionization are another. Finally, efficiency-wage theories suggest that, for various reasons, firms may find it profitable to keep wages high despite an excess supply of labour.

4. Whether we conclude that most unemployment is short-term or long-term depends on how we look at the data. Most spells of unemployment are short. Yet most weeks of unemployment are attributable to the small number of long-term unemployed.

5. The unemployment rates among demographic groups and among Canada's regions differ substantially. In particular, the unemployment rates for younger workers are much greater than for older workers. This difference results from a difference in the rate of job separation rather than from a difference in the rate of job finding. Unemployment in the Maritimes is very high, and this is largely due to a lower rate of job finding.

6. The unemployment rate gradually drifted upward over the second half of the twentieth century. Various explanations have been proposed, including the changing demographic composition of the labour force, an increase in sectoral shifts, and skill-biased technological change. The natural unemployment rule has started drifting down again since the turn of the century.

7. American and European labour markets exhibit significant differences. In recent years, Europe has experienced considerably more unemployment than the United States, and employed Europeans work fewer hours than employed Americans.

KEY CONCEPTS

Natural rate of unemployment	Employment insurance (EI)	Insiders versus outsiders
Frictional unemployment	Wage rigidity	Efficiency wages
Sectoral shift	Structural unemployment	Discouraged workers

QUESTIONS FOR REVIEW

1. What determines the natural rate of unemployment?

2. Describe the difference between frictional unemployment and wait unemployment.

3. Give three explanations why the real wage may remain above the level that equilibrates labour supply and labour demand.

4. Is most unemployment long-term or short-term? Explain your answer.

5. How do economists explain the high natural rate of unemployment in the 1970s and 1980s? How do they explain the fall in the natural rate in the 1990s and early 2000s?

PROBLEMS AND APPLICATIONS

1. Answer the following questions about your own experience in the labour force:

   a. When you or one of your friends is looking for a part-time job, how many weeks does it typically take? After you find a job, how many weeks does it typically last?

   b. From your estimates, calculate (in a rate per week) your rate of job finding f and your rate of job separation s. (*Hint:* If f is the rate of job finding, then the average spell of unemployment is $1/f$.)

   c. What is the natural rate of unemployment for the population you represent?

2. In this chapter we saw that the steady-state rate of unemployment is $U/L = s/(s + f)$. Suppose that the unemployment rate does not begin at this level. Show that unemployment will evolve over time and reach this steady state. (*Hint:* Express the change in the number of unemployed as a function of $s, f,$ and U. Then show that if unemployment is above the natural rate, unemployment falls, and if unemployment is below the natural rate, unemployment rises.)

3. The residents of a certain dormitory have collected the following data: People who live in the dorm can be classified as either involved in a relationship or uninvolved. Among involved people, 10 percent experience a breakup of their relationship every month. Among uninvolved people, 5 percent will enter into a relationship every month. What is the steady-state fraction of residents who are uninvolved?

4. Suppose that the government passes legislation making it more difficult for firms to fire workers. (An example is a law requiring severance pay for fired workers.) If this legislation reduces the rate of job separation without affecting the rate of job finding, how would the natural rate of unemployment change? Do you think that it is plausible that the legislation would not affect the rate of job finding? Why or why not?

5. Consider an economy with the following Cobb–Douglas production function:

$$Y = K^{1/3}L^{2/3}.$$

The economy has 1,000 units of capital and a labour force of 1,000 workers.

   a. Derive the equation describing labour demand in this economy as a function of the real wage and the capital stock. (*Hint:* Review the appendix to Chapter 3.)

   b. If the real wage can adjust to equilibrate labour supply and labour demand, what is the real wage? In this equilibrium, what are employment, output, and the total amount earned by workers?

   c. Now suppose that the government, concerned about the welfare of the working class, passes a law requiring firms to pay workers a real wage of 1 unit of output. How does this wage compare to the equilibrium wage?

   d. The government cannot dictate how many workers firms hire at the mandated wage. Given this fact, what are the effects of this law? Specifically, what happens to employment, output, and the total amount earned by workers?

e. Will the government succeed in its goal of helping the working class? Explain.

f. Do you think that this analysis provides a good way of thinking about a minimum-wage law? Why or why not?

6. Suppose that a country experiences a reduction in productivity—that is, an adverse shock to the production function.

   a. What happens to the labour demand curve?

   b. How would this change in productivity affect the labour market—that is, employment, unemployment, and real wages—if the labour market were always in equilibrium?

   c. How would this change in productivity affect the labour market if unions prevented real wages from falling?

7. When workers' wages rise, their decision on how much time to spend working is affected in two conflicting ways, as you may have learned in courses in microeconomics. The *income effect* is the impulse to work less, because greater incomes mean workers can afford to consume more leisure. The *substitution effect* is the impulse to work more, because the reward to working an additional hour has risen (equivalently, the opportunity cost of leisure has gone up). Apply these concepts to Blanchard's hypothesis about American and European tastes for leisure. On which side of the Atlantic do income effects appear larger than substitution effects? On which side do the two effects approximately cancel? Do you think it is a reasonable hypothesis that tastes for leisure vary by geography? Why or why not?

8. In any city at any time, some of the stock of usable office space is vacant. This vacant office space is unemployed capital. How would you explain this phenomenon? Is it a social problem?

APPENDIX

Unemployment, Inequality, and Government Policy

The efficiency-wage model is one theory of unemployment that was discussed in the main body of this chapter. In this appendix, we describe a specific version of this model that can be used as a vehicle to assess some common presumptions—such as "payroll taxes are job killers" and "globalization makes rising income inequality inevitable."

As explained earlier, one common version of the efficiency-wage model is based on the assumption of asymmetric information. Employees know whether they are shirking, but employers cannot be sure. To mention just one consideration, it is impossible for employers to verify fully whether individual employees can be believed when they call in sick. Firms can lessen this worker-productivity problem by making it more expensive for employees to lose their jobs. By paying a wage that exceeds each worker's alternative option, employers can ensure that their employees work hard to avoid being fired. But when all firms raise payments in this way, the overall level of wages exceeds what would obtain in a competitive market. With labour more expensive, firms hire fewer workers in total, and there is unemployment, as shown in Figure 6-3.

It is worthwhile formalizing this model of the labour market. Let w and b stand for the wage a worker receives from her employer and the income she can expect if she leaves that firm, respectively. With the firm's incomplete monitoring process, there is a probability that the worker can be fired for low productivity. That probability can be reduced by putting forth more effort, but this effort decreases the utility that the employee receives while at work. Let fraction a times the wage represent the income equivalent of the loss in utility that stems from this extra effort.

The worker faces two options: either she stays on the job with a net return of $(1 - a)w$, or she is fired, in which case she receives b. Firms will get high productivity from workers as long as $(1 - a)w$ is greater than or equal to b. But in the interest of minimizing wage costs, firms do not want to meet this constraint with any unnecessary payment, so they set

$$w = b/(1 - a).$$

Since a is a fraction, this equation verifies that firms set wages above the workers' alternative.

How is b, the workers' alternative, determined? Again, there are two options. A fired worker may get employed by another firm (and the probability of this outcome is the economy's employment rate, $(1 - u)$), or she may go without work (and the probability of this happening is the unemployment rate, u). In a full equilibrium, all firms have to pay the same wage to keep their workers. Finally, for simplicity, let us assume that there is an employment-insurance program that pays workers fraction c of their former wage if they are out of work. All this means that each worker's alternative is

$$b = (1 - u)w + u(cw).$$

When this definition of the alternative option is substituted into the wage-setting rule, $w = b/(1 - a)$, the result can be simplified to

$$u = a/(1 - c).$$

This expression for the full-equilibrium structural unemployment rate indicates three things. First, if workers do not find hard work distasteful at all (that is, if $a = 0$), firms would not need to set wages above the competitive level to limit any shirking problem, so there would be no unemployment. (Implicitly, this is what we assumed in Chapter 3.) Second, since there is no variable relating to worker skill or education levels in the unemployment-rate equation, changes in these factors do *not* affect employment. If workers are more skilled, both their current employer and other potential employers are prepared to pay them more. So wages rise generally and there are no changes in the incentive to shirk. The model is consistent with experience in this regard. Labour productivity increased dramatically over the twentieth century and, just as the model predicts, we observed a vast increase in real wages and no long-term trend in the unemployment rate.

The third implication of this model is that the unemployment problem is accentuated by a more generous employment-insurance program (a higher value for c). The reason? More generous support for unemployment lowers the cost of being fired. Workers react by shirking more, so firms react by raising wages. With higher wages, firms find it profitable to hire fewer workers. Since unemployment insurance is a form of income redistribution, the model illustrates the standard tradeoff involved: the size of the overall economic pie shrinks when we try to redistribute. This fact does not mean that redistribution should be rejected. Society may prefer a higher unemployment rate if each individual involved is better protected from hardship.

Let us extend this model to allow for payroll and personal income taxes. Employees pay tax rate t times their wages, while employment-insurance receipts are not taxed. Since workers keep only proportion $(1 - t)$ of each dollar earned on the job, the revised expressions are $w(1 - t)(1 - a) = b$ and $b = (1 - u)w(1 - t) + u(cw)$. These relationships lead to a revised expression for the steady-state unemployment rate:

$$u = a(1 - t)/(1 - c - t).$$

We see that the unemployment rate depends on the tax rate faced by employees. Higher taxes lower the return from working. To counteract the resulting increased propensity to shirk, firms raise wages and fewer individuals find jobs.

An important insight can be gained by inserting representative numerical values for each term in the unemployment-rate equation. Initially, let us assume a tax rate of 15 percent ($t = 0.15$), an employment insurance program that pays each former worker one-half of what she previously earned ($c = 0.5$), and a shirking parameter value ($a = 0.02$) that yields a representative value for unemployment of 5 percent ($u = 0.05$). Now we investigate how much the unemployment rate rises as we consider higher values for the tax rate (and the other parameters, c and a, are fixed). You can verify that as the tax rate rises by equal amounts, first from 15 to 25 percent and then from 25 to 35 percent, the unemployment rate rises, first by 1 percentage point, from 5 to 6 percent, and then by 2.67 percentage points, from 6 to 8.67 percent. Clearly, the unemployment rate rises much more when taxes are already high. The model is consistent with the widespread drive to lower taxes.

It is noteworthy that the *employer* payroll tax rate does not affect unemployment. Just like an increase in general productivity, a lower employer payroll tax rate raises both the firms' willingness to pay higher wages and the workers' wage claims. As a result, unemployment can be reduced by a revenue-neutral cut in the employee payroll tax rate (financed by an increase in the employer payroll tax rate).

The major payroll taxes in Canada are the contributions to employment insurance (EI) and to the public pension programs (the CPP and QPP). During the late 1990s, the contributions to EI were reduced by a small amount each year (because the EI account was in surplus), but the contributions to the CPP/QPP were increased a great deal more (because this is how the government chose to keep the public pension system from going bankrupt as the baby-boom generation ages). Since, on balance, payroll taxes have risen, there has been upward pressure on unemployment. It is unfortunate that the government has not decreased its reliance on the employee portion of this levy, since (as this model illustrates) such a change in policy could reverse this upward pressure on the unemployment rate.

Inequality

Many people fear that globalization is leading to higher unemployment. Compared to many low-wage countries, Canada has an abundance of skilled workers and a relatively small proportion of the population in the unskilled category. The opposite is the case in the developing countries. With increased integration among the world economies, Canada specializes in the production of goods that emphasize our relatively abundant factor, skilled labour, so it is the wages of skilled workers that are bid up by increased foreign trade. The other side of this development is that Canada relies more on imports to supply goods that only require unskilled labour, and this means that the demand for unskilled labour falls in Canada. The result is either lower wages for the unskilled in Canada (if there is no legislation that puts a floor on wages here) or rising unemployment among the unskilled (if there is a floor on wages—such as that imposed by minimum-wage laws). In either case, unskilled individuals can lose in the new global economy.

As noted in the main text of this chapter, a second hypothesis concerning rising income inequality is that, during the last several decades, technological change has been decidedly skill-biased—with the result that the demand for skilled workers has risen while that for the unskilled has fallen. Just as with the globalization hypothesis, the effects of these shifts in demand depend on whether it is possible for wages in the unskilled sector to fall. The United States and

Europe are often cited as illustrations of the possible outcomes. The United States has only a limited welfare state, so there is little to stop increased wage inequality from emerging, as indeed it has in recent decades. European governments, on the other hand, maintain floors below which the wages of the unskilled cannot be pushed. When technological change decreases the demand for unskilled labour, firms have no freedom to do anything but reduce their employment of these individuals. Thus, Europe has avoided large increases in wage inequality, but the unemployment rate has been very high there for many years.

Government Policy

Most economists favour the second hypothesis for explaining rising income inequality. This is because inequality has increased so much *within* each industry and occupation, in ways that are unrelated to foreign trade. But whatever the cause, the plight of the less skilled is a dire one. Figure 6-6 allows us to consider policy options.

Panel (a) in Figure 6-6 depicts the skilled labour market, while panel (b) illustrates the unskilled market. There is unemployment in both sectors. In the skilled labour market, unemployment is due to incomplete information and efficiency wages. In the unskilled market, unemployment is due to minimum wages. Let us consider a reduction in employer payroll taxes. Cutting the tax that employers

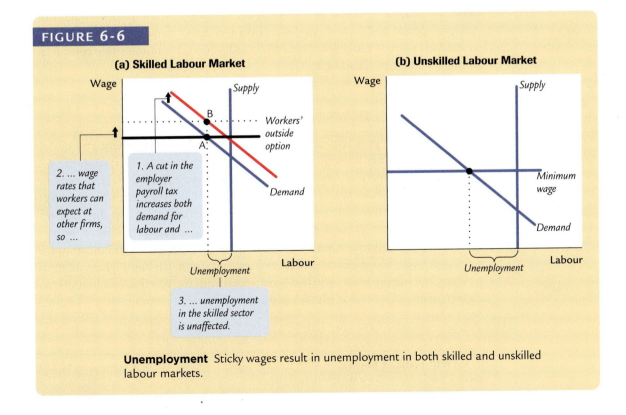

FIGURE 6-6

(a) Skilled Labour Market

Wage

Supply

B

A

Workers' outside option

2. ... wage rates that workers can expect at other firms, so ...

1. A cut in the employer payroll tax increases both demand for labour and ...

Demand

Unemployment

Labour

3. ... unemployment in the skilled sector is unaffected.

(b) Unskilled Labour Market

Wage

Supply

Minimum wage

Demand

Unemployment

Labour

Unemployment Sticky wages result in unemployment in both skilled and unskilled labour markets.

must pay when hiring skilled workers results in a shift up in the demand for skilled labour. But since all firms react in this same way, the workers' outside option rises to the same extent, so the market outcome moves from a point A to point B in panel (a) of Figure 6-6. No jobs are created. Indeed, some jobs may be destroyed. If the value of the minimum wage is set as some fixed proportion of wages in the skilled sector, there is one further effect. The minimum-wage line shifts up in panel (b) of the figure, and unemployment among the unskilled is higher. So this model does not support cutting the employer payroll tax associated with skilled workers.

Cutting the tax that employers must pay when hiring unskilled workers results in an upward shift in the demand for unskilled labour. Since the position of no other curve in either market is affected by this policy, it is obvious—without our showing it in panel (b)—that this initiative reduces unemployment in the unskilled sector. Thus, the elimination of payroll taxes levied on employers for hiring *unskilled* workers *is* supported by the model. Indeed, offering employment subsidies (a negative employer payroll tax) for (only) low-wage workers has been recommended by all leading economists who have addressed the issue of rising income inequality.

This proposal respects the proposition that lasting jobs are best generated through the private sector, and that market failure is a precondition for governments to adjust market signals. It has been shown[21] that even revenue-neutral versions of this initiative generate favourable spillover outcomes—higher wages for skilled workers and higher investment—in addition to lower unemployment for the less skilled. In contrast to "trickle-down" measures (which involve direct benefits for the well-to-do and indirect benefits for others), the low-wage subsidy is a "percolate-up" strategy (which confers direct benefits for the less well-to-do and indirect benefits for others). Trickle-down economics was considered in the appendix to Chapter 5.

The Globalization Challenge

Our discussion of policies that can lower the natural unemployment rate raises a general issue that has been much in the news in recent years. Every time there is a meeting of country representatives to such organizations as the International Monetary Fund or the World Bank, there is a major demonstration in the streets by antiglobalization protesters. These individuals resent the fact that the "neoconservative" world bodies focus on keeping capital free to move between countries. These institutions favour capital mobility on the grounds that world incomes will be maximized only if capital is free to locate where it has the highest marginal product. But the protesters are more concerned with the position of labourers, not capital owners. They want labour's income—not overall income—to be higher.

---

[21] See W.M. Scarth, *A Job-Creation Strategy for Governments with No Money* (Commentary No. 92) (Toronto: C.D. Howe Institute, 1997).

The antiglobalization protesters focus on the following concern: how can the government in a small open economy provide low-income support policies for its citizens? We can address this issue by thinking of labour as the low-income or "poor" individuals and by thinking of capital owners as the "rich." If the government is to make transfers payments to the "poor," they must raise the necessary revenue by trying to tax the "rich." But if the rich can costlessly transfer their capital to be employed in low-tax countries, our government will not be able to make the tax stick on capitalists. It would seem that there is no way to help the economic position of labour if capital cannot be taxed. The protesters' answer to this problem is to restrict the mobility of capital (that is, to limit globalization). But there is another way out of the dilemma.

We use Figure 6-7 to analyze the options available to the government. This analysis is similar to the discussion on trickle-down economics in the appendix to Chapter 5. So if you find that you do not understand the present analysis fully, review the material in the previous chapter. In panel (a) of Figure 6-7, we see a picture of the economy's capital market. Since it is profit-maximizing for firms to hire capital as long as its marginal product exceeds the rent that must be paid, the downward-sloping marginal product relationship is the demand curve for capital. The perfectly elastic supply curve indicates that the owners of capital will supply capital to this economy in unlimited amounts *if* they receive the return that is available in the rest of the world. This means that capital is withdrawn from this economy if the after-tax return is at all below the yield available elsewhere. The fact that this supply curve is horizontal is the globalization constraint that the domestic policymaker must contend with.

With no tax on the owners of capital, the economy is observed at point A—the intersection of supply and demand. Since the area under the marginal product curve represents total product, the country's GDP is given by the coloured trapazoid in panel (a). Capitalists receive a total income equal to the light blue rectangle, and labour receives the rest of national income—the light beige triangle. We are assuming that the government wants to increase what labour gets. If the government levies a tax on the earnings of capital, the owners react by demanding a higher pretax return. Indeed, if the pretax return does not rise by just enough to leave the after-tax yield equal to what is available elsewhere, then capitalists will withdraw from this country. Geometrically, we impose this reaction by shifting the capital supply curve up by just the amount of the tax [as shown in panel (b)]. The intersection of the now relevant supply and demand curves is at point B. By comparing the before-tax and after-tax outcome points (*A* and *B*), we see that some capital has left the country. As a result, the GDP is smaller; with the tax it is just the sum of the light-beige, light-green, and light-blue areas.

Not all the capital leaves the country. Once some units have left, what remains is more scarce, so it has a higher marginal product—just enough to generate a payment that covers the tax obligation. The capital that remains gets after-tax income equal to the light blue area, exactly what it received before the tax. The capital that leaves the country receives the dark blue area (elsewhere), exactly what it used to receive here. So capitalists are totally unaffected by the tax. This is the globalization constraint.

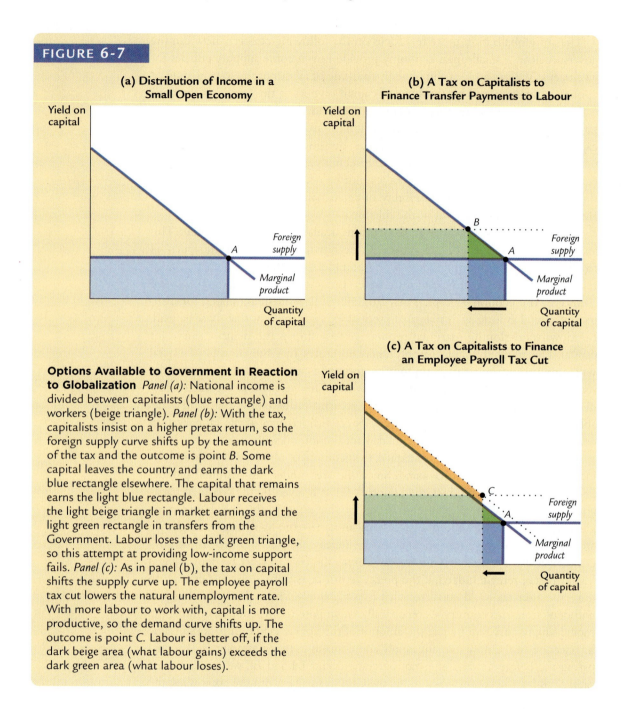

FIGURE 6-7

(a) Distribution of Income in a Small Open Economy

(b) A Tax on Capitalists to Finance Transfer Payments to Labour

(c) A Tax on Capitalists to Finance an Employee Payroll Tax Cut

Options Available to Government in Reaction to Globalization *Panel (a):* National income is divided between capitalists (blue rectangle) and workers (beige triangle). *Panel (b):* With the tax, capitalists insist on a higher pretax return, so the foreign supply curve shifts up by the amount of the tax and the outcome is point *B*. Some capital leaves the country and earns the dark blue rectangle elsewhere. The capital that remains earns the light blue rectangle. Labour receives the light beige triangle in market earnings and the light green rectangle in transfers from the Government. Labour loses the dark green triangle, so this attempt at providing low-income support fails. *Panel (c):* As in panel (b), the tax on capital shifts the supply curve up. The employee payroll tax cut lowers the natural unemployment rate. With more labour to work with, capital is more productive, so the demand curve shifts up. The outcome is point *C*. Labour is better off, if the dark beige area (what labour gains) exceeds the dark green area (what labour loses).

The government collects tax revenue equal to the light green rectangle. Since this comes out of the triangle that labour used to receive before the tax, it is labour that truly bears the burden of the tax. But since the whole point of levying the tax is to make a transfer payment to labour, this group both pays out and gets back the light green area. So labour is neither helped nor hurt by the transfers. But labour *is* worse off on balance because there is still the loss of the dark green triangle (that used to be—but is no longer—part of labour's receipts). This loss exists because labour has less capital to work with. This makes workers less productive, and lower productivity leads to lower wages. So this standard supply-demand analysis supports the concern of the antiglobalization protesters. It appears that the attempt to help the "poor" has failed; indeed, they are *worse off* after the government's attempt to help them!

But before you get too excited about joining the protesters in the streets, consider the fact that our analysis has so far involved the assumption that the government intervention has had no effect on the natural unemployment rate. As we learned earlier in this appendix, the unemployment rate can be lowered if the government uses the revenue to cut the employee payroll tax. Panel (c) in Figure 6-7 shows how the analysis is altered when the government does use the revenue in this way, rather than by making a straight transfer payment to labour.

As before, a tax that is intended to be borne by capitalists is levied to give the government the necessary revenue to finance the payroll tax cut. Thus, the supply curve shifts up by the amount of the tax in panel (c). But with the payroll tax cut leading to lower unemployment, capital now has more labour to work with, and this increases capital's productivity. We show this in the diagram by shifting capital's marginal product curve out to the right. The intersection of the now relevant supply and demand curves is at point *C*. Comparing the locations of outcome points *B* and *C,* we can appreciate that less capital leaves the country when the policy package involves a reduction in unemployment. This means that labour's net loss in the previous scenario—the dark green triangle—is now smaller in panel (c). And this is not the only piece of good news. There is an area indicating a gain in the size of labour's triangle—the dark beige band in panel (c). This region represents the additional output that was not being produced before, when more individuals were out of work.

It is too messy to show here, but labour's gain (the dark beige band) is almost certainly bigger than labour's loss (the dark green triangle). Specifically, we can combine a Cobb–Douglas production function and the efficiency-wage model of unemployment discussed earlier in the appendix. If the analysis is repeated in an algebraic mode (with these components), it can be shown that this tax substitution (a higher tax on capital combined with a lower payroll tax) *must* lead to an improvement in labour's position.

So the antiglobalization protesters have been premature in reaching the view that governments are unable to provide low-income support policy in a globalized setting. Our analysis supports their contention that the government cannot make taxes stick on the capitalists. This means that redistribution—taking from the rich and giving to the poor—is not possible. But as we have seen, there is another way to help the poor. Instead of trying to redistribute income, the government can simply decrease wastage by reducing structural unemployment. This increases the overall size of the economic pie, so that the poor can get a bigger slice without our having to reduce the size of the slice that the rich receive. The moral of the story is that the provision of low-income support in a globalized setting requires that the government focus on initiatives that can be expected to reduce structural unemployment. As a result, the analysis in this chapter is central to the challenges that will face Canada's policymakers in the coming years.

It should now be clearer why economists are applauding Canadian policymakers for introducing the Working Income Tax Benefit, rather than relying exclusively on standard welfare programs and employment insurance. Transfers to those on lower incomes can be made in three broad ways. First, the transfer can be conditional on the individual being unemployed (as in EI). This transfer has the unfortunate side effect of raising unemployment. The second option is welfare in the form of a guaranteed annual income. This policy involves a low-income transfer that is independent of an individual's employment status, so it does not have the unfortunate side effect of raising unemployment. The third option is some form of low-income employment subsidy (a negative payroll tax). This transfer payment only goes to those who are working, so the side effect in this case is a desirable one—a *lower* unemployment rate.

MORE PROBLEMS AND APPLICATIONS

1. Explain why a generous EI system raises unemployment, but may still be desirable.

2. Consider investments in education. What effect do you expect such investments to have on the unemployment rate if they are limited to programs that generate increases in the productivity of workers who are already skilled? What effect on unemployment would you expect if these investments are focused on unskilled individuals? Explain your reasoning.

3. What do the antiglobalization protesters argue about the scope that governments have to provide support for their citizens on low incomes? Explain which parts of the protesters' views you support, and which you do not support.

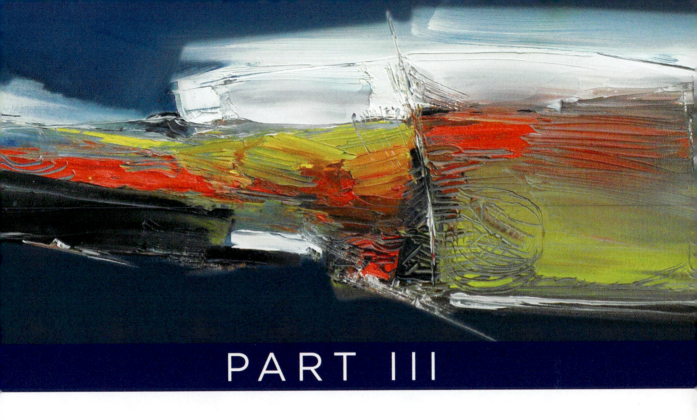

PART III

Growth Theory:
The Economy in the
Very Long Run

CHAPTER 7

Economic Growth I: Capital Accumulation and Population Growth

The question of growth is nothing new but a new disguise for an age-old issue, one which has always intrigued and preoccupied economics: the present versus the future.

— *James Tobin*

If you have ever spoken with your grandparents about what their lives were like when they were young, most likely you learned an important lesson about economic growth: material standards of living have improved substantially over time for most families in most countries. This advance comes from rising incomes, which have allowed people to consume greater quantities of goods and services.

To measure economic growth, economists use data on gross domestic product, which measures the total income of everyone in the economy. The real GDP of Canada in 2008 was 7.5 times its 1950 level, and real GDP per person was 4.4 times its 1950 level. In any given year, we can also observe large differences in the standard of living among countries. Table 7-1 shows income per person in 2007 of the world's 14 most populous countries. The United States tops the list with an income of $45,790 per person. Bangladesh has an income per person of only $1,242—less than 3 percent of the figure for the United States. (While not included in Table 7-1 since we are not one of the more populated countries, it is interesting to note that Canada's GDP per person—in U.S. dollars—was $32,273 in 2007.)

Our goal in this chapter and the next is to understand what causes these differences in income over time and across countries. In Chapter 3 we identified the factors of production—capital and labour—and the production technology as the sources of the economy's output and, thus, of its total income. Differences in income, then, must come from differences in capital, labour, and technology.

Our primary task in this chapter and the next is to develop a theory of economic growth in per-capita income called the **Solow growth model.** Our analysis in Chapter 3 enabled us to describe how the economy produces and

TABLE **7-1**

International Differences in the Standard of Living

Country	Income per Person (2007)	Country	Income per Person (2007)
United States	$45,790	Indonesia	3,728
Japan	33,525	Philippines	3,410
Germany	33,154	India	2,753
Russia	14,743	Vietnam	2,600
Mexico	12,780	Pakistan	2,525
Brazil	9,570	Nigeria	1,977
China	5,345	Bangladesh	1,242

Source: The World Bank.

uses its output at one point in time. The analysis was static—a snapshot of the economy. To explain why our national income grows, and why some economies grow faster than others, we must broaden our analysis so that it describes changes in the economy over time. By developing such a model, we make our analysis dynamic—more like a movie than a photograph. The Solow growth model shows how saving, population growth, and technological progress affect the level of an economy's output and its growth over time. In this chapter we analyze the roles of saving and population growth. In the next chapter we introduce technological progress.[1]

7-1 The Accumulation of Capital

The Solow growth model is designed to show how growth in the capital stock, growth in the labour force, and advances in technology interact in an economy, and how they affect a nation's total output of goods and services. We build this model in a series of steps. Our first step is to examine how the supply and demand for goods determine the accumulation of capital. In this first step, we assume that the labour force and technology are fixed. We then relax these assumptions, by introducing changes in the labour force later in this chapter and by introducing changes in technology in the next.

---

[1] The Solow growth model is named after economist Robert Solow and was developed in the 1950s and 1960s. In 1987 Solow won the Nobel Prize in economics for his work in economic growth. The model was introduced in Robert M. Solow, "A Contribution to the Theory of Economic Growth," *Quarterly Journal of Economics* (February 1956): 65–94.

The Supply and Demand for Goods

The supply and demand for goods played a central role in our static model of the economy in Chapter 3. The same is true for the Solow model. By considering the supply and demand for goods, we can see what determines how much output is produced at any given time and how this output is allocated among alternative uses.

The Supply of Goods and the Production Function

The supply of goods in the Solow model is based on the production function, which states that output depends on the capital stock and the labour force:

$$Y = F(K, L).$$

The Solow growth model assumes that the production function has constant returns to scale. This assumption is often considered realistic, and as we will see shortly, it helps simplify the analysis. Recall that a production function has constant returns to scale if

$$zY = F(zK, zL)$$

for any positive number z. That is, if both capital and labour are multiplied by z, the amount of output is also multiplied by z.

Production functions with constant returns to scale allow us to analyze all quantities in the economy relative to the size of the labour force. To see that this is true, set $z = 1/L$ in the equation above to obtain

$$Y/L = F(K/L, 1).$$

This equation shows that the amount of output per worker Y/L is a function of the amount of capital per worker K/L. (The number "1" is, of course, constant and thus can be ignored.) The assumption of constant returns to scale implies that the size of the economy—as measured by the number of workers—does not affect the relationship between output per worker and capital per worker.

Because the size of the economy does not matter, it will prove convenient to denote all quantities in per-worker terms. We designate quantities per worker with lowercase letters, so $y = Y/L$ is output per worker, and $k = K/L$ is capital per worker. We can then write the production function as

$$y = f(k),$$

where we define $f(k) = F(k, 1)$. Figure 7-1 illustrates this production function.

The slope of this production function shows how much extra output a worker produces when given an extra unit of capital. This amount is the marginal product of capital MPK. Mathematically, we write

$$MPK = f(k + 1) - f(k).$$

Note that in Figure 7-1, as the amount of capital increases, the production function becomes flatter, indicating that the production function exhibits diminishing marginal product of capital. When k is low, the average worker has only a little capital to work with, so an extra unit of capital is very useful and produces

FIGURE 7-1

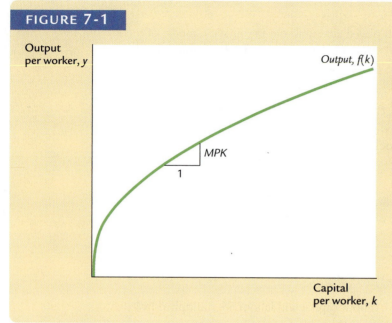

FIGURE 7-1

Output per worker, y

Output, $f(k)$

MPK

1

Capital per worker, k

The Production Function The production function shows how the amount of capital per worker k determines the amount of output per worker $y = f(k)$. The slope of the production function is the marginal product of capital: if k increases by 1 unit, y increases by MPK units. The production function becomes flatter as k increases, indicating diminishing marginal product of capital.

a lot of additional output. When k is high, the average worker already has a lot of capital, so an extra unit increases production only slightly.

The Demand for Goods and the Consumption Function The demand for goods in the Solow model comes from consumption and investment. In other words, output per worker y is divided between consumption per worker c and investment per worker i:

$$y = c + i.$$

This equation is the per-worker version of the national accounts identity for the economy. Notice that it omits government purchases (which for present purposes we can ignore) and net exports (because we are assuming a closed economy).

The Solow model assumes that each year people save a fraction s of their income and consume a fraction $(1 - s)$. We can express this idea with the following consumption function:

$$c = (1 - s)y,$$

where s, the saving rate, is a number between zero and one. Keep in mind that various government policies can potentially influence a nation's saving rate, so one of our goals is to find what saving rate is desirable. For now, however, we just take the saving rate s as given.

To see what this consumption function implies for investment, substitute $(1 - s)y$ for c in the national accounts identity:

$$y = (1 - s)y + i.$$

Rearrange the terms to obtain

$$i = sy.$$

This equation shows that investment equals saving, as we first saw in Chapter 3. Thus, the rate of saving s is also the fraction of output devoted to investment.

We have now introduced the two main ingredients of the Solow model—the production function and the consumption function—which describe the economy at any moment in time. For any given capital stock k, the production function $y = f(k)$ determines how much output the economy produces, and the saving rate s determines the allocation of that output between consumption and investment.

Growth in the Capital Stock and the Steady State

At any moment, the capital stock is a key determinant of the economy's output, but the capital stock can change over time, and those changes can lead to economic growth. In particular, two forces influence the capital stock: investment and depreciation. *Investment* is expenditure on new plant and equipment, and it causes the capital stock to rise. *Depreciation* is the wearing out of old capital, and it causes the capital stock to fall. Let's consider each of these forces in turn.

As we have already noted, investment per worker i equals sy. By substituting the production function for y, we can express investment per worker as a function of the capital stock per worker:

$$i = sf(k).$$

This equation relates the existing stock of capital k to the accumulation of new capital i. Figure 7-2 shows this relationship. This figure illustrates how, for any

FIGURE 7-2

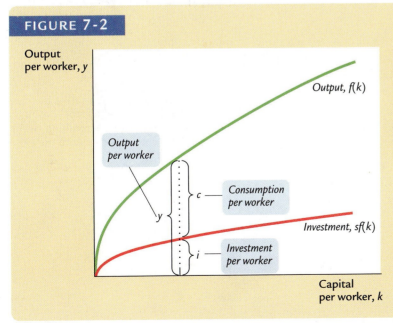

Output per worker, y

Output per worker

Output, $f(k)$

c — Consumption per worker

y

Investment, $sf(k)$

i — Investment per worker

Capital per worker, k

Output, Consumption, and Investment The saving rate s determines the allocation of output between consumption and investment. For any level of capital k, output is $f(k)$, investment is $sf(k)$, and consumption is $f(k) - sf(k)$.

value of k, the amount of output is determined by the production function $f(k)$, and the allocation of that output between consumption and saving is determined by the saving rate s.

To incorporate depreciation into the model, we assume that a certain fraction δ of the capital stock wears out each year. Here δ (the lowercase Greek letter delta) is called the *depreciation rate*. For example, if capital lasts an average of 25 years, then the depreciation rate is 4 percent per year ($\delta = 0.04$). The amount of capital that depreciates each year is δk. Figure 7-3 shows how the amount of depreciation depends on the capital stock.

We can express the impact of investment and depreciation on the capital stock with this equation:

$$\text{Change in Capital Stock} = \text{Investment} - \text{Depreciation}$$

$$\Delta k \qquad = \qquad i \qquad - \qquad \delta k,$$

where Δk is the change in the capital stock between one year and the next. Because investment i equals $sf(k)$, we can write this as

$$\Delta k = sf(k) - \delta k.$$

Figure 7-4 graphs the terms of this equation—investment and depreciation—for different levels of the capital stock k. The higher the capital stock, the greater are the amounts of output and investment. Yet the higher the capital stock, the greater also is the amount of depreciation.

As Figure 7-4 shows, there is a single capital stock k^* at which the amount of investment equals the amount of depreciation. If the economy finds itself at this level of the capital stock, the capital stock will not change because the two forces acting on it—investment and depreciation—just balance. That is, at k^*, $\Delta k = 0$, so the capital stock k and output $f(k)$ are steady over time (rather than growing or shrinking). We therefore call k^* the **steady-state** level of capital.

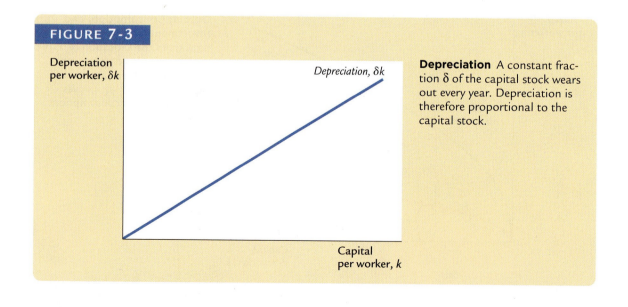

FIGURE 7-3

Depreciation per worker, δk

Depreciation, δk

Capital per worker, k

Depreciation A constant fraction δ of the capital stock wears out every year. Depreciation is therefore proportional to the capital stock.

FIGURE 7-4

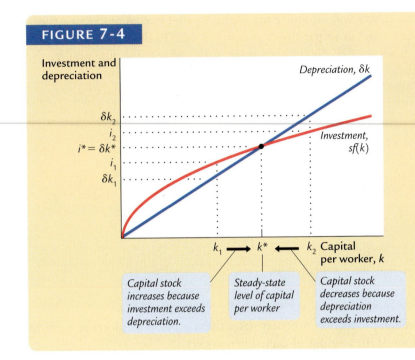

Investment, Depreciation, and the Steady State The steady-state level of capital k^* is the level at which investment equals depreciation, indicating that the amount of capital will not change over time. Below k^*, investment exceeds depreciation, so the capital stock grows. Above k^* investment is less than depreciation, so the capital stock shrinks.

Capital stock increases because investment exceeds depreciation.

Steady-state level of capital per worker

Capital stock decreases because depreciation exceeds investment.

The steady state is significant for two reasons. As we have just seen, an economy at the steady state will stay there. In addition, and just as important, an economy not at the steady state will go there. That is, regardless of the level of capital with which the economy begins, it ends up with the steady-state level of capital. In this sense, *the steady state represents the long-run equilibrium of the economy.*

To see why an economy always ends up at the steady state, suppose that the economy starts with less than the steady-state level of capital, such as level k_1 in Figure 7-4. In this case, the level of investment exceeds the amount of depreciation. Over time, the capital stock will rise and will continue to rise—along with output $f(k)$—until it approaches the steady state k^*.

Similarly, suppose that the economy starts with more than the steady-state level of capital, such as level k_2. In this case, investment is less than depreciation: capital is wearing out faster than it is being replaced. The capital stock will fall, again approaching the steady-state level. Once the capital stock reaches the steady state, investment equals depreciation, and there is no pressure for the capital stock to increase or decrease.

Approaching the Steady State: A Numerical Example

Let's use a numerical example to see how the Solow model works and how the economy approaches the steady state. For this example, we assume that the production function is

$$Y = K^{1/2}L^{1/2}.$$

From Chapter 3, you will recognize this as the Cobb–Douglas production function with the capital share parameter α equal to 1/2. To derive the per-worker production function $f(k)$, divide both sides of the production function by the labour force L:

$$\frac{Y}{L} = \frac{K^{1/2}L^{1/2}}{L}.$$

Rearrange to obtain

$$\frac{Y}{L} = \left(\frac{K}{L}\right)^{1/2}.$$

Because $y = Y/L$ and $k = K/L,$ this becomes

$$y = k^{1/2}.$$

This equation can also be written as

$$y = \sqrt{k}.$$

This form of the production function states that output per worker is equal to the square root of the amount of capital per worker.

To complete the example, let's assume that 30 percent of output is saved ($s = 0.3$), that 10 percent of the capital stock depreciates every year ($\delta = 0.1$), and that the economy starts off with 4 units of capital per worker ($k = 4$). Given these numbers, we can now examine what happens to this economy over time.

We begin by looking at the production and allocation of output in the first year, when the economy has 4 units of capital. Here are the steps we follow:

- According to the production function, the 4 units of capital per worker (k) produce 2 units of output per worker.
- Because 30 percent of output is saved and invested and 70 percent is consumed, $i = 0.6$ and $c = 1.4$.
- Because 10 percent of the capital stock depreciates, $\delta k = 0.4$.
- With investment of 0.6 and depreciation of 0.4, the change in the capital stock is $\Delta k = 0.2$.

Thus, the economy begins its second year with 4.2 units of capital per worker. We can do the same calculations for each subsequent year. Table 7-2 shows how the economy progresses year by year. Every year, because investment exceeds depreciation, new capital is added and output grows. Over many years, the economy approaches a steady state with 9 units of capital per worker. In this steady state, investment of 0.9 exactly offsets depreciation of 0.9, so that the capital stock and output are no longer growing.

Following the progress of the economy for many years is one way to find the steady-state capital stock, but there is another way that requires fewer calculations. Recall that

$$\Delta k = sf(k) - \delta k.$$

TABLE 7-2

Approaching the Steady State: A Numerical Example

Assumptions: $y = \sqrt{k}$; $s = 0.3$; $\delta = 0.1$; initial $k = 4.0$

Year	k	y	c	i	δk	Δk
1	4.000	2.000	1.400	0.600	0.400	0.200
2	4.200	2.049	1.435	0.615	0.420	0.195
3	4.395	2.096	1.467	0.629	0.440	0.189
4	4.584	2.141	1.499	0.642	0.458	0.184
5	4.768	2.184	1.529	0.655	0.477	0.178
.						
.						
.						
10	5.602	2.367	1.657	0.710	0.560	0.150
.						
.						
.						
25	7.321	2.706	1.894	0.812	0.732	0.080
.						
.						
.						
100	8.962	2.994	2.096	0.898	0.896	0.002
.						
.						
.						
∞	9.000	3.000	2.100	0.900	0.900	0.000

This equation shows how k evolves over time. Because the steady state is (by definition) the value of k at which $\Delta k = 0$, we know that

$$0 = sf(k^*) - \delta k^*,$$

or, equivalently,

$$\frac{k^*}{f(k^*)} = \frac{s}{\delta}.$$

This equation provides a way of finding the steady-state level of capital per worker, k^*. Substituting in the numbers and production function from our example, we obtain

$$\frac{k^*}{\sqrt{k^*}} = \frac{0.3}{0.1}.$$

Now square both sides of this equation to find

$$k^* = 9.$$

The steady-state capital stock is 9 units per worker. This result confirms the calculation of the steady state in Table 7-2.

The Miracle of Japanese and German Growth

Japan and Germany are two success stories of economic growth. Although today they are economic superpowers, in 1945 the economies of both countries were in shambles. World War II had destroyed much of their capital stocks. In the decades after the war, however, these two countries experienced some of the most rapid growth rates on record. Between 1948 and 1972, output per person grew at 8.2 percent per year in Japan and 5.7 percent per year in Germany, compared to only 4.1 percent per year in Canada.

Are the postwar experiences of Japan and Germany so surprising from the standpoint of the Solow growth model? Consider an economy in steady state. Now suppose that a war destroys some of the capital stock. (That is, suppose the capital stock drops from k^* to k_1 in Figure 7-4.) Not surprisingly, the level of output falls immediately. But if the saving rate—the fraction of output devoted to saving and investment—is unchanged, the economy will then experience a period of high growth. Output grows because, at the lower capital stock, more capital is added by investment than is removed by depreciation. This high growth continues until the economy approaches its former steady state. Hence, although destroying part of the capital stock immediately reduces output, it is followed by higher than normal growth. The "miracle" of rapid growth in Japan and Germany, as it is often described in the business press, is what the Solow model predicts for countries in which war has greatly reduced the capital stock. ■

How Saving Affects Growth

The explanation of Japanese and German growth after World War II is not quite as simple as suggested in the preceding case study. Another relevant fact is that both Japan and Germany save and invest a higher fraction of their output than does the United States—the country to which the performance of others is usually compared. To understand more fully the international differences in economic performance, we must consider the effects of different saving rates.

Consider what happens to an economy when its saving rate increases. Figure 7-5 shows such a change. The economy is assumed to begin in a steady state with saving rate s_1 and capital stock k_1^*. When the saving rate increases from s_1 to s_2, the $sf(k)$ curve shifts upward. At the initial saving rate s_1 and the initial capital stock k_1^*, the amount of investment just offsets the amount of depreciation. Immediately after the saving rate rises, investment is higher, but the capital stock and depreciation are unchanged. Therefore, investment exceeds depreciation. The capital stock will gradually rise until the economy reaches the new steady state k_2^*, which has a higher capital stock and a higher level of output than the old steady state.

FIGURE 7-5

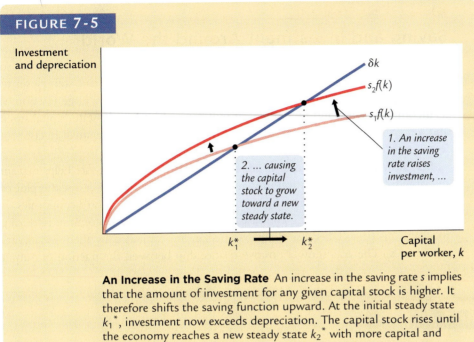

Investment and depreciation

δk

$s_2 f(k)$

$s_1 f(k)$

1. An increase in the saving rate raises investment, ...

2. ... causing the capital stock to grow toward a new steady state.

k_1^* k_2^*

Capital per worker, k

An Increase in the Saving Rate An increase in the saving rate s implies that the amount of investment for any given capital stock is higher. It therefore shifts the saving function upward. At the initial steady state k_1^*, investment now exceeds depreciation. The capital stock rises until the economy reaches a new steady state k_2^* with more capital and output.

The Solow model shows that the saving rate is a key determinant of the steady-state capital stock. *If the saving rate is high, the economy will have a large capital stock and a high level of output in the steady state. If the saving rate is low, the economy will have a small capital stock and a low level of output in the steady state.* This conclusion sheds light on many discussions of fiscal policy. As we saw in Chapter 3, a government budget deficit can reduce national saving and crowd out investment. Now we can see that the long-run consequences of a reduced saving rate are a lower capital stock and lower national income. This is why many economists are critical of persistent budget deficits.

What does the Solow model say about the relationship between saving and economic growth? Higher saving leads to faster growth in the Solow model, but only temporarily. An increase in the rate of saving raises growth until the economy reaches the new steady state. If the economy maintains a high saving rate, it will also maintain a large capital stock and a high level of output, but it will not maintain a high rate of growth forever. Policies that alter the steady-state growth rate of income per person are said to have a *growth effect;* we will see examples of such policies in the next chapter. By contrast, a higher saving rate is said to have a *level effect,* because only the level of income per person—not its growth rate—is influenced by the saving rate in the steady state.

Now that we understand how saving and growth interact, we can more fully explain the impressive economic performance of Germany and Japan after World War II. Not only were their initial capital stocks low because of the war, but their steady-state capital stocks were high because of their high saving rates. Both of these facts help explain the rapid growth of these two countries in the 1950s and 1960s.

CASE STUDY

Saving and Investment Around the World

We started this chapter with an important question: Why are some countries so rich while others are mired in poverty? Our analysis has taken us a step closer to the answer. According to the Solow model, if a nation devotes a large fraction of its income to saving and investment, it will have a high steady-state capital stock and a high level of income. If a nation saves and invests only a small fraction of its income, its steady-state capital and income will be low.

Let's now look at some data to see if this theoretical result in fact helps explain the large international variation in standards of living. Figure 7-6 is a scatterplot of data from 96 countries. (The figure includes most of the world's economies. It excludes major oil-producing countries and countries that were communist during much of this period, because their experiences are explained by their special circumstances.) The data show a positive relationship between the fraction of output

FIGURE 7-6

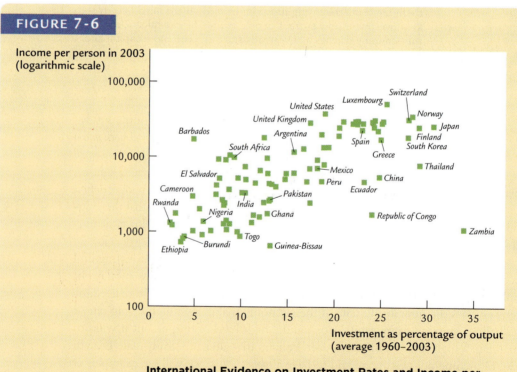

International Evidence on Investment Rates and Income per Person This scatterplot shows the experience of 96 countries, each represented by a single point. The horizontal axis shows the country's rate of investment, and the vertical axis shows the country's income per person. High investment is associated with high income per person, as the Solow model predicts.

Source: Alan Heston, Robert Summers and Bettina Aten, Penn World Table Version 6.1, Center for International Comparisons at the University of Pennsylvania, September 2006.

devoted to investment and the level of income per person. That is, countries with high rates of investment, such as Canada and Japan, usually have high incomes, whereas countries with low rates of investment, such as Eithiopia and Burundi, have low incomes. Thus, the data are consistent with the Solow model's prediction that the investment rate is a key determinant of whether a country is rich or poor.

The strong correlation shown in this figure is an important fact, but it raises as many questions as it resolves. One might naturally ask, why do rates of saving and investment vary so much from country to country? There are many potential answers, such as tax policy, retirement patterns, the development of financial markets, and cultural differences. In addition, political stability may play a role: not surprisingly, rates of saving and investment tend to be low in countries with frequent wars, revolutions, and coups. Saving and investment also tend to be low in countries with poor political institutions, as measured by estimates of official corruption. A final interpretation of the evidence in Figure 7-6 is reverse causation: perhaps high levels of income somehow foster high rates of saving and investment. Unfortunately, there is no consensus among economists about which of the many possible explanations is most important.

The association between investment rates and income per person is strong, and it is an important clue to why some countries are rich and others poor, but it is not the whole story. The correlation between these two variables is far from perfect. The United States and Peru, for instance, have had similar investment rates, but income per person is more than eight times higher in the United States. There must be other determinants of living standards beyond saving and investment. Later in this chapter and in the next one, we return to the international differences in income per person to see what other variables enter the picture. ■

7-2 The Golden Rule Level of Capital

So far, we have used the Solow model to examine how an economy's rate of saving and investment determines its steady-state levels of capital and income. This analysis might lead you to think that higher saving is always a good thing, because it always leads to greater income. Yet suppose a nation had a saving rate of 100 percent. That would lead to the largest possible capital stock and the largest possible income. But if all of this income is saved and none is ever consumed, what good is it?

This section uses the Solow model to discuss the optimal amount of capital accumulation from the standpoint of economic well-being. In the next chapter, we discuss how government policies influence a nation's saving rate. But first, in this section, we present the theory behind these policy decisions.

Comparing Steady States

To keep our analysis simple, let's assume that a policymaker can set the economy's saving rate at any level. By setting the saving rate, the policymaker determines the economy's steady state. What steady state should the policymaker choose?

When choosing a steady state, the policymaker's goal is to maximize the well-being of the individuals who make up the society. Individuals themselves do not care about the amount of capital in the economy, or even the amount of output. They care about the amount of goods and services they can consume. Thus, a benevolent policymaker would want to choose the steady state with the highest level of consumption. The steady-state value of k that maximizes consumption is called the **Golden Rule level of capital** and is k^*_{gold}.[2]

How can we tell whether an economy is at the Golden Rule level? To answer this question, we must first determine steady-state consumption per worker. Then we can see which steady state provides the most consumption.

To find steady-state consumption per worker, we begin with the national accounts identity

$$y = c + i$$

and rearrange it as

$$c = y - i.$$

Consumption is output minus investment. Because we want to find steady-state consumption, we substitute steady-state values for output and investment. Steady-state output per worker is $f(k^*)$, where k^* is the steady-state capital stock per worker. Furthermore, because the capital stock is not changing in the steady state, investment is equal to depreciation δk^*. Substituting $f(k^*)$ for y and δk^* for i, we can write steady-state consumption per worker as

$$c^* = f(k^*) - \delta k^*.$$

According to this equation, steady-state consumption is what's left of steady-state output after paying for steady-state depreciation. This equation shows that an increase in steady-state capital has two opposing effects on steady-state consumption. On the one hand, more capital means more output. On the other hand, more capital also means that more output must be used to replace capital that is wearing out.

Figure 7-7 graphs steady-state output and steady-state depreciation as a function of the steady-state capital stock. Steady-state consumption is the gap between output and depreciation. This figure shows that there is one level of the capital stock—the Golden Rule level k^*_{gold}—that maximizes consumption.

When comparing steady states, we must keep in mind that higher levels of capital affect both output and depreciation. If the capital stock is below the Golden Rule level, an increase in the capital stock raises output more than depreciation, so that consumption rises. In this case, the production function is steeper than the δk^* line, so the gap between these two curves—which equals consumption—grows as k^* rises. By contrast, if the capital stock is above the Golden Rule level, an increase in the capital stock reduces consumption, since

[2] Edmund Phelps, "The Golden Rule of Accumulation: A Fable for Growthmen," *American Economic Review* 51 (September 1961): 638–643.

FIGURE 7-7

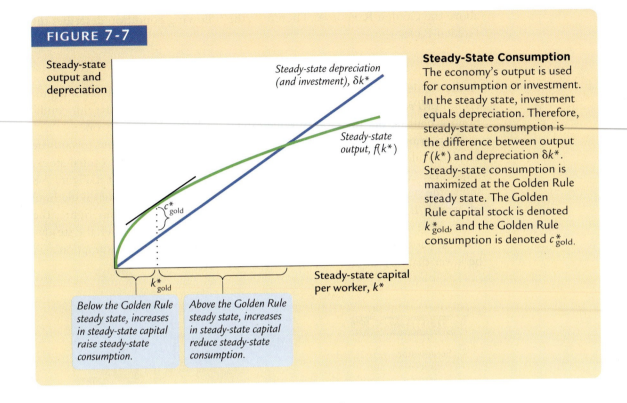

Steady-state output and depreciation

Steady-state depreciation (and investment), δk^*

Steady-state output, $f(k^*)$

c^*_{gold}

k^*_{gold}

Steady-state capital per worker, k^*

Below the Golden Rule steady state, increases in steady-state capital raise steady-state consumption.

Above the Golden Rule steady state, increases in steady-state capital reduce steady-state consumption.

Steady-State Consumption The economy's output is used for consumption or investment. In the steady state, investment equals depreciation. Therefore, steady-state consumption is the difference between output $f(k^*)$ and depreciation δk^*. Steady-state consumption is maximized at the Golden Rule steady state. The Golden Rule capital stock is denoted k^*_{gold}, and the Golden Rule consumption is denoted c^*_{gold}.

the increase in output is smaller than the increase in depreciation. In this case, the production function is flatter than the δk^* line, so the gap between the curves—consumption—shrinks as k^* rises. At the Golden Rule level of capital, the production function and the δk^* line have the same slope, and consumption is at its greatest level.

We can now derive a simple condition that characterizes the Golden Rule level of capital. Recall that the slope of the production function is the marginal product of capital MPK. The slope of the δk^* line is δ. Because these two slopes are equal at k^*_{gold}, the Golden Rule is described by the equation

$$MPK = \delta.$$

At the Golden Rule level of capital, the marginal product of capital equals the depreciation rate.

To make the point somewhat differently, suppose that the economy starts at some steady-state capital stock k^* and that the policymaker is considering increasing the capital stock to $k^* + 1$. The amount of extra output from this increase in capital would be $f(k^* + 1) - f(k^*)$, which is the marginal product of capital MPK. The amount of extra depreciation from having 1 more unit of capital is the depreciation rate δ. Thus, the net effect of this extra unit of capital on consumption is then $MPK - \delta$. If $MPK - \delta > 0$, then increases in capital increase consumption, so k^* must be below the Golden Rule level. If $MPK - \delta < 0$, then increases in capital decrease consumption, so k^* must be above the Golden Rule level. Therefore, the following condition describes the Golden Rule:

$$MPK - \delta = 0.$$

At the Golden Rule level of capital, the marginal product of capital net of depreciation ($MPK - \delta$) equals zero. As we will see, a policymaker can use this condition for figuring out the Golden Rule capital stock for any given economy.[3]

Keep in mind that the economy does not automatically gravitate toward the Golden Rule steady state. If we want any particular steady-state capital stock, such as the Golden Rule, we need a particular saving rate to support it. Figure 7-8 shows the steady state if the saving rate is set to produce the Golden Rule level of capital. If the saving rate is higher than the one used in this figure, the steady-state capital stock will be too high. If the saving rate is lower, the steady-state capital stock will be too low. In either case, steady-state consumption will be lower than it is at the Golden Rule steady state.

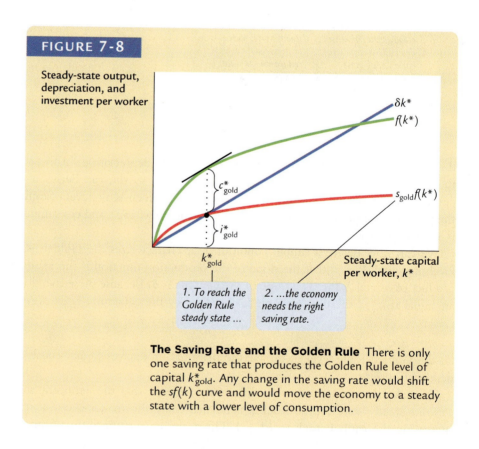

FIGURE 7-8

Steady-state output, depreciation, and investment per worker

δk^*

$f(k^*)$

$s_{gold}f(k^*)$

$\left. \right\} c^*_{gold}$

$\left. \right\} i^*_{gold}$

k^*_{gold}

Steady-state capital per worker, k^*

1. To reach the Golden Rule steady state ...

2. ...the economy needs the right saving rate.

The Saving Rate and the Golden Rule There is only one saving rate that produces the Golden Rule level of capital k^*_{gold}. Any change in the saving rate would shift the $sf(k)$ curve and would move the economy to a steady state with a lower level of consumption.

---

[3] *Mathematical note:* Another way to derive the condition for the Golden Rule uses a bit of calculus. Recall that $c^* = f(k^*) - \delta k^*$. To find the k^* that maximizes c^*, differentiate to find $dc^*/dk^* = f'(k^*) - \delta$ and set this derivative equal to zero. Noting that $f'(k^*)$ is the marginal product of capital, we obtain the Golden Rule condition in the text.

Finding the Golden Rule Steady State: A Numerical Example

Consider the decision of a policymaker choosing a steady state in the following economy. The production function is the same as in our earlier example:

$$y = \sqrt{k}.$$

Output per worker is the square root of capital per worker. Depreciation δ is again 10 percent of capital. This time, the policymaker chooses the saving rate s and thus the economy's steady state.

To see the outcomes available to the policymaker, recall that the following equation holds in the steady state:

$$\frac{k^*}{f(k^*)} = \frac{s}{\delta}.$$

In this economy, this equation becomes

$$\frac{k^*}{\sqrt{k^*}} = \frac{s}{0.1}.$$

Squaring both sides of this equation yields a solution for the steady-state capital stock. We find

$$k^* = 100s^2.$$

Using this result, we can compute the steady-state capital stock for any saving rate.

Table 7-3 presents calculations showing the steady states that result from various saving rates in this economy. We see that higher saving leads to a higher capital stock, which in turn leads to higher output and higher depreciation. Steady-state consumption, the difference between output and depreciation, first rises with higher saving rates and then declines. Consumption is highest when the saving rate is 0.5. Hence, a saving rate of 0.5 produces the Golden Rule steady state.

Recall that another way to identify the Golden Rule steady state is to find the capital stock at which the net marginal product of capital ($MPK - \delta$) equals zero. For this production function, the marginal product is[4]

$$MPK = \frac{1}{2\sqrt{k}}.$$

Using this formula, the last two columns of Table 7-3 present the values of MPK and $MPK - \delta$ in the different steady states. Note that the net marginal product of capital is exactly zero when the saving rate is at its Golden Rule value of 0.5. Because of diminishing marginal product, the net marginal product of capital is

---

[4] *Mathematical note:* To derive this formula, note that the marginal product of capital is the derivative of the production function with respect to k.

TABLE 7-3

Finding the Golden Rule Steady State: A Numerical Example

Assumptions: $y = \sqrt{k}$; $\delta = 0.1$

s	k^*	y^*	δk^*	c^*	MPK	MPK $- \delta$
0.0	0.0	0.0	0.0	0.0	•	•
0.1	1.0	1.0	0.1	0.9	0.500	0.400
0.2	4.0	2.0	0.4	1.6	0.250	0.150
0.3	9.0	3.0	0.9	2.1	0.167	0.067
0.4	16.0	4.0	1.6	2.4	0.125	0.025
0.5	**25.0**	**5.0**	**2.5**	**2.5**	**0.100**	**0.000**
0.6	36.0	6.0	3.6	2.4	0.083	−0.017
0.7	49.0	7.0	4.9	2.1	0.071	−0.029
0.8	64.0	8.0	6.4	1.6	0.062	−0.038
0.9	81.0	9.0	8.1	0.9	0.056	−0.044
1.0	100.0	10.0	10.0	0.0	0.050	−0.050

---

greater than zero whenever the economy saves less than this amount, and it is less than zero whenever the economy saves more.

This numerical example confirms that the two ways of finding the Golden Rule steady state—looking at steady-state consumption or looking at the marginal product of capital—give the same answer. If we want to know whether an actual economy is currently at, above, or below its Golden Rule capital stock, the second method is usually more convenient, because it is relatively straightforward to estimate the marginal product of capital. By contrast, evaluating an economy with the first method requires estimates of steady-state consumption at many different saving rates; such information is hard to obtain. Thus, when we apply this kind of analysis to the Canadian economy in the next chapter, we will evaluate Canadian saving by examining the marginal product of capital. Before engaging in that policy analysis, however, we need to proceed further in our development and understanding of the Solow model.

The Transition to the Golden Rule Steady State

Let's now make our policymaker's problem more realistic. So far, we have been assuming that the policymaker can simply choose the economy's steady state and jump there immediately. In this case, the policymaker would choose the steady state with highest consumption—the Golden Rule steady state. But now suppose that the economy has reached a steady state other than the Golden Rule. What happens to consumption, investment, and capital when the economy makes the transition between steady states? Might the impact of the transition deter the policymaker from trying to achieve the Golden Rule?

We must consider two cases: the economy might begin with more capital than in the Golden Rule steady state, or with less. It turns out that the two cases offer very different problems for policymakers. (As we will see in the next chapter, the second case—too little capital—describes most actual economies, including that of Canada.)

Starting with Too Much Capital We first consider the case in which the economy begins at a steady state with more capital than it would have in the Golden Rule steady state. In this case, the policymaker should pursue policies aimed at reducing the rate of saving in order to reduce the capital stock. Suppose that these policies succeed and that at some point—call it time t_0—the saving rate falls to the level that will eventually lead to the Golden Rule steady state.

Figure 7-9 shows what happens to output, consumption, and investment when the saving rate falls. The reduction in the saving rate causes an immediate increase in consumption and a decrease in investment. Because investment and depreciation were equal in the initial steady state, investment will now be less than depreciation, which means the economy is no longer in a steady state. Gradually, the capital stock falls, leading to reductions in output, consumption, and investment. These variables continue to fall until the economy reaches the new steady state. Because we are assuming that the new steady state is the Golden Rule steady state, consumption must be higher than it was before the change in the saving rate, even though output and investment are lower.

Note that, compared to the old steady state, consumption is higher not just in the new steady state but also along the entire path to it. When the capital stock exceeds the Golden Rule level, reducing saving is clearly a good policy, for it increases consumption at every point in time.

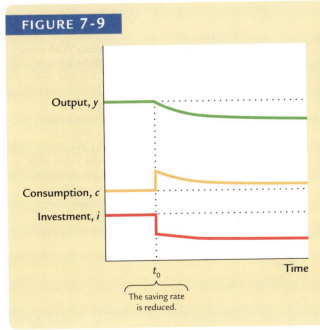

FIGURE 7-9

Output, y

Consumption, c

Investment, i

t_0

The saving rate
is reduced.

Time

Reducing Saving When Starting With More Capital Than in the Golden Rule Steady State This figure shows what happens over time to output, consumption, and investment when the economy begins with more capital than the Golden Rule level and the saving rate is reduced. The reduction in the saving rate (at time t_0) causes an immediate increase in consumption and an equal decrease in investment. Over time, as the capital stock falls, output, consumption, and investment fall together. Because the economy began with too much capital, the new steady state has a higher level of consumption than the initial steady state.

Starting with Too Little Capital When the economy begins with less capital than in the Golden Rule steady state, the policymaker must raise the saving rate to reach the Golden Rule. Figure 7-10 shows what happens. The increase in the saving rate at time t_0 causes an immediate fall in consumption and a rise in investment. Over time, higher investment causes the capital stock to rise. As capital accumulates, output, consumption, and investment gradually increase, eventually approaching the new steady-state levels. Because the initial steady state was below the Golden Rule, the increase in saving eventually leads to a higher level of consumption than that which prevailed initially.

Does the increase in saving that leads to the Golden Rule steady state raise economic welfare? Eventually it does, because the new steady-state level of consumption is higher than the initial level. But achieving that new steady state requires an initial period of reduced consumption. Note the contrast to the case in which the economy begins above the Golden Rule. *When the economy begins above the Golden Rule, reaching the Golden Rule produces higher consumption at all points in time. When the economy begins below the Golden Rule, reaching the Golden Rule requires initially reducing consumption to increase consumption in the future.*

When deciding whether to try to reach the Golden Rule steady state, policymakers have to take into account that current consumers and future consumers are not always the same people. Reaching the Golden Rule achieves the highest steady-state level of consumption and thus benefits future generations. But when the economy is initially below the Golden Rule, reaching the Golden Rule requires raising investment and thus lowering the consumption of current generations. Thus, when choosing whether to increase capital accumulation, the policymaker faces a tradeoff among the welfare of different

---

FIGURE 7-10

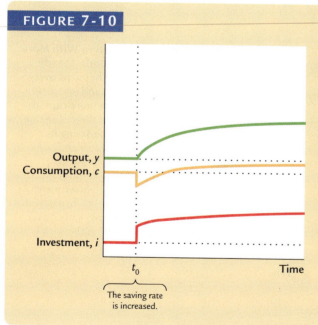

Increasing Saving When Starting With Less Capital Than in the Golden Rule Steady State This figure shows what happens over time to output, consumption, and investment when the economy begins with less capital than the Golden Rule, and the saving rate is increased. The increase in the saving rate (at time t_0) causes an immediate drop in consumption and an equal jump in investment. Over time, as the capital stock grows, output, consumption, and investment increase together. Because the economy began with less capital than the Golden Rule, the new steady state has a higher level of consumption than the initial steady state.

generations. A policymaker who cares more about current generations than about future generations may decide not to pursue policies to reach the Golden Rule steady state. By contrast, a policymaker who cares about all generations equally will choose to reach the Golden Rule. Even though current generations will consume less, an infinite number of future generations will benefit by moving to the Golden Rule.

Thus, optimal capital accumulation depends crucially on how we weigh the interests of current and future generations. The biblical Golden Rule tells us, "do unto others as you would have them do unto you." If we heed this advice, we give all generations equal weight. In this case, it is optimal to reach the Golden Rule level of capital—which is why it is called the "Golden Rule."

7-3 Population Growth

The basic Solow model shows that capital accumulation, by itself, cannot explain sustained economic growth: high rates of saving lead to high growth temporarily, but the economy eventually approaches a steady state in which capital and output are constant. To explain the sustained economic growth that we observe in most parts of the world, we must expand the Solow model to incorporate the other two sources of economic growth—population growth and technological progress. In this section we add population growth to the model.

Instead of assuming that the population is fixed, as we did in Sections 7-1 and 7-2, we now suppose that the population and the labour force grow at a constant rate n. For example, in Canada during the last 80 years, the population grew about 1.6 percent per year, so $n = 0.016$. This means that if 16 million people are working one year, then 16.26 million (1.016×16) are working the next year, and 16.5 million (1.016×16.26) the year after that, and so on.

The Steady State with Population Growth

How does population growth affect the steady state? To answer this question, we must discuss how population growth, along with investment and depreciation, influences the accumulation of capital per worker. As we noted before, investment raises the capital stock, and depreciation reduces it. But now there is a third force acting to change the amount of capital per worker: the growth in the number of workers causes capital per worker to fall.

We continue to let lowercase letters stand for quantities per worker. Thus, $k = K/L$ is capital per worker, and $y = Y/L$ is output per worker. Keep in mind, however, that the number of workers is growing over time.

The change in the capital stock per worker is

$$\Delta k = i - (\delta + n)k.$$

This equation shows how new investment, depreciation, and population growth influence the per-worker capital stock. New investment increases k, whereas depreciation and population growth decrease k. We have seen this equation earlier in this chapter for the special case of a constant population ($n = 0$).

We can think of the term $(\delta + n)k$ as defining *break-even investment*—the amount of investment necessary to keep the capital stock per worker constant. Break-even investment includes the depreciation of existing capital, which equals δk. It also includes the amount of investment necessary to provide new workers with capital. The amount of investment necessary for this purpose is nk, because there are n new workers for each existing worker, and because k is the amount of capital for each worker. The equation shows that population growth reduces the accumulation of capital per worker much the way depreciation does. Depreciation reduces k by wearing out the capital stock, whereas population growth reduces k by spreading the capital stock more thinly among a larger population of workers.[5]

Our analysis with population growth now proceeds much as it did previously. First, we substitute $sf(k)$ for i. The equation can then be written as

$$\Delta k = sf(k) - (\delta + n)k.$$

To see what determines the steady-state level of capital per worker, we use Figure 7-11, which extends the analysis of Figure 4-4 to include the effects of population growth. An economy is in a steady state if capital per worker k is

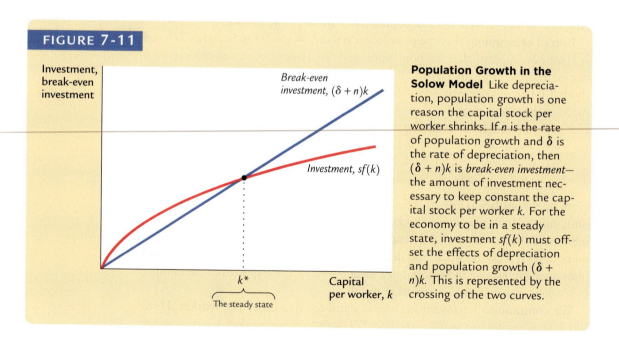

FIGURE 7-11

Break-even investment, $(\delta + n)k$

Investment, $sf(k)$

Investment, break-even investment

k^*

The steady state

Capital per worker, k

Population Growth in the Solow Model Like depreciation, population growth is one reason the capital stock per worker shrinks. If n is the rate of population growth and δ is the rate of depreciation, then $(\delta + n)k$ is *break-even investment*—the amount of investment necessary to keep constant the capital stock per worker k. For the economy to be in a steady state, investment $sf(k)$ must offset the effects of depreciation and population growth $(\delta + n)k$. This is represented by the crossing of the two curves.

---

[5] *Mathematical note:* Formally deriving the equation for the change in k requires a bit of calculus. Note that the change in k per unit of time is $dk/dt = d(K/L)/dt$. After applying the chain rule, we can write this as $dk/dt = (1/L)(dK/dt) - (K/L^2)(dL/dt)$. Now use the following facts to substitute in this equation: $dK/dt = I - \delta K$ and $(dL/dt)/L = n$. After a bit of manipulation, this produces the equation in the text.

unchanging. As before, we designate the steady-state value of k as k^*. If k is less than k^*, investment is greater than break-even investment, so k rises. If k is greater than k^*, investment is less than break-even investment, so k falls.

In the steady state, the positive effect of investment on the capital stock per worker just balances the negative effects of depreciation and population growth. That is, at k^*, $\Delta k = 0$ and $i^* = \delta k^* + nk^*$. Once the economy is in the steady state, investment has two purposes. Some of it (δk^*) replaces the depreciated capital, and the rest (nk^*) provides the new workers with the steady-state amount of capital.

The Effects of Population Growth

Population growth alters the basic Solow model in three ways. First, it brings us closer to explaining sustained economic growth. In the steady state with population growth, capital per worker and output per worker are constant. Because the number of workers is growing at rate n, however, *total* capital and *total* output must also be growing at rate n. Hence, while population growth cannot explain sustained growth in the standard of living (because output per worker is constant in the steady state), it can help explain sustained growth in total output.

Second, population growth gives us another explanation for why some countries are rich and others are poor. Consider the effects of an increase in population growth. Figure 7-12 shows that an increase in the rate of population

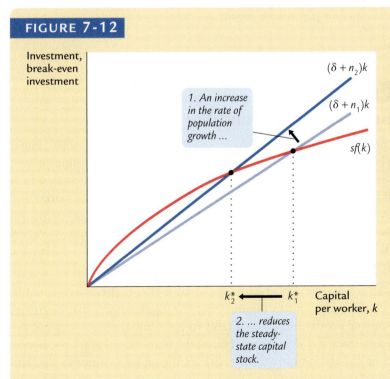

FIGURE 7-12

Investment, break-even investment

$(\delta + n_2)k$

1. An increase in the rate of population growth ...

$(\delta + n_1)k$

$sf(k)$

k_2^* ← k_1^* Capital per worker, k

2. ... reduces the steady-state capital stock.

The Impact of Population Growth An increase in the rate of population growth from n_1 to n_2 shifts the line representing population growth and depreciation upward. The new steady state k_2^* has a lower level of capital per worker than the initial steady state k_1^*. Thus, the Solow model predicts that economies with higher rates of population growth will have lower levels of capital per worker and therefore lower incomes.

growth from n_1 to n_2 reduces the steady-state level of capital per worker from k_1^* to k_2^*. Because k^* is lower, and because $y^* = f(k^*)$, the level of output per worker y^* is also lower. Thus, the Solow model predicts that countries with higher population growth will have lower levels of GDP per person. Notice that a change in the population growth rate, like a change in the saving rate, has a level effect on income per person, but it does not affect the steady-state growth rate of income per person.

Finally, population growth affects our criterion for determining the Golden Rule (consumption-maximizing) level of capital. To see how this criterion changes, note that consumption per worker is

$$c = y - i.$$

Because steady-state output is $f(k^*)$ and steady-state investment is $(\delta + n)k^*$, we can express steady-state consumption as

$$c^* = f(k^*) - (\delta + n)k^*.$$

Using an argument largely the same as before, we conclude that the level of k^* that maximizes consumption is the one at which

$$MPK = \delta + n,$$

or equivalently,

$$MPK - \delta = n.$$

In the Golden Rule steady state, the marginal product of capital net of depreciation equals the rate of population growth.

CASE STUDY

Population Growth Around the World

Let's return now to the question of why standards of living vary so much around the world. The analysis we have just completed suggests that population growth may be one of the answers. According to the Solow model, a nation with a high rate of population growth will have a low steady-state capital stock per worker and thus also a low level of income per worker. In other words, high population growth tends to impoverish a country because it is hard to maintain a high level of capital per worker when the number of workers is growing quickly. To see whether the evidence supports this conclusion, we again look at cross-country data.

Figure 7-13 is a scatterplot of data for the same 96 countries examined in the previous case study (and in Figure 7-6). The figure shows that countries with high rates of population growth tend to have low levels of income per person. The international evidence is consistent with our model's prediction that the rate of population growth is one determinant of a country's standard of living.

FIGURE 7-13

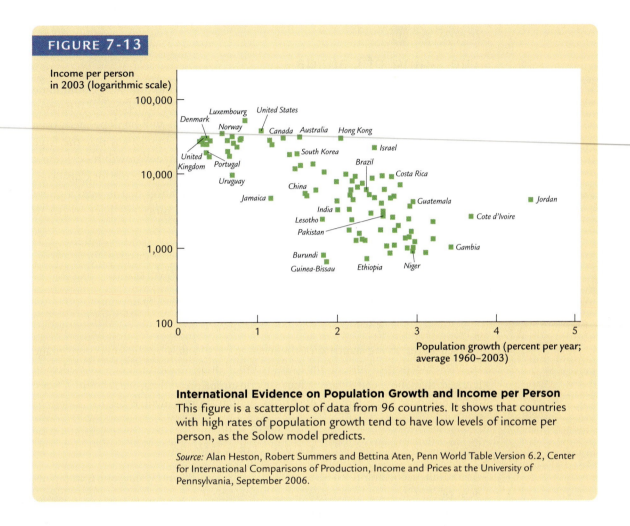

International Evidence on Population Growth and Income per Person
This figure is a scatterplot of data from 96 countries. It shows that countries
with high rates of population growth tend to have low levels of income per
person, as the Solow model predicts.

Source: Alan Heston, Robert Summers and Bettina Aten, Penn World Table Version 6.2, Center
for International Comparisons of Production, Income and Prices at the University of
Pennsylvania, September 2006.

This conclusion is not lost on policymakers. Those trying to pull the world's
poorest nations out of poverty, such as the advisers sent to developing nations by
the World Bank, often advocate reducing fertility by increasing education about
birth-control methods and expanding women's job opportunities. Toward the
same end, China has followed the totalitarian policy of allowing only one child
per couple. These policies to reduce population growth should, if the Solow
model is right, raise income per person in the long run.

In interpreting the cross-country data, however, it is important to keep in mind
that correlation does not imply causation. The data show that low population
growth is typically associated with high levels of income per person, and the Solow
model offers one possible explanation for this fact, but other explanations are also
possible. It is conceivable that high income encourages low population growth,
perhaps because birth-control techniques are more readily available in richer countries. The international data can help us evaluate a theory of growth, such as the
Solow model, because they show us whether the theory's predictions are borne out
in the world. But often more than one theory can explain the same facts. ■

CASE STUDY

The Aging of Canada

Over the first 35 years of the present century, the ratio of the Canadian labour force to the Canadian population is expected to fall from 0.525 to 0.475—a 10 percent reduction. As a result, a higher proportion of Canadians will be dependent on a smaller group of workers. The main reason for this development is that the large baby-boom generation is growing older. We can use the Solow growth model to get some idea about how much stress this demographic change will cause for Canadians.

Let β and LS stand for the proportion of the population that is working and the living standard of the average citizen, respectively. Since we have used c to denote consumption per worker, then

$$LS = \frac{\text{Total Consumption}}{\text{Population}} = \frac{\text{Consumption per Worker}}{\text{Population per Worker}} = c\beta.$$

If the level of c is independent of β, this equation implies that

$$\Delta LS/LS = \Delta \beta/\beta.$$

That is, the living standard of the average person falls by the same percentage as does the proportion of the population that is working.[6] We have already learned that the steady-state values of consumption and capital, c^* and k^*, are determined by the following equations (which do not involve β):

$$sf(k^*) = (\delta + n)k^*$$
$$c^* = f(k^*) - (\delta + n)k^*$$

As a result, according to the Solow model, the steady-state value of c *is* independent of β.

As noted, Canada's β will fall by 10 percent over the next 30 years. According to the Solow growth model, this development will lower the average living standard to a level that is 10 percent below what it would otherwise have reached. It turns out that the estimated drop in living standards is smaller when the Solow model is extended to allow for forward-looking behaviour in the savings function (that is, when the model is enriched by including the theory of consumption and saving that we discuss in Chapter 17). This is because forward-looking households save more in anticipation of the coming labour shortage, and the resulting increase in wealth gives households the means to sustain higher levels of consumption when the old-age dependency is high. Nevertheless, this calculation, based on the fundamental version of the Solow model, can make sense of why many Canadians are becoming increasingly concerned about the aging population that is part of the postwar baby boom generation getting older. ■

---

[6] To help in understanding this relationship, see the primer on products and percentage changes on page 29. To read more about the implications of our aging population for average living standards, see W. Scarth, "Some Macroeconomic Effects of Population Aging on Productivity Growth and Living Standards," in Abbott, Beach, Boadway and MacKinnon, eds., *Retirement Policy Issues in Canada*, (Kingston:McGill-Queen's University Press) 2009.

Alternative Perspectives on Population Growth

The Solow growth model highlights the interaction between population growth and capital accumulation. In this model, high population growth reduces output per worker because rapid growth in the number of workers forces the capital stock to be spread more thinly; so in the steady state each worker is equipped with less capital. The model omits some other potential effects of population growth. Here we consider two—one emphasizing the interaction of population with natural resources, the other emphasizing the interaction of population with technology.

The Malthusian Model In his book *An Essay on the Principle of Population as It Affects the Future Improvement of Society,* the early economist Thomas Robert Malthus (1766–1834) offered what may be history's most chilling forecast. Malthus argued that an ever increasing population would continually strain society's ability to provide for itself. Humankind, he predicted, would forever live in poverty.

Malthus began by noting that "food is necessary to the existence of man" and that "the passion between the sexes is necessary and will remain nearly in its present state." He concluded that "the power of population is infinitely greater than the power in the earth to produce subsistence for man." According to Malthus, the only check on population growth was "misery and vice." Attempts by charities or governments to alleviate poverty are counterproductive, he argued, because they merely allow the poor to have more children, placing even greater strains on society's productive capabilities.

Although the Malthusian model may have described the world when Malthus lived, its prediction that humankind would remain in poverty forever has proven very wrong. The world population has increased about sixfold over the past two centuries, but average living standards are much higher. Because of economic growth, chronic hunger and malnutrition are less common now than they were in Malthus's day. Famines occur from time to time, but they are more often the result of unequal income distribution or political instability than the inadequate production of food.

Malthus failed to see that the growth in humankind's ingenuity would more than offset the effects of a larger population. Pesticides, fertilizers, mechanized farm equipment, new crop varieties, and other technological advances that Malthus never imagined have allowed each farmer to feed ever greater numbers of people. Even with more mouths to feed, fewer farmers are necessary because each farm is so productive. Today, fewer than 2 percent of North Americans work on farms, producing enough food to feed the nation and some excess to export as well.

In addition, although the "passion between the sexes" is just as strong now as it was in Malthus's day, the link between passion and population growth that Malthus assumed has been broken by modern birth control. Many advanced nations, such as those in Western Europe, are now experiencing fertility below replacement rates. Over the next century, shrinking populations may be more likely than rapidly expanding ones. There is now little reason to think that an ever expanding population will overwhelm food production and doom mankind to poverty.[7]

There has been a revival of Malthus-like reasoning in recent decades. In the present version, the concern is not that higher population will pull living standards back down to subsistence levels. Instead, it is the running out of nonrenewable resources that is cited as something that will lead to the same outcome, as well as to a vastly altered planet, with global warming and destroyed ecosystems. As in Malthus' time, the pessimists in the current debate put little faith in the self-correcting mechanisms of the market system. Both optimists and pessimists are aware that the increased scarcity of key raw materials and the increased concern for the environment will create profit opportunities for firms to address these concerns. Optimists expect that technological progress will rescue humankind from our sustainability concerns, just as it did when the agricultural revolution answered Malthus's worries. Further, optimists stress that economic growth gives society the ability to meet these challenges. Pessimists are not nearly so sure; they see the environmental costs of economic growth as much bigger than the benefits. Unfortunately, further discussion of this central issue is beyond the scope of this book.

The Kremerian Model While Malthus saw population growth as a threat to rising living standards, economist Michael Kremer has suggested that world population growth is a key driver of advancing economic prosperity. If there are more people, Kremer argues, then there are more scientists, inventors, and engineers to contribute to innovation and technological progress.

As evidence for this hypothesis, Kremer begins by noting that, over the broad span of human history, world growth rates have increased together with world population. For example, world growth was more rapid when the world population was 1 billion (which occurred around the year 1800) than it was when the population was only 100 million (around 500 B.C.). This fact is consistent with the hypothesis that having more people induces more technological progress.

Kremer's second, more compelling piece of evidence comes from comparing regions of the world. The melting of the polar ice caps at the end of the ice age around 10,000 B.C. flooded the land bridges and separated the world into several distinct regions that could not communicate with one another for thousands of years. If technological progress is more rapid when there are more people to discover things, then the more populous regions should have experienced more rapid growth.

And indeed they did. The most successful region of the world in 1500 (when Columbus reestablished technological contact) included the Old World civilizations of the large Eurasia-Africa region. Next in technological development were

[7] For modern analyses of the Malthusian model, see Oded Galor and David N. Weil, "Population, Technology, and Growth: From Malthusian Stagnation to the Demographic Transition and Beyond," *American Economic Review* 90 (September 2000): 806–828, and Gary D. Hansen and Edward C. Prescott, "Malthus to Solow," *American Economic Review* 92 (September 2002): 1205–1217.

the Aztec and Mayan civilizations in the Americas, followed by the hunter-gatherers of Australia, and then the primitive people of Tasmania, who lacked even fire making and most stone and bone tools.

The least populous isolated region was Flinders Island, a tiny island between Tasmania and Australia. With few people to contribute new innovations, Flinders Island had the least technological advance and in fact seemed to regress. Around 3000 B.C., human society on Flinders Island died out completely.

Kremer concludes from this evidence that a large population is a prerequisite for technological advance.[8]

7-4 Conclusion

This chapter has started the process of building the Solow growth model. The model as developed so far shows how saving and population growth determine the economy's steady-state capital stock and its steady-state level of income per person. As we have seen, it sheds light on many features of actual growth experiences—why Germany and Japan grew so rapidly after being devastated by World War II, why countries that save and invest a high fraction of their output have higher material living standards than countries that save and invest a smaller fraction, and why countries with high rates of population growth are poorer than countries with low rates of population growth.

What the model cannot do, however, is explain the persistent growth in living standards we observe in most countries. In the model we have developed so far, output per worker stops growing when the economy reaches its steady state. To explain persistent growth, we need to introduce technological progress into the model. That is our first job in the next chapter.

Summary

1. The Solow growth model shows that in the long run, an economy's rate of saving determines the size of its capital stock and thus its level of production. The higher the rate of saving, the higher the stock of capital and the higher the level of output.

2. In the Solow model, an increase in the rate of saving has a level effect on income per person: it causes a period of rapid growth, but eventually that growth slows as the new steady state is reached. Thus, although a high

---

[8] Michael Kremer, "Population Growth and Technological Change: One Million B.C. to 1990," *Quarterly Journal of Economics* 108 (August 1993): 681–716.

saving rate yields a high steady-state level of output, saving by itself cannot generate persistent economic growth.

3. The level of capital that maximizes steady-state consumption is called the Golden Rule level. If an economy has more capital than in the Golden Rule steady state, then reducing saving will increase consumption at all points in time. By contrast, if the economy has less capital than in the Golden Rule steady state, then reaching the Golden Rule requires increased investment and thus lower consumption for current generations.

4. The Solow model shows that an economy's rate of population growth is another long-run determinant of the standard of living. According to the Solow model, the higher the rate of population growth, the lower the steady-state levels of capital per worker and output per worker. Other theories highlight other effects of population growth. Malthus suggested that population growth will strain the natural resources necessary to produce food; Kremer suggested that a large population may promote technological progress.

KEY CONCEPTS

Solow growth model   Steady state   Golden Rule level of capital

QUESTIONS FOR REVIEW

1. In the Solow model, how does the saving rate affect the steady-state level of income? How does it affect the steady-state rate of growth?

2. Why might an economic policymaker choose the Golden Rule level of capital?

3. Might a policymaker choose a steady state with more capital than in the Golden Rule steady state? With less capital than in the Golden Rule steady state? Explain your answers.

4. In the Solow model, how does the rate of population growth affect the steady-state level of income? How does it affect the steady-state rate of growth?

PROBLEMS AND APPLICATIONS

1. Country A and country B both have the production function

$$Y = F(K, L) = K^{1/2}L^{1/2}.$$

a. Does this production function have constant returns to scale? Explain.

b. What is the per-worker production function, $y = f(k)$?

c. Assume that neither country experiences population growth or technological progress and that 5 percent of capital depreciates each year. Assume further that country A saves 10 percent of output each year and country B saves 20 percent of output each year. Using your answer from part (b) and the steady-state condition that investment equals depreciation, find the steady-state level of capital per worker for each country. Then find the steady-state levels of income per worker and consumption per worker.

d. Suppose that both countries start off with a capital stock per worker of 2. What are the levels of income per worker and consumption per worker? Remembering that the change in the capital stock is investment less depreciation, use a calculator or a computer spreadsheet to show how the capital stock per worker will evolve over time in both countries. For each year, calculate income per worker and consumption per worker. How many years will it be before the consumption in country B is higher than the consumption in country A?

2. In the discussion of German and Japanese postwar growth, the text describes what happens when part of the capital stock is destroyed in a war. By contrast, suppose that a war does not directly affect the capital stock, but that casualties reduce the labour force. Assume that the economy was in a steady state before the war, the savings rate is unchanged, and the rate of population growth after the war returns to normal.

a. What is the immediate impact of the war on total output and on output per person?

b. What happens subsequently to output per worker in the postwar economy? Is the growth rate of output per worker after the war smaller or greater than normal?

3. Consider an economy described by the production function: $Y = F(K, L) = K^{0.3}L^{0.7}$.

a. What is the per-worker production function?

b. Assuming no population growth or technological progress, find the steady-state capital stock per worker, output per worker, and consumption per worker as a function of the saving rate and the depreciation rate.

c. Assume that the depreciation rate is 10 percent per year. Make a table showing steady-state capital per worker, output per worker, and consumption per worker for saving rates of 0 percent, 10 percent, 20 percent, 30 percent, and so on. (You will need a calculator with an exponent key for this.) What saving rate maximizes output per worker? What saving rate maximizes consumption per worker?

d. (Harder) Use calculus to find the marginal product of capital. Add to your table the marginal product of capital net of depreciation for each of the saving rates. What does your table show?

4. "Devoting a larger share of national output to investment would help restore rapid productivity growth and rising living standards." Do you agree with this claim? Explain.

5. One view of the consumption function is that workers have high propensities to consume and capitalists have low propensities to consume. To explore the implications of this view, suppose that an economy consumes all wage income and saves all capital income. Show that if the factors of production earn their marginal product, this economy reaches the Golden Rule level of capital. (*Hint:* Begin with the identity that saving equals investment. Then use the steady-state condition that investment is just enough to keep up with depreciation and population growth, and the fact that saving equals capital income in this economy.)

6. Many demographers predict that Canada will have zero population growth in the twenty-first century, in contrast to average population growth of about 1.6 percent per year in the last 75 years. Use the Solow model to forecast the effect of this slowdown in population growth on the growth of total output and the growth of output per person. Consider the effects both in the steady state and in the transition between steady states.

7. In the Solow model, population growth leads to steady-state growth in total output, but not in output per worker. Do you think this would still be true if the production function exhibited increasing or decreasing returns to scale? Explain. (For the definitions of increasing and decreasing returns to scale, see Chapter 3, "Problems and Applications," Problem 2.)

8. Consider how unemployment would affect the Solow growth model. Suppose that output is produced according to the production function $Y = K^{\alpha}[(1 - u)L]^{1-\alpha}$, where K is capital, L is the labour force, and u is the natural rate of unemployment. The national saving rate is s,

the labour force grows at rate n, and capital depreciates at rate δ.

a. Express output per worker ($y = Y/L$) as a function of capital per worker ($k = K/L$) and the natural rate of unemployment. Describe the steady state of this economy.

b. Suppose that some change in government policy reduces the natural rate of unemployment. Describe how this change affects output both immediately and over time. Is the steady-state effect on output larger or smaller than the immediate effect? Explain.

9. Choose two countries that interest you—one rich and one poor. What is the income per person in each country? Find some data on country characteristics that might help explain the difference in income: investment rates, population growth rates, educational attainment, and so on. (*Hint:* The Website of the World Bank, www.worldbank.org, is one place to find such data.) How might you figure out which of these factors is most responsible for the observed income difference?

CHAPTER 8

Economic Growth II: Technology, Empirics, and Policy

> *Is there some action a government of India could take that would lead the Indian economy to grow like Indonesia's or Egypt's? If so, what, exactly? If not, what is it about the "nature of India" that makes it so? The consequences for human welfare involved in questions like these are simply staggering: Once one starts to think about them, it is hard to think about anything else.*
>
> — *Robert E. Lucas, Jr., 1988*

This chapter continues our analysis of the forces governing long-run economic growth. With the basic version of the Solow growth model as our starting point, we take on four new tasks.

Our first task is to make the Solow model more general and realistic. In Chapter 3 we saw that capital, labour, and technology are the key determinants of a nation's production of goods and services. In Chapter 7 we developed the Solow model to show how changes in capital (through saving and investment) and changes in the labour force (through population growth) affect the economy's output. We are now ready to add the third source of growth—changes in technology—into the mix. The Solow model does not explain technological progress but instead takes it as exogenously given and shows how it interacts with other variables in the process of economic growth.

Our second task is to move from theory to empirics. That is, we consider how well the Solow model fits the facts. Over the past two decades, a large literature has examined the predictions of the Solow model and other models of economic growth. It turns out that the glass is both half full and half empty. The Solow model can shed much light on international growth experiences, but it is far from the last word on the subject.

Our third task is to examine how a nation's public policies can influence the level and growth of its citizens' standard of living. In particular, we address five questions: Should our society save more or save less? How can policy influence the rate of saving? Are there some types of investment that policy should especially encourage? What institutions ensure that the economy's resources are put to their best use? How can policy increase the rate of technological progress? The Solow growth model provides the theoretical framework within which we consider these policy issues.

Our fourth task is to consider what the Solow model leaves out. As we have discussed previously, models help us understand the world by simplifying it. After completing an analysis of a model, therefore, it is important to consider whether we have oversimplified matters. In this last section, we examine a new set of theories, called *endogenous growth theories,* that hope to explain the technological progress that the Solow model takes as exogenous.

8-1 Technological Progress in the Solow Model

So far, our model has assumed an unchanging relationship between the inputs of capital and labour and the output of goods and services. Yet the model can be modified to include exogenous technological progress, which over time expands society's production capabilities.

The Efficiency of Labour

To incorporate technological progress, we must return to the production function that relates total capital K and total labour L to total output Y. Thus far, the production function has been

$$Y = F(K, L).$$

We now write the production function as

$$Y = F(K, L \times E),$$

where E is a new (and somewhat abstract) variable called the **efficiency of labour.** The efficiency of labour is meant to reflect society's knowledge about production methods: as the available technology improves, the efficiency of labour rises, and each hour of work contributes more to the production of goods and services. For instance, the efficiency of labour rose when assembly-line production transformed manufacturing in early twentieth century, and it rose again when computerization was introduced in the the late twentieth century. The efficiency of labour also rises when there are improvements in the health, education, or skills of the labour force, and when institutions develop that better allow individual initiative to be harnessed.

The term $L \times E$ can be interpreted as measuring the *effective* number of workers. It takes into account the number of actual workers L and the efficiency of each worker E. In other words, L measures the number of workers in the labour force, whereas $L \times E$ measures both the workers and the technology with which the typical worker is equipped. This new production function states that total output Y depends on the number of units of capital K and on the effective number of workers, $L \times E$. The essence of this approach to modeling technological progress is that increases in the efficiency of labour E are analogous to increases in the labour force L. Suppose, for example, that an advance in production methods makes the efficiency of labour E double between 1980 and 2010. This means that a single worker in 2010 is, *in effect,* as productive as two workers were in 1980. That is, even if the actual number of workers (L) stays the same from 1980 to 2010, the effective number of workers ($L \times E$) doubles, and the economy benefits from an increased production of goods and services.

The simplest assumption about technological progress is that it causes the efficiency of labour E to grow at some constant rate g. For example, if $g = 0.02$, then each unit of labour becomes 2 percent more efficient each year: output increases as if the labour force had increased by 2 percent more than it really did. This form of technological progress is called *labour augmenting,* and g is called the rate of **labour-augmenting technological progress.** Because the labour force L is growing at rate n, and the efficiency of each unit of labour E is growing at rate g, the effective number of workers $L \times E$ is growing at rate $n + g$.

The Steady State with Technological Progress

Because technological progress is modeled here as labour augmenting, it fits into the Solow model much the same as population growth does. Although technological progress does not cause the actual number of workers to increase, each worker in effect comes with more units of labour over time. Thus, technological progress causes the effective number of workers to increase. As a result, the analytic tools we used in Chapter 7 to study the Solow model with population growth are easily adapted to study the Solow model with labour-augmenting technological progress.

We begin by reconsidering our notation. Previously, when there was no technological progress, we analyzed the economy in terms of quantities per worker; now we can generalize that approach by analyzing the economy in terms of quantities per effective worker. We now let $k = K/(L \times E)$ stand for capital per effective worker, and $y = Y/(L \times E)$ stand for output per effective worker. With these definitions, we can again write $y = f(k)$.

Our analysis of the economy proceeds just as it did when we examined population growth. The equation showing the evolution of k over time becomes

$$\Delta k = sf(k) - (\delta + n + g)k.$$

As before, the change in the capital stock Δk equals investment $sf(k)$ minus break-even investment $(\delta + n + g)k$. Now, however, because $k = K/EL$, break-even investment includes three terms: to keep k constant, δk is needed to replace depreciating capital, nk is needed to provide capital for new workers, and gk is needed to provide capital for the new "effective workers" created by technological progress.[1]

---

[1] *Mathematical note:* This model with technological progress is a strict generalization of the model analyzed in Chapter 7. In particular, if the efficiency of labour is constant at $E = 1$, then $g = 0$, and the definitions of k and y reduce to our previous definitions. In this case, the more general model considered here simplifies precisely to the Chapter 7 version of the Solow model.

FIGURE 8-1

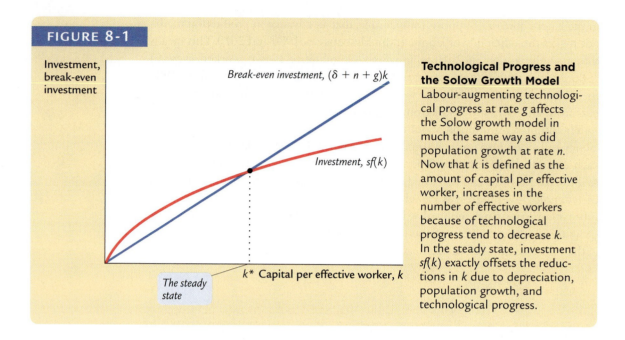

Investment, break-even investment

Break-even investment, $(\delta + n + g)k$

Investment, $sf(k)$

k^* Capital per effective worker, k

The steady state

Technological Progress and the Solow Growth Model
Labour-augmenting technological progress at rate g affects the Solow growth model in much the same way as did population growth at rate n. Now that k is defined as the amount of capital per effective worker, increases in the number of effective workers because of technological progress tend to decrease k. In the steady state, investment $sf(k)$ exactly offsets the reductions in k due to depreciation, population growth, and technological progress.

As shown in Figure 8-1, the inclusion of technological progress does not substantially alter our analysis of the steady state. There is one level of k, denoted k^*, at which capital per effective worker and output per effective worker are constant. As before, this steady state represents the long-run equilibrium of the economy.

The Effects of Technological Progress

Table 8-1 shows how four key variables behave in the steady state with technological progress. As we have just seen, capital per effective worker k is constant in the steady state. Because $y = f(k)$, output per effective worker is also constant. These quantities per effective worker are steady in the steady state.

TABLE 8-1

Steady-State Growth Rates in the Solow Model with Technological Progress

Variable	Symbol	Steady-State Growth Rate
Capital per effective worker	$k = K/(E \times L)$	0
Output per effective worker	$y = Y/(E \times L) = f(k)$	0
Output per worker	$Y/L = y \times E$	g

From this information, we can also infer what's happening to variables that are not expressed in per-effective-worker units. For instance, consider output per actual worker $Y/L = y \times E$. Because y is constant in the steady state and E is growing at rate g, output per worker must also be growing at rate g in the steady state. Similarly, the economy's total output is $Y = y \times (E \times L)$. Because y is constant in the steady state, E is growing at rate g, and L is growing at rate n, total output grows at rate $n + g$ in the steady state.

With the addition of technological progress, our model can finally explain the sustained increases in standards of living that we observe. That is, we have shown that technological progress can lead to sustained growth in output per worker. By contrast, a high rate of saving leads to a high rate of growth only until the steady state is reached. Once the economy is in steady state, the rate of growth of output per worker depends only on the rate of technological progress. *According to the Solow model, only technological progress can explain sustained growth and persistently rising living standards.*

The introduction of technological progress also modifies the criterion for the Golden Rule. The Golden Rule level of capital is now defined as the steady state that maximizes consumption per effective worker. Following the same arguments that we have used before, we can show that steady-state consumption per effective worker is

$$c^* = f(k^*) - (\delta + n + g)k^*.$$

Steady-state consumption is maximized if

$$MPK = \delta + n + g,$$

or

$$MPK - \delta = n + g.$$

That is, at the Golden Rule level of capital, the net marginal product of capital, $MPK - \delta$, equals the rate of growth of total output, $n + g$. Because actual economies experience both population growth and technological progress, we must use this criterion to evaluate whether they have more or less capital than they would at the Golden Rule steady state.

8-2 From Growth Theory to Growth Empirics

So far in this chapter we have introduced exogenous technological progress into the Solow model to explain sustained growth in standards of living. Let's now discuss what happens when the theory is forced to confront the facts. Since the Solow model is intended to describe a closed economy, and since the United States is the most important developed Western economy that trades a relatively small percentage of its GDP with the rest of the world, it is customary to evaluate the Solow model by comparing its predictions to outcomes in the United States.

Balanced Growth

According to the Solow model, technological progress causes the values of many variables to rise together in the steady state. This property, called *balanced growth,* does a good job of describing the long-run data for the U.S. economy.

Consider first output per worker Y/L and the capital stock per worker K/L. According to the Solow model, in the steady state, both of these variables grow at g, the rate of technological progress. U.S. data for the past half century show that output per worker and the capital stock per worker have in fact grown at approximately the same rate—about 2 percent per year. To put it another way, the capital-output ratio has remained approximately constant over time.

Technological progress also affects factor prices. Problem 3(d) at the end of the chapter asks you to show that, in the steady state, the real wage is predicted to grow at the rate of technological progress. The real rental price of capital, how-ever, is predicted to stay constant over time. Again, these predictions hold true for the United States. Over the past 50 years, the real wage has increased about 2 percent per year; it has increased by about the same amount as real GDP per worker. Yet the real rental price of capital (measured as real capital income divided by the capital stock) has remained about the same.

The Solow model's prediction about factor prices—and the success of this prediction—is especially noteworthy when contrasted with Karl Marx's theory of the development of capitalist economies. Marx predicted that the return to capital would decline over time and that this would lead to economic and polit-ical crisis. Economic history has not supported Marx's prediction, which partly explains why we now study Solow's theory of growth rather than Marx's.

Convergence

If you travel around the world, you will see tremendous variation in living stan-dards. The world's poor countries have average levels of income per person that are less than one-tenth the average levels in the world's rich countries. These differences in income are reflected in almost every measure of the quality of life—from the number of televisions and telephones per household to the infant mortality rate and life expectancy.

Much research has been devoted to the question of whether economies converge over time to one another. In particular, do economies that start off poor subsequently grow faster than economies that start off rich? If they do, then the world's poor economies will tend to catch up with the world's rich economies. This property of catch-up is called *convergence*. If convergence does not occur, then countries that start off behind are likely to remain poor.

The Solow model makes clear predictions about when convergence should occur. According to the model, whether two economies will converge depends on why they differ in the first place. On the one hand, suppose two economies happen by historical accident to start off with different capital stocks, but they have the same steady state, as determined by their saving rates, population growth rates, and the efficiency of labour. In this case, we should expect the two economies to converge; the poorer economy with the smaller capital stock will naturally grow more quickly to reach the steady state. (In a case study in Chapter 7, we applied this logic to explain rapid growth in Germany and Japan after World War II.) On the other hand, if two economies have different steady states, perhaps because the economies have different rates of saving, then we should not expect convergence. Instead, each economy will approach its own steady state.

Experience is consistent with this analysis. In samples of economies with similar cultures and policies, studies find that economies converge to one another at a rate of about 2 percent per year. That is, the gap between rich and poor economies closes by about 2 percent each year. An example is the economies of individual American states. For historical reasons, such as the U.S. Civil War of the 1860s, income levels varied greatly among states a century ago. Yet these differences have slowly disappeared over time.

In international data, a more complex picture emerges. When researchers examine only data on income per person, they find little evidence of convergence: countries that start off poor do not grow faster on average than countries that start off rich. This finding suggests that different countries have different steady states. If statistical techniques are used to control for some of the determinants of the steady state, such as saving rates, population growth rates, and accumulation of human capital (education), then once again the data show convergence at a rate of about 2 percent per year. In other words, the economies of the world exhibit *conditional convergence:* they appear to be converging to their own steady states, which in turn are determined by such variables as saving, population growth, and human capital.[2]

Factor Accumulation Versus Production Efficiency

As a matter of accounting, international differences in income per person can be attributed to either (1) differences in the factors of production, such as the quantities of physical and human capital, or (2) differences in the efficiency with which economies use their factors of production. That is, workers in a poor country may be poor because they lack tools and skills or because the tools and skills they have are not being put to the best use. To describe this issue in terms of the Solow model, the question is whether the large gap between rich and poor is explained by differences in capital accumulation (including human capital) or differences in the production function.

[2] Robert Barro and Xavier Sala-i-Martin, "Convergence across States and Regions," *Brookings Papers on Economic Activity* (1991, no. 1): 107–182; N. Gregory Mankiw, David Romer, and David N. Weil, "A Contribution to the Empirics of Economic Growth," *Quarterly Journal of Economics* (May 1992): 407–437.

Much research has attempted to estimate the relative importance of these two sources of income disparities. The exact answer varies from study to study, but both factor accumulation and production efficiency appear important. Moreover, a common finding is that they are positively correlated: nations with high levels of physical and human capital also tend to use those factors efficiently.[3]

There are several ways to interpret this positive correlation. One hypothesis is that an efficient economy may encourage capital accumulation. For example, a person in a well functioning economy may have greater resources and incentive to stay in school and accumulate human capital. Another hypothesis is that capital accumulation may induce greater efficiency. If there are positive externalities to physical and human capital, then countries that save and invest more will appear to have better production functions (unless the research study accounts for these externalities, which is hard to do). Thus, greater production efficiency may cause greater factor accumulation, or the other way around.

A final hypothesis is that both factor accumulation and production efficiency are driven by a common third variable. Perhaps the common third variable is the quality of the nation's institutions, including the government's policymaking process. As one economist put it, when governments screw up, they screw up big time. Multiple bad policies, such as high inflation, excessive budget deficits, widespread market interference, and rampant corruption, often go hand in hand. We should not be surprised that economies exhibiting these maladies both accumulate less capital and fail to use the capital they have as efficiently as they might.

CASE STUDY

Is Free Trade Good for Economic Growth?

At least since Adam Smith, economists have advocated free trade as a policy that promotes national prosperity. Here is how Smith put the argument in his 1776 classic, *The Wealth of Nations*:

> It is a maxim of every prudent master of a family, never to attempt to make at home what it will cost him more to make than to buy. The tailor does not attempt to make his own shoes, but buys them of the shoemaker. The shoemaker does not attempt to make his own clothes but employs a tailor. . . .
>
> What is prudence in the conduct of every private family can scarce be folly in that of a great kingdom. If a foreign country can supply us with a commodity cheaper than we ourselves can make it, better buy it of them with some part of the produce of our own industry employed in a way in which we have some advantage.

Today, economists make the case with greater rigour, relying on David Ricardo's theory of comparative advantage as well as more modern theories of international trade. According to these theories, a nation open to trade can achieve

---

[3] Robert E. Hall and Charles I. Jones, "Why Do Some Countries Produce So Much More Output Per Worker Than Others?" *Quarterly Journal of Economics* 114, (February 1999), 83–116; Peter J. Klenow and Andres Rodriguez-Clare, "The Neoclassical Revival in Growth Economics: Has It Gone Too Far?" *NBER Macroeconomics Annual* (1997): 73–103.

greater production efficiency and a higher standard of living by specializing in goods for which it has a comparative advantage.

A skeptic might point out that this is just a theory. What about the evidence? Do nations that permit free trade in fact enjoy greater prosperity? A large body of literature addresses precisely this question.

One approach is to look at international data to see if countries that are open to trade typically enjoy greater prosperity. The evidence shows that they do. Economists Andrew Warner and Jeffrey Sachs studied this question for the period from 1970 to 1989. They report that among developed nations, the open economies grew at 2.3 percent per year, while the closed economies grew at 0.7 percent per year. Among developing nations, the open economies grew at 4.5 percent per year, while the closed economies again grew at 0.7 percent per year. These findings are consistent with Smith's view that trade enhances prosperity, but they are not conclusive. Correlation does not prove causation. Perhaps being closed to trade is correlated with various other restrictive government policies, and the other policies retard growth.

A second approach is to look at what happens when closed economies remove their trade restrictions. Once again, Smith's hypothesis fairs well. Throughout history, when nations open themselves up to the world economy, the typical result is a subsequent increase in economic growth. This occurred in Japan in the 1850s, South Korea in the 1960s, and Vietnam in the 1990s. But once again, correlation does not prove causation. Trade liberalization is often accompanied by other reforms, and it is hard to disentangle the effects of trade from the effects of the other reforms.

A third approach to measuring the impact of trade on growth, proposed by economists Jeffrey Frankel and David Romer, is to look at the impact of geography. Some countries trade less simply because they are geographically disadvantaged. For example, New Zealand is disadvantaged compared to Belgium because it is farther from other populous countries. Similarly, landlocked countries are disadvantaged compared to countries with their own seaports. Because these geographical characteristics are correlated with trade but arguably uncorrelated with other determinants of economic prosperity, they can be used to identify the causal impact of trade on income. (The statistical technique, which you may have studied in an econometrics course, is called *instrumental variables.*) After analyzing the data, Frankel and Romer conclude that "a rise of one percentage point in the ratio of trade to GDP increases income per person by at least one-half percentage point. Trade appears to raise income by spurring the accumulation of human and physical capital and by increasing output for given levels of capital."

The overwhelming weight of the evidence from this body of research is that Adam Smith was right. Openness to international trade is good for economic growth.[4] ■

---

[4] Jeffrey D. Sachs, and Andrew Warner, "Economic Reform and the Process of Global Integration," *Brookings Papers on Economic Activity* (1995): 1–95; Jeffrey A. Frankel and David Romer, "Does Trade Cause Growth?" *American Economics Review* 89 (June 1999): 379–399.

8-3 Policies to Promote Growth

So far we have used the Solow model to uncover the relationships among the different sources of economic growth and we have discussed some of the empirical work that describes actual growth experiences. We can now use the theory to help guide our thinking about economic policy.

Evaluating the Rate of Saving

According to the Solow growth model, how much a nation saves and invests is a key determinant of its citizens' standard of living. So let's begin our policy discussion with a natural question: Is the rate of saving in the Canadian economy too low, too high, or about right?

As we have seen, the saving rate determines the steady-state levels of capital and output. One particular saving rate produces the Golden Rule steady state, which maximizes consumption per worker and thus economic well-being. The Golden Rule provides the benchmark against which we can compare the Canadian economy.

To decide whether the Canadian economy is at, above, or below the Golden Rule steady state, we need to compare the marginal product of capital net of depreciation ($MPK - \delta$) with the growth rate of total output ($n + g$). As we established in Section 8.1, at the Golden Rule steady state, $MPK - \delta = n + g$. If the economy is operating with less capital than in the Golden Rule steady state, then diminishing marginal product tells us that $MPK - \delta > n + g$. In this case, increasing the rate of saving will increase capital accumulation and economic growth, and eventually lead to a steady state with higher consumption (although consumption will be lower for part of the transition to the new steady state). On the other hand, if the economy is operating with too much capital, then $MPK - \delta < n + g$. In this case, capital accumulation is excessive: reducing the rate of saving would lead to higher consumption, both immediately and in the long run.

To make this comparison for a real economy, such as the Canadian economy, we need an estimate of the growth rate ($n + g$) and an estimate of the net marginal product of capital ($MPK - \delta$). Real GDP in Canada has grown at just under 4 percent per year since 1950, so $n + g = 0.04$. We can estimate the net marginal product of capital from the following three facts:

1. The capital stock is about 3 times one year's GDP.

2. Depreciation of capital is about 10 percent of GDP.

3. Capital income is about 33 percent of GDP.

Using the notation of our model (and the result from Chapter 3 that capital owners earn income of MPK for each unit of capital), we can write these facts as

1. $k = 3y$.

2. $\delta k = 0.1y$.

3. $MPK \times k = 0.33y$.

We solve for the rate of depreciation δ by dividing equation 2 by equation 1:

$$\frac{\delta k}{k} = \frac{0.1y}{3y}$$

$$\delta = 0.033.$$

And we solve for the marginal product of capital MPK by dividing equation 3 by equation 1:

$$\frac{MPK \times k}{k} = \frac{0.33y}{3y}$$

$$MPK = 0.11.$$

Thus, about 3.33 percent of the capital stock depreciates each year, and the marginal product of capital is about 11 percent per year. The net marginal product of capital, $MPK - \delta$, is 7.67 percent per year.

We can now see that the return to capital ($MPK - \delta = 7.67$ percent per year) is well in excess of the economy's average growth rate ($n + g = 4$ percent per year). This fact, together with our previous analysis, indicates that the capital stock in the Canadian economy is well below the Golden Rule level. In other words, if Canada saved and invested a higher fraction of its income, it would grow more rapidly and eventually reach a steady state with higher consumption. This finding suggests that policymakers should want to increase the rate of saving and investment. In fact, for many years, increasing capital formation has been a high priority of economic policy.

This conclusion is not unique to the Canadian economy. When calculations similar to preceding ones are done for other economies, the results are similar. The possibility of excessive saving and capital accumulation beyond the Golden Rule level is intriguing as a matter of theory, but it appears not to be a problem that actual economies face. In practice, economists are more often concerned with insufficient saving. This kind of calculation provides the intellectual foundation for this concern.[5]

Changing the Rate of Saving

The preceding calculations show that to move the Canadian economy toward the Golden Rule steady state, policymakers should increase national saving. But how can they do that? We saw in Chapter 3 that, as a matter of sheer accounting, higher national saving means higher public saving, higher private saving, or some combination of the two. Much of the debate over policies to increase growth centers on which of these is likely to be most effective.

---

[5] For more on this topic and some international evidence, see Andrew B. Abel, N. Gregory Mankiw, Lawrence H. Summers, and Richard J. Zeckhauser, "Assessing Dynamic Efficiency: Theory and Evidence," *Review of Economic Studies* 56 (1989): 1–19.

The most direct way in which the government affects national saving is through public saving—the difference between what the government receives in tax revenue and what it spends. When the government's spending exceeds its revenue, the government runs a *budget deficit,* which represents negative public saving. As we saw in Chapter 3, a budget deficit raises interest rates and crowds out investment; the resulting reduction in the capital stock is part of the burden of the national debt on future generations. Conversely, if the government spends less than it raises in revenue, it runs a *budget surplus.* It can then retire some of the national debt and stimulate investment. This influence of government budget policy on capital accumulation explains why our federal government made reducing the budget deficit an important priority during the 1990s, and why there is much public concern about the federal government's record annual budget deficit of $50 billion in 2009. As this book goes to press, the government is running this deficit for short-run cyclical reasons—to help stimulate the level of economic activity during a recession. It is encountering a trade-off between its short-run and its long-run objectives—deficits help to end the recession in the short run, but they are undesirable in the long run because they limit capital formation.

The government also affects national saving by influencing private saving—the saving done by households and firms. In particular, how much people decide to save depends on the incentives they face, and these incentives are altered by a variety of public policies. Many economists argue that high tax rates on capital income—including the corporate income tax and the personal income tax—discourage private saving by reducing the rate of return that savers earn. On the other hand, tax-exempt savings plans, such as RRSPs for retirement planning and the recently introduced tax-free savings accounts, are designed to encourage private saving by giving preferential treatment to income that is saved. Some economists have proposed increasing the incentive to save by replacing the current system of income taxation with a system of consumption taxation.

Many disagreements among economists over public policy are rooted in different views about how much private saving responds to incentives. For example, suppose that the government were to expand the amount that people can put into RRSPs. Would people respond to the increased incentive to save by saving more? Or would people merely transfer saving done in other forms into this form—reducing tax revenue and thus public saving without any stimulus to private saving? Clearly, the desirability of the policy depends on the answers to these questions. Unfortunately, despite much research on this issue, no consensus has emerged.

CASE STUDY

Tax Incentives for Saving and Investment

The Canadian government has long believed that Canada's capital/labour ratio is below the Golden Rule value. This has been the motivation behind a series of policies that were designed to raise domestic saving and to make investment more profitable for firms.

On the saving side, we have had tax-free savings accounts, RRSPs, the goods and services tax (GST), and the capital gains exemption from income taxes. All savings that are deposited within an RRSP involve two tax breaks. First, the amount contributed can be deducted from taxable income (so individuals in a 50 percent tax bracket are effectively earning interest on twice the funds that they would have without an RRSP). Second, all interest earned within the plan is tax deferred. Eventually, when the RRSP is closed out, the individuals must pay taxes on all funds withdrawn. But this does not remove the tax advantage. For one thing, the tax rate is often lower during one's retirement. For another thing, even when this is not the case, people prefer to pay taxes later. By allowing people to defer taxes, RRSPs involve the government in extending an interest-free loan to individuals (for many years). The government has been willing to give up all the associated revenue in an attempt to increase national saving.

The GST was introduced in 1988. One rationale for this tax is that sales taxes stimulate saving (compared to income taxes). With an income tax, individuals pay taxes whether they spend their income on consumption or saving. With a sales tax, people can avoid the tax by saving, since the tax is only levied when people spend.

The tax exemption on capital gains income was removed in the 1994 federal budget. With the government budget deficit running out of control, the government felt it had no option but to end this tax incentive. But its original intent was the same as with RRSPs. Prior to the 1994 budget, all individuals were exempt from tax on the first $100,000 of capital gains they had received on their saving. It is still the case that dividend and capital-gain income is taxed at lower rates than wage income.

Although many government policies are designed to encourage saving, one important policy is often thought to reduce saving: the public pension system. These transfers to the elderly are financed with a payroll tax on the working-age population. This system is thought to reduce private saving because it reduces individuals' need to provide for their own retirement.

To counteract the reduction in national saving attributed to public pensions, some economists have proposed reforms. The system is now largely *pay-as-you-go:* most of the current tax receipts are paid out to the current elderly population. One suggestion is that the system should be *fully funded.* Under this plan, the government would put aside in a trust fund the payments a generation makes when it is young and working; the government would then pay out the principal and accumulated interest to this same generation when it is older and retired. Under a fully funded pension system, an increase in public saving would offset the reduction in private saving.

A closely related proposal is *privatisation,* which means turning this government program for the elderly into a system of mandatory private savings accounts, much like private pension plans. In principle, the issues of funding and privatisation are distinct. A fully funded system could be either public (in which case the government holds the funds) or private (in which case private financial institutions hold the funds). In practice, however, the issues are often linked. Some economists have argued that a fully funded public system is problematic. They note that such a system would end up holding a large share of the nation's wealth, which would increase the role of the government in allocating capital. In addition, they fear that a large publicly controlled fund would tempt politicians to cut taxes or increase spending, which could deplete the fund and cause the system to revert to pay-as-you-go status.

These issues rose to prominence in the late 1990s, as policymakers became aware that the current public pension system was not sustainable. That is, the amount of revenue being raised by the payroll tax appeared insufficient to pay all the benefits being promised. According to most projections, this problem was to become acute as the large baby-boom generation retired during the early decades of the twenty-first century. Various solutions were proposed. One possibility was to maintain the current system with some combination of smaller benefits and higher taxes. Other possibilities included movements toward a fully funded system, perhaps also including private accounts. The federal government opted for higher payroll taxes.

In addition to its attempts to stimulate private saving, the government also tries to raise investment by giving interest-free loans directly to firms, in the form of "accelerated depreciation allowances." Again, the purpose is to increase capital accumulation in the economy. When firms fill out their corporate tax forms, they deduct expenses from gross sales to calculate their tax base (profits). One aspect of these calculations is particularly arbitrary—how the expenses of the firm's machines and equipment are treated. Firms would like to claim (for tax purposes) that equipment fully wears out (depreciates) during the purchase year. Firms can then claim the entire cost of the equipment immediately. This makes recorded profits low, and so keeps initial tax payments low. In fact, equipment wears out over a period of years. By having no equipment-purchase expenses left to claim in those later years, firms have bigger tax obligations later on. But, as with households, firms like paying taxes later, since by doing so they have received an interest-free loan from the government.

Vast amounts of tax revenue are forgone because of these tax incentives, so it should not be surprising to learn that some have been controversial. One class of policies that is particularly "expensive" is the set of corporate tax breaks that are available to all firms operating in Canada, whether or not they are branch plants of multinational companies. International tax agreements make our tax initiatives useless for these firms. Multinationals are allowed a tax credit for taxes already paid in other countries when they calcuate their corporate tax obligations in the country where the parent company is based. For example, a company based in the United States is allowed to deduct the taxes its affiliate has already paid in Canada from what taxes it would otherwise owe to the U.S. government. Thus, a tax break offered by the Canadian government makes the tax credit in the United States precisely that much smaller. The Canadian government is simply transferring revenue to the U.S. government. Since these firms are no better off as a result of the Canadian government's generosity, we cannot expect the policy to stimulate investment spending on the part of these firms.

This is not the place to evaluate more fully the Canadian attempts to raise saving and investment. However successful these schemes have been, the main point to be appreciated is *why* these initiatives were taken. The purpose has been to move Canada closer to the Golden Rule outcome. ∎

Allocating the Economy's Investment

The Solow model makes the simplifying assumption that there is only one type of capital. In the world, of course, there are many types. Private businesses invest in traditional types of capital, such as bulldozers and steel plants, and newer types of capital, such as computers and robots. The government invests in various forms of public capital, called *infrastructure,* such as roads, bridges, and sewer systems.

In addition, there is *human capital*—the knowledge and skills that workers acquire through education, from early childhood programs to on-the-job training for adults in the labour force. Although the captial variable in the Solow model is usually interpreted as including only physical capital, in many ways human capital is analogous to physical capital. Like physical capital, human capital raises our ability to produce goods and services. Raising the level of human capital requires investment in the form of teachers, libraries, and student time. Recent research on economic growth has emphasized that human capital is at least as important as physical capital in explaining international differences in standards of living. One way of modeling this fact is to give the variable we call "capital" a broader definition that includes both human and physical capital.[6]

Policymakers trying to stimulate economic growth must confront the issue of what kinds of capital the economy needs most. In other words, what kinds of capital yield the highest marginal products? To a large extent, policymakers can rely on the marketplace to allocate the pool of saving to alternative types of investment. Those industries with the highest marginal products of capital will naturally be most willing to borrow at market interest rates to finance new investment. Many economists advocate that the government should merely create a "level playing field" for different types of capital—for example, by ensuring that the tax system treats all forms of capital equally. The government can then rely on the market to allocate capital efficiently.

Other economists have suggested that the government should actively encourage particular forms of capital. Suppose, for instance, that technological advance occurs as a by-product of certain economic activities. This would happen if new and improved production processes are devised during the process of building capital (a phenomenon called *learning by doing*) and if these ideas become part of society's pool of knowledge. Such a by-product is called a *technological externality* (or a *knowledge spillover*). In the presence of such externalities, the social returns to capital exceed the private returns, and the benefits of

---

[6] Earlier in this chapter, when we were interpreting K as only physical capital, human capital was folded into the efficiency-of-labour parameter E. The alternative approach suggested here is to include human capital as part of K, so that E represents technology but not human capital. If K is given this broader interpretation, then much of what we call labour income is really the return to human capital. As a result, the true capital share is much larger than the traditional Cobb–Douglas value of about one-third. For more on this topic, see N. Gregory Mankiw, David Romer, and David N. Weil, "A Contribution to the Empirics of Economic Growth," *Quarterly Journal of Economics* (May 1992): 407–437.

increased capital accumulation to society are greater than the Solow model suggests.[7] Moreover, some types of capital accumulation may yield greater externalities than others. If, for example, installing robots yields greater technological externalities than building a new steel mill, then perhaps the government should use the tax laws to encourage investment in robots. The success of such an *industrial policy*, as it is sometimes called, requires that the government be able to measure accurately the externalities of different economic activities so it can give the correct incentive to each activity.

Most economists are skeptical about industrial policies, for two reasons. First, measuring the externalities from different sectors is so difficult as to be virtually impossible. If policy is based on poor measurements, its effects might be close to random and, thus, worse than no policy at all. Second, the political process is far from perfect. Once the government gets in the business of rewarding specific industries with subsidies and tax breaks, the rewards are as likely to be based on political clout as the magnitude of externalties.

One type of capital that necessarily involves the government is public capital. Municipal, provincial, and federal governments are always deciding if and when they should borrow to finance new roads, bridges, and transit systems. In 2009, one of U.S. President Barack Obama's first economic proposals was to increase spending on such infrastructure. This policy was motivated partly by a desire to increase short-run aggregate demand (a goal we will examine later in this book) and partly by a desire to provide public capital and enhance long-run economic growth. Many politicians have argued that here in Canada we have been investing too little in infrastructure as well. They claim that a higher level of infrastructure investment would make the economy substantially more productive. Among economists, this claim has had both defenders and critics. Yet all of them agree that measuring the marginal product of public capital is difficult. Private capital generates an easily measured rate of profit for the firm owning the capital, whereas the benefits of public capital are more diffuse. Moreover, while private capital investment is made by investors spending their own money, the allocation of resources for public capital involves the political process and taxpayer funding. It is all too common to see essentially useless projects being built simply because the local member of parliament has the political muscle to get funds approved.

Establishing the Right Institutions

As discussed earlier, economists who study international differences in the standard of living attribute some of these differences to the inputs of physical and human capital and some to the productivity with which these inputs are used. One reason that nations may have different levels of production efficiency is that they have different institutions that guide the allocation of scarce resources. Creating the right institutions is important for ensuring that resources are allocated to their best use.

[7] Paul Romer, "Crazy Explanations for the Productivity Slowdown," NBER *Macroeconomics Annual* 2 (1987): 163–201.

A nation's legal tradition is an example of such an institution. Some countries, such as Canada, the United States, Australia, India, and Singapore, are former colonies of the United Kingdom and therefore have English-style common law systems. Other nations, such as Italy, Spain, and most of Latin America, have legal traditions that evolved from the French Napoleonic Codes. Studies have found that legal protections for shareholders and creditors are stronger in the English-style legal systems than in the French-style systems. As a result, the English-style countries have better developed capital markets. Nations with more developed capital markets, in turn, experience more rapid growth because it is easier for small and start-up companies to finance investment projects, leading to a more efficient allocation of the nation's capital.[8]

Another important institutional difference across countries is the quality of government itself. Ideally, governments should provide a "helping hand" to the market system, protecting property rights, enforcing contracts, promoting competition, prosecuting fraud, and so on. Yet governments sometimes diverge from this ideal and act more like a "grabbing hand," using the authority of the state to enrich a few powerful individuals at the expense of the broader community. Empirical studies have shown that the extent of corruption in a nation is indeed a significant determinant of economic growth.[9]

Adam Smith, the great eighteenth-century economist, was well aware of the role of institutions in economic growth. He once wrote, "Little else is requisite to carry a state to the highest degree of opulence from the lowest barbarism but peace, easy taxes, and a tolerable administration of justice: all the rest being brought about by the natural course of things." Sadly, many nations do not enjoy these three simple advantages.

CASE STUDY

The Colonial Origins of Modern Institutions

International data show a remarkable correlation between latitude and economic prosperity: nations closer to the equator typically have lower levels of income per person than nations farther from the equator. This fact is true in both the northern and southern hemispheres.

What explains the correlation? Some economists have suggested that the tropical climates near the equator have a direct negative impact on productivity. In the heat of the tropics, agriculture is more difficult, and disease is more prevalent. This makes the production of goods and services more difficult.

Although the direct impact of geography is one reason tropical nations tend to be poor, it is not the whole story. Recent research by Daron Acemoglu, Simon

---

[8] Rafael La Porta, Florencio Lopez-de-Silanes, Andrei Shleifer, and Robert Vishny, "Law and Finance," *Journal of Political Economy* 106, (1998): 1113–1155; Ross Levine and Robert G. King, "Finance and Growth: Schumpeter Might Be Right," *Quarterly Journal of Economics* 108 (1993): 717–737.

[9] Paulo Mauro, "Corruption and Growth," *Quarterly Journal of Economics* 110 (1995): 681–712.

Johnson, and James Robinson has suggested an indirect mechanism—the impact of geography on institutions. Here is their explanation, presented in several steps:

1. In the seventeenth, eighteenth, and nineteenth centuries, tropical climates presented European settlers with an increased risk of disease, especially from malaria and yellow fever. As a result, when Europeans were colonizing much of the rest of the world, they avoided settling in tropical areas, such as most of Africa and Central America. The European settlers preferred areas with more moderate climates and better health conditions, such as the regions that are now Canada, the United States, and New Zealand.

2. In areas where Europeans settled in large numbers, the settlers established European-like institutions that protected individual property rights and limited the power of government. By contrast, in tropical climates, the colonial powers often set up "extractive" institutions, including authoritarian governments, so that they could take advantage of the area's natural resources. These institutions enriched the colonizers, but they did little to foster economic growth.

3. Although the era of colonial rule is now over, the early institutions that the European colonizers established are strongly correlated with the modern institutions in the former colonies. In tropical nations, where the colonial powers set up extractive institutions, there is typically less protection of property rights even today. When the colonizers left, the extractive institutions remained and were simply taken over by new ruling elites.

4. The quality of institutions is a key determinant of economic performance. Where property rights are well protected, people have more incentive to make the investments that lead to economic growth. Where property rights are less respected, as is typically the case in tropical nations, investment and growth tend to lag behind.

This research suggests that much of the international variation in living standards we observe today is a result of the long reach of history.[10] ∎

Encouraging Technological Progress

The Solow model shows that sustained growth in income per worker must come from technological progress. The Solow model, however, takes technological progress as exogenous; it does not explain it. Unfortunately, the determinants of technological progress are not well understood.

Despite this limited understanding, many public policies are designed to stimulate technological progress. Most of these policies encourage the private sector to devote resources to technological innovation. For example, the patent system gives a temporary monopoly to inventors of new products; the tax code offers tax breaks for firms engaging in research and development; and government

---

[10] Daron Acemoglu, Simon Johnson, and James A. Robinson, "The Colonial Origins of Comparative Development: An Empirical Investigation," *American Economic Association* 91 (December 2001): 1369–1401.

funding agencies directly subsidize basic research. In addition, as discussed above, proponents of industrial policy argue that the government should take a more active role in promoting specific industries that are key for rapid technological advance. In recent years, the encouragement of technological progress has taken on an international dimension. Many of the companies that engage in research to advance technology are located in the United States and other developed nations. Developing nations such as China have an incentive to "free ride" on this research by not strictly enforcing intellectual property rights. That is, Chinese companies often use the ideas developed abroad without compensating the patent holders. The United States has strenuously objected to this practice, and China has promised to step up enforcement. If intellectual property rights were better enforced around the world, firms would have more incentive to engage in research, and this would promote worldwide technological progress.

CASE STUDY

The Worldwide Slowdown in Economic Growth: 1972–1995

Beginning in the early 1970s and lasting until the mid-1990s, world policymakers faced a perplexing problem: a global slowdown in economic growth. Table 8-2 presents data on the growth in real GDP per person for seven major world economies. Growth in Canada fell from 2.9 percent before 1972 to 1.8 percent from 1972 to 1995. Other countries experienced similar or more severe declines. Accumulated over many years, even a small change in the rate of growth has a large effect on economic well-being. Indeed, real income in Canada in 2008 was 28 percent lower than it would have been had growth remained at its previous

TABLE 8-2			
	Growth Around the World		
	GROWTH IN OUTPUT PER PERSON (PERCENT PER YEAR)		
Country	1948–1972	1972–1995	1995–2007
Canada	2.9	1.8	2.2
France	4.3	1.6	1.7
West Germany	5.7	2.0	
Germany			1.5
Italy	4.9	2.3	1.2
Japan	8.2	2.6	1.2
United Kingdom	2.4	1.8	2.6
United States	2.2	1.5	2.0

Source: Angus Maddison, *Phases of Capitalist Development* (Oxford: Oxford University Press, 1982); *OECD National Accounts;* and *World Bank: World Development Indicators.*

level. (Incidentally, it is worth emphasizing that Table 8-2 focuses on growth in GDP *per person*. Since Canada's population grew more rapidly than our real GDP during these periods, these reported growth rates are lower than the 4 percent output growth mentioned earlier in this chapter.)

Why did the productivity growth slowdown occur? Studies have shown that the slowdown in growth is attributable to a slowdown in the rate at which the production function is improving over time. The appendix to this chapter explains how economists measure changes in the production function with a variable called *total factor productivity,* which is closely related to the efficiency of labour in the Solow model. Our understanding of why the growth in total factor productivity slowed is still quite incomplete. This is frustrating since, as just noted, accumulated over many years, even a small change in productivity growth has a large effect on economic welfare.

Many economists have attempted to explain this adverse change. Let's consider some of their explanations.

Measurement Problems One possibility is that the productivity slowdown did not really occur and that it shows up in the data simply because the data are flawed. As you may recall from Chapter 2, one problem in measuring inflation is correcting for changes in the quality of goods and services. The same issue arises when measuring output and productivity. For instance, if technological advance leads to *more* computers being built, then the increase in output and productivity is easy to measure. But if technological advance leads to *faster* computers being built, then output and productivity have in effect increased, but that increase is more subtle and harder to measure. Government statisticians try to correct for changes in quality, but despite their best efforts, the resulting data are far from perfect.

Unmeasured quality improvements mean that our standard of living is rising more rapidly than the official data indicate. This issue should make us suspicious of the data, but by itself it cannot explain the productivity slowdown. To explain a *slowdown* in growth, one must argue that the measurement problems have gotten *worse*. There is some indication that this might be so. Over time, fewer people are working in industries with tangible and easily measured output, such as agriculture, and more people are working in industries with intangible and less easily measured output, such as medical services. Yet few economists believe that measurement problems are the full story.

Oil Prices When the productivity slowdown began around 1973, the obvious hypothesis to explain it was the large increase in oil prices caused by the actions of the OPEC oil cartel. The primary piece of evidence was the timing: productivity growth slowed at almost exactly the same time that oil prices skyrocketed. Over time, however, this explanation has appeared less likely. One reason is that the accumulated shortfall in productivity seems too large to be explained by an increase in oil prices—petroleum-based products are not that large a fraction of a typical firm's costs. In addition, if this explanation were right, productivity should have sped up when political turmoil in OPEC caused oil prices to plummet in 1986. Unfortunately, that did not happen.

Worker Quality Some economists have suggested that the productivity slowdown might be attributable to changes in the labour force. In the early 1970s, the large baby-boom generation started leaving school and taking jobs. At the same time, changing social norms encouraged many women to leave full-time housework and enter the labour force. Both of these developments lowered the average level of experience among workers, which in turn lowered average productivity.

Other economists point to changes in worker quality due to human capital. Although the educational attainment of the labour force is now as high as it has ever been, educational attainment is not increasing as rapidly as it has in the past. In addition, declining performance on some standardized tests suggests that the quality of education has been declining over time. If so, this could explain slowing productivity growth.

The Depletion of Ideas Still other economists have suggested that the world has started to run out of new ideas about how to produce and, as a result, we have entered an age of slower technological progress. These economists often argue that the anomaly is not the period since 1970 but the two decades before that. In the late 1940s, the economy had a large backlog of ideas that had not been fully implemented because of the Great Depression of the 1930s and World War II in the first half of 1940s. After the economy used up this backlog, the argument goes, a slowdown in productivity growth was inevitable. Indeed, while recent growth rates are disappointing compared to those of the 1950s and 1960s, they are not any lower than average growth rates from 1870 to 1950. Perhaps lower productivity growth is something we just have to get used to.

As any good doctor will tell you, sometimes a patient's illness goes away on its own, even if the doctor has failed to come up with an accurate diagnosis and an effective remedy. This situation seems—at least partially—to be the outcome of the productivity slowdown. In the mid-1990s, economic growth rebounded, at least in some English-speaking countries and in particular in the United States. As with the slowdown in economic growth in the 1970s, the acceleration in the 1990s is hard to explain definitively. But at least part of the credit goes to advances in computer and information technology, including the Internet.[11]

You might wonder why it took so long for computers to seem to contribute to rising productivity. In this regard, it is useful to recall that similar lags have been common throughout history. For example, the electric light bulb was invented in 1879, but it took several decades for electricity to have a big economic impact. For businesses to reap large productivity gains, they had to do more than just replace steam engines with electric motors; they had to rethink the entire organization of factories. Similarly, replacing the typewriters on desks with computers and word processing programs, as was common in the 1980s, may have had small productivity effects. Only later, when the Internet and other advanced applications were invented, did the computers yield large economic gains.[12] ∎

---

[11] For various views on the growth slowdown, see "Symposium: The Slowdown in Productivity Growth," *The Journal of Economic Perspectives* 2 (Fall 1988): 3–98.

[12] For more on this topic, see the symposium on "Computers and Productivity," *The Journal of Economic Perspectives* (Fall 2000). On the parallel between electricity and computers, see Paul A. David, "The Dynamo and the Computer: A Historical Perspective on the Modern Productivity Paradox," *American Economic Review* 80, no. 2 (May 1990): 355–361.

8-4 Beyond the Solow Model: Endogenous Growth Theory

A chemist, a physicist, and an economist are all trapped on a desert island, trying to figure out how to open a can of food.

"Let's heat the can over the fire until it explodes," says the physicist.

"No, no," says the engineer, "Let's drop the can onto the rocks from the top of a high tree."

"I have an idea," says the economist. "First, we assume a can opener . . . ."

This old joke takes aim at how economists use assumptions to simplify—and sometimes oversimplify—the problems they face. It is particularly apt when evaluating the theory of economic growth. One goal of growth theory is to explain the persistent rise in living standards that we observe in most parts of the world. The Solow growth model shows that such persistent growth must come from technological progress. But where does technological progress come from? In the Solow model, it is just assumed!

The preceding Case Study on the productivity slowdown of the 1970s and speedup of the 1990s suggests that changes in the pace of technological progress are tremendously important. To understand fully the process of economic growth, we need to go beyond the Solow model and develop models that explain technological advance. Models that do this often go by the label **endogenous growth theory** because they reject the Solow model's assumption of exogenous technological change. Although the field of endogenous growth theory is large and sometimes complex, here we get a quick taste of this modern research.[13]

The Basic Model

To illustrate the idea behind endogenous growth theory, let's start with a particularly simple production function:

$$Y = AK,$$

where Y is output, K is the capital stock, and A is a constant measuring the amount of output produced for each unit of capital. Notice that this production function does not exhibit the property of diminishing returns to capital. One extra unit of capital produces A extra units of output, regardless of how much capital there is. This absence of diminishing returns to capital is the key difference between this model and the Solow model.

---

[13] This section provides a brief introduction to the large and fascinating literature on endogenous growth theory. Early and important contributions to this literature include Paul M. Romer, "Increasing Returns and Long-Run Growth," *Journal of Political Economy* 94 (October 1986): 1002–1037; and Robert E. Lucas, Jr., "On the Mechanics of Economic Development," *Journal of Monetary Economics* 22 (1988): 3–42. The reader can learn more about this topic in the undergraduate textbook by Charles I. Jones, *Introduction to Economic Growth,* 2d ed. (New York: Norton, 2002) or David N. Weil, *Economic Growth* (Upper Saddle River, NJ: Pearson, 2005).

Now let's see what this production function says about economic growth. As before, we assume a fraction s of income is saved and invested. We therefore describe capital accumulation with an equation similar to those we used previously:

$$\Delta K = sY - \delta K.$$

This equation states that the change in the capital stock (ΔK) equals investment (sY) minus depreciation (δK). (For simplicity in this derivation, we abstract from population growth.) Combining this equation with the $Y = AK$. production function, we obtain after a bit of manipulation

$$\Delta Y/Y = \Delta K/K = sA - \delta.$$

This equation shows what determines the growth rate of output $\Delta Y/Y$. Notice that, as long as $sA > \delta$, the economy's income grows forever, even without the assumption of exogenous technological progress.

Thus, a simple change in the production function can alter dramatically the predictions about economic growth. In the Solow model, saving leads to growth temporarily, but diminishing returns to capital eventually force the economy to approach a steady state in which growth depends only on exogenous technological progress. By contrast, in this endogenous growth model, saving and investment can lead to persistent growth.

But is it reasonable to abandon the assumption of diminishing returns to capital? The answer depends on how we interpret the variable K in the production function $Y = AK$. If we take the traditional view that K includes only the economy's stock of plants and equipment, then it is natural to assume diminishing returns. Giving 10 computers to a worker does not make that worker ten times as productive as he or she is with one computer.

Advocates of endogenous growth theory, however, argue that the assumption of constant (rather than diminishing) returns to capital is more palatable if K is interpreted more broadly. Earlier in this chapter, we interpreted K as only physical capital, and the level of knowledge was part of what was incorporated into the efficiency of labour parameter E. Here we are suggesting an alternative interpretation. Perhaps the best case for the endogenous growth model is to view knowledge as a type of capital. Clearly, knowledge is an important input into the economy's production—both its production of goods and services and its production of new knowledge. Compared to other forms of capital, however, it is less natural to assume that knowledge exhibits the property of diminishing returns. (Indeed, the increasing pace of scientific and technological innovation over the past few centuries has led some economists to argue that there are increasing returns to knowledge.) If we accept the view that knowledge is a type of capital, then this endogenous growth model with its assumption of constant returns to capital becomes a more plausible description of long-run economic growth.

The policy implications of this basic endogenous growth model are worth illustrating quantitatively. To do so, however, we need to rely on the more advanced theory of household consumption behaviour covered in Chapter 17.2. As a result, readers may wish to reread the remainder of this subsection after covering Chapter 17, but it is worth skim-reading this material at this stage, because the general idea can still be appreciated.

We learn in Chapter 17 that forward-looking households optimize by setting the marginal rate of substitution between current and future consumption equal to the ratio of the prices of present and future consumption. Since postponing consumption allows the household to earn the after-tax interest rate, $r(1 - t)$, on those funds, the household has more resources if it waits to consume in the future. Thus, the present-to-future price ratio equals $[1 + r(1 - t)]$. The marginal rate of substitution is the ratio of current marginal utility to future marginal utility. The simplest function that involves diminishing marginal utility of consumption at each point in time and impatience across time is

$$\text{Utility} = \log(\text{Present Consumption}) + \frac{1}{(1 + i)}\log(\text{Future Consumption}),$$

where i is the household's rate of impatience. For this utility function, current marginal utility is (1/Present Consumption) and future marginal utility is (1/Future Consumption)$[1/(1 + i)]$. Equating the resulting expression for the marginal rate of substitution to the price ratio, we have

$$\frac{\text{Future Consumption}}{\text{Present Consumption}} (1 + i) = [1 + r(1 - t)].$$

We can simplify this optimal consumption rule by moving the $(1 + i)$ term to the denominator on the right-hand side, by subtracting one from both sides, and by denoting present and future consumption by C_1 and C_2 respectively. The result is

$$(C_2 - C_1)/C_1 = (1 + r(1 - t) - 1 - i)/(1 + i).$$

For any reasonable value for the annual rate of impatience, such as 0.04, the value of $(1 + i)$ is very close to unity, so we can make this approximation. With this simplification, the optimal purchase rule amounts to saying that—to optimize—households must arrange their affairs so that the percentage growth in consumption equals the excess of the after-tax interest they receive on their saving over their rate of impatience. Using the symbols we have used in this chapter to represent the growth rate of income and consumption, $n + g$, we have

$$n + g = \text{Growth Rate} = r(1 - t) - i.$$

We now use this relationship to illustrate how much government policy can affect the growth rate.

In the $Y = AK$ model, the marginal product of capital r is a constant A. The household's rate of impatience i is also independent of fiscal policy. Thus, the government's tax rate is the only variable on the right-hand side of the equation that changes. For an illustration of the effect of tax policy on the growth rate, let us assume that capital's marginal product is 8 percent, the household rate of impatience is 4 percent, and the tax rate is 25 percent ($r = 0.08$, $i = 0.04$, $t = 0.25$). These assumptions make the growth rate 2 percent ($n + g = 0.02$). Now consider the tax rate being reduced by just two percentage points (to 0.23). The right-hand side of our growth-rate equation rises by r times 0.02, or by 0.0016. We conclude that the annual growth rate for consumption rises by about one-sixth of one percentage point. Is this a significant increase? It doesn't seem like much, but it represents more consumption for households—*every* year *forever*. We now calculate the *present value* of this ongoing series of small improvements in living standards.

Let us choose units so that present consumption is unity. The present value of all present and future consumption is then one divided by the excess of the household's rate of impatience over the rate at which consumption is growing: $1/[i - (n + g)]$. Initially, before the tax cut, this expression equals $1/(0.04 - 0.02) = 50$. After the tax cut, this expression equals $1/(0.04 - 0.0216) = 54.3$. So a small cut in the tax rate—just two percentage points—raises consumption by a one-time equivalent amount that is four and one-third times as big as an entire year's consumption! That represents a lot of hospitals, day care centres, and social benefits.

We conclude that the basic endogenous growth model has a very exciting property. It suggests that even small tax changes—ones that are well within the range of what can be executed from a political point of view—can have rather dramatic effects on material living standards. This explains Robert Lucas's expression of excitement in the quotation that starts this chapter and explains why macroeconomists have devoted a lot of research effort to investigating whether such results are found in more elaborate versions of endogenous growth theory.

A Two-Sector Model

Although the $Y = AK$ model is the simplest example of endogenous growth, the theory has gone well beyond this. One line of research has tried to develop models with more than one sector of production in order to offer a better description of the forces that govern technological progress. To see what we might learn from such models, let's sketch out an example.

The economy has two sectors, which we can call manufacturing firms and research universities. Firms produce goods and services, which are used for consumption and investment in physical capital. Universities produce a factor of production called "knowledge," which is then freely used in both sectors. The economy is described by the production function for firms, the production function for universities, and the capital-accumulation equation:

$Y = F[K,(1 - u)LE]$ (production function in manufacturing firms),

$\Delta E = g(u)E$ (production function in research universities),

$\Delta K = sY - \delta K$ (capital accumulation),

where u is the fraction of the labour force in universities (and $1 - u$ is the fraction in manufacturing), E is the stock of knowledge (which in turn determines the efficiency of labour), and g is a function that shows how the growth in knowledge depends on the fraction of the labour force in universities. The rest of the notation is standard. As usual, the production function for the manufacturing firms is assumed to have constant returns to scale: if we double both the amount of physical capital (K) and the number of effective workers in manufacturing [$(1 - u)EL$], we double the output of goods and services (Y).

This model is a cousin of the $Y = AK$ model. Most important, this economy exhibits constant (rather than diminishing) returns to capital, as long as capital is broadly defined to include knowledge. In particular, if we double both physical capital K and knowledge E, then we double the output of both sectors in the economy. As a result, like the $Y = AK$ model, this model can generate persistent growth without the assumption of exogenous shifts in the production function. Here persistent growth arises endogenously because the creation of knowledge in universities never slows down.

At the same time, however, this model is also a cousin of the Solow growth model. If u, the fraction of the labour force in universities, is held constant, then the efficiency of labour E grows at the constant rate $g(u)$. This result of constant growth in the efficiency of labour at rate g is precisely the assumption made in the Solow model with technological progress. Moreover, the rest of the model—the manufacturing production function and the capital-accumulation equation—also resembles the rest of the Solow model. As a result, for any given value of u, this endogenous growth model works just like the Solow model.

There are two key decision variables in this model. As in the Solow model, the fraction of output used for saving and investment, s, determines the steady-state stock of physical capital. In addition, the fraction of labour in universities, u, determines the growth in the stock of knowledge. Both s and u affect the level of income, although only u affects the steady-state growth rate of income. Thus, this model of endogenous growth takes a small step in the direction of showing which societal decisions determine the rate of technological change.

The Microeconomics of Research and Development

The two-sector endogenous growth model just presented takes us closer to understanding technological progress, but it still tells only a rudimentary story about the creation of knowledge. If one thinks about the process of research and development for even a moment, three facts become apparent. First, although knowledge is largely a public good (that is, a good freely available to everyone), much research is done in firms that are driven by the profit motive. Second, research is profitable because innovations give firms temporary monopolies, either because of the patent system or because there is an advantage to being the first firm on the market with a new product. Third, when one firm innovates, other firms build on that innovation to produce the next generation of innovations. These (essentially microeconomic) facts are not easily connected with the (essentially macroeconomic) growth models we have discussed so far.

Some endogenous growth models try to incorporate these facts about research and development. Doing this requires modeling both the decisions that firms face as they engage in research and the interactions among firms that have some degree of monopoly power over their innovations. Going into more detail about these models is beyond the scope of this book. But it should be clear already that one virtue of these endogenous growth models is that they offer a more complete description of the process of technological innovation.

One question these models are designed to address is whether, from the standpoint of society as a whole, private profit-maximizing firms tend to engage in too little or too much research. In other words, is the social return to research (which is what society cares about) greater or smaller than the private return (which is what motivates individual firms)? It turns out that, as a theoretical matter, there are effects in both directions. On the one hand, when a firm creates a new technology, it makes other firms better off by giving them a base of knowledge on which to build in future research. As Isaac Newton famously remarked, "If I have seen farther than others, it is because I was standing on the shoulder of giants." On the other hand, when one firm invests in research, it can also make other firms worse off by making that earlier invention obsolete. This negative outcome has been called the "stepping on toes" effect. Whether firms left to their own devices do too little or too much research depends on whether the positive "standing on shoulders" externality or the negative "stepping on toes" externality is more prevalent.

Although theory alone is ambiguous about whether research effort is more or less than optimal, the empirical work in this area is usually less so. Many studies have suggested the "standing on shoulders" externality is important and, as a result, the social return to research is large—often in excess of 40 percent per year. This is an impressive rate of return, especially when compared to the return to physical capital, which we earlier estimated to be just under 8 percent per year. In the judgment of some economists, this finding justifies substantial government subsidies to research.[14]

CASE STUDY

The Process of Creative Destruction

In his 1942 book, *Capitalism, Socialism, and Democracy,* economist Joseph Schumpeter suggested that economic progress comes through a process of "creative destruction." According to Schumpeter, the driving force behind progress is the entrepreneur with an idea for a new product, a new way to produce an old product, or some other innovation. When the entrepreneur's firm enters the market, it has some degree of monopoly power over its innovation; indeed, the prospect of monopoly profits motivates the entrepreneur. The entry of the new firm is good for consumers, who now have an expanded range of choices, but it is often bad for incumbent producers, who may find it hard to compete with the entrant. If the new product is sufficiently better than old ones, the incumbents may even be driven out of business. Over time, the process keeps renewing itself. The entrepreneur's firm becomes an incumbent, enjoying high profitability until its product is displaced by another entrepreneur with the next generation of innovation.

History coΩnfirms Schumpeter's thesis that technological progress produces winners and losers. For example, in England in the early nineteenth century, an important innovation was the invention and spread of machines that could

---

[14] For an overview of the empirical literature on the effects of research, see Zvi Griliches, "The Search for R&D Spillovers," *Scandinavian Journal of Economics* 94 (1991): 29–47.

produce textiles using unskilled workers at low cost. This technological advance was good for consumers who could clothe themselves more cheaply. Yet skilled knitters in England saw their jobs threatened by new technology, and they responded by organizing violent revolts. The rioting workers, called Luddites, smashed the weaving machines used in the wool and cotton mills and set the homes of the mill owners on fire (a less than creative form of destruction). Today, the term "Luddite" refers to anyone who opposes technological progress.

A more recent example of creative destruction entails the retailing giant Wal-Mart. Although retailing may seem like a relatively static activity, in fact it is a sector that has seen sizable rates of technological progress over the past several decades. Through better inventory-control, marketing, and personnel-management techniques, for example, Wal-Mart has found ways to bring goods to consumers at lower cost than traditional retailers. These changes benefit not only consumers, who can buy goods at lower prices, but also the stockholders of Wal-Mart, who share in its profitability. But they adversely affect small family-run stores, who find it hard to compete when a Wal-Mart opens nearby.

Faced with the prospect of being the victims of creative destruction, incumbent producers often look to the political process to stop the entry of new, more efficient competitors. The original Luddites wanted the British government to save their jobs by restricting the spread of the new textile technology; instead, the Parliament sent troops to suppress the Luddite riots. Similarly, in recent years, local retailers have sometimes tried to use local land use regulations to stop Wal-Mart from entering their market. The cost of such entry restrictions, however, is to slow the pace of technological progress. In Europe, where entry regulations are stricter than they are in the United States, the economies have not seen the emergence of retailing giants like Wal-Mart; as a result, productivity growth in retailing has been much lower.[15]

Schumpeter's vision of how capitalist economies work has merit as a matter of economic history. Moreover, it has inspired some recent work in the theory of economic growth. One line of endogenous growth theory, pioneered by economists Philippe Aghion and Peter Howitt, builds on Schumpeter's insights by modeling technological advance as a process of entrepreneurial innovation and creative destruction.[16] ∎

8-5 Conclusion

Long-run economic growth is the single most important determinant of the economic well-being of a nation's citizens. Everything else that macroeconomists study—unemployment, inflation, trade deficits, and so on—pales in comparison.

---

[15] Robert J. Gordon, "Why Was Europe Left at the Station When America's Productivity Locomotive Departed?" NBER Working Paper No. 10661 (2004).

[16] Philippe Aghion and Peter Howitt, "A Model of Growth through Creative Destruction," *Econometrica* 60 (1992): 323–351.

Fortunately, economists know quite a lot about the forces that govern economic growth. The Solow growth model and the more recent endogenous growth models show how saving, population growth, and technological progress interact in determining the level of and growth in a nation's standard of living. Although these theories offer no magic recipe to ensure an economy achieves rapid growth, they do offer much insight, and they provide the intellectual framework for much of the debate over public policy aimed at promoting long-run economic growth.

Summary

1. In the steady state of the Solow growth model, the growth rate of income per person is determined solely by the exogenous rate of technological progress.

2. Many empirical studies have examined to what extent the Solow model can help explain long-run economic growth. The model can explain much of what we see in the data, such as balanced growth and conditional convergence. Recent studies have also found that international variation in standards of living is attributable to a combination of capital accumulation and the efficiency with which capital is used.

3. In the Solow model with population growth and technological progress, the Golden Rule (consumption-maximizing) steady state is characterized by equality between the net marginal product of capital ($MPK - \delta$) and the steady-state growth rate of total income ($n + g$). In the Canadian economy, the net marginal product of capital is well in excess of the growth rate, indicating that the Canadian economy has much less capital than it would have in the Golden Rule steady state.

4. Policymakers in Canada and other countries often claim that their nations should devote a larger percentage of their output to saving and investment. Increased public saving and tax incentives for private saving are two ways to encourage capital accumulation. Policymakers can also promote economic growth by setting up the right legal and financial institutions so that resources are allocated efficiently and by ensuring proper incentives to encourage research and technological progress.

5. In the early 1970s, the rate of growth of income per person fell substantially in most industrialized countries. The cause of this slowdown is not well understood. In the mid-1990s, the growth rate rebounded, most likely because of advances in information technology.

6. Modern theories of endogenous growth attempt to explain the rate of technological progress, which the Solow model takes as exogenous. These models try to explain the decisions that determine the creation of knowledge through research and development.

KEY CONCEPTS

Efficiency of labour

Labour-augmenting technological progress

Endogenous growth theory

QUESTIONS FOR REVIEW

1. In the Solow model, what determines the steady-state rate of growth of income per worker?

2. In the steady state of the Solow model, at what rate does output per person grow? At what rate does capital per person grow? How does this compare with the Canadian experience?

3. What data would you need to determine whether an economy has more or less capital than in the Golden Rule steady state?

4. How can policymakers influence a nation's saving rate?

5. What has happened to the rate of productivity growth over the past 50 years? How might you explain this phenomenon?

6. How does endogenous growth theory explain persistent growth without the assumption of exogenous technological progress? How does this differ from the Solow model?

PROBLEMS AND APPLICATIONS

1. An economy described by the Solow growth model has the following production function:

$$y = \sqrt{k}.$$

   a. Solve for the steady-state value of y as a function of s, n, g, and δ.

   b. A developed country has a saving rate of 28 percent and a population growth rate of 1 percent per year. A less-developed country has a saving rate of 10 percent and a population growth rate of 4 percent per year. In both countries, $g = 0.02$ and $\delta = 0.04$. Find the steady-state value of y for each country.

   c. What policies might the less-developed country pursue to raise its level of income?

2. In the United States, the capital share of GDP is about 30 percent; the average growth in output is about 3 percent per year; the depreciation rate is about 4 percent per year; and the capital–output ratio is about 2.5. Suppose that the production function is Cobb–Douglas, so that the capital share in output is constant, and that the United States has been in a steady state. (For a discussion of the Cobb–Douglas produc-

tion function, see the appendix to Chapter 3.)

   a. What must the saving rate be in the initial steady state? [*Hint:* Use the steady-state relationship, $sy = (\delta + n + g)k$.]

   b. What is the marginal product of capital in the initial steady state?

   c. Suppose that public policy raises the saving rate so that the economy reaches the Golden Rule level of capital. What will the marginal product of capital be at the Golden Rule steady state? Compare the marginal product at the Golden Rule steady state to the marginal product in the initial steady state. Explain.

   d. What will the capital–output ratio be at the Golden Rule steady state? (*Hint:* For the Cobb–Douglas production function, the capital–output ratio is related to the marginal product of capital.)

   e. What must the saving rate be to reach the Golden Rule steady state?

3. Prove each of the following statements about the steady state with population growth and techno-logical progress.

a. The capital–output ratio is constant.

b. Capital and labour each earn a constant share of an economy's income. [*Hint:* Recall the definition $MPK = f(k + 1) - f(k)$.]

c. Total capital income and total labour income both grow at the rate of population growth plus the rate of technological progress, $n + g$.

d. The real rental price of capital is constant, and the real wage grows at the rate of technological progress g. (*Hint:* The real rental price of capital equals total capital income divided by the capital stock, and the real wage equals total labour income divided by the labour force.)

4. Two countries, Richland and Poorland, are described by the Solow growth model. They have the same Cobb–Douglas production function, $F(K, {}^\alpha L) = A\, K^\alpha L^{1-\alpha}$, but with different quantities of capital and labour. Richland saves 32 percent of its income, while Poorland saves 10 percent. Richland has population growth of 1 percent per year, while Poorland has population growth of 3 percent. (The numbers in this problem are chosen to be approximately realistic descriptions of rich and poor nations.) Both nations have technological progress at a rate of 2 percent per year and depreciation at a rate of 5 percent per year.

a. What is the per worker production function $f(k)$?

b. Solve for the ratio of Richland's steady-state income per worker to Poorland's. (*Hint:* The parameter α will play a role in your answer.)

c. If the Cobb–Douglas parameter α takes the conventional value of about one-third, how much higher should income per worker be in Richland compared to Poorland?

d. Income per worker in Richland is actually 16 times income per worker in Poorland. Can you explain this fact by changing the value of the parameter α? What must it be? Can you think of any way of justifying such a value for this parameter? How else might you explain the large difference in income between Richland and Poorland?

5. The amount of education the typical person receives varies substantially among countries. Suppose you were to compare a country with a highly educated labour force and a country with a less educated labour force. Assume that education affects only the level of the efficiency of labour. Also assume that the countries are otherwise the same: they have the same saving rate, the same depreciation rate, the same population growth rate, and the same rate of technological progress. Both countries are described by the Solow model and are in their steady states. What would you predict for the following variables?

a. The rate of growth of total income.

b. The level of income per worker.

c. The real rental price of capital.

d. The real wage.

6. This question asks you to analyze in more detail the two-sector endogenous growth model presented in the text.

a. Rewrite the production function for manufactured goods in terms of output per effective worker and capital per effective worker.

b. In this economy, what is break-even investment (the amount of investment needed to keep capital per effective worker constant)?

c. Write down the equation of motion for k, which shows Δk as saving minus break-even investment. Use this equation to draw a graph showing the determination of steady-state k. (*Hint:* This graph will look much like those we used to analyze the Solow model.)

d. In this economy, what is the steady-state growth rate of output per worker Y/L? How do the saving rate s and the fraction of the labour force in universities u affect this steady-state growth rate?

e. Using your graph, show the impact of an increase in u. (*Hint:* This change affects both curves.) Describe both the immediate and the steady-state effects.

f. Based on your analysis, is an increase in u an unambiguously good thing for the economy? Explain.

Accounting for the Sources of Economic Growth

Real GDP in Canada has grown an average of almost 4 percent per year over the past 50 years. What explains this growth? In Chapter 3 we linked the output of the economy to the factors of production—capital and labour—and to the production technology. Here we develop a technique called *growth accounting* that divides the growth in output into three different sources: increases in capital, increases in labour, and advances in technology. This breakdown provides us with a measure of the rate of technological change.

Increases in the Factors of Production

We first examine how increases in the factors of production contribute to increases in output. To do this, we start by assuming there is no technological change, so the production function relating output Y to capital K and labour L is constant over time:

$$Y = F(K, L).$$

In this case, the amount of output changes only because the amount of capital or labour changes.

Increases in Capital First, consider changes in capital. If the amount of capital increases by ΔK units, by how much does the amount of output increase? To answer this question, we need to recall the definition of the marginal product of capital MPK:

$$MPK = F(K + 1, L) - F(K, L).$$

The marginal product of capital tells us how much output increases when capital increases by 1 unit. Therefore, when capital increases by ΔK units, output increases by approximately $MPK \times \Delta K$.[17]

For example, suppose that the marginal product of capital is 1/5; that is, an additional unit of capital increases the amount of output produced by one-fifth of a unit. If we increase the amount of capital by 10 units, we can compute the

---

[17] Note the word "approximately." This answer is only an approximation because the marginal product of capital varies: it falls as the amount of capital increases. An exact answer would take into account that each unit of capital has a different marginal product. If the change in K is not too large, however, the approximation of a constant marginal product is very accurate.

amount of additional output as follows:

$$\Delta Y = MPK \times \Delta K$$

$$= \frac{1}{5} \times \frac{\text{Units of Output}}{\text{Unit of Capital}} \times 10 \text{ Units of Capital}$$

$$= 2 \text{ Units of Output.}$$

By increasing capital by 10 units, we obtain 2 more units of output. Thus, we use the marginal product of capital to convert changes in capital into changes in output.

Increases in Labour Next, consider changes in labour. If the amount of labour increases by ΔL units, by how much does output increase? We answer this question the same way we answered the question about capital. The marginal product of labour MPL tells us how much output changes when labour increases by 1 unit—that is,

$$MPL = F(K, L + 1) - F(K, L).$$

Therefore, when the amount of labour increases by ΔL units, output increases by approximately $MPL \times \Delta L$.

For example, suppose that the marginal product of labour is 2; that is, an additional unit of labour increases the amount of output produced by 2 units. If we increase the amount of labour by 10 units, we can compute the amount of additional output as follows:

$$\Delta Y = MPL \times \Delta L$$

$$= 2 \frac{\text{Units of Output}}{\text{Unit of Labor}} \times 10 \text{ Units of Labor}$$

$$= 20 \text{ Units of Output.}$$

By increasing labour by 10 units, we obtain 20 more units of output. Thus, we use the marginal product of labour to convert changes in labour into changes in output.

Increases in Capital and Labour Finally, let's consider the more realistic case in which both factors of production change. Suppose that the amount of capital increases by ΔK and the amount of labour increases by ΔL. The increase in output then comes from two sources: more capital and more labour. We can divide this increase into the two sources using the marginal products of the two inputs:

$$\Delta Y = (MPK \times \Delta K) + (MPL \times \Delta L).$$

The first term in parentheses is the increase in output resulting from the increase in capital, and the second term in parentheses is the increase in output resulting from the increase in labour. This equation shows us how to attribute growth to each factor of production.

We now want to convert this last equation into a form that is easier to interpret and apply to the available data. First, with some algebraic rearrangement, the equation becomes[18]

$$\frac{\Delta Y}{Y} = \left(\frac{MPK \times K}{Y} \right) \frac{\Delta K}{K} + \left(\frac{MPL \times L}{Y} \right) \frac{\Delta L}{L}.$$

This form of the equation relates the growth rate of output, $\Delta Y/Y$, to the growth rate of capital, $\Delta K/K$, and the growth rate of labour, $\Delta L/L$.

Next, we need to find some way to measure the terms in parentheses in the last equation. In Chapter 3 we showed that the marginal product of capital equals its real rental price. Therefore, $MPK \times K$ is the total return to capital, and $(MPK \times K)/Y$ is capital's share of output. Similarly, the marginal product of labour equals the real wage. Therefore, $MPL \times L$ is the total compensation that labour receives, and $(MPL \times L)/Y$ is labour's share of output. Under the assumption that the production function has constant returns to scale, Euler's theorem (which we discussed in Chapter 3) tells us that these two shares sum to 1. In this case, we can write

$$\frac{\Delta Y}{Y} = \alpha \frac{\Delta K}{K} + (1 - \alpha) \frac{\Delta L}{L},$$

where α is capital's share and $(1 - \alpha)$ is labour's share.

This last equation gives us a simple formula for showing how changes in inputs lead to changes in output. In particular, we must weight the growth rates of the inputs by the factor shares. As we discussed in Chapter 3, capital's share in Canada is about 33 percent, that is, $\alpha = 0.33$. Therefore, a 10-percent increase in the amount of capital ($\Delta K/K = 0.10$) leads to a 3.3-percent increase in the amount of output ($\Delta Y/Y = 0.033$). Similarly, a 10-percent increase in the amount of labour ($\Delta L/L = 0.10$) leads to a 6.7-percent increase in the amount of output ($\Delta Y/Y = 0.067$).

Technological Progress

So far in our analysis of the sources of growth, we have been assuming that the production function does not change over time. In practice, of course, technological progress improves the production function. For any given amount of inputs, we can produce more output today than we could in the past. We now extend the analysis to allow for technological progress.

---

[18] *Mathematical note:* To see that this is equivalent to the previous equation, note that we can multiply both sides of this equation by Y and thereby cancel Y from three places in which it appears. We can cancel the K in the top and bottom of the first term on the right-hand side and the L in the top and bottom of the second term on the right-hand side. These algebraic manipulations turn this equation into the previous one.

We include the effects of the changing technology by writing the production function as

$$Y = AF(K, L),$$

where A is a measure of the current level of technology called *total factor productivity.* Output now increases not only because of increases in capital and labour but also because of increases in total factor productivity. If total factor productivity increases by 1 percent and if the inputs are unchanged, then output increases by 1 percent.

Allowing for a changing technology adds another term to our equation accounting for economic growth:

$$\frac{\Delta Y}{Y} = \alpha\frac{\Delta K}{K} + (1 - \alpha)\frac{\Delta L}{L} + \frac{\Delta A}{A}$$

$$\begin{array}{ccccc} \text{Growth in} & = & \text{Contribution} & + & \text{Contribution} & + & \text{Growth in Total} \\ \text{Output} & & \text{of Capital} & & \text{of Labour} & & \text{Factor Productivity} \end{array}.$$

This is the key equation of growth accounting. It identifies and allows us to measure the three sources of growth: changes in the amount of capital, changes in the amount of labour, and changes in total factor productivity.

Because total factor productivity is not directly observable, it is measured indirectly. We have data on the growth in output, capital, and labour; we also have data on capital's share of output. From these data and the growth-accounting equation, we can compute the growth in total factor productivity to make sure that everything adds up:

$$\frac{\Delta A}{A} = \frac{\Delta Y}{Y} - \alpha\frac{\Delta K}{K} - (1 - \alpha)\frac{\Delta L}{L}.$$

$\Delta A/A$ is the change in output that cannot be explained by changes in inputs. Thus, the growth in total factor productivity is computed as a residual—that is, as the amount of output growth that remains after we have accounted for the determinants of growth that we can measure. Indeed, $\Delta A/A$ is sometimes called the *Solow residual,* after Robert Solow, who first showed how to compute it.[19]

Total factor productivity can change for many reasons. Changes most often arise because of increased knowledge about production methods, so the Solow residual is often used as a measure of technological progress. Yet other factors, such as education and government regulation, can affect total factor productivity as well. For example, if higher public spending raises the quality of education, then workers may become more productive and output may rise, which implies higher total factor productivity. As another example, if government regulations require firms to purchase capital to reduce pollution or increase worker safety,

---

[19] Robert M. Solow, "Technical Change and the Aggregate Production Function," *Review of Economics and Statistics* 39 (1957): 312–320. It is natural to ask how growth in labour efficiency E relates to growth in total factor productivity. One can show that $\Delta A/A = (1 - \alpha)\Delta E/E$, where α is capital's share. Thus, technological change as measured by growth in the efficiency of labour is proportional to technological change as measured by the Solow residual.

then the capital stock may rise without any increase in measured output, which implies lower total factor productivity. *Total factor productivity captures anything that changes the relation between measured inputs and measured output.*

The Sources of Growth in Canada

Having learned how to measure the sources of economic growth, we now consider the data. On average, over the course of the twentieth century, Canadian output has grown at an annual rate of approximately 3 percent. Roughly speaking, over the same period, labour and capital have grown annually at 1 percentage point and 3 percentage points, respectively. Taking α at 0.33, we can provide rough estimates of the contribution to output growth of its three main determinants—growth in the labour input, growth in the capital input, and technological change. (The contribution of the latter is calculated as the residual). Table 8-3 shows the results.

We see that about 44 percent of the increase in Canadian output has been due to increases in productivity. More detailed estimates of this breakdown and evidence for subperiods within the century are available.[20] These studies show that the contribution of increased productivity to growth has been as low as 23 percent and as high as 69 percent (in particular periods), but the average is the 44 percent that we have calculated above. It is in the last quarter of the

---

TABLE 8-3

Accounting for Economic Growth in Canada

Source of Growth	Components	Data	Share of Output Growth
Output growth	$\Delta Y/Y$	3%	
Labour's share	$(1 - \alpha)$ times	0.67	
Labour growth rate	$\Delta L/L$	1%	
Contribution of labour			0.67
Capital's share	α times	0.33	
Capital growth rate	$\Delta K/K$	3%	
Contribution of capital			0.99
Contribution of productivity growth	$\Delta Y/Y - (1 - \alpha)(\Delta L/L) - \alpha(\Delta K/K)$		1.34
Proportion of growth due to increase in total factor productivity = 1.34/3 = 0.44			

Source: Authors' calculations.

---

[20] Michael Denny and Thomas Wilson, "Productivity and Growth: Canada's Competitive Roots," in *The Bell Canada Papers on Economic and Public Policy,* Vol. 1 (Kingston: John Deutsch Institute, 1993), 7–58; *Aggregate Productivity Measures* (Ottawa: Statistics Canada, 1989).

twentieth century that the contribution of productivity growth was the smallest. This means that Canada's slower average growth rate during this period had more to do with slower productivity growth than it did with a drop in the level of investment in new capital equipment. This fact makes it difficult to argue that all Canada needs to return to more rapid growth is to increase the rate of saving and investment spending.

As already noted, since the early 1970s, Canada's overall productivity performance has lagged behind that of our competitors, in particular, that of the United States. The importance of lagging productivity growth for the competitiveness of Canadian firms can be appreciated by considering the final decade of the twentieth century. Over this decade, the wages of Canadian workers increased by 3 percent more than the wages of American workers. Canadian firms are less competitive if their unit labour costs rise compared to their competitors. If our workers had become more productive, the higher wages would not have increased unit costs. However, over the decade, productivity grew by 8 percent more in the United States, so—ignoring changes in the exchange rate—Canadian unit costs rose by 11 percent. Our firms remained competitive, however, since the Canadian dollar depreciated by almost double this amount during the 1990s. There has been increased concern about the gap between U.S. and Canadian productivity growth in recent years, because the Canadian dollar has been appreciating, not depreciating. Canadians no longer have the exchange rate acting as a cushion for our weaker productivity growth performance.

CASE STUDY

Growth in the East Asian Tigers

Perhaps the most spectacular growth experiences in recent history have been those of the "Tigers" of East Asia: Hong Kong, Singapore, South Korea, and Taiwan. From 1966 to 1990, while real income per person was growing about 2 percent per year in the United States, it grew more than 7 percent per year in each of these countries. In the course of a single generation, real income per person increased fivefold, moving the Tigers from among the world's poorest countries to among the richest. (In the late 1990s, a period of pronounced financial turmoil tarnished the reputation of some of these economies. But this short-run problem, which we examine in a case study in Chapter 12, doesn't come close to reversing the spectacular long-run growth performance that the Asian Tigers have experienced.)

What accounts for these growth miracles? Some commentators have argued that the success of these four countries is hard to reconcile with basic growth theory, such as the Solow growth model, which takes technology as growing at a constant, exogenous rate. They have suggested that these countries' rapid growth is due to their ability to imitate foreign technologies. By adopting technology developed abroad, the argument goes, these countries managed to improve their production functions substantially in a relatively short period of time. If this argument is correct, these countries should have experienced unusually rapid growth in total factor productivity.

One recent study shed light on this issue by examining in detail the data from these four countries. The study found that their exceptional growth can be traced to large increases in measured factor inputs: increases in labour-force participation, increases in the capital stock, and increases in educational attainment. In South Korea, for example, the investment–GDP ratio rose from about 5 percent in the 1950s to about 30 percent in the 1980s; the percentage of the working population with at least a high-school education went from 26 percent in 1966 to 75 percent in 1991.

Once we account for growth in labour, capital, and human capital, little of the growth in output is left to explain. None of these four countries experienced unusually rapid growth in total factor productivity. Indeed, the average growth in total factor productivity in the East Asian Tigers was almost exactly the same as in the United States. Thus, although these countries' rapid growth has been truly impressive, it is easy to explain using the tools of basic growth theory.[21] ■

The Solow Residual in the Short Run

When Robert Solow introduced his famous residual, his aim was to shed light on the forces that determine technological progress and economic growth in the long run. But economist Edward Prescott has used American data to look at the Solow residual as a measure of technological change over shorter periods of time. He concludes that fluctuations in technology are a major source of short-run changes in economic activity.

Figure 8-2 shows the Solow residual and the growth in output using annual data for the United States during the period 1970 to 2007. Notice that the Solow residual fluctuates substantially. If Prescott's interpretation is correct, then we can draw conclusions from these short-run fluctuations, such as that technology worsened in 1982 and improved in 1984. Notice also that the Solow residual moves closely with output: in years when output falls, technology tends to worsen. In Prescott's view, this fact implies that recessions are driven by adverse shocks to technology. The hypothesis that technological shocks are the driving force behind short-run economic fluctuations, and the complementary hypothesis that monetary policy has no role in explaining these fluctuations, form the foundation for an approach called *real-business-cycle theory*.

Prescott's interpretation of these data is controversial, however. Many economists believe that the Solow residual does not accurately represent changes in technology over short periods of time. The standard explanation of the cyclical behaviour of the Solow residual is that it results from two measurement problems.

First, during recessions, firms may continue to employ workers they do not need so that they will have these workers on hand when the economy recovers. This phenomenon, called *labour hoarding*, means that labour input is overestimated

---

[21] Alwyn Young, "The Tyranny of Numbers: Confronting the Statistical Realities of the East Asian Growth Experience," *Quarterly Journal of Economics* 101 (August 1995): 641–680.

in recessions, because the hoarded workers are probably not working as effectively as usual. As a result, the Solow residual is more cyclical than the available production technology. In a recession, productivity as measured by the Solow residual falls even if technology has not changed simply because hoarded workers are sitting around waiting for the recession to end.

Second, when demand is low, firms may produce things that are not easily measured. In recessions, workers may clean the factory, organize the inventory, get some training, and do other useful tasks that standard measures of output fail to include. If so, then output is underestimated in recessions, which would also make the measured Solow residual cyclical for reasons other than technology.

Thus, economists can interpret the cyclical behavior of the Solow residual in different ways. Some economists point to the low productivity in recessions as evidence for adverse technology shocks. Others believe that measured productivity is low in recessions because workers are not working as hard as usual and because more of their output is not measured. Unfortunately, there is no clear evidence on the importance of labour hoarding and the cyclical mismeasurement of output. Therefore, different interpretations of Figure 8-2 persist.[22]

MORE PROBLEMS AND APPLICATIONS

1. In the economy of Solovia, the owners of capital get two-thirds of national income, and the workers receive one-third.

   a. The men of Solovia stay at home performing household chores, while the women work in factories. If some of the men started working outside the home so that the labour force increased by 5 percent, what would happen to the measured output of the economy? Does labour productivity—defined as output per worker—increase, decrease, or stay the same? Does total factor productivity increase, decrease, or stay the same?

   b. In year 1, the capital stock was 6, the labour input was 3, and output was 12. In year 2, the capital stock was 7, the labour input was 4, and output was 14. What happened to total factor productivity between the two years?

2. Labour productivity is defined as Y/L, the amount of output divided by the amount of labour input. Start with the growth-accounting equation and show that the growth in labour productivity depends on growth in total factor productivity and growth in the capital–labour ratio. In particular, show that

$$\frac{\Delta(Y/L)}{Y/L} = \frac{\Delta A}{A} + \alpha \frac{\Delta(K/L)}{K/L}.$$

(*Hint:* You may find the following mathematical trick helpful. If $z = wx$, then the growth rate of

---

[22] To learn more about this topic, consult the Appendix to Chapter 14. Also, read Edward C. Prescott, "Theory Ahead of Business Cycle Measurement," and Lawrence H. Summers, "Some Skeptical Observations on Real Business Cycle Theory," both in *Quarterly Review* 10, no. 4, Federal Reserve Bank of Minneapolis (Fall 1986): 9–27; N. Gregory Mankiw, "Real Business Cycles: A New Keynesian Perspective," *Journal of Economic Perspectives* 3 (Summer 1989): 79–90; Bennett T. McCallum, "Real Business Cycle Models," in Robert Barro, ed., Modern Business Cycle Theory (Cambridge, MA: Harvard University Press, 1989), 16–50; and Charles I. Plosser, "Understanding Real Business Cycles," *Journal of Economic Perspectives* 3 (Summer 1989): 51–77.

z is approximately the growth rate of w plus the growth rate of x. That is,

$$\Delta z / z \approx \Delta w / w + \Delta x / x.$$

3. Suppose an economy described by the Solow model is in a steady state with population growth n of 1.8 percent per year and technological progress g of 1.8 percent per year. Total output and total capital grow at 3.6 percent per year. Suppose further that the capital share of output is 1/3. If you used the growth-accounting equation to divide output growth into three sources—capital, labour, and total factor productivity—how much would you attribute to each source?

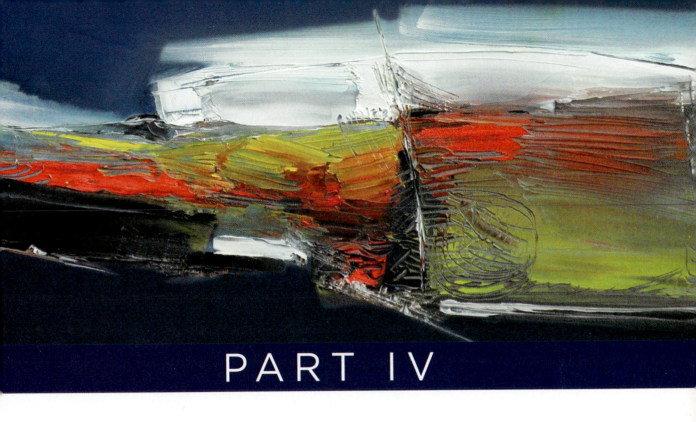

PART IV

Business Cycle Theory:
The Economy in
the Short Run

CHAPTER 9

Introduction to Economic Fluctuations

The modern world regards business cycles much as the ancient Egyptians regarded the overflowing of the Nile. The phenomenon recurs at intervals, it is of great importance to everyone, and natural causes of it are not in sight.

— *John Bates Clark, 1898*

Economic fluctuations present a recurring problem for economists and policymakers. On average, Canada's real GDP has grown at an annual rate of 3.1 percent since 1970, but this long-run average hides the fact that the economy's output of goods and services has not grown smoothly. Growth is higher in some years than in others; sometimes the economy loses ground and growth turns negative. These fluctuations in the economy's output are closely associated with fluctuations in employment. When the economy experiences a period of falling output and rising unemployment, the economy is said to be in *recession*. A recession occurred in 1991. As you can see in Figure 9.1, real GDP fell about 2 percent that year. Not surprisingly, the unemployment rate rose over this period, from 7.5 percent in 1989 to 11.3 percent in 1992. As this book goes to press, Canada is enduring its most recent recession. Real GDP growth slowed throughout 2008, and it turned negative in the fourth quarter. Once again, unemployment rose—by 2.5 percentage points between July 2008 and July 2009. Often one of the most important drivers of fluctuations in the Canadian economy is the existence of volatility in the United States. Because we export a significant fraction of our output to the Americans, when they stop buying Canadian goods, many firms in Canada need to cut production. But our economy is not a mirror image of the U.S. economy. For example, the recent recession has been much deeper there: in the fourth quarter of 2008, U.S. real GDP fell at an annualized rate of 3.8 percent. As a result, unemployment rose more dramatically south of the border. In addition to rising unemployment, recessions are also associated with shorter workweeks: more workers have part-time jobs, and fewer workers work overtime.

Economists call these fluctuations in output and employment the *business cycle*. Although this term suggests that fluctuations in the economy are regular and predictable, neither is the case, as Figure 9-1 makes clear. The historical fluctuations

FIGURE 9-1

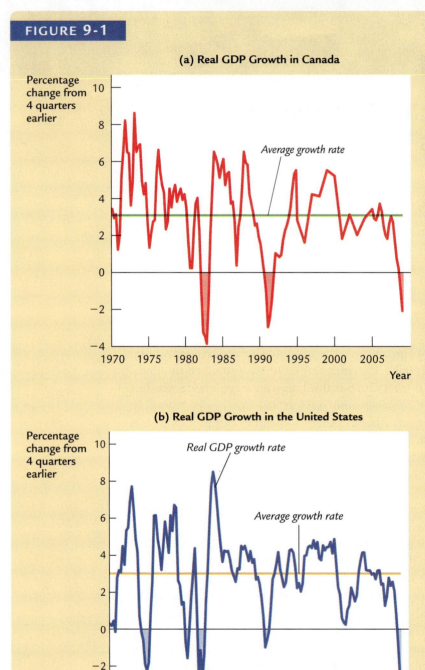

(a) Real GDP Growth in Canada

Percentage change from 4 quarters earlier

Average growth rate

Year

Real GDP Growth in Canada and the United States In Canada the growth rate in real GDP averages around 3.1 percent per year, as indicated by the green line in panel (a). But there is a wide variation around this average. Recessions are periods during which real GDP falls—that is, during which real GDP growth is negative. U.S. GDP is shown in panel (b). Clearly business cycles in the two economies are closely connected. But the state of the U.S. economy is not the only important thing for Canada.

Source: Statistics Canada, Cansim Series 1992067 and U.S. Department of Commerce.

(b) Real GDP Growth in the United States

Percentage change from 4 quarters earlier

Real GDP growth rate

Average growth rate

Year

summarized in the figure raise a variety of related questions. What causes short-run fluctuations? What model should we use to explain them? Can policymakers avoid recessions? If so, what policy levers should they use?

In Parts Two and Three of this book, we developed models to identify the long-run determinants of national income, unemployment, inflation, and other economic variables. Yet we did not examine why these variables fluctuate so much from year to year. Here in Part Four, we see how economists explain short-run fluctuations. We begin in this chapter with two tasks. First, we discuss the key differences between how the economy behaves in the long run and how it behaves in the short run. Second, we introduce the model of aggregate supply and aggregate demand, which most economists use to explain short-run fluctuations. Developing this model in more detail will be our primary job in the chapters that follow.

Because real GDP is the best single measure of economic activity, it is the focus of our model. Yet you will recall from our discussion of Okun's law near the end of Chapter 2, the business cycle is apparent not only in data from the national income accounts but also in data that describe conditions in the labour market. Put simply, when the economy heads into an economic downturn, jobs are harder to find. In Chapter 2 we saw that a temporary slowing of the GDP growth rate by 2 percentage points typically results in a 1 percentage point temporary rise in the unemployment rate. This is one of the primary reasons why policymakers are concerned about business cycles.

Okun's law is a reminder that the forces governing the short-run business cycle are very different from those shaping long-run economic growth. As we saw in Chapters 7 and 8, long-run growth in GDP is determined primarily by technological progress. The long-run trend leading to higher standards of living from generation to generation is not associated with any long-run trend in the rate of unemployment. By contrast, short-run movements in GDP are highly correlated with the utilization of the economy's labour force. The declines in the production of goods and services that occur during recessions are always associated with increases in joblessness.

Many economists, particularly those working in business and government, are engaged in the task of forecasting short-run fluctuations in the economy. Business economists are interested in forecasting to help their companies plan for changes in the economic environment. Government economists are interested in forecasting for two reasons. First, the economic environment affects the government; for example, the state of the economy influences how much tax revenue the government collects. Second, the government can affect the economy through its choice of monetary and fiscal policy. Economic forecasts are therefore an input into policy planning.

One way that economists arrive at their forecasts is by looking at *leading indicators,* which are variables that tend to fluctuate in advance of the overall economy. Forecasts can differ in part because economists hold varying opinions about which leading indicators are the most reliable. Some of the most used leading indicators are new orders, inventory levels, the number of new building permits issued, stock market indexes, money supply data, the spread between short-term and long-term interest rates, and consumer confidence surveys. These data are often used to forecast changes in economic activity about six to nine months into the future.

Other than looking at leading indicators, what can policymakers use to guide their deliberations? They can rely on the model of aggregate supply and demand that has been developed by macroeconomists. We now turn to the task of developing this framework.

Just as Egypt now controls the flooding of the Nile Valley with the Aswan Dam, modern society tries to control the business cycle with appropriate economic policies. The model we develop over the next several chapters shows how monetary and fiscal policies influence the business cycle. We will see that these policies can potentially stabilize the economy or, if poorly conducted, make the problem of economic instability even worse.

9-1 Time Horizons in Macroeconomics

Before we start building a model to explain short-run economic fluctuations, let's step back and ask a fundamental question: Why do economists need different models for different time horizons? Why can't we stop the course here and be content with the classical models developed in Chapters 3 through 8? The answer, as this book has consistently reminded its reader, is that classical macroeconomic theory applies to the long run but not to the short run. But why is this so?

How the Short Run and the Long Run Differ

Most macroeconomists believe that the key difference between the short run and the long run is the behaviour of prices. *In the long run, prices are flexible and can respond to changes in supply or demand. In the short run, many prices are "sticky" at some predetermined level.* Because prices behave differently in the short run than in the long run, economic policies have different effects over different time horizons.

To see how the short run and the long run differ, consider the effects of a change in monetary policy. Suppose that the Bank of Canada suddenly reduced the money supply by 5 percent. According to the classical model, the money supply affects nominal variables—variables measured in terms of money—but not real variables. As you may recall from Chapter 4, the theoretical separation of real and nominal variables is called the *classical dichotomy*, and the irrelevance of the money supply for the determination of real variables is called *monetary neutrality*. Most economists believe that these classical ideas explain how the economy works in the long run: a 5-percent reduction in the money supply lowers all prices (including nominal wages) by 5 percent while all real variables remain the same. Thus, in the long run, changes in the money supply do not cause fluctuations in output or employment.

In the short run, however, many prices do not respond to changes in monetary policy. A reduction in the money supply does not immediately cause all firms to cut the wages they pay, all stores to change the price tags on their goods, all mail-order firms to issue new catalogues, and all restaurants to print new menus. Instead, there is little immediate change in many prices; that is, many prices are sticky. This short-run price stickiness implies that the short-run impact of a change in the money supply is not the same as the long-run impact.

A model of economic fluctuations must take into account this short-run price stickiness. We will see that the failure of prices to adjust quickly and completely to changes in the money supply (as well as to other exogenous changes in economic conditions) means that, in the short run, output and employment must do some of the adjusting instead. In other words, during the time horizon over which prices are sticky, the classical dichotomy no longer holds: nominal variables can influence real variables, and the economy can deviate from the equilibrium predicted by the classical model.

If You Want to Know Why Firms Have Sticky Prices, Ask Them

How sticky are prices, and why are they sticky? As we have seen, these questions are at the heart of new Keynesian theories of short-run economic fluctuations (as well as of the traditional model of aggregate demand and aggregate supply). In an intriguing study, economist Alan Blinder attacked these questions directly by surveying firms about their price-adjustment decisions.

Blinder began by asking firm managers how often they change prices. The answers, summarized in Table 9-1, yielded two conclusions. First, sticky prices are

TABLE 9-1

The Frequency of Price Adjustment

This table is based on answers to the question: How often do the prices of your most important products change in a typical year?

Frequency	Percentage of Firms
Less than once	10.2
Once	39.3
1.01 to 2	15.6
2.01 to 4	12.9
4.01 to 12	7.5
12.01 to 52	4.3
52.01 to 365	8.6
More than 365	1.6

Source: Table 4.1, Alan S. Blinder, "On Sticky Prices: Academic Theories Meet the Real World," in N. G. Mankiw, ed., *Monetary Policy* (Chicago: University of Chicago Press, 1994), 117–154.

quite common. The typical firm in the economy adjusts its prices once or twice a year. Second, there are large differences among firms in the frequency of price adjustment. About 10 percent of firms change prices more often than once a week, and about the same number change prices less often than once a year.

Blinder then asked the firm managers why they don't change prices more often. In particular, he explained to the managers 12 economic theories of sticky prices and asked them to judge how well each of these theories describe their firms. Table 9-2 summarizes the theories and ranks them

TABLE 9-2

Theories of Price Stickiness

Theory and Brief Description	Percentage of Firms That Accepted Theory
Coordination failure: Firms hold back on price changes, waiting for others to go first	60.6
Cost-based pricing with lags: Price rises are delayed until costs rise	55.5
Delivery lags, service, etc.: Firms prefer to vary other product attributes, such as delivery lags, service, or product quality	54.8
Implicit contracts: Firms tacitly agree to stabilize prices, perhaps out of "fairness" to customers	50.4
Nominal contracts: Prices are fixed by explicit contracts	35.7
Costs of price adjustment: Firms incur costs by changing prices	30.0
Procyclical elasticity: Demand curves become less elastic as they shift in	29.7
Pricing points: Certain prices (e.g., $9.99) have special psychological significance	24.0
Inventories: Firms vary inventory stocks instead of prices	20.9
Constant marginal cost: Marginal cost is flat and markups are constant	19.7
Hierarchical delays: Bureaucratic delays slow down decisions	13.6
Judging quality by price: Firms fear customers will mistake price cuts for reductions in quality	10.0

Source: Tables 4.3 and 4.4, Alan S. Blinder, "On Sticky Prices: Academic Theories Meet the Real World," in N. G. Mankiw, ed., *Monetary Policy* (Chicago: University of Chicago Press, 1994), 117–154.

by the percentage of managers who accepted the theory. Notice that each of the theories was endorsed by some of the managers, and each was rejected by a large number as well. One interpretation is that different theories apply to different firms, depending on industry characteristics, and that price stickiness is a macroeconomic phenomenon without a single microeconomic explanation.

Among the 12 theories, coordination failure tops the list. According to Blinder, this is an important finding, for it suggests that the theory of coordination failure explains price stickiness, which in turn explains why the economy experiences short-run fluctuations around its natural level. He writes, "the most obvious policy implication of the model is that more coordinated wage and price setting—somehow achieved—could improve welfare. But if this proves difficult or impossible, the door is opened to activist monetary policy to cure recessions."[1] ■

The Model of Aggregate Supply and Aggregate Demand

How does introducing sticky prices change our view of how the economy works? We can answer this question by considering economists' two favourite words— supply and demand.

In classical macroeconomic theory, the amount of output depends on the economy's ability to *supply* goods and services, which in turn depends on the supplies of capital and labour and on the available production technology. This is the essence of the models developed in Chapters 3, 7, and 8. Flexible prices are a crucial assumption of classical theory. The theory posits, sometimes implicitly, that prices adjust to ensure that the quantity of output demanded equals the quantity supplied.

The economy works quite differently when prices are sticky. In this case, as we will see, output also depends on the *demand* for goods and services. Demand, in turn, is influenced by monetary policy, fiscal policy, and various other factors. Because monetary and fiscal policy can influence the economy's output over the time horizon when prices are sticky, price stickiness provides a rationale for why these policies may be useful in stabilizing the economy in the short run.

In the rest of this chapter, we develop a model that makes these ideas more precise. The model of supply and demand, which we used in Chapter 1 to discuss the market for pizza, offers some of the most fundamental insights in economics.

---

[1] To read more about this study, see Alan S. Blinder, "On Sticky Prices: Academic Theories Meet the Real World," in *Monetary Policy,* N. G. Mankiw, ed. (Chicago: University of Chicago Press, 1994): 117–154; or Alan S. Blinder, Elie R. D. Canetti, David E. Lebow, and Jeremy E. Rudd, *Asking About Prices: A New Approach to Understanding Price Stickiness* (New York: Russell Sage Foundation, 1998).

This model shows how the supply and demand for any good jointly determine the good's price and the quantity sold, and how shifts in supply and demand affect the price and quantity. In the rest of this chapter, we introduce the "economy-size" version of this model—*the model of aggregate supply and aggregate demand*. This macroeconomic model allows us to study how the aggregate price level and the quantity of aggregate output are determined. It also provides a way to contrast how the economy behaves in the long run and how it behaves in the short run.

Although the model of aggregate supply and aggregate demand resembles the model of supply and demand for a single good, the analogy is not exact. The model of supply and demand for a single good considers only one good within a large economy. By contrast, as we will see in the coming chapters, the model of aggregate supply and aggregate demand is a sophisticated model that incorporates the interactions among many markets. In the remainder of this chapter we get a first glimpse at those interactions by examining the model in its most simplified form. Our goal is not to explain the model fully but instead to introduce the its key elements and to illustrate how it can help explain short-run economic fluctuations.

9-2 Aggregate Demand

Aggregate demand (*AD*) is the relationship between the quantity of output demanded and the aggregate price level. In other words, the aggregate demand curve tells us the quantity of goods and services people want to buy at any given level of prices. We examine the theory of aggregate demand in detail in Chapters 10 through 12. Here we use the quantity theory of money to provide a simple, although incomplete, derivation of the aggregate demand curve.

The Quantity Equation as Aggregate Demand

Recall from Chapter 4 that the quantity theory says that

$$MV = PY,$$

where M is the money supply, V is the velocity of money, P is the price level, and Y is the amount of output. If the velocity of money is constant, then this equation states that the money supply determines the nominal value of output, which in turn is the product of the price level and the amount of output.

You might recall that the quantity equation can be rewritten in terms of the supply and demand for real money balances:

$$M/P = (M/P)^{\mathrm{d}} = kY,$$

where $k = 1/V$ is a parameter determining how much money people want to hold for every dollar of income. In this form, the quantity equation states that the supply of real money balances M/P equals the demand $(M/P)^{\mathrm{d}}$ and that the

FIGURE 9-2

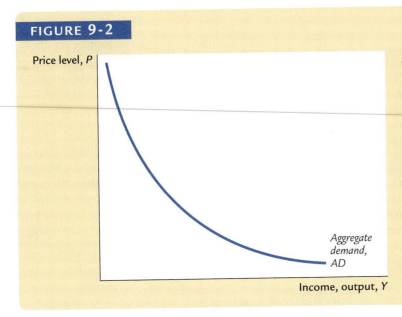

Price level, *P*

Income, output, *Y*

Aggregate demand, *AD*

The Aggregate Demand Curve
The aggregate demand curve *AD* shows the relationship between the price level *P* and the quantity of goods and services demanded *Y*. It is drawn for a given value of the money supply *M*. The aggregate demand curve slopes downward: the higher the price level *P*, the lower the level of real balances *M/P*, and therefore the lower the quantity of goods and services demanded *Y*.

demand is proportional to output *Y*. The velocity of money *V* is the "flip side" of the money demand parameter *k*.

For any fixed money supply and velocity, the quantity equation yields a negative relationship between the price level *P* and output *Y*. Figure 9-2 graphs the combinations of *P* and *Y* that satisfy the quantity equation holding *M* and *V* constant. This downward-sloping curve is called the aggregate demand curve.

Why the Aggregate Demand Curve Slopes Downward

As a strictly mathematical matter, the quantity equation explains the downward slope of the aggregate demand curve very simply. The money supply *M* and the velocity of money *V* determine the nominal value of output *PY*. Once *PY* is fixed, if *P* goes up, *Y* must go down.

What is the economic intuition that lies behind this mathematical relationship? For a complete answer, we have to wait a couple of chapters. For now, however, consider the following logic: Because we have assumed that the velocity of money is fixed, the money supply determines the dollar value of all transactions in the economy. (This conclusion should be familiar from Chapter 4.) If the price level rises for some reason, so that each transaction requires more dollars, the number of transactions and thus the quantity of goods and services purchased must fall.

We can also explain the downward slope of the aggregate demand curve by thinking about the supply and demand for real money balances. If output is higher, people engage in more transactions and need higher real balances *M/P*. For a fixed money supply *M*, higher real balances imply a lower price level. Conversely, if the price level is lower, real money balances are higher; the higher level of real balances allows a greater volume of transactions, which means a greater quantity of output is demanded.

Shifts in the Aggregate Demand Curve

The aggregate demand curve is drawn for a fixed value of the money supply. In other words, it tells us the possible combinations of P and Y for a given value of M. If the money supply changes, then the possible combinations of P and Y change, which means the aggregate demand curve shifts.

For example, consider what happens if the Bank of Canada reduces the money supply. The quantity equation, $MV = PY$, tells us that the reduction in the money supply leads to a proportionate reduction in the nominal value of output PY. For any given price level, the amount of output is lower, and for any given amount of output, the price level is lower. As in Figure 9-3, the aggregate demand curve relating P and Y shifts inward.

The opposite occurs if the Bank of Canada increases the money supply. The quantity equation tells us that an increase in M leads to an increase in PY. For any given price level, the amount of output is higher, and for any given amount of output, the price level is higher. As shown in Figure 9-4, the aggregate demand curve shifts outward.

Although the quantity theory of money gives a very simple basis for understanding the aggregate demand curve, be forewarned that reality is more complicated. Fluctuations in the money supply are not the only source of fluctuations in aggregate demand. Even if the money supply is held constant, the aggregate demand curve shifts if some event causes a change in the velocity of money. Over the next three chapters, we consider many possible reasons for shifts in the aggregate demand curve.

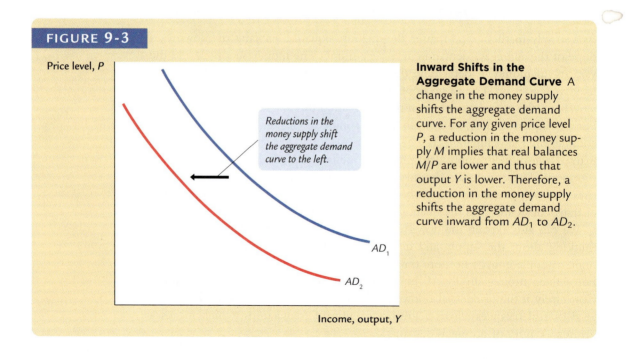

FIGURE 9-3

Price level, P

Reductions in the money supply shift the aggregate demand curve to the left.

AD_1

AD_2

Income, output, Y

Inward Shifts in the Aggregate Demand Curve A change in the money supply shifts the aggregate demand curve. For any given price level P, a reduction in the money supply M implies that real balances M/P are lower and thus that output Y is lower. Therefore, a reduction in the money supply shifts the aggregate demand curve inward from AD_1 to AD_2.

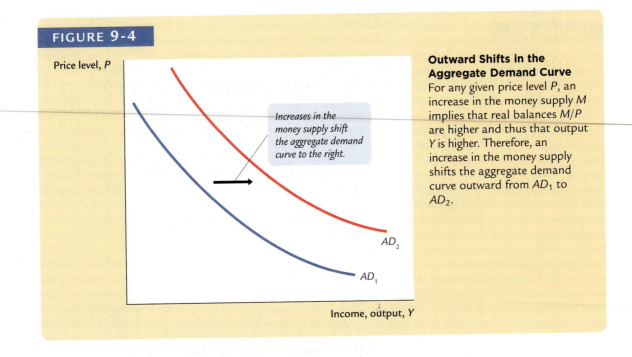

FIGURE 9-4

Price level, P

Increases in the money supply shift the aggregate demand curve to the right.

AD_2

AD_1

Income, output, Y

Outward Shifts in the Aggregate Demand Curve For any given price level P, an increase in the money supply M implies that real balances M/P are higher and thus that output Y is higher. Therefore, an increase in the money supply shifts the aggregate demand curve outward from AD_1 to AD_2.

9-3 Aggregate Supply

By itself, the aggregate demand curve does not tell us the price level or the amount of output; it merely gives a relationship between these two variables. To accompany the aggregate demand curve, we need another relationship between P and Y that crosses the aggregate demand curve—an aggregate supply curve. The aggregate demand and aggregate supply curves together pin down the economy's price level and quantity of output.

Aggregate supply (*AS*) is the relationship between the quantity of goods and services supplied and the price level. Because the firms that supply goods and services have flexible prices in the long run but sticky prices in the short run, the aggregate supply relationship depends on the time horizon. We need to discuss two different aggregate supply curves: the long-run aggregate supply curve *LRAS* and the short-run aggregate supply curve *SRAS*. We also need to discuss how the economy makes the transition from the short run to the long run.

The Long Run: The Vertical Aggregate Supply Curve

Because the classical model describes how the economy behaves in the long run, we derive the long-run aggregate supply curve from the classical model. Recall from Chapter 3 that the amount of output produced depends on the fixed amounts of capital and labour and on the available technology. To show

FIGURE 9-5

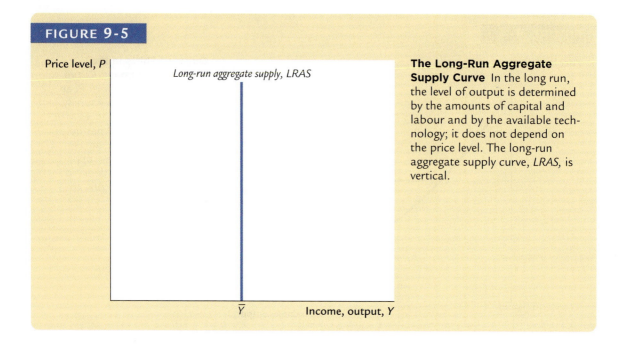

Price level, P

Long-run aggregate supply, LRAS

$\overline{Y}$

Income, output, Y

The Long-Run Aggregate Supply Curve In the long run, the level of output is determined by the amounts of capital and labour and by the available technology; it does not depend on the price level. The long-run aggregate supply curve, *LRAS*, is vertical.

this, we write

$$Y = F(\overline{K}, \overline{L})$$
$$= \overline{Y}.$$

According to the classical model, output does not depend on the price level. To show that output is the same for all price levels, we draw a vertical aggregate supply curve, as in Figure 9-5. The intersection of the aggregate demand curve with this vertical aggregate supply curve determines the price level.

If the aggregate supply curve is vertical, then changes in aggregate demand affect prices but not output. For example, if the money supply falls, the aggregate demand curve shifts downward, as in Figure 9-6. The economy moves from the old intersection of aggregate supply and aggregate demand, point *A,* to the new intersection, point *B.* The shift in aggregate demand affects only prices.

The vertical aggregate supply curve satisfies the classical dichotomy, for it implies that the level of output is independent of the money supply. This long-run level of output, $\overline{Y}$, is called the *full-employment* or *natural* level of output. It is the level of output at which the economy's resources are fully employed or, more realistically, at which unemployment is at its natural rate (which we discussed in Chapter 6).

The Short Run: The Horizontal Aggregate Supply Curve

The classical model and the vertical aggregate supply curve apply only in the long run. In the short run, some prices are sticky and, therefore, do not adjust to changes in demand. Because of this price stickiness, the short-run aggregate supply curve is not vertical.

FIGURE 9-6

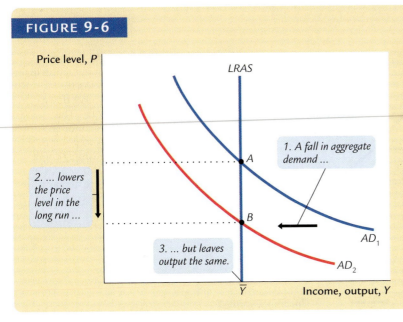

Shifts in Aggregate Demand in the Long Run A reduction in the money supply shifts the aggregate demand curve downward from AD_1 to AD_2. The equilibrium for the economy moves from point A to point B. Since the aggregate supply curve is vertical in the long run, the reduction in aggregate demand affects the price level but not the level of output.

In this chapter, we simplify things by assuming an extreme example, which we relax in later chapters. Suppose that all firms have issued price catalogues and that it is costly for them to issue new ones. Thus, all prices are stuck at predetermined levels. At these prices, firms are willing to sell as much as their customers are willing to buy, and they hire just enough labour to produce the amount demanded. Because the price level is fixed, we represent this situation in Figure 9-7 with a horizontal aggregate supply curve.

The short-run equilibrium of the economy is the intersection of the aggregate demand curve and this horizontal short-run aggregate supply curve. In this case, changes in aggregate demand do affect the level of output. For example, if the Bank of Canada suddenly reduces the money supply, the aggregate demand

FIGURE 9-7

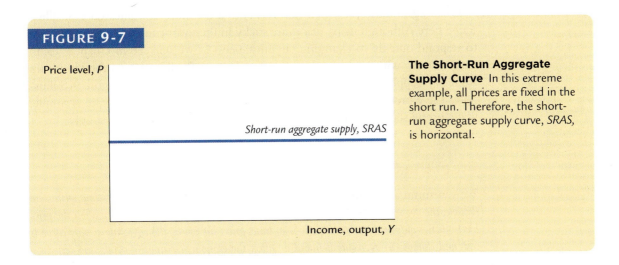

The Short-Run Aggregate Supply Curve In this extreme example, all prices are fixed in the short run. Therefore, the short-run aggregate supply curve, SRAS, is horizontal.

FIGURE 9-8

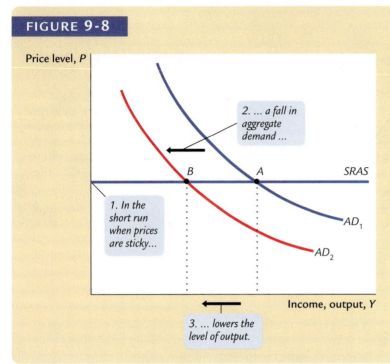

Price level, P

2. ... a fall in aggregate demand ...

B A SRAS

1. In the short run when prices are sticky...

AD_1

AD_2

Income, output, Y

3. ... lowers the level of output.

Shifts in Aggregate Demand in the Short Run A reduction in the money supply shifts the aggregate demand curve downward from AD_1 to AD_2. The equilibrium for the economy moves from point A to point B. Since the aggregate supply curve is horizontal in the short run, the reduction in aggregate demand reduces the level of output.

curve shifts inward, as in Figure 9-8. The economy moves from the old intersection of aggregate demand and aggregate supply, point A, to the new intersection, point B. The movement from point A to point B represents a decline in output at a fixed price level.

Thus, a fall in aggregate demand reduces output in the short run because prices do not adjust instantly. After the sudden fall in aggregate demand, firms are stuck with prices that are too high. With demand low and prices high, firms sell less of their product, so they reduce production and lay off workers. The economy experiences a recession.

Once again, be forewarned that reality is a bit more complicated than illustrated here. Although many prices are sticky in the short run, some prices are able to respond quickly to changing circumstances. As we will see in Chapter 13, in an economy with some sticky prices and some flexible prices, the short-run aggregate supply curve is upward sloping rather than horizontal. Figure 9-8 illustrates the extreme case in which all prices are stuck. Because this case is simple, it is a useful starting point for thinking about short-run aggregate supply.

From the Short Run to the Long Run

We can summarize our analysis so far as follows: *Over long periods of time, prices are flexible, the aggregate supply curve is vertical, and changes in aggregate demand affect the price level but not output. Over short periods of time, prices are sticky, the aggregate supply curve is flat, and changes in aggregate demand do affect the economy's output of goods and services.*

FIGURE 9-9

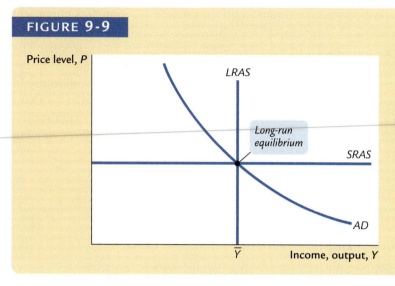

Long-Run Equilibrium In the long run, the economy finds itself at the intersection of the long-run aggregate supply curve and the aggregate demand curve. Because prices have adjusted to this level, the short-run aggregate supply curve crosses this point as well.

How does the economy make the transition from the short run to the long run? Let's trace the effects over time of a fall in aggregate demand. Suppose that the economy is initially in long-run equilibrium, as shown in Figure 9-9. In this figure, there are three curves: the aggregate demand curve, the long-run aggregate supply curve, and the short-run aggregate supply curve. The long-run equilibrium is the point at which aggregate demand crosses the long-run aggregate supply curve. Prices have adjusted to reach this equilibrium. Therefore, when the economy is in its long-run equilibrium, the short-run aggregate supply curve must cross this point as well.

Now suppose that the Bank of Canada reduces the money supply and the aggregate demand curve shifts downward, as in Figure 9-10. In the short run,

FIGURE 9-10

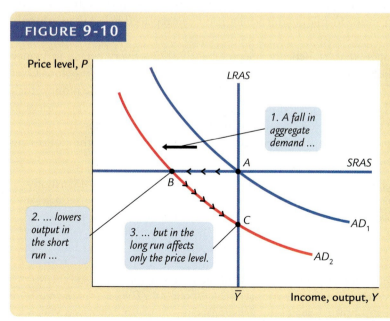

A Reduction in Aggregate Demand The economy begins in long-run equilibrium at point A. A reduction in aggregate demand, perhaps caused by a decrease in the money supply, moves the economy from point A to point B, where output is below its natural level. As prices fall, the economy gradually recovers from the recession, moving from point B to point C.

prices are sticky, so the economy moves from point *A* to point *B*. Output and employment fall below their natural levels, which means the economy is in a recession. Over time, in response to the low demand, wages and prices fall. The gradual reduction in the price level moves the economy downward along the aggregate demand curve to point *C,* which is the new long-run equilibrium. In the new long-run equilibrium (point *C*), output and employment are back to their natural levels, but prices are lower than in the old long-run equilibrium (point *A*). Thus, a shift in aggregate demand affects output in the short run, but this effect dissipates over time as firms adjust their prices.

CASE STUDY

A Monetary Lesson from French History

Finding modern examples to illustrate the lessons from Figure 9-10 is hard. The executives of modern central banks are too smart to engineer a substantial reduction in the money supply for no good reason. They know that a recession would ensue, and they usually do their best to prevent it:. Fortunately, history often fills in the gap when recent experience fails to produce a relevant experiment.

A vivid example of the effects of monetary contraction occurred in eighteenth-century France. François Velde, an economist at the Federal Reserve Bank of Chicago, recently studied this episode in French economic history.

The story begins with the unusual nature of French money at the time. The money stock in this economy included a variety of gold and silver coins that, in contrast to modern money, did not indicate a specific monetary value. Instead, the monetary value of each coin was set by government decree, and the government could easily change the monetary value and thus the money supply. Sometimes these changes would occur literally overnight. It is almost as though, while you were sleeping, every $1 bill in your wallet had been replaced by a bill worth only 80 cents.

Indeed, that is what happened on September 22, 1724. Every person in France woke up with 20 percent less money than he or she had had the night before. Over the course of seven months during that year, the nominal value of the money stock was reduced by about 45 percent. The government's goal was to reduce prices in the economy to what the government considered an appropriate level.

What happened as a result of this policy? Velde reports the following consequences:

> ...Although prices and wages did fall, they did not do so by the full 45%; moreover, it took them months, if not years, to fall that far. Real wages in fact rose, at least initially. Interest rates rose. The only market that adjusted instantaneously and fully was the foreign exchange market. Even markets that were as close to fully competitive as one can imagine, such as grain markets, failed to react initially. ....
>
> At the same time, the industrial sector of the economy (or at any rate the textile industry) went into a severe contraction, by about 30%. The onset of the recession may have occurred before the deflationary policy began, but it was widely

believed at the time that the severity of the contraction was due to monetary policy, in particular to a resulting "credit crunch" as holders of money stopped providing credit to trade in anticipation of further price declines (the "scarcity of money" frequently blamed by observers). Likewise, it was widely believed (on the basis of past experience) that a policy of inflation would halt the recession, and coincidentally or not, the economy rebounded once the nominal money supply was increased by 20% in May 1726.

This description of events from French history fits well with the lessons from modern macroeconomic theory.[2] ■

FYI

David Hume on the Real Effects of Money

As noted in Chapter 4, many of the central ideas of monetary theory have a long history. The classical theory of money discussed in that chapter dates back as far as the eighteenth-century philosopher and economist David Hume. While Hume understood that changes in the money supply ultimately leads to inflation, he also knew that money had real effects in the short run. Here is how Hume described a monetary injection in his 1752 essay "Of Money":

> To account, then, for this phenomenon, we must consider, that though the high price of commodities be a necessary consequence of the increase of gold and silver, yet it follows not immediately upon that increase; but some time is required before the money circulates through the whole state, and makes its effect be felt on all ranks of people. At first, no alteration is perceived; by degrees the price rises, first of one commodity, then of another; till the whole at last reaches a just proportion with the new quantity of specie which is in the kingdom. In my opinion, it is only in this interval or intermediate situation, between the acquisition of money and rise of prices, that the increasing quantity of gold and silver is favourable to industry. When any quantity of money is imported into a nation, it is not at first dispersed into many hands; but is confined to the coffers of a few persons, who immediately seek to employ it to advantage. Here are a set of manufacturers or merchants, we shall suppose, who have received returns of gold and silver for goods which they sent to Cadiz. They are thereby enabled to employ more workmen than formerly, who never dream of demanding higher wages, but are glad of employment from such good paymasters. If workmen become scarce, the manufacturer gives higher wages, but at first requires an increase of labour; and this is willingly submitted to by the artisan, who can now eat and drink better, to compensate his additional toil and fatigue. He carries his money to market, where he finds everything at the same price as formerly, but returns with greater quantity and of better kinds, for the use of his family. The farmer and gardener, finding that all their commodities are taken off, apply themselves with alacrity to the raising more; and at the same time can afford to take better and more cloths from their tradesmen, whose price is the same as formerly, and their industry only whetted by so much new gain. It is easy to trace the money in its progress through the whole commonwealth; where we shall find, that it must first quicken the diligence of every individual, before it increase the price of labour.

It is likely that, when writing these words, Hume was well aware of the French experience described in the preceding Case Study.

---

[2] François R. Velde, *Chronicles of a Deflation Unforetold.* (Federal Reserve Bank of Chicago, November 2006), pp. 40–41.

The Short Run, the Long Run, and the Very Long Run

This book discusses many models of the economy, each with its own set of simplifying assumptions. Sometimes it's hard to keep all the models straight. One way to do so is to categorize the models by the time horizon over which they apply. The models fall into three categories:

1. *The Short Run* This chapter and those that follow present the short-run theory of the economy. This theory assumes that prices are sticky and that, because of this price stickiness, capital and labour are sometimes not fully employed. Price stickiness is widely viewed as being important for explaining the economic fluctuations we observe from month to month or from year to year. Sometimes economists refer to two slightly different versions of the short run. Sometimes only one particular price—that of labour, the wage rate—is assumed to be sticky (while goods prices are flexible). In the second version of short-run models, both wages and prices are assumed to be sticky. Perhaps this case should be called the very short run. The short run aggregate supply curve drawn in this chapter is for this version of the short run. The short run aggregate supply curves drawn in Chapters 13 and 15 are positively sloped, since in those cases only wages are assumed to be sticky.

2. *The Long Run* Chapter 3 presented the basic long-run theory of the economy, called the classical model. Chapter 4 presented the classical theory of money, and Chapter 5 presented the classical theory of the open economy. These chapters assumed that prices are flexible and, therefore, that capital and labour are fully employed. These chapters also took as fixed the quantities of capital and labour, as well as the technology for turning capital and labour into output. These assumptions are best suited for a time horizon of several years. Over this period, prices can adjust to equilibrium levels, yet capital, labour, and technology are relatively constant.

3. The Very Long Run Chapters 7 and 8 presented the basic theory of economic growth, called the Solow model. This model analyzes the time horizon over which the capital stock, the labour force, and the available technology can change. This model is designed to explain how the economy works over a period of several decades. The appendix to Chapter 5 considered this time span in the open-economy case.

When analyzing economic policies, it is important to keep in mind that they influence the economy over all time horizons. We must, therefore, draw on the insights of all these models.

9-4 Stabilization Policy

Fluctuations in the economy as a whole come from changes in aggregate supply or aggregate demand. Economists call exogenous changes in these curves **shocks** to the economy. A shock that shifts the aggregate demand curve is called a **demand shock,** and a shock that shifts the aggregate supply curve is called a **supply shock.** These shocks disrupt economic well-being by pushing output and employment away from their natural levels. One goal of the model of aggregate supply and aggregate demand is to show how shocks cause economic fluctuations.

Another goal of the model is to evaluate how macroeconomic policy can respond to these shocks. Economists use the term **stabilization policy** to refer to policy actions aimed at reducing the severity of short-run economic fluctuations. Because output and employment fluctuate around their long-run natural levels, stabilization policy dampens the business cycle by keeping output and employment as close to their natural levels as possible.

In the coming chapters, we examine in detail how stabilization policy works and what practical problems arise in its use. Here we begin our analysis of stabilization policy by examining how monetary policy might respond to shocks. Monetary policy is an important component of stabilization policy because, as we have seen, the money supply has a powerful impact on aggregate demand.

Shocks to Aggregate Demand

Consider an example of a demand shock: the introduction and expanded availability of credit cards. Because credit cards are often a more convenient way to make purchases than using cash, they reduce the quantity of money that people choose to hold. This reduction in money demand is equivalent to an increase in the velocity of money. When each person holds less money, the money demand parameter k falls. This means that each dollar of money moves from hand to hand more quickly, so velocity $V\,(=1/k)$ rises.

If the money supply is held constant, the increase in velocity causes nominal spending to rise and the aggregate demand curve to shift outward, as in Figure 9-11. In the short run, the increase in demand raises the output of the economy—it causes an economic boom. At the old prices, firms now sell more output. Therefore, they hire more workers, ask their existing workers to work longer hours, and make greater use of their factories and equipment.

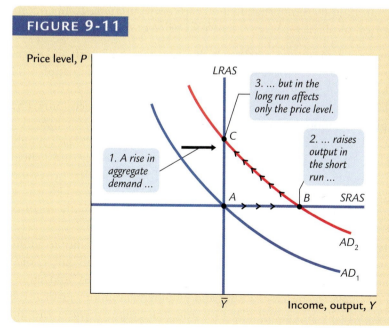

FIGURE 9-11

Price level, P

LRAS

3. ... but in the long run affects only the price level.

C

2. ... raises output in the short run ...

1. A rise in aggregate demand ...

A   B   SRAS

AD_2

AD_1

$\overline{Y}$ Income, output, Y

An Increase in Aggregate Demand The economy begins in long-run equilibrium at point A. An increase in aggregate demand, due to an increase in the velocity of money, moves the economy from point A to point B, where output is above its natural level. As prices rise, output gradually returns to its natural level, and the economy moves from point B to point C.

Over time, the high level of aggregate demand pulls up wages and prices. As the price level rises, the quantity of output demanded declines, and the economy gradually approaches the natural rate of production. But during the transition to the higher price level, the economy's output is higher than the natural rate.

What can the the Bank of Canada do to dampen this boom and keep output closer to the natural level? The Bank of Canada might reduce the money supply to offset the increase in velocity. Offsetting the change in velocity would stabilize aggregate demand. Thus, the Bank of Canada can reduce or even eliminate the impact of demand shocks on output and employment if it can skillfully control the money supply. Whether the Bank of Canada in fact has the necessary skill is a more difficult question, which we take up in Chapters 14 and 15.

Shocks to Aggregate Supply

Shocks to aggregate supply can also cause economic fluctuations. A supply shock is a shock to the economy that alters the cost of producing goods and services and, as a result, the prices that firms charge. Because supply shocks have a direct impact on the price level, they are sometimes called *price shocks*. Here are some examples:

- A drought that destroys crops. The reduction in food supply pushes up food prices.
- A new environmental protection law that requires firms to reduce their emissions of pollutants. Firms pass on the added costs to customers in the form of higher prices.
- An increase in union aggressiveness. This pushes up wages and the prices of the goods produced by union workers.
- The organization of an international oil cartel. By curtailing competition, the major oil producers can raise the world price of oil.

All these events are *adverse* supply shocks, which means they push costs and prices upward. A *favourable* supply shock, such as the breakup of an international oil cartel, reduces costs and prices.

Figure 9-12 shows how an adverse supply shock affects the economy. The short-run aggregate supply curve shifts upward. (The supply shock may also lower the natural level of output and thus shift the long-run aggregate supply curve to the left, but we ignore that effect here.) If aggregate demand is held constant, the economy moves from point *A* to point *B:* the price level rises and the amount of output falls below the natural level. An experience like this is called *stagflation,* because it combines stagnation (falling output) with inflation (rising prices).

Faced with an adverse supply shock, a policymaker with the ability to influence aggregate demand, such as the Bank of Canada, has a difficult choice between two options. The first option, implicit in Figure 9-12, is to hold aggregate demand constant. In this case, output and employment are lower than the natural level. Eventually, prices will fall to restore full employment at the old price level (point *A*). But the cost of this process is a painful recession.

FIGURE 9-12

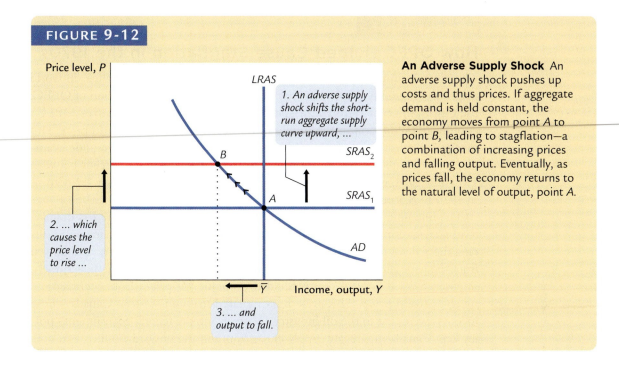

Price level, *P*

1. An adverse supply shock shifts the short-run aggregate supply curve upward, ...

LRAS

SRAS₂

B

A

SRAS₁

2. ... which causes the price level to rise ...

AD

$\overline{Y}$ Income, output, *Y*

3. ... and output to fall.

An Adverse Supply Shock An adverse supply shock pushes up costs and thus prices. If aggregate demand is held constant, the economy moves from point A to point B, leading to stagflation—a combination of increasing prices and falling output. Eventually, as prices fall, the economy returns to the natural level of output, point A.

The second option, illustrated in Figure 9-13, is to expand aggregate demand to bring the economy toward the natural level more quickly. If the increase in aggregate demand coincides with the shock to aggregate supply, the economy goes immediately from point *A* to point *C*. In this case, the Bank of Canada is said to *accommodate* the supply shock. The drawback of this option, of course, is that the price level is permanently higher. There is no way to adjust aggregate demand both to maintain full employment and to keep the price level stable.

FIGURE 9-13

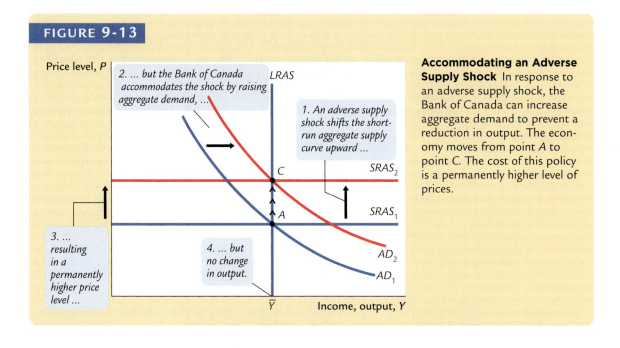

Price level, *P*

2. ... but the Bank of Canada accommodates the shock by raising aggregate demand, ...

LRAS

1. An adverse supply shock shifts the short-run aggregate supply curve upward ...

C

SRAS₂

A

SRAS₁

3. ... resulting in a permanently higher price level ...

4. ... but no change in output.

AD₂

AD₁

$\overline{Y}$ Income, output, *Y*

Accommodating an Adverse Supply Shock In response to an adverse supply shock, the Bank of Canada can increase aggregate demand to prevent a reduction in output. The economy moves from point A to point C. The cost of this policy is a permanently higher level of prices.

CASE STUDY

How OPEC Helped Cause Stagflation in the 1970s

The most disruptive supply shocks in recent history are due to changes in world primary commodity prices. The first of these was due to the formation of OPEC, the Organization of Petroleum Exporting Countries. In the early 1970s, OPEC's coordinated reduction in the supply of oil nearly doubled the world price. This increase in oil prices caused stagflation in most industrial countries. For example, in the United States, inflation rose from 6.2 percent to 11 percent between 1973 and 1974, while the unemployment rate almost doubled, from 4.9 percent in 1973 to 8.5 percent in 1975.

The unemployment effects of the OPEC oil-price increase were less dramatic in Canada for two reasons. First, using expansionary aggregate demand policies, the federal government cushioned the recession that would have followed from the large drop in export sales to the United States. Second, the government imposed a price control that precluded domestic oil prices from increasing as much as world prices. This price limit irritated many in western Canada whose incomes were tied to the oil industry. In any event, the federal government's policy kept Canada's aggregate supply curve from shifting upward as much as it otherwise would have. Canada's inflation rate only went up by 3.3 percentage points in 1974 (compared to 4.8 percentage points in the United States), and Canada's unemployment rate increased by only 1.5 percentage points in the 1973–1975 period (compared to 3.6 percentage points in the United States).

A few years later, when the world economy had nearly recovered from the first OPEC recession, almost the same thing happened again. OPEC raised oil prices, causing further stagflation. The average increase in world oil prices in the 1979–1981 period was almost 40 percent. U.S. inflation rose from 7.7 percent in 1978 to 10.3 percent by 1981, while unemployment rose from 6.1 percent to 7.5 percent over the same period. In Canada, the federal government did not attempt the same insulation of the Canadian economy from this world event, so responses were more dramatic than in the mid-1970s. Inflation rose from 8.9 percent in 1978 to 12.5 percent in 1981, while unemployment rose from 8.3 percent to 11 percent. When less protected from an adverse supply-side shock, Canada suffered a bigger bout of stagflation.[3]

More recently, OPEC has not been such a major cause of economic fluctuations. Conservation efforts and technological changes have made Western economies less susceptible to oil shocks. Our economy today is more service-based and less manufacturing-based, and services typically use less energy to produce than do manufactured goods. Because the amount of oil consumed per unit of real GDP has fallen by more than half since 1980, it takes a much larger oil price change to have the impact on the economy that we observed in the 1970s. And, of course, Canada is increasingly a producer, not just a user, of oil. ∎

---

[3] Some economists have suggested that changes in oil prices played a major role in economic fluctuations even before the 1970s. See James D. Hamilton, "Oil and the Macroeconomy Since World War II," *Journal of Political Economy* 91 (April 1983): 228–248.

9-5 Conclusion

This chapter has introduced a framework to study economic fluctuations: the model of aggregate supply and aggregate demand. The model is built on the assumption that prices are sticky in the short run and flexible in the long run. It shows how shocks to the economy cause output to deviate temporarily from the level implied by the classical model.

The model also highlights the role of monetary policy. Poor monetary policy can be a source of shocks to the economy. A well-run monetary policy can respond to shocks and stabilize the economy.

In the chapters that follow, we refine our understanding of this model and our analysis of stabilization policy. Chapters 10 through 12 go beyond the quantity equation to refine our theory of aggregate demand. This refinement shows that aggregate demand depends on fiscal policy as well as monetary policy. Chapter 13 examines aggregate supply in more detail. Chapter 14 brings these elements together in a dynamic model of aggregate demand and supply. Chapter 15 examines the debate over the virtues and limits of stabilization policy.

Summary

1. Economies experience short-run fluctuations in economic activity, measured most broadly by real GDP. These fluctuations (business cycles) are evident in many macroeconomic variables. In particular, when GDP growth declines, the unemployment rate rises above its natural rate. Some economists look at various leading indicators in an attempt to predict these fluctuations.

2. The crucial difference between how the economy works in the long run and how it works in the short run is that prices are flexible in the long run but sticky in the short run. The model of aggregate supply and aggregate demand provides a framework to analyze economic fluctuations and see how the impact of policies varies over different time horizons.

3. The aggregate demand curve slopes downward. It tells us that the lower the price level, the greater the aggregate quantity of goods and services demanded.

4. In the long run, the aggregate supply curve is vertical because output is determined by the amounts of capital and labour and by the available technology, but not by the level of prices. Therefore, shifts in aggregate demand affect the price level but not output or employment.

5. In the short run, the aggregate supply curve is horizontal, because wages and prices are sticky at predetermined levels. Therefore, shifts in aggregate demand affect output and employment.

6. Shocks to aggregate demand and aggregate supply cause economic fluctuations. Because the Bank of Canada can shift the aggregate demand curve, it can attempt to offset these shocks to maintain output and employment at their natural levels.

KEY CONCEPTS

Aggregate demand

Aggregate supply

Shocks

Demand shocks

Supply shocks

Stabilization policy

QUESTIONS FOR REVIEW

1. When GDP declines during a recession, explain what typically happens to the unemployment rate.

2. Give an example of a price that is sticky in the short run and flexible in the long run.

3. Why does the aggregate demand curve slope downward?

4. Explain the impact of an increase in the money supply in the short run and in the long run.

5. Why is it easier for the Bank of Canada to deal with demand shocks than with supply shocks?

PROBLEMS AND APPLICATIONS

1. An economy begins in long-run equilibrium, and than a change in government regulations allows banks to start paying interest on chequing accounts. Recall that the money stock is the sum of currency and demand deposits, including chequing accounts, so this regulatory change makes holding money more attractive.

  a. How does this change affect the demand for money?

  b. What happens to the velocity of money?

  c. If the central bank keeps the money supply constant, what will happen to output and prices in the short run and in the long run?

  d. If the goal of the central bank is to stabilize the price level, should the bank keep the money supply constant in response to this regulatory change? If not, what should it do? Why?

  e. If the goal of the central bank is to stabilize output, how would your answer to part (d) change?

2. Suppose the Bank of Canada reduces the money supply by 5 percent.

  a. What happens to the aggregate demand curve?

  b. What happens to the level of output and the price level in the short run and in the long run?

  c. According to Okun's law, what happens to unemployment in the short run and in the long run? (*Hint:* Okun's law is the relationship between output and unemployment discussed in Chapter 2.)

  d. What happens to the real interest rate in the short run and in the long run? (*Hint:* Use the model of the real interest rate in Chapter 3 to see what happens when output changes.)

3. Let's examine how the goals of the Bank of Canada influence its response to shocks. Suppose central bank A cares only about keeping the price level stable, and central bank B cares only about keeping output and employment at their natural rates. Explain how each central bank would respond to

  a. An exogenous decrease in the velocity of money.

  b. An exogenous increase in the price of oil.

CHAPTER 10

Aggregate Demand I: Building the *IS-LM* Model

I shall argue that the postulates of the classical theory are applicable to a special case only and not to the general case. . . . Moreover, the characteristics of the special case assumed by the classical theory happen not to be those of the economic society in which we actually live, with the result that its teaching is misleading and disastrous if we attempt to apply it to the facts of experience.

— *John Maynard Keynes,* The General Theory

Of all the economic fluctuations in world history, the one that stands out as particularly large, painful, and intellectually significant is the Great Depression of the 1930s. During this time, Canada and many other countries experienced massive unemployment and greatly reduced incomes. In the worst year, 1933, over one-fifth of the Canadian labour force was unemployed, and real GDP was 28 percent below its 1929 level.

This devastating episode caused many economists to question the validity of classical economic theory—the theory we examined in Chapters 3 through 8. Classical theory seemed incapable of explaining the Depression. According to that theory, national income depends on factor supplies and the available technology, neither of which changed substantially from 1929 to 1933. After the onset of the Depression, many economists believed that a new model was needed to explain such a large and sudden economic downturn and to suggest government policies that might reduce the economic hardship so many people faced.

In 1936 the British economist John Maynard Keynes revolutionized economics with his book *The General Theory of Employment, Interest, and Money*. Keynes proposed a new way to analyze the economy, which he presented as an alternative to classical theory. His vision of how the economy works quickly became a center of controversy. Yet, as economists debated *The General Theory*, a new understanding of economic fluctuations gradually developed.

Keynes proposed that low aggregate demand is responsible for the low income and high unemployment that characterize economic downturns. He criticized classical theory for assuming that aggregate supply alone—capital, labour, and technology—determines national income. Economists today reconcile these two views with the model of aggregate demand and aggregate supply introduced in Chapter 9. In the long run, prices are flexible, and aggregate supply determines income. But in the short run, prices are sticky, so changes in aggregate demand influence income. In 2008 and 2009, as all market economies descended into a recession, the Keynesian theory of business cycles was often in the news. Policymakers around the world debated how best to increase aggregate demand and put their economies on the road to recovery.

In this chapter and the next, we continue our study of economic fluctuations by looking more closely at aggregate demand. Our goal is to identify the variables that shift the aggregate demand curve, causing fluctuations in national income. We also examine more fully the tools policymakers can use to influence aggregate demand. In Chapter 9 we derived the aggregate demand curve from the quantity theory of money, and we showed that monetary policy can shift the aggregate demand curve. In this chapter we see that the government can influence aggregate demand with both monetary and fiscal policy.

The model of aggregate demand developed in this chapter, called the **IS–LM model,** is the leading interpretation of Keynes's theory. The goal of the model is to show what determines national income for any given price level. There are two ways to interpret this exercise. We can view the IS–LM model as showing what causes income to change in the short run when the price level is fixed. Or we can view the model as showing what causes the aggregate demand curve to shift. These two interpretations of the model are equivalent: as Figure 10-1 shows, in the short run when the price level is fixed, shifts in the aggregate demand curve lead to changes in national income.

The two parts of the IS–LM model are, not surprisingly, the **IS curve** and the **LM curve.** IS stands for "investment" and "saving," and the IS curve represents

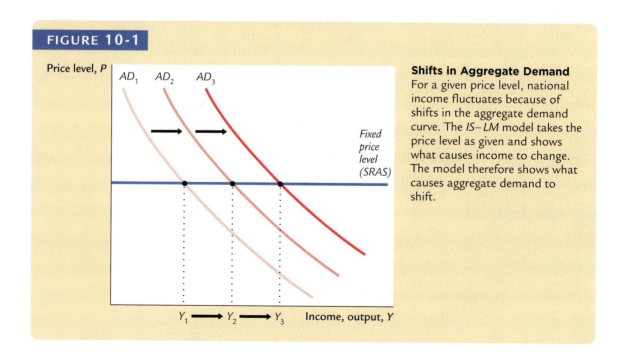

FIGURE 10-1

Shifts in Aggregate Demand
For a given price level, national income fluctuates because of shifts in the aggregate demand curve. The IS–LM model takes the price level as given and shows what causes income to change. The model therefore shows what causes aggregate demand to shift.

what's going on in the market for goods and services (which we first discussed in Chapter 3). *LM* stands for "liquidity" and "money," and the *LM* curve represents what's happening to the supply and demand for money (which we first discussed in Chapter 4). Because the interest rate influences both investment and money demand, it is the variable that links the two halves of the *IS–LM* model. The model shows how interactions between these markets determine the position and slope of the aggregate demand curve and, therefore, the level of national income in the short run.[1]

10-1 The Goods Market and the *IS* Curve

The *IS* curve plots the relationship between the interest rate and the level of income that arises in the market for goods and services. To develop this relationship, we start with a basic model called the **Keynesian cross.** This model is the simplest interpretation of Keynes's theory of how national income is determined, and it is also a building block for the more complex and realistic *IS–LM* model.

The Keynesian Cross

In *The General Theory* Keynes proposed that an economy's total income was, in the short run, determined largely by the desire to spend by households, firms, and the government. The more people want to spend, the more goods and services firms can sell. The more firms can sell, the more output they will choose to produce and the more workers they will choose to hire. Thus, the problem during recessions and depressions, according to Keynes, was inadequate spending. The Keynesian cross is an attempt to model this insight.

Planned Expenditure We begin our derivation of the Keynesian cross by drawing a distinction between actual and planned expenditure. *Actual expenditure* is the amount households, firms, and the government spend on goods and services, and as we first saw in Chapter 2, it equals the economy's gross domestic product (GDP). *Planned expenditure* is the amount households, firms, and the government would like to spend on goods and services.

Why would actual expenditure ever differ from planned expenditure? The answer is that firms might engage in unplanned inventory investment because their sales do not meet their expectations. When firms sell less of their product than they planned, their stock of inventories automatically rises; conversely, when firms sell more than planned, their stock of inventories falls. Because these unplanned changes in inventory are counted as investment spending by firms, actual expenditure can be either above or below planned expenditure.

Now consider the determinants of planned expenditure. In this chapter, we simplify by assuming that the economy is closed, so that net exports are zero. Of course, Canada is an open economy that exports a significant portion of our GDP.

---

[1] The *IS–LM* model was introduced in a classic article by the Nobel-prize–winning economist John R. Hicks, "Mr. Keynes and the Classics: A Suggested Interpretation," *Econometrica* 5 (1937): 147–159.

Thus, while our simplifying assumption is very helpful in getting the discussion of aggregate demand theory started, we must extend it to the open-economy case later on. We devote an entire chapter (Chapter 12) to doing just that. In the meantime, we write planned expenditure PE as the sum of consumption C, planned investment I, and government purchases G:

$$PE = C + I + G.$$

To this equation, we add the consumption function

$$C = C(Y - T).$$

This equation states that consumption depends on disposable income $(Y - T)$, which is total income Y minus taxes T. To keep things simple, for now we take planned investment as exogenously fixed:

$$I = \bar{I}.$$

And as in Chapter 3, we assume that fiscal policy—the levels of government purchases and taxes—is fixed:

$$G = \overline{G},$$
$$T = \overline{T}.$$

Combining these five equations, we obtain

$$PE = C(Y - \overline{T}) + \bar{I} + \overline{G}.$$

This equation shows that planned expenditure is a function of income Y, the level of planned investment $\bar{I}$, and the fiscal policy variables $\overline{G}$ and $\overline{T}$.

Figure 10-2 graphs planned expenditure as a function of the level of income. This line slopes upward because higher income leads to higher consumption and thus higher planned expenditure. The slope of this line is the marginal propensity to consume, the MPC: it shows how much planned expenditure increases when income rises by $1. This planned-expenditure function is the first piece of the model called the Keynesian cross.

FIGURE 10-2

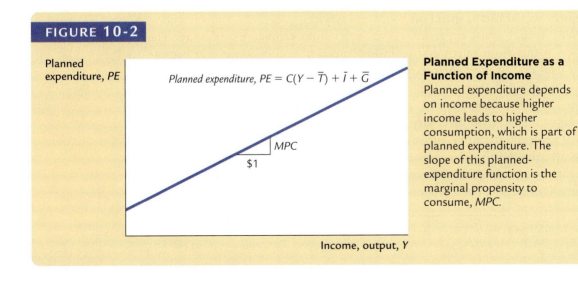

Planned expenditure, PE

Planned expenditure, $PE = C(Y - \overline{T}) + \bar{I} + \overline{G}$

MPC

$1

Income, output, Y

Planned Expenditure as a Function of Income
Planned expenditure depends on income because higher income leads to higher consumption, which is part of planned expenditure. The slope of this planned-expenditure function is the marginal propensity to consume, MPC.

The Economy in Equilibrium The next piece of the Keynesian cross is the assumption that the economy is in equilibrium when actual expenditure equals planned expenditure. This assumption is based on the idea that when people's plans have been realized, they have no reason to change what they are doing. Recalling that Y as GDP equals not only total income but also total actual expenditure on goods and services, we can write this equilibrium condition as

Actual Expenditure = Planned Expenditure

$$Y = PE.$$

The 45-degree line in Figure 10-3 plots the points where this condition holds. With the addition of the planned-expenditure function, this diagram becomes the Keynesian cross. The equilibrium of this economy is at point A, where the planned-expenditure function crosses the 45-degree line.

How does the economy get to the equilibrium? In this model, inventories play an important role in the adjustment process. Whenever the economy is not in equilibrium, firms experience unplanned changes in inventories, and this induces them to change production levels. Changes in production in turn influence total income and expenditure, moving the economy toward equilibrium.

For example, suppose the economy were ever to find itself with GDP at a level greater than the equilibrium level, such as the level Y_1 in Figure 10-4. In this case, planned expenditure PE_1 is less than production Y_1, so firms are selling less than they are producing. Firms add the unsold goods to their stock of inventories. This unplanned rise in inventories induces firms to lay off workers and reduce production, and these actions in turn reduce GDP. This process of unintended inventory accumulation and falling income continues until income Y falls to the equilibrium level.

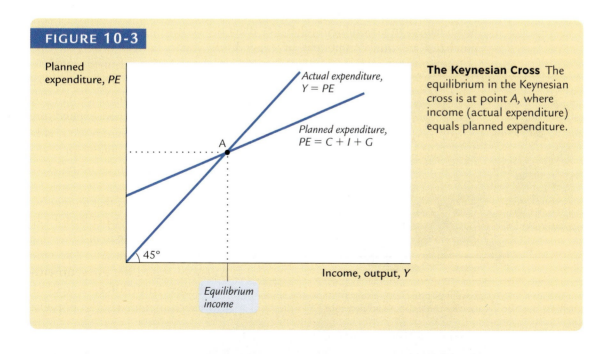

FIGURE 10-3

Planned expenditure, PE

Actual expenditure, $Y = PE$

Planned expenditure, $PE = C + I + G$

A

45°

Equilibrium income

Income, output, Y

The Keynesian Cross The equilibrium in the Keynesian cross is at point A, where income (actual expenditure) equals planned expenditure.

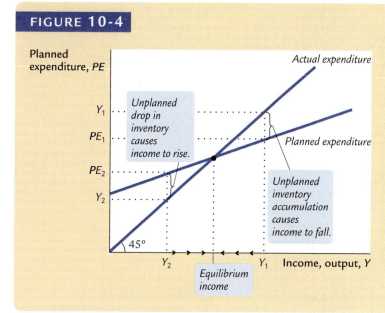

FIGURE 10-4

Planned expenditure, *PE*

Actual expenditure

Y_1

Unplanned drop in inventory causes income to rise.

PE_1

Planned expenditure

PE_2

Y_2

Unplanned inventory accumulation causes income to fall.

45°

Y_2 *Equilibrium income* Y_1 Income, output, *Y*

The Adjustment to Equilibrium in the Keynesian Cross If firms were producing at level Y_1, then planned expenditure PE_1 would fall short of production, and firms would accumulate inventories. This inventory accumulation would induce firms to reduce production. Similarly, if firms were producing at level Y_2, then planned expenditure PE_2 would exceed production, and firms would run down their inventories. This fall in inventories would induce firms to raise production. In both cases, the firms' decisions drive the economy toward equilibrium.

Similarly, suppose GDP were at a level lower than the equilibrium level, such as the level Y_2 in Figure 10-4. In this case, planned expenditure PE_2 is greater than production Y_2. Firms meet the high level of sales by drawing down their inventories. But when firms see their stock of inventories dwindle, they hire more workers and increase production. GDP rises, and the economy approaches the equilibrium.

In summary, the Keynesian cross shows how income Y is determined for given levels of planned investment I and fiscal policy G and T. We can use this model to show how income changes when one of these exogenous variables changes.

Fiscal Policy and the Multiplier: Government Purchases Consider how changes in government purchases affect the economy. Because government purchases are one component of expenditure, higher government purchases result in higher planned expenditure for any given level of income. If government purchases rise by ΔG, then the planned-expenditure schedule shifts upward by ΔG, as in Figure 10-5. The equilibrium of the economy moves from point A to point B.

This graph shows that an increase in government purchases leads to an even greater increase in income. That is, ΔY is larger than ΔG. The ratio $\Delta Y/\Delta G$ is called the **government-purchases multiplier;** it tells us how much income rises in response

"Your Majesty, my voyage will not only forge a new route to the spices of the East but also create over three thousand new jobs."

FIGURE 10-5

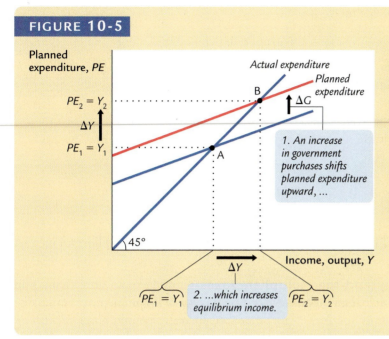

Planned expenditure, *PE*

Actual expenditure

Planned expenditure

B

ΔG

$PE_2 = Y_2$

ΔY

$PE_1 = Y_1$

A

1. An increase in government purchases shifts planned expenditure upward, ...

45°

ΔY

Income, output, *Y*

$PE_1 = Y_1$

2. ...which increases equilibrium income.

$PE_2 = Y_2$

An Increase in Government Purchases in the Keynesian Cross An increase in government purchases of ΔG raises planned expenditure by that amount for any given level of income. The equilibrium moves from point *A* to point *B*, and income rises from Y_1 to Y_2. Note that the increase in income ΔY exceeds the increase in government purchases ΔG. Thus, fiscal policy has a multiplied effect on income.

to a $1 increase in government purchases. An implication of the Keynesian cross is that the government-purchases multiplier is larger than 1.

Why does fiscal policy have a multiplied effect on income? The reason is that, according to the consumption function, $C = C(Y - T)$, higher income causes higher consumption. When an increase in government purchases raises income, it also raises consumption, which further raises income, which further raises consumption, and so on. Therefore, in this model, an increase in government purchases causes a greater increase in income.

How big is the multiplier? To answer this question, we trace through each step of the change in income. The process begins when expenditure rises by ΔG, which implies that income rises by ΔG as well. This increase in income in turn raises consumption by $MPC \times \Delta G$, where *MPC* is the marginal propensity to consume. This increase in consumption raises expenditure and income once again. This second increase in income of $MPC \times \Delta G$ again raises consumption, this time by $MPC \times (MPC \times \Delta G)$, which again raises expenditure and income, and so on. This feedback from consumption to income to consumption continues indefinitely. The total effect on income is

Initial Change in Government Purchases = ΔG

First Change in Consumption $= MPC \times \Delta G$

Second Change in Consumption $= MPC^2 \times \Delta G$

Third Change in Consumption $= MPC^3 \times \Delta G$

$\vdots \qquad\qquad\qquad\qquad \vdots$

$$\Delta Y = (1 + MPC + MPC^2 + MPC^3 + \cdots)\Delta G.$$

The government-purchases multiplier is

$$\Delta Y/\Delta G = 1 + MPC + MPC^2 + MPC^3 + \cdots$$

This expression for the multiplier is an example of an *infinite geometric series*. A result from algebra allows us to write the multiplier as[2]

$$\Delta Y/\Delta G = 1/(1 - MPC).$$

For example, if the marginal propensity to consume is 0.6, the multiplier is

$$\Delta Y/\Delta G = 1 + 0.6 + 0.6^2 + 0.6^3 + \cdots$$
$$= 1/(1 - 0.6)$$
$$= 2.5.$$

In this case, a $1.00 increase in government purchases raises equilibrium income by $2.50.[3]

Fiscal Policy and the Multiplier: Taxes Consider now how changes in taxes affect equilibrium income. A decrease in taxes of ΔT immediately raises disposable income $Y - T$ by ΔT and, therefore, increases consumption by $MPC \times \Delta T$. For any given level of income Y, planned expenditure is now higher. As

---

[2] *Mathematical note:* We prove this algebraic result as follows. Let

$$z = 1 + x + x^2 + \cdots.$$

Multiply both sides of this equation by x:

$$xz = x + x^2 + x^3 + \cdots.$$

Subtract the second equation from the first:

$$z - xz = 1.$$

Rearrange this last equation to obtain

$$z(1 - x) = 1,$$

which implies

$$z = 1/(1 - x).$$

This completes the proof.

[3] *Mathematical note:* The government-purchases multiplier is most easily derived using a little calculus. Begin with the equation

$$Y = C(Y - T) + I + G.$$

Holding T and I fixed, differentiate to obtain

$$dY = C'dY + dG,$$

and then rearrange to find

$$dY/dG = 1/(1 - C').$$

This is the same as the equation in the text.

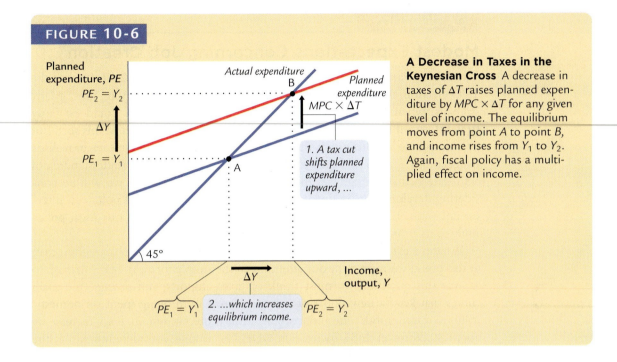

FIGURE 10-6

A Decrease in Taxes in the Keynesian Cross A decrease in taxes of ΔT raises planned expenditure by $MPC \times \Delta T$ for any given level of income. The equilibrium moves from point A to point B, and income rises from Y_1 to Y_2. Again, fiscal policy has a multiplied effect on income.

Figure 10-6 shows, the planned-expenditure schedule shifts upward by $MPC \times \Delta T$. The equilibrium of the economy moves from point A to point B.

Just as an increase in government purchases has a multiplied effect on income, so does a decrease in taxes. As before, the initial change in expenditure, now $MPC \times \Delta T$, is multiplied by $1/(1 - MPC)$. The overall effect on income of the change in taxes is

$$\Delta Y/\Delta T = -MPC/(1 - MPC).$$

This expression is the **tax multiplier,** the amount income changes in response to a $1 change in taxes. For example, if the marginal propensity to consume is 0.6, then the tax multiplier is

$$\Delta Y/\Delta T = -0.6/(1 - 0.6) = -1.5.$$

In this example, a \$1.00 cut in taxes raises equilibrium income by \$1.50.[4]

---

[4] *Mathematical note:* As before, the multiplier is most easily derived using a little calculus. Begin with the equation

$$Y = C(Y - T) + I + G.$$

Holding I and G fixed, differentiate to obtain

$$dY = C'(dY - dT),$$

and then rearrange to find

$$dY/dT = -C'/(1 - C').$$

This is the same as the equation in the text.

CASE STUDY

Modest Expectations Concerning Job Creation

The Liberal Party formed Canada's Government from 1993 to 2006. During the 1993 election, the Liberals campaigned on a platform of "jobs, jobs, jobs." Many students, when hearing the term "multiplier," expect that it could be fairly straightforward for governments to fulfull job-creation promises of this sort. But economists now believe that the multiplier terminology may create unrealistic expectations. This trend in thinking will become clearer as our understanding of aggregate demand progresses through this book. For example, we will be considering developments in financial markets—the effects of fiscal policy on interest rates and the exchange rate. We will learn that the size of our fiscal policy multipliers is much reduced by these considerations.

What is a plausible value for the government spending multiplier—given that, at this point, we must limit our attention to the simple formula $1/1 - MPC$)? To answer this question, we must think of taxes, imports, and saving—the main things that keep a new dollar of income earned from being spent on domestically produced goods. The first consideration is the tax system; taxes increase by about $0.25 for each $1 increase in GDP. The second consideration is that the transfer payments people receive from the government decrease as their income increases, and in aggregate this variation means that transfer payments fall by about $0.15 for each $1 increase in GDP. Since "taxes" in our model stand for *net* payments by individuals to government—taxes less transfer receipts—we must take the overall "tax rate" to be 0.25 plus 0.15, or 0.40. Thus the proportion of income not taxed is 0.60. Finally, Canadians tend to import about one-quarter of all goods consumed. With a propensity to spend about 75 percent of each extra dollar of disposable income, we have an overall marginal propensity to consume domestically produced goods (out of each dollar of pretax income, GDP) equal to:

Proportion of Income Not Taxed	×	Proportion of Spending Not Spent on Imports	×	Propensity to Spend	=	MPC
(0.60)		(0.75)		(0.75)	=	0.34

With the *MPC* estimated at 0.34, the spending multiplier, $1/1 - MPC$), is 1.5.

The federal government's deficit elimination program in the 1990s was the largest fiscal initiative undertaken in Canadian history—until that record was broken in 2009. During the 1994–1999 period, federal budgets involved an average cut in government spending of about $8 billion per year compared to what spending would have been if it had remained a constant fraction of GDP. Thus, we can take $\Delta G = \$8$ billion as representing the magnitude of the government's fiscal policy during this period. The multiplier formula then predicts that ΔY is $12 billion. Since Canada's GDP averaged $835 billion during these years, this fiscal policy involved changing output by about 1.4 percent.

How much could this initiative be expected to change unemployment? The answer to this question can be had by relying on Okun's law, which was explained in Chapter 2. Okun's law states that unemployment usually rises by about one-half the percentage fall in GDP. Thus, the effect of the fiscal policy of the 1990s is estimated to be a change in the unemployment rate of three-quarters of 1 percentage point. While that represented a little more than 100,000 jobs, with an average unemployment rate over this period of 9 percent, not many would summarize this change as "jobs, jobs, jobs." We must also keep in mind that the simple formula, $1/(1 - MPC)$, *over*estimates the effects of policy.

It is also important to realize that a small multiplier was exactly what the government wanted during this period. Since the government was cutting expenditures to reduce the budget deficit, it did not want to destroy many jobs. A small fiscal multiplier was just what was needed in that case.

So the "jobs, jobs, jobs" electoral refrain was misleading for two reasons. First, because our fiscal policy multiplier is small, we must have modest expectations when governments use expansionary fiscal policy. Second, since the Liberals conducted a contractionary—not an expansionary—fiscal policy after being elected, jobs were destroyed, not created! ∎

CASE STUDY

The 2009 Stimulus Package

A world-wide recession developed in late 2008 (and we discuss the causes of this recession in a case study in the next chapter). In the face of this slow-down in economic activity, our federal government reversed its earlier promise to avoid running *any* budget deficit; in fact, its budget of January 2009 included a major fiscal stimulus. Along with the funds that provincial governments would spend as part of the programs, the government promised just over $50 billion of new program spending and tax cuts over the next two years—a total representing 3.5 percent of GDP. Roughly three-quarters of the initiatives involved increased government spending, and the remaining quarter was made up of tax cuts. An even larger fiscal initiative amounting to 5 percent of GDP was introduced at the same time in the United States, where President Obama's full commitment to Keynesian analysis held sway.

We can use our analysis to assess whether the size of our government's initiative was appropriate. Recalling from the previous case study that the fiscal-policy multiplier is certainly no larger than 1.5, we can appreciate that, while leading to a record budget deficit, our government's stimulus was barely big enough to cope with the magnitude of the recession. Assuming that the $50 billion would be dispersed evenly over the two years, and ignoring the fact that the tax-multiplier is smaller than the spending multiplier, each annual initiative of $25 billion could be expected to raise GDP by (1.5 times $25 billion) = $37.5 billion—roughly 2.6 percent of GDP. During the final quarter of 2008 and the first quarter of 2009,

Canadian GDP shrank by 3 percent, measured at annual rates. Thus, if policy-makers were expecting at least two more quarters of recession, the policy in the budget could be assessed as barely adequate.

Much debate centred on whether the government should have stressed spending increases so much more than tax cuts. Advocates of the government's decision argued that increased spending was better than reduced taxes because, according to standard Keynesian theory, the government-purchases multiplier exceeds the tax multiplier. The reason for this difference is simple: when the government spends one dollar, that dollar gets spent, whereas when the government gives households a tax cut of one dollar, that dollar or some of it might be saved. Thus, advocates argued, increased government spending on roads, schools, and other infrastructure was the better route to increase aggregate demand and create jobs. Other economists were more skeptical. One concern was that spending on infrastructure would take time, whereas tax cuts could occur more quickly. Infrastructure spending requires taking bids and signing contracts, and even after the projects begin, they can take years to complete. Past estimates indicate that, on average, it takes 18 months for the spending to start! With such lags, by the time much of the stimulus goes into effect, the recession might be long over.

In addition, some economists thought that using infrastructure spending to promote employment might conflict with the goal of obtaining the infrastructure that was most needed. Here is how Gary Becker, a Nobel Prize-winning economist, explained the concern on his blog:

> Putting new infrastructure spending in depressed areas like Detroit might have a big stimulating effect since infrastructure building projects in these areas can utilize some of the considerable unemployed resources there. However, many of these areas are also declining because they have been producing goods and services that are not in great demand, and will not be in demand in the future. Therefore, the overall value added by improving their roads and other infrastructure is likely to be a lot less than if the new infrastructure were located in growing areas that might have relatively little unemployment, but do have great demand for more roads, schools, and other types of long-term infrastructure.

In its budget, the government stressed the three desirable features of a fiscal initiative—that it be *timely, targeted,* and *temporary.* Finance Canada officials argued that spending initiatives could be targeted more easily on depressed sectors or regions than could general tax cuts. Admittedly, however, some tax cuts, such as the expansion of the Working Income Tax Benefit which was part of the 2009 budget, are easily targeted on the least well-off working Canadians. Nevertheless, while the infrastructure projects score well on the targeted criterion overall, they score lower on being timely, as we have already noted. Finally, there is the temporary criterion—a question of how easy or difficult it is to reverse an initiative. The whole point of a policy of aggregate-demand management is that it is temporary. We want a stimulus only during the recession phase of the business cycle, a limitation that is very difficult to maintain with tax cuts. Once a tax cut is enacted, it is politically very hard to end. It is much easier to end infrastructure spending simply by not starting an additional project once the previous one has been completed.

Although the government did not make a persuasive case that it had struck a perfect balance between the advantages and disadvantages of spending increases versus tax cuts—in terms of all three of the important timely, targeted and temporary criteria—we can at least appreciate the nature of the compromises it faced. But whatever the details, policy-makers clearly have accepted the economic intuition provided by our basic short-run model of aggregate demand. The logic that actual fiscal-policy practitioners use is quintessentially Keynesian: when the economy sinks into recession, most governments seem to embrace the notion to act as demanders of last resort, despite small fiscal-policy multipliers and challenges of timing and reversibility.

In future chapters we will return to the broad question of whether governments should conduct an active stabilization policy—after we identify several other challenges by extending the theory of aggregate supply and demand. ■

The Interest Rate, Investment, and the *IS* Curve

The Keynesian cross is only a steppingstone on our path to the *IS–LM* model. The Keynesian cross is useful because it shows how the spending plans of households, firms, and the government determine the economy's income. Yet it makes the simplifying assumption that the level of planned investment I is fixed. As we discussed in Chapter 3, an important macroeconomic relationship is that planned investment depends on the interest rate r.

To add this relationship between the interest rate and investment to our model, we write the level of planned investment as

$$I = I(r).$$

This investment function is graphed in panel (a) of Figure 10-7. Because the interest rate is the cost of borrowing to finance investment projects, an increase in the interest rate reduces planned investment. As a result, the investment function slopes downward.

To determine how income changes when the interest rate changes, we can combine the investment function with the Keynesian-cross diagram. Because investment is inversely related to the interest rate, an increase in the interest rate from r_1 to r_2 reduces the quantity of investment from $I(r_1)$ to $I(r_2)$. The reduction in planned investment, in turn, shifts the planned-expenditure function downward, as in panel (b) of Figure 10-7. The shift in the planned-expenditure function causes the level of income to fall from Y_1 to Y_2. Hence, an increase in the interest rate lowers income.

The *IS* curve, shown in panel (c) of Figure 10-7, summarizes this relationship between the interest rate and the level of income. In essence, the *IS* curve combines the interaction between r and I expressed by the investment function and the interaction between I and Y demonstrated by the Keynesian cross. Because an increase in the interest rate causes planned investment to fall, which in turn causes income to fall, the *IS* curve slopes downward.

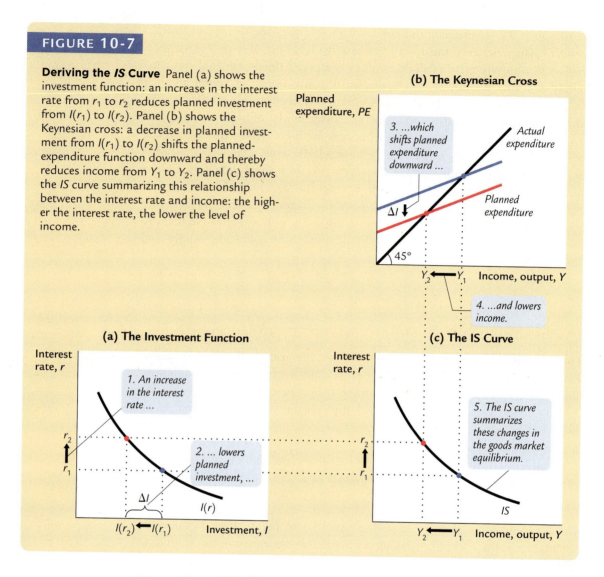

FIGURE 10-7

Deriving the *IS* Curve Panel (a) shows the investment function: an increase in the interest rate from r_1 to r_2 reduces planned investment from $I(r_1)$ to $I(r_2)$. Panel (b) shows the Keynesian cross: a decrease in planned investment from $I(r_1)$ to $I(r_2)$ shifts the planned-expenditure function downward and thereby reduces income from Y_1 to Y_2. Panel (c) shows the *IS* curve summarizing this relationship between the interest rate and income: the higher the interest rate, the lower the level of income.

How Fiscal Policy Shifts the *IS* Curve

The *IS* curve shows us, for any given interest rate, the level of income that brings the goods market into equilibrium. As we learned from the Keynesian cross, the level of income also depends on fiscal policy. The *IS* curve is drawn for a given fiscal policy; that is, when we construct the *IS* curve, we hold G and T fixed. When fiscal policy changes, the *IS* curve shifts.

Figure 10-8 uses the Keynesian cross to show how an increase in government purchases from G_1 to G_2 shifts the *IS* curve. This figure is drawn for a given interest rate $\bar{r}$ and thus for a given level of planned investment. The Keynesian cross shows that this change in fiscal policy raises planned expenditure and thereby increases equilibrium income from Y_1 to Y_2. Therefore, an increase in government purchases shifts the *IS* curve outward.

We can use the Keynesian cross to see how other changes in fiscal policy shift the *IS* curve. Because a decrease in taxes also expands expenditure and income,

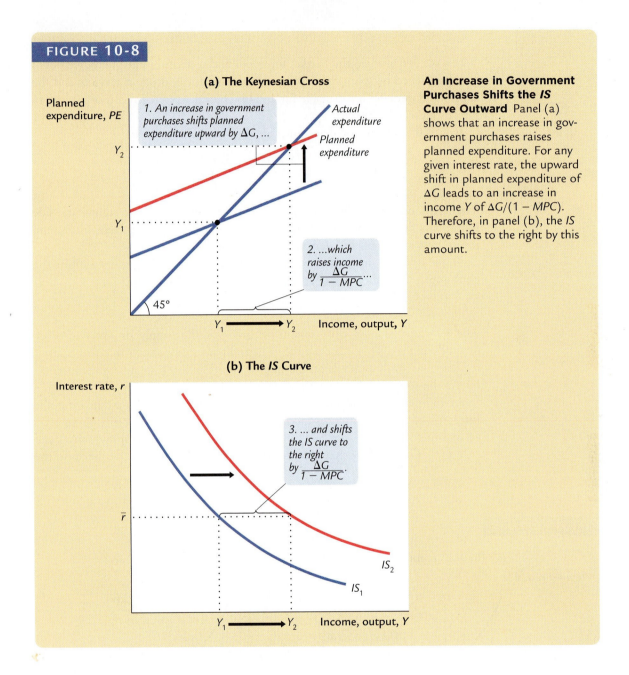

FIGURE 10-8

(a) The Keynesian Cross

Planned expenditure, *PE*

1. An increase in government purchases shifts planned expenditure upward by ΔG, ...

Actual expenditure

Planned expenditure

Y_2

Y_1

2. ...which raises income by $\frac{\Delta G}{1 - MPC}$...

45°

$Y_1 \longrightarrow Y_2$ Income, output, *Y*

(b) The *IS* Curve

Interest rate, *r*

3. ... and shifts the IS curve to the right by $\frac{\Delta G}{1 - MPC}$.

$\bar{r}$

IS_2

IS_1

$Y_1 \longrightarrow Y_2$ Income, output, *Y*

An Increase in Government Purchases Shifts the *IS* Curve Outward Panel (a) shows that an increase in government purchases raises planned expenditure. For any given interest rate, the upward shift in planned expenditure of ΔG leads to an increase in income *Y* of ΔG/(1 − MPC). Therefore, in panel (b), the *IS* curve shifts to the right by this amount.

it too shifts the *IS* curve outward. A decrease in government purchases or an increase in taxes reduces income; therefore, such a change in fiscal policy shifts the *IS* curve inward.

In summary, the IS *curve shows the combinations of the interest rate and the level of income that are consistent with equilibrium in the market for goods and services. The* IS *curve is drawn for a given fiscal policy. Changes in fiscal policy that raise the demand for goods and services shift the* IS *curve to the right. Changes in fiscal policy that reduce the demand for goods and services shift the* IS *curve to the left.*

A Loanable-Funds Interpretation of the *IS* Curve

When we first studied the market for goods and services in Chapter 3, we noted an equivalence between the supply and demand for goods and services and the supply and demand for loanable funds. This equivalence provides another way to interpret the *IS* curve.

Recall that the national accounts identity can be written as

$$Y - C - G = I$$
$$S = I.$$

The left-hand side of this equation is national saving S, and the right-hand side is investment I. National saving represents the supply of loanable funds, and investment represents the demand for these funds.

To see how the market for loanable funds produces the *IS* curve, substitute the consumption function for C and the investment function for I:

$$Y - C(Y - T) - G = I(r).$$

The left-hand side of this equation shows that the supply of loanable funds depends on income and fiscal policy. The right-hand side shows that the demand for loanable funds depends on the interest rate. The interest rate adjusts to equilibrate the supply and demand for loans.

As Figure 10-9 illustrates, we can interpret the *IS* curve as showing the interest rate that equilibrates the market for loanable funds for any given level of income. When income rises from Y_1 to Y_2, national saving, which equals $Y - C - G$, increases. (Consumption rises by less than income, because the

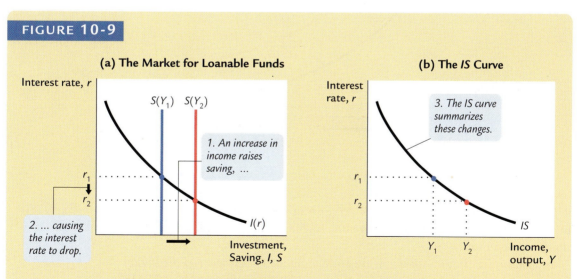

FIGURE 10-9

A Loanable-Funds Interpretation of the *IS* Curve Panel (a) shows that an increase in income from Y_1 to Y_2 raises saving and thus lowers the interest rate that equilibrates the supply and demand for loanable funds. The *IS* curve in panel (b) expresses this negative relationship between income and the interest rate.

marginal propensity to consume is less than 1.) As panel (a) shows, the increased supply of loanable funds drives down the interest rate from r_1 to r_2. The *IS* curve in panel (b) summarizes this relationship: higher income implies higher saving, which in turn implies a lower equilibrium interest rate. For this reason, the *IS* curve slopes downward.

This alternative interpretation of the *IS* curve also explains why a change in fiscal policy shifts the *IS* curve. An increase in government purchases or a decrease in taxes reduces national saving for any given level of income. The reduced supply of loanable funds raises the interest rate that equilibrates the market. Because the interest rate is now higher for any given level of income, the *IS* curve shifts upward in response to the expansionary change in fiscal policy.

Finally, note that the *IS* curve does not determine either income Y or the interest rate r. Instead, the *IS* curve is a relationship between Y and r arising in the market for goods and services or, equivalently, the market for loanable funds. Recall that our goal in this chapter is to understand aggregate demand; that is, we want to find what determines equilibrium income Y for a given price level P. The *IS* curve is just half the story. To complete the story, we need another relationship between Y and r, to which we now turn.

10-2 The Money Market and the *LM* Curve

The *LM* curve plots the relationship between the interest rate and the level of income that arises in the market for money balances. To understand this relationship, we begin by looking at a theory of the interest rate, called the **theory of liquidity preference.**

The Theory of Liquidity Preference

In his classic work *The General Theory*, Keynes offered his view of how the interest rate is determined in the short run. His explanation is called the theory of liquidity preference, because it posits that the interest rate adjusts to balance the supply and demand for the economy's most liquid asset—money. Just as the Keynesian cross is a building block for the *IS* curve, the theory of liquidity preference is a building block for the *LM* curve.

To develop this theory, we begin with the supply of real money balances. If M stands for the supply of money and P stands for the price level, then M/P is the supply of real money balances. The theory of liquidity preference assumes there is a fixed supply of real balances. That is,

$$(M/P)^s = \overline{M}/\overline{P}.$$

The money supply M is an exogenous policy variable chosen by a central bank, such as the Bank of Canada. The price level P is also an exogenous variable in this model. (We take the price level as given because the *IS–LM* model—our ultimate goal in this chapter—explains the short run when the price level is

FIGURE 10-10

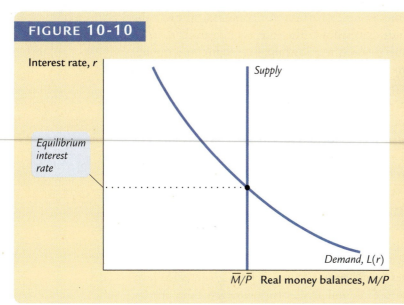

The Theory of Liquidity Preference The supply and demand for real money balances determine the interest rate. The supply curve for real money balances is vertical because the supply does not depend on the interest rate. The demand curve is downward-sloping because a higher interest rate raises the cost of holding money and thus lowers the quantity demanded. At the equilibrium interest rate, the quantity of real money balances demanded equals the quantity supplied.

fixed.) These assumptions imply that the supply of real balances is fixed and, in particular, does not depend on the interest rate. Thus, when we plot the supply of real money balances against the interest rate in Figure 10-10, we obtain a vertical supply curve.

Next, consider the demand for real money balances. The theory of liquidity preference posits that the interest rate is one determinant of how much money people choose to hold. The underlying reason is that the interest rate is the opportunity cost of holding money: it is what you forgo by holding some of your assets as money, which does not bear interest, instead of as interest-bearing bank deposits or bonds. When the interest rate rises, people want to hold less of their wealth in the form of money. Thus, we can write the demand for real money balances as

$$(M/P)^d = L(r),$$

where the function $L(\ )$ shows that the quantity of money demanded depends on the interest rate. The demand curve in Figure 10-10 illustrates this relationship. This demand curve slopes downward because higher interest rates reduce the quantity of real balances demanded.[5]

According to the theory of liquidity preference, the interest rate adjusts to equilibrate the money market. As Figure 10-10 shows, at the equilibrium interest rate, the quantity of real balances demanded equals the quantity supplied.

---

[5] Note that r is being used to denote the interest rate here, as it was in our discussion of the *IS* curve. More accurately, it is the nominal interest rate that determines money demand and the real interest rate that determines investment. To keep things simple, we are ignoring expected inflation, which creates the difference between the real and nominal interest rates. The role of expected inflation in the *IS–LM* model is explored in Chapter 11.

How does the interest rate get to this equilibrium of money supply and money demand? The adjustment occurs because whenever the money market is not in equilibrium, people try to adjust their portfolios of assets and, in the process, alter the interest rate. For instance, if the interest rate is above the equilibrium level, the quantity of real balances supplied exceeds the quantity demanded. Individuals holding the excess supply of money try to convert some of their non–interest-bearing money into interest-bearing bank deposits or bonds. Banks and bond issuers, who prefer to pay lower interest rates, respond to this excess supply of money by lowering the interest rates they offer. Conversely, if the interest rate is below the equilibrium level, so that the quantity of money demanded exceeds the quantity supplied, individuals try to obtain money by selling bonds or making bank withdrawals. To attract now scarcer funds, banks and bond issuers respond by increasing the interest rates they offer. Eventually, the interest rate reaches the equilibrium level, at which people are content with their portfolios of monetary and nonmonetary assets.

Now that we have seen how the interest rate is determined, we can use the theory of liquidity preference to show how the interest rate responds to changes in the supply of money. Suppose, for instance, that the Bank of Canada suddenly decreases the money supply. A fall in M reduces M/P, because P is fixed in the model. The supply of real balances shifts to the left, as in Figure 10-11. The equilibrium interest rate rises from r_1 to r_2, and the higher interest rate makes people satisfied to hold the smaller quantity of real money balances. The opposite would occur if the Bank of Canada had suddenly increased the money supply. Thus, according to the theory of liquidity preference, a decrease in the money supply raises the interest rate, and an increase in the money supply lowers the interest rate.

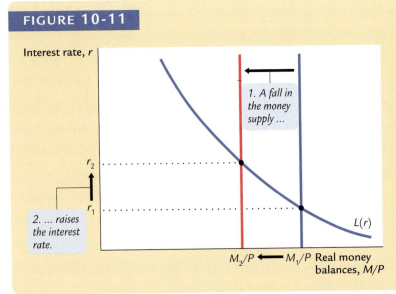

FIGURE 10-11

A Reduction in the Money Supply in the Theory of Liquidity Preference If the price level is fixed, a reduction in the money supply from M_1 to M_2 reduces the supply of real balances. The equilibrium interest rate therefore rises from r_1 to r_2.

Tight Money and Rising Interest Rates

The early 1980s saw a large and speedy reduction in North American inflation rates. During the 1980–1982 period, Canada's CPI increased at an average annual rate of 11.2 percent; during the next three years, that rate of increase slowed to 4.7 percent. This 6.5-percentage-point reduction in inflation was achieved by a dramatic tightening of monetary policy.

During the 1970s, the quantity of real money balances ($M1$ divided by the CPI) had been growing at an average rate of 2.8 percent per year. Then, during the 1980–1982 period, Canadian real money growth was pushed down to an average of −7.8 percent per year. After that, monetary policy was eased significantly; average growth in real balances was 1.7 percent per year in the 1983–1985 period.

How does such a monetary tightening influence interest rates? The answer depends on the time horizon. Our analysis of the Fisher effect in Chapter 4 suggests that the change in monetary policy would lower inflation in the long run, which, in turn, would lead to lower nominal interest rates. Yet the theory of liquidity preference that we have considered in the present chapter predicts that, in the short run when prices are sluggish, anti-inflationary monetary policy involves a leftward shift of the money supply curve and higher nominal interest rates.

Both conclusions are consistent with experience. Nominal interest rates did fall in the 1980s as inflation fell. For example, the three-month treasury bill rate fell from an average of 14.7 percent in the 1980–1982 period to an average of 10 percent in the 1983–1985 period. But it is instructive to consider the year-to-year sequence. The interest rate rose from 12.7 percent in 1980 to 17.8 percent in 1981, and it did not fall below 12.7 percent until 1983. The moral of the story is that both our short-run and our long-run analyses of interest-rate determination help us to understand the real world. ■

Income, Money Demand, and the *LM* Curve

Having developed the theory of liquidity preference as an explanation for how the interest rate is determined, we can now use the theory to derive the *LM* curve. We begin by considering the following question: how does a change in the economy's level of income Y affect the market for real money balances? The answer (which should be familiar from Chapter 4) is that the level of income affects the demand for money. When income is high, expenditure is high, so people engage in more transactions that require the use of money. Thus, greater income implies greater money demand. We can express these ideas by writing the money demand function as

$$(M/P)^{\mathrm{d}} = L(r, Y).$$

The quantity of real money balances demanded is negatively related to the interest rate and positively related to income.

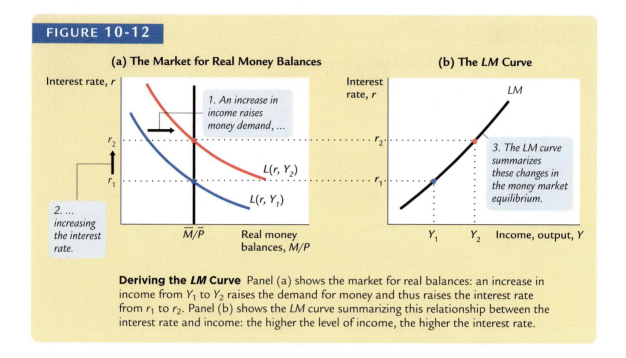

FIGURE 10-12

Deriving the *LM* Curve Panel (a) shows the market for real balances: an increase in income from Y_1 to Y_2 raises the demand for money and thus raises the interest rate from r_1 to r_2. Panel (b) shows the *LM* curve summarizing this relationship between the interest rate and income: the higher the level of income, the higher the interest rate.

Using the theory of liquidity preference, we can figure out what happens to the equilibrium interest rate when the level of income changes. For example, consider what happens in Figure 10-12 when income increases from Y_1 to Y_2. As panel (a) illustrates, this increase in income shifts the money demand curve to the right. With the supply of real money balances unchanged, the interest rate must rise from r_1 to r_2 to equilibrate the money market. Therefore, according to the theory of liquidity preference, higher income leads to a higher interest rate.

The *LM* curve plots this relationship between the level of income and the interest rate. The higher the level of income, the higher the demand for real money balances, and the higher the equilibrium interest rate. For this reason, the *LM* curve slopes upward, as in panel (b) of Figure 10-12.

How Monetary Policy Shifts the *LM* Curve

The *LM* curve tells us the interest rate that equilibrates the money market at any level of income. Yet, as we saw earlier, the equilibrium interest rate also depends on the supply of real balances, M/P. This means that the *LM* curve is drawn for a *given* supply of real money balances. If real balances change—for example, if the Central Bank alters the money supply—the *LM* curve shifts.

We can use the theory of liquidity preference to understand how monetary policy shifts the *LM* curve. Suppose that the Bank of Canada decreases the monetary base, which leads to a decrease in the money supply from M_1 to M_2. This development causes the supply of real balances to fall from M_1/P to M_2/P.

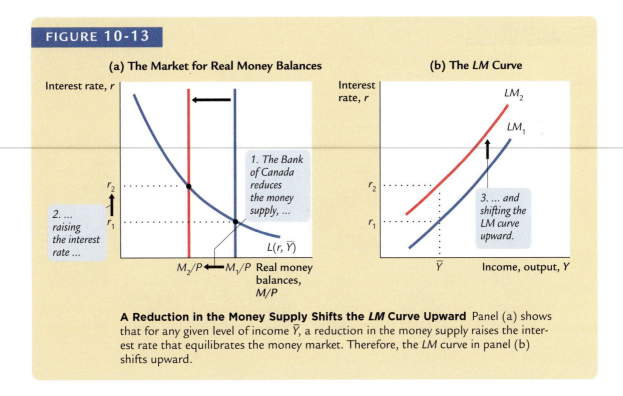

FIGURE 10-13

(a) The Market for Real Money Balances

Interest rate, r

1. The Bank of Canada reduces the money supply, ...

r_2

2. ... raising the interest rate ...

r_1

$L(r, \overline{Y})$

$M_2/P \longleftarrow M_1/P$ Real money balances, M/P

(b) The LM Curve

Interest rate, r

LM_2

LM_1

r_2

3. ... and shifting the LM curve upward.

r_1

$\overline{Y}$ Income, output, Y

A Reduction in the Money Supply Shifts the LM Curve Upward Panel (a) shows that for any given level of income $\overline{Y}$, a reduction in the money supply raises the interest rate that equilibrates the money market. Therefore, the LM curve in panel (b) shifts upward.

Figure 10-13 shows what happens. Holding constant the amount of income and thus the demand curve for real balances, we see that a reduction in the supply of real balances raises the interest rate that equilibrates the money market. Hence, a decrease in real balances shifts the LM curve upward.

In summary, the LM *curve shows the combinations of the interest rate and the level of income that are consistent with equilibrium in the market for real money balances. The* LM *curve is drawn for a given supply of real money balances. Decreases in the supply of real money balances shift the* LM *curve upward. Increases in the supply of real money balances shift the* LM *curve downward.*

A Quantity-Equation Interpretation of the LM Curve

When we first discussed aggregate demand and the short-run determination of income in Chapter 9, we derived the aggregate demand curve from the quantity theory of money. We described the money market with the quantity equation,

$$MV = PY,$$

and assumed that velocity V is constant. This assumption implies that, for any given price level P, the supply of money M by itself determines the level of income Y. Because the level of income does not depend on the interest rate, the quantity theory is equivalent to a vertical LM curve.

We can derive the more realistic upward-sloping LM curve from the quantity equation by relaxing the assumption that velocity is constant. The assumption

of constant velocity is based on the assumption that the demand for real money balances depends only on the level of income. Yet, as we have noted in our discussion of the liquidity-preference model, the demand for real money balances also depends on the interest rate: a higher interest rate raises the cost of holding money and reduces money demand. When people respond to a higher interest rate by holding less money, each dollar they do hold must be used more often to support a given volume of transactions—that is, the velocity of money must increase. We can write this as

$$MV(r) = PY.$$

The velocity function $V(r)$ indicates that velocity is positively related to the interest rate.

This form of the quantity equation yields an *LM* curve that slopes upward. Because an increase in the interest rate raises the velocity of money, it raises the level of income for any given money supply and price level. The *LM* curve expresses this positive relationship between the interest rate and income.

This equation also shows why changes in the money supply shift the *LM* curve. For any given interest rate and price level, the money supply and the level of income must move together. Thus, increases in the money supply shift the *LM* curve to the right, and decreases in the money supply shift the *LM* curve to the left.

Keep in mind that the quantity equation is merely another way to express the theory behind the *LM* curve. This quantity-theory interpretation of the *LM* curve is substantively the same as that provided by the theory of liquidity preference. In both cases, the *LM* curve represents a positive relationship between income and the interest rate that arises from the money market.

Finally, remember that the *LM* curve by itself does not determine either income Y or the interest rate r that will prevail in the economy. Like the *IS* curve, the *LM* curve is only a relationship between these two endogenous variables. To understand the economy's overall equilibrium for a given price level, we must consider both equilibrium in the goods market and equilibrium in the money market. That is, we need to use the *IS* and *LM* curves together.

10-3 Conclusion: The Short-Run Equilibrium

We now have all the pieces of the *IS–LM* model. The two equations of this model are

$$Y = C(Y - T) + I(r) + G \qquad IS,$$

$$M/P = L(r, Y) \qquad\qquad\qquad LM.$$

The model takes fiscal policy, G and T, monetary policy M, and the price level P as exogenous. Given these exogenous variables, the *IS* curve provides the combinations of r and Y that satisfy the equation representing the goods market, and the *LM* curve provides the combinations of r and Y that satisfy the

FIGURE 10-14

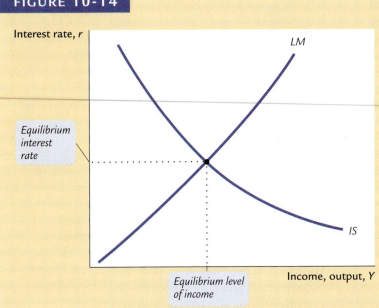

Interest rate, r

LM

Equilibrium interest rate

IS

Equilibrium level of income

Income, output, Y

Equilibrium in the *IS-LM* Model The intersection of the *IS* and *LM* curves represents simultaneous equilibrium in the market for goods and services and in the market for real money balances for given values of government spending, taxes, the money supply, and the price level.

FIGURE 10-15

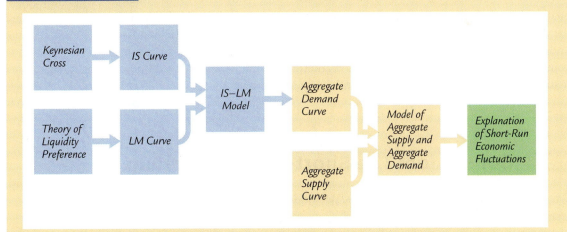

Keynesian Cross → IS Curve

Theory of Liquidity Preference → LM Curve

IS–LM Model

Aggregate Demand Curve

Aggregate Supply Curve

Model of Aggregate Supply and Aggregate Demand

Explanation of Short-Run Economic Fluctuations

The Theory of Short-Run Fluctuations This schematic diagram shows how the different pieces of the theory of short-run fluctuations fit together. The Keynesian cross explains the *IS* curve, and the theory of liquidity preference explains the *LM* curve. The *IS* and *LM* curves together yield the *IS-LM* model, which explains the aggregate demand curve. The aggregate demand curve is part of the model of aggregate supply and aggregate demand, which economists use to explain short-run fluctuations in economic activity.

equation representing the money market. These two curves are shown together in Figure 10-14.

The equilibrium of the economy is the point at which the *IS* curve and the *LM* curve cross. This point gives the interest rate *r* and the level of income *Y* that satisfy conditions for equilibrium in both the goods market and the money market. In other words, at this intersection, actual expenditure equals planned expenditure, and the demand for real money balances equals the supply.

As we conclude this chapter, let's recall that our ultimate goal in developing the *IS–LM* model is to analyze short-run fluctuations in economic activity. Figure 10-15 illustrates how the different pieces of our theory fit together. In this chapter we developed the Keynesian cross and the theory of liquidity preference as building blocks for the *IS–LM* model. As we see more fully in the next chapter, the *IS–LM* model helps explain the position and slope of the aggregate demand curve. The aggregate demand curve, in turn, is a piece of the model of aggregate supply and aggregate demand, which economists use to explain the short-run effects of policy changes and other events on national income.

Summary

1. The Keynesian cross is a basic model of income determination. It takes fiscal policy and planned investment as exogenous and then shows that there is one level of national income at which actual expenditure equals planned expenditure. It shows that changes in fiscal policy have a multiplied impact on income.

2. Once we allow planned investment to depend on the interest rate, the Keynesian cross yields a relationship between the interest rate and national income. A higher interest rate lowers planned investment, and this in turn lowers national income. The downward-sloping *IS* curve summarizes this negative relationship between the interest rate and income.

3. The theory of liquidity preference is a basic model of the determination of the interest rate. It takes the money supply and the price level as exogenous and assumes that the interest rate adjusts to equilibrate the supply and demand for real money balances. The theory implies that increases in the money supply lower the interest rate.

4. Once we allow the demand for real balances to depend on national income, the theory of liquidity preference yields a relationship between income and the interest rate. A higher level of income raises the demand for real balances, and this in turn raises the interest rate. The upward-sloping *LM* curve summarizes this positive relationship between income and the interest rate.

5. The *IS–LM* model combines the elements of the Keynesian cross and the elements of the theory of liquidity preference. The *IS* curve shows the points

that satisfy equilibrium in the goods market, and the *LM* curve shows the points that satisfy equilibrium in the money market. The intersection of the *IS* and *LM* curves shows the interest rate and income that satisfy equilibrium in both markets for a given price level.

KEY CONCEPTS

IS–LM model

IS curve

LM curve

Keynesian cross

Government-purchases multiplier

Tax multiplier

Theory of liquidity preference

QUESTIONS FOR REVIEW

1. Use the Keynesian cross to explain why fiscal policy has a multiplied effect on national income.

2. Use the theory of liquidity preference to explain why an increase in the money supply lowers the interest rate. What does this explanation assume about the price level?

3. Why does the *IS* curve slope downward?

4. Why does the *LM* curve slope upward?

PROBLEMS AND APPLICATIONS

1. Use the Keynesian cross to predict the impact on equilibrium GDP of

   a. An increase in government purchases.

   b. An increase in taxes.

   c. An equal increase in both government purchases and taxes.

2. In the Keynesian cross, assume that the consumption function is given by

   $$C = 200 + 0.75 \ (Y - T).$$

   Planned investment is 100; government purchases and taxes are both 100.

   a. Graph planned expenditure as a function of income.

   b. What is the equilibrium level of income?

   c. If government purchases increase to 125, what is the new equilibrium income?

   d. What level of government purchases is needed to achieve an income of 1,600?

3. Although our development of the Keynesian cross in this chapter assumes that taxes are a fixed amount, in many countries taxes depend on income. Let's represent the tax system by writing tax revenue as

   $$T = \overline{T} + tY,$$

   where $\overline{T}$ and t are parameters of the tax code. The parameter t is the marginal tax rate: if income rises by \$1, taxes rise by $t \times \$1$.

   a. How does this tax system change the way consumption responds to changes in GDP?

   b. In the Keynesian cross, how does this tax system alter the government-purchases multiplier?

   c. In the *IS–LM* model, how does this tax system alter the slope of the *IS* curve?

4. Consider the impact of an increase in thriftiness in the Keynesian cross. Suppose the consumption function is

$$C = \overline{C} + c(Y - T),$$

where $\overline{C}$ is a parameter called *autonomous consumption* and c is the marginal propensity to consume.

a. What happens to equilibrium income when the society becomes more thrifty, as represented by a decline in $\overline{C}$?

b. What happens to equilibrium saving?

c. Why do you suppose this result is called the *paradox of thrift?*

d. Does this paradox arise in the classical model of Chapter 3? Why or why not?

5. Suppose that the money demand function is

$$(M/P)^{\text{d}} = 1,000 - 100r,$$

where r is the interest rate in percent. The money supply M is 1,000 and the price level P is 2.

a. Graph the supply and demand for real money balances.

b. What is the equilibrium interest rate?

c. Assume that the price level is fixed. What happens to the equilibrium interest rate if the supply of money is raised from 1,000 to 1,200?

d. If the central bank wishes to raise the interest rate to 7 percent, what money supply should it set?

CHAPTER 11

Aggregate Demand II: Applying the *IS–LM* Model

> *Science is a parasite: the greater the patient population the better the advance in physiology and pathology; and out of pathology arises therapy. The year 1932 was the trough of the great depression, and from its rotten soil was belatedly begot a new subject that today we call macroeconomics.*
>
> — *Paul Samuelson*

In Chapter 10 we assembled the pieces of the *IS–LM* model as a step toward understanding short-run economic fluctuations. We saw that the *IS* curve represents the equilibrium in the market for goods and services, that the *LM* curve represents the equilibrium in the market for real money balances, and that the *IS* and *LM* curves together determine the interest rate and national income in the short run when the price level is fixed. Now we turn our attention to applying the *IS–LM* model to analyze three issues.

First, we examine the potential causes of fluctuations in national income. We use the *IS–LM* model to see how changes in the exogenous variables (government purchases, taxes, and the money supply) influence the endogenous variables (the interest rate and national income) for a given price level. We also examine how various shocks to the goods markets (the *IS* curve) and the money market (the *LM* curve) affect the interest rate and national income in the short run.

Second, we discuss how the *IS–LM* model fits into the model of aggregate supply and aggregate demand we introduced in Chapter 9. In particular, we examine how the *IS–LM* model provides a theory to explain the slope and position of the aggregate demand curve. Here we relax the assumption that the price level is fixed, and we show that the *IS–LM* model implies a negative relationship between the price level and national income. The model can also tell us what events shift the aggregate demand curve and in what direction.

Third, we examine the Great Depression of the 1930s. As this chapter's opening quotation indicates, this episode gave birth to short-run macroeconomic theory, for it led Keynes and his many followers to think that aggregate demand was the key to understanding fluctuations in national income. With the benefit of hindsight, we can use the *IS–LM* model to discuss the various explanations of

343

this traumatic economic downturn. And, as we will see throughout this chapter, the model can also be used to shed light on more recent recessions, such as the one that began in 2008.

11-1 Explaining Fluctuations With the *IS–LM* Model

The intersection of the *IS* curve and the *LM* curve determines the level of national income. When one of these curves shifts, the short-run equilibrium of the economy changes, and national income fluctuates. In this section we examine how changes in policy and shocks to the economy can cause these curves to shift.

How Fiscal Policy Shifts the *IS* Curve and Changes the Short-Run Equilibrium

We begin by examining how changes in fiscal policy (government purchases and taxes) alter the economy's short-run equilibrium. Recall that changes in fiscal policy influence planned expenditure and thereby shift the *IS* curve. The *IS–LM* model shows how these shifts in the *IS* curve affect income and the interest rate.

Changes in Government Purchases Consider an increase in government purchases of ΔG. The government-purchases multiplier in the Keynesian cross tells us that, this change in fiscal policy raises the level of income at any given interest rate by $\Delta G/(1 - MPC)$. Therefore, as Figure 11-1 shows, the *IS* curve shifts to the right by this amount. The equilibrium of the economy moves from point *A* to point *B*. The increase in government purchases raises both income and the interest rate.

To understand fully what's happening in Figure 11-1, it helps to keep in mind the building blocks for the *IS–LM* model from the preceding chapter—the Keynesian cross and the theory of liquidity preference. Here is the story. When the government increases its purchases of goods and services, the economy's planned expenditure rises. The increase in planned expenditure stimulates the production of goods and services, which causes total income *Y* to rise. These effects should be familiar from the Keynesian cross.

Now consider the money market, as described by the theory of liquidity preference. Because the economy's demand for money depends on income, the rise in total income increases the quantity of money demanded at every interest rate. The supply of money has not changed, however, so higher money demand causes the equilibrium interest rate *r* to rise.

The higher interest rate arising in the money market, in turn, has ramifications back in the goods market. When the interest rate rises, firms cut back on their investment plans. This fall in investment partially offsets the expansionary effect of the increase in government purchases. Thus, the increase in income in response to a fiscal expansion is smaller in the *IS–LM* model than it is in the Keynesian cross (where investment is assumed to be fixed). You can see this in Figure 11-1. The

FIGURE 11-1

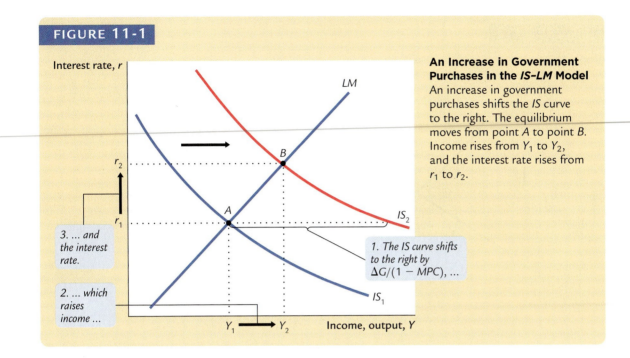

An Increase in Government Purchases in the *IS–LM* Model An increase in government purchases shifts the *IS* curve to the right. The equilibrium moves from point *A* to point *B*. Income rises from Y_1 to Y_2, and the interest rate rises from r_1 to r_2.

Interest rate, *r*

LM

r_2

B

A

r_1

IS$_2$

3. ... and the interest rate.

1. The IS curve shifts to the right by $\Delta G/(1 - MPC)$, ...

2. ... which raises income ...

IS$_1$

Y_1 → Y_2 Income, output, *Y*

horizontal shift in the *IS* curve equals the rise in equilibrium income in the Keynesian cross. This amount is larger than the increase in equilibrium income here in the *IS–LM* model. The difference is explained by the crowding out of investment due to a higher interest rate.

Changes in Taxes In the *IS–LM* model, changes in taxes affect the economy much the same as changes in government purchases do, except that taxes affect expenditure through consumption. Consider, for instance, a decrease in taxes of ΔT. The tax cut encourages consumers to spend more and, therefore, increases planned expenditure. The tax multiplier in the Keynesian cross tells us that this change in policy raises the level of income at any given interest rate by $\Delta T \times MPC/(1 - MPC)$. Therefore, as Figure 11-2 illustrates, the *IS* curve shifts to the right by this amount. The equilibrium of the economy moves from point A to point B. The tax cut raises both income and the interest rate. Once again, because the higher interest rate depresses investment, the increase in income is smaller in the *IS–LM* model than it is in the Keynesian cross.

How Monetary Policy Shifts the *LM* Curve and Changes the Short-Run Equilibrium

We now examine the effects of monetary policy. Recall that a change in the money supply alters the interest rate that equilibrates the money market for any given level of income and, thus, shifts the *LM* curve. The *IS–LM* model shows how a shift in the *LM* curve affects income and the interest rate.

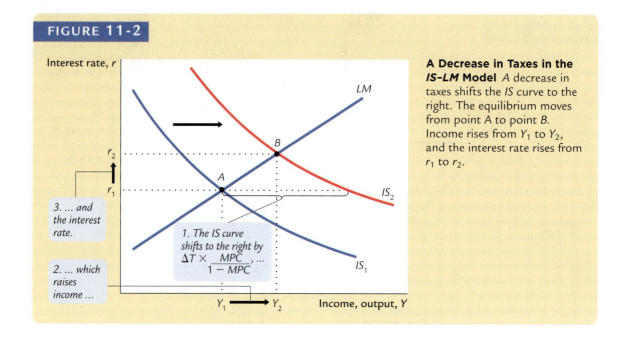

A Decrease in Taxes in the IS–LM Model A decrease in taxes shifts the IS curve to the right. The equilibrium moves from point A to point B. Income rises from Y_1 to Y_2, and the interest rate rises from r_1 to r_2.

Consider an increase in the money supply. An increase in M leads to an increase in real money balances M/P, because the price level P is fixed in the short run. The theory of liquidity preference shows that for any given level of income, an increase in real money balances leads to a lower interest rate. Therefore, the LM curve shifts downward, as in Figure 11–3. The equilibrium moves from point A to point B. The increase in the money supply lowers the interest rate and raises the level of income.

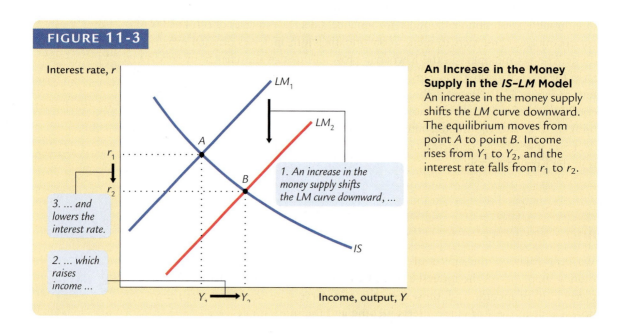

An Increase in the Money Supply in the IS–LM Model An increase in the money supply shifts the LM curve downward. The equilibrium moves from point A to point B. Income rises from Y_1 to Y_2, and the interest rate falls from r_1 to r_2.

Once again, to tell the story that explains the economy's adjustment from point *A* to point *B,* we rely on the building blocks of the *IS–LM* model—the Keynesian cross and the theory of liquidity preference. This time, we begin with the money market, where the monetary policy action occurs. When the central bank increases the supply of money, people have more money than they want to hold at the prevailing interest rate. As a result, they start depositing this extra money in banks or use it to buy bonds. The interest rate *r* then falls until people are willing to hold all the extra money that the central bank has created; this brings the money market to a new equilibrium. The lower interest rate, in turn, has ramifications for the goods market. A lower interest rate stimulates planned investment, which increases planned expenditure, production, and income *Y.*

Thus, the *IS–LM* model shows that monetary policy influences income by changing the interest rate. This conclusion sheds light on our analysis of monetary policy in Chapter 9. In that chapter we showed that in the short run, when prices are sticky, an expansion in the money supply raises income. But we did not discuss *how* a monetary expansion induces greater spending on goods and services—a process that is called the **monetary transmission mechanism.** The *IS–LM* model shows an important part of that mechanism: *an increase in the money supply lowers the interest rate, which stimulates investment and thereby expands the demand for goods and services.* The next chapter shows that in open economies, the exchange rate also has a major role in the monetary transmission mechanism.

The Interaction Between Monetary and Fiscal Policy

When analyzing any change in monetary or fiscal policy, it is important to keep in mind that the policymakers who control these policy tools are aware of what the other policymakers are doing. A change in one policy, therefore, may influence the other, and this interdependence may alter the impact of a policy change.

For example, consider the federal government policy of eliminating the budget deficit during the 1990s by cutting government spending. What effect should this policy have on the economy? According to the *IS–LM* model, the answer depends on how the Bank of Canada responds to the spending cut.

Figure 11-4 shows three of the many possible outcomes that can follow from either a spending cut or a tax increase. In panel (a), the Bank of Canada holds the money supply constant. The spending cut shifts the *IS* curve to the left. Income falls (because lower spending reduces overall demand), and the interest rate falls (because lower income shifts downward the demand for money). The fall in income indicates that the fiscal policy causes a recession.

In panel (b), the Bank of Canada wants to hold the interest rate constant. In this case, when the spending cut shifts the *IS* curve to the left, the Bank of Canada must decrease the money supply to keep the interest rate at its original level. This fall in the money supply shifts the *LM* curve upward. The interest rate does not fall, but income falls by a larger amount than if the Bank of Canada had held the money supply constant. Whereas in panel (a) the lower interest rate stimulated investment and partially offset the contractionary effect of the spending cut, in panel (b) the Bank of Canada deepens the recession by keeping the interest rate high.

FIGURE 11-4

(a) Bank of Canada Holds Money Supply Constant

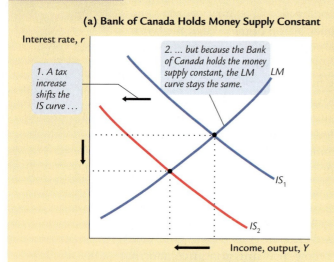

Interest rate, r

1. A tax increase shifts the IS curve . . .

2. . . . but because the Bank of Canada holds the money supply constant, the LM curve stays the same.

LM

IS_1

IS_2

Income, output, Y

(b) Bank of Canada Holds Interest Rate Constant

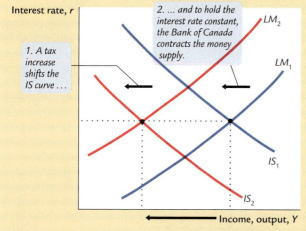

Interest rate, r

1. A tax increase shifts the IS curve . . .

2. . . . and to hold the interest rate constant, the Bank of Canada contracts the money supply.

LM_2

LM_1

IS_1

IS_2

Income, output, Y

(c) Bank of Canada Holds Income Constant

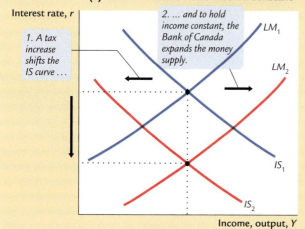

Interest rate, r

1. A tax increase shifts the IS curve . . .

2. . . . and to hold income constant, the Bank of Canada expands the money supply.

LM_1

LM_2

IS_1

IS_2

Income, output, Y

The Response of the Economy to a Tax Increase How the economy responds to a tax increase depends on how the monetary authority responds. In panel (a) the Bank of Canada holds the money supply constant. In panel (b) the Bank of Canada holds the interest rate constant by reducing the money supply. In panel (c) the Bank of Canada holds the level of income constant by raising the money supply.

In panel (c), the Bank of Canada wants to prevent the spending cut from lowering income. It must, therefore, raise the money supply and shift the *LM* curve downward enough to offset the shift in the *IS* curve. In this case, the spending cut does not cause a recession, but it does cause a large fall in the interest rate. Although the level of income is not changed, the combination of a spending cut and a monetary expansion does change the allocation of the economy's resources. The spending cut shrinks the government sector, while the lower interest rate stimulates investment. Income is not affected because these two effects exactly balance.

From this example we can see that the impact of a change in fiscal policy depends on the policy the Bank of Canada pursues—that is, on whether it holds the money supply, the interest rate, or the level of income constant. More generally, whenever analyzing a change in one policy, we must make an assumption about its effect on the other policy. What assumption is most appropriate depends on the case at hand and the many political considerations that lie behind economic policymaking.

Perhaps the most significant interaction between monetary and fiscal policy occurs in the case of a small open economy. In that case, the fundamental choice for monetary policy is whether to fix the exchange rate or to allow a flexible exchange rate. As we shall see in Chapter 12, this choice dramatically affects the power of fiscal policy. With a flexible exchange rate (and this has been Canada's policy for years), the effect of fiscal policy on real GDP is very much blunted. This is good news for those who do not want spending cuts to raise unemployment very much, as was the case for our government in the 1990s, but this is bad news for those who want to use expansionary fiscal policy to create jobs, as was the case for our government in the recession of 2008–2009. We will explore these issues more fully in Chapter 12, after we have completed our development of the closed-economy model of aggregate demand.

CASE STUDY

Policy Analysis With Macroeconometric Models

The *IS–LM* model shows how monetary and fiscal policy influence the equilibrium level of income. The predictions of the model, however, are qualitative, not quantitative. The *IS–LM* model shows that increases in government purchases raise GDP and that increases in taxes lower GDP. But when economists analyze specific policy proposals, they need to know not just the direction of the effect but the size as well. For example, if the federal government cuts spending by $5 billion and if monetary policy is not altered, how much will GDP fall? To answer this question, economists need to go beyond the graphical representation of the *IS–LM* model.

Macroeconometric models of the economy provide one way to evaluate policy proposals. A macroeconometric model is a model that describes the economy quantitatively, rather than just qualitatively. Many of these models are essentially more complicated and more realistic versions of our *IS–LM* model. The economists who build macroeconometric models use historical data to estimate parameters such as the marginal propensity to consume, the sensitivity of investment to the interest rate, and the sensitivity of money demand to the interest rate. Once a model is built, economists can simulate the effects of alternative policies with the help of a computer.

It is interesting to note that estimates of Canada's one-year government spending multiplier have changed substantially over the years. In the situation in which the Bank of Canada keeps the money supply constant, $\Delta Y / \Delta G$ was estimated to be 1.42 twenty-five years ago.[1] This estimate meant that an increase in government spending of $1 billion was expected to raise overall GDP by $1.42 billion after one year. By 1986, multiplier estimates had fallen to 0.77.[2] Finally, by the early 1990s, those using macroeconometric models were reporting government spending multipliers in the 0.50–0.67 range.[3] This wide variation in estimates for $\Delta Y / \Delta G$, all involving the same behaviour on the part of the Bank of Canada, implies a great deal of imprecision in the planning of fiscal policy. Why do the estimates of the power of fiscal policy keep shrinking as more research proceeds? Economists believe there are two reasons for this trend.

The first concerns the role of expectations on the part of households and firms. To see the importance of expectations, compare a temporary increase in government spending to a permanent one. The *IS* curve shifts out to the right in both cases, so interest rates rise, and this causes some cutback in the investment component of aggregate demand. But the size of this investment response depends on how permanent firms expect the rise in interest rates to be. If the increase in government spending is temporary, the rise in interest rates should be temporary as well, so firms' investment spending is not curtailed to a very great extent. But if the increase in government spending is expected to be permanent, the rise in interest rates matters much more in firms' long-range planning decisions, and there is a much bigger cutback in investment spending. Thus, the government spending multiplier is smaller when the change in spending is expected to last a long time.

You might think that, since changes in investment spending lag behind interest rate changes, this expectations issue cannot matter much for determining the multiplier value for a time horizon of just one year. But such a view amounts to assuming that individuals cannot see the interest changes coming. Anyone who understands the *IS–LM* model knows that permanently higher government spending raises interest rates. They also know that the value of existing financial assets (stocks and bonds) will fall when newly issued bonds promising higher yields are issued. No one wants to hold an asset with a low yield when better yields are expected. Thus, in an attempt to avoid a capital loss on existing financial assets, owners sell them the moment they expect a capital loss. That moment occurs as soon as they see a reason for interest rate increases—that is, *just* after the

[1] John Helliwell, T. Maxwell, and H.E.L. Waslander, "Comparing the Dynamics of Canadian Macro Models," *Canadian Journal of Economics* 12 (May 1979): 133–138.

[2] John Bossons, "Issues in the Analysis of Government Deficits," in John Sargent, ed., *Fiscal and Monetary Policy,* Research Studies of the Royal Commission on the Economic Union and Development Prospects for Canada 21 (Toronto: University of Toronto Press, 1986): 85–112.

[3] John Helliwell, "What's Left for Macroeconomic and Growth Policies?" *Bell Canada Papers on Economic and Public Policy* 2 (1994): 5–48.

government spending increase has been *announced* (even before it is implemented). But if everyone tries to sell financial assets at the same time, the price of those assets drops quickly. As a result, the effective yield that a new purchaser can earn on them—the going rate of interest—rises immediately. The moral of the story is that when individuals react to well-informed expectations, their reactions have the effect of bringing the long-run implications of fiscal policy forward in time.

Over the last twenty-five years, economists have made major strides in their ability to model and simulate how individuals form expectations. Because of this development, the estimated econometric models have done a much better job of including the short-run implications of future government policies. This is a fundamental reason why the estimates of $\Delta Y/\Delta G$ have shrunk so much over time as research methods have improved.

The second explanation for the decrease in $\Delta Y/\Delta G$ estimates follows from increased globalization. With financial markets becoming ever more integrated throughout the world, there has developed an ever-expanding pool of "hot money." These funds move into or out of a country like Canada the moment that the interest rate rises above or sinks below interest rate levels in other countries. This flow of funds dominates the trading in the foreign exchange markets, and so it results in large changes in exchange rates. We must wait until Chapter 12 to learn how these exchange-rate changes reduce the power of fiscal policy. But it is worth noting now that globalization has increased the size and speed of these exchange-rate effects, and so it is not surprising that estimated fiscal policy multipliers have shrunk over time.

It is interesting that, when introducing its "Action Plan" in the 2009 budget, our federal government based its deficit and job-creation plans on the assumption that the government spending multiplier is 1.5. As already noted, the evidence shows that this presumption will likely mean that the government's projection concerning economic stimulus will have been overly optimistic. Nevertheless, the government tried to ensure low government spending on imports by concentrating on programs such as home renovation grants. ∎

Shocks in the *IS–LM* Model

Because the *IS–LM* model shows how national income is determined in the short run, we can use the model to examine how various economic disturbances affect income. So far we have seen how changes in fiscal policy shift the *IS* curve and how changes in monetary policy shift the *LM* curve. Similarly, we can group other disturbances into two categories: shocks to the *IS* curve and shocks to the *LM* curve.

Shocks to the *IS* curve are exogenous changes in the demand for goods and services. Some economists, including Keynes, have emphasized that such changes in demand can arise from investors' *animal spirits*—exogenous and perhaps self-fulfilling waves of optimism and pessimism. For example, suppose that firms become pessimistic about the future of the economy and that this pessimism causes them to build fewer new factories. This reduction in the demand for investment goods causes a contractionary shift in the investment function: at every interest rate, firms want to invest less. The fall in investment reduces planned

Calvin and Hobbes © 1992 Watterson.
Dist. by Universal Press Syndicate.

expenditure and shifts the *IS* curve to the left, reducing income and employment. This fall in equilibrium income in part validates the firms' initial pessimism.

Shocks to the *IS* curve may also arise from changes in the demand for consumer goods. Suppose that consumer confidence rises, as people become less worried about losing their jobs. This induces consumers to save less for the future

FYI

What Is the Bank of Canada's Policy Instrument— the Money Supply or the Interest Rate? And What Is Quantitative Easing?

Our analysis of monetary policy has been based on the assumption that the Bank of Canada influences the economy by controlling the money supply. By contrast, when you hear about Bank of Canada policy in the media, the policy instrument mentioned most often is the Bank Rate. It is the rate charged by the Bank of Canada when loaning reserves to the chartered banks, and it affects the overnight rate charged by the chartered banks when making overnight loans to each other. Which is the correct way of discussing policy? The answer is both.

For many years, the Bank of Canada has used the interest rate as its short-term policy instrument. This means that when the Bank decides on a target for the interest rate, the Bank's bond traders are told to conduct the open-market operations necessary to hit that target. These open-market operations change the money supply and shift the *LM* curve so that the equilibrium interest rate (determined by the intersection of the *IS* and *LM* curves) equals the target interest rate that the Bank's governing council has chosen.

As a result of this operating procedure, Bank of Canada policy is often discussed in terms of

changing interest rates. Keep in mind, however, that behind these changes in interest rates are the necessary changes in the money supply. A newspaper might report, for instance, that "the Bank of Canada has lowered interest rates." To be more precise, we can translate this statement as meaning "the Bank has instructed its bond traders to buy bonds in open-market operations and to pay for these bond purchases by issuing new money. This increases the money supply, shifts the *LM* curve to the right, and therefore reduces the equilibrium interest rate to hit a new lower target."

Why has the Bank of Canada chosen to use an interest rate, rather than the money supply, as its short-term policy instrument? One possible answer is that shocks to the *LM* curve are more prevalent than shocks to the *IS* curve. If so, a policy of targeting the interest rate leads to greater macroeconomic stability than a policy of targeting the money supply. (Problem 7 at the end of this chapter asks you to analyze this issue.) Another possible answer is that interest rates are easier to measure than the money supply. As we saw in Chapter 4, the Bank of Canada has several different measures of money—*M*1, *M*2, and so on—which sometimes move in different directions. Rather than deciding which measure is best, the Bank of Canada avoids the question by using the interest rate as its short-term policy instrument. When the Bank of Canada imposes a value for the interest rate, the *LM* curve becomes unnecessary for determining the level of aggregate demand. We no longer need both the *IS* and *LM* relationships to jointly determine *Y* and *r*. Instead, we are in a situation in which the central bank sets *r*, the *IS* relationship determines aggregate demand, and the only role for the *LM* relationship is (residually) to indicate what value of the money supply was needed to deliver the target value of the rate of interest. We provide formal analyses of this no–*LM*-curve version of aggregate demand theory in the appendix to this chapter, and in Chapter 14.

Understanding the Bank of Canada's short-term policy instrument became an even bigger challenge in 2009, after the Bank had lowered its overnight lending rate all the way to zero. Because no one will pay someone else to take money off his or her hands, there is a lower bound of zero on nominal interest rates. This same limit had been reached in North America during the Depression in the 1930s and during the prolonged slump in Japan during the 1990s. When that limit was reached in Canada,

people questioned how it was then possible for the Bank of Canada to perform expansionary monetary policy. The short-term interest rate could not be lowered any more. The answer involved returning to a focus on the money supply instead of the interest rate, and arguing that the *IS–LM* model takes too narrow a view of the way money affects spending. In a broader view, households manage a portfolio of assets including money, financial claims and consumer durables. When portfolios become out of balance—with too much money—households reallocate by acquiring more financial claims *and* durables. According to this view, money affects the goods market *without* having to "go through" interest rates, because there are direct money-to-goods reallocations within the portfolio. Consequently, the quantity of money has a direct effect on consumption, so a higher quantity of money shifts *both* the *IS* and *LM* curves to the right—not just the latter. "Quantitative Easing" refers to the Bank of Canada's stimulation of aggregate demand in this way. In its *Monetary Policy Report* of April 2009, the Bank explained that it remains ready to buy longer term bonds as a way of implementing this strategy. If it does so, the Bank will have returned to using the money supply, not the short-term interest rate, as its instrument (item of focus) for conducting policy.

and consume more today. We can interpret this change as an upward shift in the consumption function. This shift in the consumption function increases planned expenditure and shifts the *IS* curve to the right, and this raises income.

Shocks to the *LM* curve arise from exogenous changes in the demand for money. For example, suppose that the demand for money increases substantially, as it does when people become worried about the security of holding wealth in less liquid forms—a sensible worry if they expect a recession or a stock market crash. According to the theory of liquidity preference, when money demand rises, the interest rate necessary to equilibrate the money market is higher (for any given level of income and money supply). Hence, an increase in money demand shifts the *LM* curve upward, which tends to raise the interest rate and depress income— that is, to cause the very recession that individuals had feared.

In summary, several kinds of events can cause economic fluctuations by shifting the *IS* curve or the *LM* curve. Remember, however, that such fluctuations are not inevitable. Policymakers can try to use the tools of monetary and fiscal policy to offset exogenous shocks. If policymakers are sufficiently quick and skillful (admittedly, a big if), shocks to the *IS* or *LM* curves need not lead to fluctuations in income or employment.

11-2 *IS–LM* as a Theory of Aggregate Demand

We have been using the *IS–LM* model to explain national income in the short run when the price level is fixed. To see how the *IS–LM* model fits into the model of aggregate supply and aggregate demand introduced in Chapter 9, we now examine what happens in the *IS–LM* model if the price level is allowed to change. By examining the effects of a changing price level, we can finally deliver what was promised when we began our study of the *IS–LM* model: a theory to explain the position and slope of the aggregate demand curve.

From the *IS–LM* Model to the Aggregate Demand Curve

Recall from Chapter 9 that the aggregate demand curve describes a relationship between the price level and the level of national income. In Chapter 9 this relationship was derived from the quantity theory of money. The analysis showed that for a given money supply, a higher price level implies a lower level of income. Increases in the money supply shift the aggregate demand curve to the right, and decreases in the money supply shift the aggregate demand curve to the left.

To understand the determinants of aggregate demand more fully, we now use the *IS–LM* model, rather than the quantity theory, to derive the aggregate demand curve. First, we use the *IS–LM* model to show why national income falls as the price level rises—that is, why the aggregate demand curve is downward sloping. Second, we examine what causes the aggregate demand curve to shift.

To explain why the aggregate demand curve slopes downward, we examine what happens in the *IS–LM* model when the price level changes. This is done in Figure 11-5. For any given money supply M, a higher price level P reduces the supply of real money balances M/P. A lower supply of real money balances shifts the *LM* curve upward, which raises the equilibrium interest rate and lowers the equilibrium level of income, as shown in panel (a). Here the price level rises from P_1 to P_2, and income falls from Y_1 to Y_2. The aggregate demand curve in panel (b) plots this negative relationship between national income and the price level. In other words, the aggregate demand curve shows the set of equilibrium points that arise in the *IS–LM* model as we vary the price level and see what happens to income.

What causes the aggregate demand curve to shift? Because the aggregate demand curve summarizes the results from the *IS–LM* model, events that shift the *IS* curve or the *LM* curve (for a given price level) cause the aggregate demand curve to shift. For instance, an increase in the money supply raises income in the *IS–LM* model for any given price level; it thus shifts the aggregate demand curve to the right, as shown in panel (a) of Figure 11-6. Similarly, an increase in government purchases or a decrease in taxes raises income in the *IS–LM* model for a given price level; it also shifts the aggregate demand curve to the right, as

FIGURE 11-5

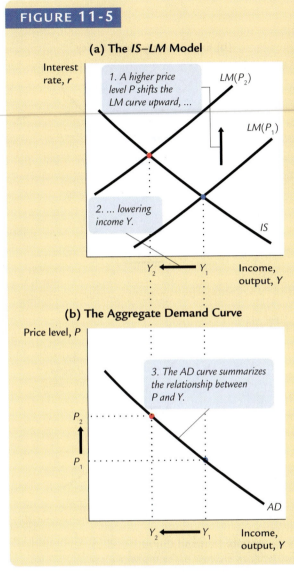

(a) The *IS–LM* Model

Interest rate, *r*

1. A higher price level P shifts the LM curve upward, ...

$LM(P_2)$

$LM(P_1)$

2. ... lowering income Y.

IS

Y_2 ← Y_1 Income, output, *Y*

(b) The Aggregate Demand Curve

Price level, *P*

3. The AD curve summarizes the relationship between P and Y.

P_2

P_1

AD

Y_2 ← Y_1 Income, output, *Y*

Deriving the Aggregate Demand Curve With the *IS–LM* Model Panel (a) shows the *IS–LM* model: an increase in the price level from P_1 to P_2 lowers real money balances and thus shifts the *LM* curve upward. The shift in the *LM* curve lowers income from Y_1 to Y_2. Panel (b) shows the aggregate demand curve summarizing this relationship between the price level and income: the higher the price level, the lower the level of income.

shown in panel (b) of Figure 11-6. Conversely, a decrease in the money supply, a decrease in government purchases, or an increase in taxes lowers income in the *IS–LM* model and shifts the aggregate demand curve to the left. Anything that changes income in the *IS–LM* model other than a change in the price level caus- es a shift in the aggregate demand curve. The factors shifting aggregate demand include not only monetary and fiscal policy but also shocks to the goods market (the *IS* curve) and shocks to the money market (the *LM* curve).

We can summarize these results as follows: *a change in income in the IS–LM model resulting from a change in the price level represents a movement along the aggregate demand curve. A change in income in the IS–LM model for a fixed price level represents a shift in the position of the aggregate demand curve.*

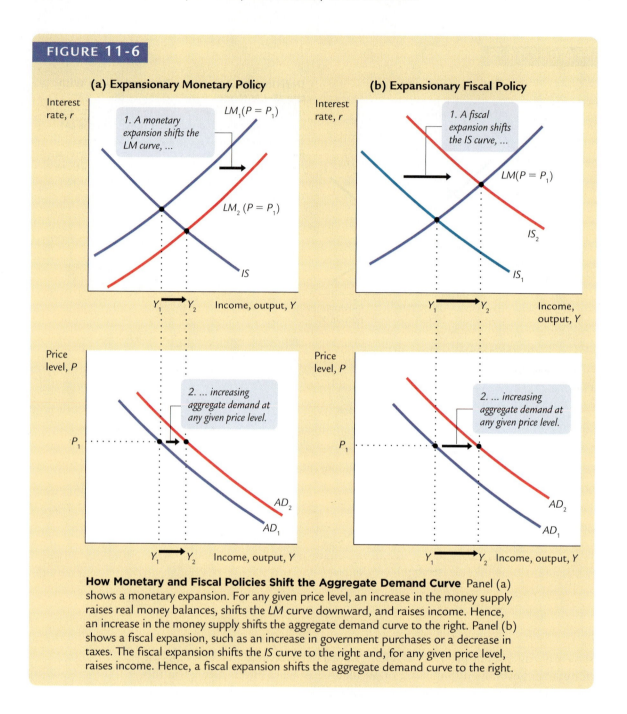

How Monetary and Fiscal Policies Shift the Aggregate Demand Curve Panel (a) shows a monetary expansion. For any given price level, an increase in the money supply raises real money balances, shifts the *LM* curve downward, and raises income. Hence, an increase in the money supply shifts the aggregate demand curve to the right. Panel (b) shows a fiscal expansion, such as an increase in government purchases or a decrease in taxes. The fiscal expansion shifts the *IS* curve to the right and, for any given price level, raises income. Hence, a fiscal expansion shifts the aggregate demand curve to the right.

The *IS–LM* Model in the Short Run and the Long Run

The *IS–LM* model is designed to explain the economy in the short run when the price level is fixed. Yet, now that we have seen how a change in the price level influences the equilibrium in the *IS–LM* model, we can also use the model to describe the economy in the long run when the price level adjusts to ensure that

FIGURE 11-7

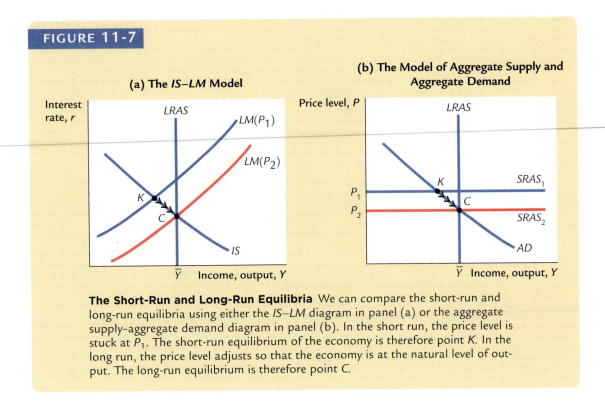

The Short-Run and Long-Run Equilibria We can compare the short-run and long-run equilibria using either the *IS–LM* diagram in panel (a) or the aggregate supply–aggregate demand diagram in panel (b). In the short run, the price level is stuck at P_1. The short-run equilibrium of the economy is therefore point *K*. In the long run, the price level adjusts so that the economy is at the natural level of output. The long-run equilibrium is therefore point C.

the economy produces at its natural rate. By using the *IS–LM* model to describe the long run, we can show clearly how the Keynesian model of income determination differs from the classical model of Chapter 3.

Panel (a) of Figure 11-7 shows the three curves that are necessary for understanding the short-run and long-run equilibria: the *IS* curve, the *LM* curve, and the vertical line representing the natural level of output $\overline{Y}$, which we label the full-employment output line. As explained in Chapter 3, this is the level of output that emerges when the market-clearing level of labour employment is inserted into the production function. Since neither the labour demand nor supply functions depend on the interest rate, this full-employment level of output is independent of *r*. That is why the full-employment output line is vertical in panel (a) of Figure 11-7. The *LM* curve is, as always, drawn for a fixed price level, P_1. The short-run equilibrium of the economy is point *K*, where the *IS* curve crosses the *LM* curve. Notice that in this short-run equilibrium, the economy's income is less than its natural level.

Panel (b) of Figure 11-7 shows the same situation in the diagram of aggregate supply and aggregate demand. At the price level P_1, the quantity of output demanded is below the natural level. In other words, at the existing price level, there is insufficient demand for goods and services to keep the economy producing at its potential.

In these two diagrams we can examine the short-run equilibrium at which the economy finds itself and the long-run equilibrium toward which the economy gravitates. Point K describes the short-run equilibrium, because it assumes that the price level is stuck at P_1. Eventually, the low demand for goods and services causes prices to fall, and the economy moves back toward its natural rate. When the price level reaches P_2, the economy is at point C, the long-run equilibrium. The diagram of aggregate supply and aggregate demand shows that at point C, the quantity of goods and services demanded equals the natural level of output. This long-run equilibrium is achieved in the IS–LM diagram by a shift in the LM curve: the fall in the price level raises real money balances and therefore shifts the LM curve to the right.

We can now see the key difference between the Keynesian and classical approaches to the determination of national income. The Keynesian assumption (represented by point K) is that the price level is stuck. Depending on monetary policy, fiscal policy, and the other determinants of aggregate demand, output may deviate from its natural level. The classical assumption (represented by point C) is that the price level is fully flexible. The price level adjusts to ensure that national income is always at its natural level.

To make the same point somewhat differently, we can think of the economy as being described by three equations. The first two are the IS and LM equations:

$$Y = C(Y - T) + I(r) + G \quad IS,$$

$$M/P = L(r, Y) \quad LM.$$

The IS equation describes the equilibrium in the goods market, and the LM equation describes the equilibrium in the money market. These two equations contain three endogenous variables: Y, P, and r. To complete the system, we need a third equation. The Keynesian approach completes the model with the assumption of fixed prices, so the Keynesian third equation is

$$P = P_1.$$

This assumption implies that the remaining two variables r and Y must adjust to satisfy the remaining two equations IS and LM. The classical approach completes the model with the assumption that output reaches its natural level, so the classical third equation is

$$Y = \overline{Y}.$$

This assumption implies that the remaining two variables r and P must adjust to satisfy the remaining two equations IS and LM. Thus, the classical approaches fixes output and allows the price level to adjust to satisfy the goods and money market equilibrium conditions, whereas the Keynesian approach fixes the price level and lets output move to satisfy the equilibrium conditions.

Which assumption is most appropriate? The answer depends on the time horizon. The classical assumption best describes the long run. Hence, our long-run analysis of national income in Chapter 3 and prices in Chapter 4 assumes that output equals the natural level. The Keynesian assumption best describes the short run. Therefore, our analysis of economic fluctuations relies on the assumption of a fixed price level.

11-3 The Great Depression

Now that we have developed the model of aggregate demand, let's use it to address the question that originally motivated Keynes: what caused the Great Depression in the United States? For Canada, there is not such a puzzle. Since Canada exports such a large fraction of Canadian GDP to the United States, a depression in that country means a very big decrease in aggregate demand in Canada. Canada had no bank failures, so there is every reason to suspect that the loss in export sales was the dominant event. But what caused the Great Depression in the United States? Even today, more than half a century after the event, economists continue to debate the cause of this major economic downturn in the world's most powerful economy. The Great Depression provides an extended case study to show how economists use the *IS–LM* model to analyze economic fluctuations.[4]

The Spending Hypothesis: Shocks to the *IS* Curve

Since the decline in U.S. income in the early 1930s coincided with falling interest rates, some economists have suggested that the cause of the decline was a contractionary shift in the *IS* curve. This view is sometimes called the *spending hypothesis,* because it places primary blame for the Depression on an exogenous fall in spending on goods and services. Economists have attempted to explain this decline in spending in several ways.

Some argue that a downward shift in the consumption function caused the contractionary shift in the *IS* curve. The stock market crash of 1929 may have been partly responsible for this decline in consumption. By reducing wealth and increasing uncertainty, the crash may have induced consumers to save more of their income.

Others explain the decline in spending by pointing to the large drop in investment in housing. Some economists believe that the residential investment boom of the 1920s was excessive, and that once this "overbuilding" became apparent, the demand for residential investment declined drastically. Another possible explanation for the fall in residential investment is the reduction in immigration in the 1930s: a more slowly growing population demands less new housing.

Once the Depression began, several events occurred that could have reduced spending further. First, the widespread bank failures in the United States (some 9,000 banks failed in the 1930–1933 period) may have reduced investment. Banks play the crucial role of getting the funds available for investment to those investors who can best use them. The closing of many banks in the early 1930s,

---

[4] For a flavour of the debate, see Milton Friedman and Anna J. Schwartz, *A Monetary History of the United States, 1867–1960* (Princeton, NJ: Princeton University Press, 1963); Peter Temin, *Did Monetary Forces Cause the Great Depression?* (New York: W. W. Norton, 1976); the essays in Karl Brunner, ed., *The Great Depression Revisited* (Boston: Martinus Nijhoff Publishing, 1981); and the symposium on the Great Depression in the Spring 1993 issue of the *Journal of Economic Perspectives*.

with depositors losing their wealth, may have prevented some investors from getting the funds they needed and thus may have led to a further contractionary shift in the investment function.[5]

In addition, U.S. fiscal policy of the 1930s caused a contractionary shift in the *IS* curve. Politicians at that time were more concerned with balancing the budget than with using fiscal policy to stimulate the economy. The Revenue Act of 1932 increased various taxes, especially those falling on lower- and middle-income consumers.[6] The Democratic platform of that year expressed concern about the budget deficit and advocated an "immediate and drastic reduction of governmental expenditures." In the midst of historically high unemployment, policymakers searched for ways to raise taxes and reduce government spending.

There are, therefore, several ways to explain a contractionary shift in the *IS* curve. Keep in mind that these different views are not inconsistent with one another. There may be no single explanation for the decline in spending. It is possible that all of these changes coincided, and together they led to a major reduction in spending.

The Money Hypothesis: A Shock to the *LM* Curve

The U.S. money supply fell 25 percent from 1929 to 1933, during which time the unemployment rate rose from 3.2 percent to 25.2 percent. This fact provides the motivation and support for what is called the *money hypothesis,* which places primary blame for the Depression on the Federal Reserve for allowing the money supply to fall by such a large amount.[7] The best known advocates of this interpretation are Milton Friedman and Anna Schwartz, who defend it in their treatise on U.S. monetary history. Friedman and Schwartz argue that contractions in the money supply have caused most economic downturns and that the Great Depression is a particularly vivid example.

Using the *IS–LM* model, we might interpret the money hypothesis as explaining the Depression by a contractionary shift in the *LM* curve. Seen in this way, however, the money hypothesis runs into two problems.

The first problem is the behaviour of *real* money balances. Monetary policy leads to a contractionary shift in the *LM* curve only if real money balances fall. Yet from 1929 to 1931, real money balances rose slightly, since the fall in the money supply was accompanied by an even greater fall in the price level. Although the monetary contraction may be responsible for the rise in unemployment from 1931 to 1933, when real money balances did fall, it probably should not be blamed for the initial downturn from 1929 to 1931.

---

[5] Ben Bernanke, "Non-Monetary Effects of the Financial Crisis in the Propagation of the Great Depression," *American Economic Review* 73 (June 1983): 257–276.

[6] E. Cary Brown, "Fiscal Policy in the 'Thirties: A Reappraisal," *American Economic Review* 46 (December 1956): 857–879.

[7] We discuss the reason for this large decrease in the money supply in Chapter 18, where we examine the money supply process in more detail (case study "Bank Failures and Deposit Insurance.")

The second problem for the money hypothesis is the behaviour of interest rates. If a contractionary shift in the *LM* curve triggered the Depression, we should have observed higher interest rates. Yet nominal interest rates fell continuously from 1929 to 1933.

These two reasons appear sufficient to reject the view that the Depression was instigated by a contractionary shift in the *LM* curve. But was the fall in the money stock irrelevant? Next, we turn to another mechanism through which monetary policy might have been responsible for the severity of the Depression—the deflation of the 1930s.

The Money Hypothesis Again: The Effects of Falling Prices

From 1929 to 1933 the U.S. price level fell 25 percent. Many economists blame this deflation for the severity of the Great Depression. They argue that the deflation may have turned what in 1931 was a typical economic downturn into an unprecedented period of high unemployment and depressed income. If correct, this argument gives new life to the money hypothesis. Since the falling money supply was, plausibly, responsible for the falling price level, it could have been responsible for the severity of the Depression. To evaluate this argument, we must discuss how changes in the price level affect income in the *IS–LM* model.

The Stabilizing Effects of Deflation
In the *IS–LM* model we have developed so far, falling prices raise income. For any given supply of money *M,* a lower price level implies higher real money balances *M/P.* An increase in real money balances causes an expansionary shift in the *LM* curve, leading to higher income.

Another channel through which falling prices expand income is called the **Pigou effect.** Arthur Pigou, a prominent classical economist in the 1930s, pointed out that real money balances are part of households' wealth. As prices fall and real money balances rise, consumers should feel wealthier and spend more. This increase in consumer spending should cause an expansionary shift in the *IS* curve, also leading to higher income.

These two reasons led some economists in the 1930s to believe that falling prices would help the economy restore itself to full employment. Yet other economists were less confident in the economy's ability to correct itself. They pointed to other effects of falling prices, to which we now turn.

The Destabilizing Effects of Deflation
Economists have proposed two theories to explain how falling prices could depress income rather than raise it. The first, called the **debt–deflation theory,** concerns the effects of *unexpected* falls in the price level. The second concerns the effects of *expected* deflation.

The debt-deflation theory begins with an observation that should be familiar from Chapter 4: unanticipated changes in the price level redistribute wealth between debtors and creditors. If a debtor owes a creditor $1,000, then the real amount of this debt is $1,000/P, where P is the price level. A fall in the price level raises the real amount of this debt—the amount of purchasing power the debtor must repay the creditor. Therefore, an unexpected deflation enriches creditors and impoverishes debtors.

The debt-deflation theory then posits that this redistribution of wealth affects spending on goods and services. In response to the redistribution from debtors to creditors, debtors spend less and creditors spend more. If these two groups have equal spending propensities, there is no aggregate impact. But it seems reasonable to assume that debtors have higher propensities to spend than creditors—perhaps that is why the debtors are in debt in the first place. In this case, debtors reduce their spending by more than creditors raise theirs. The net effect is a reduction in spending, a contractionary shift in the *IS* curve, and lower national income.

To understand how *expected* changes in prices can affect income, we need to add a new variable to the *IS–LM* model. Our discussion of the model so far has not distinguished between the nominal and real interest rates. Yet we know from previous chapters that investment depends on the real interest rate and that money demand depends on the nominal interest rate. If i is the nominal interest rate and $E\pi$ is expected inflation, then the *ex ante* real interest rate $r = i - E\pi$. We can now write the *IS–LM* model as

$$Y = C(Y - T) + I(i - E\pi) + G \quad IS,$$

$$M/P = L(i, Y) \quad\quad\quad LM.$$

Expected inflation enters as a variable in the *IS* curve. Thus, changes in expected inflation shift the *IS* curve, when it is drawn with the *nominal* interest rate on the vertical axis—as in Figure 11-8.

Let's use this extended *IS–LM* model to examine how changes in expected inflation influence the level of income. We begin by assuming that everyone expects the price level to remain the same. In this case, there is no expected

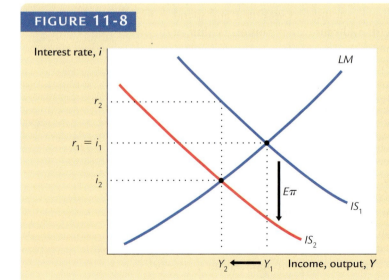

FIGURE 11-8

Expected Deflation in the IS-LM Model An expected deflation (a negative value of $E\pi$) raises the real interest rate for any given nominal interest rate, and this depresses investment spending. The reduction in investment shifts the *IS* curve downward (measuring vertically, by an amount equal to the expected deflation). The level of income falls from Y_1 to Y_2. The nominal interest rate falls from i_1 to i_2, and the real interest rate rises from r_1 to r_2.

inflation ($E\pi = 0$), and these two equations produce the familiar *IS–LM* model. Now suppose that everyone suddenly expects that the price level will fall in the future, so that $E\pi$ becomes negative. Figure 11-8 shows what happens. At any given nominal interest rate, the real interest rate is higher by the amount that $E\pi$ has dropped. Thus, the *IS* curve shifts down by this amount, as investment spending is reduced. An expected deflation thus leads to a reduction in national income from Y_1 to Y_2. The nominal interest rate falls from i_1 to i_2, and since this is less than the drop in $E\pi$, the real interest rate rises from r_1 to r_2.

The logic behind this figure is straight—forward. When firms come to expect deflation, they become reluctant to borrow to buy investment goods because they believe they will have to repay these loans later in more valuable dollars. The fall in investment depresses planned expenditure, which in turn depresses income. The fall in income reduces the demand for money, and this reduces the nominal interest rate that equilibrates the money market. The nominal interest rate falls by less than the expected deflation, so the real interest rate rises.

Note that there is a common thread in these two reasons for destabilizing deflation. In both, falling prices depress national income by causing a contractionary shift in the *IS* curve. Because a deflation of the size observed from 1929 to 1933 is unlikely except in the presence of a major contraction in the money supply, these two explanations give some of the responsibility for the Depression—especially its severity—to the Federal Reserve in the United States. In other words, if falling prices are destabilizing, then a contraction in the money supply can lead to a fall in income, even without a decrease in real money balances or a rise in nominal interest rates.

Could the Depression Happen Again?

Economists study the Depression both because of its intrinsic interest as a major economic event and to provide guidance to policymakers so that it will not happen again. To state with confidence whether this event could recur, we would need to know why it happened. Because there is not yet agreement on the causes of the Great Depression, it is impossible to rule out with certainty another depression of this magnitude.

Yet most economists believe that the mistakes that led to the Great Depression are unlikely to be repeated. Central banks seem unlikely to allow the money supply to fall by one-fourth. Many economists believe that the deflation of the early 1930s was responsible for the depth and length of the Depression. And it seems likely that such a prolonged deflation was possible only in the presence of a falling money supply.

The fiscal-policy mistakes of the Depression are also unlikely to be repeated. Fiscal policy in the 1930s not only failed to help but actually further depressed aggregate demand. Few economists today would advocate such a rigid adherence to a balanced budget in the face of massive unemployment.

In addition, there are many institutions today that would help prevent the events of the 1930s from recurring. The system of deposit insurance (now available in both Canada and the United States, and discussed in Chapter 19) makes widespread bank failures less likely. Central banks are committed to providing price stability. The income tax causes an automatic reduction in taxes when income falls, which stabilizes the economy. Finally, economists know more today than they did in the 1930s. Our knowledge of how the economy works, limited as it still is, should help policymakers formulate better policies to combat such widespread unemployment.

CASE STUDY

The Financial Crisis and Economic Downturn of 2008 and 2009

In 2008, a financial crisis developed in the United States. Both the crisis and the ensuing recession spread to many countries. Several developments during this time were reminiscent of events during the 1930s; as a result, many observers feared a severe downturn in economic activity and a substantial rise in unemployment.

The story of the 2008 crisis begins a few years earlier with a substantial boom in the U.S. housing market. The boom had several origins. In part, it was fueled by low interest rates, which made getting a mortgage less expensive for Americans and enabled them to buy higher priced homes. In addition, developments in the mortgage market made it easier for subprime borrowers—those borrowers with a higher risk of default based on their income and credit history—to get mortgages to buy homes. One of these developments was *securitization*, the process by which a financial institution (a mortgage originator) makes loans and then bundles them together into a variety of investment instruments called *mortgage-backed securities*. These mortgage-backed securities are then sold to other institutions (banks or insurance companies), which may not fully appreciate the risks they are taking. Some economists blame insufficient regulation for these high-risk loans. Others believe that, rather than too little regulation, the problem was the wrong kind of regulation: some government policies encouraged this high-risk lending to make the goal of home ownership more attainable for low-income families. Together, these forces drove up housing demand, and from 1995 to 2006, average housing prices in the United States more than doubled.

The high price of housing, however, proved unsustainable. From 2006 to 2008, housing prices fell about 20 percent nationwide in the United States. Such price fluctuations should not necessarily be a problem in a market economy. After all, price movements are how markets equilibrate supply and demand. Moreover, the price of housing in 2008 was merely a return to the level that had prevailed in 2004. But in this case, the price decline led to a series of problematic repercussions.

The first of these repercussions was a substantial rise in mortgage defaults and home foreclosures. During the housing boom, many homeowners had bought their homes with mostly borrowed money and minimal down payments. When housing prices declined, these homeowners were *underwater:* they owed more on their mortgages than their homes were worth. Many of these homeowners stopped paying their loans. The banks servicing the mortgages responded to these defaults by repossessing the houses in foreclosure procedures and then selling them. The banks wanted to recoup whatever they could. The increase in the number of homes for sale, however, exacerbated the downward spiral of housing prices.

A second repercussion was large losses at the various financial institutions that owned mortgage-backed securities. In essence, by borrowing large sums to buy high-risk mortgages, these companies had bet that housing prices would keep rising; when this bet turned bad, they found themselves at or near the point of bankruptcy. Even healthy banks stopped trusting one another and avoided inter-bank lending, because it was hard to discern which institution would be the next to go out of business. Due to these large losses at financial institutions and the widespread fear and distrust, the ability of the financial system to make loans even to creditworthy customers was impaired.

A third repercussion was a substantial rise in stock market volatility. Many companies rely on the financial system to get the resources they need for business expansion or to help them manage their short-term cash flows. With the financial system less able to perform its normal operations, the profitability of many companies was called into question. Because it was hard to know how bad things would get, stock market volatility reached levels not seen since the 1930s.

Higher stock market volatility, in turn, led to a fourth repercussion: a decline in consumer confidence. In the midst of all the uncertainty, households started putting off spending plans. Expenditures for durable goods in particular plummeted. As a result of all these events, the economy experienced a large contractionary shift in the *IS* curve.

The U.S. government responded vigorously as the crisis unfolded. First, the Fed cut its target for the federal funds rate from 5.25 percent in September 2007 to almost zero in December 2008. Second, in an even more unusual move in October 2008, the U.S. Congress appropriated $700 billion for the Treasury to use to rescue the financial system. Much of these funds were used for equity injections into banks. That is, the Treasury put funds into the banking system, and the banks could use these funds to make loans. In exchange for the funds, the U.S. government became a part owner of these banks, at least temporarily. The goal of the rescue (or "bailout," as it was sometimes called) was to stem the financial crisis on Wall Street and prevent it from causing a depression on every other street in America. Finally, as noted in Chapter 10, when Barack Obama became president in January 2009, one of his first proposals was a major increase in government spending to expand aggregate demand.

Canada did not have a significant financial crisis in 2008, and several differences in institutional arrangements contributed to this much preferred outcome. First, Canada has a *branch* banking system with just a few banks operating throughout the country, and these banks are regulated in a coordinated fashion. The United States has a *unit* banking system with thousands of individual banks, many of them operating only within particular states. These individual banks do not have the advantage of pooling risks that larger banks do. Close to one-third of the banks failed in the United States during the first four years of the Depression in the 1930s, while none failed in Canada. This ongoing difference in industrial structure has continued to serve Canada well.

A second difference is that, until recently, the three main fields within our financial sector—banking, stock brokerage services, and insurance—were kept quite separate. This arrangement made it difficult for a "shadow" banking system to develop as it did in the United States. With shadow banking, institutions that are not covered by deposit insurance, such as stock brokerages, end up serving as people's banks. This situation comes close to duplicating the fragility that existed before we introduced deposit insurance in the mid 1930s.

A third difference is the level of regulation. Canada's banks must have $1 of underlying risk-free capital for every $18 of more risky assets they acquire by making loans. Under U.S. regulations before the crisis, each dollar of underlying capital permitted $25 of risky assets to be acquired. This freedom allowed U.S. banks to become overextended.

There is one final difference that made Canada less prone to a financial crisis. The crisis in the United States started in the housing/mortgage sector. Canadian institutional arrangements in this sector are quite different. For one thing, home ownership is not as heavily promoted north of the border. For example, mortgage payments are not deductible in the Canadian personal income tax system, and zero down payments are not permitted in Canada. Down payments of 20 percent are common here, and all mortgages with a loan-to-value ratio greater than 80 percent must be insured with a federal government agency (the Canada Mortgage and Housing Corporation), which applies strict standards.

Despite the fact that Canada avoided the U.S. financial crisis, Canadians still feared a serious domestic recession in 2008. This fear was based on the fact that we export such a large proportion of our GDP to the United States. A serious recession there means a big drop in Canadian exports, and consequently, a noticeable leftward shift in the position of Canada's *IS* curve. For this reason, the Bank of Canada took action similar to the Fed's, cutting the overnight lending rate all the way essentially to zero, and committing itself to a policy of quantitative easing if necessary (see the earlier *FYI* box in this chapter). Also, on the fiscal policy front, the federal government tabled a budget in 2009 that involved the biggest annual deficit in Canadian history. Both monetary policy and fiscal policy were being used to stimulate aggregate demand with the goal of keeping the recession from developing into anything like what we endured in the 1930s.

These policy initiatives were controversial. Some argued that the Bank of Canada's readiness to pursue quantitative easing meant that the zero lower bound on nominal interest rates was not a problem, so the return to large fiscal deficits was ill advised. In the end, the government disagreed with this view. Readers who are interested in pursuing this debate in a way that integrates *IS–LM* theory and Canadian application can read a more detailed analysis provided elsewhere by one of the authors.[8]

---

[8] See William Scarth, "Stabilization Policy Debates: Assessing the Case for Fiscal Stimulus," in The 2009 Federal Budget: Challenge, Response and Retrospect, C. Beach, B. Dahlby and P. Hobson, eds., (Kingston: John Deutsch Institute for the Study of Economic Policy, 2009.)

FYI

The Liquidity Trap

Short-term interest rates fell to zero throughout much of the western world in the 2008–2009 recession, just as they had in North America during the Great Depression in the 1930s and as they had during the prolonged slump in Japan during the 1990s.

Some economists describe this situation as a *liquidity trap.* According to the *IS–LM* model, expansionary monetary policy works by reducing interest rates and stimulating investment spending. But if interest rates have already fallen almost to zero, then perhaps monetary policy is no longer effective. Nominal interest rates cannot fall below zero: rather than making a loan at a negative nominal interest rate, a person would just hold cash. In this environment, expansionary monetary policy raises the supply of money, making the public more liquid, but because interest rates can't fall any further, the extra liquidity might not have any effect. Aggregate demand, production, and employment may be "trapped" at low levels.

Other economists are skeptical about the relevance of liquidity traps and believe that central banks continue to have tools to expand the economy, even after its interest rate target hits zero. One possibility is that the central bank could raise inflation expectations by committing itself to future monetary expansion. Even if nominal interest rates cannot fall any further, higher expected inflation can lower *real* interest rates by making them negative, which would stimulate investment spending. A second possibility is that monetary expansion could cause the currency to lose value in the market for foreign currency exchange. This depreciation would make the nation's goods cheaper abroad, stimulating export demand. This mechanism goes beyond the closed-economy *IS–LM* model we have used in this chapter, but it has merit in the open-economy version of the model developed in the next chapter. A third possibility is that the central bank could conduct expansionary open-market operations in a wider variety of financial instruments than it normally does. For example, it could buy mortgages and corporate debt and thereby lower the interest rates on these kinds of loans. The Federal Reserve in the United States actively pursued this last option during the downturn of 2008.

Is the liquidity trap something monetary policymakers need to worry about? Might the tools of monetary policy at times lose their power to influence the economy? There is no consensus about the answers. Skeptics say we shouldn't worry about the liquidity trap. But others say the possibility of a liquidity trap argues for a target rate of inflation greater than zero. Under zero inflation, the real interest rate, like the nominal interest, can never fall below zero. But if the normal rate of inflation is, say, 3 percent, then the central bank can easily push the real interest rate to negative 3 percent by lowering the nominal interest rate toward zero. Thus, moderate inflation gives monetary policymakers more room to stimulate the economy when needed, reducing the risk of falling into a liquidity trap.[9]

A more detailed analysis of liquidity traps, which explains how aggregate supply and demand diagramatic analysis is affected, is available in the Appendix to this chapter.

11-4 Conclusion

The purpose of this chapter and the previous one has been to deepen our understanding of aggregate demand. We now have the tools to analyze the effects of monetary and fiscal policy in the long run and in the short run. In the long run, prices are flexible, and we use the classical analysis of Part Two of this book.

---

[9] To read more about the liquidity trap, see Paul R. Krugman, "It's Baaack: Japan's Slump and the Return of the Liquidity Trap," *Brookings Panel on Economic Activity* 1998:2, 137-205.

In the short run, prices are sticky, and we use the *IS–LM* model to examine how changes in policy influence the economy.

Although the model in this chapter and the previous chapter provides the basic framework for analyzing the economy in the short run, it is not the whole story. Future chapters refine the theory. In Chapter 12 we examine how international interactions affect the theory of aggregate demand; in Chapter 13 we examine the theory behind short-run aggregate supply; and in Chapter 14 we bring these various elements of aggregate demand and aggregate supply together to study more precisely the dynamic response of the economy over time. In Chapter 15 we consider the how this theoretical framework should be applied to the making of stabilization policy. In addition, in later chapters, we examine in more detail the elements of the *IS–LM* model, thereby refining our understanding of aggregate demand. In Chapter 17, for example, we study theories of consumption. Because the consumption function is a crucial piece of the *IS–LM* model, a deeper analysis of consumption may modify our view of the impact of monetary and fiscal policy on the economy. The simple *IS–LM* model presented in Chapters 10 and 11 provides the starting point for this further analysis.

Summary

1. The *IS–LM* model is a general theory of the aggregate demand for goods and services. The exogenous variables in the model are fiscal policy, monetary policy, and the price level. The model explains two endogenous variables: the interest rate and the level of national income.

2. The *IS* curve represents the negative relationship between the interest rate and the level of income that arises from equilibrium in the market for goods and services. The *LM* curve represents the positive relationship between the interest rate and the level of income that arises from equilibrium in the market for real money balances. Equilibrium in the *IS–LM* model—the intersection of the *IS* and *LM* curves—represents simultaneous equilibrium in the market for goods and services and in the market for real money balances.

3. The aggregate demand curve summarizes the results from the *IS–LM* model by showing equilibrium income at any given price level. The aggregate demand curve slopes downward because a lower price level increases real money balances, lowers the interest rate, stimulates investment spending, and thereby raises equilibrium income.

4. Expansionary fiscal policy—an increase in government purchases or a decrease in taxes—shifts the *IS* curve to the right. This shift in the *IS* curve increases the interest rate and income. The increase in income represents a rightward shift in the aggregate demand curve. Similarly, contractionary

fiscal policy shifts the *IS* curve to the left, lowers the interest rate and income, and shifts the aggregate demand curve to the left.

5. Expansionary monetary policy shifts the *LM* curve downward. This shift in the *LM* curve lowers the interest rate and raises income. The increase in income represents a rightward shift of the aggregate demand curve. Similarly, contractionary monetary policy shifts the *LM* curve upward, raises the interest rate, lowers income, and shifts the aggregate demand curve to the left.

KEY CONCEPTS

Monetary transmission mechanism	Pigou effect	Debt-deflation theory

QUESTIONS FOR REVIEW

1. Explain why the aggregate demand curve slopes downward.

2. What is the impact of an increase in taxes on the interest rate, income, consumption, and investment?

3. What is the impact of a decrease in the money supply on the interest rate, income, consumption, and investment?

4. Describe the possible effects of falling prices on equilibrium income.

PROBLEMS AND APPLICATIONS

1. According to the IS–LM model, what happens in the short run to the interest rate, income, consumption, and investment under the following circumstances?

   a. The central bank increases the money supply.

   b. The government increases government purchases.

   c. The government increases taxes.

   d. The government increases government purchases and taxes by equal amounts.

2. Use the *IS–LM* model to predict the effects of each of the following shocks on income, the interest rate, consumption, and investment.

In each case, explain what the central bank should do to keep income at its initial level.

   a. After the invention of a new high-speed computer chip, many firms decide to upgrade their computer systems.

   b. A wave of credit-card fraud increases the frequency with which people make transactions in cash.

   c. A best-seller entitled *Retire Rich* convinces the public to increase the percentage of their income devoted to saving.

3. Consider the economy of Hicksonia.

   a. The consumption function is given by

$$C = 200 + 0.75(Y - T).$$

The investment function is

$$I = 200 - 25r.$$

Government purchases and taxes are both 100. For this economy, graph the IS curve for r ranging from 0 to 8.

b. The money demand function in Hicksonia is

$$(M/P)^d = Y - 100r.$$

The money supply M is 1,000 and the price level P is 2. For this economy, graph the LM curve for r ranging from 0 to 8.

c. Find the equilibrium interest rate r and the equilibrium level of income Y.

d. Suppose that government purchases are raised from 100 to 150. How much does the IS curve shift? What are the new equilibrium interest rate and level of income?

e. Suppose instead that the money supply is raised from 1,000 to 1,200. How much does the LM curve shift? What are the new equilibrium interest rate and level of income?

f. With the initial values for monetary and fiscal policy, suppose that the price level rises from 2 to 4. What happens? What are the new equilibrium interest rate and level of income?

g. Derive and graph an equation for the aggregate demand curve. What happens to this aggregate demand curve if fiscal or monetary policy changes, as in parts (d) and (e)?

4. Explain why each of the following statements is true. Discuss the impact of monetary and fiscal policy in each of these special cases.

a. If investment does not depend on the interest rate, the IS curve is vertical.

b. If money demand does not depend on the interest rate, the LM curve is vertical.

c. If money demand does not depend on income, the LM curve is horizontal.

d. If money demand is extremely sensitive to the interest rate, the LM curve is horizontal.

5. Suppose that the government wants to raise investment but keep output constant. In the IS–LM model, what mix of monetary and fiscal policy will achieve this goal? In the 1980s, the Canadian government ran budget deficits

while the Bank of Canada pursued a tight monetary policy. What effect should this policy mix have?

6. Use the IS–LM diagram to describe the short-run and long-run effects of the following changes on national income, the interest rate, the price level, consumption, investment, and real money balances.

a. An increase in the money supply.

b. An increase in government purchases.

c. An increase in taxes.

7. The central bank is considering two alternative monetary policies:

- holding the money supply constant and letting the interest rate adjust, or

- adjusting the money supply to hold the interest rate constant.

In the IS–LM model, which policy will better stabilize output under the following conditions?

a. All shocks to the economy arise from exogenous changes in the demand for goods and services.

b. All shocks to the economy arise from exogenous changes in the demand for money.

8. Suppose that the demand for real money balances depends on disposable income. That is, the money demand function is

$$M/P = L(r, Y - T).$$

Using the IS–LM model, discuss whether this change in the money demand function alters the following:

a. The analysis of changes in government purchases.

b. The analysis of changes in taxes.

9. This problem asks you to analyze the IS–LM model algebraically. Suppose consumption is a linear function of disposable income:

$$C(Y - T) = a + b(Y - T),$$

where $a > 0$ and $0 < b < 1$. Suppose also that investment is a linear function of the interest rate:

$$I(r) = c - dr,$$

where $c > 0$ and $d > 0$.

a. Solve for Y as a function of r, the exogenous variables G and T, and the model's parameters $a, b, c,$ and d.

b. How does the slope of the *IS* curve depend on the parameter d, the interest rate sensitivity of investment? Refer to your answer to part (a), and explain the intuition.

c. Which will cause a bigger horizontal shift in the *IS* curve, a $100 tax cut or a $100 increase in government spending? Refer to your answer to part (a), and explain the intuition.

   Now suppose demand for real money balances is a linear function of income and the interest rate:

$$L(r, Y) = eY - fr,$$

where $e > 0$ and $f > 0$.

d. Solve for r as a function of Y, M, and P and the parameters e and f.

e. Using your answer to part (d), determine whether the *LM* curve is steeper for large or small values of f, and explain the intuition.

f. How does the size of the shift in the *LM* curve resulting from a $100 increase in M depend on

   i. the value of the parameter e, the income sensitivity of money demand?

   ii. the value of the parameter f, the interest rate sensitivity of money demand?

g. Use your answers to parts (a) and (d) to derive an expression for the aggregate demand curve. Your expression should show Y as a function of P; of exogenous policy variables M, G, and T; and of the model's parameters. Your expression should not contain r.

h. Use your answer to part (g) to prove that the aggregate demand curve has a negative slope.

i. Use your answer to part (g) to prove that increases in G and M, and decreases in T, shift the aggregate demand curve to the right. How does this result change if the parameter f, the interest sensitivity of money demand, equals zero?

Aggregate Demand Theory Without the *LM* Curve

Aggregate Demand in a Closed Economy

Some readers may find the two-quadrant diagrammatic derivation of the aggregate demand curve in Figure 11-5 confusing. The algebraic derivation presented in this appendix offers a second chance to understand this topic. A second purpose of this appendix is to eliminate the gap between news media reports that talk of the Bank of Canada "setting interest rates" and the discussion in Chapters 10 and 11 about the Bank setting the money supply. A third purpose of this appendix is to provide a more explicit discussion of how a liquidity trap can affect the power of monetary policy. For simplicity, as in Chapters 10 and 11, the algebraic treatment begins by abstracting from foreign trade. The small open economy case (in which foreign trade is central) is considered at the end of the appendix.

In the closed-economy setting, the relationships that define the components of aggregate demand are as follows:

$$Y = C + I + G$$
$$C = C^* + c(Y - T)$$
$$I = I^* - br$$
$$r = r^* + a(P - P^*)$$

The first equation states that the total of all goods produced, the GDP, must be purchased by households (C), firms (I), or the government (G). The household consumption function is the second equation (see Figure 10.2). C^* stands for the vertical intercept in that figure, and c denotes the marginal propensity to consume (the slope of the line shown in Figure 10.2). As noted earlier, c is (realistically) assumed to be a positive fraction.

Firms' investment spending on new plant and equipment depends inversely on the cost of borrowing. To capture this fact, we specify investment as an inverse function of the interest rate, r, in the third equation. I^* is the intercept of this equation, and b is a positive parameter that defines the magnitude of the firms' reaction to changes in the interest rate that they must pay on their loans.

Finally, the fourth equation defines the behaviour of the central bank. The bank's goal is stable prices—that is, the bank wants to keep the price level, P, from either rising or falling. To pursue this goal, the bank adjusts the nation's interest rate—so that the current value is above (or below) its long-run average value, r^*—whenever the observed price level is above (or below) its target value, P^*. The bank assumes that, by raising the interest rate, it will induce firms to cut back their spending. This reduction in aggregate demand is intended to induce firms to lower prices (and to bring the overall price index back to the bank's target path). Parameter a defines the degree of aggressiveness that the central bank displays as it pursues this price stability objective.

When the four equations are combined (eliminating variables C, I, and r by substitution), the one remaining relationship is the equation that defines the nation's aggregate demand function

$$Y = \frac{(A - abP)}{(1 - c)},$$

where $A = (C^* + I^* + G - cT - br^* + abP^*)$. Since the slope of the aggregate demand curve (in price-output space) is rise/run $= \Delta P / \Delta Y$, the expression that defines this slope is

$$\text{Slope of the Aggregate Demand Curve} = \frac{-(1 - c)}{ab}.$$

This expression confirms that the slope of the demand curve is negative as long as the marginal propensity to consume is a fraction and as long as parameters a and b are both positive. The only one of these propositions that is in doubt is the one concerning the central bank parameter a. In some cases, the bank cannot manipulate the interest rate, and we must acknowledge this possibility by setting the bank's reaction parameter to zero ($a = 0$) in some instances. The aggregate demand curve becomes vertical, not negatively sloped, in this situation, which we refer to as the "impotent" central bank case. We wish to explore both this and the opposite extreme possibility, which we call the "aggressive" central bank case.

With an aggressive central bank, monetary policy involves adjusting the interest rate so much and so quickly that the price level never departs from its target value. This approach means that the central bank's reaction coefficient (parameter a) must be infinitely large. The equations just presented can be checked to verify that as parameter a tends to infinity, the equation of the aggregate demand relationship reduces to

$$P = P^*$$

and the slope expression equals zero. So the aggregate demand relationship tends to a horizontal line at height P^* as the central bank becomes ever more aggressive in targeting price stability. In the limit, the position of this line is not affected at all by changes in expenditure (changes in variables such as G and T), so fiscal policy is useless for affecting economic activity in this case. This is "bad news" if the government wants to create jobs with what is intended to be an "expansionary" fiscal policy. The reason this policy does not work is that, to avoid the upward pressure on the price level, the central bank raises the interest rate. This increase creates what is known as a "crowding out effect": preexisting investment spending falls to make room for the higher public spending. But this outcome is "good news" if the government is cutting spending with a view to deficit reduction and it does not want to cause a recession in the process. In this case, the central bank response is lower interest rates, and this induces higher investment spending to take the place of the previously higher public spending. This analysis suggests that it was fortunate that Canada had a central bank that was actively committed to price stability when the fight against the deficit was proceeding during the 1990s.

The second extreme specification of monetary policy that we consider is one in which the central bank is unable to adjust the interest rate in the downward direction at all. This specification is relevant when the interest rate is already approximately zero, since it is impossible for nominal interest rates to become negative. (As explained at the end of Chapter 11, individuals always have the option of putting their money under their mattress). The equations just presented imply that the aggregate demand curve is vertical in this opposite extreme case.

We now consider how a situation that approaches each of these extremes can affect the ability of the economy to cure itself of a recession (Figure 11.9). There are two aggregate demand curves in this figure, and both intersect the short-run aggregate supply curve at point K. The price level (at value P_1) is too high to generate enough demand to secure full employment. The fairly flat demand curve is relevant when the central bank can and does adjust the interest rate fairly aggressively with a view to achieving price stability, while the much steeper demand curve is relevant when the central bank cannot adjust the interest rate significantly. In the first case, as prices fall, the economy moves from its Keynesian initial point (K) to the classical long-run outcome (point C) without too much deflation. But in the other case, deflation can continue indefinitely, without the economy ever getting back to full employment. As noted near the end of Chapter 11, a number of people feel that this "impotent central banker" case applied directly to the United States in the 1930s and to Japan in the 1990s. In both cases, the central bank could not lower interest rates (since yields were already essentially zero), and deflation did not eliminate the general stagnation of economic activity.

As already noted, Keynes called this outcome a "liquidity trap": the central bank is trapped. It cannot decrease loan rates (by increasing the money supply), since households do not accept negative nominal interest rates. Keynes applied

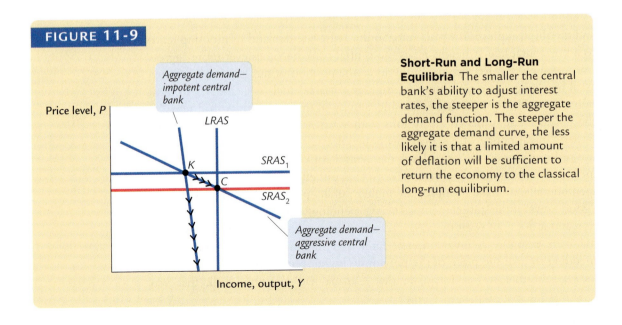

FIGURE 11-9

Aggregate demand—
impotent central
bank

Price level, P

LRAS

K

$SRAS_1$

C

$SRAS_2$

Aggregate demand—
aggressive central
bank

Income, output, Y

Short-Run and Long-Run Equilibria The smaller the central bank's ability to adjust interest rates, the steeper is the aggregate demand function. The steeper the aggregate demand curve, the less likely it is that a limited amount of deflation will be sufficient to return the economy to the classical long-run equilibrium.

this analysis to the Great Depression of the 1930s. At that time, households had no desire to turn extra currency into stocks and bonds. They simply hoarded additional currency, and (as a result) central banks lost their ability to lower interest rates and affect aggregate demand. Consequently, Keynes called for expansionary fiscal policy during the Great Depression.

Aggregate Demand in a Small Open Economy

We now return to the algebraic derivation of the aggregate demand curve, but this time we introduce a slightly different reaction function on the part of the central bank—one that more closely matches the behaviour of the Bank of Canada. Readers may wish to postpone reading this section of the appendix until after they have studied Chapter 12. That chapter covers the version of aggregate demand theory suitable for a small economy that is integrated with the rest of the world in its trading relationship.

In an open economy, there is a net exports component of demand:

$$Y = C + I + G + NX.$$

We continue to assume that household consumption and firms' investment spending depend on disposable income and the interest rate, respectively,

$$C = C^* + c(Y - T),$$
$$I = I^* - br.$$

We assume that net exports depend inversely on the relative price of domestic goods. From the point of view of foreigners, the cost of our goods depends on both the domestic currency price and the price of the Canadian dollar (the exchange rate, e). The following net export relationship embodies this assumption:

$$NX = X^* - d(P + e).$$

In Chapter 18 (page 571) we note that the Bank of Canada focuses on a weighted average of the interest rate and the exchange rate, known as the monetary conditions index (MCI). Defining the MCI as the Bank of Canada does,

$$MCI = r + (d/b)e,$$

and redefining the policy reaction function in the open-economy setting as

$$MCI = MCI^* + a(P - P^*),$$

we derive a summary aggregate demand relationship:

$$Y = C^* + c(Y - T) + I^* + G + X^* - b[r + (d/b)e] - dP$$
$$= C^* + c(Y - T) + I^* + G + X^* - b(MCI) - dP$$
$$= C^* + c(Y - T) + I^* + G + X^* - b[MCI^* + a(P - P^*)] - dP$$
$$= \frac{A - (ab + d)P}{(1 - c)}$$

where A is now defined as $C^* - cT + I^* + G + X^* - b(MCI^*) + abP^*$.

This summary expression for aggregate demand is similar to the one we have derived for the closed economy. As in that environment, we consider two polar cases. The first involves flexible exchange rates—a situation in which the central bank has no commitment to target any particular value for the exchange rate. As before, we assume that the central bank uses this independence to aggressively target domestic price stability. In this case, the central bank parameter *a* tends to infinity. The second situation involves a commitment to fix the exchange rate. With an ongoing obligation to buy and sell foreign exchange in whatever quantities dictated by market outcomes, the central bank has no independence to pursue any other policy objective. This impotence is imposed by setting central bank parameter *a* to zero. It can be readily verified that switching between these two cases (case 1—flexible exchange rates with the central bank imposing price stability and case 2—fixed exchange rates) has a big effect on the nature of the country's aggregate demand curve. We consider each case in turn.

With flexible exchange rates, the aggregate demand equation tends toward a horizontal line defined by $P = P^*$ as the central bank pursues price stability ever more aggressively. Since variables such as G, T, and X^* drop out of the equation, aggregate demand is completely unaffected by domestic fiscal policy or developments in the rest of the world. This is "bad news" for the government if it wants to use changes in its budget to conduct a stabilization policy. However, it is "good news" from the point of view that the economy is insulated from shocks that occur in the rest of the world (such as a recession in the United States, which would cause a drop in Canadian exports). The intuition behind these results is provided in Chapter 12.

With fixed exchange rates, the central bank is unable to target the price level. But since the slope of the aggregate demand curve (equal to $-(1 - c)/d$)) remains negative, Keynes's liquidity trap concern represents a less serious problem for a small open economy. A recession can end via a change in the exchange rate, so a change in the interest rate is not necessary.

This result suggests that a flexible exchange rate is a shock absorber; when aggregate demand falls, a depreciating Canadian dollar provides one way for demand to increase again, and this degree of freedom is lost if the exchange rate is fixed. Figure 11-9 can be used to illustrate this feature of a flexible exchange rate policy, if we reinterpret the two aggregate demand curves. The steep curve must be relabeled "aggregate demand with a fixed exchange rate" and the flatter demand curve must be relabeled "aggregate demand with a flexible exchange rate." Then we assume that the same loss in demand has pushed both the fixed-exchange-rate economy and the flexible-exchange-rate economy to point *K* in the short run. According to Figure 11-9, the deflation that occurs naturally when there is insufficient aggregate demand will eliminate the recession fairly readily under flexible exchange rates, but it will not do so with a fixed exchange rate. This analysis leads officials at the Bank of Canada to argue that Canada is well served by having a currency that is independent from the U.S. dollar (via a flexible exchange rate policy).

CHAPTER 12

The Open Economy Revisited: The Mundell-Fleming Model and the Exchange-Rate Regime

> *The world is still a closed economy, but its regions and countries are becoming increasingly open. . . . The international economic climate has changed in the direction of financial integration, and this has important implications for economic policy.*
>
> — *Robert Mundell, 1963*

When conducting monetary and fiscal policy, policymakers often look beyond their own country's borders. Even if domestic prosperity is their sole objective, it is necessary for them to consider the rest of the world. The international flow of goods and services (measured by net exports) and the international flow of capital (measured by net foreign investment) can affect an economy in profound ways. Policymakers ignore these effects at their peril.

In this chapter we extend our analysis of aggregate demand to include international trade and finance. The model developed in this chapter is called the **Mundell–Fleming model.** This model has been described as "the dominant policy paradigm for studying open-economy monetary and fiscal policy." In 1999, Robert Mundell, a Canadian, was awarded the Nobel Prize for his work in open-economy macroeconomics, including this model.[1]

The Mundell-Fleming model is a close relative of the *IS–LM* model. Both models stress the interaction between the goods market and the money market. Both models assume that the price level is fixed and then show what causes short-run fluctuations in aggregate income (or, equivalently, shifts in the aggregate

---

[1] The quotation is from Maurice Obstfeld and Kenneth Rogoff, *Foundations of International Finance* (Cambridge, MA: MIT Press, 1996), a leading graduate-level textbook in open-economy macro-economics. The Mundell–Fleming model was developed in the early 1960s. Mundell's contributions are collected in Robert A. Mundell, *International Economics* (New York: Macmillan, 1968). For Fleming's contribution, see J. Marcus Fleming, "Domestic Financial Policies Under Fixed and Under Floating Exchange Rates," *IMF Staff Papers* 9 (November 1962): 369–379. Fleming died in 1976; so he was not eligible to share in the Nobel award.

demand curve). The key difference is that the *IS–LM* model assumes a closed economy, whereas the Mundell–Fleming model assumes an open economy. The Mundell–Fleming model extends the short-run model of national income from Chapters 10 and 11 by including the effects of international trade and finance discussed in Chapter 5.

The Mundell–Fleming model makes one important and extreme assumption: it assumes that the economy being studied is a small open economy with perfect capital mobility. That is, the economy can borrow or lend as much as it wants in world financial markets and, as a result, the economy's interest rate is determined by the world interest rate. Here is how Mundell himself motivated this assumption in his original 1963 article:

> In order to present my conclusions in the simplest possible way and to bring the implications for policy into sharpest relief, I assume the extreme degree of mobility that prevails when a country cannot maintain an interest rate different from the general level prevailing abroad. This assumption will overstate the case but it has the merit of posing a stereotype towards which international financial relations seem to be heading. At the same time it might be argued that the assumption is not far from the truth in those financial centers, of which Zurich, Amsterdam, and Brussels may be taken as examples, where the authorities already recognize their lessening ability to dominate money market conditions and insulate them from foreign influences. It should also have a high degree of relevance to a country like Canada whose financial markets are dominated to a great degree by the vast New York market.

As we will see, Mundell's assumption of a small open economy with perfect capital mobility will prove useful in developing a tractable and illuminating model. With the interest rate determined, we can concentrate our attention on the role of the exchange rate.

One lesson from the Mundell–Fleming model is that the behaviour of an economy depends on the exchange-rate system it has adopted. Indeed, the model was first developed in large part to understand how alternative exchange-rate regimes work and how the choice of exchange-rate regime impinges on monetary and fiscal policy. We begin by assuming that the economy operates with a flexible, or floating, exchange rate. That is, we assume that the central bank allows the exchange rate to adjust to changing economic conditions. We then examine how the economy operates under a fixed exchange rate, and we discuss whether a floating or fixed exchange rate is better. This question has been extraordinarily important in recent years, as many nations around the world have debated what exchange-rate system to adopt.

12-1 The Mundell-Fleming Model

In this section we build the Mundell–Fleming model, and in the following sections we use the model to examine the impact of various policies. As you will see, the Mundell–Fleming model is built from components we have used in previous chapters. But these pieces are put together in a new way to address a new set of questions.

Components of the Model

The Mundell–Fleming model is made up of components that should be familiar. We begin by simply stating the three equations that make up the model. They are

$$Y = C(Y - T) + I(r) + G + NX(e) \qquad IS,$$

$$M/P = L(r, Y) \qquad\qquad LM,$$

$$r = r^*.$$

Before putting these equations together to make a short-run model of a small open economy, let's review each of them in turn.

The first equation describes the goods market. It states that aggregate supply Y is equal to aggregate demand—the sum of consumption C, investment I, government purchases G, and net exports NX. Consumption depends positively on disposable income $Y - T$. Investment depends negatively on the interest rate r. Net exports depend negatively on the exchange rate e.

Recall that we define the exchange rate e as the amount of foreign currency per unit of domestic currency—for example, e might be $0.90 (U.S.) per Canadian dollar. For the purposes of the Mundell–Fleming model, we do not need to distinguish between the real and nominal exchange rates. In Chapter 5 we related net exports to the real exchange rate ϵ, which equals eP/P^*, where P is the domestic price level and P^* is the foreign price level. Because the Mundell–Fleming model assumes that prices are fixed, changes in the real exchange rate are proportional to changes in the nominal exchange rate. That is, when the nominal exchange rate rises, foreign goods become less expensive compared to domestic goods, which depresses exports and stimulates imports.

The second equation describes the money market. It states that the supply of real money balances, M/P, equals the demand, $L(r, Y)$. The demand for real balances depends negatively on the interest rate and positively on overall output. As long as we have a floating exchange rate, the money supply M is an exogenous variable controlled by the central bank. Like the *IS–LM* model, the Mundell–Fleming model takes the price level P as an exogenous variable, so there is no difference between nominal and real interest rates.

The third equation states that the world interest rate r^* determines the interest rate in this economy. This equation holds because we are examining a small open economy. That is, the economy is sufficiently small relative to the world economy that it can borrow or lend as much as it wants in world financial markets without affecting the world interest rate.

Although the idea of perfect capital mobility is expressed mathematically with a simple equation, it is important not to lose sight of the sophisticated process that this equation represents. Imagine that some event were to occur that would normally raise the interest rate (such as a decline in domestic saving). In a small open economy, the domestic interest rate might rise by a little bit for a short time, but as soon as it did, foreigners would see the higher interest rate and start lending to this country (by, for instance, buying this country's bonds). The capital inflow would drive the domestic interest rate back toward r^*. Similarly, if any event were ever to start driving the domestic interest rate downward, capital would flow out of the country to earn a higher return abroad, and this capital outflow would pull the domestic interest rate back upward toward r^*. Hence, the $r = r^*$ equation represents the assumption that the international flow of capital is sufficiently rapid and large as to keep the domestic interest rate equal to the world interest rate.

It should be recalled from our discussion in Chapter 5 (in particular from Figure 5-2) that there are deviations of the Canadian interest rate from the world interest rate. One form of departure is a risk premium that depends on such factors as international concern about political instability in Canada (for example, Quebec separation). We consider risk premiums later on in this chapter, but initially they are ignored. The second reason for departures from the $r = r^*$ condition is that it takes some time for international lenders to react to yield differentials (and in doing so, to eliminate them). Thus, we view $r = r^*$ as representing full equilibrium, and we can consider temporary deviations from this full equilibrium while discussing the time sequence involved in the Mundell–Fleming model.

These three equations fully describe the Mundell–Fleming model. Our job is to examine the implications of these equations for short-run fluctuations in a small open economy. If you do not understand the equations, you should review Chapters 5 and 10 before continuing.

The Model on a *Y–r* Graph

One way to depict the Mundell–Fleming model is to use a graph in which income Y is on the horizontal axis and the interest rate r is on the vertical axis. This presentation is comparable to our analysis of the closed economy in the *IS–LM* model. As Figure 12-1 shows, the *IS* curve slopes downward, and the *LM* curve slopes upward. New in this graph is the horizontal line representing the world interest rate.

FIGURE 12-1

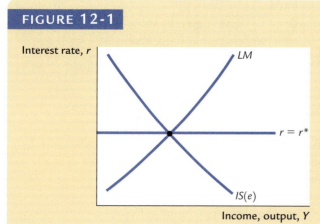

The Mundell-Fleming Model on a *Y–r* Graph This presentation of the Mundell-Fleming model is similar to that of the closed-economy *IS–LM* model. In the small open economy, however, the position of the *IS* curve depends on the exchange rate. The exchange rate adjusts to ensure that the *IS* curve crosses the point where the *LM* curve intersects the horizontal line that represents the world interest rate r^*.

Two features of this graph deserve special attention. First, because the exchange rate influences the demand for goods, the *IS* curve is drawn for a given value of the exchange rate (say, $0.90 (U.S.) per Canadian dollar). An increase in the exchange rate (say, to $0.95 (U.S.) per Canadian dollar) makes Canadian goods more expensive for foreigners to purchase, relative to foreign goods, which reduces net exports. Hence, an increase in the value of our dollar shifts the *IS* curve to the left. To remind us that the position of the *IS* curve depends on the exchange rate, the *IS* curve is labeled *IS(e)*.

Second, the three curves in Figure 12-1 all intersect at the same point. This might seem an unlikely coincidence. But, in fact, the exchange rate adjusts to ensure that all three curves pass through the same point.

To see why all three curves must intersect at a single point, let's imagine a hypothetical situation in which they did not, as in panel (a) of Figure 12-2. Here, the domestic interest rate—the point where the *IS* and *LM* curves intersect— would be higher than the world interest rate. Since Canada would be offering a

---

FIGURE 12-2

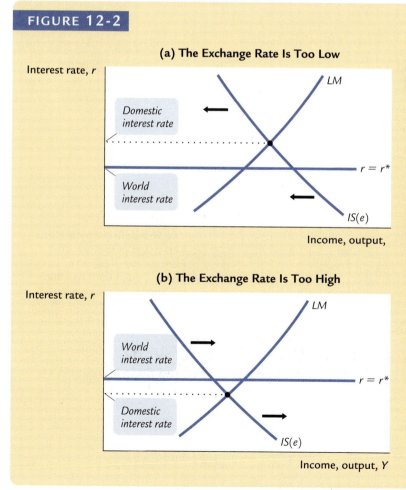

(a) The Exchange Rate Is Too Low

Interest rate, *r*

Domestic interest rate

World interest rate

LM

r = *r**

IS(e)

Income, output,

(b) The Exchange Rate Is Too High

Interest rate, *r*

World interest rate

Domestic interest rate

LM

r = *r**

IS(e)

Income, output, *Y*

The Mundell-Fleming Model With the Exchange Rate at the Wrong Level This figure shows why the *IS* curve must intersect at the point at which the *LM* curve and the *r* = *r** line cross. In panel (a), because the three curves do not cross at the same point, the domestic interest rate would exceed the world interest rate. Foreign investors would try to invest their funds in Canada. In the process, they would bid up the Canadian dollar and shift the *IS* curve downward. In panel (b), the domestic interest rate would be less than the world interest rate. Investors would try to invest their funds abroad. In the process, they would sell Canadian dollars, depressing its value. This shifts the *IS* curve upward.

higher rate of return than is available in world financial markets, investors from around the world would want to buy Canadian financial assets. But first these foreign investors must convert their funds into dollars. In the process, they would bid up the value of the Canadian dollar. This rise in the exchange rate would shift the *IS* curve downward until the domestic interest rate equaled the world interest rate.

Alternatively, imagine that the *IS* and *LM* curves intersect at a point where the domestic interest rate is below the world interest rate, as in panel (b) of Figure 12-2. Since Canada would be offering a lower rate of return, investors would want to invest in world financial markets. But, to be able to buy foreign financial assets, they must convert their Canadian dollars into foreign currency. In the process of doing so, they would depress the value of the Canadian dollar. The fall in the exchange rate would stimulate Canadian export sales and so shift the *IS* curve upward until the domestic interest rate equaled the world interest rate.

To sum up, the equilibrium in this graph is found where the *LM* curve crosses the line representing the world interest rate. The exchange rate then adjusts and shifts the *IS* curve so that the *IS* curve crosses this point as well.

The Model on a *Y-e* Graph

The second way to depict the model is to use a graph in which income is on the horizontal axis and the exchange rate is on the vertical axis, as in Figure 12-3. This graph is drawn holding the interest rate constant at the world interest rate.

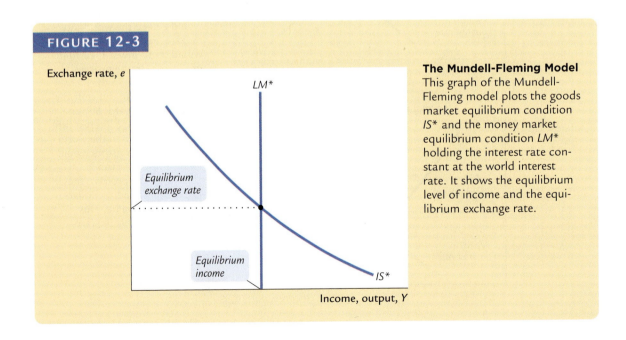

FIGURE 12-3

Exchange rate, *e*

LM*

Equilibrium exchange rate

Equilibrium income

IS*

Income, output, *Y*

The Mundell-Fleming Model This graph of the Mundell-Fleming model plots the goods market equilibrium condition *IS** and the money market equilibrium condition *LM** holding the interest rate constant at the world interest rate. It shows the equilibrium level of income and the equilibrium exchange rate.

The two equations in this figure are

$$Y = C(Y - T) + I(r^*) + G + NX(e) \qquad IS^*,$$

$$M/P = L(r^*, Y) \qquad\qquad\qquad LM^*.$$

We label these curves IS^* and LM^* to remind us that we are holding the interest rate constant at the world interest rate r^*. The equilibrium of the economy is found where the IS^* curve and the LM^* curve intersect. This intersection determines the exchange rate and the level of income.

The IS^* curve slopes downward because a higher exchange rate lowers net exports and thus lowers aggregate income. To show how this works, Figure 12-4 combines the net-exports schedule and the Keynesian–cross diagram to derive the IS^* curve. An increase in the Canadian dollar from e_1 to e_2 lowers net exports

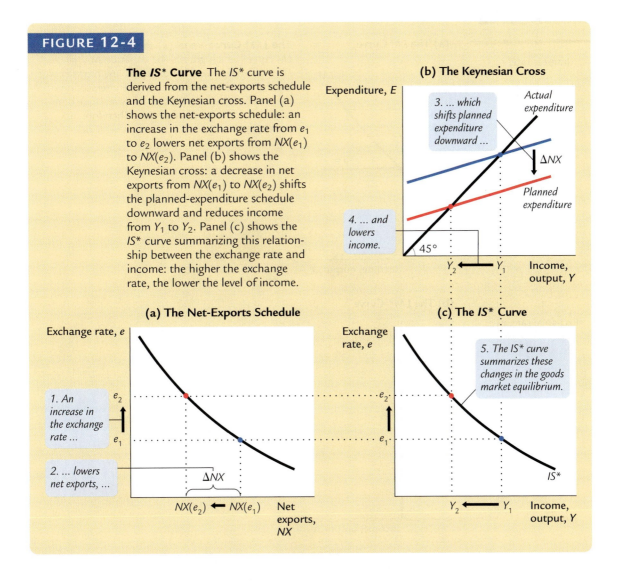

FIGURE 12-4

The IS^* Curve The IS^* curve is derived from the net-exports schedule and the Keynesian cross. Panel (a) shows the net-exports schedule: an increase in the exchange rate from e_1 to e_2 lowers net exports from $NX(e_1)$ to $NX(e_2)$. Panel (b) shows the Keynesian cross: a decrease in net exports from $NX(e_1)$ to $NX(e_2)$ shifts the planned-expenditure schedule downward and reduces income from Y_1 to Y_2. Panel (c) shows the IS^* curve summarizing this relationship between the exchange rate and income: the higher the exchange rate, the lower the level of income.

(b) The Keynesian Cross

Expenditure, E

Actual expenditure

3. ... which shifts planned expenditure downward ...

ΔNX

Planned expenditure

4. ... and lowers income.

45°

$Y_2 \leftarrow Y_1$ Income, output, Y

(a) The Net-Exports Schedule

Exchange rate, e

1. An increase in the exchange rate ...

e_2

e_1

2. ... lowers net exports, ...

ΔNX

$NX(e_2) \leftarrow NX(e_1)$ Net exports, NX

(c) The IS^* Curve

Exchange rate, e

5. The IS^* curve summarizes these changes in the goods market equilibrium.

e_2

e_1

IS^*

$Y_2 \leftarrow Y_1$ Income, output, Y

from $NX(e_1)$ to $NX(e_2)$. The reduction in net exports reduces planned expenditure and thus lowers income. Just as the standard IS curve combines the investment schedule and the Keynesian cross, the IS^* curve combines the net-exports schedule and the Keynesian cross.

The LM^* curve is vertical because the exchange rate does not enter into the LM^* equation. Given the world interest rate, the LM^* equation determines aggregate income, regardless of the exchange rate. Figure 12-5 shows how the LM^* curve arises from the world interest rate and the LM curve, which relates the interest rate and income.

We can now use the $IS^*–LM^*$ diagram (Figure 12-3). The equilibrium for the economy is found where the IS^* curve and the LM^* curve intersect. This intersection shows the exchange rate and the level of income at which the goods

FIGURE 12-5

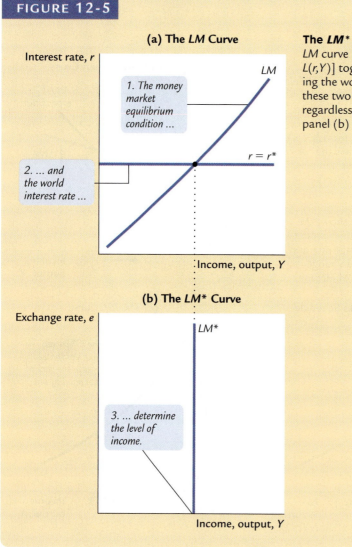

(a) The LM Curve

Interest rate, r

1. The money market equilibrium condition ...

2. ... and the world interest rate ...

LM

$r = r^*$

Income, output, Y

(b) The LM* Curve

Exchange rate, e

LM^*

3. ... determine the level of income.

Income, output, Y

The LM* Curve Panel (a) shows the standard LM curve [which graphs the equation $M/P = L(r, Y)$] together with a horizontal line representing the world interest rate r^*. The intersection of these two curves determines the level of income, regardless of the exchange rate. Therefore, as panel (b) shows, the LM^* curve is vertical.

market and the money market are both in equilibrium. With this diagram, we can use the Mundell–Fleming model to show how aggregate income Y and the Canadian dollar e respond to changes in policy.

12-2 The Small Open Economy Under Floating Exchange Rates

Before analyzing the impact of policies in an open economy, we must specify the international monetary system in which the country has chosen to operate. That is, we must consider how people engaged in international trade and finance can convert the currency of one country into the currency of another.

We start with the system relevant for most major economies today: **floating exchange rates.** Under a system of floating, or flexible, exchange rates, the exchange rate is set by market forces and is allowed to fluctuate in response to changing economic conditions. In this case, the exchange rate e adjusts to achieve simultaneous equilibrium in the goods market and the money market. When something happens to change that equilibrium, the exchange rate is allowed to move to a new equilibrium value, since the central bank does not intervene in the foreign exchange market.

Let's now consider three policies that can change the equilibrium: fiscal policy, monetary policy, and trade policy. Our goal is to use the Mundell–Fleming model to show the impact of policy changes and to understand the economic forces at work as the economy moves from one equilibrium to another.

Fiscal Policy

Suppose that the government stimulates domestic spending by increasing government purchases or by cutting taxes. Because such expansionary fiscal policy increases planned expenditure, it shifts the IS^* curve to the right, as in Figure 12-6. As a result, the exchange rate appreciates, while the level of income remains the same.

Notice that fiscal policy has very different effects in a small open economy than it does in a closed economy. In the closed-economy IS–LM model, a fiscal expansion raises income, whereas in a small open economy with a floating exchange rate and, as the interest rate rises, because higher income increases the demand for money. That is not possible in a small open economy because, as soon as the interest rate starts to rise above the world interest rate r^*, capital quickly flows in from abroad to take advantage of the higher return. This capital inflow not only pushes the interest rate back to r^* but it also has another effect: because foreign investors need to buy the domestic currency to invest in the domestic economy, the capital inflow increases the demand for the domestic currency in the market for foreign-currency exchange, bidding up the value of the domestic currency. The appreciation of the domestic currency makes domestic goods expensive relative to foreign goods, reducing net exports. The fall in net exports exactly offsets the effects of the expansionary fiscal policy on income. Thus, in a small open economy with a floating exchange rate, a fiscal expansion leaves income at the same level.

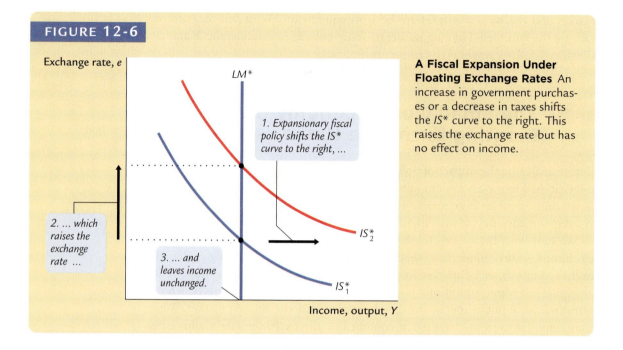

FIGURE 12-6

Exchange rate, *e*

1. Expansionary fiscal policy shifts the *IS** curve to the right, ...

2. ... which raises the exchange rate ...

3. ... and leaves income unchanged.

IS*₂

IS*₁

LM*

Income, output, *Y*

A Fiscal Expansion Under Floating Exchange Rates An increase in government purchases or a decrease in taxes shifts the *IS** curve to the right. This raises the exchange rate but has no effect on income.

Why is the fall in net exports so great as to render fiscal policy completely powerless to influence income? To answer this question, consider the equation that describes the money market:

$$M/P = L(r, Y).$$

In both closed and open economies, the quantity of real money balances supplied M/P is fixed by the central bank (which sets M) and the assumption of sticky prices (which fixes P). The quantity demanded (determined by r and Y) must equal this fixed supply. In a closed economy, a fiscal expansion causes the equilibrium interest rate to rise. This increase in the interest rate (which reduces the quantity of money demanded) implies an increase in equilibrium income (which raises the quantity of money demanded). These two effects together maintain equilibrium in the money market. By contrast, in a small open economy, r is fixed at r^*, so there is only one level of income that can satisfy this equation, and this level of income does not change when fiscal policy changes. Thus, when the government increases spending or cuts taxes, the appreciation of the exchange rate and the fall in net exports must be exactly large enough to offset fully the normal expansionary effect of the policy on income.

Monetary Policy

Suppose now that the Bank of Canada increases the money supply. Because the price level is assumed to be fixed, the increase in the money supply means an increase in real balances. The increase in real balances shifts the *LM** curve to the right, as in Figure 12-7. Hence, an increase in the money supply raises income and lowers the exchange rate.

FIGURE 12-7

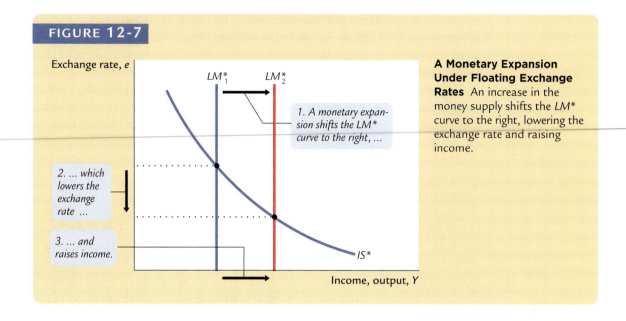

Exchange rate, e

LM^*_1 LM^*_2

1. A monetary expansion shifts the LM* curve to the right, ...

2. ... which lowers the exchange rate ...

3. ... and raises income.

IS^*

Income, output, Y

A Monetary Expansion Under Floating Exchange Rates An increase in the money supply shifts the LM^* curve to the right, lowering the exchange rate and raising income.

Although monetary policy influences income in an open economy, as it does in a closed economy, the monetary transmission mechanism is different. Recall that in a closed economy an increase in the money supply increases spending because it lowers the interest rate and stimulates investment. In a small open economy, this channel of monetary transmission is not available because the interest rate is fixed by the world interest rate. So how does monetary policy influence spending? To answer this question, once again we need to think about the international flow of capital and its implications for the domestic economy.

The interest rate and the exchange are again the key variables. As soon as an increase in the money supply puts downward pressure on the domestic interest rate, capital flows out of the economy, as investors seek a higher return elsewhere. This capital outflow prevents the domestic interest rate from falling below the world interest rate r^*. It also has another effect: because investing abroad requires converting domestic currency into foreign currency, the capital outflow increases the supply of the domestic currency in the market for foreign-currency exchange, causing the domestic currrency to fall in value. This depreciation in the exchange rate makes domestic goods inexpensive relative to foreign goods and, thereby, stimulates net exports and overall demand. Hence, in a small open economy, monetary policy influences income by altering the exchange rate rather than the interest rate.

CASE STUDY

Tight Monetary Policy Combined With Loose Fiscal Policy

During the late 1980s, Canada experienced a combination of tight monetary policy and loose fiscal policy. The Governor of the Bank of Canada, John Crow, was committed to bringing inflation down, and his success earned him quite a reputation among the world central bankers. But both the federal and provincial governments were following an expansionary fiscal policy; their expenditures were far in excess of their tax revenues. Government deficits were increasing at record rates.

The Mundell–Fleming model predicts that both policies would raise the value of the Canadian dollar, and, indeed, Canadian currency did rise. In 1985 1 Canadian dollar could be purchased for $0.71 (U.S.), and by 1991 its price had risen to $0.89 (U.S.). This rise in the Canadian dollar made imported goods less expensive, and it made Canadian industries that compete against these foreign sellers less competitive. It is no wonder that this period witnessed a dramatic increase in "cross-border shopping by Canadians."

Many analysts have noted that it was unfortunate that Canada's monetary-fiscal policy mix during this period was so counterproductive for Canadian firms' gaining a foothold in the U.S. markets following the signing of the Free Trade Agreement in January 1989. At the very time Canadian producers were becoming more competitive in the United States, because of the removal of U.S. tariffs on Canadian exports, these firms were becoming less competitive because of the dramatic rise in the value of the Canadian dollar.

Canada witnessed a similar mix of tight money and loose fiscal policy some 30 years earlier. John Diefenbaker, Canada's prime minister at the time, was trying to reduce unemployment during the worst postwar recession up to that point by raising government spending and cutting taxes (the same set of policies used by our government as this book goes to press—as officials struggle to limit the 2009 recession). But James Coyne, the Governor of the Bank of Canada during Diefenbaker's time, was focused exclusively on keeping the inflation rate close to zero. Thus, Coyne refused to print any new currency to help finance the government's deficit. The result was just what the Mundell–Fleming model predicts. Funds flowed into Canada, and the value of the Canadian dollar increased dramatically. This put a further profit squeeze on Canadian exporting firms, so that as rapidly as the government was creating jobs in the government sector, the rising Canadian dollar was destroying jobs in the exporting and import-competing sectors.

The dispute between the government and the Bank of Canada Governor became so bitter during the Coyne affair that the Bank of Canada Act was changed following this incident. Now the Governor must resign immediately if he or she is issued a written directive from the Minister of Finance that directs monetary policy to be other than what the Governor thinks is appropriate. Many analysts speculated that a directive might be issued in late 1993, when the Liberal government of Jean Chrétien came to power. The Liberals had campaigned on a platform of expansionary fiscal policy to create jobs, and they had been critical of John Crow's tight monetary policy. But as it turned out, a directive was not necessary, because Crow's seven-year appointment ended in February 1994. The Liberals simply waited out John Crow's tenure and then appointed Gordon Thiesson, Crow's senior deputy governor. This appointment signalled that the Liberals supported the Bank of Canada's low-inflation policy after all. There was no speculation in 2009, since the Bank of Canada's policy was very expansionary then—working to support, not negate, the government's fiscal policy. ■

Trade Policy

Suppose that the government reduces the demand for imported goods by imposing an import quota or a tariff. What happens to aggregate income and the
exchange rate? How does the economy reach its new equilibrium?

Because net exports equal exports minus imports, a reduction in imports
means an increase in net exports. That is, the net-exports schedule shifts to the
right, as in Figure 12-8. This shift in the net-exports schedule increases planned

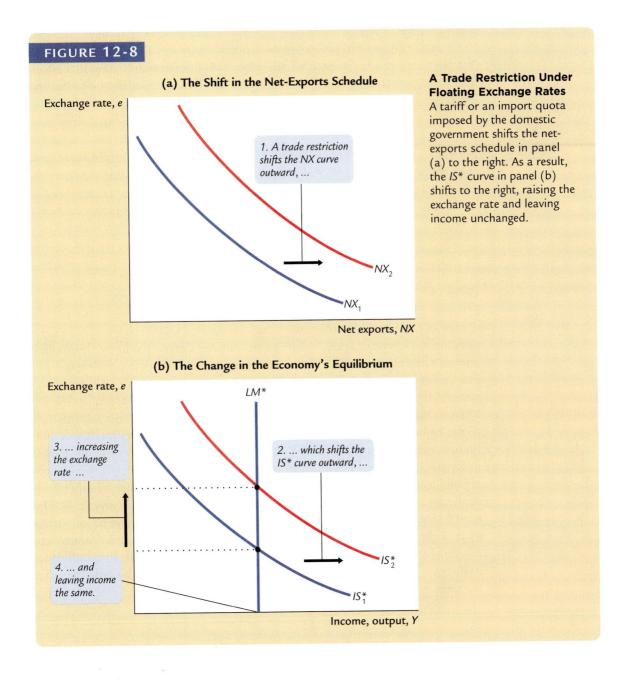

FIGURE 12-8

(a) The Shift in the Net-Exports Schedule

Exchange rate, e

1. A trade restriction shifts the NX curve outward, ...

NX_2

NX_1

Net exports, NX

(b) The Change in the Economy's Equilibrium

Exchange rate, e

LM^*

3. ... increasing the exchange rate ...

2. ... which shifts the IS^* curve outward, ...

IS_2^*

4. ... and leaving income the same.

IS_1^*

Income, output, Y

A Trade Restriction Under Floating Exchange Rates
A tariff or an import quota imposed by the domestic government shifts the net-exports schedule in panel (a) to the right. As a result, the IS^* curve in panel (b) shifts to the right, raising the exchange rate and leaving income unchanged.

expenditure and thus moves the IS^* curve to the right. Because the LM^* curve is vertical, the trade restriction raises the exchange rate but does not affect income.

The economic forces behind this transition are similar to the case of expansionary fiscal policy. Because net exports are a component of GDP, the rightward shift in the net-exports schedule, other things equal, puts upward pressure on income Y; an increase in Y, in turn, increases money demand and puts upward pressure on the interest rate r. Foreign capital quickly responds by flowing into the domestic economy, pushing the interest rate back to the world interest rate r^* and causing the domestic currency to appreciate in value. Finally, the appreciation of the currency makes domestic goods more expensive relative to foreign goods, which decreases net exports NX and returns income Y to its initial level.

Often a stated goal of policies to restrict trade is to alter the trade balance NX. Yet, as we first saw in Chapter 5, such policies do not necessarily have that effect. The same conclusion holds in the Mundell–Fleming model under floating exchange rates. Recall that

$$NX(e) = Y - C(Y - T) - I(r^*) - G.$$

Because a trade restriction does not affect income, consumption, investment, or government purchases, it does not affect the trade balance. Although the shift in the net-exports schedule tends to raise NX, the increase in the exchange rate reduces NX by the same amount. The overall effect is simply *less trade*. The domestic economy imports less than it did before the trade restriction, but it exports less as well.

World Interest-Rate Changes

Consider an increase in the general level of world interest rates. In the Mundell–Fleming model, this means that Canadian interest rates must rise (as the law of one price operates in the world bond markets). But will this cause a rise or fall in the level of aggregate demand in Canada? Clearly, the higher borrowing cost will depress the investment spending component of aggregate demand, but can the exchange-rate change insulate aggregate demand from this depressing effect of higher interest rates? We now use the model to answer this question.

From Figure 12-5 we know that higher world interest rates cause LM^* to shift to the right. Also, since higher interest rates depress firms' investment spending on new plant and equipment, IS^* shifts back to the left. These shifts are shown in Figure 12-9, where equilibrium moves from point A to point B. With funds initially leaving the country in pursuit of the high yields available in other parts of the world, the domestic currency depreciates, as shown in Figure 12-9. The model shows that this depreciation in the Canadian dollar must be of such a magnitude that aggregate demand rises. New exports are stimulated more than investment expenditure is reduced.[2] Thus, one advantage of allowing a floating exchange rate is that we do not have to suffer a recession just because there are increases in either world tariffs or world interest rates.

---

[2] This strong prediction is not maintained as the Mundell–Fleming model is made more general— as we explain in the appendix to this chapter.

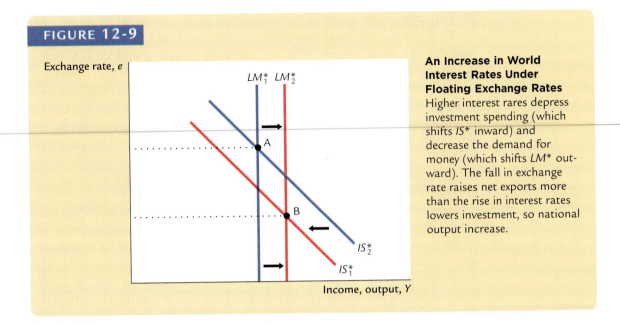

FIGURE 12-9

Exchange rate, *e*

LM_1^* LM_2^*

A

B

IS_2^*

IS_1^*

Income, output, *Y*

An Increase in World Interest Rates Under Floating Exchange Rates Higher interest rares depress investment spending (which shifts *IS** inward) and decrease the demand for money (which shifts *LM** outward). The fall in exchange rate raises net exports more than the rise in interest rates lowers investment, so national output increase.

12-3 The Small Open Economy Under Fixed Exchange Rates

We now turn to the second type of exchange-rate system: **fixed exchange rates.** Under a fixed exchange rate, the central bank announces a value for the exchange rate and stands ready to buy and sell the domestic currency to keep the exchange rate at its announced level. In the 1950s and 1960s, most of the world's major economies operated within the Bretton Woods system—an international monetary system under which most governments agreed to fix exchange rates. The world abandoned this system in the early 1970s, and most exchange rates were allowed to float freely. Yet fixed exchange rates are not merely of historical interest. Some European countries have reinstated a system of fixed exchange rates among themselves (as a common currency, the euro, was introduced in 1999). More recently, China fixed the value of its currency against the U.S. dollar—a policy that, as we will see, was a source of some tension between the two countries. In this section we discuss how such a system works, and we examine the impact of economic policies on an economy with a fixed exchange rate. Later in the chapter we examine the pros and cons of fixed exchange rates.

How a Fixed-Exchange-Rate System Works

Under a system of fixed exchange rates, a central bank stands ready to buy or sell the domestic currency for foreign currencies at a predetermined price. Suppose, for example, that the Bank of Canada announced that it was going to fix the exchange rate at $0.90 (U.S.) per dollar. It would then stand ready to give

$1 (Canadian) in exchange for $0.90 (U.S.) or to give $0.90 (U.S.) in exchange for $1 (Canadian). To carry out this policy, the Bank of Canada would need a reserve of Canadian dollars (which it can print) and a reserve of U.S. dollars (which it must have accumulated in past transactions).

A fixed exchange rate dedicates a country's monetary policy to the single goal of keeping the exchange rate at the announced level. In other words, the essence of a fixed-exchange-rate system is the commitment of the central bank to allow the money supply to adjust to whatever level will ensure that the equilibrium exchange rate equals the announced exchange rate. Moreover, as long as the central bank stands ready to buy or sell foreign currency at the fixed exchange rate, the money supply adjusts automatically to the necessary level.

To see how fixing the exchange rate determines the money supply, consider the following example. Suppose that the Bank of Canada announces that it will fix the exchange rate at $0.90 (U.S.) per dollar, but, in the current equilibrium with the current money supply, the exchange rate is $0.95 (U.S.) per dollar. This situation is illustrated in panel (a) of Figure 12-10. Notice that there is a profit opportunity: an arbitrageur could buy $95 (U.S.) in the marketplace for $100 (Canadian), and then sell the U.S. dollars to the Bank of Canada for $105.55 ($95/$0.90); making a profit of $5.55. When the Bank of Canada buys these

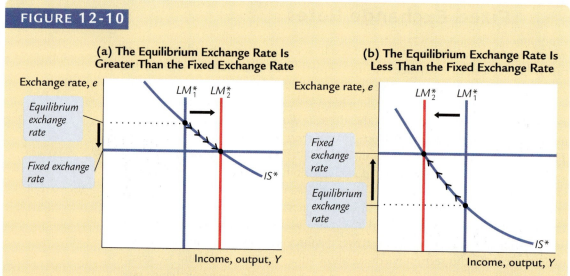

FIGURE 12-10

(a) The Equilibrium Exchange Rate Is Greater Than the Fixed Exchange Rate

(b) The Equilibrium Exchange Rate Is Less Than the Fixed Exchange Rate

How a Fixed Exchange Rate Governs the Money Supply In panel (a), the equilibrium exchange rate initially exceeds the fixed level. Arbitrageurs will buy foreign currency in foreign-exchange markets and sell it to the Bank of Canada for a profit. This process automatically increases the money supply, shifting the LM^* curve to the right and lowering the exchange rate. In panel (b), the equilibrium exchange rate is below the fixed level. Arbitrageurs will buy dollars in foreign-exchange markets and use them to buy foreign currency from the Bank of Canada. This process automatically reduces the money supply, shifting the LM^* curve to the left and raising the exchange rate.

U.S. dollars from the arbitrageur, the Canadian dollars it pays for them automatically increase the domestic money supply. The rise in the money supply shifts the LM^* curve to the right, lowering the equilibrium exchange rate. In this way, the money supply continues to rise until the equilibrium exchange rate falls to the announced level.

Conversely, suppose that the Bank of Canada announces that it will fix the exchange rate at $0.90 (U.S.) per dollar, when the equilibrium is $0.80 (U.S.) per dollar. Panel (b) of Figure 12-10 shows this situation. In this case, an arbitrageur could make a profit by buying $90 (U.S.) from the Bank of Canada for $100 and then selling the U.S. dollars in the marketplace for $112.50 Canadian ($90/$0.80). When the Bank of Canada sells these U.S. dollars, the Canadian dollars it receives are no longer circulating among private transactors, so this policy automatically reduces the money supply. The fall in the money supply shifts the LM^* curve to the left, raising the equilibrium exchange rate. The money supply continues to fall until the equilibrium exchange rate rises to the announced level.

These examples make clear that fixing the exchange rate requires a commitment on the part of the Bank of Canada to either buy or sell whatever amount of foreign exchange is demanded by private participants in foreign-currency markets. Fixing a Canadian dollar price below the free-market equilibrium can be done indefinitely, because all the Bank of Canada needs is an unlimited supply of Canadian dollars (which it can print). Nevertheless, this policy is limited by the willingness of Canadians to tolerate the inflation that eventually accompanies rapid growth in the domestic money supply.

Fixing the Canadian dollar at a price above the free-market equilibrium, on the other hand, cannot be done indefinitely. This follows from the basic fact that the Bank of Canada cannot print foreign exchange. Private traders know this, and they can easily determine how rapidly the Bank of Canada's reserves of foreign exhange are running out. Canada's balance of payments data record precisely this—the amount by which the country's foreign exchange reserves have been depleted each period. Armed with this information, private traders can readily guess when the Bank of Canada will have to give up fixing the exchange rate at such a high value. It is in this situation that we hear about a "speculative run against the currency" in the media. Once private traders see that a country's currency is about to fall in value, they sell off that currency to avoid the almost certain capital loss. This very action hastens the exchange-rate change and verifies the speculator's expectations.

It is important to understand that this exchange-rate system fixes the nominal exchange rate. Whether it also fixes the real exchange rate depends on the time horizon under consideration. If prices are flexible, as they are in the long run, then the real exchange rate can change even while the nominal exchange rate is fixed. Therefore, in the long run described in Chapter 5, a policy to fix the nominal exchange rate would not influence any real variable, including the real exchange rate. A fixed nominal exchange rate would influence only the money supply and the price level. Yet in the short run described by the Mundell–Fleming model, prices are fixed, so a fixed nominal exchange rate implies a fixed real exchange rate as well.

The International Gold Standard

During the late nineteenth and early twentieth centuries, most of the world's major economies operated under a gold standard. Each country maintained a reserve of gold and agreed to exchange one unit of its currency for a specified amount of gold. Through the gold standard, the world's economies maintained a system of fixed exchange rates.

To see how an international gold standard fixes exchange rates, suppose that the U.S. Treasury stands ready to buy or sell 1 ounce of gold for $100, and the Bank of England stands ready to buy or sell 1 ounce of gold for 100 pounds. Together, these policies fix the rate of exchange between dollars and pounds: $1 must trade for 1 pound. Otherwise, the law of one price would be violated, and it would be profitable to buy gold in one country and sell it in the other.

Suppose, for example, that the market exchange rate were 2 pounds per dollar. In this case, an arbitrageur could buy 200 pounds for $100, use the pounds to buy 2 ounces of gold from the Bank of England, bring the gold to the United States, and sell it to the Treasury for $200—making a $100 profit. Moreover, by bringing the gold to the United States from England, the arbitrageur would increase the money supply in the United States and decrease the money supply in England.

Thus, during the era of the gold standard, the international transport of gold by arbitrageurs was an automatic mechanism adjusting the money supply and stabilizing exchange rates. This system did not completely fix exchange rates, because shipping gold across the Atlantic was costly. Yet the international gold standard did keep the exchange rate within a range dictated by transportation costs. It thereby prevented large and persistent movements in exchange rates.[3] ∎

Fiscal Policy

Let's now examine how economic policies affect a small open economy with a fixed exchange rate. Suppose that the government stimulates domestic spending by increasing government purchases or by cutting taxes. This policy shifts the *IS** curve to the right, as in Figure 12-11, putting upward pressure on the market exchange rate. But because the central bank stands ready to trade foreign and domestic currency at the fixed exchange rate, arbitrageurs quickly respond to the rising exchange rate by selling foreign currency to the central bank, leading to an automatic monetary expansion. The rise in the money supply shifts the *LM** curve to the right. Thus, in contrast to the situation under floating exchange rates, a fiscal expansion under fixed exchange rates raises aggregate income.

---

[3] For more on how the gold standard worked, see the essays in Barry Eichengreen, ed., *The Gold Standard in Theory and History* (New York: Methuen, 1985).

FIGURE 12-11

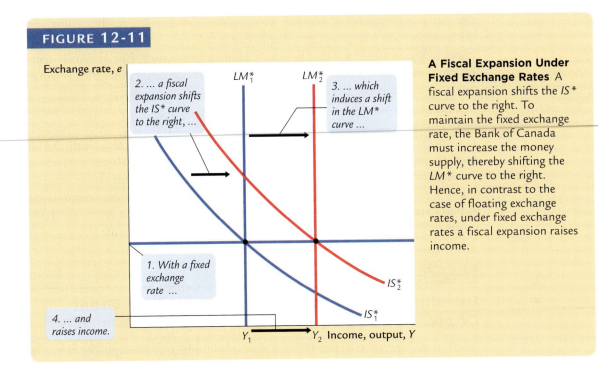

Exchange rate, *e*

2. ... a fiscal expansion shifts the IS* curve to the right, ...

LM_1^* LM_2^*

3. ... which induces a shift in the LM* curve ...

1. With a fixed exchange rate ...

4. ... and raises income.

IS_2^*

IS_1^*

Y_1 Y_2 Income, output, *Y*

A Fiscal Expansion Under Fixed Exchange Rates A fiscal expansion shifts the *IS** curve to the right. To maintain the fixed exchange rate, the Bank of Canada must increase the money supply, thereby shifting the *LM** curve to the right. Hence, in contrast to the case of floating exchange rates, under fixed exchange rates a fiscal expansion raises income.

Monetary Policy

Imagine that a central bank operating with a fixed exchange rate were to try to increase the money supply—for example, by buying bonds from the public. What would happen? The initial impact of this policy is to shift the *LM** curve to the right, lowering the exchange rate, as in Figure 12-12. But, because the central bank is committed to trading foreign and domestic currency at a fixed exchange

FIGURE 12-12

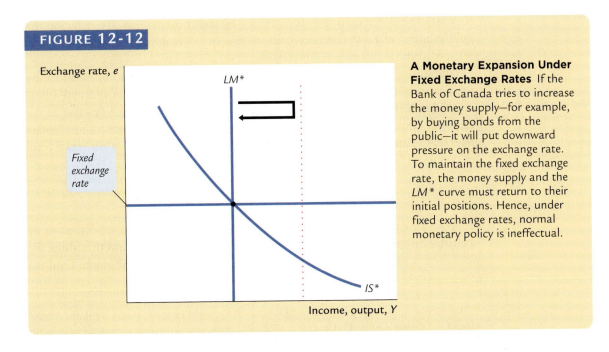

Exchange rate, *e*

LM*

Fixed exchange rate

IS*

Income, output, *Y*

A Monetary Expansion Under Fixed Exchange Rates If the Bank of Canada tries to increase the money supply—for example, by buying bonds from the public—it will put downward pressure on the exchange rate. To maintain the fixed exchange rate, the money supply and the *LM** curve must return to their initial positions. Hence, under fixed exchange rates, normal monetary policy is ineffectual.

rate, arbitrageurs quickly respond to the falling exchange rate by selling the domestic currency to the central bank, causing the money supply and the LM^* curve to return to their initial positions. Hence, monetary policy as usually conducted is ineffectual under a fixed exchange rate. By agreeing to fix the exchange rate, the central bank gives up its control over the money supply.

A country with a fixed exchange rate can, however, conduct a type of monetary policy: it can decide to change the level at which the exchange rate is fixed. A reduction in the official value of the currency is called a **devaluation,** and an increase in its official value is called a **revaluation.** In the Mundell–Fleming model, a devaluation shifts the LM^* curve to the right; it acts like an increase in the money supply under a floating exchange rate. A devaluation thus expands net exports and raises aggregate income. Conversely, a revaluation shifts the LM^* curve to the left, reduces net exports, and lowers aggregate income.

CASE STUDY

Devaluation and the Recovery From the Great Depression

The Great Depression of the 1930s was a global problem. Although events in the United States may have precipitated the downturn for many other Western countries like Canada, all of the world's major economies experienced huge declines in production and employment. Yet not all governments responded to this calamity in the same way.

One key difference among governments was how committed they were to the fixed exchange rate set by the international gold standard. Some countries, such as France, Germany, Italy, and the Netherlands, maintained the old rate of exchange between gold and currency. Other countries, such as Denmark, Finland, Norway, Sweden, and the United Kingdom, reduced the amount of gold they would pay for each unit of currency by about 50 percent. By reducing the gold content of their currencies, these governments devalued their currencies relative to those of other countries.

The subsequent experience of these two groups of countries conforms to the prediction of the Mundell–Fleming model. Those countries that pursued a policy of devaluation recovered quickly from the Depression. The lower value of the currency stimulated exports and expanded production. By contrast, those countries that maintained the old exchange rate suffered longer with a depressed level of economic activity.[4] ■

Trade Policy

Suppose that the government reduces imports by imposing an import quota or a tariff. This policy shifts the net-exports schedule to the right and thus shifts the IS^* curve to the right, as in Figure 12-13. The shift in the IS^* curve tends to

---

[4] Barry Eichengreen and Jeffrey Sachs, "Exchange Rates and Economic Recovery in the 1930s," *Journal of Economic History* 45 (December 1985): 925–946.

FIGURE 12-13

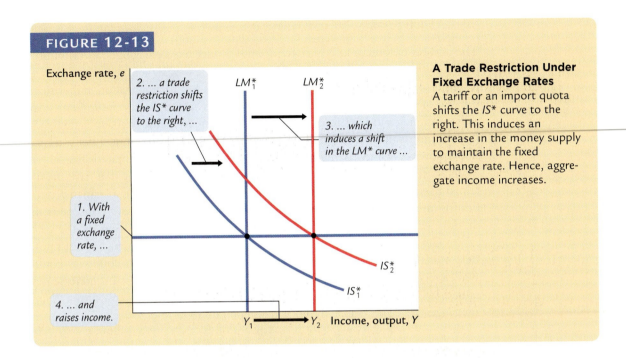

Exchange rate, e

2. ... a trade restriction shifts the IS* curve to the right, ...

LM_1^* LM_2^*

3. ... which induces a shift in the LM* curve ...

1. With a fixed exchange rate, ...

IS_2^*

IS_1^*

4. ... and raises income.

Y_1 Y_2 Income, output, Y

A Trade Restriction Under Fixed Exchange Rates A tariff or an import quota shifts the IS* curve to the right. This induces an increase in the money supply to maintain the fixed exchange rate. Hence, aggregate income increases.

raise the exchange rate. To keep the exchange rate at the fixed level, the money supply must rise, shifting the LM^* curve to the right.

The result of a trade restriction under a fixed exchange rate is very different from that under a floating exchange rate. In both cases, a trade restriction shifts the net-exports schedule to the right, but only under a fixed exchange rate does a trade restriction increase net exports NX. The reason is that a trade restriction under a fixed exchange rate induces monetary expansion rather than an appreciation of the exchange rate. The monetary expansion, in turn, raises aggregate income. Recall the accounting identity

$$NX = S - I.$$

When income rises, saving also rises, and this implies an increase in net exports.

This analysis can be used to consider tariffs levied by foreigners as well. In that case, our net exports are reduced so the shifts in IS^* and LM^* are to the left, instead of to the right (as they are in Figure 12-13). In contrast to the floating-exchange-rate case, then, Canada must suffer a recession following the imposition of foreign trade restrictions, if the exchange rate is fixed.

Similarly, if we have a fixed exchange rate, we must suffer a recession if world commodity prices change—as they did in the 1990s during the Asian crisis—to reduce Canadian net exports. At the time of the Asian crisis, Canada had a floating exchange rate. While the dip in the Canadian dollar (down to $0.63 (U.S.) in mid-1998) caused concern, it did provide Canada some insulation from this major event. While our exports of primary commodities suffered during the Asian crisis, at least our manufacturing exports were stimulated by the lower domestic currency. Many analysts concluded that it was fortunate that Canada had not opted for a fixed exchange rate at this time.

World Interest-Rate Changes

The analysis of foreign interest-rate increases under fixed exchange rates is similar to that for trade restrictions imposed by other countries. Higher interest rates lower investment spending by firms, so IS^* shifts to the left for this reason, rather than because of a reduction in net exports. However, whatever causes the IS^* curve to shift is insignificant; LM^* must still shift to the left to keep the exchange rate fixed. (Just picture Figure 12-13 running in reverse.) Thus, Canada must suffer a recession following an increase in world interest rates if the exchange rate is fixed.

This same analysis applies to small open economies in Europe that have maintained fixed exchange rates with one another. In the early 1990s, German reunification meant a big increase in government spending to improve conditions in the former East Germany. Given the commitment to low inflation on the part of the German central bank, this spending led to higher German interest rates. Our model shows that the only way that the other European countries could avoid a recession—that would otherwise accompany this increase in interest rates caused by the changes happening in Germany—was to shift away from fixed exchange rates. This is exactly what happened in 1992.

Policy in the Mundell–Fleming Model: A Summary

The Mundell–Fleming model shows that the effect of almost any economic policy on a small open economy depends on whether the exchange rate is floating or fixed. Table 12-1 summarizes our analysis of the short-run effects of fiscal, monetary, and trade policies, and world interest rate changes, on income, the

---

TABLE 12-1

The Mundell-Fleming Model: Summary of Policy Effects and the Impact of Events in the Rest of the World

	EXCHANGE-RATE REGIME					
	FLOATING			FIXED		
	IMPACT ON:					
Policy/World Event	Y	e	NX	Y	e	NX
Fiscal expansion	0	≠	↓	≠	0	0
Monetary expansion	≠	↓	≠	0	0	0
Import restriction	0	≠	0	≠	0	≠
Export restriction	0	↓	0	↓	0	↓
Higher interest rates	≠	↓	≠	↓	0	0

Note: This table shows the direction of impact of various economic policies on income Y, the exchange rate e, and the trade balance NX. A "≠" indicates that the variable increases; a "↓" indicates that it decreases; a "0" indicates no effect. Remember that the exchange rate is defined as the amount of foreign currency per unit of domestic currency (for example, $0.90 (U.S.)/Canadian dollar).

exchange rate, and the trade balance. What is most striking is that all of the results are different under floating and fixed exchange rates.

To be more specific, the Mundell–Fleming model shows that the power of monetary and fiscal policy to influence aggregate income depends on the exchange-rate regime. Under floating exchange rates, only monetary policy can affect income. The usual expansionary impact of fiscal policy is offset by a rise in the value of the currency and a decrease in net exports. Under fixed exchange rates, only fiscal policy can affect income. The normal potency of monetary policy is lost because the money supply is dedicated to maintaining the exchange rate at the announced level.

CASE STUDY

Regional Tensions Within Canada

The Mundell–Fleming model can be used to help explain why regional tensions increased in Canada during the late 1980s. At that time, the Ontario government was running an expansionary fiscal policy. We now know that the overall impact of such a policy (throughout the country) is that it has no effect on aggregate demand. Instead it creates a higher Canadian dollar, which forces net exports to be reduced by the same amount as government spending is increased. But consider the distribution of these two effects within the country.

The increase in the government spending component of aggregate demand is concentrated entirely within Ontario, whereas the crowding out of preexisting net export demand is felt in all provinces. The result is that demand in Ontario is increased, while that in the rest of the country is decreased. The two effects add up to zero as far as overall demand in the entire country is concerned. Thus, fiscal policy *does* work under floating exchange rates after all, but only from one province's point of view. Ontario can reduce its unemployment problem, but *only* by worsening the same problem for the other regions! ■

12-4 Interest-Rate Differentials

So far, our analysis in this chapter has assumed that the interest rate in a small open economy is equal to the world interest rate: $r = r^*$. To some extent, however, as we noted in Chapter 5, interest rates differ around the world. We now extend our analysis by considering the causes and effects of international interest-rate differentials.

Country Risk and Exchange-Rate Expectations

When we assumed earlier that the interest rate in our small open economy is determined by the world interest rate, we were applying the law of one price. We reasoned that if the domestic interest rate were above the world interest rate, people from abroad would lend to that country, driving the domestic interest rate down. And if the domestic interest rate were below the world interest rate, domestic residents would lend abroad to earn a higher return, driving the domestic interest rate up. In the end, the domestic interest rate would equal the world interest rate.

Why doesn't this logic always apply? There are two reasons.

One reason is country risk. When investors buy Canadian government bonds or make loans to Canadian corporations, they are fairly confident that they will be repaid with interest. By contrast, in some less-developed countries, it is plausible to fear that a revolution or other political upheaval might lead to a default on loan repayments. Borrowers in such countries often have to pay higher interest rates to compensate lenders for this risk.

Another reason interest rates differ across countries is expected changes in the exchange rate. For example, suppose that people expect the Mexican peso to fall in value relative to the U.S. dollar. Then loans made in pesos will be repaid in a less valuable currency than loans made in dollars. To compensate for this expected fall in the Mexican currency, the interest rate in Mexico will be higher than the interest rate in the United States.

Thus, because of both country risk and expectations of exchange-rate changes, the interest rate of a small open economy can differ from interest rates in other economies around the world. Let's now see how this fact affects our analysis.

Differentials in the Mundell–Fleming Model

As outlined in Chapter 5, to incorporate interest-rate differentials into the Mundell–Fleming model, we assume that the interest rate in our small open economy is determined by the world interest rate plus a risk premium θ:

$$r = r^* + \theta.$$

The risk premium is determined by the perceived political risk of making loans in a country and the expected change in the real exchange rate. For our purposes here, we can take the risk premium as exogenous in order to examine how changes in the risk premium affect the economy.

The model is largely the same as before. The two equations are

$$Y = C(Y - T) + I(r^* + \theta) + G + NX(e) \qquad IS^*,$$

$$M/P = L(r^* + \theta, Y) \qquad LM^*.$$

For any given fiscal policy, monetary policy, price level, and risk premium, these two equations determine the level of income and exchange rate that equilibrate the goods market and the money market. Holding constant the risk premium, monetary policy, fiscal policy, and trade policy work as we have already seen.

Now suppose that political turmoil causes the country's risk premium θ to rise. The effects are just like the increase in foreign interest rates that we considered earlier. The most direct effect is that the domestic interest rate r rises, so the analysis is just like our earlier discussion of world interest-rate increases. The higher interest rate has two effects. First, the IS^* curve shifts to the left, because the higher interest rate reduces investment. Second, the LM^* curve shifts to the right, because the higher interest rate reduces the demand for money, and this allows a higher level of income for any given money supply. [Recall that Y must satisfy the equation $M/P = L(r^* + \theta, Y)$.] As Figure 12-14 shows, these two shifts cause income to rise and the currency to depreciate.

This analysis has an important implication: expectations of the exchange rate are partially self-fulfilling. For example, suppose that people come to believe that the Mexican peso will not be valuable in the future. Investors will place a larger risk premium on Mexican assets: θ will rise in Mexico. This expectation will drive up Mexican interest rates and, as we have just seen, will drive down the value of the Mexican currency. *Thus, the expectation that a currency will lose value in the future causes it to lose value today.*

One surprising—and perhaps inaccurate—prediction of this analysis is that an increase in country risk as measured by θ will cause the economy's income to increase. This occurs in Figure 12-14 because of the rightward shift in the LM^* curve. Although higher interest rates depress investment, the depreciation of the currency stimulates net exports by an even greater amount. As a result, aggregate income rises.

There are three reasons why, in practice, such a boom in income does not occur. First, the central bank might want to avoid the large depreciation of the domestic currency and, therefore, may respond by decreasing the money supply M. Second, the depreciation of the domestic currency increases the price of imported goods, causing an increase in the price level P (which shrinks the

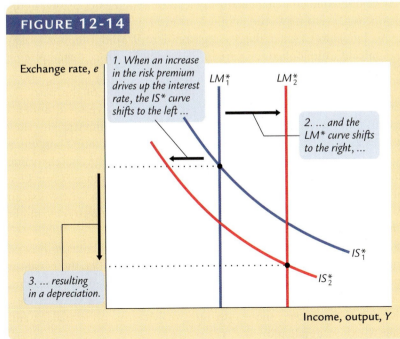

FIGURE 12-14

An Increase in the Risk Premium An increase in the risk premium associated with a country drives up its interest rate. Because the higher interest rate reduces investment, the IS^* curve shifts to the left. Because it also reduces money demand, the LM^* curve shifts to the right. Income rises, and the exchange rate depreciates.

Exchange rate, e

1. When an increase in the risk premium drives up the interest rate, the IS^* curve shifts to the left ...

LM^*_1 LM^*_2

2. ... and the LM^* curve shifts to the right, ...

IS^*_1

IS^*_2

3. ... resulting in a depreciation.

Income, output, Y

real money supply). We pursue this possibility in the appendix to this chapter. Third, when some event increases the country risk premium θ, residents of the country might respond to the same event by increasing their demand for money (for any given income and interest rate), because money is often the safest asset available. All three of these changes would tend to shift the LM^* curve toward the left, which mitigates the fall in the exchange rate but also tends to depress income.

Thus, increases in country risk are not desirable. In the short run, they typically lead to a depreciating currency and, through the three channels just described, falling aggregate income. In addition, because a higher interest rate reduces investment, the long-run implication is reduced capital accumulation and lower economic growth.

CASE STUDY

International Financial Crisis: Mexico 1994–1995

In August 1994, a Mexican peso was worth 30 U.S. cents. A year later, it was worth only 16 cents. What explains this massive fall in the value of the Mexican currency? Country risk is a large part of the story.

At the beginning of 1994, Mexico was a country on the rise. The recent passage of the North American Free Trade Agreement (NAFTA), which reduced trade barriers among the United States, Canada, and Mexico, made many people confident about the future of the Mexican economy. Investors around the world were eager to make loans to the Mexican government and to Mexican corporations.

Political developments soon changed that perception. A violent uprising in the Chiapas region of Mexico made the political situation in Mexico seem precarious. Then Luis Donaldo Colosio, the leading presidential candidate, was assassinated. The political future looked less certain, and many investors started placing a larger risk premium on Mexican assets.

At first, the rising risk premium did not affect the value of the peso, for Mexico was operating with a fixed exchange rate. As we have seen, under a fixed exchange rate, the central bank agrees to trade the domestic currency (pesos) for a foreign currency (U.S. dollars) at a predetermined rate. Thus, when an increase in the country risk premium put downward pressure on the value of the peso, the Mexican central bank had to accept pesos and pay out U.S. dollars. This automatic exchange-market intervention contracted the Mexican money supply (shifting the LM^* curve to the left) when the currency might otherwise have depreciated.

Yet Mexico's reserves of foreign currency were too small to maintain its fixed exchange rate. When Mexico ran out of dollars at the end of 1994, the Mexican government announced a devaluation of the peso. This choice had repercussions, however, because the government had repeatedly promised that it would not devalue. Investors became even more distrustful of Mexican policymakers and feared further Mexican devaluations.

Investors around the world (including those in Mexico) avoided buying Mexican assets. The country risk premium rose once again, adding to the upward pressure on interest rates and the downward pressure on the peso. The Mexican stock market plummeted. When the Mexican government needed to roll over some of its debt that was coming due, investors were unwilling to buy the new debt. Default appeared to be the government's only option. In just a few months, Mexico had gone from being a promising emerging economy to being a risky economy with a government on the verge of bankruptcy.

Then the United States stepped in. The U.S. government had three motives: to help its neighbour to the south, to prevent the massive illegal immigration that might follow government default and economic collapse, and to prevent the investor pessimism regarding Mexico from spreading to other developing countries. The U.S. government, together with the International Monetary Fund (IMF), led an international effort to bail out the Mexican government. In particular, the United States provided loan guarantees for Mexican government debt, which allowed the Mexican government to refinance the debt that was coming due. These loan guarantees helped restore confidence in the Mexican economy, thereby reducing to some extent the country risk premium.

Although the U.S. loan guarantees may well have stopped a bad situation from getting worse, they did not prevent the Mexican meltdown of 1994–1995 from being a painful experience for the Mexican people. Not only did the Mexican currency lose much of its value, but Mexico also went through a deep recession. Fortunately, by the late 1990s, the worst was over, and aggregate income was growing again. But the lesson from this experience is clear and could well apply again in the future: changes in perceived country risk, often attributable to political instability, are an important determinant of interest rates and exchange rates in small open economies. ∎

CASE STUDY

International Financial Crisis: Asia 1997–1998

Toward the end of 1997, as the Mexican economy was recovering from its financial crisis, a similar story started to unfold in several Asian economies, including Thailand, South Korea, and especially Indonesia. The symptoms were familiar: high interest rates, falling asset values, and a depreciating currency. In Indonesia, for instance, short-term nominal interest rates rose above 50 percent, the stock market lost about 90 percent of its value (measured in U.S. dollars), and the rupiah fell against the U.S. dollar by more than 80 percent. The crisis led to rising inflation in these countries (as the depreciating currency made imports more expensive) and to falling GDP (as high interest rates and reduced confidence depressed spending). Real GDP in Indonesia fell about 15 percent in 1998, making the downturn larger than any recession in North America since the Great Depression of the 1930s.

What sparked this firestorm? The problem began in the Asian banking systems. For many years, the governments in the Asian nations had been more involved in managing the allocation of resources—in particular, financial resources—than is true in Canada and other developed countries. Some commentators had applauded this "partnership" between government and private enterprise and had even suggested that Canada should follow the example. Over time, however, it became clear that many Asian banks had been extending loans to those with the most political clout rather than to those with the most profitable investment projects. Once rising default rates started to expose this "crony capitalism," as it was then called, international investors started to lose confidence in the future of these economies. The risk premiums for Asian assets rose, causing interest rates to skyrocket and currencies to collapse.

International crises of confidence often involve a vicious circle that can amplify the problem. Here is one theory about what happened in Asia:

1. Problems in the banking system eroded international confidence in these economies.

2. Loss of confidence raised risk premiums and interest rates.

3. Rising interest rates, together with the loss of confidence, depressed the prices of stock and other assets.

4. Falling asset prices reduced the value of collateral being used for bank loans.

5. Reduced collateral increased default rates on bank loans.

6. Greater defaults exacerbated problems in the banking system. Now return to step 1 to complete and continue the circle.

Some economists have used this vicious-circle argument to suggest that the Asian crisis was a self-fulfilling prophecy: bad things happened merely because people expected bad things to happen. Most economists, however, thought the political corruption of the banking system was a real problem, which was then compounded by this vicious circle of reduced confidence.

As the Asian crisis developed, the IMF and the United States tried to restore confidence, much as they had with Mexico a few years earlier. In particular, the IMF made loans to the Asian countries to help them through the crisis; in exchange for these loans, it exacted promises that the governments would reform their banking systems and eliminate crony capitalism. The IMF's hope was that the short-term loans and longer-term reforms would restore confidence, lower the risk premium, and turn the vicious circle into a virtuous one. This policy seems to have worked: the Asian economies recovered quickly from their crisis. ■

12-5 Should Exchange Rates Be Floating or Fixed?

Having analyzed how an economy works under floating and fixed exchange rates, we turn to the question of which exchange-rate regime is preferable.

Pros and Cons of Different Exchange-Rate Systems

The primary argument for a floating exchange rate is that it allows monetary policy to be used for other purposes. Under fixed rates, monetary policy is committed to the single goal of maintaining the exchange rate at its announced level. Yet the exchange rate is only one of many macroeconomic variables that monetary policy can influence. A system of floating exchange rates leaves monetary policymakers free to pursue other goals, such as stabilizing prices.

Advocates of fixed exchange rates argue that exchange-rate uncertainty makes international trade more difficult. After the world abandoned the Bretton Woods system of fixed exchange rates in the early 1970s, both real and nominal exchange rates became (and have remained) much more volatile than anyone had expected. Some economists attribute this volatility to irrational and destabilizing speculation by international investors. Business executives often claim that this volatility is harmful because it increases the uncertainty that accompanies international business transactions. Yet, despite this exchange-rate volatility, the amount of world trade has continued to rise under floating exchange rates.

Advocates of fixed exchange rates sometimes argue that a commitment to a fixed exchange rate is one way to discipline a nation's monetary authority and prevent excessive growth in the money supply. Yet there are many other policy rules to which the central bank could be committed. In Chapter 15, for

"Then it's agreed. Until the dollar firms up, we let the clamshell float."

instance, we discuss policy rules such as targets for nominal GDP or the inflation rate. Fixing the exchange rate has the advantage of being simpler to implement than these other policy rules, because the money supply adjusts automatically, but this policy may lead to greater volatility in income and employment. Indeed, in the Mundell–Fleming model, shocks to the IS^* curve *must* affect real GDP more under fixed exchange rates. In the appendix to this chapter, we explore the generality of this strong prediction. We extend the Mundell–Fleming model to allow for a direct effect of the exchange rate on the cost of living index, and for the interest rate differential to depend on the expected change in the exchange rate. In this more general setting, the shock-absorber feature of a floating rate is weakened.

In the end, the choice between floating and fixed rates is not as stark as it may seem at first. Under systems of fixed exchange rates, countries can change the value of their currency if maintaining the exchange rate conflicts too severely with other goals. Under systems of floating exchange rates, countries often use informal targets for the exchange rate when deciding whether to expand or contract the money supply. We rarely observe exchange rates that are completely fixed or completely floating. Instead, under both systems, stability of the exchange rate is usually one among many of the central bank's objectives.

CASE STUDY

Monetary Union

If you have ever driven the 6,000 kilometres from Halifax to Vancouver, you will recall that you never needed to change your money from one form of currency to another. In all provinces, local residents are happy to accept the Canadian dollar for the items you might buy. Such a *monetary union* is the most extreme form of a fixed exchange rate. The exchange rate between Nova Scotia dollars and British Columbia dollars is irrevocably fixed.

If you made a similar 6,000-kilometre trip across Europe during the 1990s, however, your experience was very different. You didn't have to travel far before needing to exchange your French francs for German marks, Dutch guilders, Spanish pesetas, or Italian lira. The large number of currencies in Europe made traveling less convenient and more expensive. Every time you crossed a border, you had to wait in line at a bank to get the local money, and you had to pay the bank a fee for the service.

Today, however, the situation in Europe is more like that in Canada. Many European countries have given up having their own currencies and have formed a monetary union that uses a common currency called the *euro*. As a result, the exchange rate between France and Germany is now as fixed as the exchange rate between Nova Scotia and British Columbia.

The introduction of a common currency has its costs. The most important is that the nations of Europe are no longer able to conduct their own monetary policies. Instead, the European Central Bank, with the participation of all member countries, sets a single monetary policy for all of Europe. The central banks of the individual countries monitor local conditions but they have no control over the money supply or interest rates. Critics of the move toward a common currency argue that the cost of losing national monetary policy is large. When a recession hits one country but not others in Europe, that country does not have the tool of monetary policy to combat the downturn. This argument is one reason some European nations, such as the United Kingdom, have chosen not to give up their own currency in favour of the euro.

Why, according to the euro critics, is monetary union a bad idea for Europe if it works so well in Canada and the United States? These economists argue that the North American economies are different from Europe in two important ways. First, labour is more mobile among Canadian provinces and among U.S. states than among European countries. This is in part because much of Canada and the United States has a common language and in part because many North Americans are descended from immigrants, who have shown a willingness to move. Therefore, when a regional recession occurs, North American workers are more likely to move from high-unemployment areas to low-unemployment ones. Second, Canada and the United States have strong central governments that can use fiscal policy to redistribute resources among regions. Because Europe does not have these two advantages, it bears a larger cost when it restricts itself to a single monetary policy.

Advocates of a common currency believe that the loss of national monetary policy is more than offset by other gains. With a single currency in all of Europe, travelers and businesses no longer need to worry about exchange rates, and this encourages international trade. In addition, a common currency may have the political advantage of making Europeans feel more connected to one another. The twentieth century was marked by two world wars, both of which were sparked by European discord. If a common currency makes the nations of Europe more harmonious, it benefits the entire world. ■

Speculative Attacks, Currency Boards, and Dollarization

Imagine that you are a central banker of a small country. You and your fellow policymakers decide to fix your currency—let's call it the peso—at par against the U.S. dollar. From now on, one peso will sell for one dollar.

As discussed earlier, you now have to stand ready to buy and sell pesos for a dollar each. The money supply will adjust automatically to make the equilibrium exchange rate equal your target. There is, however, one potential problem with this plan: you might run out of dollars. If people come to the central bank to sell large quantities of pesos, the central bank's dollar reserves might dwindle to zero. In this case, the central bank has no choice but to abandon the fixed exchange rate and let the peso depreciate.

This fact raises the possibility of a *speculative attack*—a change in investors' perceptions that makes the fixed exchange rate untenable. Suppose that, for no good reason, a rumor spreads that the central bank is going to abandon the exchange-rate peg. People would respond by rushing to the central bank to convert pesos into dollars before the pesos lose value. This rush would drain the central bank's reserves and could force the central bank to abandon the peg. In this case, the rumor would prove self-fulfilling.

To avoid this possibility, some economists argue that a fixed exchange rate should be supported by a *currency board,* such as that used by Argentina in the 1990s. A currency board is an arrangement by which the central bank holds enough foreign currency to back each and every unit of the domestic currency. In our example, the central bank would hold one U.S. dollar (or one dollar invested in a U.S. government bond) for every peso. No matter how many pesos turned up at the central bank to be exchanged, the central bank would never run out of dollars. Despite this fact, countries with currency boards still suffer from speculative attacks. The reason is that, when previously circulating pesos are turned in for foreign exchange, the country's money supply is automatically reduced. With a severe attack, this development can recess the domestic economy so much that the government loses the political will to maintain the currency board. This is what speculators are testing when a run against such a country's currency occurs.

To avoid any possibility of a speculative attack, once a central bank has decided to adopt a currency board, it might just as well consider the natural next step:

it can abandon the peso altogether and let its country use the U.S. dollar. Such a plan is called *dollarization*. It happens on its own in high-inflation economies, where foreign currencies offer a more reliable store of value than the domestic currency. But it can also occur as a matter of public policy, as in Panama. If a country really wants its currency to be irrevocably fixed to the dollar, the most reliable method is to make its currency the dollar. The only loss from dollarization is the seigniorage revenue that a government gives up by relinquishing its control over the printing press. The U.S. government then gets the revenue generated by growth in the money supply.[5]

The Impossible Trinity

The analysis of exchange-rate regimes leads to a simple conclusion: you can't have it all. To be more precise, it is impossible for a nation to have free capital flows, a fixed exchange rate, and independent monetary policy. This fact, often called the *impossible trinity,* is illustrated in Figure 12-15. A nation must choose one side of this triangle, giving up the institutional feature at the opposite corner.

The first option is to allow free flows of capital and to conduct an independent monetary policy, as Canada has done since 1970. In this case, it is impossible to have a fixed exchange rate. Instead, the exchange rate must float to equilibrate the market for foreign-currency exchange.

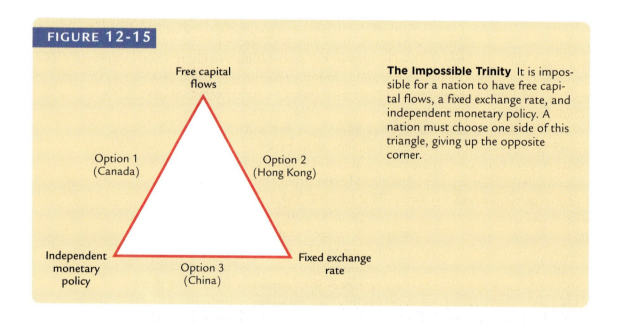

FIGURE 12-15

The Impossible Trinity It is impossible for a nation to have free capital flows, a fixed exchange rate, and independent monetary policy. A nation must choose one side of this triangle, giving up the opposite corner.

Free capital flows

Option 1 (Canada)

Option 2 (Hong Kong)

Independent monetary policy

Option 3 (China)

Fixed exchange rate

---

[5] Dollarization may also lead to a loss in national pride from seeing American portraits on the currency. If it wanted, the U.S. government could fix this problem by leaving blank the center space that now has George Washington's portrait. Each nation using the U.S. dollar could insert the face of its own local hero.

The second option is to allow free flows of capital and to fix the exchange rate, as Hong Kong has done in recent years. In this case, the nation loses the ability to run an independent monetary policy. The money supply must adjust to keep the exchange rate at its predetermined level. In effect, when a nation fixes its currency to that of another nation, it is adopting that other nation's monetary policy.

The third option is to restrict the international flow of capital in and out the country, as China has done in recent years. In this case, the interest rate is no longer fixed by world interest rates but is determined by domestic forces, much as is the case in a completely closed economy. In this case, it is possible to both fix the exchange rate and conduct an independent monetary policy.

History has shown that nations can, and do, choose different sides of the trinity. Every nation must ask itself the following question: does it want to live with exchange-rate volatility (option one), does it want to give up the use of monetary policy for purposes of domestic stabilization (option two), or does it want to restrict its citizens from participating in world financial markets (option three)? The impossible trinity says that no nation can avoid making one of these choices.

CASE STUDY

The Chinese Currency Controversy

From 1995 to 2005 the Chinese currency, the yuan, was pegged to the U.S. dollar at an exchange rate of 8.28 yuan per U.S. dollar. In other words, the Chinese central bank stood ready to buy and sell yuan at this price. This policy of fixing the exchange rate was combined with a policy of restricting international capital flows. Chinese citizens were not allowed to convert their savings into dollars or euros and invest abroad.

Many observers believed that, by the early 2000s, the yuan was significantly undervalued. They suggested that if the yuan were allowed to float, it would increase in value relative to the U.S. dollar. The evidence in favour of this hypothesis was that China was accumulating large dollar reserves in its efforts to maintain the fixed exchange rate. That is, the Chinese central bank had to supply yuan and demand dollars in foreign-exchange markets to keep the yuan at the pegged level. If this intervention in the currency market ceased, the yuan would rise in value compared to the dollar.

The pegged yuan became a contentious political issue in the United States. U.S. producers that competed against Chinese imports complained that the undervalued yuan made Chinese goods cheaper, putting the U.S. producers at a disadvantage. (Of course, U.S. consumers benefited from inexpensive imports, but in the politics of international trade, producers usually shout louder than consumers.) In response to these concerns, President George W. Bush called on China to let its currency float. Senator Charles Schumer from New York proposed a more drastic step—a tariff of 27.5 percent on Chinese imports until China adjusted the value of its currency.

In July 2005 China announced that it would move in the direction of a floating exchange rate. Under the new policy, it would still intervene in foreign-exchange markets to prevent large and sudden movements in the exchange rate, but it would permit gradual changes. Moreover, it would judge the value of the yuan not just relative to the dollar but relative to a broad basket of currencies. By January 2009, the exchange rate had moved to 6.84 yuan per dollar—a 21 percent appreciation of the yuan.

Despite this large change in the exchange rate, China's critics continued to complain about that nation's intervention in foreign-exchange markets. In January 2009, the new U.S. Treasury Secretary Timothy Geithner said, "President Obama—backed by the conclusions of a broad range of economists—believes that China is manipulating its currency. . . . President Obama has pledged as president to use aggressively all diplomatic avenues open to him to seek change in China's currency practices." As this book was going to press, it was unclear how successful those efforts would be. ■

12-6 From the Short Run to the Long Run: The Mundell-Fleming Model With a Changing Price Level

So far we have used the Mundell–Fleming model to study the small open economy in the short run when the price level is fixed. We now consider what happens when the price level changes. Doing so will show how the Mundell-Fleming model provides a theory of the aggregate demand curve in a small open economy. It will also show how this short-run model relates to the long-run model of the open economy we examined in Chapter 5.

Because we now want to consider changes in the price level, the nominal and real exchange rate in the economy will no longer be moving in tandem. Thus, we must distinguish between these two variables. The nominal exchange rate is e and the real exchange rate is ϵ, which equals eP/P^*, as you should recall from Chapter 5. We can write the Mundell–Fleming model as

$$Y = C(Y - T) + I(r^*) + G + NX(e) \qquad IS^*,$$

$$M/P = L(r^*, Y) \qquad LM^*.$$

These equations should be familiar by now. The first equation describes the IS^* curve, and the second equation describes the LM^* curve. Note that net exports depend on the real exchange rate.

Figure 12-16 shows what happens when the price level falls. Because a lower price level raises the level of real money balances, the LM^* curve shifts to the right, as in panel (a) of Figure 12-16. The real exchange rate depreciates, and the equilibrium level of income rises. The aggregate demand curve summarizes this negative relationship between the price level and the level of income, as shown in panel (b) of Figure 12-16.

The levels of income at point K and point C are both of interest. Our central concern in this chapter has been how policy influences point K, the short-run equilibrium. In Chapter 5 we examined the determinants of point C, the long-run equilibrium. Whenever policymakers consider any change in policy, they need to consider both the short-run and long-run effects of their decision.

12-7 A Concluding Reminder

In this chapter we have examined how a small open economy works in the short run when prices are sticky. We have seen how how monetary, fiscal, and trade policy influence income and the exchange rate, and how the behaviour of the economy depends on whether the exchange rate is floating or fixed. Since Canada is a small open economy, the Mundell–Fleming model applies very well—as we have seen in earlier sections of this chapter. In closing, however, we should note that many countries, including the United States, are neither closed economies nor small open economies: they lie somewhere in between.

A large open economy like the United States combines the behaviour of a closed economy and the behavior of a small open economy. When analyzing policies in a large open economy, we need to consider both the closed-economy logic of Chapter 11 and the open-economy logic developed in this chapter. The results are, as one would guess, a mixture of the two polar cases we have already examined.

To see how we can draw on the logic of both the closed and small open economies and apply these insights to the United States, consider how a monetary contraction affects the economy in the short run. In a closed economy, a monetary contraction raises the interest rate, lowers investment, and thus lowers aggregate income. In a small open economy with a floating exchange rate, a monetary contraction raises the exchange rate, lowers net exports, and thus lowers aggregate income. The interest rate is unaffected, however, because it is determined by world financial markets.

The U.S. economy contains elements of both cases. Because the United States is large enough to affect the world interest rate, a monetary contraction does raise the interest rate and depress investment. At the same time, a monetary contraction also raises the value of the U.S. dollar, thereby depressing net exports. Hence, although the Mundell–Fleming model does not precisely describe an economy like that of the United States, it does predict correctly what happens to international variables such as the exchange rate, and it shows how international interactions alter the effects of monetary and fiscal policies.

Summary

1. The Mundell–Fleming model is the *IS–LM* model for a small open economy. It takes the price level as given and then shows what causes fluctuations in income and the exchange rate.

2. The Mundell–Fleming model shows that fiscal policy does not influence aggregate income under floating exchange rates. A fiscal expansion causes the currency to appreciate, reducing net exports and offsetting the usual expansionary impact on aggregate income. Fiscal policy does influence aggregate income under fixed exchange rates.

3. The Mundell–Fleming model shows that monetary policy does not influence aggregate income under fixed exchange rates. Any attempt to expand the money supply is futile, because the money supply must adjust to ensure that the exchange rate stays at its announced level. Monetary policy does influence aggregate income under floating exchange rates.

4. If investors are wary of holding assets in a country, the interest rate in that country may exceed the world interest rate by some risk premium. According to the Mundell–Fleming model, an increase in the risk premium causes the interest rate to rise and the currency of that country to depreciate.

5. There are advantages to both floating and fixed exchange rates. Floating exchange rates leave monetary policymakers free to pursue objectives other than exchange-rate stability. Fixed exchange rates reduce some of the uncertainty in international business transactions, and they remove the negative spillover effects to other regions of the country that result from provincial-level fiscal policies that are undertaken with a flexible exchange rate.

6. When deciding on an exchange-rate regime, policymakers are constrained by the fact that it is impossible for a nation to have free capital flows, a fixed exchange rate, and independent monetary policy.

KEY CONCEPTS

Mundell–Fleming model

Floating exchange rates

Fixed exchange rates

Devaluation

Revaluation

QUESTIONS FOR REVIEW

1. In the Mundell–Fleming model with floating exchange rates, explain what happens to aggregate income, the exchange rate, and the trade balance when taxes are raised. What would happen if exchange rates were fixed rather than floating?

2. In the Mundell–Fleming model with floating exchange rates, explain what happens to aggregate income, the exchange rate, and the trade balance when the money supply is reduced. What would happen if exchange rates were fixed rather than floating?

3. In the Mundell–Fleming model with floating exchange rates, explain what happens to aggregate income, the exchange rate, and the trade balance when a quota on imported cars is removed. What would happen if exchange rates were fixed rather than floating?

4. What are the advantages of floating exchange rates and fixed exchange rates?

5. Describe the impossible trinity.

PROBLEMS AND APPLICATIONS

1. Use the Mundell–Fleming model to predict what would happen to aggregate income, the exchange rate, and the trade balance under both floating and fixed exchange rates in response to each of the following shocks:

   a. A fall in consumer confidence about the future induces consumers to spend less and save more.

   b. The introduction of a stylish line of Volkswagens makes some consumers prefer foreign cars over domestic cars.

   c. The introduction of automatic teller machines reduces the demand for money.

2. A small open economy with a floating exchange rate is in recession with balanced trade. If policymakers want to reach full employment while maintaining balanced trade, what combination of monetary and fiscal policy should they choose?

3. The Mundell–Fleming model takes the world interest rate r^* as an exogenous variable. Let's consider what happens when this variable changes.

   a. What might cause the world interest rate to rise?

   b. In the Mundell–Fleming model with a floating exchange rate, what happens to aggregate income, the exchange rate, and the trade balance when the world interest rate rises?

   c. In the Mundell–Fleming model with a fixed exchange rate, what happens to aggregate income, the exchange rate, and the trade balance when the world interest rate rises?

4. Business executives and policymakers are often concerned about the "competitiveness" of Canadian industry (the ability of Canadian industries to sell their goods profitably in world markets).

   a. How would a change in the nominal exchange rate affect competitiveness in the short-run when prices are sticky?

   b. Suppose you wanted to make domestic industries more competitive but did not want to alter aggregate income. According to the Mundell–Fleming model, what combination of monetary and fiscal policies should you pursue?

5. Suppose that higher income implies higher imports and thus lower net exports. That is, the net exports function is

   $$NX = NX(e, Y).$$

   Examine the effects in a small open economy of a fiscal expansion on income and the trade balance under

   a. A floating exchange rate.

   b. A fixed exchange rate.

   How does your answer compare to the results in Table 12-1?

6. Suppose that money demand depends on disposable income, so that the equation for the money market becomes

   $$M/P = L(r, Y - T).$$

   Analyze the impact of a tax cut in a small open economy on the exchange rate and income under both floating and fixed exchange rates.

7. Suppose that the price level relevant for money demand includes the price of imported goods and that the price of imported goods depends on the exchange rate. That is, the money market is described by

   $$M/P = L(r, Y),$$

   where

   $$P = \lambda P_d + (1 - \lambda)P_f/e.$$

   The parameter λ is the share of domestic goods in the price index P. Assume that the price of domestic goods P_d and the price of foreign goods measured in foreign currency P_f are fixed.

   a. Suppose we graph the LM^* curve for given values of P_d and P_f (instead of the usual P). Is this LM^* curve still vertical? Explain.

   b. What is the effect of expansionary fiscal policy under floating exchange rates in this model? Explain. Contrast with the standard Mundell–Fleming model.

   c. Suppose that political instability increases the country risk premium and, thereby, the interest rate. What is the effect on the exchange rate, the price level, and aggregate income in this model? Contrast with the standard

Mundell–Fleming model. This question anticipates part of what is covered in the appendix of this chapter.

8. Use the Mundell–Fleming model to answer the following questions about the province of Alberta (a small open economy).

   a. What kind of exchange-rate system does Alberta have with its major trading partners (the provinces of British Columbia and Ontario)?

   b. If Alberta suffers from a recession, should the provincial government use monetary or fiscal policy to stimulate employment? Explain. (*Note:* For this question, assume that the provincial government can print dollar bills.)

   c. If Alberta prohibited the import of wines from the province of Ontario, what would happen to income, the exchange rate, and the trade balance? Consider both the short-run and the long-run impacts.

Extensions to the Mundell–Fleming Model

One of the most important properties of the Mundell–Fleming model is the insulation a flexible exchange rate provides in the face of demand shocks. As we discovered in the main text of this chapter, a reduction in demand leads to a lower domestic currency, which stimulates net exports. With new jobs created in the export- and import-competing sectors—to replace those lost due to the initial drop in demand—a floating exchange rate provides the economy with an automatic stabilizer. Why is it that a number of countries are prepared to give up this automatic stabilizer? Perhaps policymakers in these countries feel that the Mundell–Fleming model is too simplified. We explore this question in this appendix by examining whether the property of insulation from demand shocks remains as the model is extended.

Three extensions are considered. First, since the exchange rate is an important determinant of the domestic price of imports, we allow the exchange rate to have a direct effect on the consumer price index (CPI). Second, we allow domestic prices and wages to be endogenous. Third, we consider endogenous exchange-rate expectations.

The Exchange Rate and the CPI

Households buy both domestically produced goods and imports. If we use P^d, P^f, and λ to denote the price of domestically produced goods, the price of foreign goods (denominated in foreign currency), and the proportion of each household budget that is devoted to domestically produced goods, the consumer price index can be written as

$$P = \lambda P^d + (1 - \lambda)P^f/e.$$

(P^f/e) is the price of imports in domestic currency units.

With respect to prices, two simplifications are involved in the Mundell–Fleming model. First, fixed prices—both at home and abroad—are assumed. This simplification involves setting $P^d = P^f = 1$. Second, the price of domestically produced goods, P^d, and the overall consumer price index, P, are assumed to be the same thing. By focusing on the formal definition of the CPI, we can see that this second simplification is inappropriate. Even with $P^d = P^f = 1$, the consumer price index is not constant. Indeed, it must change whenever the exchange rate does:

$$P = \lambda + (1 - \lambda)/e.$$

The revised model becomes

$$Y = C(Y - T) + I(r^*) + G + NX(e),$$

$$M/P = L(Y, r^*),$$

$$P = \lambda + \frac{(1 - \lambda)}{e}.$$

Compared to the basic Mundell–Fleming model, this extension involves the exchange rate affecting the money market. (Once the third equation is used to replace P in the LM^* equation, we can see that e becomes an important part of that relationship.) Given this complication, we must re-derive the LM^* locus. This is accomplished in Figure 12-18. There we see that, because a lower domestic currency makes imports more expensive, the CPI is higher when e is lower. As a result, the real money supply is smaller when the domestic currency falls in

FIGURE 12-18

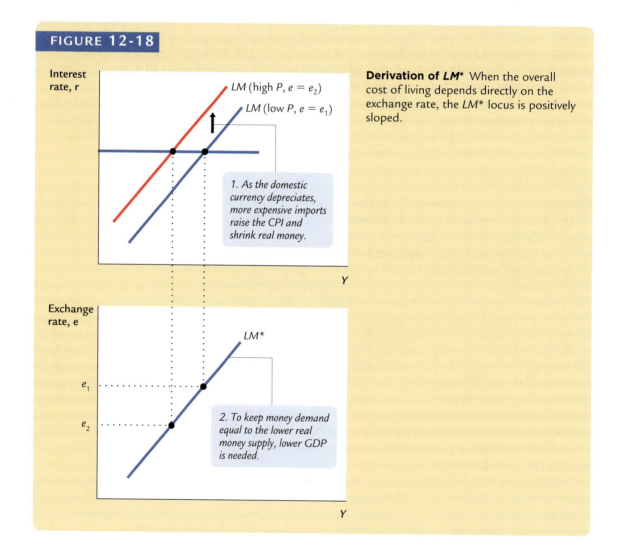

Derivation of LM^* When the overall cost of living depends directly on the exchange rate, the LM^* locus is positively sloped.

Interest rate, r

LM (high P, e = e₂)

LM (low P, e = e₁)

1. As the domestic currency depreciates, more expensive imports raise the CPI and shrink real money.

Y

Exchange rate, e

LM*

e₁

e₂

2. To keep money demand equal to the lower real money supply, lower GDP is needed.

Y

FIGURE 12-19

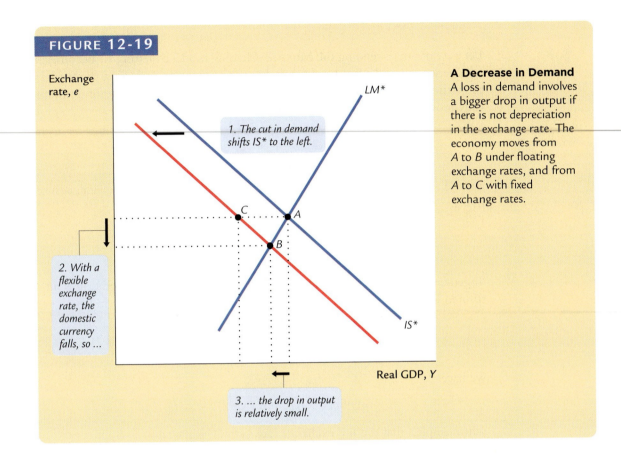

Exchange rate, e

LM*

1. The cut in demand shifts IS* to the left.

C   A

B

2. With a flexible exchange rate, the domestic currency falls, so ...

IS*

Real GDP, Y

3. ... the drop in output is relatively small.

A Decrease in Demand
A loss in demand involves a bigger drop in output if there is not depreciation in the exchange rate. The economy moves from A to B under floating exchange rates, and from A to C with fixed exchange rates.

value, and the *LM* curve in panel (a) shifts to the left. The positive slope of the *LM** locus in panel (b) summarizes this outcome.

We are now in a position to reassess the insulation property. A drop in demand—perhaps caused by lower government spending—shifts *IS** to the left as usual. The revised result is shown in Figure 12-19. With a floating exchange rate, the economy moves from A to B; with a fixed exchange rate, the central bank must move *LM** to the left and the economy moves from A to C. (Only the final outcome, not the shift in *LM**, is shown in Figure 12-19.) Since output falls in both scenarios, a floating exchange rate no longer provides complete insulation from demand shocks. Nevertheless, since the fall in output is less with a floating rate, some insulation still remains. It is important to note a second difference between the fixed- and flexible-exchange-rate cases. The CPI is not affected under fixed rates, while the CPI must rise under floating rates. This is one reason why some countries have opted for fixed exchange rates. A floating rate provides some (but reduced) insulation for real output, but that insulation is "purchased" at the expense of having to accept an increase in the general cost of living. In short, under floating rates, a decrease in spending is like an oil price increase—it is *stagflationary.*

Flexible Domestic Prices

Let us continue extending the Mundell–Fleming model by letting P^d become an endogenous variable. Just to illustrate how this extension can affect the model's properties, we focus on one special case. We assume that the price of domestically produced goods adjusts one-for-one with changes in wages,

$$\frac{\Delta P^d}{P^d} = \frac{\Delta W}{W},$$

and we assume that wages adjust one-for-one with changes in the overall cost of living,

$$\frac{\Delta W}{W} = \frac{\Delta P}{P},$$

Together, these relationships imply $\Delta P^d/P^d = \Delta P/P$. When this condition is substituted into the percentage-change version of the consumer price index,

$$\frac{\Delta P}{P} = \lambda \frac{\Delta P^d}{P^d} + (1 - \lambda) \left(\frac{\Delta P^f}{P^f} - \frac{\Delta e}{e} \right),$$

we have

$$\Delta P^d/P^d = \Delta P/P = (\Delta P^f/P^f - \Delta e/e),$$

which implies that the *real* exchange rate, eP^d/P^f, is *constant*.

The revised *IS* relationship is

$$Y = C(Y - T) + I(r^*) + G + NX\left(\frac{eP^d}{P^f} \right)$$

Since the real exchange rate is fixed, the *IS** locus that follows from this relationship is *vertical,* and the effect of a drop in government spending is shown in Figure 12-20. The economy moves from point A to B under flexible exchange rates, and from A to C with a fixed rate. Since the effect on real output is the same, the insulation feature of a floating exchange rate is lost completely. While the direct effect of a falling domestic currency remains favourable (it stimulates demand for domestically produced goods), the model now contains an indirect effect that is unfavourable (the falling domestic currency raises the general cost of living, and therefore wages). Higher domestic costs make the economy less competitive. In this specific model, the direct and indirect effects of the falling dollar just cancel.

This version of the model gives even more support for those who choose a fixed exchange rate. In this case, a fixed exchange rate does not involve giving up any built-in stability, and we avoid the increase in the cost of living (which accompanies a drop in spending only in the flexible-exchange-rate case).

The choice with respect to the exchange-rate regime seems to depend on whether a country's labour-market institutions lead to sticky nominal wages or sticky real wages in the short run. In many European countries there is a synchronized annual adjustment in most nominal wage rates (and this adjustment reflects the

FIGURE 12-20

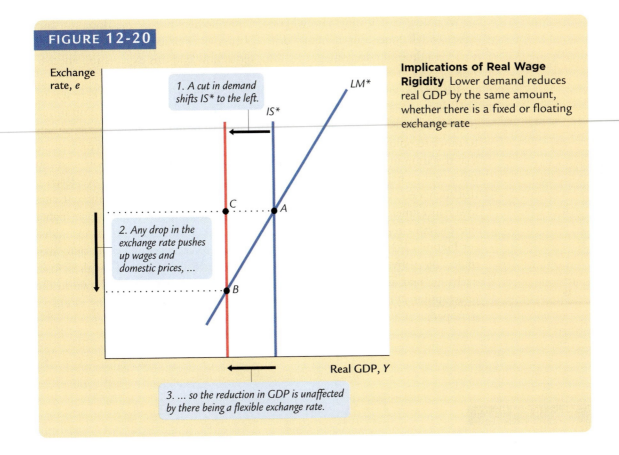

Implications of Real Wage Rigidity Lower demand reduces real GDP by the same amount, whether there is a fixed or floating exchange rate

(Figure labels: Exchange rate, e; 1. A cut in demand shifts IS* to the left.; LM*; IS*; C; A; 2. Any drop in the exchange rate pushes up wages and domestic prices, ...; B; Real GDP, Y; 3. ... so the reduction in GDP is unaffected by there being a flexible exchange rate.)

previous year's increase in the CPI). As a result, the present version of our model seems particularly suited to European countries, and their adoption of a common currency is therefore supported by the analysis. In North America, on the other hand, many workers have wage contracts that stipulate the nominal wage for a considerable time into the future. As a result, most economists are more comfortable assuming sticky *nominal* wages, not sticky real wages, for Canada and the United States. This presumption makes the earlier version of the Mundell–Fleming model more appropriate for Canada; and this analysis supports our decision to reject currency union with the United States (fixed exchange rates).

Exchange-Rate Expectations

To keep things relatively straightforward in this discussion of exchange-rate expectations, let us revert to the $P^d = P^f = 1$ simplification. In the main text of this chapter we noted that perfect capital mobility forces the domestic interest rate to equal the foreign rate plus the risk premium:

$$r = r^* + \theta.$$

Thus far, we have limited our attention to exogenous changes in θ. The purpose of this part of the appendix is to consider θ as an endogenous variable.

We know that θ must rise whenever asset holders expect the domestic currency to fall. Since our currency does fall (under flexible exchange rates) when there is a drop in government spending, let us now add this expectation effect to our analysis of fiscal retrenchment.

We saw the outcome of a reduction in G in Figure 12-19—when there was no risk-premium effect. At least as far as avoiding part of an undesirable drop in real output is concerned, a floating exchange rate is appealing; it allows the economy to move to point B, not point C. But since well-informed individuals understand that this drop in the domestic currency will occur, they will adjust their expectations, and θ will rise accordingly. In the main text of this chapter, we learned that such a rise in θ must shift the IS^* locus to the left (since higher interest rates lower investment spending) and shift the LM^* locus to the right (since higher interest rates reduce money demand). Once these additional shifts are added (in Figure 12-21), we see that the more complete comparison of the outcomes under alternative exchange-rate regimes is a move from A to C with a fixed exchange rate, and a move from A to D under flexible rates. As is shown in the figure, point D may be just as far to the left as point C. If so, a floating rate does not operate as a built-in stabilizer with respect to real output outcomes.

FIGURE 12-21

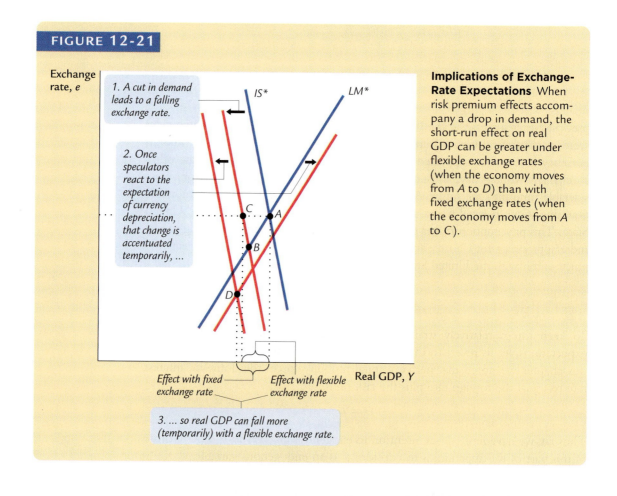

1. A cut in demand leads to a falling exchange rate.

2. Once speculators react to the expectation of currency depreciation, that change is accentuated temporarily, ...

Exchange rate, e

IS^* LM^*

Effect with fixed exchange rate

Effect with flexible exchange rate

Real GDP, Y

3. ... so real GDP can fall more (temporarily) with a flexible exchange rate.

Implications of Exchange-Rate Expectations When risk premium effects accompany a drop in demand, the short-run effect on real GDP can be greater under flexible exchange rates (when the economy moves from A to D) than with fixed exchange rates (when the economy moves from A to C).

Of course, these additional shifts in the IS^* and LM^* loci are only temporary, since once the exchange rate stops changing, θ will return to zero. This consideration leads many policymakers to opt for a floating exchange rate but to intervene in an ongoing fashion to smooth out the short-run variations in the exchange rate. (This is called managed floating.) But it is easy to see that such an attempt to smooth the exchange rate may backfire. To appreciate this fact, consider rewriting the interest arbitrage condition, $r = r^* + \theta$.

Let θ be represented by the expected depreciation in the domestic currency, which we can denote as $-(e - e^{\exp})$, where $e^{\exp}$ stands for the expected exchange rate. Also, let the interest-rate deviation $(r^* - r)$ be represented by the random variable v. The interest-arbitrage relationship then becomes:

$$e_t = e_t^{\exp} + v_t.$$

The t subscripts denote the current time period. In forming expectations about the exchange rate, it is reasonable to assume that individuals will put some weight on where they expect the exchange rate to be going (its full equilibrium value, e^*) and some weight on where the exchange rate has been (its value in the previous time period, e_{t-1}). Letting those weights be $(1 - \gamma)$ and γ, expectation formation is given by

$$e_t^{\exp} = (1 - \gamma)e^* + \gamma e_{t-1}.$$

Substituting this expression into the interest arbitrage condition, we have

$$e_t = (1 - \gamma)e^* + \gamma e_{t-1} + v_t.$$

Simple examination of this relationship indicates that exchange-rate volatility is smallest when γ is zero. Suppose that the random disturbance term, v_t, is nonzero for just one period. If γ is zero, the exchange rate will be affected for just that one period. But if γ is positive, the effect of that one disturbance will last for many periods. For example, if γ is one-half, the exchange rate will still be affected by one-half of the original amount one period later, and by one-quarter of the original amount two periods later, and so on.

So low volatility in the exchange rate requires a low value of γ. But if individuals know that the central bank is smoothing the exchange rate, they have every reason to put a large weight on the previous period's value when forming expectations. Thus, the more the central bank tries to smooth the exchange rate, the more rational it is for individuals to choose a high value for γ, and the more volatile is the exchange rate after all.

This conclusion is an example of the Lucas critique (discussed in Chapter 15 p. 517). Exchange-rate smoothing makes sense if the direct effect of policy on expectation formation is ignored, but not otherwise. Partly because of this ambiguity, many central banks have opted for stabilizing the rate of inflation, not the exchange rate.

An Attempt at Perspective

In a world of capital mobility, with speculators constantly on the lookout for fixed-exchange-rate promises to "test," the most credible form of fixed exchange rates is currency union. In Canada's case, this means eliminating the Canadian dollar and using the U.S. dollar as our currency. This choice has been hotly debated in the media.

The main advantage of currency union is the possibility that a lower risk premium could bring lower interest rates and a higher capital/labour ratio. However, with the U.S. Fed pursuing roughly the same inflation rate as the Bank of Canada, there is little basis for choice on this criterion. Without negotiation, however, Canadians would relinquish seigniorage revenue (a small consideration) and lender-of-last-resort facilities for financial crises (a significant consideration, as the events of 2008 have reminded us) by choosing currency union. The final issue concerns whether a separate currency imparts built-in stability to the economy. The basic answer to this question, which follows from our series of extensions to the Mundell–Fleming model, is that a floating rate does act as a buffer. This shock-absorber property is often exaggerated to a significant degree, but as long as Canada approximates what Mundell has called an "optimum currency area," it is likely that *some* of this property of flexible exchange rates will remain.

To appreciate what is meant by an optimum currency area, it is instructive to think of North America divided in two ways—first between north and south, and second between west and east. First, assume that the north produces wheat and the south produces cars. A shift in tastes (higher demand for cars and lower demand for wheat) results in inflation in the south and unemployment in the north. If there is a separate currency for the north and a floating exchange rate, a depreciating northern currency can reduce both the inflation and unemployment problems. Now assume that the west produces wheat and the east produces cars. The same shift in tastes causes inflation in the east and unemployment in the west. As before, if there is a separate currency for the west, a flexible exchange rate is a substitute for factor mobility, so it can decrease the costs of adjusting to the change in tastes.

In the first scenario, north and south are the areas for which it would be helpful to have separate currencies; in the second scenario, it is the east and west that represent optimum currency areas. The problem in North America is that—over time—the second scenario is becoming the more relevant one, while currencies are still based on our national border (north versus south). The greater this mismatch is, the less sense it makes (on short-run macroeconomic stability grounds) to maintain a separate Canadian currency. As a result, we can expect the debate on Canada's exchange-rate policy to continue. It is interesting to note that, as Mundell has contributed to the development of open-economy macroeconomics following his original model, he has argued—increasingly over time—for a return to fixed exchange rates.

MORE PROBLEMS AND APPLICATIONS

1. Explain how the imposition of a tariff by foreign governments (on our exports) affects real GDP and the overall price level (under flexible exchange rates) in each of the extended versions of the Mundell–Fleming model.

2. Explain how the imposition of a tariff by the domestic government (on our imports) affects real GDP and the overall price level (under flexible exchange rates) in each of the extended versions of the Mundell–Fleming model.

3. Explain how an increase in world interest rates affects real GDP and the overall price level (under flexible exchange rates) in each of the extended versions of the Mundell–Fleming model.

Aggregate Supply and the Short-Run Tradeoff Between Inflation and Unemployment

Probably the single most important macroeconomic relationship is the Phillips curve.

— *George Akerlof*

There is always a temporary tradeoff between inflation and unemployment; there is no permanent tradeoff. The temporary tradeoff comes not from inflation per se, but from unanticipated inflation, which generally means, from a rising rate of inflation.

— *Milton Friedman*

Most economists analyze short-run fluctuations in national income and the price level using the model of aggregate demand and aggregate supply. In the previous three chapters, we examined aggregate demand in some detail. The *IS–LM* model—along with its open-economy cousin the Mundell–Fleming model—shows how changes in monetary and fiscal policy and shocks to the money and goods markets shift the aggregate demand curve. In this chapter, we turn our attention to aggregate supply and develop theories that explain the position and slope of the aggregate supply curve.

When we introduced the aggregate supply curve in Chapter 9, we established that aggregate supply behaves very differently in the short run than in the long run. In the long run, prices are flexible, and the aggregate supply curve is vertical. When the aggregate supply curve is vertical, shifts in the aggregate demand curve affect the price level, but the output of the economy remains at its natural level. By contrast, in the short run, prices are sticky, and the aggregate supply curve is not vertical. In this case, shifts in aggregate demand do cause fluctuations in output. In Chapter 9 we took a simplified view of price stickiness by drawing the short-run aggregate supply curve as a horizontal line, representing the extreme situation in which all prices are fixed. Our task now is to refine this understanding of short-run aggregate supply to better reflect the real world in which some prices are sticky and others are not.

After examining the basic theory of the short-run aggregate supply curve, we establish a key implication. We show that this curve implies a tradeoff between two measures of economic performance—inflation and unemployment. This tradeoff, called the *Phillips* curve, tells us that to reduce the rate of inflation policymakers must temporarily raise unemployment and that to reduce unemployment they must accept higher inflation. But, as the quotation from Milton Friedman at the beginning of the chapter suggests, the tradeoff between inflation and unemployment is only temporary. One goal of this chapter is to explain why policymakers face such a tradeoff in the short run and, just as important, why they do not face it in the long run.

13-1 The Basic Theory of Aggregate Supply

When students in physics classes study balls rolling down inclined planes, they often begin by assuming away the existence of friction. This assumption makes the problem simpler and is useful in many circumstances, but no good engineer would ever take this assumption as a literal description of how the world works. Similarly, this book began with classical macroeconomic theory, but it would be a mistake to assume that this model is true in all circumstances. Our job now is to look more deeply into the "frictions" of macroeconomics.

We do this by examining two prominent models of aggregate supply. In both models, some market imperfection (that is, some type of friction) causes the output of the economy to deviate from its natural level. As a result, the short-run aggregate supply curve is upward sloping, rather than vertical, and shifts in the aggregate demand curve cause output to fluctuate. These temporary deviations of output from its natural level represent the booms and busts of the business cycle.

Each of the two models takes us down a different theoretical route, but each route ends up in the same place. That final destination is a short-run aggregate supply equation of the form

$$Y = \overline{Y} + \alpha(P - EP), \qquad \alpha > 0,$$

where Y is output, $\overline{Y}$ is the natural level of output, P is the price level, and EP is the expected price level. This equation states that output deviates from its natural level when the price level deviates from the expected price level. The parameter α indicates how much output responds to unexpected changes in the price level; $1/\alpha$ is the slope of the aggregate supply curve.

Each of the models tells a different story about what lies behind this short-run aggregate supply equation. In other words, each model highlights a particular reason why unexpected movements in the price level are associated with fluctuations in aggregate output.

The Sticky-Price Model

The most widely accepted explanation for the upward-sloping short-run aggregate supply curve is called the **sticky-price model.** This model emphasizes that firms do not instantly adjust the prices they charge in response to changes in demand. Sometimes prices are set by long-term contracts between firms and customers. Even without formal agreements, firms may hold prices steady to avoid annoying their regular customers with frequent price changes. Some prices are sticky because of the way markets are structured: once a firm has printed and distributed its catalogue or price list, it is costly to alter prices. And sometimes sticky prices can be a reflection of sticky wages: firms base their prices on the costs of production, and wages may depend on social norms and notions of fairness that evolve only slowly over time.

There are various ways to formalize the idea of sticky prices to show how they can help explain an upward-sloping aggregate supply curve. Here we examine an especially simple model. We first consider the pricing decisions of individual firms and then add together the decisions of many firms to explain the behaviour of the economy as a whole. To fully understand the model, we have to depart from the assumption of perfect competition, which we have used since Chapter 3. Perfectly competitive firms are price takers rather than price setters. If we want to consider how firms set prices, it is natural to assume that these firms have at least some monopolistic control over the prices they charge.

Consider the pricing decision facing a typical firm. The firm's desired price p depends on two macroeconomic variables:

- The overall level of prices P. A higher price level implies that the firm's costs are higher. Hence, the higher the overall price level, the more the firm would like to charge for its product.

- The level of aggregate income Y. A higher level of income raises the demand for the firm's product. Because marginal cost increases at higher levels of production, the greater the demand, the higher the firm's desired price.

We write the firm's desired price as

$$p = P + a(Y - \overline{Y}).$$

This equation says that the desired price p depends on the overall level of prices P and on the level of aggregate output relative to the natural level $Y - \overline{Y}$. The parameter a (which is greater than zero) measures how much the firm's desired price responds to the level of aggregate output.[1]

Now assume that there are two types of firms. Some have flexible prices: they always set their prices according to this equation. Others have sticky prices: they announce their prices in advance based on what they expect economic conditions to be. Firms with sticky prices set prices according to

$$p = EP + a(EY - E\overline{Y}),$$

---

[1] *Mathematical note:* The firm cares most about its relative price, which is the ratio of its nominal price to the overall price level. If we interpret p and P as the logarithms of the firm's price and the price level, then this equation states that the desired relative price depends on the deviation of output from the natural level.

where, as before, an "E" represents the expected value of a variable. For simplicity, assume that these firms expect output to be at its natural rate, so that the last term, $a(EY - E\overline{Y})$, is zero. Then these firms set the price

$$p = EP.$$

That is, firms with sticky prices set their prices based on what they expect other firms to charge.

We can use the pricing rules of the two groups of firms to derive the aggregate supply equation. To do this, we find the overall price level in the economy, which is the weighted average of the prices set by the two groups. If s is the fraction of firms with sticky prices and $1 - s$ the fraction with flexible prices, then the overall price level is

$$P = sEP + (1 - s)[P + a(Y - \overline{Y})].$$

The first term is the price of the sticky-price firms weighted by their fraction in the economy, and the second term is the price of the flexible-price firms weighted by their fraction. Now subtract $(1 - s)P$ from both sides of this equation to obtain

$$sP = sEP + (1 - s)[a(Y - \overline{Y})].$$

Divide both sides by s to solve for the overall price level:

$$P = EP + [(1 - s)a/s](Y - \overline{Y}).$$

The two terms in this equation are explained as follows:

- When firms expect a high price level, they expect high costs. Those firms that fix prices in advance set their prices high. These high prices cause the other firms to set high prices also. Hence, a high expected price level EP leads to a high actual price level P.

- When output is high, the demand for goods is high. Those firms with flexible prices set their prices high, which leads to a high price level. The effect of output on the price level depends on the proportion of firms with flexible prices.

Hence, the overall price level depends on the expected price level and on the level of output.

Algebraic rearrangement puts this aggregate pricing equation into a more familiar form:

$$Y = \overline{Y} + \alpha(P - EP),$$

where $\alpha = s/[(1 - s)a]$. Like the other models, the sticky-price model says that the deviation of output from the natural level is positively associated with the deviation of the price level from the expected price level.[2]

---

[2] For a more advanced development of the sticky-price model, see Julio Rotemberg, "Monopolistic Price Adjustment and Aggregate Output," *Review of Economic Studies* 49 (1982): 517–531; and Guillermo Calvo, "Staggered Prices in a Utility-Maximizing Framework," *Journal of Monetary Economics* 12, no. 3 (1983): 383–398.

An Alternative Theory: The Imperfect-Information Model

Another explanation for the upward slope of the short-run aggregate supply curve is called the **imperfect-information model.** Unlike the previous model, this one assumes that markets clear—that is, all prices are free to adjust to balance supply and demand. In this model, the short-run and long-run aggregate supply curves differ because of temporary misperceptions about prices.

The imperfect-information model assumes that each supplier in the economy produces a single good and consumes many goods. Because the number of goods is so large, suppliers cannot observe all prices at all times. They monitor closely the prices of what they produce but less closely the prices of all the goods they consume. Because of imperfect information, they sometimes confuse changes in the overall level of prices with changes in relative prices. This confusion influences decisions about how much to supply, and it leads to a short-run relationship between the price level and output.

Consider the decision facing a single supplier—a wheat farmer, for instance. Because the farmer earns income from selling wheat and uses this income to buy goods and services, the amount of wheat she chooses to produce depends on the price of wheat relative to the prices of other goods and services in the economy. If the relative price of wheat is high, the farmer is motivated to work hard and produce more wheat, because the reward is great. If the relative price of wheat is low, she prefers to enjoy more leisure and produce less wheat.

Unfortunately, when the farmer makes her production decision, she does not know the relative price of wheat. As a wheat producer, she monitors the wheat market closely and always knows the nominal price of wheat. But she does not know the prices of all the other goods in the economy. She must, therefore, estimate the relative price of wheat using the nominal price of wheat and her expectation of the overall price level.

Consider how the farmer responds if all prices in the economy, including the price of wheat, increase. One possibility is that she expected this change in prices. When she observes an increase in the price of wheat, her estimate of its relative price is unchanged. She does not work any harder.

The other possibility is that the farmer did not expect the price level to increase (or to increase by this much). When she observes the increase in the price of wheat, she is not sure whether other prices have risen (in which case wheat's relative price is unchanged) or whether only the price of wheat has risen (in which case its relative price is higher). The rational inference is that some of each has happened. In other words, the farmer infers from the increase in the nominal price of wheat that its relative price has risen somewhat. She works harder and produces more.

Our wheat farmer is not unique. Her decisions are similar to those of her neighbours, who produce broccoli, cauliflower, dill, endive, and zucchini. When the price level rises unexpectedly, all suppliers in the economy observe increases in the prices of the goods they produce. They all infer, rationally but mistakenly, that the relative prices of the goods they produce have risen. They work harder and produce more.

To sum up, the imperfect-information model says that when prices exceed expected prices, suppliers raise their output. The model implies an aggregate supply curve that is now familiar:

$$Y = \overline{Y} + \alpha(P - EP).$$

Output deviates from the natural level when the price level deviates from the expected price level.

The imperfect-information story described above is the version developed originally by Nobel Prize–winning economist Robert Lucas in the 1970s. Recent work on imperfect-information models of aggregate supply has taken a somewhat different approach. Rather than emphasizing confusion about relative prices and the absolute price level, as Lucas did, this new work stresses the limited ability of individuals to incorporate information about the economy into their decisions. In this case, the friction that causes the short-run aggregate supply curve to be upward sloping is not the limited availability of information; it is, instead, the limited ability of people to absorb and process information that is widely available. This information-processing constraint causes price-setters to respond slowly to macroeconomic news. The resulting equation for short-run aggregate supply is similar to those from the two models we have seen, even though the microeconomic foundations are somewhat different.[3]

CASE STUDY

International Differences in the Aggregate Supply Curve

Although all countries experience economic fluctuations, these fluctuations are not exactly the same everywhere. International differences are intriguing puzzles in themselves, and they often provide a way to test alternative economic theories. Examining international differences has been especially fruitful in research on aggregate supply.

When Robert Lucas proposed the imperfect-information model, he derived a

---

[3] To read Lucas's description of his model, see Robert E. Lucas, "Understanding Business Cycles," *Carnegie-Rochester Conference Series on Public Policy* 5 (1977): 7–29. Lucas was building on the work of Milton Friedman, another Nobel Prize winner. See Milton Friedman, "The Role of Monetary Policy," *American Economic Review* 58 (March 1968): 1–17. For recent work emphasizing the role of information-processing constraints, see Michael Woodford, "Imperfect Common Knowledge and the Effects of Monetary Policy," in Philippe Aghion, Roman Frydman, Joseph Stiglitz, and Michael Woodford, eds., *Knowledge, Information, and Expectations in Modern Macroeconomics: In Honor of Edmund S. Phelps* (Princeton, N.J.: Princeton University Press, 2003); and N. Gregory Mankiw and Ricardo Reis, "Sticky Information Versus Sticky Prices: A Proposal to Replace the New Keynesian Phillips Curve," *Quarterly Journal of Economics* 107 (November 2002): 1295–1328.

surprising interaction between aggregate demand and aggregate supply: according to his model, the slope of the aggregate supply curve should depend on the variability of aggregate demand. In countries where aggregate demand fluctuates widely, the aggregate price level fluctuates widely as well. Because most movements in prices in these countries do not represent movements in relative prices, suppliers should have learned not to respond much to unexpected changes in the price level. Therefore, the aggregate supply curve should be relatively steep (that is, α will be small). Conversely, in countries where aggregate demand is relatively stable, suppliers should have learned that most price changes are relative price changes. Accordingly, in these countries, suppliers should be more responsive to unexpected price changes, making the aggregate supply curve relatively flat (that is, α will be large).

Lucas tested this prediction by examining international data on output and prices. He found that changes in aggregate demand have the biggest effect on output in those countries where aggregate demand and prices are most stable. Lucas concluded that the evidence supports the imperfect-information model.[4]

The sticky-price model also makes predictions about the slope of the short-run aggregate supply curve. In particular, it predicts that the average rate of inflation should influence the slope of the short-run aggregate supply curve. When the average rate of inflation is high, it is very costly for firms to keep prices fixed for long intervals. Thus, firms adjust prices more frequently. More frequent price adjustment in turn allows the overall price level to respond more quickly to shocks to aggregate demand. Hence, a high rate of inflation should make the short-run aggregate supply curve steeper.

International data support this prediction of the sticky-price model. In countries with low average inflation, the short-run aggregate supply curve is relatively flat: fluctuations in aggregate demand have large effects on output and are only slowly reflected in prices. High-inflation countries have steep short-run aggregate supply curves. In other words, high inflation appears to erode the frictions that cause prices to be sticky.[5]

Note that the sticky-price model can also explain Lucas's finding that countries with variable aggregate demand have steep aggregate supply curves. If the price level is highly variable, few firms will commit to prices in advance (s will be small). Hence, the aggregate supply curve will be steep (α will be small). ∎

Implications

We have seen two models of aggregate supply and the market imperfection that each uses to explain why the short-run aggregate supply curve is upward sloping. One model assumes the prices of some goods are sticky; the second assumes information about prices is imperfect. Keep in mind that these models are not

[4] Robert E. Lucas, Jr., "Some International Evidence on Output-Inflation Tradeoffs," *American Economic Review* 63 (June 1973): 326–334.

[5] Laurence Ball, N. Gregory Mankiw, and David Romer, "The New Keynesian Economics and the Output-Inflation Tradeoff," *Brookings Papers on Economic Activity* (1988:1): 1–65.

incompatible with one another. We need not accept one model and reject the others. The world may contain both of these market imperfections, as well as some others, and all of them may contribute to the behaviour of short-run aggregate supply.

The two models of aggregate supply differ in their assumptions and emphases, but their implications for aggregate output are similar. Both can be summarized by the equation

$$Y = \overline{Y} + \alpha(P - EP).$$

This equation states that deviations of output from the natural level are related to deviations of the price level from the expected price level. *If the price level is higher than the expected price level, output exceeds its natural level. If the price level is lower than the expected price level, output falls short of its natural level.* Figure 13-1 graphs this equation. Notice that the short-run aggregate supply curve is drawn for a given expectation EP and that a change in EP would shift the curve.

Now that we have a better understanding of aggregate supply, let's put aggregate supply and aggregate demand back together. Figure 13-2 uses our aggregate supply equation to show how the economy responds to an unexpected increase in aggregate demand attributable, say, to an unexpected monetary expansion. In the short run, the equilibrium moves from point A to point B. The increase in aggregate demand raises the actual price level from P_1 to P_2. Because people did not expect this increase in the price level, the expected price level remains at EP_2, and output rises from Y_1 to Y_2, which is above the natural level $\overline{Y}$. Thus, the unexpected expansion in aggregate demand causes the economy to boom.

Yet the boom does not last forever. In the long run, the expected price level rises to catch up with reality, causing the short-run aggregate supply curve to shift upward. As the expected price level rises from EP_2 to EP_3, the equilibrium of the

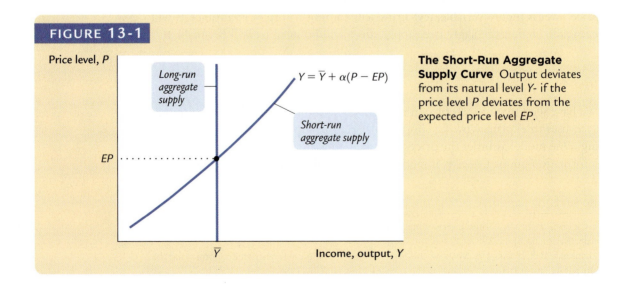

FIGURE 13-1

Price level, P

Long-run aggregate supply

$Y = \overline{Y} + \alpha(P - EP)$

Short-run aggregate supply

EP

$\overline{Y}$

Income, output, Y

The Short-Run Aggregate Supply Curve Output deviates from its natural level Y- if the price level P deviates from the expected price level EP.

FIGURE 13-2

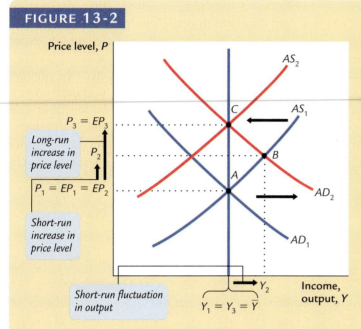

How Shifts in Aggregate Demand Lead to Short-Run Fluctuations Here the economy begins in a long-run equilibrium, point A. When aggregate demand increases unexpectedly, the price level rises from P_1 to P_2. Because the price level P_2 is above the expected price level EP_2, output rises temporarily above the natural level, as the economy moves along the short-run aggregate supply curve from point A to point B. In the long run, the expected price level rises to EP_3, causing the short-run aggregate supply curve to shift upward. The economy returns to a new long-run equilibrium, point C, where output is back at its natural level.

economy moves from point B to point C. The actual price level rises from P_2 to P_3, and output falls from Y_2 to Y_3. In other words, the economy returns to the natural level of output in the long run, but at a much higher price level.

This analysis shows an important principle, which holds for both models of aggregate supply: long-run monetary neutrality and short-run monetary *non*neutrality are perfectly compatible. Short-run nonneutrality is represented here by the movement from point *A* to point *B,* and long-run monetary neutrality is represented by the movement from point *A* to point *C.* We reconcile the short-run and long-run effects of money by emphasizing the adjustment of expectations about the price level.

13-2 Inflation, Unemployment, and the Phillips Curve

Two goals of economic policymakers are low inflation and low unemployment, but often these goals conflict. Suppose, for instance, that policymakers were to use monetary or fiscal policy to expand aggregate demand. This policy would move the economy along the short-run aggregate supply curve to a point of higher output and a higher price level. (Figure 13-2 shows this as the change from point A to point B.) Higher output means lower unemployment, because firms employ more workers when they produce more. A higher price level, given the previous year's price level, means higher inflation. Thus, when policymakers move the economy up along the short-run aggregate supply curve, they reduce the unemployment rate and raise the inflation rate. Conversely, when they contract aggregate demand and move the economy down the short-run aggregate supply curve, unemployment rises and inflation falls.

This tradeoff between inflation and unemployment, called the *Phillips curve,* is our topic in this section. As we have just seen (and will derive more formally in a moment), the Phillips curve is a reflection of the short-run aggregate supply curve: as policymakers move the economy along the short-run aggregate supply curve, unemployment and inflation move in opposite directions. The Phillips curve is a useful way to express aggregate supply because inflation and unemployment are such important measures of economic performance.

Deriving the Phillips Curve from the Aggregate Supply Curve

The **Phillips curve** in its modern form states that the inflation rate depends on three forces:

- Expected inflation
- The deviation of unemployment from the natural rate, called *cyclical unemployment*
- Supply shocks.

These three forces are expressed in the following equation:

$$\pi = E\pi - \beta(u - u^{n}) + v$$

$$\text{Inflation} = \frac{\text{Expected}}{\text{Inflation}} - (\beta \times \frac{\text{Cyclical}}{\text{Unemployment}}) + \frac{\text{Supply}}{\text{Shock}},$$

where β is a parameter measuring the response of inflation to cyclical unemployment. Notice that there is a minus sign before the cyclical unemployment term: other things equal, higher unemployment is associated with lower inflation.

Where does this equation for the Phillips curve come from? Although it may not seem familiar, we can derive it from our equation for aggregate supply. To see how, write the aggregate supply equation as

$$P = EP + \frac{1}{\alpha}(Y - \overline{Y}).$$

With one addition, one subtraction, and one substitution, we can transform this equation into the Phillips curve—a relationship between inflation and unemployment.

Here are the three steps. First, add to the right-hand side of the equation a supply shock v to represent exogenous events (such as a change in world oil prices) that alter the price level and shift the short-run aggregate supply curve:

$$P = EP + \frac{1}{\alpha}(Y - \overline{Y}) + v.$$

Next, to go from the price level to inflation rates, subtract last year's price level P_{-1} from both sides of the equation to obtain

$$(P - P_{-1}) = (EP - P_{-1}) + \frac{1}{\alpha}(Y - \overline{Y}) + v.$$

The term on the left-hand side, $P - P_{-1}$, is the difference between the current price level and last year's price level, which is inflation π.[6] The term on the right-hand side, $EP - P_{-1}$, is the difference between the expected price level and last year's price level, which is expected inflation $E\pi$. Therefore, we can replace $P - P_{-1}$ with π and $EP - P_{-1}$ with $E\pi$:

$$\pi = E\pi + \frac{1}{\alpha}(Y - \overline{Y}) + v.$$

Third, to go from output to unemployment, recall from Chapter 2 that Okun's law gives a relationship between these two variables. One version of Okun's law states that the deviation of output from its natural level is inversely related to the deviation of unemployment from its natural rate; that is, when output is higher than the natural level of output, unemployment is lower than the natural rate of unemployment. We can write this as

$$\frac{1}{\alpha}(Y - \overline{Y}) = -\beta(u - u^n).$$

Using this Okun's law relationship, we can substitute $-\beta(u - u^n)$ for $(1/\alpha)(Y - \overline{Y})$ in the previous equation to obtain:

$$\pi = E\pi - \beta(u - u^n) + v.$$

Thus, we can derive the Phillips curve equation from the aggregate supply equation.

All this algebra is meant to show one thing: the Phillips curve equation and the short-run aggregate supply equation represent essentially the same macroeconomic ideas. In particular, both equations show a link between real and nominal variables that causes the classical dichotomy (the theoretical separation of real and nominal variables) to break down in the short run. According to the short-run aggregate supply equation, output is related to unexpected movements in the price level. According to the Phillips curve equation, unemployment is related to unexpected movements in the inflation rate. The aggregate supply curve is more

---

[6] *Mathematical note:* This statement is not precise, because inflation is really the *percentage* change in the price level. To make the statement more precise, interpret P as the logarithm of the price level. By the properties of logarithms, the change in P is roughly the inflation rate. The reason is that $dP = d(\log \text{price level}) = d(\text{price level})/\text{price level}$.

The History of the Modern Phillips Curve

The Phillips curve is named after New Zealand-born economist A. W. Phillips. In 1958 Phillips observed a negative relationship between the unemployment rate and the rate of wage inflation in data for the United Kingdom.[7] The Phillips curve that economists use today differs in three ways from the relationship Phillips examined.

First, the modern Phillips curve substitutes price inflation for wage inflation. This difference is not crucial, because price inflation and wage inflation are closely related. In periods when wages are rising quickly, prices are rising quickly as well.

Second, the modern Phillips curve includes expected inflation. This addition is due to the work of Milton Friedman and Edmund Phelps. In developing early versions of the imperfect information model in the 1960s, these two economists emphasized the importance of expectations for aggregate supply.

Third, the modern Phillips curve includes supply shocks. Credit for this addition goes to OPEC, the Organization of Petroleum Exporting Countries. In the 1970s OPEC caused large increases in the world price of oil, which made economists more aware of the importance of shocks to aggregate supply.

convenient when we are studying output and the price level, whereas the Phillips curve is more convenient when we are studying unemployment and inflation. But we should not lose sight of the fact that the Phillips curve and the aggregate supply curve are merely two sides of the same coin.

Adaptive Expectations and Inflation Inertia

To make the Phillips curve useful for analyzing the choices facing policymakers, we need to specify what determines expected inflation. A simple and often plausible assumption is that people form their expectations of inflation based on recently observed inflation. This assumption is called **adaptive expectations.** For example, suppose that people expect prices to rise this year at the same rate as they did last year. Then expected inflation $E\pi$ equals last year's inflation π_{-1}:

$$E\pi = \pi_{-1}.$$

In this case, we can write the Phillips curve as

$$\pi = \pi_{-1} - \beta(u - u^n) + v,$$

---

[7] A. W. Phillips, "The Relationship Between Unemployment and the Rate of Change of Money Wages in the United Kingdom, 1861–1957," *Economica* 25 (November 1958): 283–299.

which states that inflation depends on past inflation, cyclical unemployment, and a supply shock. When the Phillips curve is written in this form, the natural rate of unemployment is sometimes called the *Nonaccelerating Inflation Rate of Unemployment (NAIRU)*.

The first term in this form of the Phillips curve, π_{-1}, implies that inflation has inertia. That is, like an object moving through space, inflation keeps going unless something acts to stop it. In particular, if unemployment is at the NAIRU and if there are no supply shocks, the price level will continue to rise at the rate it has been rising. This inertia arises because past inflation influences expectations of future inflation and because these expectations influence the wages and prices that people set. Robert Solow captured the concept of inflation inertia well when, during the high inflation of the 1970s, he wrote, "Why is our money ever less valuable? Perhaps it is simply that we have inflation because we expect inflation, and we expect inflation because we've had it."

In the model of aggregate supply and aggregate demand, inflation inertia is interpreted as persistent upward shifts in both the aggregate supply curve and the aggregate demand curve. Consider first aggregate supply. If prices have been rising quickly, people will expect them to continue to rise quickly. Because the position of the short-run aggregate supply curve depends on the expected price level, the short-run aggregate supply curve will shift upward over time. It will continue to shift upward until some event, such as a recession or a supply shock, changes inflation and thereby changes expectations of inflation.

The aggregate demand curve must also shift upward to confirm the expectations of inflation. Most often, the continued rise in aggregate demand is due to persistent growth in the money supply. If the Bank of Canada suddenly halted money growth, aggregate demand would stabilize, and the upward shift in aggregate supply would cause a recession. The high unemployment in the recession would reduce inflation and expected inflation, causing inflation inertia to subside.

Two Causes of Rising and Falling Inflation

The second and third terms in the Phillips curve equation show the two forces that can change the rate of inflation.

The second term, $\beta(u - u^n)$, shows that cyclical unemployment—the deviation of unemployment from its natural rate—exerts upward or downward pressure on inflation. Low unemployment pulls the inflation rate up. This is called **demand-pull inflation** because high aggregate demand is responsible for this type of inflation. High unemployment pulls the inflation rate down. The parameter β measures how responsive inflation is to cyclical unemployment.

The third term, v, shows that inflation also rises and falls because of supply shocks. An adverse supply shock, such as the rise in world oil prices in the 1970s, implies a positive value of v and causes inflation to rise. This is called **cost-push inflation** because adverse supply shocks are typically events that push up the costs of production. A beneficial supply shock, such as the oil glut that led to a fall in oil prices in the 1980s, makes v negative and causes inflation to fall.

The Short-Run Tradeoff Between Inflation and Unemployment

Consider the options the Phillips curve gives to a policymaker who can influence aggregate demand with monetary or fiscal policy. At any moment, expected inflation and supply shocks are beyond the policymaker's immediate control. Yet, by changing aggregate demand, the policymaker can alter output, unemployment, and inflation. The policymaker can expand aggregate demand to lower unemployment and raise inflation. Or the policymaker can depress aggregate demand to raise unemployment and lower inflation.

Figure 13-3 plots the Phillips curve equation and shows the short-run tradeoff between inflation and unemployment. When unemployment is at its natural rate ($u = u^n$), inflation depends on expected inflation and the supply shock ($\pi = E\pi + v$). The parameter β determines the slope of the tradeoff between inflation and unemployment. In the short run, for a given level of expected inflation, policymakers can manipulate aggregate demand to choose any combination of inflation and unemployment on this curve, called the *short-run Phillips curve*.

Notice that the position of the short-run Phillips curve depends on the expected rate of inflation. If expected inflation rises, the curve shifts upward, and the policymaker's tradeoff becomes less favourable: inflation is higher for any level of unemployment. Figure 13-4 shows how the tradeoff depends on expected inflation.

Because people adjust their expectations of inflation over time, the tradeoff between inflation and unemployment holds only in the short run. The policymaker cannot keep inflation above expected inflation (and thus unemployment below its natural rate) forever. Eventually, expectations adapt to whatever inflation rate the policymaker has chosen. In the long run, the classical dichotomy holds, unemployment returns to its natural rate, and there is no tradeoff between inflation and unemployment.

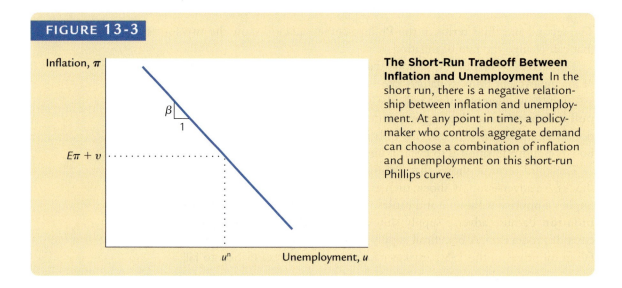

FIGURE 13-3

The Short-Run Tradeoff Between Inflation and Unemployment In the short run, there is a negative relationship between inflation and unemployment. At any point in time, a policymaker who controls aggregate demand can choose a combination of inflation and unemployment on this short-run Phillips curve.

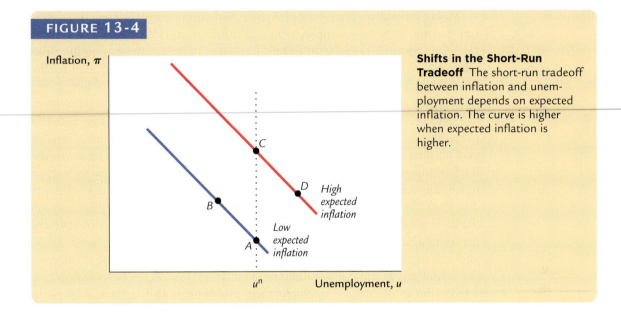

FIGURE 13-4

Inflation, π

C

D High expected inflation

B

Low expected inflation

A

u^n Unemployment, u

Shifts in the Short-Run Tradeoff The short-run tradeoff between inflation and unemployment depends on expected inflation. The curve is higher when expected inflation is higher.

To follow this process explicitly, assume that the economy is initially at point *A* in Figure 13-4—a point at which actual and expected inflation coincide. Then, assume that expansionary monetary or fiscal policy is used to move the economy from point *A* to point *B*. The short-run tradeoff is operating; there are lower unemployment and higher inflation. But the economy cannot stay at point *B* since it involves actual inflation being greater than peoples' expectations of inflation. As individuals revise their expectations upward, there is a tendency for the point showing the economy's outcome to move up in Figure 13-4. Often, in this situation, the government begins to contract aggregate demand—now that it realizes that the inflationary consequences of its previous policy are larger than first assumed. This reaction creates a tendency for the point showing the economy's outcome to move back to the right in Figure 13-4. The net effect of these two tendencies—the upward revision in inflationary expectations and the backing off of aggregate demand policy—is an upward-sloping move from point *B* to point *C*. At this stage, there is not a tradeoff; both unemployment and inflation are rising.

Point *C* is sustainable in the long run. Unemployment has returned to the natural rate and actual and expected inflation are consistent (they are both high). When the government wants to fight inflation, contractionary monetary and fiscal policy move the outcome from point *C* to point *D*. Again we see a short-run tradeoff—inflation falling but unemployment rising. But because actual inflation is less than expected inflation at point *D*, expectations are revised down. The economy spends a long time at point *D* if people are slow to adjust expectations, and there will be a significant sacrifice involved in fighting inflation—a prolonged period of high unemployment.

We can summarize the options for policymakers quite simply. There is a short-run tradeoff between unemployment and inflation, and this fact is indicated by the set of *negatively sloped* relationships in Figure 13-4. But there is no long-run relationship between unemployment and inflation, and this is indicated by the fact that all long-run-sustainable points in Figure 13-4 occur on a *vertical* line (denoted by *AC*). Another way to appreciate the temporary nature of the short-run tradeoff is to focus on the fact that it describes a relationship between *cyclical* unemployment and inflation. Because, by definition, the average level of cyclical unemployment is zero, that average level cannot be dependent on the level of inflation. If policymakers wish to lower the long-run average level of unemployment (that is, if they wish to lower *structural* unemployment—the natural rate), they must not look to monetary policy. Instead they must rely on the fiscal policies that were explored in Chapter 6. If the natural unemployment rate can be lowered by such policies, the increased level of employment would raise the natural level of output $\bar{Y}$. As a result, Okun's law would be unaffected: the output gap would still be related to the unemployment gap. Graphically, then, a reduction in the natural unemployment rate shifts both the vertical long-run Phillips curve and the family of short-run Phillips (with their negative slope unaltered) to the left.

CASE STUDY

Inflation and Unemployment in Canada

Figure 13-5 depicts the history of inflation and unemployment in Canada since 1956. We see that the pre-1970 observations (all squares without a date label) are well summarized by the negatively sloped Phillips curve. During this period, there were few large supply shocks, and the government never allowed aggregate demand to expand so much that a sustained inflation developed. As a result, inflationary expectations played little role.

Then, in the 1970s, things changed. The large supply shock of the OPEC oil-price increases and the government's shift to more expansionary monetary and fiscal policy caused inflation to shoot up with little reduction in unemployment. The time path for the early 1970s is shown by the upward-pointing arrows in Figure 13-5. In the later 1970s, aggregate demand policy was tightened somewhat, and wage and price controls were imposed for the 1975–1978 period. As a result, the economy slid down its short-run Phillips curve; but with inflationary expectations much higher by then, that short-run Phillips curve was farther out from the origin than the earlier one.

The second OPEC shock occurred in 1979. Again, given that demand policy was used to try to insulate unemployment from this event, inflation shot up (see the second set of arrows pointing up in Figure 13-5). By 1981, concern about high inflation peaked, and the Bank of Canada embarked on an enthusiastic disinflation. The contractionary monetary policy pushed the economy down its short-run Phillips curve once again (see the arrows that are farthest to the right in Figure 13-5). But, after two bouts of high inflation, inflationary expectations

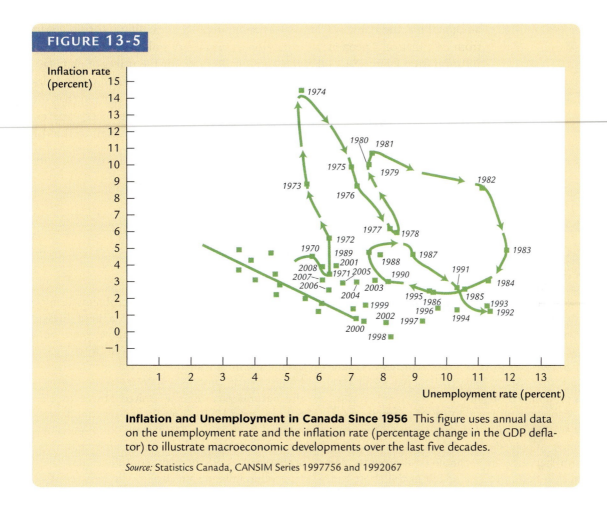

FIGURE 13-5

Inflation and Unemployment in Canada Since 1956 This figure uses annual data on the unemployment rate and the inflation rate (percentage change in the GDP deflator) to illustrate macroeconomic developments over the last five decades.

Source: Statistics Canada, CANSIM Series 1997756 and 1992067

had ratcheted up to very high levels. As a result the short-run Phillips curve was even farther out from the origin.

Both actual and expected inflation came down during the 1981–1985 period. Perhaps because the inflation problem had become less severe, there was a partial reverse of policy in the 1986–1990 period, so unemployment fell and inflation started rising again. The arrows for this period in Figure 13-5 indicate that Canada's short-run Phillips curve had returned part of the way back toward the origin by then (and this is consistent with the fact that lower inflationary expectations had become widespread by then).

Beginning in 1990, the second contractionary monetary policy was initiated. Again, inflation dropped quite dramatically, while unemployment was pushed higher again. By 1993, the battle against inflation had been won, but it took the remainder of the decade for unemployment to come down significantly. With the recession of 2009, the unemployment rate shot up by 2.5 percentage points in the first half of the year, and—as predicted by the Phillips curve—inflation came down a little. There were two reasons why inflation receded by only a small amount. First, the Bank of Canada was committed to not letting inflation depart from its target of 2 percent, so expansionary monetary policy was used to keep inflation from falling. Second, while the inflation rate for the prices of manufactured goods did fall, this was cancelled out—in terms of the overall GDP deflator inflation rate—by rising commodity prices. All in all, we can see that the modern Phillips curve (augmented by supply shocks and inflationary expectations) is a very useful vehicle for interpreting Canada's unemployment and inflation experience of the last 50 years. ■

FYI

How Precise Are Estimates of the Natural Rate of Unemployment?

Ask an astronomer how far a particular star is from our sun, and you'll get a number, but it won't be accurate. Our ability to measure astronomical distances is still limited. An astronomer might well take better measurements and conclude that a star is really twice or half as far away as previously thought.

Estimates of natural rate of unemployment, or NAIRU, are also far from precise. One problem is supply shocks. Shocks to oil supplies, farm harvests, or technological progress can cause inflation to rise or fall in the short run. When we observe rising inflation, therefore, we cannot be sure if it is evidence that the unemployment rate is below the natural rate or evidence that the economy is experiencing an adverse supply shock.

A second problem is that the natural rate changes over time. Demographic changes (such as the aging of the baby boom generation), policy changes (such as in the generosity of employment insurance), and institutional changes (such as the declining role of unions) all influence the economy's normal level of unemployment. Estimating the natural rate is like hitting a moving target.

Economists deal with these problems using statistical techniques that yield a best guess about the natural rate and allow them to gauge the uncertainty associated with their estimates. In one such study, Douglas Staiger, James Stock, and Mark Watson estimated the natural rate for the United States to be 6.2 percent in 1990, with a 95 percent confidence interval from 5.1 to 7.7 percent. A 95 percent confidence interval is a range such that the statistician is 95 percent confident that the true value falls in that range. The large confidence interval here of 2.6 percentage points shows that estimates of the natural rate are not at all precise. While the Canadian studies of the natural rate have not been quite as explicit presenting the confidence interval involved, the results are similar. In 2005, the point estimate for Canada's NAIRU was 6 percent (see Figure 6-1).

This conclusion has profound implications. Policymakers may want to keep unemployment close to its natural rate, but their ability to do so is limited by the fact that they cannot be sure what the natural rate is.[8]

---

[8] Douglas Staiger, James H. Stock, and Mark W. Watson, "How Precise Are Estimates of the Natural Rate of Unemployment?" in Christina D. Romer and David H. Romer, eds., *Reducing Inflation: Motivation and Strategy* (Chicago: University of Chicago Press, 1997).

Disinflation and the Sacrifice Ratio

Imagine an economy in which unemployment is at its natural rate and inflation is running at 6 percent. What would happen to unemployment and output if the central bank pursued a policy to reduce inflation from 6 to 2 percent?

The Phillips curve shows that in the absence of a beneficial supply shock, lowering inflation requires a period of high unemployment and reduced output. But by how much and for how long would unemployment need to rise above the natural rate? Before deciding whether to reduce inflation, policymakers must know how much output would be lost during the transition to lower inflation. This cost can then be compared with the benefits of lower inflation.

Much research has used the available data to examine the Phillips curve quantitatively. The results of these studies are often summarized in a number called the **sacrifice ratio,** the percentage of a year's real GDP that must be forgone to reduce inflation by 1 percentage point. Estimates of the sacrifice ratio vary substantially—between 2 percent and 5 percent. These estimates mean that, for every percentage point that inflation is to fall, something between 2 percent and 5 percent of one year's GDP must be sacrificed.[9]

We can also express the sacrifice ratio in terms of unemployment. Okun's law says that a change of 1 percentage point in the unemployment rate translates into a change of 2 percentage points in GDP. Therefore, reducing inflation by 1 percentage point requires between 1 percentage point and 2.5 percentage points of cyclical unemployment.

We can use the midrange values for the sacrifice ratio to estimate by how much and for how long unemployment must rise to reduce inflation. If reducing inflation by 1 percentage point requires a sacrifice of 3.5 percent of a year's GDP, reducing inflation by 4 percentage points requires a sacrifice of 14 percent of a year's GDP. Equivalently, this reduction in inflation requires a sacrifice of 7 percentage points of cyclical unemployment.

This disinflation could take various forms, each totaling the same sacrifice of 14 percent of a year's GDP. For example, a rapid disinflation would lower output by 7 percent for 2 years: this is sometimes called the *cold-turkey* solution to inflation. A gradual disinflation would depress output by 2 percent for 7 years.

Rational Expectations and the Possibility of Painless Disinflation

Because the expectation of inflation influences the short-run tradeoff between inflation and unemployment, it is crucial to understand how people form expectations. So far, we have been assuming that expected inflation depends on recently observed

[9] Barry Cozier and G. Wilkinson, *Some Evidence on Hysteresis and the Costs of Disinflation in Canada,* Technical Report No. 55 (Ottawa: Bank of Canada, 1991); William M. Scarth, "Fighting Inflation: Are the Costs of Getting to Zero Too High?," in Robert C. York, ed., *Taking Aim: The Debate on Zero Inflation,* Study No. 10 (Toronto: C.D. Howe Institute, 1990): 81–103.

inflation. Although this assumption of adaptive expectations is plausible, it is probably too simple to apply in all circumstances.

An alternative approach is to assume that people have **rational expectations.** That is, we might assume that people optimally use all the available information, including information about current government policies, to forecast the future. Because monetary and fiscal policies influence inflation, expected inflation should also depend on the monetary and fiscal policies in effect. According to the theory of rational expectations, a change in monetary or fiscal policy will change expectations, and an evaluation of any policy change must incorporate this effect on expectations. If people do form their expectations rationally, then inflation may have less inertia than it first appears.

Here is how Thomas Sargent, a prominent advocate of rational expectations, describes its implications for the Phillips curve:

> An alternative "rational expectations" view denies that there is any inherent momentum to the present process of inflation. This view maintains that firms and workers have now come to expect high rates of inflation in the future and that they strike inflationary bargains in light of these expectations. However, it is held that people expect high rates of inflation in the future precisely because the government's current and prospective monetary and fiscal policies warrant those expectations. . . . Thus inflation only seems to have a momentum of its own; it is actually the long-term government policy of persistently running large deficits and creating money at high rates which imparts the momentum to the inflation rate. An implication of this view is that inflation can be stopped much more quickly than advocates of the "momentum" view have indicated and that their estimates of the length of time and the costs of stopping inflation in terms of foregone output are erroneous. . . . [Stopping inflation] would require a change in the policy regime: there must be an abrupt change in the continuing government policy, or strategy, for setting deficits now and in the future that is sufficiently binding as to be widely believed. . . . How costly such a move would be in terms of foregone output and how long it would be in taking effect would depend partly on how resolute and evident the government's commitment was.[10]

Thus, advocates of rational expectations argue that the short-run Phillips curve does not accurately represent the options that policymakers have available. They believe that if policymakers are credibly committed to reducing inflation, rational people will understand the commitment and will quickly lower their expectations of inflation. Inflation can then come down without a rise in unemployment and fall in output. According to the theory of rational expectations, traditional estimates of the sacrifice ratio are not useful for evaluating the impact of alternative policies. Under a credible policy, the costs of reducing inflation may be much lower than estimates of the sacrifice ratio suggest.

In the most extreme case, one can imagine reducing the rate of inflation without causing any recession at all. A painless disinflation has two requirements.

---

[10] Thomas J. Sargent, "The Ends of Four Big Inflations," in Robert E. Hall, ed., *Inflation: Causes and Effects* (Chicago: University of Chicago Press, 1982).

First, the plan to reduce inflation must be announced before the workers and firms who set wages and prices have formed their expectations. Second, the workers and firms must believe the announcement; otherwise, they will not reduce their expectations of inflation. If both requirements are met, the announcement will immediately shift the short-run tradeoff between inflation and unemployment downward, permitting a lower rate of inflation without higher unemployment.

Although the rational-expectations approach remains controversial, almost all economists agree that expectations of inflation influence the short-run tradeoff between inflation and unemployment. The credibility of a policy to reduce inflation is therefore one determinant of how costly the policy will be. Unfortunately, it is often difficult to predict whether the public will view the announcement of a new policy as credible. The central role of expectations makes forecasting the results of alternative policies far more difficult.

CASE STUDY

The Sacrifice Ratio in Practice

The Phillips curve with adaptive expectations implies that reducing inflation requires a period of high unemployment and low output. By contrast, the rational-expectations approach suggests that reducing inflation can be much less costly. What happens during actual disinflations?

Consider the Canadian disinflation in the 1980s. This decade began with inflation over 10 percent. Yet because of the tight monetary policies pursued by the Bank of Canada, the rate of inflation fell substantially in the first few years of the decade. This episode provides a natural experiment with which to estimate how much output is lost during the process of disinflation.

The first question is, how much did inflation fall? As measured by the GDP deflator, inflation reached a peak of 10.8 percent in 1981 and then hit a low of 2.5 percent by the end of 1985. Thus, we can estimate that the Bank of Canada engineered a reduction in inflation of 8.3 points over four years.

The second question is, how much output was lost during this period? Table 13-1 shows the unemployment rate from 1982 to 1985. Assuming that the natural rate of unemployment in the early 1980s was 8.5 percent (see Figure 6-1), we can compute the amount of cyclical unemployment in each year. In total over this period, there were 11.5 point-years of cyclical unemployment. Okun's law says that 1 percentage point of unemployment implies 2 percentage points of GDP. Therefore, 22 percentage points of annual GDP were lost during the disinflation.

Now we can compute the sacrifice ratio for this episode. We know that 22 percentage points of GDP were lost, and that inflation fell by 8.3 percentage points. Hence, 22/8.3, or 2.7, percentage points of GDP were lost for each percentage-point reduction in inflation. The estimate of the sacrifice ratio from the disinflation of the 1980s is 2.7.

TABLE 13-1

Unemployment During the Disinflation of the 1980s

Year	Unemployment Rate	Natural Rate	Cyclical Unemployment
1982	11.0%	8.5%	2.5%
1983	11.8	8.5	3.3
1984	11.2	8.5	3.7
1985	10.5	8.5	2.0
			Total 11.5%

This estimate of the sacrifice ratio is at the low end of the estimates made before this episode. Why is it that inflation was reduced at a smaller cost than many economists had predicted? One explanation is that the contractionary monetary policy of the early 1980s was far more dramatic than the earlier less-concerted attempts to reduce inflation. Perhaps the Bank of Canada's tough stand was credible enough to influence expectations of inflation directly. Yet the change in expectations was not large enough to make the disinflation painless: in 1983 unemployment reached its highest level since the Great Depression.

Another interpretation of our estimate of the sacrifice ratio is that it is a miscalculation. In the three years previous to the disinflation policy, the unemployment rate was 7.5 percent, and this value was what most Canadian economists (including those working at the Bank of Canada) had been estimating the natural unemployment rate to be back then. If we change the third column of Table 13-1 to a series of 7.5 percent entries, instead of a column of 8.5 percent entries, the total point-years of cyclical unemployment over this period rises from 11.5 percent to 15.5 percent. The estimated sacrifice ratio jumps to 3.7 percent, not 2.7 percent. Furthermore, since unemployment did not return to 7.5 percent until 1989, it can be argued that the cyclical unemployment in the 1986–1988 period should also be attributed to the disinflation policy. During the 1986–1988 years there was an additional 3.6 point-years of cyclical unemployment, and counting this additional excess capacity boosts the overall sacrifice ratio to 4.6. Thus, disinflation is seen as much more costly if a lower estimate of the natural unemployment rate is used in the calculations.

Which estimate of the natural rate is more credible? A glance back at Figure 6-1 suggests that the natural rate *did* rise form 7.5 percent to 8.5 percent over this period. But the important issue is *why*. If this rise is due to such things as increased generosity of the employment-insurance system, as some believe, then our first estimate of the sacrifice ratio using the 8.5 percent natural rate is the better one. But if the natural unemployment rate rose *only because* the actual unemployment rate did, then our second estimate of the sacrifice ratio is more accurate.

The possibility that the natural rate could depend on the actual rate is discussed more fully in the next section of this chapter. It remains a controversial topic of current research. At this point, economists must simply admit that their estimates of the sacrifice ratio are not pinned down with a great degree of accuracy.

Another controversy concerning estimates of the sacrifice ratio stems from the fact that the contractionary monetary policy in the early 1980s forced the federal government's debt–to–GDP ratio to rise dramatically in the latter half of the 1980s. By raising interest rates, the Bank of Canada magnified the government's debt service payment obligations, and by slowing economic growth the Bank cut government revenues. Both these developments increased the budget deficit. Since unemployment then had to be pushed up during the 1990s, as contractionary fiscal policy was used to eliminate the deficit, it can be argued that some of this excess unemployment should be attributed to the disinflation. Allowing for this, the estimated sacrifice ratio is very large.

Although the Canadian disinflation of the 1980s is only one historical episode, this kind of analysis can be applied to other disinflations. One study documented the results of 65 disinflations in 19 countries. In almost all these episodes, the reduction in inflation came at the cost of temporarily lower output. Yet the size of the output loss varied from episode to episode. Rapid disinflations usually had smaller sacrifice ratios than slower ones. That is, in contrast to what the Phillips curve with adaptive expectations suggests, a cold-turkey approach appears less costly than a gradual one. Moreover, countries with more flexible wage-setting institutions, such as shorter labour contracts, had smaller sacrifice ratios. These findings indicate that reducing inflation always has some cost, but that policies and institutions can affect its magnitude.[11] ∎

Challenges to the Natural-Rate Hypothesis

Our discussion of the cost of disinflation—and indeed our entire discussion of economic fluctuations in the past four chapters—has been based on an assumption called the **natural-rate hypothesis.** This hypothesis is summarized in the following statement:

> *Fluctuations in aggregate demand affect output and employment only in the short run. In the long run, the economy returns to the levels of output, employment, and unemployment described by the classical model.*

The natural-rate hypothesis allows macroeconomists to study separately short-run and long-run developments in the economy. It is one expression of the classical dichotomy.

Recently, three challenges have been posed for the natural-rate hypothesis. First, it has been pointed out that the observations on inflation and unemployment in the 1990s are, at first blush, puzzling when interpreted within this model. In Canada, for example, by 1993, inflation was essentially a constant at

---

[11] Laurence Ball, "What Determines the Sacrifice Ratio?" in N. Gregory Mankiw, ed., *Monetary Policy* (Chicago: University of Chicago Press, 1994).

about 1.5–2.0 percent. The Bank of Canada's target was being met on a consistent basis. Surely, argue the critics, in such a situation, expectations of inflation must have settled at about this same number without too much of a time lag. If so, the natural-rate model implies that the observed unemployment rate must be the natural rate. But since Canada's unemployment rate remained above 9 percent until 1998, this reasoning means that Canada's natural rate was this very high number for much of the decade. Since few economists can think of structural reasons why this should be so, the natural-rate hypothesis seems to be threatened.

We should not be too quick to jump to this conclusion, however. After all, for simplicity's sake, our derivation of the expectations-augmented Phillips curve has abstracted from open-economy considerations. Let us briefly indicate how things change when this simplification is not involved. In a closed-economy model, with labour as the only variable factor in the short run, markup pricing involves prices rising by the same amount as wages: $\Delta P/P = \Delta W/W$. In an open economy, with both labour and imported intermediate products as variable factors in the short run, markup pricing involves

$$\frac{\Delta P}{P} = \frac{\Delta W}{W} + \gamma \frac{\Delta R}{R}$$

where R denotes the raw material price that must be paid for these imported inputs and γ stands for the importance of intermediate imports in the production of final goods. Combining this markup pricing relationship with a Phillips curve determining wage changes, where the 'e' superscript denotes expectations.

$$\frac{\Delta W}{W} = \left(\frac{\Delta P}{P}\right)^{e} - \beta(u - u^{n}),$$

we have

$$\frac{\Delta P}{P} = \left(\frac{\Delta P}{P}\right)^{e} - \beta(u - u^{n}) + \gamma \frac{\Delta R}{R}.$$

Even when expectations are fully realized, this relationship does not imply that the actual unemployment rate equals the natural rate. Instead, unemployment is given by

$$u = u^{n} + \left(\frac{\gamma}{\beta}\right) \left(\frac{\Delta R}{R}\right).$$

Since the price Canadian firms must pay for intermediate imports rises whenever our real exchange rate falls, and since Canada's real exchange rate was falling significantly through the 1990s, the last term in this equation was positive throughout this period. Thus, the open-economy version of the natural-rate hypothesis implies that Canada's actual unemployment rate exceeded our natural rate during this period after all.

This reasoning helps makes sense of the American experience in the 1990s as well. Given the closed-economy version of the natural-rate hypothesis, analysts

FIGURE 13-6

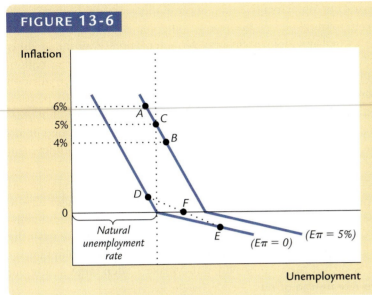

Implications of a Nonlinear Short-Run Phillips Curve Shocks push the economy between points *A* and *B* (with an average outcome given by *C*) if a high inflation target is adopted. Shocks push the economy between points *D* and *E* (with an average outcome of *F*) if a low inflation target is chosen. The low target makes higher average unemployment possible.

were puzzled as to why U.S. inflation did not accelerate in the late 1990s when the U.S. unemployment rate fell below 4 percent. Many thought that the natural rate was not this low and, with actual and expected inflation likely coinciding at the time, the model predicts rising inflation. But, once again, the last equation directs our attention to the real exchange rate. The Americans' real exchange rate was rising through the 1990s, and the equation indicates that—with no inflation surprises—the actual unemployment rate must fall below the natural rate. So exchange-rate considerations can go a long way toward answering this challenge to the natural-rate hypothesis.

The second challenge stems from the proposition that the family of short-run Phillips curves may be *curves,* not straight lines as shown in earlier figures in this chapter. The reason why this might be the case is that wages tend to be less sticky in the upward direction than they are when market pressures are pushing wages down. Statistical studies lend some support to this concern, and Figure 13-6 indicates why this can be important. Figure 13-6 shows two short-run Phillips curves that embody this relative downward rigidity hypothesis in a dramatic way; each Phillips curve is steep when positive inflation is involved and quite flat when negative inflation is involved. One short-run Phillips curve corresponds to underlying expectations of inflation equal to 5 percent, and the other is relevant for zero inflationary expectations.

We compare two long-run situations. First, suppose that the economy has average inflation of 5 percent, but shocks push the economy back and forth between points *A* and *B*. Half the time inflation is 6 percent, and the other half of the time inflation is 4 percent. Because the average is 5 percent, it is reasonable to assume inflationary expectations of 5 percent. What are the implications of this volatility for unemployment? Again, because the economy bounces back and forth between points A and B, the average outcome is point C, which corresponds to the natural unemployment rate. Now let us see how things differ when the volatility shifts the outcome between the steep and the flatter regions of a short-run Phillips curve. This occurs in Figure 13-6 if the average inflation rate is zero. In this case, if inflation fluctuates between plus and minus 1 percent, the economy moves between points D and E. Average inflation is zero, but average unemployment is given by the intersection of the straight line joining points D and E and the horizontal axis—that is, by point F. The average unemployment rate exceeds the natural rate.

Thus, as long as the Phillips curve is flatter at low inflation rates and the economy is subject to ongoing shocks, then there is a long-run tradeoff after all—in an average outcomes sense. It appears that we can have lower average unemployment if we choose a small positive inflation rate—enough to make what the evidence shows is a small degree of nonlinearity in the short-run Phillips curves not matter. This is one of the reasons why policymakers often target a low but positive inflation rate instead of zero.

There is one other argument that some economists have stressed to explain why aggregate demand may affect output and employment even in the long run. They have pointed out a number of mechanisms through which recessions might leave permanent scars on the economy by altering the natural rate of unemployment. **Hysteresis** is the term used to describe the long-lasting influence of history on the natural rate, and hysteresis is the third challenge to the natural-rate hypothesis.

A recession can have permanent effects if it changes the people who become unemployed. For instance, workers might lose valuable job skills when unemployed, lowering their ability to find a job even after the recession ends. Alternatively, a long period of unemployment may change an individual's attitude toward work and reduce his desire to find employment. In either case, the recession permanently inhibits the process of job search and raises the amount of frictional unemployment.

Another way in which a recession can permanently affect the economy is by changing the process that determines wages. Those who become unemployed may lose their influence on the wage-setting process. Unemployed workers may lose their status as union members, for example. More generally, some of the *insiders* in the wage-setting process become *outsiders*. If the smaller group of insiders cares more about high real wages and less about high employment, then the recession may permanently push real wages further above the equilibrium level and raise the amount of wait unemployment.

Hysteresis remains a controversial theory. Some economists believe the theory helps explain persistently high unemployment in Europe, for the rise in European unemployment starting in the early 1980s coincided with disinflation but continued after inflation stabilized. Moreover, the increase in unemployment tended to be larger for those countries that experienced the greatest reductions in inflations, such as Ireland, Italy, and Spain. Yet there is still no consensus whether the hysteresis phenomenon is significant, or why it might be more pronounced in some countries than in others. (Other explanations of high European unemployment, discussed in Chapter 6, give little role to the disinflation.) If true, however, the theory is important, because hysteresis greatly increases the cost of recessions. Put another way, hysteresis raises the sacrifice ratio, because output is lost even after the period of disinflation is over.[12]

13-3 Conclusion

We began this chapter by discussing two models of aggregate supply, each of which focuses on a different reason why in the short run, output rises above its natural level when the price level rises above the level that people had expected. Both models explain why the short-run aggregate supply curve is upward sloping, and both yield a short-run tradeoff between inflation and unemployment. A convenient way to express and analyze that tradeoff is with the Phillips-curve equation, according to which inflation depends on expected inflation, cyclical unemployment, and supply shocks.

Keep in mind that not all economists endorse all the ideas discussed here. There is widespread disagreement, for instance, about the practical importance of rational expectations and the relevance of hysteresis. If you find it difficult to fit all the pieces together, you are not alone. The study of aggregate supply remains one of the most unsettled—and therefore one of the most exciting—research areas in macroeconomics.

Summary

1. The two theories of aggregate supply—the sticky-price, and imperfect-information models—attribute deviations of output and employment from their natural levels to various market imperfections. According to both theories, output rises above the natural level when the price level exceeds the expected price level, and output falls below the natural level when the price level is less than the expected price level.

2. Economists often express aggregate supply in a relationship called the Phillips curve. The Phillips curve says that inflation depends on expected inflation, the deviation of unemployment from its natural rate, and supply

---

[12] Olivier J. Blanchard and Lawrence H. Summers, "Beyond the Natural Rate Hypothesis," *American Economic Review* 78 (May 1988): 182–187; Laurence Ball, "Disinflation and the NAIRU," in Christina D. Romer and David H. Romer, eds., *Reducing Inflation: Motivation and Strategy* (Chicago: University of Chicago Press, 1997): 167–185.

shocks. According to the Phillips curve, policymakers who control aggregate demand face a short-run tradeoff between inflation and unemployment.

3. If expected inflation depends on recently observed inflation, then inflation has inertia, which means that reducing inflation requires either a beneficial supply shock or a period of high unemployment and reduced output. If people have rational expectations, however, then a credible announcement of a change in policy might be able to influence expectations directly and, therefore, reduce inflation without causing a recession.

4. Most economists accept the natural-rate hypothesis, according to which fluctuations in aggregate demand have only short-run effects on output and unemployment. Yet some economists have suggested ways in which recessions can leave permanent scars on the economy by raising the natural rate of unemployment.

KEY CONCEPTS

Sticky-price model

Imperfect-information model

Phillips curve

Adaptive expectations

Demand-pull inflation

Cost-push inflation

Sacrifice ratio

Rational expectations

Natural-rate hypothesis

Hysteresis

QUESTIONS FOR REVIEW

1. Explain the two theories of aggregate supply. On what market imperfection does each theory rely? What do the theories have in common?

2. How is the Phillips curve related to aggregate supply?

3. Why might inflation be inertial?

4. Explain the differences between demand-pull inflation and cost-push inflation.

5. Under what circumstances might it be possible to reduce inflation without causing a recession?

6. Explain two ways in which a recession might raise the natural rate of unemployment.

PROBLEMS AND APPLICATIONS

1. In the sticky-price model, describe the aggregate supply curve in the following special cases. How do these cases compare to the short-run aggregate supply curve we discussed in Chapter 9?

   a. No firms have flexible prices ($s = 1$).

   b. The desired price does not depend on aggregate output ($a = 0$).

2. Suppose that an economy has the Phillips curve

$$\pi = \pi_{-1} - 0.5(u - 0.06).$$

   a. What is the natural rate of unemployment?

   b. Graph the short-run and long-run relationships between inflation and unemployment.

c. How much cyclical unemployment is necessary to reduce inflation by 5 percentage points? Using Okun's law, compute the sacrifice ratio.

d. Inflation is running at 10 percent. The Fed wants to reduce it to 5 percent. Give two scenarios that will achieve that goal.

3. According to the rational-expectations approach, if everyone believes that policymakers are committed to reducing inflation, the cost of reducing inflation—the sacrifice ratio—will be lower than if the public is skeptical about the policymakers' intentions. Why might this be true? How might credibility be achieved?

4. Suppose that the economy is initially at a long-run equilibrium. Then the central bank increases the money supply.

   a. Assuming any resulting inflation to be unexpected, explain any changes in GDP, unemployment, and inflation that are caused by the monetary expansion. Explain your conclusions using three diagrams: one for the *IS–LM* model, one for the *AD–AS* model, and one for the Phillips curve.

   b. Assuming instead that any resulting inflation is expected, explain any changes in GDP, unemployment, and inflation that are caused by the monetary expansion. Once again, explain your conclusions using three diagrams: one for the *IS–LM* model, one for the *AD–AS* model, and one for the Phillips curve.

5. Assume that people have rational expectations and that the economy is described by the sticky-price model. Explain why each of the following propositions is true:

   a. Only unanticipated changes in the money supply affect real GDP. Changes in the money supply that were anticipated when prices were set do not have any real effects.

   b. If the Bank of Canada chooses the money supply at the same time as people are setting prices, so that everyone has the same information about the state of the economy, then monetary policy cannot be used systematically to stabilize output. Hence, a policy of keeping the money supply constant will have

the same real effects as a policy of adjusting the money supply in response to the state of the economy. (This is called the *policy irrelevance proposition*.)

   c. If the Bank of Canada sets the money supply well after people have set prices, so the Bank of Canada has collected more information about the state of the economy, then monetary policy can be used systematically to stabilize output.

6. Suppose that an economy has the Phillips curve

$$\pi = \pi_{-1} - 0.5(u - u^n),$$

and that the natural rate of unemployment is given by an average of the past two years' unemployment:

$$u^n = 0.5(u_{-1} + u_{-2}).$$

   a. Why might the natural rate of unemployment depend on recent unemployment (as is assumed in the above equation)?

   b. Suppose that the Bank of Canada follows a policy to reduce permanently the inflation rate by 1 percentage point. What effect will that policy have on the unemployment rate over time?

   c. What is the sacrifice ratio in this economy? Explain.

   d. What do these equations imply about the short-run and long-run tradeoffs between inflation and unemployment?

7. Some economists believe that taxes have an important effect on labour supply. They argue that higher taxes cause people to want to work less and that lower taxes cause them to want to work more. Consider how this effect alters the macroeconomic analysis of tax changes.

   a. If this view is correct, how does a tax cut affect the natural rate of output?

   b. How does a tax cut affect the aggregate demand curve? The long-run aggregate supply curve? The short-run aggregate supply curve?

   c. What is the short-run impact of a tax cut on output and the price level? How does your answer differ from the case without the labour-supply effect?

d. What is the long-run impact of a tax cut on output and the price level? How does your answer differ from the case without the labour-supply effect?

8. Princeton economist Alan Blinder, who has served as Vice Chairman of the U.S. Federal Reserve, once wrote the following:

> The costs that attend the low and moderate inflation rates experienced in the United States and in other industrial countries appear to be quite modest— more like a bad cold than a cancer on society. . . . As rational individuals, we do not volunteer for a lobotomy to cure a head cold. Yet, as a collectivity, we routinely prescribe the economic equivalent of lobotomy (high unemployment) as a cure for the inflationary cold.[13]

What do you think Blinder meant by this? What are the policy implications of the viewpoint Blinder is advocating? Do you agree? Why or why not?

9. Go to the website of Statistics Canada (www.statcan.ca). For each of the past five years, find the inflation rate as measured by the consumer price index (all items)—sometimes called *headline inflation*—and as measured by the CPI excluding food and energy—sometimes called *core inflation*. Compare these two measures of inflation. Why might they be different? What might the difference tell you about shifts in the aggregate supply curve and in the short-run Phillips curve?

---

[13] Alan Blinder, *Hard Heads, Soft Hearts: Tough-Minded Economics for a Just Society* (Reading, MA: Addison-Wesley, 1987): 51.

A Big, Comprehensive Model

In the previous chapters, we have seen many models of how the economy works. When learning these models, it can be hard to see how they are related. Now that we have finished developing the model of aggregate demand and aggregate supply, this is a good time to look back at what we have learned. This appendix sketches a large comprehensive model that incorporates much of the theory we have already seen, including the classical theory presented in Part Two and the business cycle theory presented in Part Four. The notation and equations should be familiar from previous chapters. The goal is to put much of our previous analysis into a common framework to clarify the relationships among the various models.

The model has seven equations:

$$Y = C(Y - T) + I(r) + G + NX(\epsilon) \qquad \textit{IS: Goods Market Equilibrium}$$

$$M/P = L(i, Y) \qquad \textit{LM: Money Market Equilibrium}$$

$$NX(\epsilon) = CF(r - r^*) \qquad \textit{Foreign Exchange Market Equilibrium}$$

$$i = r + E\pi \qquad \textit{Relationship Between Real and Nominal Interest Rates}$$

$$\epsilon = eP/P^* \qquad \textit{Relationship Between Real and Nominal Exchange Rates}$$

$$Y = \overline{Y} + \alpha(P - EP) \qquad \textit{Aggregate Supply}$$

$$\overline{Y} = F(\overline{K}, \overline{L}) \qquad \textit{Natural Level of Output}$$

These seven equations determine the equilibrium values of seven endogenous variables: output Y, the natural level of output $\overline{Y}$, the real interest rate r, the nominal interest rate i, the real exchange rate ϵ, the nominal exchange rate e, and the price level P.

There are many exogenous variables that influence these endogenous variables. They include the money supply M, government purchases G, taxes T, the capital stock K, the labour force L, the world price level P^*, and the world real interest rate r^*. In addition, there are two expectation variables: the expectation of future inflation $E\pi$ and the expectation of the current price level formed in the past EP. As written, the model takes these expectations as exogenous, although additional equations could be added to make them endogenous.

Although mathematical techniques are available to analyze this seven-equation model, they are beyond the scope of this book. But this large model is still useful, because we can use it to see how the smaller models we have examined are related to one another. In particular, *many of the models we have been studying are special cases of this large model.* Let's consider six special cases in particular. (A problem at the end of this section examines a few more.)

Special Case 1: The Classic Closed Economy

Suppose that $EP = P$, $L(i, Y) = (1/V)Y$ and $CF(r - r^*) = 0$. In words, these equations mean that expectations of the price level adjust so that expectations are correct, that money demand is proportional to income, and that there are no international capital flows. In this case, output is always at its natural level, the real interest rate adjusts to equilibrate the goods market, the price level moves parallel with the money supply, and the nominal interest rate adjusts one-for-one with expected inflation. This special case corresponds to the economy analyzed in Chapters 3 and 4.

Special Case 2: The Classic Small Open Economy

Suppose that $EP = P$, $L(i, Y) = (1/V)Y$, and $CF(r - r^*)$ is infinitely elastic. Now we are examining the special case when international capital flows respond greatly to any differences between the domestic and world interest rates. This means that $r = r^*$ and that the trade balance NX equals the difference between saving and investment at the world interest rate. This special case corresponds to the economy analyzed in Chapter 5.

Special Case 3: The Basic Model of Aggregate Demand and Aggregate Supply

Suppose that α is infinite and $L(i, Y) = (1/V)Y$. In this case, the short-run aggregate supply curve is horizontal, and the aggregate demand curve is determined only by the quantity equation. This special case corresponds to the economy analyzed in Chapter 9.

Special Case 4: The *IS-LM* Model

Suppose that α is infinite and $CF(r - r^*) = 0$. In this case, the short-run aggregate supply curve is horizontal, and there are no international capital flows. For any given level of expected inflation $E\pi$, the level of income and interest rate must adjust to equilibrate the goods market and the money market. This special case corresponds to the economy analyzed in Chapter 10 and 11.

Special Case 5: The Mundell–Fleming Model with a Floating Exchange Rate

Suppose that α is infinite and $CF(r - r^*)$ infinitely elastic. In this case, the short-run aggregate supply curve is horizontal, and international capital flows are so great as to ensure that $r = r^*$. The exchange rate floats freely to reach its equilibrium level. This special case corresponds to the first economy analyzed in Chapter 12.

Special Case 6: The Mundell-Fleming Model with a Fixed Exchange Rate

Suppose that α is infinite, $CF(r - r^*)$ is infinitely elastic, and the nominal exchange rate e is fixed. In this case, the short-run aggregate supply curve is horizontal, huge international capital flows ensure that $r = r^*$, but the exchange rate is set by the central bank. The exchange rate is now an exogenous policy variable, but the money supply M is an endogenous variable that must adjust to ensure the exchange rate hits the fixed level. This special case corresponds to the second economy analyzed in Chapter 12.

You should now see the value in this big model. Even though the model is too large to be useful in developing an intuitive understanding of how the economy works, it shows that the different models we have been studying are closely related. In each chapter, we made some simplifying assumptions to make the big model smaller and easier to understand.

Figure 13-7 presents a schematic diagram that illustrates how various models are related. In particular, it shows how, starting with the mother of all models above, you can arrive at some of the models examined in previous chapters. Here are the steps:

1. *Classical or Keynesian?* You decide whether you want a classical special case (which occurs when $EP = P$ or when α equals zero, so output is at its natural level) or a Keynesian special case (which occurs when α equals infinity, so the price level is completely fixed).

2. *Closed or Open?* You decide whether you want a closed economy (which occurs when the capital flow CF always equals zero) or an open economy (which allows CF to differ from zero).

3. *Floating or Fixed?* If you are examining a small open economy, you decide whether the exchange rate is floating (in which case the central bank sets the money supply) or fixed (in which case the central bank allows the money supply to adjust).

4. *Fixed velocity?* If you are considering a closed economy with the Keynesian assumption of fixed prices, you decide whether you want to focus on the special case in which velocity is exogenously fixed.

By making this series of modeling decisions, you move from the more complete and complex model to a simpler, more narrowly focused special case that is easier to understand and use.

When thinking about the real world, it is important to keep in mind all the models and their simplifying assumptions. Each of these models provides insight into some facet of the economy.

FIGURE 13-7

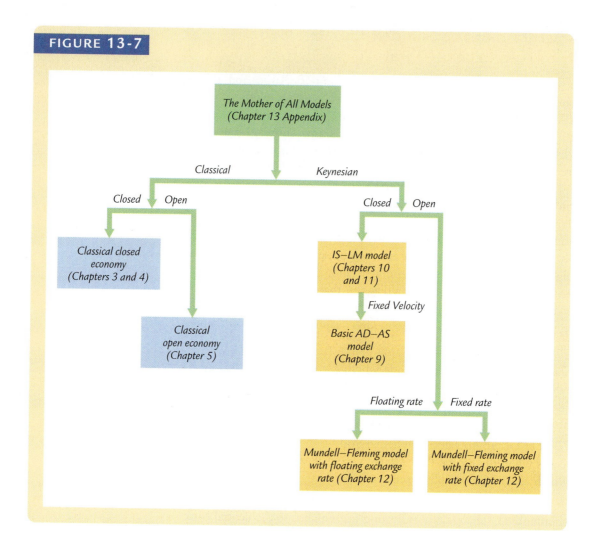

MORE PROBLEMS AND APPLICATIONS

1. Let's consider more special cases of this large model. Starting with the large model, what extra assumptions would you need to yield each of the following models?

   a. The model of the classical large open economy in the appendix to Chapter 5

   b. The Keynesian cross in the first half of Chapter 10

   c. The *IS–LM* model for the large open economy in the appendix to Chapter 12

CHAPTER 14

A Dynamic Model of Aggregate Demand and Aggregate Supply

The important thing in science is not so much to obtain new facts as to discover new ways of thinking about them.

— *William Bragg*

This chapter continues our analysis of short-run economic fluctuations. It presents a model that we will call the *dynamic model of aggregate demand and aggregate supply.* This model offers another lens through which to view the business cycle and the effects of monetary and fiscal policy.

As the name suggests, this new model emphasizes the dynamic nature of economic fluctuations. The dictionary defines the word "dynamic" as "relating to energy or objects in motion, characterized by continuous change or activity." This definition applies readily to economic activity. The economy is continually bombarded by various shocks. These shocks have an immediate impact on the economy's short-run equilibrium, and they also affect the subsequent path of output, inflation, and many other variables. The dynamic *AD–AS* model focuses attention on how output and inflation respond over time to exogenous changes in the economic environment.

In addition to placing greater emphasis on dynamics, the model differs from our previous models in another significant way: it explicitly incorporates the response of monetary policy to economic conditions. In previous chapters, we followed the conventional simplification that the central bank sets the money supply, which in turn is one determinant of the equilibrium interest rate. In the real world, however, many central banks set a target for the interest rate and allow the money supply to adjust to whatever level is necessary to achieve that target. Moreover, the target interest rate set by the central bank depends on economic conditions, including both inflation and output. The dynamic *AD–AS* model builds in these realistic features of monetary policy.

Although the dynamic *AD–AS* model is new to the reader, most of its components are not. Many of the building blocks of this model will be familiar from previous chapters, even though they sometimes take on slightly different forms. More important, these components are assembled in new ways. You can think of this model as a new recipe that mixes familiar ingredients to

459

create a surprisingly original meal. In this case, we will mix familiar economic relationships in a new way to produce deeper insights into the nature of short-run economic fluctuations.

Compared to the models in preceding chapters, the dynamic AD–AS model is closer to those studied by economists at the research frontier. Moreover, economists involved in setting macroeconomic policy, including those working in central banks around the world, often use versions of this model when analyzing the impact of economic events on output and inflation.

14-1 Elements of the Model

Before examining the components of the dynamic AD–AS model, we need to introduce one piece of notation: Throughout this chapter, the subscript t on a variable represents time. For example, Y is used to represent total output and national income, as it has been throughout this book. But now it takes the form Y_t, which represents national income in time period t. Similarly, Y_{t-1} represents national income in period $t - 1$, and Y_{t+1} represents national income in period $t + 1$. This new notation will allow us to keep track of variables as they change over time.

Let's now look at the five equations that make up the dynamic AD–AS model.

Output: The Demand for Goods and Services

The demand for goods and services is given by the equation

$$Y_t = \overline{Y}_t - \alpha \, (r_t - \rho) + \epsilon_t,$$

where Y_t is the total output of goods and services, $\overline{Y}_t$ is the economy's natural level of output, r_t is the real interest rate, ϵ_t is a random demand shock, and α and ρ are parameters greater than zero. This equation is similar in spirit to the demand for goods and services equation in Chapter 3 and the IS equation in Chapter 10. Because this equation is so central to the dynamic AD–AS model, let's examine each of the terms with some care.

The key feature of this equation is the negative relationship between the real interest rate r_t and the demand for goods and services Y_t. When the real interest rate increases, borrowing becomes more expensive, and saving yields a greater reward. As a result, firms engage in fewer investment projects, and consumers save more and spend less. Both of these effects reduce the demand for goods and services. (In addition, the high interest rate may attract foreign funds into the country so that our dollar might appreciate in foreign-exchange markets, causing net exports to fall, but for our purposes in this chapter these open-economy effects need not play a central role and can largely be ignored.) The parameter α tells us how sensitive demand is to changes in the real interest rate. The larger the value of α, the more the demand for goods and services responds to a given change in the real interest rate.

The first term on the right-hand side of the equation, $\overline{Y}_t$, implies that the demand for goods and services rises with the economy's natural level of output. In most cases, we can simplify matters by taking this variable to be constant; that is, $\overline{Y}_t$ will be assumed to be the same for every time period t. We will, however, examine how this model can incorporate long-run growth, represented by exogenous increases in $\overline{Y}_t$ over time. A key piece of that analysis is apparent in this demand equation: as long-run growth makes the economy richer, the demand for goods and services grows proportionately.

The last term in the demand equation, ϵ_t, represents exogenous shifts in demand. Think of ϵ_t as a *random variable*—a variable whose values are determined by chance. It is zero on average but fluctuates over time. For example, if (as Keynes famously suggested) investors are driven in part by "animal spirits"— irrational waves of optimism and pessimism—those changes in sentiment would be captured by ϵ_t. When investors become optimistic, they increase their demand for goods and services, represented here by a positive value of ϵ_t. When they become pessimistic, they cut back on spending, and ϵ_t is negative.

The variable ϵ_t also captures changes in fiscal policy that affect the demand for goods and services. A temporary increase in government spending or a tax cut that stimulates consumer spending means a positive value of ϵ_t. A cut in government spending or a tax hike means a negative value of ϵ_t. Thus, this variable captures a variety of exogenous influences on the demand for goods and services.

Finally, consider the parameter ρ. From a mathematical perspective, ρ is just a constant, but it has a useful economic interpretation. It is the real interest rate at which, in the absence of any shock ($\epsilon_t = 0$), the demand for goods and services equals the natural level of output. We can call ρ the *natural rate of interest*. Throughout this chapter, the natural rate of interest is assumed to be constant (although Problem 7 at the end of the chapter examines what happens if it changes). As we will see, in this model, the natural rate of interest plays a key role in the setting of monetary policy.

The Real Interest Rate: The Fisher Equation

The real interest rate in this model is defined as it has been in earlier chapters. The real interest rate r_t is the nominal interest rate i_t minus the expected rate of future inflation $E_t\pi_{t+1}$. That is,

$$r_t = i_t - E_t\pi_{t+1}.$$

This Fisher equation is similar to the one we first saw in Chapter 4. Here, $E_t\pi_{t+1}$ represents the expectation formed in period t of inflation in period $t + 1$. The variable r_t is the *ex ante* real interest rate: the real interest rate that people anticipate based on their expectation of inflation.

A word on the notation and timing convention should clarify the meaning of these variables. The variables r_t and i_t are interest rates that prevail at time t and, therefore, represent a rate of return between periods t and $t + 1$. The variable π_t

denotes the current inflation rate, which is the percentage change in the price level between periods $t - 1$ and t. Similarly, π_{t+1} is the percentage change in the price level that will occur between periods t and $t + 1$. As of time period t, π_{t+1} represents a future inflation rate and therefore is not yet known.

Note that the subscript on a variable tells us when the variable is determined. The nominal and *ex ante* real interest rates between t and $t + 1$ are known at time t, so they are written as i_t and r_t. By contrast, the inflation rate between t and $t + 1$ is not known until time $t + 1$, so it is written as π_{t+1}.

This subscript rule also applies when the expectations operator E precedes a variable, but here you have to be especially careful. As in previous chapters, the operator E in front of a variable denotes the expectation of that variable prior to its realization. The subscript on the expectations operator tells us when that expectation is formed. So $E_t\pi_{t+1}$ is the expectation of what the inflation rate will be in period $t + 1$ (the subscript on π) based on information available in period t (the subscript on E). While the inflation rate π_{t+1} is not known until period $t + 1$, the expectation of future inflation, $E_t\pi_{t+1}$, is known at period t. As a result, even though the *ex post* real interest rate, which is given by $i_t - \pi_{t+1}$, will not be known until period $t + 1$, the *ex ante* real interest rate, $r_t = i_t - E_t\pi_{t+1}$, is known at time t.

Inflation: The Phillips Curve

Inflation in this economy is determined by a conventional Phillips curve augmented to include roles for expected inflation and exogenous supply shocks. The equation for inflation is

$$\pi_t = E_{t-1}\pi_t + \phi(Y_t - \overline{Y}_t) + v_t.$$

This piece of the model is similar to the Phillips curve and short-run aggregate supply equation introduced in Chapter 13. According to this equation, inflation π_t depends on previously expected inflation $E_{t-1}\pi_t$, the deviation of output from its natural level $(Y_t - \overline{Y}_t)$, and an exogenous supply shock v_t.

Inflation depends on expected inflation because some firms set prices in advance. When these firms expect high inflation, they anticipate that their costs will be rising quickly and that their competitors will be implementing substantial price hikes. The expectation of high inflation thereby induces these firms to announce significant price increases for their own products. These price increases in turn cause high actual inflation in the overall economy. Conversely, when firms expect low inflation, they forecast that costs and competitors' prices will rise only modestly. In this case, they keep their own price increases down, leading to low actual inflation.

The parameter ϕ, which is greater than zero, tells us how much inflation responds when output fluctuates around its natural level. Other things equal, when the economy is booming and output rises above its natural level, firms experience increasing marginal costs, and so they raise prices. When the economy is in recession and output is below its natural level, marginal cost falls, and firms cut prices. The parameter ϕ reflects both how much marginal cost responds to the state of economic activity and how quickly firms adjust prices in response to changes in cost.

In this model, the state of the business cycle is measured by the deviation of output from its natural level $(Y_t - \overline{Y}_t)$. The Phillips curves in Chapter 13 sometimes emphasized the deviation of unemployment from its natural rate. This difference is not significant, however. Recall Okun's law from Chapter 2: Short-run fluctuations in output and unemployment are strongly and negatively correlated. When output is above its natural level, unemployment is below its natural rate, and vice versa. As we continue to develop this model, keep in mind that unemployment fluctuates along with output, but in the opposite direction.

The supply shock v_t is a random variable that averages to zero but could, in any given period, be positive or negative. This variable captures all influences on inflation other than expectations of inflation (which is captured in the first term, $E_{t-1}\pi_t$) and short-run economic conditions [which are captured in the second term, $\phi(Y_t - \overline{Y}_t)$]. For example, if an aggressive oil cartel pushes up world oil prices, thus increasing overall inflation, that event would be represented by a positive value of v_t. Similarly, if a hurricane destroys a number of the oil rigs in the Gulf of Mexico, raising world oil prices and causing inflation to rise, v_t would also be positive. Similar events with effects moving in the opposite direction would make v_t negative. In short, v_t reflects all exogenous events that directly influence inflation.

Expected Inflation: Adaptive Expectations

As we have seen, expected inflation plays a key role in both the Phillips curve equation for inflation and the Fisher equation relating nominal and real interest rates. To keep the dynamic *AD–AS* model simple, we assume that people form their expectations of inflation based on the inflation they have recently observed. That is, people expect prices to continue rising at the same rate they have been rising. This is sometimes called the assumption of *adaptive expectations*. It can be written as

$$E_t\pi_{t+1} = \pi_t.$$

When forecasting in period t what inflation rate will prevail in period $t + 1$, people simply look at inflation in period t and extrapolate it forward.

The same assumption applies in every period. Thus, when inflation was observed in period $t - 1$, people expected that rate to continue. This implies that $E_{t-1}\pi_t = \pi_{t-1}$.

This assumption about inflation expectations is admittedly crude. Many people are probably more sophisticated in forming their expectations. As we discussed in Chapter 13, some economists advocate an approach called *rational expectations,* according to which people optimally use all available information when forecasting the future. Incorporating rational expectations into the model is, however, beyond the scope of this book. (Moreover, the empirical validity of rational expectations is open to dispute.) The assumption of adaptive expectations greatly simplifies the exposition of the theory without losing many of the model's insights.

The Nominal Interest Rate: The Monetary-Policy Rule

The last piece of the model is the equation for monetary policy. We assume that the central bank sets a target for the nominal interest rate i_t based on inflation and output using this rule:

$$i_t = \pi_t + \rho + \theta_\pi(\pi_t - \pi_t^*) + \theta_Y(Y_t - \overline{Y}_t).$$

In this equation, π_t^* is the central bank's target for the inflation rate. (For most purposes, target inflation can be assumed to be constant, but we will keep a time subscript on this variable so we can examine later what happens when the central bank changes its target.) Two key policy parameters are θ_π and θ_Y, which are both assumed to be greater than zero. They indicate how much the central bank allows the interest rate target to respond to fluctuations in inflation and output. The larger the value of θ_π, the more responsive the central bank is to the deviation of inflation from its target; the larger the value of θ_Y, the more aggressive the central bank is in responding to the deviation of output from its natural level. Recall that ρ, the constant in this equation, is the *natural rate of interest* (the real interest rate at which, in the absence of any shock, the demand for goods and services equals the natural level of output). This equation tells us how the central bank uses monetary policy to respond to any situation it faces. That is, it tells us how the target for the nominal interest rate chosen by the central bank responds to macroeconomic conditions.

To interpret this equation, it is best to focus not just on the nominal interest rate i_t but also on the real interest rate r_t. Recall that the real interest rate, rather than the nominal interest rate, influences the demand for goods and services. So, although the central bank sets a target for the nominal interest rate i_t, the bank's influence on the economy works through the real interest rate r_t. By definition, the real interest rate is $r_t = i_t - E_t\pi_{t+1}$, but with our expectation equation $E_t\pi_{t+1} = \pi_t$, we can also write the real interest rate as $r_t = i_t - \pi_t$. According to the equation for monetary policy, if inflation is at its target ($\pi_t = \pi_t^*$) and output is at its natural level ($Y_t = \overline{Y}_t$), the last two terms in the equation are zero, and so the real interest rate equals the natural rate of interest ρ. As inflation rises above its target ($\pi_t > \pi_t^*$) or output rises above its natural level ($Y_t > \overline{Y}_t$), the central bank takes steps to ensure that the real interest rate rises. And as inflation falls below its target ($\pi_t < \pi_t^*$) or output falls below its natural level ($Y_t < \overline{Y}_t$), the central bank engineers a reduction in the real interest rate.

At this point, one might naturally ask: what about the money supply? In previous chapters, such as Chapters 10 and 11, the money supply was typically taken to be the policy instrument of the central bank, and the interest rate adjusted to bring money supply and money demand into equilibrium. Here, we turn that logic on its head. The central bank is assumed to set a target for the nominal interest rate. It then adjusts the money supply to whatever level is necessary to ensure that the equilibrium interest rate (which balances money supply and demand) hits the target.

The main advantage of using the interest rate, rather than the money supply, as the policy instrument in the dynamic *AD–AS* model is that it is more realistic. Today, most central banks, including the Bank of Canada, set a short-term target for the nominal interest rate. Keep in mind, though, that hitting that target requires adjustments in the money supply. For this model, we do not need to specify the

equilibrium condition for the money market, but we should remember that it is lurking in the background. When a central bank decides to change the interest rate, it is also committing itself to adjust the money supply accordingly.

CASE STUDY

The Taylor Rule

If you wanted to set interest rates to achieve low, stable inflation while avoiding large fluctuations in output and employment, how would you do it? This is exactly the question that the members of the governing council at the Bank of Canada must ask themselves every week. The short-term policy instrument that the Bank now sets is the *overnight rate*—the short-term interest rate at which banks make loans to one another. On eight pre-arranged dates each year, the Bank announces its current target for the overnight rate. The Bank's overnight-loan traders are then told to conduct buy and sell orders so that the desired target is met.

The hard part of the Bank's job is choosing the target for the overnight rate. Two general guidelines are clear. First, when inflation heats up, the overnight rate should rise. An increase in the interest rate will mean a smaller money supply and, eventually, lower investment, lower output, higher unemployment, and reduced inflation. Second, when real economic activity slows—as reflected in real GDP or unemployment—the overnight rate should fall. A decrease in the interest rate will mean a larger money supply and, eventually, higher investment, higher output, and lower unemployment. These two guidelines are represented by the monetary-policy equation in the dynamic *AD–AS* model.

The Bank of Canada needs to go beyond these general guidelines, however, and determine its exact response to changes in inflation and real economic activity. Stanford University economist John Taylor has proposed the following rule for setting the similar interest rate in the United States— known as the federal funds rate[1]:

$$\text{Nominal Federal Funds Rate} = \text{Inflation} + 2.0$$
$$+ \; 0.5 \; (\text{Inflation} - 2.0) + 0.5 \; (\text{GDP gap}).$$

The *GDP gap* is the percentage by which real GDP deviates from an estimate of its natural level. (For consistency with our dynamic *AD–AS* model, the GDP gap here is taken to be positive if GDP rises above its natural level and negative if it falls below it.)

According to the **Taylor rule,** the real federal funds rate—the nominal rate minus inflation—responds to inflation and the GDP gap. According to this rule, the real federal funds rate equals 2 percent when inflation is 2 percent and GDP is at its natural level. The first constant of 2 percent in this equation can be interpreted as an estimate of the natural rate of interest ρ, and the second

---

[1] John B. Taylor, "Discretion Versus Policy Rules in Practice," *Carnegie-Rochester Conference Series on Public Policy* 39 (1993): 195–214.

constant of 2 percent subtracted from inflation can be interpreted as the Fed's inflation target π_t^*. For each percentage point that inflation rises above 2 percent, the real federal funds rate rises by 0.5 percent. For each percentage point that real GDP rises above its natural level, the real federal funds rate rises by 0.5 percent. If inflation falls below 2 percent or GDP moves below its natural level, the real federal funds rate falls accordingly.

In addition to being simple and reasonable, the Taylor rule for monetary policy also resembles actual Fed behavior in recent years. Figure 14–1 shows the actual nominal federal funds rate and the target rate as determined by Taylor's proposed rule. Notice how the two series tend to move together. John Taylor's monetary rule may be more than an academic suggestion. To some degree, it may be the rule that the Federal Reserve governors have been subconsciously following.

Canadian monetary policy is conducted in a similar fashion. As in the Taylor rule, the Bank of Canada's target inflation rate has been 2 percent for

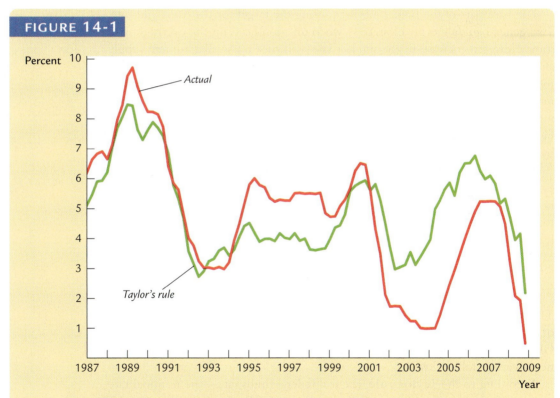

FIGURE 14-1

The Federal Funds Rate: Actual and Suggested This figure shows the federal funds rate set by the Federal Reserve in the United States and the target rate that John Taylor's rule for monetary policy would recommend. Notice that the two series move closely together.

Source: Federal Reserve Board, U.S. Department of Commerce, U.S. Department of Labor, and author's calculations. To implement the Taylor rule, the inflation rate is measured as the percentage change in the GDP deflator over the previous four quarters, and the GDP gap is measured as negative two times the deviation of the unemployment rate from its natural rate (as shown in Figure 6-1).

a number of years. While the Bank has no similar explicit mandate concerning the output gap, Bank officials focus on keeping *future* inflation on target, and they know that—given the Phillips curve—this objective will not be met if the current output gap is allowed to become large. So the Bank reacts to variations in the output gap as well.

As this book went to press, researchers at the Bank of Canada were debating whether it would be better if they targeted the *price level*, not just its rate of change through time—the *inflation rate*. Historical evidence has shown that—perhaps unintentionally—the Bank has actually delivered a time path for Canada's price level that is without any long-term drift away from a growth path of 2 percent. So, as a matter of fact, Canada's performance has been consistent with what would emerge with a price-level target. This is why, in the Appendix to Chapter 11, we investigated a macro model with the central bank being an interest-rate setter (as in the present chapter) but without the dynamics that we are dealing with here. By modeling the central bank as targeting the price level rather than its time derivative, the inflation rate, the analysis in the Chapter 11 Appendix was much simpler and only slightly less realistic. One of the reasons for including the present chapter is to reassure readers that our Chapter 11 simplification avoiding explicit dynamics did not lead us astray. The more complete dynamic analysis in the present chapter is what provides this reassurance, and what permits readers to get a more complete glimpse of what current research-level analysis of monetary policy is actually like. ■

14-2 Solving the Dynamic Model

We have now looked at each of the pieces of the dynamic *AD–AS* model. To summarize, here are the five equations that make up the model:

$$Y_t = \overline{Y}_t - \alpha\,(r_t - \rho) + \epsilon_t \qquad\qquad \text{The Demand for Goods and Services}$$

$$r_t = i_t - E_t\pi_{t+1} \qquad\qquad \text{The Fisher Equation}$$

$$\pi_t = E_{t-1}\pi_t + \phi(Y_t - \overline{Y}_t) + v_t \qquad\qquad \text{The Phillips Curve}$$

$$E_t\pi_{t+1} = \pi_t \qquad\qquad \text{Adaptive Expectations}$$

$$i_t = \pi_t + \rho + \theta_\pi(\pi_t - \pi_t^*) + \theta_Y(Y_t - \overline{Y}_t) \qquad \text{The Monetary-Policy Rule}$$

These five equations determine the paths of the model's five endogenous variables: output Y_t, the real interest rate r_t, inflation π_t, expected inflation $E_t\pi_{t+1}$, and the nominal interest rate i_t.

Table 14-1 lists all the variables and parameters in the model. In any period, the five endogenous variables are influenced by the four exogenous variables in the equations as well as the previous period's inflation rate. Lagged inflation π_{t-1} is called a *predetermined variable*. That is, it is a variable that was endogenous in the past but, because it is fixed by the time when we arrive in period *t,* is essentially exogenous for the purposes of finding the current equilibrium.

TABLE 14-1

The Variables and Parameters in the Dynamic *AD–AS* Model

Endogenous Variables

Y_t	Output
π_t	Inflation
r_t	Real interest rate
i_t	Nominal interest rate
$E_t\pi_{t+1}$	Expected inflation

Exogenous Variables

$\overline{Y}_t$	Natural level of output
π_t^*	Central bank's target for inflation
ϵ_t	Shock to the demand for goods and services
v_t	Shock to the Phillips curve (supply shock)

Predetermined Variable

π_{t-1}	Previous period's inflation

Parameters

α	The responsiveness of the demand for goods and services to the real interest rate
ρ	The natural rate of interest
ϕ	The responsiveness of inflation to output in the Phillips curve
θ_π	The responsiveness of the nominal interest rate to inflation in the monetary-policy rule
θ_Y	The responsiveness of the nominal interest rate to output in the monetary-policy rule

We are almost ready to put these pieces together to see how various shocks to the economy influence the paths of these variables over time. Before doing so, however, we need to establish the starting point for our analysis: the economy's long-run equilibrium.

The Long-Run Equilibrium

The long-run equilibrium represents the normal state around which the economy fluctuates. It occurs when there are no shocks ($\epsilon_t = v_t = 0$) and inflation has stabilized ($\pi_t = \pi_{t-1}$).

Straightforward algebra applied to the above five equations can be used to verify these long-run values:

$$Y_t = \overline{Y}_t.$$

$$r_t = \rho.$$

$$\pi_t = \pi_t^*.$$

$$E_t \pi_{t+1} = \pi_t^*.$$

$$i_t = \rho + \pi_t^*.$$

In words, the long-run equilibrium is described as follows: output and the real interest rate are at their natural values, inflation and expected inflation are at the target rate of inflation, and the nominal interest rate equals the natural rate of interest plus target inflation.

The long-run equilibrium of this model reflects two related principles: the classical dichotomy and monetary neutrality. Recall that the classical dichotomy is the separation of real from nominal variables, and monetary neutrality is the property according to which monetary policy does not influence real variables. The equations immediately above show that the central bank's inflation target π_t^* influences only inflation π_t, expected inflation $E_t \pi_{t+1}$, and the nominal interest rate i_t. If the central bank raises its inflation target, then inflation, expected inflation, and the nominal interest rate all increase by the same amount. The real variables—output Y_t and the real interest rate r_t—do not depend on monetary policy. In these ways, the long-run equilibrium of the dynamic AD–AS model mirrors the classical models we examined in Chapters 3 to 8.

The Dynamic Aggregate Supply Curve

To study the behaviour of this economy in the short run, it is useful to analyze the model graphically. Because graphs have two axes, we need to focus on two variables. We will use output Y_t and inflation π_t as the variables on the two axes because these are the variables of central interest. As in the conventional AD–AS model, output will be on the horizontal axis. But because the price level has faded into the background in this dynamic presentation, the vertical axis in our graphs will now represent the inflation rate.

To generate this graph, we need two equations that summarize the relationships between output Y_t and inflation π_t. These equations are derived from the five equations of the model we have already seen. To isolate the relationships between Y_t and π_t, however, we need to use a bit of algebra to eliminate the other three endogenous variables (r_t, i_t, and $E_{t-1} \pi_t$).

The first relationship between output and inflation comes almost directly from the Phillips curve equation. We can get rid of the one extra endogenous variable in the equation ($E_{t-1} \pi_t$) by using the expectations equation ($E_{t-1} \pi_t = \pi_{t-1}$) to substitute past inflation π_{t-1} for expected inflation $E_{t-1} \pi_t$. With this substitution, the equation for the Phillips curve becomes

$$\pi_t = \pi_{t-1} + \phi(Y_t - \overline{Y}_t) + v_t. \qquad (DAS)$$

This equation relates inflation π_t and output Y_t for given values of two exogenous variables ($\overline{Y}_t$ and v_t) and a predetermined variable (π_{t-1}).

Figure 14-2 graphs the relationship between inflation π_t and output Y_t described by this equation. We call this upward-sloping curve the *dynamic aggregate supply curve,* or *DAS*. The dynamic aggregate supply curve is similar to the aggregate supply curve we saw in Chapter 13, except that inflation

FIGURE 14-2

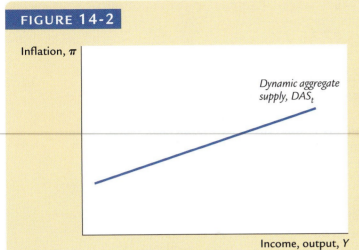

Inflation, π

Dynamic aggregate supply, DAS_t

Income, output, Y

The Dynamic Aggregate Supply Curve The dynamic aggregate supply curve DAS_t shows a positive association between output Y_t and inflation π_t. Its upward slope reflects the Phillips curve relationship: Other things equal, high levels of economic activity are associated with high inflation. The dynamic aggregate supply curve is drawn for given values of past inflation π_{t-1}, the natural level of output $\overline{Y}_t$, and the supply shock v_t. When these variables change, the curve shifts.

rather than the price level is on the vertical axis. The *DAS* curve shows how inflation is related to output in the short run. Its upward slope reflects the Phillips curve: Other things equal, high levels of economic activity are associated with high inflation.

The *DAS* curve is drawn for given values of past inflation π_{t-1}, the natural level of output $\overline{Y}_t$, and the supply shock v_t. If any one of these three variables changes, the *DAS* curve shifts. One of our tasks ahead is to trace out the implications of such shifts. But first, we need another curve.

The Dynamic Aggregate Demand Curve

The dynamic aggregate supply curve is one of the two relationships between output and inflation that determine the economy's short-run equilibrium. The other relationship is (no surprise) the dynamic aggregate demand curve. We derive it by combining four equations from the model and then eliminating all the endogenous variables other than output and inflation.

We begin with the demand for goods and services:

$$Y_t = \overline{Y}_t - \alpha\,(r_t - \rho) + \epsilon_t.$$

To eliminate the endogenous variable r_t, the real interest rate, we use the Fisher equation to substitute $i_t - E_t\pi_{t+1}$ for r_t:

$$Y_t = \overline{Y}_t - \alpha\,(i_t - E_t\pi_{t+1} - \rho) + \epsilon_t.$$

To eliminate another endogenous variable, the nominal interest rate i_t, we use the monetary-policy equation to substitute for i_t:

$$Y_t = \overline{Y}_t - \alpha\,[\pi_t + \rho + \theta_\pi(\pi_t - \pi_t^*) + \theta_Y(Y_t - \overline{Y}_t) - E_t\pi_{t+1} - \rho] + \epsilon_t.$$

Next, to eliminate the endogenous variable expected inflation $E_t\pi_{t+1}$, we use our equation for inflation expectations to substitute π_t for $E_t\pi_{t+1}$:

$$Y_t = \overline{Y}_t - \alpha \left[\pi_t + \rho + \theta_\pi(\pi_t - \pi_t^*) + \theta_Y(Y_t - \overline{Y}_t) - \pi_t - \rho\right] + \epsilon_t.$$

Notice that the positive π_t and ρ inside the brackets cancel the negative ones. The equation simplifies to

$$Y_t = \overline{Y}_t - \alpha \left[\theta_\pi(\pi_t - \pi_t^*) + \theta_Y(Y_t - \overline{Y}_t)\right] + \epsilon_t.$$

If we now bring like terms together and solve for Y_t, we obtain

$$Y_t = \overline{Y}_t - [\alpha\theta_\pi/(1 + \alpha\theta_Y)](\pi_t - \pi_t^*) + [1/(1 + \alpha\theta_Y)]\,\epsilon_t. \qquad (DAD)$$

This equation relates output Y_t to inflation π_t for given values of three exogenous variables ($\overline{Y}_t$, π_t^*, and ϵ_t).

Figure 14-3 graphs the relationship between inflation π_t and output Y_t described by this equation. We call this downward-sloping curve the *dynamic aggregate demand curve*, or *DAD*. The *DAD* curve shows how the quantity of output demanded is related to inflation in the short run. It is drawn holding constant the natural level of output $\overline{Y}_t$, the inflation target π_t^*, and the demand shock ϵ_t. If any one of these three variables changes, the *DAD* curve shifts. We will examine the effect of such shifts shortly.

It is tempting to think of this dynamic aggregate demand curve as nothing more than the standard aggregate demand curve from Chapter 11 with inflation, rather than the price level, on the vertical axis. In some ways, they are similar: they both embody the link between the interest rate and the demand for goods and services. But there is an important difference. The conventional aggregate demand curve in Chapter 11 is drawn for a given money supply. By contrast, because the monetary-policy rule was used to derive the dynamic aggregate demand equation,

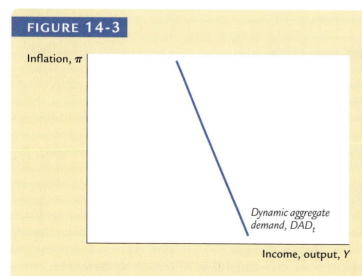

FIGURE 14-3

Inflation, π

Dynamic aggregate demand, DAD_t

Income, output, Y

The Dynamic Aggregate Demand Curve The dynamic aggregate demand curve shows a negative association between output and inflation. Its downward slope reflects monetary policy and the demand for goods and services: a high level of inflation causes the central bank to raise nominal and real interest rates, which in turn reduces the demand for goods and services. The dynamic aggregate demand curve is drawn for given values of the natural level of output $\overline{Y}_t$, the inflation target π_t^*, and the demand shock ϵ_t. When these exogenous variables change, the curve shifts.

472 | PART IV Business Cycle Theory: The Economy in the Short Run

the dynamic aggregate demand curve is drawn for a given rule for monetary policy. Under that rule, the central bank sets the interest rate based on macroeconomic conditions, and it allows the money supply to adjust accordingly.

The dynamic aggregate demand curve is downward sloping because of the following mechanism. When inflation rises, the central bank follows its rule and responds by increasing the nominal interest rate. Because the rule specifies that the central bank raise the nominal interest rate by more than the increase in inflation, the real interest rate rises as well. The increase in the real interest rate reduces the quantity of goods and services demanded. This negative association between inflation and quantity demanded, working through central bank policy, makes the dynamic aggregate demand curve slope downward.

The dynamic aggregate demand curve shifts in response to changes in fiscal and monetary policy. As we noted earlier, the shock variable ϵ_t reflects changes in government spending and taxes (among other things). Any change in fiscal policy that increases the demand for goods and services means a positive value of ϵ_t and a shift of the *DAD* curve to the right. Any change in fiscal policy that decreases the demand for goods and services means a negative value of ϵ_t and a shift of the *DAD* curve to the left.

Monetary policy enters the dynamic aggregate demand curve through the target inflation rate π_t^*. The *DAD* equation shows that, other things equal, an increase in π_t^* raises the quantity of output demanded. (There are two negative signs in front of π_t^* so the effect is positive.) Here is the mechanism that lies behind this mathematical result: When the central bank raises its target for inflation, it pursues a more expansionary monetary policy by reducing the nominal interest rate. The lower nominal interest rate in turn means a lower real interest rate, which stimulates spending on goods and services. Thus, output is higher for any given inflation rate, so the dynamic aggregate demand curve shifts to the right. Conversely, when the central bank reduces its target for inflation, it raises nominal and real interest rates, thereby dampening demand for goods and services and shifting the dynamic aggregate demand curve to the left.

The Short-Run Equilibrium

The economy's short-run equilibrium is determined by the intersection of the dynamic aggregate demand curve and the dynamic aggregate supply curve. The economy can be represented algebraically using the two equations we have just derived:

$$Y_t = \overline{Y}_t - [\alpha\theta_\pi/(1 + \alpha\theta_Y)](\pi_t - \pi_t^*) + [1/(1 + \alpha\theta_Y)]\epsilon_t. \qquad (DAD)$$

$$\pi_t = \pi_{t-1} + \phi(Y_t - \overline{Y}_t) + v_t. \qquad (DAS)$$

In any period t, these equations together determine two endogenous variables: inflation π_t and output Y_t. The solution depends on five other variables that are exogenous (or at least determined prior to period t). These exogenous (and predetermined) variables are the natural level of output $\overline{Y}_t$, the central bank's target inflation rate π_t^*, the shock to demand ϵ_t, the shock to supply v_t, and the previous period's rate of inflation π_{t-1}.

FIGURE 14-4

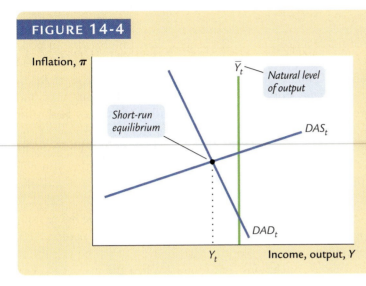

The Short-Run Equilibrium The short-run equilibrium is determined by the intersection of the dynamic aggregate demand curve and the dynamic aggregate supply curve. This equilibrium determines the inflation rate and level of output that prevail in period t. In the equilibrium shown in this figure, the short-run equilibrium level of output Y_t falls short of the economy's natural level of output $\overline{Y}_t$.

Taking these exogenous variables as given, we can illustrate the economy's short-run equilibrium as the intersection of the dynamic aggregate demand curve and the dynamic aggregate supply curve, as in Figure 14-4. The short-run equilibrium level of output Y_t can be less than its natural level $\overline{Y}_t$, as it is in this figure, greater than its natural level, or equal to it. As we have seen, when the economy is in long-run equilibrium, output is at its natural level ($Y_t = \overline{Y}_t$).

The short-run equilibrium determines not only the level of output Y_t but also the inflation rate π_t. In the subsequent period ($t + 1$), this inflation rate will become the lagged inflation rate that influences the position of the dynamic aggregate supply curve. This connection between periods generates the dynamic patterns that we will examine below. That is, one period of time is linked to the next through expectations about inflation. A shock in period t affects inflation in period t, which in turn affects the inflation that people expect for period $t + 1$. Expected inflation in period $t + 1$ in turn affects the position of the dynamic aggregate supply curve in that period, which in turn affects output and inflation in period $t + 1$, which then affects expected inflation in period $t + 2$, and so on.

These linkages of economic outcomes across time periods will become clear as we work through a series of examples.

14-3 Using the Model

Let's now use the dynamic AD–AS model to analyze how the economy responds to changes in the exogenous variables. The four exogenous variables in the model are the natural level of output $\overline{Y}_t$, the supply shock v_t, the demand shock ϵ_t, and the central bank's inflation target π_t^*. To keep things simple, we will assume that the economy always begins in long-run equilibrium and is then subject to a change in one of the exogenous variables. Within each particular scenario, we also assume that the other exogenous variables are held constant.

Long-Run Growth

The economy's natural level of output $\overline{Y}_t$ changes over time because of population growth, capital accumulation, and technological progress, as discussed in Chapters 7 and 8. Figure 14-5 illustrates the effect of an increase in $\overline{Y}_t$. Because this variable affects both the dynamic aggregate demand curve and the dynamic aggregate supply curve, both curves shift. In fact, they both shift to the right by exactly the amount that $\overline{Y}_t$ has increased. In the case of the dynamic aggregate supply curve, this is most easily appreciated by inverting its equation so that Y_t, not π_t, is on the left-hand side. When you do this, you will see that the coefficient on $\overline{Y}_t$ is unity—just as it is in the equation of the dynamic aggregate demand curve.

The shifts in these curves move the economy's equilibrium in the figure from point A to point B. Output Y_t increases by exactly as much as the natural level $\overline{Y}_t$. Inflation is unchanged.

The story behind these conclusions is as follows: When the natural level of output increases, the economy can produce a larger quantity of goods and services. This is represented by the rightward shift in the dynamic aggregate supply curve. At the same time, the increase in the natural level of output makes people richer. Other things equal, they want to buy more goods and services. This is represented by the rightward shift in the dynamic aggregate demand curve. The simultaneous shifts in supply and demand increase the economy's output without putting either upward or downward pressure on inflation. In this way, the economy can experience long-run growth and a stable inflation rate.

FIGURE 14-5

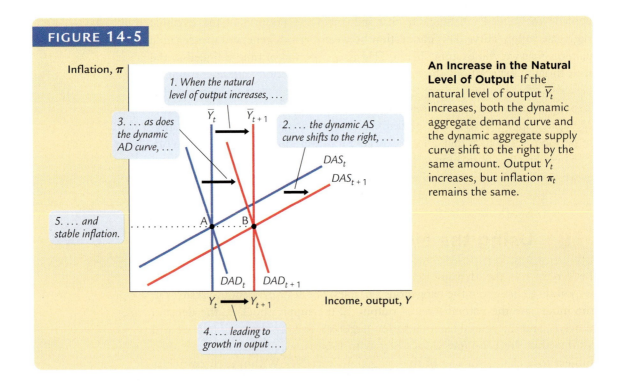

An Increase in the Natural Level of Output If the natural level of output $\overline{Y}_t$ increases, both the dynamic aggregate demand curve and the dynamic aggregate supply curve shift to the right by the same amount. Output Y_t increases, but inflation π_t remains the same.

A Shock to Aggregate Supply

Consider now a shock to aggregate supply. In particular, suppose that v_t rises to 1 percent for one period and subsequently returns to zero. This shock to the Phillips curve might occur, for example, because a hurricane destroys some oil rigs, causing energy costs to rise and prices to be pushed up, or because new union agreements raise wages and, thereby, the costs of production. In general, the supply shock v_t captures any event that influences inflation beyond expected inflation $E_{t-1}\pi_t$ and current economic activity, as measured by $Y_t - \overline{Y}_t$.

Figure 14-6 shows the result. In period t, when the shock occurs, the dynamic aggregate supply curve shifts upward from DAS_{t-1} to DAS_t. To be precise, the curve shifts upward by exactly the size of the shock, which we assumed to be 1 percentage point. Because the supply shock v_t is not a variable in the dynamic aggregate demand equation, the DAD curve is unchanged. Therefore, the economy moves along the dynamic aggregate demand curve from point A to point B. As the figure illustrates, the supply shock in period t causes inflation to rise to π_t and output to fall to Y_t.

These effects work in part through the reaction of monetary policy to the shock. When the supply shock causes inflation to rise, the central bank responds by following its policy rule and raising nominal and real interest rates. The higher real interest rate reduces the quantity of goods and services demanded, which depresses output below its natural level. (This series of events is represented by the movement along the DAD curve from point A to point B.) The lower level

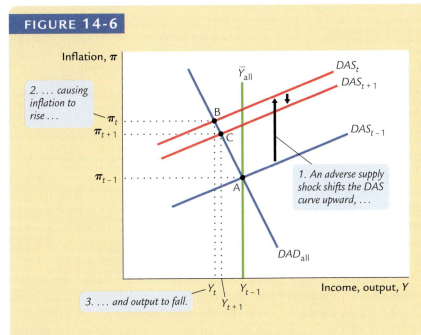

FIGURE 14-6

A Supply Shock A supply shock in period t shifts the dynamic aggregate supply curve upward from DAS_{t-1} to DAS_t. The dynamic aggregate demand curve is unchanged. The economy's short-run equilibrium moves from point A to point B. Inflation rises and output falls. In the subsequent period ($t + 1$), the dynamic aggregate supply curve shifts to DAS_{t+1} and the economy moves to point C. The supply shock has returned to its normal value of zero, but inflation expectations remain high. As a result, the economy returns only gradually to its initial equilibrium, point A.

The Numerical Calibration and Simulation

FYI

The text presents some numerical simulations of the dynamic *AD–AS* model. When interpreting these results, it is easiest to think of each period as representing one year. We examine the impact of the change in the year of the shock (period t) and over the subsequent 12 years.

The simulations use these parameter values:

$$\overline{Y}_t = 100.$$

$$\pi_t^* = 2.0.$$

$$\alpha = 1.0.$$

$$\rho = 2.0.$$

$$\phi = 0.25.$$

$$\theta_\pi = 0.5.$$

$$\theta_Y = 0.5.$$

Here is how to interpret these numbers. The natural level of output $\overline{Y}_t$ is 100; as a result of choosing this convenient number, fluctuations in $Y_t - \overline{Y}_t$ can be viewed as percentage deviations of output from its natural level. The central bank's inflation target π_t^* is 2 percent. The parameter $\alpha = 1.0$ implies that a 1-percentage-point increase in the real interest rate reduces output demand by 1, which is 1 percent of its natural level. The econo-

my's natural rate of interest ρ is 2 percent. The Phillips curve parameter $\phi = 0.25$ implies that when output is 1 percent above its natural level, inflation rises by 0.25 percentage point. The parameters for the monetary policy rule $\theta_\pi = 0.5$ and $\theta_Y = 0.5$ are those suggested by John Taylor and, as we saw earlier, are reasonable approximations of the behaviour of the actual central bank.

In all cases, the simulations assume a change of 1 percentage point in the exogenous variable of interest. Larger shocks would have qualitatively similar effects, but the magnitudes would be proportionately greater. For example, a shock of 3 percentage points would affect all the variables in the same way as a shock of 1 percentage point, but the movements would be three times as large as in the simulation shown.

The graphs of the time paths of the variables after a shock (shown in Figures 14-7, 14-9, and 14-11) are called *impulse response functions*. The word "impulse" refers to the shock, and "response function" refers to how the endogenous variables respond to the shock over time. These simulated impulse response functions are one way to illustrate how the model works. They show how the endogenous variables move when a shock hits the economy, how these variables adjust in subsequent periods, and how they are correlated with one another over time.

---

of output dampens the inflationary pressure to some degree, so inflation rises somewhat less than the initial shock.

In the periods after the shock occurs, expected inflation is higher because expectations depend on past inflation. In period $t + 1$, for instance, the economy is at point C. Even though the shock variable v_t returns to its normal value of zero, the dynamic aggregate supply curve does not immediately return to its initial position. Instead, it slowly shifts back downward toward its initial position DAS_{t-1} as a lower level of economic activity reduces inflation and thereby expectations of future inflation. Throughout this process, output remains below its natural level.

Figure 14–7 shows the time paths of the key variables in the model in response to the shock. (These simulations are based on realistic parameter values: see the nearby FYI box for their description.) As panel (a) shows, the shock v_t spikes upward by 1 percentage point in period t and then returns to zero in subsequent

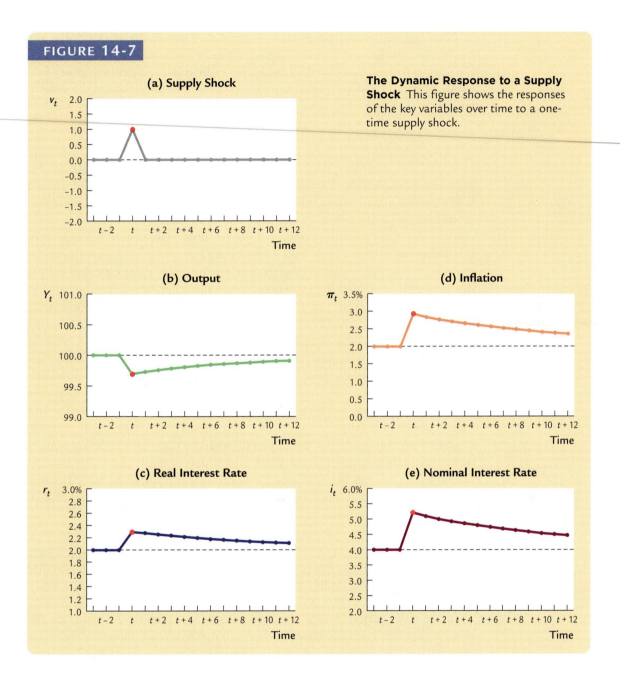

FIGURE 14-7

(a) Supply Shock

The Dynamic Response to a Supply Shock This figure shows the responses of the key variables over time to a one-time supply shock.

(b) Output

(d) Inflation

(c) Real Interest Rate

(e) Nominal Interest Rate

periods. Inflation, shown in panel (d), rises by 0.9 percentage point and gradually returns to its target of 2 percent over a long period of time. Output, shown in panel (b), falls in response to the supply shock but also eventually returns to its natural level.

The figure also shows the paths of nominal and real interest rates. In the period of the supply shock, the nominal interest rate, shown in panel (e), increases by 1.2 percentage points, and the real interest rate, in panel (c), increases by 0.3 percentage points. Both interest rates return to their normal values as the economy returns to its long-run equilibrium.

These figures illustrate the phenomenon of *stagflation* in the dynamic *AD–AS* model. An adverse supply shock causes inflation to rise, which in turn increases expected inflation. As the central bank applies its rule for monetary policy and responds by raising interest rates, it gradually squeezes inflation out of the system, but only at the cost of a prolonged downturn in economic activity.

A Shock to Aggregate Demand

Now let's consider a shock to aggregate demand. To be realistic, if the disturbance is to represent a major fiscal stimulus like the one introduced in 2009, the shock is assumed to persist over several periods. In particular, for our illustration, we suppose that $\epsilon_t = 1$ for five periods and then returns to its normal value of zero. In addition to a major fiscal policy, the positive shock ϵ_t might represent, for example, a war that increases government purchases or a stock market bubble that increases wealth and thereby consumption spending. In general, the demand shock captures any event that influences the demand for goods and services for given values of the natural level of output $\overline{Y}_t$ and the real interest rate r_t.

Figure 14-8 shows the result. In period t, when the shock occurs, the dynamic aggregate demand curve shifts to the right from DAD_{t-1} to DAD_t. Because the demand shock ϵ_t is not a variable in the dynamic aggregate supply equation, the *DAS* curve is unchanged from period $t-1$ to period t. The economy moves along the dynamic aggregate supply curve from point A to point B. Output and inflation both increase.

Once again, these effects work in part through the reaction of monetary policy to the shock. When the demand shock causes output and inflation to rise, the central bank responds by increasing the nominal and real interest rates. Because a higher real interest rate reduces the quantity of goods and services demanded, it partly offsets the expansionary effects of the demand shock.

In the periods after the shock occurs, expected inflation is higher because expectations depend on past inflation. As a result, the dynamic aggregate supply curve shifts upward repeatedly; as it does so, it continually reduces output and increases inflation. In the figure, the economy goes from point B in the initial period of the shock to points C, D, E, and F in subsequent periods.

In the sixth period $(t + 5)$, the demand shock disappears. At this time, the dynamic aggregate demand curve returns to its initial position. However, the economy does not immediately return to its initial equilibrium, point A. The period of high demand has increased inflation and thereby expected inflation. High expected inflation keeps the dynamic aggregate supply curve higher than it was initially. As a result, when demand falls off, the economy's equilibrium moves to point G, and output falls to Y_{t+5}, which is below its natural level. The economy then gradually recovers, as the higher-than-target inflation is squeezed out of the system.

Figure 14-9 shows the time path of the key variables in the model in response to the demand shock. Note that the positive demand shock increases real and nominal interest rates. When the demand shock disappears, both interest rates fall. These responses occur because when the central bank sets the nominal interest rate, it takes into account both inflation rates and deviations of output from its natural level.

FIGURE 14-8

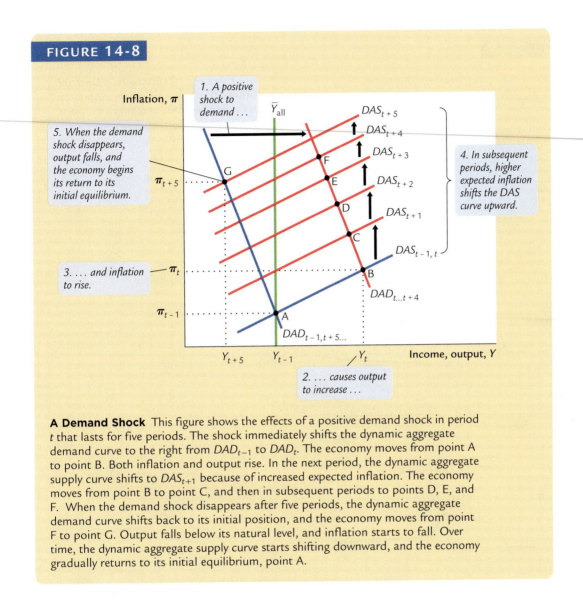

A Demand Shock This figure shows the effects of a positive demand shock in period *t* that lasts for five periods. The shock immediately shifts the dynamic aggregate demand curve to the right from DAD_{t-1} to DAD_t. The economy moves from point A to point B. Both inflation and output rise. In the next period, the dynamic aggregate supply curve shifts to DAS_{t+1} because of increased expected inflation. The economy moves from point B to point C, and then in subsequent periods to points D, E, and F. When the demand shock disappears after five periods, the dynamic aggregate demand curve shifts back to its initial position, and the economy moves from point F to point G. Output falls below its natural level, and inflation starts to fall. Over time, the dynamic aggregate supply curve starts shifting downward, and the economy gradually returns to its initial equilibrium, point A.

A Shift in Monetary Policy

Suppose that the central bank decides to reduce its target for the inflation rate. Specifically, imagine that, in period *t*, π_t^* falls from 2 percent to 1 percent and thereafter remains at that lower level. Let's consider how the economy will react to this change in monetary policy.

Recall that the inflation target enters the model as an exogenous variable in the dynamic aggregate demand curve. When the inflation target falls, the *DAD* curve shifts to the left, as shown in Figure 14-10. (To be precise, it shifts downward by exactly 1 percentage point.) Because target inflation does not enter the dynamic aggregate supply equation, the *DAS* curve does not shift initially. The economy moves from its initial equilibrium, point A, to a new equilibrium, point B. Output and inflation both fall.

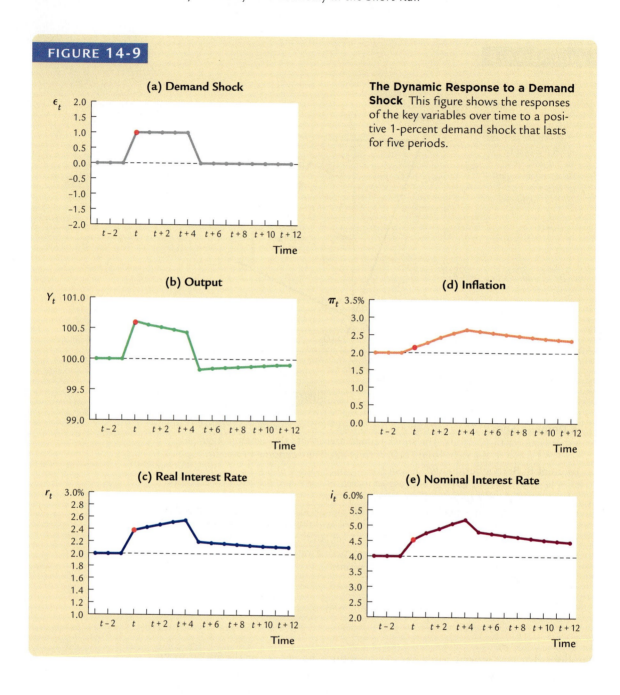

FIGURE 14-9

(a) Demand Shock

The Dynamic Response to a Demand Shock This figure shows the responses of the key variables over time to a positive 1-percent demand shock that lasts for five periods.

(b) Output

(d) Inflation

(c) Real Interest Rate

(e) Nominal Interest Rate

Monetary policy is, not surprisingly, key to the explanation of this outcome. When the central bank lowers its target for inflation, current inflation is now above the target, so the central bank follows its policy rule and raises real and nominal interest rates. The higher real interest rate reduces the demand for goods and services. When output falls, the Phillips curve tells us that inflation falls as well.

Lower inflation, in turn, reduces the inflation rate that people expect to prevail in the next period. In period $t + 1$, lower expected inflation shifts the dynamic aggregate supply curve downward, to DAS_{t+1}. (To be precise, the curve shifts

FIGURE 14-10

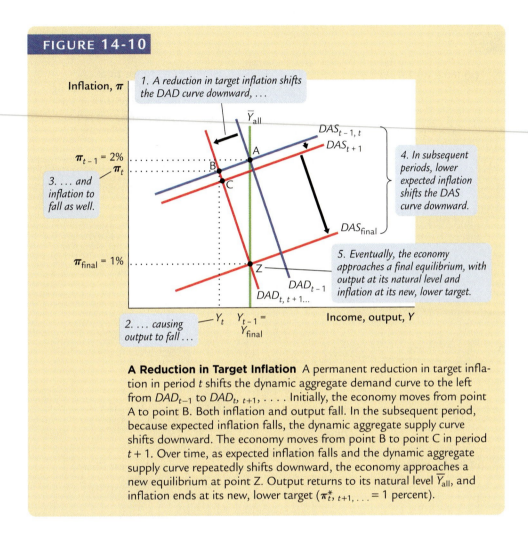

A Reduction in Target Inflation A permanent reduction in target inflation in period t shifts the dynamic aggregate demand curve to the left from DAD_{t-1} to $DAD_{t,\ t+1},\ \ldots$. Initially, the economy moves from point A to point B. Both inflation and output fall. In the subsequent period, because expected inflation falls, the dynamic aggregate supply curve shifts downward. The economy moves from point B to point C in period $t+1$. Over time, as expected inflation falls and the dynamic aggregate supply curve repeatedly shifts downward, the economy approaches a new equilibrium at point Z. Output returns to its natural level $\overline{Y}_{all}$, and inflation ends at its new, lower target ($\pi^*_{t,\ t+1,\ \ldots} = 1$ percent).

downward by exactly the fall in expected inflation.) This shift moves the economy from point B to point C, further reducing inflation and expanding output. Over time, as inflation continues to fall and the DAS curve continues to shift toward DAS_{final}, the economy approaches a new long-run equilibrium at point Z, where output is back at its natural level ($Y_{final} = \overline{Y}_{all}$) and inflation is at its new lower target ($\pi^*_{t,t+1,\ldots} = 1$ percent).

Figure 14-11 shows the response of the variables over time to a reduction in target inflation. Note in panel (e) the time path of the nominal interest rate i_t. Before the change in policy, the nominal interest rate is at its long-run value of 4.0 percent (which equals the natural real interest rate ρ of 2 percent plus target inflation π^*_{t-1} of 2 percent). When target inflation falls to 1 percent, the nominal interest rate rises to 4.2 percent. Over time, however, the nominal interest rate falls as inflation and expected inflation fall toward the new target rate; eventually, i_t approaches its new long-run value of 3.0 percent. Thus, a shift toward a lower inflation target increases the nominal interest rate in the short run but decreases it in the long run.

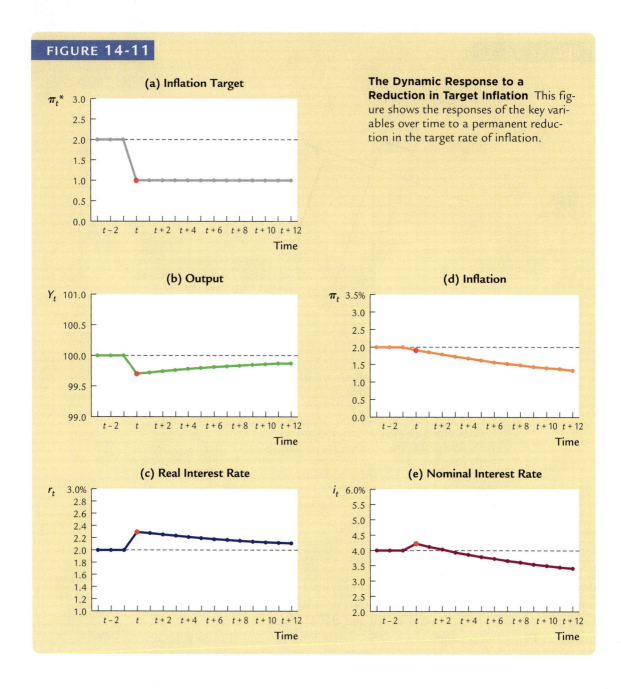

FIGURE 14-11

(a) Inflation Target

The Dynamic Response to a Reduction in Target Inflation This figure shows the responses of the key variables over time to a permanent reduction in the target rate of inflation.

(b) Output

(d) Inflation

(c) Real Interest Rate

(e) Nominal Interest Rate

We close with a caveat: Throughout this analysis we have maintained the assumption of adaptive expectations. That is, we have assumed that people form their expectations of inflation based on the inflation they have recently experienced. It is possible, however, that if the central bank makes a credible announcement of its new policy of lower target inflation, people will respond by altering their expectations of inflation immediately. That is, they may form expectations rationally, based on the policy announcement, rather than adaptively, based on what they have experienced. (We discussed this possibility in Chapter 13.) If so, the dynamic aggregate supply curve will shift downward immediately upon the change in policy, just when the dynamic aggregate demand curve shifts downward. In this case, the economy will instantly reach its new long-run equilibrium. By contrast, if people do not believe an announced policy of low inflation until they see it, then the assumption of adaptive expectations is appropriate, and the transition path to lower inflation will involve a period of lost output, as shown in Figure 14-11.

14-4 Two Applications: Lessons for Monetary Policy

So far in this chapter, we have assembled a dynamic model of inflation and output and used it to show how various shocks affect the time paths of output, inflation, and interest rates. We now use the model to shed light on the design of monetary policy.

It is worth pausing at this point to consider what we mean by the phrase "the design of monetary policy." So far in this analysis, the central bank has had a simple role: it merely had to adjust the money supply to ensure that the nominal interest rate hit the target level prescribed by the monetary-policy rule. The two key parameters of that policy rule are θ_π (the responsiveness of the target interest rate to inflation) and θ_Y (the responsiveness of the target interest rate to output). We have taken these parameters as given without discussing how they are chosen. Now that we know how the model works, we can consider a deeper question: what should the parameters of the monetary policy rule be?

The Tradeoff Between Output Variability and Inflation Variability

Consider the impact of a supply shock on output and inflation. According to the dynamic AD–AS model, the impact of this shock depends crucially on the slope of the dynamic aggregate demand curve. In particular, the slope of the DAD curve determines whether a supply shock has a large or small impact on output and inflation.

This phenomenon is illustrated in Figure 14-12. In the two panels of this figure, the economy experiences the same supply shock. In panel (a), the dynamic aggregate demand curve is nearly flat, so the shock has a small effect on inflation but a large effect on output. In panel (b), the dynamic aggregate demand curve is steep, so the shock has a large effect on inflation but a small effect on output.

Why is this important for monetary policy? Because the central bank can influence the slope of the dynamic aggregate demand curve. Recall the equation for the DAD curve:

$$Y_t = \overline{Y}_t - [\alpha\theta_\pi/(1 + \alpha\theta_Y)](\pi_t - \pi_t^*) + [1/(1 + \alpha\theta_Y)]\,\epsilon_t.$$

Two key parameters here are θ_π and θ_Y, which govern how much the central bank's interest rate target responds to changes in inflation and output. When the

FIGURE 14-12

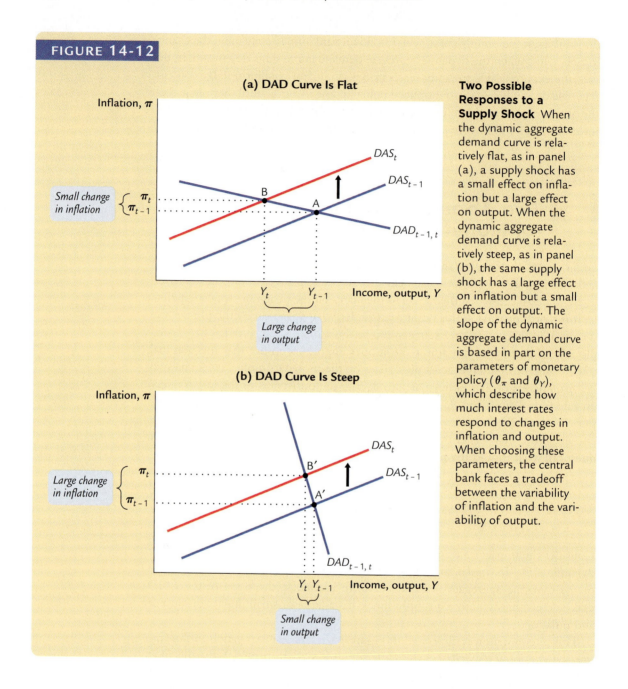

(a) DAD Curve Is Flat

Inflation, π

DAS_t

DAS_{t-1}

B

A

Small change in inflation $\begin{cases} \pi_t \\ \pi_{t-1} \end{cases}$

$DAD_{t-1,t}$

Y_t Y_{t-1} Income, output, Y

Large change in output

(b) DAD Curve Is Steep

Inflation, π

DAS_t

B'

DAS_{t-1}

A'

Large change in inflation $\begin{cases} \pi_t \\ \pi_{t-1} \end{cases}$

$DAD_{t-1,t}$

Y_t Y_{t-1} Income, output, Y

Small change in output

Two Possible Responses to a Supply Shock When the dynamic aggregate demand curve is relatively flat, as in panel (a), a supply shock has a small effect on inflation but a large effect on output. When the dynamic aggregate demand curve is relatively steep, as in panel (b), the same supply shock has a large effect on inflation but a small effect on output. The slope of the dynamic aggregate demand curve is based in part on the parameters of monetary policy (θ_π and θ_Y), which describe how much interest rates respond to changes in inflation and output. When choosing these parameters, the central bank faces a tradeoff between the variability of inflation and the variability of output.

central bank chooses these policy parameters, it determines the slope of the DAD curve and thus the economy's short-run response to supply shocks.

On the one hand, suppose that, when setting the interest rate, the central bank responds strongly to inflation (θ_π is large) and weakly to output (θ_Y is small). In this case, the coefficient on inflation in the above equation is large. That is, a small change in inflation has a large effect on output. As a result, the dynamic aggregate demand curve is relatively flat, and supply shocks have large effects on output but small effects on inflation. The story goes like this: When the economy experiences a supply shock that pushes up inflation, the central bank's policy rule has it respond vigorously with higher interest rates. Sharply higher interest rates significantly reduce the quantity of goods and services demanded, thereby leading to a large recession that dampens the inflationary impact of the shock (which was the purpose of the monetary policy response).

On the other hand, suppose that, when setting the interest rate, the central bank responds weakly to inflation (θ_π is small) but strongly to output (θ_Y is large). In this case, the coefficient on inflation in the above equation is small, which means that even a large change in inflation has only a small effect on output. As a result, the dynamic aggregate demand curve is relatively steep, and supply shocks have small effects on output but large effects on inflation. The story is just the opposite as before: Now, when the economy experiences a supply shock that pushes up inflation, the central bank's policy rule has it respond with only slightly higher interest rates. This small policy response avoids a large recession but accommodates the inflationary shock.

In its choice of monetary policy, the central bank determines which of these two scenarios will play out. That is, when setting the policy parameters θ_π and θ_Y, the central bank chooses whether to make the economy look more like panel (a) or more like panel (b) of Figure 14-12. When making this choice, the central bank faces a tradeoff between output variability and inflation variability. The central bank can be a hard-line inflation fighter, as in panel (a), in which case inflation is stable but output is volatile. Alternatively, it can be more accommodative, as in panel (b), in which case inflation is volatile but output is more stable. It can also choose some position in between these two extremes.

One job of a central bank is to promote economic stability. There are, however, various dimensions to this charge. When there are tradeoffs to be made, the central bank has to determine what kind of stability to pursue. The dynamic $AD-AS$ model shows that one fundamental tradeoff is between the variability in inflation and the variability in output.

Note that this tradeoff is very different from a simple tradeoff between inflation and output. In the long run of this model, inflation goes to its target, and output goes to its natural level. Consistent with classical macroeconomic theory, policymakers do not face a long-run tradeoff between inflation and output. Instead, they face a choice about which of these two measures of macroeconomic performance they want to stabilize. When deciding on the parameters of the monetary-policy rule, they determine whether supply shocks lead to inflation variability, output variability, or some combination of the two.

CASE STUDY

The United States Fed Versus the European Central Bank

According to the dynamic $AD-AS$ model, a key policy choice facing any central bank concerns the parameters of its policy rule. The monetary parameters θ_π and θ_Y determine how much the interest rate responds to macroeconomic conditions.

As we have just seen, these responses in turn determine the volatility of inflation and output.

The U.S. Federal Reserve (Fed) and the European Central Bank (ECB) appear to have different approaches to this decision. The legislation that created the Fed states explicitly that its goal is "to promote effectively the goals of maximum employment, stable prices, and moderate long-term interest rates." Because the Fed is supposed to stabilize both employment and prices, it is said to have a *dual mandate*. (The third goal—moderate long-term interest rates—should follow naturally from stable prices.) By contrast, the ECB says on its Web site that "the primary objective of the ECB's monetary policy is to maintain price stability. The ECB aims at inflation rates of below, but close to, 2% over the medium term." All other macroeconomic goals, including stability of output and employment, appear to be secondary. As far as its mandate is concerned, the Bank of Canada is very similar to the ECB, not the Fed.

We can interpret these differences in central bank mandates in light of our model. Compared to the Fed, the ECB seems to give more weight to inflation stability and less weight to output stability. This difference in objectives should be reflected in the parameters of the monetary-policy rules. To achieve its dual mandate, the Fed would respond more to output and less to inflation than the ECB would.

A case in point occurred in 2008 when the world economy was experiencing rising oil prices, a financial crisis, and a slowdown in economic activity. The Fed responded to these events by lowering interest rates from about 5 percent to a range of 0 to 0.25 percent over the course of a year. The ECB, facing a similar situation, also cut interest rates—but by much less. The ECB was less concerned about recession and more concerned about keeping inflation in check.

The dynamic *AD–AS* model predicts that, other things equal, the policy of the ECB should, over time, lead to more variable output and more stable inflation. Testing this prediction, however, is difficult for two reasons. First, because the ECB was established only in 1998, there is not yet enough data to establish the long-term effects of its policy. Second, and perhaps more important, other things are not always equal. Europe and the United States differ in many ways beyond the policies of their central banks, and these other differences may affect output and inflation in ways unrelated to differences in monetary-policy priorities. ■

The Taylor Principle

How much should the nominal interest rate set by the central bank respond to changes in inflation? The dynamic *AD–AS* model does not give a definitive answer, but it does offer an important guideline.

Recall the equation for monetary policy:

$$i_t = \pi_t + \rho + \theta_\pi(\pi_t - \pi_t^*) + \theta_Y(Y_t - \overline{Y}_t).$$

According to this equation, a 1-percentage-point increase in inflation π_t induces an increase in the nominal interest rate i_t of $1 + \theta_\pi$ percentage points. Because we assume that that θ_π is greater than zero, whenever inflation increases, the central bank raises the nominal interest rate by an even larger amount.

Imagine, however, that the central bank behaved differently and, instead, increased the nominal interest rate by less than the increase in inflation. In this case, the monetary policy parameter θ_π would be less than zero. This change would profoundly alter the model. Recall that the dynamic aggregate demand equation is:

$$Y_t = \overline{Y}_t - [\alpha\theta_\pi/(1 + \alpha\theta_Y)](\pi_t - \pi_t^*) + [1/(1 + \alpha\theta_Y)]\,\epsilon_t.$$

If θ_π is negative, then an increase in inflation would increase the quantity of output demanded, and the dynamic aggregate demand curve would be upward sloping.

An upward-sloping DAD curve leads to unstable inflation, as illustrated in Figure 14-13. Suppose that in period t there is a one-time positive shock to aggregate demand. That is, for one period only, the dynamic aggregate demand curve shifts to the right, to DAD_t; in the next period, it returns to its original position. In period t, the economy moves from point A to point B. Output and inflation rise. In the next period, because higher inflation has increased expected inflation, the dynamic aggregate supply curve shifts upward, to DAS_{t+1}.

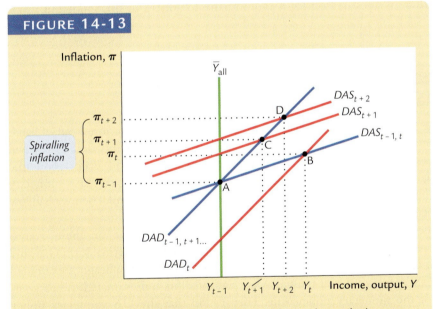

FIGURE 14-13

The Importance of the Taylor Principle This figure shows the impact of a demand shock in an economy that does not satisfy the Taylor principle, so the dynamic aggregate demand curve is upward sloping. A demand shock moves the DAD curve to the right for one period, to DAD_t, and the economy moves from point A to point B. Both output and inflation increase. The rise in inflation increases expected inflation and, in the next period, shifts the dynamic aggregate supply curve upward to DAS_{t+1}. Therefore, in period $t+1$, the economy then moves from point B to point C. Because the DAD curve is upward sloping, output is still above the natural level, so inflation continues to increase. In period $t+2$, the economy moves to point D, where output and inflation are even higher. Inflation spirals out of control.

The economy moves from point B to point C. But because we are assuming in this case that the dynamic aggregate demand curve is upward sloping, output remains above the natural level, even though demand shock has disappeared. Thus, inflation rises yet again, shifting the *DAS* curve farther upward in the next period, moving the economy to point D. And so on. Inflation continues to rise with no end in sight.

The economic intuition may be easier to understand than the geometry. A positive demand shock increases output and inflation. If the central bank does not increase the nominal interest rate sufficiently, the real interest rate falls. A lower real interest rate increases the quantity of goods and services demanded. Higher output puts further upward pressure on inflation, which in turn lowers the real interest rate yet again. The result is inflation spiraling out of control.

The dynamic *AD−AS* model leads to a strong conclusion: *For inflation to be stable, the central bank must respond to an increase in inflation with an even greater increase in the nominal interest rate.* This conclusion is sometimes called the **Taylor principle,** after economist John Taylor, who emphasized its importance in the design of monetary policy. Most of our analysis in this chapter assumed that the Taylor principle holds (that is, we assumed that $\theta_\pi > 0$). We can see now that there is good reason for a central bank to adhere to this guideline.

CASE STUDY

What Caused the Great Inflation?

In the 1970s, inflation in all western countries, including Canada, got out of hand. As we saw in previous chapters, the inflation rate during this decade reached double-digit levels. Rising prices were widely considered the major economic problem of the time. Beginning in the early 1980s, contractionary monetary policy was used to eventually bring inflation back under control. Then we had low and stable inflation for the next quarter century.

The dynamic *AD−AS* model offers a new perspective on these events. According to research by monetary economists Richard Clarida, Jordi Gali, and Mark Gertler, the key is the Taylor principle. Clarida and colleagues examined the U.S. data on interest rates, output, and inflation and estimated the parameters of the monetary policy rule. They found that the U.S. monetary policy obeyed the Taylor principle after 1980, whereas earlier monetary policy did not. In particular, the parameter θ_π was estimated to be 0.72 after 1980, close to Taylor's proposed value of 0.5, but it was -0.14 during the 1960s and 1970s.[2] The negative value of θ_π during the earlier era means that monetary policy did not satisfy the Taylor principle.

[2] These estimates are derived from Table VI of Richard Clarida, Jordi Gali, and Mark Gertler, "Monetary Policy Rules and Macroeconomic Stability: Evidence and Some Theory," *Quarterly Journal of Economics* 115, number 1 (February 2000): 147–180.

This finding suggests a potential cause of the great inflation of the 1970s. When the U.S. economy was hit by demand shocks (such as government spending on the Vietnam War) and supply shocks (such as the OPEC oil-price increases), the Fed raised nominal interest rates in response to rising inflation but not by enough. Therefore, despite the increase in nominal interest rates, real interest rates fell. The insufficient monetary response not only failed to squash the inflationary pressures but actually exacerbated them. The problem of spiraling inflation was not solved until the monetary-policy rule was changed to include a more vigorous response of interest rates to inflation.

An open question is why policymakers were so passive in the earlier era. Here are some conjectures from Clarida, Gali, and Gertler:

> Why is it that during the pre-1979 period the Federal Reserve followed a rule that was clearly inferior? Another way to look at the issue is to ask why it is that the Fed maintained persistently low short-term real rates in the face of high or rising inflation. One possibility . . . is that the Fed thought the natural rate of unemployment at this time was much lower than it really was (or equivalently, that the output gap was much smaller). . . .
>
> Another somewhat related possibility is that, at that time, neither the Fed nor the economics profession understood the dynamics of inflation very well. Indeed, it was not until the mid-to-late 1970s that intermediate textbooks began emphasizing the absence of a long-run trade-off between inflation and output. The ideas that expectations may matter in generating inflation and that credibility is important in policymaking were simply not well established during that era. What all this suggests is that in understanding historical economic behavior, it is important to take into account the state of policymakers' knowledge of the economy and how it may have evolved over time. ∎

14-5 Conclusion: Toward DSGE Models

If you go on to take more advanced courses in macroeconomics, you will likely learn about a class of models called dynamic, stochastic, general equilibrium models, often abbreviated as DSGE models. These models are *dynamic* because they trace the path of variables over time. They are *stochastic* because they incorporate the inherent randomness of economic life. They are *general equilibrium* because they take into account the fact that everything depends on everything else. In many ways, they are the state-of-the-art models in the analysis of short-run economic fluctuations.

The dynamic *AD–AS* model we have presented in this chapter is a simplified version of these DSGE models. Unlike analysts using advanced DSGE models, we have not started with the household and firm optimizing decisions that underlie the macroeconomic relationships. But the macro relationships that this chapter has posited are similar to those found in more sophisticated DSGE models. The dynamic *AD–AS* model is a good stepping-stone between the basic model of aggregate demand and aggregate supply we saw in earlier chapters and the more complex DSGE models you will see in a more advanced course.

There is one subset of the DSGE models—one that is summarized by just as few equations as our dynamic *AD–AS* model—that has become known as the *New Neo-Classical Synthesis* model. It gives equal billing to important Classical and Keynesian ideas. On the Classical side, the synthesis model involves long-run monetary neutrality and rational expectations, and it respects the maxim that the behavioural rules followed by all households and firms in the model be explicitly derived as optimal responses to the challenges that these agents face. On the Keynesian side, the synthesis model stresses the volatility trade-off that follows from the existence of some market failure. It is by allowing for market failure that the synthesis model provides a rigorous micro foundation for the proposition that the government attempts to stabilize the economy *may* be formally justified. Our dynamic, but simplified, analysis in this chapter is meant to introduce students to this important synthesis of Classical and Keynesian ideas that has emerged over the last decade.[3] In the Appendix to this chapter, we introduce students to a few of the recent developments on each of the Classical and Keynesian sides of this synthesis.

Beyond paving the way for more advanced work, our dynamic *AD–AS* model also yields some important lessons. It shows how various macroeconomic variables—output, inflation, and real and nominal interest rates—respond to shocks and interact with one another over time. It demonstrates that, in the design of monetary policy, central banks face a tradeoff between variability in inflation and variability in output. Finally, it suggests that central banks need to respond vigorously to inflation to prevent it from getting out of control. If you ever find yourself running a central bank, these are good lessons to keep in mind.

Summary

1. The dynamic model of aggregate demand and aggregate supply combines five economic relationships: an equation for the goods market, which relates quantity demanded to the real interest rate; the Fisher equation, which relates real and nominal interest rates; the Phillips curve equation, which determines inflation; an equation for expected inflation; and a rule for monetary policy, according to which the central bank sets the nominal interest rate as a function of inflation and output.

2. The long-run equilibrium of the model is classical. Output and the real interest rate are at their natural levels, independent of monetary policy. The central bank's inflation target determines inflation, expected inflation, and the nominal interest rate.

---

[3] Related contributions to pedagogy on this topic are: David Romer, "Keynesian Macroeconomics Without the LM Curve," *Journal of Economic Perspectives* 14, no. 2, (2000): 149–169; Carl Walsh, "Teaching Inflation Targeting: An Analysis for Intermediate Macro," *Journal of Economic Education* 33, no. 4 (2002): 333–346; and the Chapter 11 Appendix that has appeared in the previous two editions of this book.

3. The dynamic AD–AS model can be used to determine the immediate impact on the economy of any shock and can also be used to trace out the effects of the shock over time.

4. Because the parameters of the monetary-policy rule influence the slope of the dynamic aggregate demand curve, they determine whether a supply shock has a greater effect on output or inflation. When choosing the parameters for monetary policy, a central bank faces a tradeoff between output variability and inflation variability.

5. The dynamic AD–AS model typically assumes that the central bank responds to a 1-percentage-point increase in inflation by increasing the nominal interest rate by more than 1 percentage point, so the real interest rate rises as well. If the central bank responds less vigorously to inflation, the economy becomes unstable. A shock can send inflation spiraling out of control.

KEY CONCEPTS

Taylor rule	Taylor principle	Inflation–Real output volatility trade-off

QUESTIONS FOR REVIEW

1. On a carefully labeled graph, draw the dynamic aggregate supply curve. Explain why it has the slope it has.

2. On a carefully labeled graph, draw the dynamic aggregate demand curve. Explain why it has the slope it has.

3. A central bank has a new head, who decides to raise the target inflation rate from 2 to 3 percent. Using a graph of the dynamic AD–AS model, show the effect of this change. What happens to the nominal interest rate immediately upon the change in policy and in the long run? Explain.

4. A central bank has a new head, who decides to increase the response of interest rates to inflation. How does this change in policy alter the response of the economy to a supply shock? Give both a graphical answer and a more intuitive economic explanation.

PROBLEMS AND APPLICATIONS

1. Derive the long-run equilibrium for the dynamic AD–AS model. Assume there are no shocks to demand or supply ($\epsilon_t = v_t = 0$) and inflation has stabilized ($\pi_t = \pi_{t-1}$), and then use the five equations to derive the value of each variable in the model. Be sure to show each step you follow.

2. Suppose the monetary-policy rule has the wrong natural rate of interest. That is, the central bank follows this rule:

$$i_t = \pi_t + \rho' + \theta_\pi(\pi_t - \pi_t^*) + \theta_Y(Y_t - \overline{Y}_t)$$

where ρ' does not equal ρ, the natural rate of interest in the equation for goods demand. The rest of the dynamic AD–AS model is the same as in the chapter. Solve for the long-run equilibrium under this policy rule. Explain in words the intuition behind your solution.

3. "If a central bank wants to achieve lower nominal interest rates, it has to raise the nominal interest rate." Explain in what way this statement makes sense.

4. The *sacrifice ratio* is the accumulated loss in output that results when the central bank lowers its target for inflation by 1 percentage point. For the parameters used in the text simulation, what is the implied sacrifice ratio? Explain.

5. The text analyzes the case of a temporary shock to the demand for goods and services. Suppose, however, that ϵ_t were to increase permanently. What would happen to the economy over time? In particular, would the inflation rate return to its target in the long run? Why or why not? (*Hint:* It might be helpful to solve for the long-run equilibrium without the assumption that ϵ_t equals zero.) How might the central bank alter its policy rule to deal with this issue?

6. Suppose a central bank does not satisfy the Taylor principle; that is, θ_π is less than zero. Use a graph to analyze the impact of a supply shock. Does this analysis contradict or reinforce the Taylor principle as a guideline for the design of monetary policy?

7. The text assumes that the natural rate of interest ρ is a constant parameter. Suppose instead that it varies over time, so now it has to be written as ρ_t.

   a. How would this change affect the equations for dynamic aggregate demand and dynamic aggregate supply?

   b. How would a shock to ρ_t affect output, inflation, the nominal interest rate, and the real interest rate?

   c. Can you see any practical difficulties that a central bank might face if ρ_t varied over time?

8. Suppose that people's expectations of inflation are subject to random shocks. That is, instead of being merely adaptive, expected inflation in period t, as seen in period $t - 1$, is $E_{t-1}\pi_t = \pi_{t-1} + \eta_{t-1}$, where η_{t-1} is a random shock. This shock is normally zero, but it deviates from zero when some event beyond past inflation causes expected inflation to change. Similarly, $E_t\pi_{t+1} = \pi_t + \eta_t$.

   a. Derive the two equations for dynamic aggregate demand and dynamic aggregate supply in this slightly more general model.

   b. Suppose that the economy experiences an *inflation scare*. That is, in period t, for some reason people come to believe that inflation in period $t + 1$ is going to be higher, so η_t is greater than zero (for this period only). What happens to the DAD and DAS curves in period t? What happens to output, inflation, and nominal and real interest rates in that period? Explain.

   c. What happens to the DAD and DAS curves in period $t + 1$? What happens to output, inflation, and nominal and real interest rates in that period? Explain.

   d. What happens to the economy in subsequent periods?

   e. In what sense are inflation scares self-fulfilling?

9. Use the dynamic AD–AS model to solve for inflation as a function of only lagged inflation and the supply and demand shocks. (Assume target inflation is a constant.)

   a. According to the equation you have derived, does inflation return to its target after a shock? Explain. (*Hint:* Look at the coefficient on lagged inflation.)

   b. Suppose the central bank does not respond to changes in output but only to changes in inflation, so that $\theta_Y = 0$. How, if at all, would this fact change your answer to part (a)?

   c. Suppose the central bank does not respond to changes in inflation but only to changes in output, so that $\theta_\pi = 0$. How, if at all, would this fact change your answer to part (a)?

   d. Suppose the central bank does not follow the Taylor principle but instead raises the nominal interest rate only 0.8 percentage point for each percentage-point increase in inflation. In this case, what is θ_π? How does a shock to demand or supply influence the path of inflation?

APPENDIX

Components of the Synthesis

As explained in this chapter's conclusion, our dynamic *AD–AS* model is a simplified version of what is now known as the New Neo-Classical Synthesis. This synthesis is a version of business-cycle theory that blends the microeconomic rigour favoured by Classical economists with the recognition of some market failure that is the essence of the Keynesian view. The two approaches that are synthesized are called the New Classical and the New Keynesian schools of thought. This Appendix gives you a bit more detail on each of these components of the synthesis.

As a matter of logic, the output of the economy can fluctuate either because the natural level of output fluctuates or because the output of the economy has deviated from its natural level. Throughout most of this book, we have presumed that the natural rate of output grows smoothly over time (as explained by the Solow growth model) and that most short-run fluctuations are deviations from the natural level (as explained by the model of aggregate demand and aggregate supply). **New Keynesian theory** accepts these presumptions. By contrast, what is known as **New Classical theory,** or **Real Business Cycle theory,** suggests that deviations from the natural level are not the whole story and that a significant part of actual fluctuations should be viewed as changes in the natural, or equilibrium, level of output.

According to this theory, short-run economic fluctuations can be explained while maintaining the assumptions of the classical model, which we have used to study the long run. Most important, real business cycle theory assumes that prices are fully flexible, even in the short run. Almost all microeconomic analysis is based on the premise that prices adjust to clear markets. Advocates of real business cycle theory argue that macroeconomic analysis should be based on the same assumption.

Because real business cycle theory assumes complete price flexibility, it is consistent with the classical dichotomy: in this theory, nominal variables, such as the money supply and the price level, do not influence real variables, such as output and employment. To explain fluctuations in real variables, real business cycle theory emphasizes real changes in the economy, such as changes in production technologies, that can alter the economy's natural level. The "real" in real business cycle theory refers to the theory's exclusion of nominal variables in explaining short-run economic fluctuations.

By contrast, new Keynesian economics is based on the premise that market-clearing models such as real business cycle theory cannot explain short-run economic fluctuations. In *The General Theory,* Keynes urged economists to abandon the classical presumption that wages and prices adjust quickly to equilibrate markets. He emphasized that aggregate demand is a primary determinant of national income in the short run. New Keynesian economists accept these basic conclusions, and so they advocate models with sticky wages and prices.

In their research, new Keynesian economists try to develop more fully the Keynesian approach to economic fluctuations. Many new Keynesians accept an extended version of the *IS-LM* model as their theory of aggregate demand—one that is based on the intertemporal approach to household consumption behaviour that we discuss in Chapter 17 and that has been pioneered by real business cycle theorists. On the supply side, new Keynesians are working to provide a similar theory—an intertemporal-optimization base for the Phillips curve. This work tries to explain how wages and prices behave in the short run by identifying more precisely the market imperfections that make wages and prices sticky and that cause output to deviate from its natural level. We discuss some of this research in the second half of this appendix.

In presenting the work of these two schools of thought, this appendix takes an approach that is more descriptive than analytic. Studying recent theoretical developments in detail would require more mathematics than is appropriate for this book. Yet, even without the formal models, we can discuss the direction of this research and get a sense of how different economists are applying microeconomic thinking to better understand macroeconomic fluctuations.[4]

The Theory of Real Business Cycles

When we studied economic growth in Chapters 7 and 8, we described a relatively smooth process. Output grew as population, capital, and the available technology evolved over time. In the Solow growth model, the economy approaches a steady state in which most variables grow together at a rate determined by the constant rate of technological progress.

But is the process of economic growth necessarily as steady as the Solow model assumes? Perhaps technological progress and economic growth occur unevenly. Perhaps there are shocks to the economy that induce short-run fluctuations in the natural level of output and employment. To see how this might be so, we consider a famous allegory which economists have borrowed from author Daniel Defoe.

The Economics of Robinson Crusoe

Robinson Crusoe is a sailor stranded on a desert island. Because Crusoe lives alone, his life is simple. Yet he has to make many economic decisions. Considering Crusoe's decisions—and how they change in response to changing circumstances—sheds light on the decisions that people face in larger, more complex economies.

To keep things simple, imagine that Crusoe engages in only a few activities. Crusoe spends some of his time enjoying leisure, perhaps swimming at his island's

[4] For a more formal treatment of the issues discussed here, see David Romer, *Advanced Macroeconomics,* 3rd. ed. (New York: McGraw-Hill, 2006), and William Scarth, *Macroeconomics: An Introduction to Advanced Methods,* Third ed. (Toronto: Thomson Custom Publishing, 2007).

beaches. He spends the rest of his time working, either catching fish or collecting vines to make into fishing nets. Both forms of work produce a valuable good: fish are Crusoe's consumption, and nets are Crusoe's investment. If we were to compute GDP for Crusoe's island, we would add together the number of fish caught and the number of nets made (weighted by some "price" to reflect Crusoe's relative valuation of these two goods).

Crusoe allocates his time among swimming, fishing, and making nets based on his preferences and the opportunities available to him. It is reasonable to assume that Crusoe optimizes. That is, he chooses the quantities of leisure, consumption, and investment that are best for him given the constraints that nature imposes.

Over time, Crusoe's decisions change as shocks impinge on his life. For example, suppose that one day a big school of fish passes by the island. GDP rises in the Crusoe economy for two reasons. First, Crusoe's productivity rises: with a large school in the water, Crusoe catches more fish per hour of fishing. Second, Crusoe's employment rises. That is, he decides to reduce temporarily his enjoyment of leisure in order to work harder and take advantage of this unusual opportunity to catch fish. The Crusoe economy is booming.

Similarly, suppose that a storm arrives one day. Because the storm makes outdoor activity difficult, productivity falls: each hour spent fishing or making nets yields a smaller output. In response, Crusoe decides to spend less time working and to wait out the storm in his hut. Consumption of fish and investment in nets both fall, so GDP falls as well. The Crusoe economy is in recession.

Suppose that one day Crusoe is attacked by natives. While he is defending himself, Crusoe has less time to enjoy leisure. Thus, the increased demand for defense spurs employment in the Crusoe economy, especially in the "defense industry." To some extent, Crusoe spends less time fishing for consumption. To a larger extent, he spends less time making nets, because this task is easy to put off for a while. Thus, defense spending crowds out investment. Because Crusoe spends more time at work, GDP (which now includes the value of national defense) rises. The Crusoe economy is experiencing a wartime boom.

What is notable about this story of booms and recessions is its simplicity. *In this story, fluctuations in output, employment, consumption, investment, and productivity are all the natural and desirable response of an individual to the inevitable changes in his environment.* In the Crusoe economy, fluctuations have nothing to do with monetary policy, sticky prices, or any type of market failure.

According to the theory of real business cycles, fluctuations in our economy are much the same as fluctuations in Robinson Crusoe's. Shocks to our ability to produce goods and services (like the changing weather on Crusoe's island) alter the natural levels of employment and output. These shocks are not necessarily desirable, but they are inevitable. Once the shocks occur, it is desirable for GDP, employment, and other real macroeconomic variables to fluctuate in response.

The parable of Robinson Crusoe, like any model in economics, is not intended to be a literal description of how the economy works. Instead, it tries to get at the essence of the complex phenomenon that we call the business cycle. Does the parable achieve this goal? Are the booms and recessions in modern industrial economies really like the fluctuations on Robinson Crusoe's island? Economists disagree about the answer to this question and, therefore, disagree about the validity of real business cycle theory. At the heart of the debate are four basic issues:

- The interpretation of the labour market: Do fluctuations in employment reflect voluntary changes in the quantity of labour supplied?

- The importance of technology shocks: Does the economy's production function experience large, exogenous shifts in the short run?

- The neutrality of money: Do changes in the money supply have only nominal effects?

- The flexibility of wages and prices: Do wages and prices adjust quickly and completely to balance supply and demand?

Whether or not you view the parable of Robinson Crusoe as a plausible allegory for the business cycle, considering these four issues is instructive, for each of them raises fundamental questions about how the economy works.

The Interpretation of the Labour Market

Real business cycle theory emphasizes the idea that the quantity of labour supplied at any given time depends on the incentives that workers face. Just as Robinson Crusoe changes his work effort voluntarily in response to changing circumstances, workers are willing to work more hours when they are well rewarded and are willing to work fewer hours when they are poorly rewarded. Sometimes, if the reward for working is sufficiently small, workers choose to forgo working altogether—at least temporarily. This willingness to reallocate hours of work over time is called the **intertemporal substitution of labour.**

To see how intertemporal substitution affects labour supply, consider the following example. A university student finishing her second year has two summer vacations left before graduation. She wishes to work for one of these summers (so she can buy a car after she graduates) and to relax at the beach during the other summer. How should she choose which summer to work?

Let W_1 be her real wage in the first summer and W_2 the real wage she expects in the second summer. To choose which summer to work, the student compares these two wages. Yet, because she can earn interest on money earned earlier, a dollar earned in the first summer is more valuable than a dollar earned in the second summer. Let r be the real interest rate. If the student works in the first summer and saves her earnings, she will have $(1 + r)W_1$ a year later. If she works in the second summer, she will have W_2. The intertemporal relative wage—that is, the earnings from working the first summer relative to the earnings from working the second summer—is

$$\text{Intertemporal Relative Wage} = \frac{(1 + r)W_1}{W_2}.$$

Working the first summer is more attractive if the interest rate is high or if the wage is high relative to the wage expected to prevail in the future.

According to real business cycle theory, all workers perform this cost–benefit analysis when deciding whether to work or to enjoy leisure. If the wage is temporarily high or if the interest rate is high, it is a good time to work. If the wage is temporarily low or if the interest rate is low, it is a good time to enjoy leisure.

Real business cycle theory uses the intertemporal substitution of labour to explain why employment and output fluctuate. Shocks to the economy that cause the interest rate to rise or the wage to be temporarily high cause people to want to work more. The increase in work effort raises employment and production. Shocks that cause the interest rate to fall or the wage to be temporarily low decrease employment and production.

Critics of real business cycle theory believe that fluctuations in employment do not reflect changes in the amount people want to work. They believe that *desired* employment is not very sensitive to the real wage and the real interest rate. They point out that the unemployment rate fluctuates substantially over the business cycle. The high unemployment in recessions suggests that the labour market does not clear: if people were voluntarily choosing not to work in recessions, they would not call themselves unemployed. These critics conclude that wages do not adjust to equilibrate labour supply and labour demand, as real business cycle models assume.

In reply, advocates of real business cycle theory argue that unemployment statistics are difficult to interpret. The mere fact that the unemployment rate is high does not mean that intertemporal substitution of labour is unimportant. Individuals who voluntarily choose not to work may call themselves unemployed so they can collect employment-insurance benefits. Or they may call themselves unemployed because they would be willing to work if they were offered the wage they receive in most years.

The Importance of Technology Shocks

The Crusoe economy fluctuates because of changes in the weather, which induce Crusoe to alter his work effort. In real business cycle theory, the analogous variable is technology, which determines an economy's ability to turn inputs (capital and labour) into output (goods and services). The theory assumes that our economy experiences fluctuations in technology and that these fluctuations in technology, that are called **technology shocks,** cause fluctuations in output and employment. When the available production technology improves, the economy produces more output, and real wages rise. Because of intertemporal substitution of labour, the improved technology also leads to greater employment. Real business cycle theorists often explain recessions as periods of "technological regress." According to these models, output and employment fall during recessions because the available production technology deteriorates, lowering output and reducing the incentive to work.

Critics of real business cycle theory are skeptical that the economy experiences large shocks to technology. It is a more common presumption that technological progress occurs gradually. Critics argue that technological regress is especially implausible: the accumulation of technological knowledge may slow down, but it is hard to imagine that it would go in reverse.

Advocates respond by taking a broad view of shocks to technology. They argue that there are many events that, although not literally technological, affect the economy much as technology shocks do. For example, bad weather, the passage of strict environmental regulations, or increases in raw material prices have effects similar to adverse changes in technology: they all reduce our ability to turn capital and labour into goods and services. Whether such events are sufficiently common to explain the frequency and magnitude of business cycles is an open question.

The Neutrality of Money

Just as money has no role in the Crusoe economy, real business cycle theory assumes that money in our economy is neutral, even in the short run. That is, monetary policy is assumed not to affect real variables such as output and employment. Not only does the neutrality of money give real business cycle theory its name, but neutrality is also the theory's most radical assumption.

Critics argue that the evidence does not support short-run monetary neutrality. They point out that reductions in money growth and inflation are almost always associated with periods of high unemployment. Monetary policy appears to have a strong influence on the real economy.

Advocates of real business cycle theory argue that their critics confuse the direction of causation between money and output. These advocates claim that the money supply is endogenous: fluctuations in output might cause fluctuations in the money supply. For example, when output rises because of a beneficial technology shock, the quantity of money demanded rises. The Bank of Canada may respond by raising the money supply to accommodate the greater demand. This endogenous response of money to economic activity may give the illusion of monetary non-neutrality.[5]

CASE STUDY

Testing for Monetary Neutrality

The direction of causation between fluctuations in the money supply and fluctuations in output is hard to establish. The only sure way to determine cause and effect would be to conduct a controlled experiment. Imagine that the central bank set the money supply according to some random process. Every January, the Governor of the Bank of Canada would flip a coin. Heads would mean an expansionary monetary policy for the coming year; tails a contractionary one. After a number of years we would know with confidence the effects of monetary policy. If output and employment usually rose after the coin came up heads and usually fell after it came up tails, then we would conclude that monetary

[5] Robert G. King and Charles I. Plosser, "Money, Credit, and Prices in a Real Business Cycle," *American Economic Review* 74 (June 1984): 363–380.

policy has real effects. On the other hand if the flip of the coin were unrelated to subsequent economic performance, then we would conclude that real business cycle theorists are right about the neutrality of money.

Unfortunately for scientific progress, but fortunately for the economy, economists are not allowed to conduct such experiments. Instead, we must glean what we can from the data that history gives us.

One classic study in the history of monetary policy is the 1963 book by Milton Friedman and Anna Schwartz, *A Monetary History of the United States, 1867–1960.* This book describes the historical events that shaped decisions over monetary policy and the economic events that resulted from those decisions. Friedman and Schwartz claim, for instance, that the death in 1928 of Benjamin Strong, the president of the New York Federal Reserve Bank, was one cause of the Great Depression of the 1930s: Strong's death left a power vacuum at the Fed, which prevented the Fed from responding vigorously as economic conditions deteriorated. In other words, Strong's death, like the Fed's coin coming up tails, was a random event leading to more contractionary monetary policy.[6]

A more recent study by Christina Romer and David Romer follows in the footsteps of Friedman and Schwartz. The Romers carefully read through the minutes of the meetings of the Federal Reserve's Open Market Committee, which sets monetary policy in the United States. From these minutes, they identified dates when the Fed appears to have shifted its policy toward reducing the rate of inflation. The Romers argue that these dates are, in essence, the equivalent of the Fed's coin coming up tails. They then show that the economy experienced a decline in output and employment after each of these dates. Thus, the Romers' evidence appears to establish the short-run non-neutrality of money.[7]

Interpretations of history, however, are always open to dispute. No one can be sure what would have happened during the 1930s had Benjamin Strong lived. Similarly, not everyone is convinced that the Romers' dates are as exogenous as a coin's flip: perhaps the Fed was actually responding to events that would have caused declining output and employment even without Fed action. Thus, while most economists are convinced that monetary policy has an important role in the business cycle, this judgment is based on the accumulation of evidence from many studies. There is no "smoking gun" that convinces absolutely everyone. ■

The Flexibility of Wages and Prices

Real business cycle theory assumes that wages and prices adjust quickly to clear markets, just as Crusoe always achieves his optimal level of GDP without any impediment from a market imperfection. Advocates of this theory believe that the market imperfection of sticky wages and prices is not important for understanding

[6] Milton Friedman and Anna J. Schwartz, *A Monetary History of the United States, 1867–1960* (Princeton, NJ: Princeton University Press, 1960).
[7] Christina Romer and David Romer, "Does Monetary Policy Matter? A New Test in the Spirit of Friedman and Schwartz," *NBER Macroeconomics Annual* (1989): 121–170.

economic fluctuations. They also believe that the assumption of flexible prices is superior methodologically to the assumption of sticky prices, because it ties macroeconomic theory more closely to microeconomic theory.

Critics point out that many wages and prices are not flexible. They believe that this inflexibility explains both the existence of unemployment and the non-neutrality of money. To explain why prices are sticky, they rely on the various new Keynesian theories that we discuss in the next section.[8]

New Keynesian Economics

Most economists are skeptical of the basic version of the theory of real business cycles and believe that short-run fluctuations in output and employment involve deviations from the economy's natural levels of these variables. They think these deviations occur because wages and prices are slow to adjust to changing economic conditions. As we have discussed in Chapters 9, 13, and earlier in the present chapter, this stickiness makes the short-run aggregate supply curve upward sloping rather than vertical. As a result, fluctuations in aggregate demand cause short-run fluctuations in output and employment. The most recent generation of real business cycle models have embraced the hypothesis of sticky prices, so that both demand and technology shocks play a role in determining cycles. As a result, as noted already, a synthesis has developed in modern research in macroeconomics.[9]

But why exactly are prices sticky? New Keynesian research has attempted to answer this question by examining the microeconomics behind short-run price adjustment. By doing so, it tries to put the traditional theories of short-run fluctuations on a firmer theoretical foundation.

Small Menu Costs and Aggregate-Demand Externalities

One reason prices do not adjust immediately in the short run is that there are costs to price adjustment. To change its prices, a firm may need to send out a new catalogue to customers, distribute new price lists to its sales staff, or, in the case of a restaurant, print new menus. These costs of price adjustment, called **menu costs,** lead firms to adjust prices intermittently rather than continuously.

---

[8] For a textbook that emphasizes the real business cycle approach, see Stephen Williamson, *Macro-economics Canadian Edition* (Toronto: Pearson, Addison-Wesley, 2004). To read more about real business cycle theory, see N. Gregory Mankiw, "Real Business Cycles: A New Keynesian Perspective," *Journal of Economic Perspectives* 3 (Summer 1989): 79–90; Bennett T. McCallum, "Real Business Cycle Models," in R. Barro, ed., *Modern Business Cycle Theory* (Cambridge, MA: Harvard University Press, 1989), 16–50; and Charles I. Plosser, "Understanding Real Business Cycles," *Journal of Economic Perspectives* 3 (Summer 1989): 51–77.

[9] See Marvin Goodfriend and Robert G. King, "The New Neoclassical Synthesis and the Role of Monetary Policy," *NBER Macroeconomics Annual* 1997, pp. 231–283.

Economists disagree about whether menu costs explain the short-run stickiness of prices. Skeptics point out that menu costs are usually very small. How can small menu costs help to explain recessions, which are very costly for society? Proponents reply that small does not mean inconsequential: even though menu costs are small for the individual firm, they can have large effects on the economy as a whole.

According to proponents of the menu-cost hypothesis, to understand why prices adjust slowly, we must acknowledge that there are externalities to price adjustment: a price reduction by one firm benefits other firms in the economy. When a firm lowers the price it charges, it slightly lowers the average price level and thereby raises real money balances. The increase in real money balances expands aggregate income (by shifting the *LM* curve outward). The economic expansion in turn raises the demand for the products of all firms. This macroeconomic impact of one firm's price adjustment on the demand for all other firms' products is called an **aggregate-demand externality.**

In the presence of this aggregate-demand externality, small menu costs can make prices sticky, and this stickiness can have a large cost to society. Suppose that a firm originally sets its price too high and later must decide whether to cut its price. The firm makes this decision by comparing the benefit of a price cut—higher sales and profit—to the cost of price adjustment. Yet because of the aggregate-demand externality, the benefit to society of the price cut would exceed the benefit to the firm. The firm ignores this externality when making its decision, so it may decide not to pay the menu cost and cut its price even though the price cut is socially desirable. *Hence, sticky prices may be optimal for those setting prices, even though they are undesirable for the economy as a whole.*[10]

CASE STUDY

How Large are Menu Costs?

When microeconomists discuss a firm's costs, they usually emphasize the labour, capital, and raw materials needed to produce the firm's output. The cost of changing prices is rarely mentioned. For many purposes, this omission is a reasonable simplification. Yet the cost of changing prices is not zero, as was established by a study of price changes in five large supermarket chains.

In this study, a group of economists examined a unique store-level data set to determine how large menu costs really are. They found that price adjustment "is a complex process, requiring dozens of steps and a nontrivial amount of resources."

---

[10] For more on this topic, see N. Gregory Mankiw, "Small Menu Costs and Large Business Cycles: A Macroeconomic Model of Monopoly," *Quarterly Journal of Economics* 100 (May 1985): 529–537; George A. Akerlof and Janet L. Yellen, "A Near Rational Model of the Business Cycle, With Wage and Price Inertia," *Quarterly Journal of Economics* 100 (Supplement 1985): 823–838; and Olivier Jean Blanchard and Nobuhiro Kiyotaki, "Monopolistic Competition and the Effects of Aggregate Demand," *American Economic Review* 77 (September 1987): 647–666. These three articles are reprinted in N. Gregory Mankiw and David Romer, eds., *New Keynesian Economics* (Cambridge, MA: MIT Press, 1991).

These resources include the labour cost of changing shelf prices, the costs of printing and delivering new price tags, and the cost of supervising the process. The data included detailed measurements of these costs; when necessary, a stop-watch was used to measure the labour input.

The study reported that, for a typical store in a supermarket chain, menu costs add up to $105,887 a year. This amount equals 0.70 percent of a store's revenue, or 35 percent of net profits. If that total is divided by the number of price changes that a store institutes in a given year on all of its products, the result is that each price change costs $0.52.

A notable finding from this research is that the cost of changing prices depends on the legal environment. One supermarket chain examined in the study was operating in a state with an item-pricing law, which required that a separate price tag be placed on each individual item sold (in addition to the price tag on the shelf). The law raised the estimated cost of a price change from $0.52 to $1.33. As one would expect, the higher cost of changing prices reduced the frequency of price adjustment: the supermarket chain operating under the item-pricing law changed 6.3 percent of product prices per week, compared to 15.6 percent for other chains.

These findings apply to only a single industry, so one should be cautious about extrapolating the results to the entire economy. Nonetheless, the authors of the study conclude that "the magnitude of the menu costs we find is large enough to be capable of having macroeconomic significance."[11] ∎

Recessions as Coordination Failure

Some new Keynesian economists suggest that recessions result from a failure of coordination among economic decisionmakers. In recessions, output is low, workers are unemployed, and factories sit idle. It is possible to imagine allocations of resources in which everyone is better off—for example, the high output and employment of the 1920s were clearly preferable to the low output and employment of the 1930s. If society fails to reach an outcome that is feasible and that everyone prefers, then the members of society have failed to coordinate their behaviour in some way.

Coordination problems can arise in the setting of wages and prices because those who set them must anticipate the actions of other wage and price setters. Union leaders negotiating wages are concerned about the concessions other unions will win. Firms setting prices are mindful of the prices other firms will charge.

To see how a recession could arise as a failure of coordination, consider the following parable. The economy is made up of two firms. After a fall in the money supply, each firm must decide whether to cut its price, based on its goal of maximizing profit. Each firm's profit, however, depends not only on its pricing decision but also on the decision made by the other firm.

---

[11] Daniel Levy, Mark Bergen, Shantanu Dutta, and Robert Venable, "The Magnitude of Menu Costs: Direct Evidence from Large Supermarket Chains," *Quarterly Journal of Economics* 112 (August 1997): 791–825. All dollar figures in this case study are expressed in 1991 dollars, since that is the year when the data were collected. If expressed in 2005 dollars, they would be about 40 percent larger.

TABLE 14-2

		Firm 2	
		Cut Price	Keep High Price
Firm 1	Cut Price	**Firm 1** makes $30 **Firm 2** makes $30	**Firm 1** makes $5 **Firm 2** makes $15
	Keep High Price	**Firm 1** makes $15 **Firm 2** makes $5	**Firm 1** makes $15 **Firm 2** makes $15

Price Setting and Coordination Failure This table shows a hypothetical "game" between two firms, each of which is deciding whether to cut prices after a fall in the money supply. Each firm must choose a strategy without knowing the strategy the other firm will choose. What outcome would you expect?

The choices facing each firm are listed in Table 14-2, which shows how the profits of the two firms depend on their actions. If neither firm cuts its price, real money balances are low, a recession ensues, and each firm makes a profit of only $15. If both firms cut their prices, real money balances are high, a recession is avoided, and each firm makes a profit of $30. Although both firms prefer to avoid a recession, neither can do so by its own actions. If one firm cuts its price while the other does not, a mild recession follows. The firm making the price cut gains customers but gets less revenue from each one. If demand is inelastic, the price-cutting firm will lose; in the example depicted in Table 14-2, this firm makes only $5, while the other firm makes $15.

The essence of this parable is that each firm's decision influences the set of outcomes available to the other firm. When one firm cuts its price, it improves the position of the other firm, because the other firm can then act to avoid the recession. This positive impact of one firm's price cut on the other firm's profit opportunities might arise from an aggregate-demand externality.

What outcome should we expect in this economy? On the one hand, if each firm expects the other to cut its price, both will cut prices, resulting in the preferred outcome in which each makes $30. On the other hand, if each firm expects the other to maintain its price, both will maintain their prices, resulting in the inferior result in which each makes $15. Either of these outcomes is possible: economists say that there are *multiple equilibria*.

The inferior outcome, in which each firm makes $15, is an example of a **coordination failure.** If the two firms could coordinate, they would both cut their price and reach the preferred outcome. In the real world, unlike in our parable, coordination is often difficult because the number of firms setting prices is large. *The moral of the story is that prices can be sticky simply because people expect them to be sticky, even though stickiness is in no one's interest.*[12]

---

[12] For more on coordination failure, see Russell Cooper and Andrew John, "Coordinating Coordination Failures in Keynesian Models," *Quarterly Journal of Economics* 103 (1988): 441–463; and Laurence Ball and David Romer, "Sticky Prices as Coordination Failure," *American Economic Review* 81 (June 1991): 539–552.

Experimental Evidence on Coordination Games

What happens when economic actors, such as the firms in our parable, face a problem of coordination? Do they somehow manage to choose the preferred outcome, knowing that this outcome makes them both better off? Or do they fail to coordinate?

One way to answer this question is by experimentation. In two research studies, student volunteers were asked to play coordination games, such as the "game" in Table 14-2. To maintain anonymity, the students played each other through computer terminals. To ensure earnest play, the students were rewarded with small amounts of money depending on how many points they won in the game.

Consider what strategy you would choose if you were playing the game in Table 14-2. Remember that you don't know the strategy of the other player: you only know that the other player is facing the same decision you are. Would you cut your price or keep it high? Would your strategy change if the payoffs in the upper left corner were $100 instead of $30? Or if they were only $16?

The experimental evidence shows that economic actors do not always coordinate by choosing the preferred outcome. Whether coordination occurs depends on the specific payoff numbers and, therefore, varies from game to game. But, in some games, coordination failure is the most common outcome, while in other games there is strong support for cooperation as firms and workers exchange gifts—high wages for a high level of worker effort—just as predicted in efficiency-wage theory (Chapter 6).[13] ∎

The Staggering of Wages and Prices

Not everyone in the economy sets new wages and prices at the same time. Instead, the adjustment of wages and prices throughout the economy is staggered. Staggering slows the process of coordination and price adjustment. In particular, *staggering makes the overall level of wages and prices adjust gradually, even when individual wages and prices change frequently.*

Consider the following example, which, for simplicity, involves no aggregate-demand externality. Suppose first that price setting is synchronized: every firm adjusts its price on the first day of every month. If the money supply and aggregate demand rise on May 10, output will be higher from May 10 to June 1 because prices are fixed during this interval. But on June 1 all firms will raise their prices in response to the higher demand, ending the boom.

---

[13] Russell Cooper, Douglas V. DeJong, Robert Forsythe, and Thomas W. Ross, "Selection Criteria in Coordination Games: Some Experimental Results," *American Economic Review* 80 (March 1990): 218–233; John B. Van Huyck, Raymond C. Battalio, and Richard O. Beil, "Tacit Coordination Games, Strategic Uncertainty, and Coordination Failure," *American Economic Review* 80 (March 1990): 234–248. Martin Brown, Armin Falk and Ernst Fehr, "Relational Contracts and the Nature of Market Interactions," *Econometrica* 72 (May 2004): 747–780.

Now suppose that price setting is staggered: half the firms set prices on the first of each month and half on the fifteenth. If the money supply rises on May 10, then half the firms can raise their prices on May 15. But if the demand for their product is elastic, these firms will probably not raise their prices very much. Because half the firms will not be changing their prices on the fifteenth, a price increase by any firm will raise that firm's *relative* price, causing it to lose customers. (By contrast, if all firms are synchronized, all firms can raise prices together, leaving relative prices unaffected.) If the May 15 price setters make little adjustment in their prices, then the other firms will make little adjustment when their turn comes on June 1, because they also want to avoid relative price changes. And so on. The price level rises slowly as the result of small price increases on the first and the fifteenth of each month. Hence, staggering makes the overall price level adjust sluggishly, because no firm wishes to be the first to post a substantial price increase.

Staggering also affects wage determination. Consider, for example, how a fall in the money supply works its way through the economy. A smaller money supply reduces aggregate demand, which in turn requires a proportionate fall in nominal wages to maintain full employment. Each worker might be willing to take a lower nominal wage if all other wages were to fall proportionately. The worker could then reasonably expect a reduction in the overall level of goods prices. But each worker is reluctant to be the first to take a pay cut, knowing that this means, at least temporarily, a fall in his or her relative wage. Since the setting of wages is staggered, the reluctance of each worker to reduce his or her wage first makes the overall level of wages slow to respond to changes in aggregate demand. In other words, the staggered setting of individual wages makes the overall level of wages sticky.[14]

Conclusion

Recent developments in the theory of short-run economic fluctuations remind us that we do not understand economic fluctuations as well as we would like. Fundamental questions about the economy remain open to dispute. Is the stickiness of wages and prices a key to understanding economic fluctuations? Does monetary policy have real effects?

The way economists answer these questions affects how they view the role of economic policy. Economists who believe that wages and prices are sticky, such as those pursuing new Keynesian theories, often believe that monetary and fiscal policy should be used to try to stabilize the economy. Price stickiness is a type of market imperfection, and so it is *possible,* but not necessarily the case that stabilization policies can raise economic well-being for society as a whole.

---

[14] For more on the effects of staggering, see John Taylor, "Staggered Price Setting in a Macro Model," *American Economic Review* 69 (May 1979): 108–113; and Olivier J. Blanchard, "Price Asynchronization and Price Level Inertia," in R. Dornbusch and Mario Henrique Simonsen, eds., *Inflation, Debt, and Indexation* (Cambridge, MA: MIT Press, 1983), 3–24.

By contrast, the basic version of the real business cycle theory suggests that the government's influence on the economy is limited and that even if the government could stabilize the economy, it should not try to do so. According to this theory, the ups and downs of the business cycle are the natural and efficient response of the economy to changing technological possibilities. The standard real business cycle model does not include any type of market imperfection. In this model, the "invisible hand" of the marketplace guides the economy to an optimal allocation of resources.

Although this appendix has divided recent research into two distinct camps, not all economists fall entirely into one camp or the other. Over time, more economists have been trying to incorporate the strengths of both approaches into their research. Real business cycle theory places a heavy emphasis on intertemporal optimization and forward-looking behaviour, while new Keynesian theory stresses the importance of sticky prices and other market imperfections. Increasingly, theories at the research frontier meld many of these elements to advance our understanding of economic fluctuations. It is this kind of work that makes macroeconomics an exciting field of study.[15]

Summary

1. The theory of real business cycles is an explanation of short-run economic fluctuations built on the assumptions of the classical model, including the classical dichotomy and the flexibility of wages and prices. According to this theory, economic fluctuations are the natural and efficient response of the economy to changing economic circumstances, especially changes in technology.

2. Advocates and critics of real business cycle theory disagree about whether employment fluctuations represent intertemporal substitution of labour, whether technology shocks cause most economic fluctuations, whether monetary policy affects real variables, and whether the short-run stickiness of wages and prices is important for understanding economic fluctuations.

---

[15] As noted earlier in the chapter, the combined approach is called the new neoclassical synthesis. Here is a more complete list of references: Marvin Goodfriend, "Monetary Policy in the New Neo-classical Synthesis: A Primer," Federal Reserve Bank of Richmond *Quarterly Review 90* (Summer 2004): 21–45; Julio Rotemberg and Michael Woodford, "An Optimization-Based Econometric Framework for the Evaluation of Monetary Policy," *NBER Macroeconomics Annual* (1997): 297–346; Richard Clarida, Jordi Gali, and Mark Gertler, "The Science of Monetary Policy: A New Keynesian Perspective," *Journal of Economic Literature* 37 (December 1999): 1661–1707. These papers examine models in which both forward-looking optimizing behaviour and sticky prices play central roles in explaining the business cycle and the short-run effects of monetary policy, and so they go beyond the simplified synthesis model that we presented in the main text of this chapter.

3. New Keynesian research on short-run economic fluctuations builds on the traditional model of aggregate demand and aggregate supply and tries to provide a better explanation of why wages and prices are sticky in the short run. One new Keynesian theory suggests that even small costs of price adjustment can have large macroeconomic effects because of aggregate-demand externalities. Another theory suggests that recessions occur as a type of coordination failure. A third theory suggests that staggering in price adjustment makes the overall price level sluggish in response to changing economic conditions.

4. Modern macroeconomics combines the real business cycle and new Keynesian approaches in what is called the new neoclassical synthesis.

KEY CONCEPTS

New Keynesian economics

Real business cycle theory

Intertemporal substitution of labour

Technology shocks

Menu costs

Aggregate-demand externality

Coordination failure

QUESTIONS FOR REVIEW

1. How does real business cycle theory explain fluctuations in employment?

2. What are the four central disagreements in the debate over real business cycle theory?

3. How does staggering of price adjustment by individual firms affect the adjustment of the overall price level to a monetary contraction?

MORE PROBLEMS AND APPLICATIONS

1. According to real business cycle theory, permanent and transitory shocks to technology should have very different effects on the economy. Use the parable of Robinson Crusoe to compare the effects of a transitory shock (good weather expected to last only a few days) and a permanent shock (a beneficial change in weather patterns). Which shock would have a greater effect on Crusoe's work effort? On GDP? Is it possible that one of these shocks might reduce work effort?

2. Suppose that prices are fully flexible and that the output of the economy fluctuates because of

shocks to technology, as real business cycle theory claims.

a. If the central bank holds the money supply constant, what will happen to the price level as output fluctuates?

b. If the central bank adjusts the money supply to stabilize the price level, what will happen to the money supply as output fluctuates?

c. Many economists have observed that fluctuations in the money supply are positively correlated with fluctuations in output. Is this evidence against real business cycle theory?

3. Coordination failure is an idea with many applications. Here is one: Andy and Ben are running a business together. If both work hard, the business is a success, and they each earn $100 in profit. If one them fails to work hard, the business is less successful, and they each earn $70. If neither works hard, the business is even less successful, and they each earn $60 in profit. Working hard takes $20 worth of effort.

 a. Set up this "game" as in Table 14-2.

 b. What outcome would Andy and Ben prefer?

 c. What outcome would occur if each expected his partner to work hard?

 d. What outcome would occur if each expected his partner to be lazy?

 e. Is this a good description of the relationship among partners? Why or why not?

4. (This problem uses basic microeconomics.) The chapter discussed the price-adjustment decisions of firms with menu costs. This problem asks you to consider that issue more analytically in the simple case of a single firm.

 a. Draw a diagram describing a monopoly firm, including a downward-sloping demand curve and a cost curve. (For simplicity, assume that marginal cost is constant, so the cost curve is a horizontal line.) Show the profit-maximizing price and quantity. Show the areas that represent profit and consumer surplus at this optimum.

 b. Now suppose the firm has previously announced a price slightly above the optimum. Show this price and the quantity sold. Show the area representing the lost profit from the excessive price. Show the area representing the lost consumer surplus.

 c. The firm decides whether to cut its price by comparing the extra profit from a lower price to the menu cost. In making this decision, what externality is the firm ignoring? In what sense is the firm's price-adjustment decision inefficient?

PART V

Macroeconomic Policy Debates

Stabilization Policy

*The Federal Reserve's job is to take away the punch bowl just as the party
gets going.*

— *William McChesney Martin*

*What we need is not a skilled monetary driver of the economic vehicle
continuously turning the steering wheel to adjust to the unexpected
irregularities of the route, but some means of keeping the monetary passenger
who is in the back seat as ballast from occasionally leaning over and giving the
steering wheel a jerk that threatens to send the car off the road.*

— *Milton Friedman*

How should government policymakers respond to the business cycle? The
two quotations above—the first from a former chairman of the Federal
Reserve (the U.S. central bank), the second from a prominent critic of
central banks—show the diversity of opinion over how this question is best
answered.

Some economists, such as William McChesney Martin, view the economy as
inherently unstable. They argue that the economy experiences frequent shocks
to aggregate demand and aggregate supply. Unless policymakers use monetary
and fiscal policy to stabilize the economy, these shocks will lead to unnecessary
and inefficient fluctuations in output, unemployment, and inflation. According
to the popular saying, macroeconomic policy should "lean against the wind,"
stimulating the economy when it is depressed and slowing the economy when
it is overheated.

Other economists, such as Milton Friedman, view the economy as naturally
stable. They blame bad economic policies for the large and inefficient fluctuations we have sometimes experienced. They argue that economic policy should
not try to "fine-tune" the economy. Instead, economic policymakers should
admit their limited abilities and be satisfied if they do no harm.

This debate has persisted for decades with numerous protagonists advancing
various arguments for their positions. It became especially relevant as economies

around the world sank into recession in 2008. The fundamental issue is how policymakers should use the theory of short-run economic fluctuations developed in the preceding chapters.

In this chapter we ask two questions that arise in this debate. First, should monetary and fiscal policy take an active role in trying to stabilize the economy, or should policy remain passive? Second, should policymakers be free to use their discretion in responding to changing economic conditions, or should they be committed to following a fixed policy rule?

15-1 Should Policy Be Active or Passive?

Policymakers in the federal government view economic stabilization as one of their primary responsibilities. The analysis of macroeconomic policy is a regular duty of the Department of Finance and the Bank of Canada. When the government is considering a major change in either fiscal or monetary policy, foremost in the discussion are how the change will influence inflation and unemployment and whether aggregate demand needs to be stimulated or restrained.

Although the government has long conducted monetary and fiscal policy, the view that it should use these policy instruments to try to stabilize the economy is more recent. The federal *White Paper* of 1945 was the landmark document in which the government first held itself accountable for macroeconomic performance. The *White Paper* states that the "government will be prepared, in periods when unemployment is threatening, to incur deficits and increases in the national debt resulting from its employment and income policy." This policy commitment was written when the memory of the Great Depression was still fresh. The lawmakers who wrote it believed, as many economists do, that in the absence of an active government role in the economy, events like the Great Depression could occur regularly.

To many economists the case for active government policy is clear and simple. Recessions are periods of high unemployment, low incomes, and increased economic hardship. The model of aggregate demand and aggregate supply shows how shocks to the economy can cause recessions. It also shows how monetary and fiscal policy can limit recessions by responding to these shocks. These economists consider it wasteful not to use these policy instruments to stabilize the economy.

Other economists are critical of the government's attempts to stabilize the economy. These critics argue that the government should take a hands-off approach to macroeconomic policy. At first, this view might seem surprising. If our model shows how to prevent or reduce the severity of recessions, why do these critics want the government to refrain from using monetary and fiscal policy for economic stabilization? To find out, let's consider some of their arguments.

Lags in the Implementation and Effects of Policies

Economic stabilization would be easy if the effects of policy were immediate. Making policy would be like driving a car: policymakers would simply adjust their instruments to keep the economy on the desired path.

Making economic policy, however, is less like driving a car than it is like piloting a large ship. A car changes direction almost immediately after the steering wheel is turned. By contrast, a ship changes course long after the pilot adjusts the rudder, and once the ship starts to turn, it continues turning long after the rudder is set back to normal. A novice pilot is likely to oversteer and, after noticing the mistake, overreact by steering too much in the opposite direction. The ship's path could become unstable, as the novice responds to previous mistakes by making larger and larger corrections.

Like a ship's pilot, economic policymakers face the problem of long lags. Indeed, the problem for policymakers is even more difficult, because the lengths of the lags are hard to predict. These long and variable lags greatly complicate the conduct of monetary and fiscal policy.

Economists distinguish between two lags that are relevant to the conduct of stabilization policy: the inside lag and the outside lag. The **inside lag** is the time between a shock to the economy and the policy action responding to that shock. This lag arises because it takes time for policymakers first to recognize that a shock has occurred and then to put appropriate policies into effect. The **outside lag** is the time between a policy action and its influence on the economy. This lag arises because policies do not immediately influence spending, income, and employment.

Fiscal policy can have a long inside lag, since changes in spending or taxes must be voted through both the House of Commons and the Senate. The process of parliamentary committee hearings can be slow and cumbersome. An additional problem concerning fiscal policy is that provincial governments sometimes want to push the economy in the opposite direction from what is intended by the federal government. (This coordination problem was discussed more fully in Chapter 12.)

Monetary policy has a much shorter inside lag than fiscal policy, for a central bank can decide on and implement a policy change in less than a day, but monetary policy has a substantial outside lag. Monetary policy works by changing the money supply and thereby interest rates and the exchange rate, which in turn influence the investment and net-exports components of aggregate demand. But many firms make investment, import, and export plans far in advance. Therefore, a change in monetary policy is thought not to affect economic activity until about six months after it is made.

The long and variable lags associated with monetary and fiscal policy certainly make stabilizing the economy more difficult. Advocates of passive policy argue that, because of these lags, successful stabilization policy is almost impossible. Indeed, attempts to stabilize the economy can be destabilizing. Suppose that the economy's condition changes between the beginning of a policy action and its impact on the economy. In this case, active policy may end up stimulating the economy when it is heating up or depressing the economy when it is cooling off. Advocates of active policy admit that such lags do require policymakers to be cautious. But, they argue, these lags do not necessarily mean that policy should be completely passive, especially in the face of a severe and protracted economic downturn, such as the recession that began in 2008.

Some policies, called **automatic stabilizers,** are designed to reduce the lags associated with stabilization policy. Automatic stabilizers are policies that stimulate or depress the economy when necessary *without* any deliberate policy change. For example, the system of income taxes automatically reduces taxes when the economy goes into a recession, without any change in the tax laws, because individuals and corporations pay less tax when their incomes fall. Similarly, the employment-insurance and welfare systems automatically raise transfer payments when the economy moves into a recession, because more people apply for benefits. One can view these automatic stabilizers as a type of fiscal policy without any inside lag.

CASE STUDY

Profit Sharing as an Automatic Stabilizer

Economists often propose policies to improve the automatic-stabilizing powers of the economy. The economist Martin Weitzman has made one of the most intriguing suggestions: profit sharing. Today, most labour contracts specify a fixed wage. For example, a manufacturing firm might pay assembly-line workers $30 an hour. Weitzman recommends that the workers' total pay should depend on their firm's profits. A profit-sharing contract for this firm might pay workers $15 for each hour of work, but in addition the workers would divide among themselves a share of the firm's profit.

Weitzman argues that profit sharing would act as an automatic stabilizer. Under the current wage system, a fall in demand for a firm's product causes the firm to lay off workers: it is no longer profitable to employ them at the old wage. The firm will rehire these workers only if the wage falls or if demand recovers. Under a profit-sharing system, Weitzman argues, firms would be more likely to maintain employment after a fall in demand. Under the profit-sharing contract for our hypothetical manufacturing firm, for example, each additional hour of work would cost the firm only $15; the rest of the compensation for additional workers would come from the workers' share of profits. Because the marginal cost of labour would be so much lower under profit sharing, a fall in demand would not normally cause a firm to lay off workers.

To provide evidence for the advantages of profit sharing, Weitzman points to Japan. Most Japanese workers receive a large fraction of their compensation in the form of year-end bonuses. Weitzman argues that, because of these bonuses, Japanese workers "think of themselves more as permanently employed partners than as hired hands."

The *New York Times* dubbed Weitzman's proposal "the best idea since Keynes." Advocates of his theory want the government to provide tax incentives to encourage firms to adopt profit-sharing plans. Others, however, have expressed skepticism. They wonder why, if profit sharing is such a good idea, firms and workers don't sign such contracts without prodding from the government. Whether profit sharing would help stabilize the economy, as Weitzman suggests, remains an open question.[1] ■

---

[1] Martin L. Weitzman, *The Share Economy* (Cambridge, MA: Harvard University Press, 1984).

The Difficult Job of Economic Forecasting

Because policy influences the economy only after a substantial lag, successful stabilization policy requires the ability to predict accurately future economic conditions. If we cannot predict whether the economy will be in a boom or a recession in six months or a year, we cannot evaluate whether monetary and fiscal policy should now be trying to expand or contract aggregate demand. Unfortunately, economic developments are often unpredictable, at least given our current understanding of the economy.

One way forecasters try to look ahead is with the index of leading indicators. This index, called the composite index, is composed of 10 data series—such as stock prices, the number of housing starts, firms' inventories, the U.S. leading indicator, the value of orders for new plants and equipment, and the money supply—that often fluctuate in advance of the economy. A large fall in a leading indicator signals that a recession is more likely.

"It's true, Caesar. Rome is declining, but I expect it to pick up in the next quarter."

Drawing by Dana Fradon; © 1988
The New Yorker Magazine, Inc.

Another way forecasters look ahead is with macroeconometric models, which have been developed both by government agencies and by private firms for forecasting and policy analysis. As we discussed in Chapter 11, these large-scale computer models are made up of many equations, each representing a part of the economy. After making assumptions about the path of the exogenous variables, such as monetary policy, fiscal policy, and foreign variables such as oil prices and trade restrictions, these models yield predictions about unemployment, inflation, and other endogenous variables. Keep in mind, however, that the validity of these predictions is only as good as the model and the forecasters' assumptions about the exogenous variables.

CASE STUDY

Two Episodes in Economic Forecasting

"Light showers, bright intervals, and moderate winds." This was the forecast offered by the renowned British national weather service on October 14, 1987. The next day Britain was hit by the worst storm in over two centuries.

Like weather forecasts, economic forecasts are a crucial input to private and public decisionmaking. Business executives rely on economic forecasts when deciding how much to produce and how much to invest in plant and equipment. Government policymakers also rely on them when developing economic policies. Yet also like weather forecasts, economic forecasts are far from precise.

Even the most severe economic downturn, the Great Depression of the 1930s, caught economic forecasters completely by surprise. Even after the stock market crash of 1929, they remained confident that the economy would not suffer a substantial setback. In late 1931, when the economy was clearly in bad shape, the eminent economist Irving Fisher predicted that it would recover quickly. Subsequent events showed that these forecasts were much too optimistic.[2]

Forecasting success is still an elusive goal, as the recession of the early 1990s illustrates. On average, during the first three years of the decade, Canada's real GDP fell by 0.4 percentage points each year. Throughout this period, the federal government surveyed private forecasters to ensure that their own projections of GDP growth agreed with the existing consensus. One of the reasons the government's budget deficit increased so much during the 1990–1992 period is that Finance Department officials (and other forecasters) overestimated GDP growth by over 3 percentage points per year! (With lower levels of income being earned, the existing set of tax rates did not generate the amount of revenue that the government expected.)

This low level of forecasting accuracy is discouraging for those who favour an active stabilization policy. Furthermore, there is significant disparity among the various forecasters' estimates. For example, in the federal budget of 1994 (delivered in February of that year), it was noted that the private forecasts for real GDP growth in that year ranged from 2.9 percent to 4.3 percent. More important, Statistics Canada (one of the most respected statistical agencies in the world) finds that it must revise its estimates of real GDP *several* times—even *after* the period in question has become a matter of history. Journalist Bruce Little used the graph shown in Figure 15-1 to indicate how much data revision goes on. For example, in just the nine months between June 1992 and March 1993, the estimate for GDP growth during the first quarter of 1992 was revised downward *four* times, with the final estimate's being a growth rate that is only *one-sixth* of the initial measurement. And this is just getting recorded history straight—this is not forecasting at all. Although less well

FIGURE 15-1

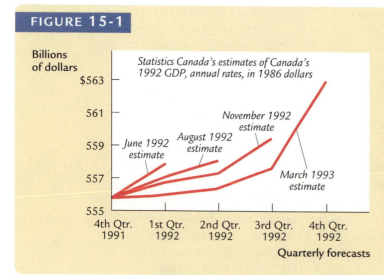

Recording the Recession of the Early 1990s Forecasting is particularly difficult if the figure being forecasted is constantly being revised. This graph shows how often Statistics Canada data for real GDP are revised during the year following the issue of their preliminary estimates.

Source: Bruce Little, "Revised Recovery Not So Robust," *The Globe and Mail,* March 13, 1993, p. B21.

---

[2] Kathryn M. Dominguez, Ray C. Fair, and Matthew D. Shapiro, "Forecasting the Depression: Harvard Versus Yale," *American Economic Review* 78 (September 1988): 595–612. This article shows how badly economic forecasters did during the Great Depression, and it argues that they could not have done any better with the modern forecasting techniques available today.

documented, the recession of 2008–2009 was underestimated initially as well. More specifically, in October 2008, most professional forecasters predicted that Canadian GDP growth in 2009 would be 1 percent. Just six months later, in March 2009, those same forecasters predicted the 2009 growth rate at minus 2 percent. Thus, while economic forecasts are an essential input to private and public decisionmaking, they have been, and continue to be, very uncertain. ■

Ignorance, Expectations, and the Lucas Critique

The prominent economist Robert Lucas once wrote, "As an advice-giving profession we are in way over our heads." Even many of those who advise policymakers would agree with this assessment. Economics is a young science, and there is still much that we do not know. Economists cannot be completely confident when they assess the effects of alternative policies. This ignorance suggests that economists should be cautious when offering policy advice.

In his writing on macroeconomic policymaking, Lucas has emphasized that economists need to pay more attention to the issue of how people form expectations of the future. Expectations play a crucial role in the economy because they influence all sorts of behaviour. For instance, households decide how much to consume based on how much they expect to earn in the future, and firms decide how much to invest based on their expectations of future profitability. These expectations depend on many things, but one factor, according to Lucas, is especially important: the economic policies being pursued by the government. When policymakers estimate the effect of any policy change, therefore, they need to know how people's expectations will respond to the policy change. Lucas has argued that traditional methods of policy evaluation—such as those that rely on standard macroeconometric models—do not adequately take into account this impact of policy on expectations. This criticism of traditional policy evaluation is known as the **Lucas critique.**[3]

An important example of the Lucas critique arises in the analysis of disinflation. As you may recall from Chapter 13, the cost of reducing inflation is often measured by the sacrifice ratio, which is the number of percentage points of GDP that must be forgone to reduce inflation by 1 percentage point. Because estimates of the sacrifice ratio are often large, they have led some economists to argue that policymakers should learn to live with inflation, rather than incurring the large cost of reducing it.

According to advocates of the rational-expectations approach, however, these estimates of the sacrifice ratio are unreliable because they are subject to the Lucas critique. Traditional estimates of the sacrifice ratio are based on adaptive expectations, that is, on the assumption that expected inflation depends on past inflation. Adaptive expectations may be a reasonable premise in some circumstances, but if the policymakers make a credible change in policy, workers and firms setting wages and

---

[3] Robert E. Lucas, Jr., "Econometric Policy Evaluation: A Critique," *Carnegie Rochester Conference on Public Policy* 1 (Amsterdam: North-Holland, 1976), 19–46.

prices will rationally respond by adjusting their expectations of inflation appropriately. This change in inflation expectations will quickly alter the short-run tradeoff between inflation and unemployment. As a result, reducing inflation can potentially be much less costly than is suggested by traditional estimates of the sacrifice ratio.

We encounter two other examples of the Lucas critique in this book. First, in the appendix to Chapter 12, we examine whether the central bank should smooth the exchange rate or not. We find that the answer to this question depends fundamentally on whether individuals adjust their forecasts of the exchange rate to reflect this intervention by the authorities. Second, in Chapter 17, we study the household consumption function. We learn that economists have sometimes made very inaccurate predictions concerning how consumers respond to changes in personal-income tax rates. This is because analysts have ignored the effect of the government's policies on consumers' expectations. In Chapter 17, we see how economists have learned to respect the Lucas critique by modifying their theory of consumer behaviour.

The Lucas critique leaves us with two lessons. The more narrow lesson is that economists evaluating alternative policies need to consider how policy affects expectations and, thereby, behaviour. The broader lesson is that policy evaluation is hard, so economists engaged in this task should be sure to show the requisite humility.

The Historical Record

In judging whether government policy should play an active or passive role in the economy, we must give some weight to the historical record. If the economy has experienced many large shocks to aggregate supply and aggregate demand, and if policy has successfully insulated the economy from these shocks, then the case for active policy should be clear. Conversely, if the economy has experienced few large shocks, and if the fluctuations we have observed can be traced to inept economic policy, then the case for passive policy should be clear. In other words, our view of stabilization policy should be influenced by whether policy has historically been stabilizing or destabilizing. For this reason, the debate over macroeconomic policy frequently turns into a debate over macroeconomic history.

Yet history does not settle the debate over stabilization policy. Disagreements over history arise because it is not easy to identify the sources of economic fluctuations. The historical record often permits more than one interpretation.

The Great Depression is a case in point. Economists' views on macroeconomic policy are often related to their views on the cause of the Depression. Some economists believe that a large contractionary shock to private spending caused the Depression. They assert that policymakers should have responded by using the tools of monetary and fiscal policy to stimulate aggregate demand. Other economists believe that the large fall in the money supply in the United States caused the Depression. They assert that the Depression would have been avoided if the U.S. central bank, the Fed, had been pursuing a passive monetary policy of increasing the money supply at a steady rate. Hence, depending on one's beliefs about its cause, the Great Depression can be viewed either as an example of why active monetary and fiscal policy is necessary or as an example of why it is dangerous.

Is the Stabilization of the Economy a Figment of the Data?

Keynes wrote *The General Theory* in the 1930s, and in the wake of the Keynesian revolution, governments around the world began to view economic stabilization as a primary responsibility. Some economists believe that the development of Keynesian theory has had a profound influence on the behaviour of the economy. Comparing data from before World War I and after World War II, they find that real GDP and unemployment have become much more stable. This, some Keynesians claim, is the best argument for active stabilization policy: it has worked.

In a series of provocative and influential papers, economist Christina Romer has challenged this assessment of the historical record. She argues that the measured reduction in volatility reflects not an improvement in economic policy and performance but rather an improvement in the economic data. The older data are much less accurate than the newer data. Romer claims that the higher volatility of unemployment and real GDP reported for the period before World War I is largely a figment of the data.

Romer uses various techniques to make her case. One is to construct more accurate data for the earlier period. This task is difficult because data sources are not readily available. A second way is to construct *less* accurate data for the recent period—that is, data that are comparable to the older data and thus suffer from the same imperfections. After constructing new "bad" data, Romer finds that the recent period appears almost as volatile as the early period, suggesting that the volatility of the early period may be largely an artifact of how the data were assembled.

Romer's work is an important part of the continuing debate over whether macroeconomic policy has improved the performance of the economy. Although her work remains controversial, most economists now believe that the economy in the immediate aftermath of the Keynesian revolution was only slightly more stable than it had been before.[4] ∎

15-2 Should Policy Be Conducted by Rule or by Discretion?

A second topic of debate among economists is whether economic policy should be conducted by rule or by discretion. Policy is conducted by rule if policymakers announce in advance how policy will respond to various situations and commit themselves to following through on this announcement. Policy is

---

[4] To read more about this topic, see Christina D. Romer, "Spurious Volatility in Historical Unemployment Data," *Journal of Political Economy* 94 (February 1986): 1–37; Christina D. Romer, "Is the Stabilization of the Postwar Economy a Figment of the Data?" *American Economic Review* 76 (June 1986): 314–334. In 2009, Professor Romer became chair of President Obama's Council of Economic Advisors.

conducted by discretion if policymakers are free to size up events as they occur and choose whatever policy they consider appropriate at the time.

The debate over rules versus discretion is distinct from the debate over passive versus active policy. Policy can be conducted by rule and yet be either passive or active. For example, a passive policy rule might specify steady growth in the money supply of 2 percent per year. An active policy rule might specify that

$$\text{Money Growth} = 2\% + (\text{Unemployment Rate} - 7\%).$$

Under this rule, the money supply grows at 2 percent if the unemployment rate is 7 percent, but for every percentage point by which the unemployment rate exceeds 7 percent, money growth increases by an extra percentage point. This rule tries to stabilize the economy by raising money growth when the economy is in a recession.

We begin this section by discussing why policy might be improved by a commitment to a policy rule. We then examine several possible policy rules.

Distrust of Policymakers and the Political Process

Some economists believe that economic policy is too important to be left to the discretion of policymakers. Although this view is more political than economic, evaluating it is central to how we judge the role of economic policy. If politicians are incompetent or opportunistic, then we may not want to give them the discretion to use the powerful tools of monetary and fiscal policy.

Incompetence in economic policy arises for several reasons. Some economists view the political process as erratic, perhaps because it reflects the shifting power of special interest groups. In addition, macroeconomics is complicated, and politicians often do not have sufficient knowledge of it to make informed judgments. This ignorance allows charlatans to propose incorrect but superficially appealing solutions to complex problems. The political process often cannot weed out the advice of charlatans from that of competent economists.

Opportunism in economic policy arises when the objectives of policymakers conflict with the well-being of the public. Some economists fear that politicians use macroeconomic policy to further their own electoral ends. If citizens vote on the basis of economic conditions prevailing at the time of the election, then politicians have an incentive to pursue policies that will make the economy look good during election years. A new government might cause a recession soon after coming into office to lower inflation and then stimulate the economy as the next election approaches to lower unemployment; this would ensure that both inflation and unemployment are low on election day. Manipulation of the economy for electoral gain, called the **political business cycle,** has been the subject of extensive research by economists and political scientists.[5]

Politicians have not fully abided by the principles set out in the 1945 *White Paper* on income and employment. We noted earlier that this statement of government

---

[5] William Nordhaus, "The Political Business Cycle," *Review of Economic Studies* 42 (1975): 169–190; Edward Tufte, *Political Control of the Economy* (Princeton, NJ: Princeton University Press, 1978).

intent involved the government's increasing the national debt during recessions, by having spending exceed taxes when the economy might benefit from stimulation. Most politicians like this message—it excuses budget deficits. Indeed, it is based on the proposition that running a deficit *is* the responsible policy in some instances. But many politicians seem to have ignored a later section of the *White Paper,* in which it is clearly stated that "in periods of buoyant employment and income, budget plans will call for surpluses." If this part of the *White Paper*'s advice had been heeded, then Canadians would have witnessed budget surpluses as often as budget deficits. The result would have been no long-run increase in the national debt, such as what we observed from the early 1970s until the mid-1990s.

Distrust of the political process leads some economists to advocate placing economic policy outside the realm of politics. Some have proposed constitutional amendments, such as a balanced-budget amendment, that would tie the hands of legislators and insulate the economy from both incompetence and opportunism.

The Time Inconsistency of Discretionary Policy

If we assume that we can trust our policymakers, discretion at first glance appears superior to a fixed policy rule. Discretionary policy is, by its nature, flexible. As long as policymakers are intelligent and benevolent, there might appear to be little reason to deny them flexibility in responding to changing conditions.

Yet a case for rules over discretion arises from the problem of **time inconsistency** of policy. In some situations policymakers may want to announce in advance the policy they will follow in order to influence the expectations of private decisionmakers. But later, after the private decisionmakers have acted on the basis of their expectations, these policymakers may be tempted to renege on their announcement. Understanding that policymakers may be inconsistent over time, private decisionmakers are led to distrust policy announcements. In this situation, to make their announcements credible, policymakers may want to make a commitment to a fixed policy rule.

Time inconsistency is illustrated most simply in a political rather than an economic example—specifically, public policy about negotiating with terrorists over the release of hostages. The announced policy of many nations is that they will not negotiate over hostages. Such an announcement is intended to deter terrorists: if there is nothing to be gained from kidnapping hostages, rational terrorists won't kidnap any. In other words, the purpose of the announcement is to influence the expectations of terrorists and thereby their behaviour.

But, in fact, unless the policymakers are credibly committed to the policy, the announcement has little effect. Terrorists know that once hostages are taken, policymakers face an overwhelming temptation to make some concession to obtain the hostages' release. The only way to deter rational terrorists is to take away the discretion of policymakers and commit them to a rule of never negotiating. If policymakers were truly unable to make concessions, the incentive for terrorists to take hostages would be largely eliminated.

The same problem arises less dramatically in the conduct of monetary policy. Consider the dilemma of a central bank that cares about both inflation and unemployment. According to the Phillips curve, the tradeoff between inflation and unemployment depends on expected inflation. The Bank of Canada would prefer everyone to expect low inflation so that it will face a favourable tradeoff. To reduce expected inflation, the Bank of Canada often *announces* that low inflation is the paramount goal of monetary policy.

But an announcement of a policy of low inflation is by itself not credible. Once households and firms have formed their expectations of inflation and set wages and prices accordingly, the Bank of Canada has an incentive to renege on its announcement and implement expansionary monetary policy to reduce unemployment. People understand the Bank's incentive to renege and therefore do not believe the announcement in the first place. Just as a government leader facing a hostage crisis is sorely tempted to negotiate their release, a central bank with discretion is sorely tempted to inflate in order to reduce unemployment. And just as terrorists discount announced policies of never negotiating, households and firms discount announced policies of low inflation.

The surprising outcome of this analysis is that policymakers can sometimes better achieve their goals by having their discretion taken away from them. In the case of rational terrorists, fewer hostages will be taken and killed if policymakers are committed to following the seemingly harsh rule of refusing to negotiate for hostages' freedom. In the case of monetary policy, there will be lower inflation without higher unemployment if the Bank of Canada is committed to a policy of zero inflation. (This conclusion about monetary policy is modeled more explicitly in the appendix to this chapter.)

The time inconsistency of policy arises in many other contexts. Here are some examples:

- To encourage investment, the government announces that it will not tax income from capital. But after factories have been built, the government is tempted to renege on its promise because the taxation of existing capital does not distort economic incentives. (Individuals will not destroy existing capital just to avoid taxes.)

- To encourage research, the government announces that it will give a temporary monopoly to companies that discover new drugs. But after a drug has been discovered, the government is tempted to revoke the patent or to regulate the price to make the drug more affordable.

- To encourage good behaviour, a parent announces that he or she will punish a child whenever the child breaks a rule. But after the child has misbehaved, the parent is tempted to forgive this transgression, because punishment is unpleasant for the parent as well as for the child.

- To encourage you to work hard, your professor announces that this course will end with an exam. But after you have studied and learned all the material, the professor is tempted to cancel the exam so that he or she won't have to grade it.

In each case, rational agents understand the incentive for the policymaker to renege, and this expectation affects their behaviour. And in each case, the solution is to take away the policymaker's discretion with a credible commitment to a fixed policy rule.

CASE STUDY

Alexander Hamilton Versus Time Inconsistency

Time inconsistency has long been a problem associated with discretionary policy. In fact, it was one of the first problems that confronted Alexander Hamilton when President George Washington appointed him the first U.S. Secretary of the Treasury in 1789.

Hamilton faced the question of how to deal with the debts that the new nation had accumulated as it fought for its independence from Britain. When the revolutionary government incurred the debts, it promised to honour them when the war was over. But after the war, many Americans advocated defaulting on the debt because repaying the creditors would require taxation, which is always costly and unpopular.

Hamilton opposed the time-inconsistent policy of repudiating the debt. He knew that the nation would likely need to borrow again sometime in the future. In his *First Report on the Public Credit,* which he presented to Congress in 1790, he wrote

> If the maintenance of public credit, then, be truly so important, the next inquiry which suggests itself is: By what means is it to be effected? The ready answer to which question is, by good faith; by a punctual performance of contracts. States, like individuals, who observe their engagements are respected and trusted, while the reverse is the fate of those who pursue an opposite conduct.

Thus, Hamilton proposed that the nation make a commitment to the policy rule of honouring its debts.

The policy rule that Hamilton originally proposed has continued for over two centuries. Today, unlike in Hamilton's time, when most governments debate spending priorities, people do not propose defaulting on the public debt. However, there have been exceptions. For example, the provinces of Alberta and Saskatchewan defaulted on their debts in the 1930s, and several developing countries were forgiven part of their international debts in the 1980s. Nevertheless, these exceptions represent extreme situations in which alternative actions were extraordinarily difficult. In the case of public debt, almost everyone now agrees that the government should be committed to a fixed policy rule. ∎

Rules for Monetary Policy

Even if we are convinced that policy rules are superior to discretion, the debate over macroeconomic policy is not over. If the Bank of Canada were to commit to a rule for monetary policy, what rule should it choose? Let's discuss briefly three policy rules that various economists advocate.

Some economists, called **monetarists,** advocate that the Bank of Canada keep the money supply growing at a steady rate. The quotation at the beginning of this chapter from Milton Friedman—the most famous monetarist—exemplifies this view of monetary policy. Monetarists believe that fluctuations in the money supply are responsible for most large fluctuations in the economy. They argue that slow and steady growth in the money supply would yield stable output, employment, and prices.

Although a monetarist policy rule might have prevented many of the economic fluctuations we have experienced historically, most economists believe that it is not the best possible policy rule. Steady growth in the money supply stabilizes aggregate demand only if the velocity of money is stable. But the variations in velocity in the 1980s, which we discussed in Chapter 9, show that velocity is sometimes unpredictable. Most economists believe that a policy rule needs to allow the money supply to adjust to various shocks to the economy.

A second policy rule that economists widely advocate is nominal GDP targeting. Under this rule, the Bank of Canada announces a planned path for nominal GDP. If nominal GDP rises above the target, the Bank of Canada reduces money growth to dampen aggregate demand. If it falls below the target, the Bank of Canada raises money growth to stimulate aggregate demand. Since a nominal GDP target allows monetary policy to adjust to changes in the velocity of money, most economists believe it would lead to greater stability in output and prices than a monetarist policy rule.

A third policy rule that is often advocated is **inflation targeting.** Under this rule, the Bank of Canada announces a target for the inflation rate (usually a low one) and then adjusts the interest rate (and ultimately the money supply) when the actual inflation deviates from the target. Like nominal GDP targeting, inflation targeting insulates the economy from changes in the velocity of money. In addition, an inflation target has the political advantage that it is easy to explain to the public.

Notice that all these rules are expressed in terms of some nominal variable—the money supply, nominal GDP, or the price level. One can also imagine policy rules expressed in terms of real variables. For example, the Bank of Canada might try to target the unemployment rate at 5 percent. The problem with such a rule is that no one knows exactly what the natural rate of unemployment is. If the Bank of Canada chose a target for the unemployment rate below the natural rate, the result would be accelerating inflation. Conversely, if the Bank of Canada chose a target for the unemployment rate above the natural rate, the result would be accelerating deflation. For this reason, economists rarely advocate rules for monetary policy expressed solely in terms of real variables, even though real variables such as unemployment and real GDP are the best measures of economic performance.

CASE STUDY

Inflation Targeting: Rule or Constrained Discretion?

Since the late 1980s, many of the world's central banks—including those of Australia, Canada, Finland, Israel, New Zealand, Spain, Sweden, and the United Kingdom—adopted some form of inflation targeting. Sometimes inflation targeting takes the form of a central bank announcing its policy intentions. In Canada's case, the federal Minister of Finance and the governor of the Bank of Canada set a target band of 1–3 percent for the inflation rate since 1996. Initially, the target was for what was referred to as core inflation, which excludes the eight most volatile components of the CPI, as well as the effect of indirect taxes on the remaining components.

Other times the inflation target takes the form of a national law that spells out the goals of monetary policy. For example, the Reserve Bank of New Zealand Act of 1989 told the central bank "to formulate and implement monetary policy directed to the economic objective of achieving and maintaining stability in the general level of prices." The act conspicuously omitted any mention of any other competing objective, such as stability in output, employment, interest rates, or exchange rates.

Should we interpret inflation targeting as a type of precommitment to a policy rule? Not completely. In all the countries that have adopted inflation targeting, central banks are left are with a fair amount of discretion. Inflation targets are usually set as a range—for example, an inflation rate of 1 to 3 percent in Canada's case—rather than a particular number. Thus, the central bank can choose where in the range it wants to be: it can stimulate the economy and be near the top of the range, or dampen the economy and be near the bottom. In addition, the central banks are sometimes allowed to adjust their targets for inflation, at least temporarily, if some exogenous event (such as an easily identified supply shock such as the introduction of the GST or its reduction by two percentage points in recent years) pushes inflation outside of the range that was previously announced.

In light of this flexibility, what is the purpose of inflation targeting? Although inflation targeting does leave the central bank with some discretion, the policy does constrain how this discretion is used. When a central bank is told simply to "do the right thing," it is hard to hold the central bank accountable, for people can argue forever about what the right thing is in any specific circumstance. By contrast, when a central bank has announced an inflation target, the public can more easily judge whether the central bank is meeting that target. Thus, although inflation targeting does not tie the hands of the central bank, it does increase the transparency of monetary policy and, by doing so, makes central bankers more accountable for their actions.[6] ∎

CASE STUDY

Central Bank Independence

Suppose you were put in charge of writing the constitution and laws for a country. Would you give the political leader of the country authority over the policies of the central bank? Or would you allow the central bank to make decisions free from such political influence? In other words, assuming that

---

[6] See Ben S. Bernanke and Frederic S. Mishkin, "Inflation Targeting: A New Framework for Monetary Policy?" *Journal of Economic Perspectives* 11 (Spring 1997): 97–116.

monetary policy is made by discretion rather than by rule, who should exercise that discretion?

Countries vary greatly in how they choose to answer this question. In some countries, the central bank is a branch of the government; in others, the central bank is largely independent. In Canada, the Governor of the Bank of Canada is appointed for a 7-year term. The Governor must resign if he or she does not wish to implement the monetary policy of the government. But the government must put its detailed instructions in writing and on public record, so the Governor has significant power if there is a disagreement. In the United States, Fed governors are appointed by the president for 14-year terms, and they cannot be recalled if the president is unhappy with their decisions. This institutional structure gives the Fed a degree of independence similar to that of the Supreme Court.

Many researchers have investigated the effects of constitutional design on monetary policy. They have examined the laws of different countries to construct an index of central bank independence. This index is based on various characteristics, such as the length of bankers' terms, the role of government officials on the bank board, and the frequency of contact between the government and the central bank. The researchers have then examined the correlation between central bank independence and macroeconomic performance.

The results of these studies are striking: more independent central banks are strongly associated with lower and more stable inflation. Figure 15-2 shows a scatterplot of central bank independence and average inflation for the period 1955 to 1988. Countries that had an independent central bank, such as Germany, Switzerland, and the United States, tended to have low average inflation. Countries that had central banks with less independence, such as New Zealand and Spain, tended to have higher average inflation.

Researchers have also found there is no relationship between central bank independence and real economic activity. In particular, central bank independence is not correlated with average unemployment, the volatility of unemployment, the average growth of real GDP, or the volatility of real GDP. Central-bank independence appears to offer countries a free lunch: it has the benefit of lower inflation without any apparent cost. This finding has led some countries, such as New Zealand, to rewrite their laws to give their central banks greater independence.[7] ■

---

[7] For a more complete presentation of these findings and references to the large literature on central-bank independence, see Alberto Alesina and Lawrence H. Summers, "Central Bank Independence and Macroeconomic Performance: Some Comparative Evidence," *Journal of Money, Credit, and Banking* 25 (May 1993): 151–162. For a study that questions the link between inflation and central-bank independence, see Marta Campillo and Jeffrey A. Miron, "Why Does Inflation Differ Across Countries?" in Christina D. Romer and David H. Romer, eds., *Reducing Inflation: Motivation and Strategy* (Chicago: University of Chicago Press, 1997): 335–362.

FIGURE 15-2

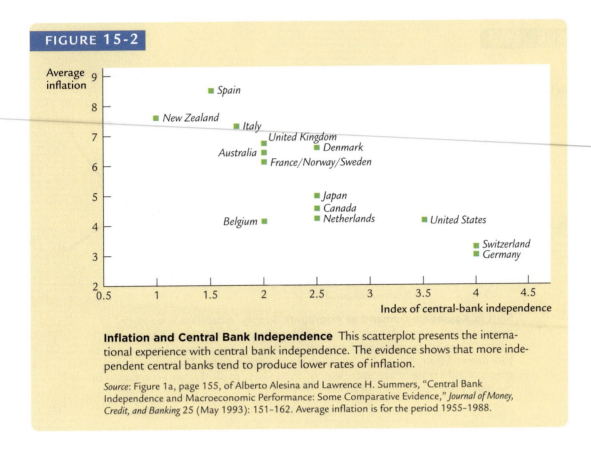

Inflation and Central Bank Independence This scatterplot presents the international experience with central bank independence. The evidence shows that more independent central banks tend to produce lower rates of inflation.

Source: Figure 1a, page 155, of Alberto Alesina and Lawrence H. Summers, "Central Bank Independence and Macroeconomic Performance: Some Comparative Evidence," *Journal of Money, Credit, and Banking* 25 (May 1993): 151–162. Average inflation is for the period 1955–1988.

CASE STUDY

The Bank of Canada's Low-Inflation Target: Implications for Fiscal Policy

In an effort to acquire credibility as an inflation-fighter, the Bank of Canada has repeatedly emphasized since 1987 that its *sole* target is price stability. In 1996, in an attempt to show its support for a slightly more flexible form of this commitment, the federal government published its (and the Bank's) inflation target for the next 5 years—that the annual rise in the CPI stay within the 1–3 percent range. The commitment to this target range has been extended since, and it still applies today.

The Bank of Canada continues to argue that reducing unemployment is *not* part of what it sees as its mandate. Many Canadians are critical of the Bank's taking this narrow view; they want the Bank of Canada to care about unemployment, too. Some of those criticizing the Bank of Canada ignore the fact that the Bank officials are not strict monetarists, and that, by pursuing an inflation rate close to zero, the Bank of Canada *will automatically help to stabilize employment.* We are now in a position to appreciate this important implication of the Bank of Canada's monetary rule.

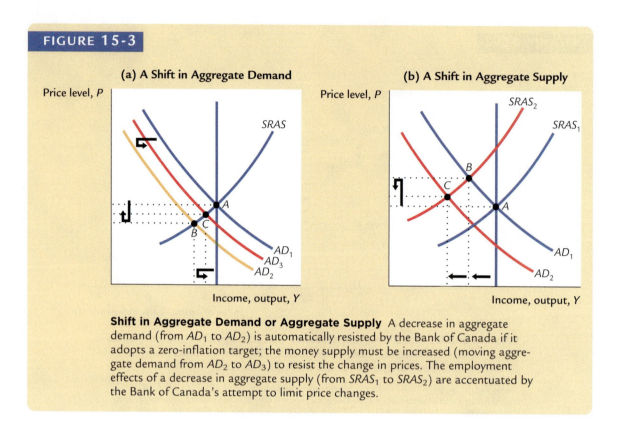

FIGURE 15-3

(a) A Shift in Aggregate Demand

Price level, P

SRAS

A

C

B

AD_1
AD_3
AD_2

Income, output, Y

(b) A Shift in Aggregate Supply

Price level, P

$SRAS_2$

$SRAS_1$

B

C

A

AD_1

AD_2

Income, output, Y

Shift in Aggregate Demand or Aggregate Supply A decrease in aggregate demand (from AD_1 to AD_2) is automatically resisted by the Bank of Canada if it adopts a zero-inflation target; the money supply must be increased (moving aggregate demand from AD_2 to AD_3) to resist the change in prices. The employment effects of a decrease in aggregate supply (from $SRAS_1$ to $SRAS_2$) are accentuated by the Bank of Canada's attempt to limit price changes.

Consider a decrease in aggregate demand, as shown in panel (a) of Figure 15-3. If the Bank of Canada holds the money supply constant, the economy moves from point A to point B in the short run, and a recession occurs. But some deflation in prices occurs as well, and this evokes an automatic reaction from the Bank of Canada if it has adopted a zero-inflation target instead of a constant money supply rule. To implement a zero-inflation target, the Bank of Canada must increase the money supply whenever there is a downward pressure on the price level (as shown in panel (a) of Figure 15-3). Even if the Bank does not fully accomplish its goal, the result is that the aggregate demand curve shifts somewhat back to the right. The economy ends up at point C, and the magnitude of the recession is reduced. Thus, as far as aggregate demand disturbances are concerned, inflation targeting involves the very built-in stabilization feature that many Bank of Canada critics want the economy to have. So the Bank of Canada *does* care about unemployment, even if indirectly.

One way of interpreting this analysis is to say that inflation targeting makes fiscal-policy multipliers smaller than they would otherwise be. Inflation targeting reduces the importance of both the undesired shifts in the aggregate demand curve *and* the shifts that are deliberately planned by fiscal policy. So a high degree of built-in stability involves good news and bad. The good news is that unforeseen events have a limited effect on unemployment; the bad news is that demand policies that are intended to lower unemployment by shifting aggregate demand to the right have limited effects as well.

In Chapter 11, we noted that the numerical estimates of fiscal-policy multipliers from macroeconometric models have been falling in recent years. We can now appreciate another reason why this trend in estimated multiplier values is not something we should find surprising. The Bank of Canada has switched from money-growth targeting to inflation targeting.

What about aggregate supply shocks? The effects of a leftward shift in the aggregate supply curve are shown in panel (b) of Figure 15-3. If the Bank of Canada holds the money supply constant in the face of this event, the economy moves from point A to point B. Again, a recession occurs, but in this case, it is accompanied by inflation, not deflation. If the Bank of Canada adopts a zero-inflation target, it must decrease the money supply in an attempt to reduce the upward pressure on prices. With this response accounted for, the economy moves to point C instead of point B, and the magnitude of the recession is made larger by monetary policy. Thus, inflation targeting is *de*stabilizing in the face of supply-side shocks.

The Bank of Canada's critics are concerned about limiting the losses in Canadian output and employment. But since this analysis shows that inflation targeting is stabilizing for demand shocks but destabilizing for supply shocks, it offers no clear verdict concerning the Bank of Canada and its critics. Because of this ambiguity, it is important to remember what was explained in the appendix to Chapter 12. The extended Mundell–Fleming analysis in that appendix indicates that a contractionary fiscal policy is like adverse *supply* shock since it generates lower output and pressure for higher prices. If the major shocks to hit our economy are spending cuts (as was the case throughout the 1990s), our analysis suggests that the critics of the Bank were correct at that time to be concerned about the employment implications of Canada's monetary and fiscal policy mix. But when fiscal policy is expansionary, as it was in the recession of 2008–2009, these same critics should applaud the Bank of Canada's commitment to price stability, since it leads the Bank to support Finance Canada's initiative. ∎

15-3 Conclusion: Making Policy in an Uncertain World

In this chapter we have examined whether policy should take an active or passive role in responding to economic fluctuations and whether policy should be conducted by rule or by discretion. There are many arguments on both sides of these questions. Perhaps the only clear conclusion is that there is no simple and compelling case for any particular view of macroeconomic policy. In the end, you must weigh the various arguments, both economic and political, and decide for yourself what kind of role the government should play in trying to stabilize the economy.

For better or worse, economists play a key role in the formulation of economic policy. Because the economy is complex, this role is often difficult. Yet it is also inevitable. Economists cannot sit back and wait until our knowledge of the economy has been perfected before giving advice. In the meantime, someone must advise economic policymakers. That job, difficult as it sometimes is, falls to economists.

The role of economists in the policymaking process goes beyond giving advice to policymakers. Even economists cloistered in academia influence policy indirectly through their research and writing. In the conclusion of *The General Theory,* John Maynard Keynes wrote that

> the ideas of economists and political philosophers, both when they are right and when they are wrong, are more powerful than is commonly understood. Indeed, the world is ruled by little else. Practical men, who believe themselves to be quite exempt from intellectual influences, are usually the slaves of some defunct economist. Madmen in authority, who hear voices in the air, are distilling their frenzy from some academic scribbler of a few years back.

This is as true today as it was when Keynes wrote it in 1936—except now that academic scribbler is often Keynes himself.

Summary

1. Advocates of active policy view the economy as subject to frequent shocks that will lead to unnecessary fluctuations in output and employment unless monetary or fiscal policy responds. Many believe that economic policy has been successful in stabilizing the economy.

2. Advocates of passive policy argue that because monetary and fiscal policies work with long and variable lags, attempts to stabilize the economy are likely to end up being destabilizing. In addition, they believe that our present understanding of the economy is too limited to be useful in formulating successful stabilization policy and that inept policy is a frequent source of economic fluctuations.

3. Advocates of discretionary policy argue that discretion gives more flexibility to policymakers in responding to various unforeseen situations.

4. Advocates of policy rules argue that the political process cannot be trusted. They believe that politicians make frequent mistakes in conducting economic policy and sometimes use economic policy for their own political ends. In addition, advocates of policy rules argue that a commitment to a fixed policy rule is necessary to solve the problem of time inconsistency.

KEY CONCEPTS

Inside and outside lags

Automatic stabilizers

Lucas critique

Political business cycle

Time inconsistency

Monetarists

Inflation Targeting

QUESTIONS FOR REVIEW

1. What are the inside lag and the outside lag? Which has the longer inside lag—monetary or fiscal policy? Which has the longer outside lag? Why?

2. Why would more accurate economic forecasting make it easier for policymakers to stabilize the economy? Describe two ways economists try to forecast developments in the economy.

3. Describe the Lucas critique.

4. How does a person's interpretation of macroeconomic history affect his view of macroeconomic policy?

5. What is meant by the "time inconsistency" of economic policy? Why might policymakers be tempted to renege on an announcement they made earlier? In this situation, what is the advantage of a policy rule?

6. List three policy rules that the Bank of Canada might follow. Which of these would you advocate? Why?

PROBLEMS AND APPLICATIONS

1. Suppose that the tradeoff between unemployment and inflation is determined by the Phillips curve:

$$u = u^n - \alpha(\pi - E\pi),$$

where u denotes the unemployment rate, π^n the natural rate of unemployment, π the rate of inflation, and $E\pi$ the expected rate of inflation. In addition, suppose that the country involves two political parties, the Left and the Right. Suppose that the Left party always follows a policy of high money growth and the Right party always follows a policy of low money growth. What "political business cycle" pattern of inflation and unemployment would you predict under the following conditions?

a. Every four years, one of the parties takes control based on a random flip of a coin. [*Hint:* What will expected inflation be prior to the election?]

b. The two parties take turns.

2. When cities pass laws limiting the rent landlords can charge on apartments, the laws usually apply to existing buildings and exempt any buildings not yet built. Advocates of rent control argue that this exemption ensures that rent control does not discourage the construction of new housing. Evaluate this argument in light of the time-inconsistency problem.

3. The *cyclically adjusted budget deficit* is the budget deficit corrected for the effects of the business cycle. In other words, it is the budget deficit that the government would be running if unemployment were at the natural rate. (It is also called the *full-employment budget deficit*.) Some economists have proposed the rule that the cyclically adjusted budget deficit always be balanced. Compare this proposal to a strict balanced-budget rule. Which is preferable? What problems do you see with the rule requiring a balanced cyclically adjusted budget?

Time Inconsistency and the Tradeoff Between Inflation and Unemployment

In this appendix, we examine more formally the time-inconsistency argument for rules rather than discretion. This analysis is relegated to an appendix because we need to use some calculus.[8]

Suppose that the Phillips curve describes the relationship between inflation and unemployment. Letting u denote the unemployment rate, u^n the natural rate of unemployment, π the rate of inflation, and $E\pi$ the expected rate of inflation, unemployment is determined by

$$u = u^n - \alpha(\pi - E\pi).$$

Unemployment is low when inflation exceeds expected inflation and high when inflation falls below expected inflation.

For simplicity, suppose also that the Bank of Canada chooses the rate of inflation. Of course, more realistically, the Bank of Canada controls inflation only imperfectly through its control of the money supply. But for the purposes of illustration, it is useful to assume that the Bank of Canada can control inflation perfectly.

The Bank of Canada likes low unemployment and low inflation. Suppose that the cost of unemployment and inflation, as perceived by the Bank of Canada, can be represented as

$$L(u, \pi) = u + \gamma\pi^2,$$

where the parameter γ represents how much the Bank of Canada dislikes inflation relative to unemployment. $L(u, \pi)$ is called the *loss function*. The Bank of Canada's objective is to make the loss as small as possible.

Having specified how the economy works and the Bank of Canada's objective, let's compare monetary policy made under a fixed rule and under discretion.

First, consider policy under a fixed rule. A rule commits the Bank of Canada to a particular level of inflation. As long as private agents understand that the Bank of Canada is committed to this rule, the expected level of inflation will be the level the Bank of Canada is committed to produce. Since expected inflation equals actual inflation ($E\pi = \pi$), unemployment will be at its natural rate ($u = u^n$).

---

[8] The material in this appendix is derived from Finn E. Kydland and Edward C. Prescott, "Rules Rather Than Discretion: The Inconsistency of Optimal Plans," *Journal of Political Economy* 85 (June 1977): 473–492; and Robert J. Barro and David Gordon, "A Positive Theory of Monetary Policy in a Natural Rate Model," *Journal of Political Economy* 91 (August 1983): 589–610. Kydland and Prescott won the Nobel prize for this and other work in 2004.

What is the optimal rule? Since unemployment is at its natural rate regardless of the level of inflation legislated by the rule, there is no benefit to having any inflation at all. Therefore, the optimal fixed rule requires that the Bank of Canada produce zero inflation.

Second, consider discretionary monetary policy. Under discretion, the economy works as follows:

1. Private agents form their expectations of inflation $E\pi$.

2. The Bank of Canada chooses the actual level of inflation π.

3. Based on expected and actual inflation, unemployment is determined.

Under this arrangement, the Bank of Canada minimizes its loss $L(u, \pi)$ subject to the constraint that the Phillips curve imposes. When making its decision about the rate of inflation, the Bank of Canada takes expected inflation as already determined.

To find what outcome we would obtain under discretionary policy, we must examine what level of inflation the Bank of Canada would choose. By substituting the Phillips curve into the Bank of Canada's loss function, we obtain

$$L(u, \pi) = u^n - \alpha(\pi - E\pi) + \gamma\pi^2.$$

Notice that the Bank of Canada's loss is negatively related to unexpected inflation (the second term in the equation) and positively related to actual inflation (the third term). To find the level of inflation that minimizes this loss, differentiate with respect to π to obtain

$$dL/d\pi = -\alpha + 2\gamma\pi.$$

The loss is minimized when this derivative equals zero[9]. Solving for p, we get

$$\pi = \alpha/(2\gamma).$$

Whatever level of inflation private agents expected, this is the "optimal" level of inflation for the Bank of Canada to choose. Of course, rational private agents understand the objective of the Bank of Canada and the constraint that the Phillips curve imposes. They therefore expect that the Bank of Canada will choose this level of inflation. Expected inflation equals actual inflation [$E\pi = \pi = \alpha/(2\gamma)$], and unemployment equals its natural rate ($u = u^n$).

Now compare the outcome under optimal discretion to the outcome under the optimal rule. In both cases, unemployment is at its natural rate. Yet discretionary policy produces more inflation than does policy under the rule. *Thus, optimal discretion is worse than the optimal rule.* This is true even though the Bank of Canada under discretion was attempting to minimize its loss, $L(u, \pi)$.

At first it may seem bizarre that the Bank of Canada can achieve a better outcome by being committed to a fixed rule. Why can't the Bank of Canada with discretion mimic the Bank of Canada committed to a zero-inflation

---

[9] *Mathematical note:* The second derivative, $d^2L/d\pi^2 = 2\gamma$, is positive, ensuring that we are solving for a minimum of the loss function rather than a maximum!

rule? The answer is that the Bank of Canada is playing a game against private decisionmakers who have rational expectations. Unless it is committed to a fixed rule of zero inflation, the Bank of Canada cannot get private agents to expect zero inflation.

Suppose, for example, that the Bank of Canada simply announces that it will follow a zero-inflation policy. Such an announcement by itself cannot be credible. After private agents have formed their expectations of inflation, the Bank of Canada has the incentive to renege on its announcement in order to decrease unemployment. (As we have just seen, once expectations are given, the Bank of Canada's optimal policy is to set inflation at $\pi = \alpha/(2\gamma)$, regardless of $E\pi$.) Private agents understand the incentive to renege and therefore do not believe the announcement in the first place.

This theory of monetary policy has an important corollary. Under one circumstance, the Bank of Canada with discretion achieves the same outcome as the Bank of Canada committed to a fixed rule of zero inflation. If the Bank of Canada dislikes inflation much more than it dislikes unemployment (so that γ is very large), inflation under discretion is near zero, since the Bank of Canada has little incentive to inflate. This finding provides some guidance to those who have the job of appointing central bankers. An alternative to imposing a fixed rule is to appoint an individual with a fervent distaste for inflation. Perhaps this is why even liberal politicians who are more concerned about unemployment than inflation sometimes appoint conservative central bankers who are more concerned about inflation.

MORE PROBLEMS AND APPLICATIONS

1. In the 1970s in Canada, the inflation rate and the natural rate of unemployment both rose. Let's use this model of time inconsistency to examine this phenomenon. Assume that policy is discretionary.

   a. In the model as developed so far, what happens to the inflation rate when the natural rate of unemployment rises?

   b. Let's now change the model slightly by supposing that the Bank of Canada's loss function is quadratic in both inflation and unemployment. That is,

   $$L(u, \pi) = u^2 + \gamma\pi^2.$$

   Follow steps similar to those in the text to solve for the inflation rate under discretionary policy.

   c. Now what happens to the inflation rate when the natural rate of unemployment rises?

   d. In 1987, Prime Minister Brian Mulroney's government appointed the conservative central banker John Crow to head the Bank of Canada. According to this model, what should have happened to inflation and unemployment?

CHAPTER 16

Government Debt and Budget Deficits

All decent people live beyond their incomes nowadays and those who aren't

respectable live beyond other people's. A few gifted individuals manage to do both.

— Saki

When a government spends more than it collects in taxes, it has a budget deficit, which it finances by borrowing from the private sector. The accumulation of past borrowing is the government debt.

Although attention to the national debt has waxed and waned over the years, it has been especially intense during the past 35 years. Expressed as a percentage of GDP, the debt doubled from 1975 to 1985, and then almost doubled again from 1985 to 1995. By the late 1990s, the budget deficit had come under control and had even turned into a budget surplus, but it took some time for the level of debt to fall. As this book goes to press, almost 40 of the 50 percentage point increase in the ratio of the debt to GDP that had occurred in the 1975–1995 period had been reversed.

The previous large increase in government debt during a period of peace and prosperity was unprecedented in Canadian history. Not surprisingly, it sparked a renewed interest among economists and policymakers in the economic effects of government debt. Some view the large budget deficits during the 1975–1995 period as the worst mistake of economic policy since the Great Depression, while others think that the deficits matter very little. This debate flared up again in 2009 when—in response to the world financial crisis and the recession—the Federal Government's budget involved the biggest deficit in Canadian history. Many Canadians viewed this increase in the deficit as fully appropriate, since they thought this was what the government had to do to keep the financial crisis from developing into something on the scale of the Great Depression of the 1930s. Others thought that any comparison of this sort was ridiculous, and so they viewed this return to big deficits as a betrayal of what they had voted for. This chapter considers various facets of this debate.

We begin simply by looking at the numbers. Section 16-1 examines the size of the Canadian government debt, comparing it to the debt of other countries and to the debt that Canada has had during its own past. It also takes a brief look at what the future may hold. Section 16-2 discusses why measuring changes in government indebtedness is not as straightforward as it might seem. Indeed, some economists have argued that traditional measures are so misleading that they should be ignored completely.

We then look at how government debt affects the economy. Section 16-3 describes the traditional view of government debt, according to which government borrowing reduces national saving, crowds out capital accumulation, and increases interest payment obligations to foreigners. This view is held by most economists and has been implicit in the discussion of fiscal policy throughout this book. Section 16-4 discusses an alternative view, called *Ricardian equivalence,* which is held by a small but influential minority of economists. According to the Ricardian view, government debt does not influence national saving and capital accumulation. As we will see, the debate between the traditional and Ricardian views of government debt arises from disagreements over how consumers respond to the government's debt policy.

Section 16-5 then looks at other facets of the debate over government debt. It begins by discussing whether the government should always try to balance its budget and, if not, when a budget deficit or surplus is desirable. It also examines the effects of government debt on monetary policy, the political process, and a nation's role in the world economy.

16-1 The Size of the Government Debt

Let's begin by putting the government debt in perspective. As this book went to press, the debt of the Canadian federal government was about $465 billion. If we divide this number by 33 million, roughly the number of people in Canada at the time, we find that each person's share of the government debt was about $14,000. Obviously, this is not a trivial number—few people sneeze at $14,000. Yet if we compare this debt to the roughly $1.5 million a typical person will earn over his or her working life, the government debt does not look like the catastrophe it is sometimes made out to be.

One way to judge the size of a government's debt is to compare it to the amount of debt other countries have accumulated. Table 16-1 shows the amount of government debt for 28 major countries expressed as a percentage of each country's GDP. On the top of the list are the heavily indebted countries of Japan and Italy, which have accumulated a debt that exceeds annual GDP. At the bottom are Australia and Luxembourg, which have accumulated relatively small debts. Canada is in the middle of the pack. By international standards, Canadian federal and provincial governments, taken as a group, are neither especially profligate nor especially frugal.

Over the course of Canadian history, the indebtedness of the federal government has varied substantially. Figure 16-1 shows the ratio of the federal debt to GDP since 1925. What explains this variation?

Focusing on just the Canadian federal government, national debt is the sum total of all the annual budget deficits incurred since confederation in 1867. As already noted, that debt reached close to the $600 billion mark at the turn of the

TABLE 16-1

How Indebted Are the World's Governments?

Country	Government Debt as a Percentage of GDP	Country	Government Debt as a Percentage of GDP
Japan	173.0	Switzerland	48.1
Italy	113.0	Norway	45.4
Greece	100.8	Sweden	44.6
Belgium	92.2	Spain	44.2
United States	73.2	Finland	39.6
France	72.5	Slovak Republic	38.0
Hungary	71.8	Czech Republic	36.1
Portugal	70.9	Ireland	32.8
Germany	64.8	Korea	32.6
Canada	63.0	Denmark	28.4
Austria	62.6	New Zealand	25.3
United Kingdom	58.7	Iceland	24.8
Netherlands	54.5	Luxembourg	18.1
Poland	52.8	Australia	14.2

Source: OECD Economic Outlook. Data are based on estimates of gross government financial liabilities and nominal GDP for 2008.

century. Most of this debt accumulated in recent years—only just over 5 percent can be attributed to the country's first 100 years of existence! The federal debt shot up during the Great Depression of the 1930s and ballooned during World War II, as Figure 16–1 shows. These developments have not been interpreted as government mismanagement, however, because people have reasoned that the government had no choice but to get involved in these crises. Most people think that because future generations have benefited from the freedom that the war ensured, it is only fair that they shoulder some of the burden. Issuing debt during the war, therefore, was the government's way of spreading some of the costs to future generations.

Following the war, the federal government's debt–GDP ratio was 110 percent. By 1970, it was less than 20 percent. The debt ratio was brought under control in three main ways. First, the government ran budget surpluses for a number of years in the 1945–1970 period, and in each of those years the debt was decreased by the amount of the surplus. Second, Canada enjoyed a long period of rapid economic growth. With real GDP growing briskly, the ratio of the outstanding debt to GDP shrank at a rapid rate. Finally, during the Korean War period in the early 1950s, and during the 1965–1980 period, Canada's inflation rate reduced the real value of the debt by a significant amount. Unexpected inflation is simply a gradual (some would say "civilized") way for a country to default on some of its debt.

By 1994, the federal debt ratio had climbed back up to 73 percent. There were two main reasons for this dramatic reversal of the postwar trend. First, Canada's average growth rate for real GDP had been lower since the mid-1970s, when

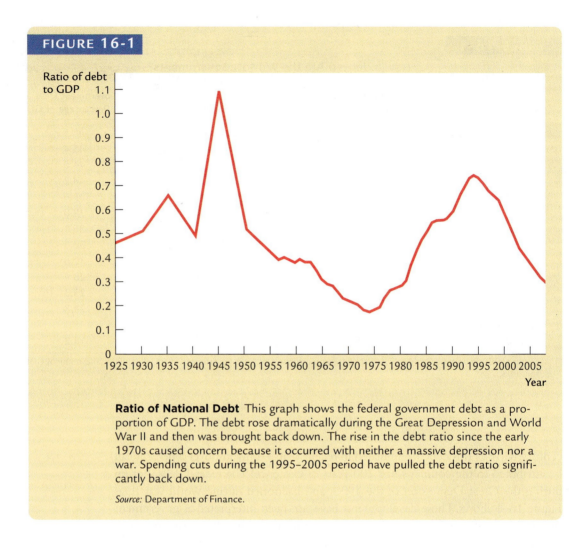

FIGURE 16-1

Ratio of debt to GDP

Ratio of National Debt This graph shows the federal government debt as a proportion of GDP. The debt rose dramatically during the Great Depression and World War II and then was brought back down. The rise in the debt ratio since the early 1970s caused concern because it occurred with neither a massive depression nor a war. Spending cuts during the 1995–2005 period have pulled the debt ratio significantly back down.

Source: Department of Finance.

most Western countries began suffering from a slowdown in productivity growth. Second, the government simply overspent. The federal government ran a deficit *every* year between 1971 and 1998.

Broadly speaking, there are three reasons why many were concerned about the resulting increase in debt. First, Canadians were more indebted to foreigners. As a proportion of GDP, Canada's net foreign debt (including all forms, not just government debt) was almost 50 percent in 1994. This put Canada in *first* place among G7 countries in foreign debt standings. (The second- and third-place finishers were Italy at 12 percent and the United States at 10 percent.) Just to pay the interest on that debt, Canadians had to give up 4.5 percent of GDP in 1994. On average, it is unrealistic to expect Canada's economy to grow at that rate in real terms, so the prospects for an improvement in the Canadian standard of living were bleak. Second, many regard debt as worrisome because it may lead to further tax increases in order to pay for the interest. The tax–GDP ratio in Canada increased from 31.5 percent in 1980 to 37.5 percent in 1993, and despite higher taxes, federal debt service costs rose from

20 percent of tax revenue to 32 percent of revenue over this same period. Finally, the existence of the debt raises issues of equity. Some regard it as immoral that one generation "spends beyond its means," thereby lowering the standard of living for future generations through such mechanisms as reduced government programs.

During the middle of the 1990s, the federal government started to get its budget deficit under control. A combination of spending cuts, rising taxes, and rapid economic growth caused the ratio of debt to GDP to stabilize and decline by about 10 percentage points by the end of the century. Our experience during most of the first decade of the new century tempted some observers to think that exploding government debt is a thing of the past. But as the 2009 recession hit, rising unemployment meant that the government's tax collections shrunk and, at the same time, the stimulus package involved higher government spending. Both these developments caused the deficit, and therefore the accumulated debt, to start rising again. As the following case study suggests, it will likely take several years for the resulting temporary rise in the debt-to-GDP ratio to be overcome. It is important that the debt ratio be put back on its previous downward trend, since some increase in this measure is likely to reappear in the years to come, as the aging baby boom generation withdraws from the labour force and demands increased health and pension benefits during their retirement.

CASE STUDY

Canadian Deficits and Debt: Past, Present, and Future

As noted earlier, between 1973 and 1993 our federal government debt ratio rose dramatically—by 50 percentage points. The Trudeau Liberals were in power for the first 10 years of this period, and the Mulroney Conservatives took over for the second half of this episode. As the size of the budget deficits grew during the Trudeau years, the Conservatives were adamant that they would stop the rise in debt if given the chance. Indeed, the Conservatives did run a more contractionary policy. Why did the debt ratio continue to explode nonetheless? When the Liberals took office again in 1993, why did they succeed in reversing the trend in the debt ratio—when the Conservatives had failed? To answer these questions, we need to understand the basic accounting relationships of deficits and debt.

The primary deficit is the excess of the government's program spending over its tax revenue. Program spending is all government expenditure except interest payments. The overall deficit is the primary deficit plus the government's interest payment obligations on its outstanding debt. To reduce the outstanding debt, the government must run an overall surplus, and this, in turn, requires a primary surplus that exceeds the existing interest payment obligations. As a first step, then, the government must eliminate its primary deficit. While this first step is not sufficient to reduce Canada's national debt, you might think that it would be enough to eliminate the explosive growth in the *ratio* of the debt to GDP. History suggests that this is not the case. Brian Mulroney's Conservative government maintained an average primary balance of zero, and was therefore much more prudent than the Trudeau Liberals, who averaged a sizable primary deficit. Despite this effort by the Conservatives, the deficit and debt problem worsened during their term of office. To appreciate why, let's carefully distinguish the primary deficit, the overall deficit, the debt, and the debt ratio.

Letting D and B stand for the government's deficit and the stock of outstanding bonds, respectively, we can summarize the key relationships as follows. The deficit is the excess of government spending over tax revenue (the primary deficit, $G - T$) plus interest payments on the outstanding bonds, rB:

$$D = G - T + rB.$$

The national debt increases by the size of the current deficit:

$$\Delta B = D.$$

Using lowercase letters to stand for the ratio of each item to GDP (i.e., $g = G/Y$, $t = T/Y$, $d = D/Y$, and $b = B/Y$), then the deficit ratio is

$$d = g - t + rb,$$

and the increase in the debt ratio is

$$\Delta b = d - nb,$$

where n stands for the long-run average growth rate in output (which takes place because of productivity increases and population growth). This last relationship may require further explanation. Since $b = B/Y$, b rises whenever its numerator grows more than its denominator does. Thus,

$$\frac{\Delta b}{b} = \frac{\Delta B}{B} - \frac{\Delta Y}{Y}.$$

If Y grows at rate n ($\Delta Y/Y = n$) and the bond stock grows by the size of the deficit ($\Delta B = D$) this relationship can be rewritten as

$$\frac{\Delta b}{b} = \frac{D}{B} - n,$$

or

$$\Delta b = d - nb.$$

If the government sets the primary deficit ratio at some target value, it is setting $(g - t)$ as an exogenous constant. The implications for the debt ratio can then be seen by eliminating d from our two key relationships:

$$\Delta b = (g - t) + (r - n)b.$$

Consider the Conservatives' policy of setting $(g - t)$ at zero. This relationship says that the debt ratio must *forever* rise—Δb is forever positive—if r exceeds n. That is, the debt ratio rises without bound if the interest rate the government pays on government bonds (the growth rate for the numerator of the debt ratio) exceeds the economy's underlying average growth rate (the growth rate for the denominator of the debt ratio).

Since r exceeded n throughout the 1970s and 1980s, it is not surprising that Canada's debt ratio rose *inexorably,* despite the Conservatives' success in keeping $(g - t)$ at zero.

The economy's average growth rate exceeded interest rates during the 1950s and 1960s in Canada, when such factors as the postwar reconstruction of industry, the shift of population to the cities, and the development of Canada's natural resources made growth particularly high. Given this temporary excess of n over r and the fact that the federal government often ran budget surpluses, it is not surprising that the debt ratio fell during these years (as shown in Figure 16-1). But considering long-run average values, we must realize that r exceeds $n,$ so it is impossible to grow out of the debt problem by keeping the primary deficit at zero.[1]

When the Liberals took over in 1993, they switched to targeting the *overall* deficit ratio instead of targeting just the *primary* deficit ratio. Could we have expected this policy to have greater success in controlling the debt ratio?

The Liberal policy involved switching the exogenous and endogenous variables. Under the previous regime, $(g - t)$ was exogenous and d was endogenous. The Liberals' plan made d exogenous, and to accomplish this, they had to allow either g or t to become endogenous. Since their plan accomplished most of the deficit reduction through expenditure cuts, not tax increases, we take g as the endogenous variable in the following illustration.

Using a subscript of -1 to stand for previous period's values, the debt-ratio growth equation can be rewritten as

$$b = (1 - n)b_{-1} + d$$

This debt-ratio growth equation says that the value of this period's debt ratio is equal to the value of last period's debt ratio plus the adjustments that indicate how both the numerator and the denominator of the debt ratio have grown over the period. The numerator has grown by the size of the deficit, and the denominator has grown by the economy's rate of growth. The debt-ratio growth equation involves both these adjustments in ratio terms.

If d is an exogenous constant, the debt-ratio growth equation states that b *cannot* keep growing forever. Except for the constant $d,$ this year's debt ratio is just a *fraction,* $(1 - n)$ of last period's value. So the Liberal plan had to work. It involved the government's "making room" in its budget by cutting programs by whatever was necessary to meet both the interest payment obligations *and* the overall deficit target. This policy succeeded, but it involved more pain in terms of lost programs.

To illustrate the magnitude of these cutbacks, Table 16-2 presents a simulation of the Liberal policy. The simulation starts with values for the deficit ratio $(d = 0.06)$, the tax ratio $(t = 0.17)$, the debt ratio $(b = 0.70)$, the program spending ratio $(g = 0.178)$, and the interest rate $(r = 0.075)$, which represent what the Liberals

[1] When evaluating whether Canada was above or below the Golden Rule level of saving (described in Chapter 8), we noted that the net marginal product of capital, $MPK - \delta$, exceeded the growth rate, here denoted simply by $n,$ by a wide margin. In Chapter 18, we will see that $MPK = r + \delta$ in full equilibrium. In terms of long-run averages, then, we conclude that r exceeds n.

TABLE 16-2

A Simulation of Federal Fiscal Policy

Fiscal Year	Deficit/GDP (d)	Debt/GDP (b)	Spending/GDP (g)
1993–1994	0.06	0.72	0.178
1994–1995	0.05	0.73	0.166
1995–1996	0.04	0.73	0.155
1996–1997	0.03	0.72	0.145
1997–1998	0	0.68	0.128
1998–1999	0	0.64	0.130
1999–2000	−0.01	0.60	0.123
2000–2001	−0.01	0.56	0.126
2001–2002	−0.01	0.52	0.132
2002–2003	−0.01	0.48	0.129
2003–2004	−0.01	0.44	0.131
2004–2005	−0.01	0.41	0.134
2005–2006	−0.01	0.37	0.130
2006–2007	−0.01	0.34	0.131
2007–2008	−0.01	0.31	0.133
2008–2009	0.005	0.32	0.146
2009–2010	0.03	0.35	0.170
2010–2011	0.03	0.36	0.166
2011–2012	0.02	0.36	0.156
2012–2013	0.015	0.36	0.147
2013–2014	0.01	0.35	0.142

inherited in 1993. These values satisfy the budget identity

$$d = g - t + rb.$$

From this starting position, the simulation involves an annual growth rate for GDP of 5.5 percent ($n = 0.055$). While actual history involved year-to-year variation in GDP growth, we simplify by taking just the average trend (3.5 percent real growth plus 2.0 percent inflation). We focus first on the top two sections of Table 16-2 (covering 1993–1999 when the government eliminated its deficit, and 1999–2008 when the government ran a surplus each year equal to roughly one percent of GDP each year.) To use the two budget accounting identities in a simulation, we need to make two more assumptions designed to reflect actual history. We insert representative values for the interest rate and the tax rate. In the former case, the 7.5 percent value is involved for the first four years, then, to reflect the general decline in interest rates through the following period, we insert 6.5 percent for four years, 6.0 percent for the next four years, and then 5 percent for three years. For the tax ratio, the 17 percent figure is assumed until the end of the 1996–1997 fiscal year; a slightly higher value, 17.5 percent, is assumed after that to reflect the fact that the government did adjust policy by approximately this amount for five years. Then, in the 2002–2008 period, the tax rate is 17 percent for three years and then 16 percent for three years—again to reflect the fact that the government cut tax rates during this period.

The second column in the table indicates the deficit ratio that the government imposed during each fiscal year that followed. We used the $b_{+1} = (1 - n)b + d$ equation to generate the third-column entry (the next year's debt ratio), and we used the $g = d + t - rb$ equation to calculate the fourth-column entry (what had to happen to program spending to meet the deficit-ratio target).

Despite our simplifications, we see that the basic accounting identities do an excellent job of simulating history. They show the debt ratio falling by 40 percentage points to 31 percent by the end of the 2007–2008 fiscal year. This figure matches the true outcome of 30 percent very closely. The same can be said for the fourth column in the table. It indicates that dramatic spending cuts were needed to achieve this debt reduction. As a proportion of GDP, program spending had to be cut by a massive 5 percentage points of GDP in the first five years of this fiscal retrenchment exercise. And a decade later, the program spending ratio could recover by just one of these five percentage points. So, although the Liberals did get control of the debt ratio, this long-term gain resulted in a lot of short-term pain for those who depended on these government programs.

As just noted, after bottoming out in the fourth year of the deficit reduction period, the program spending ratio began to recover. The rise in program spending is widely referred to as the "fiscal dividend." A fiscal dividend exists during a period of debt reduction because new room is created in the budget as the debt ratio falls. Lower debt means that the government has lower interest payment obligations, and the government can then use these funds to raise program spending, reduce taxes, or pay down debt. In the table, to match the government's actual choices, we have assumed that the government chooses a combination of increased spending and debt reduction (budget surpluses).

How big is the "fiscal dividend" likely to be in the long run? To answer this question, we consider the budgetary implications of reducing the debt ratio by 50 percentage points—that is, back to the level of the early 1970s. The interest payments term in the budget identity, rb, would fall by $r\Delta b$, and for a 6 percent interest rate, that's $(0.06)(0.5) = 0.03$. Thus, there would be 3 percentage points of GDP new room in the budget. Further, it is important to consider the full-equilibrium version of the $\Delta b = d - nb$ equation. In full equilibrium, $\Delta b = 0$, so $d = nb$. If we settle on a full equilibrium with a 20 percent debt ratio, this relationship and a 5.5 percent growth rate imply that $d = (0.055)(.2) = 0.011$. Thus, moving from a balanced budget (which characterized the Canadian situation when the fiscal dividend debate began) to a full equilibrium involving a 20 percent debt ratio *requires* an *increase* in the deficit ratio of 1.1 percentage point. (d increases from 0 to 0.011.) Thus, the overall fiscal dividend in the long run is 4.1 percentage points of GDP.

To put this in perspective, it is worth noting that the entire federal personal income tax system raises just 8 percent of GDP. Thus, as long as debt reduction is part of our fiscal plan, the fiscal dividend will be enough to cut income taxes in half! (We are not suggesting that tax cuts are better than spending increases; this illustration is intended just to show the dramatic magnitude of what can accompany debt reduction.)

Of course, the debt ratio can gradually approach any target number, like 20 percent, whether we balance the budget or run surpluses in the short run. The choice between these two options concerns the distribution of costs and benefits over time. Relative to balanced budgets, surpluses involve short-term pain for long-term gain. We postpone receiving the fiscal dividend, but we reach the full magnitude of the benefits faster. Why should we be concerned about how long this takes?

To answer this question, many people focus on the aging of the population. With the oldest group within the large baby-boom generation starting retirement in 2011, and with increases in life expectancy generally, the proportion of the Canadian population that is over 65 years of age will double over the first 30 years of the present century. This fact will put a strain on our public pension and health-care systems (since most health-care expenses occur in older age). The Auditor General has estimated that the government will need at least 4 percentage points of GDP—beyond what is now spent—to maintain these programs. And surely the government will face other challenges. To mention just three, there are widespread demands (and government promises) for significant tax relief, there is the growing problem of rising income inequality (see the appendix to Chapter 6), and the need to address environmental and climate-change concerns. Even ignoring these and all other demands on the public purse, the fiscal dividend may be just barely big enough to cover the aging problem.

These facts indicate that we will almost certainly have to return to a series of years involving budget deficits in the longer-term future. To keep this development from pushing debt levels to new heights, many feel that we have a limited number of years to get the debt ratio down if we are to make room for the future rise that will occur when the demographic shock hits.

The government has accepted this analysis. The federal finance department funded a conference in 2003, asking participants to provide guidance concerning what target the government should identify for the ratio of the outstanding debt to GDP. Research presented at the conference showed that a target of between 20 and 25 percent—reached within 10 years—would be necessary if we want to limit the threat to the growth in average living standards posed by the aging of the baby boomer generation.[2] In the 2004 Budget, the government adopted this very target. The 2005 *Economic Update* of Finance Canada contained the following statements:

- With the aging of Canada's population, the country will face increases in aging-related expenditures, such as elderly benefits and health care. In order to meet these future pressures, it is critical that the federal government maintain a strong focus on fiscal discipline and debt reduction over the next several years, before the major impacts of population aging are felt.

- In the 2004 budget, the Government set a long-run goal of reducing the debt-to-GDP ratio to 25 per cent by 2014–15.

---

[2] William Scarth, "What Should We Do About the Debt?" in *Is the Debt War Over?*, edited by C. Ragan and W. Watson (Montreal: Institute for Research on Public Policy, 2004).

By focusing on the last year for which data was available when this book went to press—the 2007–2008 fiscal year—we can see that the government was well on its way to reaching this long-term target for the debt ratio within the desired time frame. But then the 2008–2009 recession hit. To illustrate how much this development may limit the government's ability to reach its longer-term debt-reduction objective, we have extended our simulation in the bottom section of Table 16-2 into what was the future when this book was being written.

As before, to perform this projection, we must make assumptions about the economy's growth rate, the general level of interest rates, and what amount of annual budget deficit the government will allow in the future. With respect to the growth rate, we assume zero as an average for the 2008–2010 recession period, and then a return to 5.5 percent after that. For interest rates, we assume 3 percent for 2008–2010, 4 percent for 2010–2012, and 5 percent for 2012–2014. Finally, for the budget deficit ratio, we make assumptions which match the government's own projection over this six-year period: one-half of one percent, 3 percent, 3 percent, 2 percent, 1.5 percent, and 1 percent. The implications for the debt ratio appear in the bottom section of Table 16-2.

The recession can be expected to cause the long-term decline in the debt ratio to be reversed. Instead of falling by another 17 percentage points as it did in the previous six years, the debt ratio rises by five percentage points. Then the debt ratio starts to resume its downward trend four years after the recession ends. These simulations suggest that, despite its large fiscal stimulus efforts during the recession and the accompanying postponement of further reductions on the debt-reduction front, the government will not miss its ultimate target for the debt ratio (to be reached by 2015) by too much. For this reason, many observers have concluded that it was appropriate for the government to take action in an attempt to limit the recession, even though it caused some delay in returning to its target debt-reduction path. In other words, these observers do not think that the government has lost its relatively recently achieved reputation for fiscal prudence. Other observers worry that once the return to deficits has been accepted, it will be much harder for the government to return quickly to debt reduction. As a result, these individuals worry that the general level of living standards in the longer term may not be as high as otherwise, and that this may turn out to be the price we must pay for undertaking such a vigorous initiative during the 2008–2009 recession. ■

16-2 Problems in Measurement

The government budget deficit equals government spending minus government revenue, which in turn equals the amount of new debt the government needs to issue to finance its operations. This definition may sound simple enough, but in fact debates over fiscal policy sometimes arise over how the budget deficit should be measured. Some economists believe that the deficit as currently measured is not a good indicator of the stance of fiscal policy. That is, they believe that the budget deficit does not accurately gauge either the impact of fiscal policy on today's economy or the burden being placed on future generations of taxpayers. In this section we discuss four problems with the usual measure of the budget deficit.

Measurement Problem 1: Inflation

The least controversial of the measurement issues is the correction for inflation. Almost all economists agree that the government's indebtedness should be measured in real terms, not in nominal terms. The measured deficit should equal the change in the government's real debt, not the change in its nominal debt.

The budget deficit as commonly measured, however, does not correct for inflation. To see how large an error this induces, consider the following example. Suppose that the real government debt is not changing; in other words, in real terms, the budget is balanced. In this case, the nominal debt must be rising at the rate of inflation. That is,

$$\frac{\Delta B}{B} = \pi,$$

where π is the inflation rate and B is the stock of government bonds. This implies

$$\Delta B = \pi B.$$

The government would look at the change in the nominal debt ΔB and would report a budget deficit of πB. Hence, most economists believe that the reported budget deficit is overstated by the amount πB.

We can make the same argument in another way. The deficit is government expenditure minus government revenue. Part of expenditure is the interest paid on the government debt. Expenditure should include only the real interest paid on the debt rB, not the nominal interest paid iB. Because the difference between the nominal interest rate i and the real interest rate r is the inflation rate π, the budget deficit is overstated by πB.

This correction for inflation can be large, especially when inflation is high, and it can often change our evaluation of fiscal policy. For example, in 1981, the federal government reported a budget deficit of over $7 billion. But inflation was over 12 percent, and after correction for inflation, the deficit turned into a small surplus.

Measurement Problem 2: Capital Assets

Many economists believe that an accurate assessment of the government's budget deficit requires taking into account the government's assets as well as its liabilities. In particular, when measuring the government's overall indebtedness, we should subtract government assets from government debt. Therefore, the budget deficit should be measured as the change in debt minus the change in assets.

Certainly, individuals and firms treat assets and liabilities symmetrically. When a person borrows to buy a house, we do not say that he is running a budget deficit. Instead, we offset the increase in assets (the house) against the increase in debt (the mortgage) and record no change in net wealth. Perhaps we should treat the government's finances the same way.

A budget procedure that accounts for assets as well as liabilities is called **capital budgeting,** because it takes into account changes in capital. For example, suppose that the government sells one of its office buildings or some of its land and uses the proceeds to reduce the government debt. Under current budget procedures, the reported deficit would be lower. Under capital budgeting, the revenue received from the sale would not lower the deficit, because the reduction in debt would be offset by a reduction in assets. Similarly, under capital budgeting, government borrowing to finance the purchase of a capital good would not raise the deficit.

The major difficulty with capital budgeting is that it is hard to decide which government expenditures should count as capital expenditures. For example, should the highway system be counted as an asset of the government? If so, what is its value? Should spending on education be treated as expenditure on human capital? These difficult questions must be answered if the government is to adopt a capital budget.

Economists and policymakers disagree about whether the federal government should use capital budgeting. Opponents of capital budgeting argue that, although the system is superior in principle to the current system, it is too difficult to implement in practice. Proponents of capital budgeting argue that even an imperfect treatment of capital assets would be better than ignoring them altogether.

Measurement Problem 3: Uncounted Liabilities

Some economists argue that the measured budget deficit is misleading because it excludes some important government liabilities. For example, consider the Canada and Quebec Pension Plans. People pay some of their income into the system when young and expect to receive benefits when old. Perhaps accumulated future public pension benefits should be included in the government's liabilities.

One might argue that pension liabilities are different from government debt because the government can change the laws determining pension benefits. Yet, in principle, the government could always choose not to repay all of its debt: the government honours its debt only because it chooses to do so. Promises to pay the holders of government debt may not be fundamentally different from promises to pay the future recipients the public pension system. In the mid-1990s, the unfunded debt of the Canada Pension Plan was just about the same size as the entire federal government debt that is usually reported, so this measurement issue is important. The government responded to this public pension problem by scheduling a series of increases in the associated payroll taxes (employer and employee contributions to the public pension) to take effect over a 10-year period. As a result, there is no actuarial underfunding problem remaining for our public pension. Some other countries have not taken similar bold action. As a result, you will continue to read about ongoing debates in both the United States and the United Kingdom about whether they should address their underfunded pensions in the same way (by increasing contributions) or in another way (by decreasing benefits or delaying the age that citizens can begin to collect their pensions).

A particularly difficult form of government liability to measure is the *contingent liability*—the liability that is due only if a specified event occurs. For example, the government guarantees many forms of private credit, such as student loans, mortgages for low- and moderate-income families, and deposits in banks and trust companies. If the borrower repays the loan, the government pays nothing; if the borrower defaults, the government makes the repayment. When the government provides this guarantee, it undertakes a liability contingent on the borrower's default. Yet this contingent liability is not reflected in the budget deficit, in part because it is not clear what dollar value to attach to it.

CASE STUDY

Accounting for TARP

In 2008, many U.S. banks found themselves in serious trouble, and the federal government put substantial taxpayer funds into rescuing the financial system. A Case Study in Chapter 11 discusses the causes of this financial crisis, the ramifications, and the policy responses. But here we note one particular small side effect: it made measuring the federal government's budget deficit more difficult.

As part of the financial rescue package, called the Troubled Assets Relief Program (TARP), the U.S. Treasury bought preferred stock in many banks. In essence, the plan worked as follows. The Treasury borrowed money, gave the money to the banks, and in exchange became a part owner of those banks. In the future, the banks were expected to pay the Treasury a preferred dividend (similar to interest) and eventually to repay the initial investment as well. When that repayment occurred, the Treasury would relinquish its ownership share in the banks.

The question then arose: how should the government's accounting statements reflect these transactions? The U.S. Treasury under the Bush administration adopted the conventional view that these TARP expenditures should be counted as current expenses, like any other form of spending. Likewise, when the banks repaid the Treasury, these funds would be counted as revenue. Accounted for in this way, TARP caused a surge in the budget deficit when the funds were distributed to the banks, but it would lead to a smaller deficit, and perhaps a surplus, in the future when repayments were received from the banks.

The Congressional Budget Office (CBO), however, took a different view. Because most of the TARP expenditures were expected to be repaid, the CBO thought it was wrong to record this expenditure like other forms of spending. Instead, the CBO believed "the equity investments for TARP should be recorded on a net present value basis adjusted for market risk, rather than on a cash basis as recorded thus far by the Treasury." That is, for this particular program, the CBO adopted a form of capital budgeting. But it took into account the possibility that these investments would not pay off. In its estimation, every dollar spent on the TARP program cost the taxpayer only about 25 cents. If the actual cost turned out to be larger than the estimated 25 cents, the CBO would record those additional costs later; if the actual cost turned out to be less than projected, the CBO would later record a gain for the government. Because of these differences in accounting, while the TARP funds were being distributed, the budget deficit as estimated by the CBO was much smaller than the budget deficit as recorded by the U.S. Treasury.

When the Obama administration came into office, it adopted an accounting treatment more similar to the one used by the CBO, but with a larger estimate of the cost of TARP funds. The president's first budget proposal stated, "Estimates of the value of the financial assets acquired by the Federal Government to date suggest that the Government will get back approximately two-thirds of the money spent purchasing such assets—so the net cost to the Government is roughly 33 cents on the dollar. These transactions are typically reflected in the budget at this net cost, since that budgetary approach best reflects their impact on the Government's underlying fiscal position." ■

Measurement Problem 4: The Business Cycle

Many changes in the government's budget deficit occur automatically in response to a fluctuating economy. For example, when the economy goes into a recession, incomes fall, so people pay less in personal income taxes. Profits fall, so corporations pay less in corporate profit taxes. More people become eligible for government assistance, such as welfare and employment insurance, so government spending rises. Even without any change in the laws governing taxation and spending, the budget deficit increases.

These automatic changes in the deficit are not errors in measurement, for the government truly borrows more when a recession depresses tax revenue and boosts government spending. But these changes do make it more difficult to use the deficit to monitor changes in fiscal policy. That is, the deficit can rise or fall either because the government has changed policy or because the economy has changed direction. For some purposes, it would be good to know which is occurring.

Many economists believe that government spending and tax rates should be set so that the budget *would* be balanced *if* real GDP was at the natural level. If this were accomplished, we would observe deficits during recessions (when unemployment is high and the government is making more transfer payments and collecting fewer tax dollars), and we would observe surpluses during booms (when employment and tax revenue are high and employment insurance and welfare payments are low). To assess fiscal policy, then, we need to know what the deficit would be if we were not undergoing a business cycle.

To solve this problem, the Department of Finance calculates what it calls the **cyclically adjusted budget deficit**—what the excess of spending over revenue would be if Canadian GDP were at it natural-rate value. We can now clarify how these data are used. For example, in 1994, when the federal government's annual deficit was at its pre-2008–2009 biggest, the deficit was about $40 billion, while the cyclically adjusted deficit was estimated to be approximately $25 billion. According to these calculations, about $15 billion of the $40 billion total resulted from the fact that unemployment was so high in 1994. According to this approach, any attempt to push the deficit below $15 billion is regarded as inappropriate, since that part of the deficit was simply due to the state of the economy. It would vanish automatically when the economy returned to the natural rate. Efforts to eliminate it any earlier just prolong and deepen the recession. It is true that the national debt increases while we wait for this automatic elimination of that fraction of the deficit to take place. However, since there should be budget surpluses in the boom years, there should be no tendency for debt to grow over the longer run.

As the 1994 example makes clear, the cyclically adjusted deficit is a useful measure because it reflects policy changes but not the current stage of the business cycle.

Summing Up

Economists differ in the importance they place on these measurement problems. Some believe that the problems are so severe that the budget deficit as normally measured is almost meaningless. Most take these measurement problems seriously but still view the measured budget deficit as a useful indicator of fiscal policy.

The undisputed lesson is that to evaluate fully what fiscal policy is doing, economists and policymakers must look at more than just the measured budget deficit. And, in fact, they do. No economic statistic is perfect. Whenever we see a number reported in the media, we need to know what it is measuring and what it is leaving out. This is especially true for data on government debt and budget deficits.

16-3 The Traditional View of Government Debt

Imagine that you are an economist working for the Department of Finance in Ottawa. You receive a letter from a member of Parliament (MP):

> Dear Finance Canada Economist:
>
> Parliament is about to consider the govenment's proposal to cut all taxes by 20 percent. Before deciding whether to endorse the policy, I would like your analysis. I see little hope of reducing government spending any further, so the tax cut would mean an increase in the budget deficit. How would the tax cut and budget deficit affect the economy and the economic well-being of the country?
>
> Sincerely,
> Member of Parliament

Before responding to the MP, you open your favourite economics textbook—this one, of course—to see what the models predict for such a change in fiscal policy.

To analyze the long-run effects of this policy change, you turn to the models in Chapters 3 through 8. The model in Chapter 3 shows that a tax cut stimulates consumer spending and reduces national saving. The reduction in saving raises the interest rate, which crowds out investment. The Solow growth model introduced in Chapter 7 shows that lower investment eventually leads to a lower steady-state capital stock and a lower level of output. Because we concluded in Chapter 8 that the Canadian economy has less capital than in the Golden Rule steady state (the steady state with maximum consumption), the fall in steady-state capital means lower consumption and reduced economic well-being.

To analyze the short-run effects of the policy change, you use the *IS–LM* model in Chapters 10 and 11. This model shows that a tax cut stimulates consumer spending, which implies an expansionary shift in the *IS* curve. If there is no change in monetary policy, the shift in the *IS* curve leads to an expansionary shift in the aggregate demand curve. In the short run, when prices are sticky, the expansion in aggregate demand leads to higher output and lower unemployment. Over time, as prices adjust, the economy returns to the natural level of output, and the higher aggregate demand results in a higher price level.

To see how international trade affects your analysis, you turn to the open-economy models in Chapters 5 and 12. The model in Chapter 5 shows that when national saving falls, people start financing investment by borrowing from abroad, causing a trade deficit. Although the inflow of capital from abroad lessens the effect of the fiscal-policy change on capital accumulation, it leads to Canada becoming more indebted to foreign countries. The fiscal-policy change also causes the Canadian dollar to appreciate in the short run, which makes foreign goods cheaper in Canada and domestic goods more expensive abroad. The Mundell–Fleming model in Chapter 12 shows that the appreciation of the dollar and the resulting fall in net exports reduce the short-run expansionary impact of the fiscal change on output and employment.

With all these models in mind, you draft a response:

Dear MP:

A tax cut financed by government borrowing would have many effects on the economy. The immediate impact of the tax cut would be to stimulate consumer spending. Higher consumer spending affects the economy in both the short run and the long run.

In the short run, higher consumer spending would raise the demand for goods and services and thus raise output and employment. Interest rates would also rise, however, as investors competed for a smaller flow of saving and as the Bank of Canada tightens monetary policy to limit inflationary pressure. Higher interest rates would discourage investment and would encourage capital to flow in from abroad. The dollar would rise in value against foreign currencies, and Canadian firms would become less competitive in world markets.

In the long run, the smaller national saving caused by the tax cut would mean a smaller capital stock and a greater foreign debt. Therefore, the output of the nation would be smaller, and a greater share of that output would be owed to foreigners.

The overall effect of the tax cut on economic well-being is hard to judge. Current generations would benefit from higher consumption and higher employment, although inflation would likely be higher as well. Future generations would bear much of the burden of today's budget deficits: they would be born into a nation with a smaller capital stock and a larger foreign debt.

Your faithful servant,
Finance Canada Economist

The MP replies:

Dear Finance Canada Economist:

Thank you for your letter. It made sense to me. But yesterday my committee heard testimony from a prominent economist who called herself a "Ricardian" and who reached quite a different conclusion. She said that a tax cut by itself would not stimulate consumer spending. She concluded that the budget deficit would therefore not have all the effects you listed. What's going on here?

Sincerely,
MP

After studying the next section, you write back to the MP, explaining in detail the debate over Ricardian equivalence.

Taxes and Incentives

Throughout this book we have summarized the tax system with a single variable *T*. In our models, the policy instrument is the level of taxation that the government chooses; we have ignored the issue of how the government raises this tax revenue. In practice, however, taxes are not lump-sum payments but are levied on some type of economic activity. Canadian governments raise some revenue by taxing personal income, some by taxing payrolls, some by taxing corporate profits, and some by taxing purchases.

Courses in public finance spend much time studying the pros and cons of alternative types of taxes. One lesson emphasized in such courses is that taxes affect incentives. When people are taxed on their labour earnings, they have less incentive to work hard. When people are taxed on the income from owning capital, they have less incentive to save and invest in capital. As a result, when taxes change, incentives change, and this development has macroeconomic effects. If lower tax rates encourage increased work and investment, the aggregate supply of goods and services increases.

Some economists, called *supply-siders,* believe that the incentive effects of taxes are large. Some supply-siders go so far as to suggest that tax cuts can be self-financing: a cut in tax rates induces such a large increase in aggregate supply—and therefore in the nation's overall tax base—that tax revenue increases, despite the fall in tax rates. Although all economists agree that taxes affect incentives and that incentives affect aggregate supply to some degree, most believe that the incentive effects are not large enough to make tax cuts self-financing in most circumstances.

In recent years, there has been much debate about how to reform the tax system to reduce the disincentives that impede the economy from reaching it full potential. A proposal endorsed by many economists is to move from the current income tax system toward a consumption tax. Compared to an income tax, a consumption tax provides more incentives for saving, investment, and capital accumulation. One way of moving toward a consumption tax base is to raise the maximum annual contribution limits that individuals face when depositing funds into their registered retirement savings plans (RRSPs) and their tax-free savings accounts. If there were no contribution limits, current taxable income would be smaller than actual income received by the total documented saving that an individual undertakes each period. Because this difference is the individual's consumption, we would have an expenditure-based tax system. Because it would continue to be administered as an income tax, it could remain as progressive as we wish it to be. Another way of taxing consumption is to adopt a value-added tax, a tax, now used by many European countries, and by Canada in the form of the GST.[3]

Some have argued that we are already fairly close to an expenditure-based tax system. For many individuals, their net worth is not much greater than the value of their house. Since the capital gains that an individual receives as the house becomes more valuable over the years is exempt from income taxation, the rate of return on saving for many individuals may not be appreciably reduced by our income tax system as it is.

---

[3] To read more about how taxes affect the economy through incentives, the best place to start is an undergraduate textbook in public finance, such as Harvey Rosen and Ted Gayer, *Public Finance*, 8th ed. (New York: McGraw-Hill, 2007). In the more advanced literature that links public finance and macroeconomics, a classic reference is Christophe Chamley, "Optimal Taxation of Capital Income in a General Equilibrium Model with Infinite Lives," *Econometrica* 54 (May 1986): 607–622. Chamley establishes conditions under which the tax system should not distort the incentive to save (that is, conditions under which consumption taxation is superior to income taxation). The robustness of this conclusion is investigated in Andrew Atkeson, V. V. Chari, and Patrick J. Kehoe, "Taxing Capital Income: A Bad Idea," *Federal Reserve Bank of Minneapolis Quarterly Review* 23 (Summer 1999): 3–17.

16-4 The Ricardian View of Government Debt

The traditional view of government debt presumes that when the government cuts taxes and runs a budget deficit, consumers respond to their higher after-tax income by spending more. An alternative view, called **Ricardian equivalence,** questions this presumption. According to the Ricardian view, consumers are forward-looking and, therefore, base their spending decisions not only on their current income but also on their expected future income. As we explore more fully in Chapter 17, the forward-looking consumer is at the heart of many modern theories of consumption. The Ricardian view of government debt applies the logic of the forward-looking consumer to analyze the effects of fiscal policy.

The Basic Logic of Ricardian Equivalence

Consider the response of a forward-looking consumer to the tax cut that Parliament is debating. The consumer might reason as follows:

> The government is cutting taxes without any plans to reduce government spending. Does this policy alter my set of opportunities? Am I richer because of this tax cut? Should I consume more?
>
> Maybe not. The government is financing the tax cut by running a budget deficit. At some point in the future, the government will have to raise taxes to pay off the debt and accumulated interest. So the policy really represents a tax cut today coupled with a tax hike in the future. The tax cut merely gives me transitory income that eventually will be taken back. I am not any better off, so I will leave my consumption unchanged.

The forward-looking consumer understands that government borrowing today means higher taxes in the future. A tax cut financed by government debt does not reduce the tax burden; it merely reschedules it. It therefore should not encourage the consumer to spend more.

One can view this argument another way. Suppose that the government borrows $1,000 from the typical citizen to give that citizen a $1,000 tax cut. In essence, this policy is the same as giving the citizen a $1,000 government bond as a gift. One side of the bond says, "The government owes you, the bondholder, $1,000 plus interest." The other side says, "You, the taxpayer, owe the government $1,000 plus interest." Overall, the gift of a bond from the government to the typical citizen does not make the citizen richer or poorer, because the value of the bond is offset by the value of the future tax liability.

The general principle is that government debt is equivalent to future taxes, and if consumers are sufficiently forward-looking, future taxes are equivalent to current taxes. Hence, financing the government by debt is equivalent to financing it by taxes. This view is called *Ricardian equivalence* after the famous nineteenth-century economist David Ricardo, because he first noted the theoretical argument.

The implication of Ricardian equivalence is that a debt-financed tax cut leaves consumption unaffected. Households save the extra disposable income to pay the future tax liability that the tax cut implies. This increase in private saving just offsets the decrease in public saving. National saving—the sum of private and public saving—remains the same. The tax cut therefore has none of the effects that the traditional analysis predicts.

The logic of Ricardian equivalence does not mean that all changes in fiscal policy are irrelevant. Changes in fiscal policy do influence consumer spending if they influence present or future government purchases. For example, suppose that the government cuts taxes today because it plans to reduce government purchases in the future. If the consumer understands that this tax cut does not require an increase in future taxes, he feels richer and raises his consumption. But note that it is the reduction in government purchases, rather than the reduction in taxes, that stimulates consumption: the announcement of a future reduction in government purchases would raise consumption today even if current taxes were unchanged, because it would imply lower taxes at some time in the future.

Consumers and Future Taxes

The essence of the Ricardian view is that when people choose their consumption, they rationally look ahead to the future taxes implied by government debt. But how forward-looking are consumers? Defenders of the traditional view of government debt believe that the prospect of future taxes does not have as large an influence on current consumption as the Ricardian view assumes. Here are some of their arguments.[4]

Myopia Proponents of the Ricardian view of fiscal policy assume that people are rational when making decisions such as choosing how much of their income to consume and how much to save. When the government borrows to pay for current spending, rational consumers look ahead to the future taxes required to support this debt. Thus, the Ricardian view presumes that people have substantial knowledge and foresight.

One possible argument for the traditional view of tax cuts is that people are shortsighted, perhaps because they do not fully comprehend the implications of government budget deficits. It is possible that some people follow simple and not fully rational rules of thumb when choosing how much to save. Suppose, for example, that a person acts on the assumption that future taxes will be the same as current taxes. This person will fail to take account of future changes in taxes required by current government policies. A debt-financed tax cut will lead this person to believe that his lifetime income has increased, even if it hasn't. The tax cut will therefore lead to higher consumption and lower national saving.

Borrowing Constraints The Ricardian view of government debt assumes that consumers base their spending not only on current income but on their lifetime income, which includes both current and expected future income. According to the

---

[4] For a survey of the debate over Ricardian equivalence, see Douglas Bernheim, "Ricardian Equivalence: An Evaluation of Theory and Evidence," *NBER Macroeconomics Annual* (1987): 263–303. See also the symposium on budget deficits in the Spring 1989 issue of the *Journal of Economic Perspectives*.

Ricardian view, a debt-financed tax cut increases current income, but it does not alter lifetime income or consumption. Advocates of the traditional view of government debt argue that current income is more important than lifetime income for those consumers who face binding borrowing constraints. A *borrowing constraint* is a limit on how much an individual can borrow from banks or other finanical institutions.

A person who would like to consume more than his current income—perhaps because he expects higher income in the future—has to do so by borrowing. If he cannot borrow to finance current consumption, or can borrow only a limited amount, his current income determines his spending, regardless of what his lifetime income might be. In this case, a debt-financed tax cut raises current income and thus consumption, even though future income is lower. In essence, when the government cuts current taxes and raises future taxes, it is giving taxpayers a loan. For a person who wanted to obtain a loan but was unable to, the tax cut expands his opportunities and stimulates consumption.

CASE STUDY

A Test of Ricardian Equivalence

In 1994, changes in Canada's personal income tax system forced many individuals to increase the amount of taxes they paid on a quarterly installment basis (rather than paying taxes just once each year in April on income that does not involve automatic tax deductions by one's employer). Does a change of this kind affect consumer spending? Some evidence is available from a similar change that was introduced in the United States just two years earlier.

The American policy was an attempt to deal with a lingering recession by lowering the amount of income taxes that were being withheld from workers' paycheques. The policy did not reduce the amount of taxes that workers owed; it merely delayed payment. The higher take-home pay that workers received during 1992 was to be offset by higher tax payments, or smaller tax refunds, when income taxes were due in April 1993.

What effect would you have predicted for this policy? According to the logic of Ricardian equivalence, consumers should realize that their lifetime resources were unchanged and, therefore, save the extra take-home pay to meet the upcoming tax liability. Yet the first George Bush, the U.S. president at the time, claimed his policy would provide "money people can use to help pay for clothing, college, or to get a new car." That is, he believed that consumers would spend the extra income, thereby stimulating aggregate demand and helping the economy recover from the recession. Bush seemed to be assuming that consumers were shortsighted or faced binding borrowing constraints.

Gauging the actual effects of this policy is difficult with aggregate data, because many other things were happening at the same time. Yet some evidence comes from a survey two economists conducted shortly after the policy was announced. The survey asked people what they would do with the extra income. Fifty-seven percent of the respondents said they would save it, use it to repay debts, or adjust their withholding in order to reverse the effect of Bush's executive order. Forty-three percent said they would spend the extra income. Thus, for this policy change, a majority of the population was planning to act as Ricardian theory posits. Nonetheless, Bush was partly right: many people planned to spend the extra income, even though they understood that the following year's tax bill would be higher.[5]

These U.S. results suggest that the Canadian policy (which was essentially the reverse of the American initiative in 1992) would lower the government's budget deficit temporarily and dampen aggregate demand temporarily (thereby weakening Canada's recovery slightly). It is the first of these two effects that appealed to the Canadian government. ■

Future Generations Besides myopia and borrowing constraints, a third argument for the traditional view of government debt is that consumers expect the implied future taxes to fall not on them but on future generations. Suppose, for example, that the government cuts taxes today, issues 30-year bonds to finance the budget deficit, and then raises taxes in 30 years to repay the loan. In this case, the government debt represents a transfer of wealth from the next generation of taxpayers (which faces the tax hike) to the current generation of taxpayers (which gets the tax cut). This transfer raises the lifetime resources of the current generation, so it raises their consumption. In essence, a debt-financed tax cut stimulates consumption because it gives the current generation the opportunity to consume at the expense of the next generation.

Economist Robert Barro has provided a clever rejoinder to this argument to support the Ricardian view. Barro argues that because future generations are the children and grandchildren of the current generation, we should not view them as independent economic actors. Instead, he argues, the appropriate assumption is that current generations care about future generations. This altruism between generations is evidenced by the gifts that many people give their children, often in the form of bequests at the time of their death. The existence of bequests suggests that many people are not eager to take advantage of the opportunity to consume at their children's expense.

"What's this I hear about you adults mortgaging my future?"

[5] Matthew D. Shapiro and Joel Slemrod, "Consumer Response to the Timing of Income: Evidence From a Change in Tax Withholding," *American Economic Review* 85 (March 1995): 274–283.

According to Barro's analysis, the relevant decisionmaking unit is not the individual, who lives only a finite number of years, but the family, which continues forever. In other words, an individual decides how much to consume based not only on his own income but also on the income of future members of his family. A debt-financed tax cut may raise the income an individual receives in his lifetime, but it does not raise his family's overall resources. Instead of consuming the extra income from the tax cut, the individual saves it and leaves it as a bequest to his children, who will bear the future tax liability.

We can see now that the debate over government debt is really a debate over consumer behaviour. The Ricardian view assumes that consumers have a long time horizon. Barro's analysis of the family implies that the consumer's time horizon, like the government's, is effectively infinite. Yet it is possible that consumers do not look ahead to the tax liabilities of future generations. Perhaps they expect their children to be richer than they are and, therefore, welcome the opportunity to consume at their children's expense. The fact that many people leave zero or minimal bequests to their children is consistent with this hypothesis. For these zero-bequest families, a debt-financed tax cut alters consumption by redistributing wealth among generations.[6]

<hr>

CASE STUDY

Why Do Parents Leave Bequests?

The debate over Ricardian equivalence is partly a debate over how different generations are linked to one another. Robert Barro's defense of the Ricardian view is based on the assumption that parents leave their children bequests because they care about them. But is altruism really the reason that parents leave bequests?

One group of economists has suggested that parents use bequests to control their children. Parents often want their children to do certain things for them, such as phoning home regularly and visiting on holidays. Perhaps parents use the implicit threat of disinheritance to induce their children to be more attentive.

To test this "strategic bequest motive," these economists examined data on how often children visit their parents. They found that the more wealthy the parent, the more often the children visit. Even more striking was another result: only wealth that can be left as a bequest induces more frequent visits. Wealth that cannot be bequeathed, such as pension wealth, which reverts to the pension company in the event of an early death, does not encourage children to visit. These findings suggest that there may be more to the relationships among generations than mere altruism.[7] ■

<hr>

[6] Robert J. Barro, "Are Government Bonds Net Wealth?" *Journal of Political Economy* 81 (1974): 1095–1117.

[7] B. Douglas Bernheim, Andrei Shleifer, and Lawrence H. Summers, "The Strategic Bequest Motive," *Journal of Political Economy* 93 (1985): 1045–1076.

Making a Choice

Having seen the traditional and Ricardian views of government debt, you should ask yourself two sets of questions.

First, which view do you agree with? If the government cuts taxes today, runs a budget deficit, and raises taxes in the future, how will the policy affect the economy? Will it stimulate consumption, as the traditional view holds? Or will consumers understand that their lifetime income is unchanged and, therefore, offset the budget deficit with higher private saving?

Second, why do you hold the view that you do? If you agree with the traditional view of government debt, what is the reason? Do consumers fail to understand that higher government borrowing today means higher taxes

---

FYI

Ricardo on Ricardian Equivalence

David Ricardo was a millionaire stockbroker and one of the great economists of all time. His most important contribution was his 1817 book *Principles of Political Economy and Taxation,* in which he developed the theory of comparative advantage, which economists still use to explain the gains from international trade. Ricardo was also a member of the British Parliament, where he put his own theories to work and opposed the corn laws, which restricted international trade in grain.

Ricardo was interested in the alternative ways in which a government might pay for its expenditure. In an 1820 article called "Essay on the Funding System," he considered an example of a war that cost 20 million pounds. He noted that if the interest rate were 5 percent, this expense could be financed with a one-time tax of 20 million pounds, a perpetual tax of 1 million pounds, or a tax of 1.2 million pounds for 45 years. He wrote:

> In point of economy, there is no real difference in either of the modes; for twenty million in one payment, one million per annum for ever, or 1,200,0000 pounds for 45 years, are precisely of the same value.

Ricardo was aware that the issue involved the linkages among generations:

> It would be difficult to convince a man possessed of 20,000 pounds, or any other sum, that a perpetual payment of 50 pounds per annum was equally burdensome with a single tax of 1000 pounds. He would have some vague notion that the 50 pounds per annum would be paid by posterity, and would not be paid by him; but if he leaves his fortune to his son, and leaves it charged with this perpetual tax, where is the difference whether he leaves him 20,000 pounds with the tax, or 19,000 pounds without it?

Although Ricardo viewed these alternative methods of government finance as equivalent, he did not think other people would view them as such:

> The people who pay taxes . . . do not manage their private affairs accordingly. We are apt to think that the war is burdensome only in proportion to what we are at the moment called to pay for it in taxes, without reflecting on the probable duration of such taxes.

Thus, Ricardo doubted that people were rational and farsighted enough to look ahead fully to their future tax liabilities.

As a policymaker, Ricardo took seriously the government debt. Before the British Parliament, he once declared,

> This would be the happiest country in the world, and its progress in prosperity would go beyond the powers of imagination to conceive, if we got rid of two great evils—the national debt and the corn laws.

It is one of the great ironies in the history of economic thought that Ricardo rejected the theory that now bears his name!

tomorrow? Or do they ignore future taxes, either because they are borrowing-constrained or because future taxes fall on future generations with which they do not feel an economic link? If you hold the Ricardian view, do you believe that consumers have the foresight to see that government borrowing today will result in future taxes levied on them or their descendants? Do you believe that consumers will save the extra income to offset that future tax liability?

We might hope that the evidence could help us decide between these two views of government debt. Yet when economists examine historical episodes of large budget deficits, the evidence is inconclusive. History can be interpreted in different ways.

Consider, for example, the experience of the 1980s. The large budget deficits run by most Western countries seem to offer a natural experiment to test the two views of government debt. At first glance, this episode appears decisively to support the traditional view. The large budget deficits coincided with low national saving, high real interest rates, and large trade deficits. Indeed, advocates of the traditional view of government debt often claim that the experience of the 1980s confirms their position.

Yet those who hold the Ricardian view of government debt interpret these events differently. Perhaps saving was low in the 1980s because people were optimistic about future economic growth—an optimism that was also reflected in a booming stock market. Or perhaps saving was low because people expected that the tax cut would eventually lead not to higher taxes but to lower government spending instead. Because it is hard to rule out any of these interpretations, both views of government debt survive.

16-5 Other Perspectives on Government Debt

The policy debates over government debt have many facets. So far we have considered the traditional and Ricardian views of government debt. According to the traditional view, a government budget deficit expands aggregate demand and stimulates output in the short run but crowds out capital and depresses economic growth in the long run. According to the Ricardian view, a government budget deficit has none of these effects, because consumers understand that a budget deficit represents merely postponement of a tax burden. With these two theories as background, we now consider several other perspectives on government debt.

Balanced Budgets Versus Optimal Fiscal Policy

Economists and politicians frequently propose rules for fiscal policy. The rule that has received the most attention is the balanced-budget rule. Under a balanced-budget rule, the government would not be allowed to spend more than

it receives in tax revenue. In the United States, many state governments operate under such a fiscal policy rule, since state constitutions often require a balanced budget. In Canada, this issue has been a recurring topic of political
debate and several provinces adopted such a rule in the 1990s.

Most economists oppose a strict rule requiring the government to balance its
budget. There are three reasons why optimal fiscal policy may at times call for a
budget deficit or surplus.

Stabilization A budget deficit or surplus can help stabilize the economy. In
essence, a balanced-budget rule would revoke the automatic stabilizing powers of the system of taxes and transfers. When the economy goes into a recession, taxes automatically fall, and transfers automatically rise. While these
automatic responses help stabilize the economy, they push the budget into
deficit. A strict balanced-budget rule would require that the government raise
taxes or reduce spending in a recession, but these actions would further
depress aggregate demand.

Tax Smoothing A budget deficit or surplus can be used to reduce the distortion of incentives caused by the tax system. As you probably learned in
courses in microeconomics, high tax rates impose a cost on society by discouraging economic activity. A tax on labour earnings, for instance, reduces
the incentive that people have to work long hours. Because this disincentive
becomes particularly large at very high tax rates, as we learned in the appendix to Chapter 6, the total social cost of taxes is minimized by keeping tax
rates relatively stable rather than making them high in some years and low in
others. Economists call this policy tax smoothing. To keep tax rates smooth, a
deficit is necessary in years of unusually low income (recessions) or unusually high expenditure (wars).

Intergenerational Redistribution A budget deficit can be used to shift a tax
burden from current to future generations. For example, some economists
argue that if the current generation fights a war to maintain freedom, future
generations benefit as well and should bear some of the burden. To pass on
some of the war's costs, the current generation can finance the war with a budget deficit. The government can later retire the debt by levying taxes on the
next generation.

These considerations lead most economists to reject a strict balanced-
budget rule. At the very least, a rule for fiscal policy needs to take account of
the recurring episodes, such as recessions and wars, during which a budget
deficit is a reasonable policy response.

Effects on Monetary Policy

It is often argued that a large budget deficit leads to high expectations of inflation. We first discussed such a possibility in Chapter 4. As we saw, one way for a
government to finance a budget deficit is to have the central bank buy up the

newly issued government bonds—that is, simply to print money—a policy that leads to higher inflation. Indeed, when countries experience hyperinflation, the typical reason is that fiscal policymakers are relying on the inflation tax to pay for some of their spending. The ends of hyperinflations almost always coincide with fiscal reforms that include large cuts in government spending and, therefore, a reduced need for seigniorage.

In addition to this link between the budget deficit and inflation, some economists have suggested that a high level of debt might also encourage the government to create inflation. Because most government debt is specified in nominal terms, the real value of the debt falls when the price level rises. This is the usual redistribution between creditors and debtors caused by unexpected inflation—here the debtor is the government and the creditor is the private sector. But this debtor, unlike others, has access to the monetary printing press. A high level of debt might encourage the government to print money, thereby raising the price level and reducing the real value of its debts.

Despite these concerns about a possible link between government debt and monetary policy, there is little evidence that this link is important in most developed countries. In North America, for instance, inflation was high in the 1970s, even though government debt was low relative to GDP (at least by the standards of the years to follow). Monetary policymakers got inflation under control in the early 1980s, just as fiscal policymakers presided over a large increase in the debt ratio. Thus, although monetary policy might be driven by fiscal policy in some situations, such as during the classic hyperinflations, this situation appears not to be the norm in most countries today. There are several reasons for this. First, most governments can finance deficits by selling debt to the public and don't need to rely on seigniorage. Second, central banks often have enough independence to resist political pressure for more expansionary monetary policy. Third, and most important, policymakers in all parts of government know that inflation is a poor solution to fiscal problems.

Debt and the Political Process

Fiscal policy is made not by angels but by an imperfect political process. Some economists worry that the possibility of financing government spending by issuing debt makes that political process all the worse.

This idea has a long history. Nineteenth-century economist Knut Wicksell claimed that if the benefit of some type of government spending exceeded its cost, it should be possible to finance that spending in a way that would receive unanimous support from the voters. He concluded that government spending should be undertaken only when support was, in fact, nearly unanimous. In the case of debt finance, however, Wicksell was concerned that "the interests [of future taxpayers] are not represented at all or are represented inadequately in the tax-approving assembly."

Many economists have echoed this theme more recently. In their 1977 book *Democracy in Deficit,* James Buchanan and Richard Wagner argued for a balanced-budget rule for fiscal policy on the grounds that it "will have the effect of bringing the real costs of public outlays to the awareness of decision makers; it will tend to dispel the illusory 'something for nothing' aspects of fiscal choice." Similarly, Martin Feldstein, president of the National Bureau of Economic Research in the United States, argues that "only the 'hard budget constraint' of having to balance the budget" can force politicians to judge whether spending's "benefits really justify its costs."

These arguments have led some economists to favour a constitutional amendment that would require a balanced budget on an annual basis. Often these proposals have escape clauses for times of national emergency, such as wars and depressions, when a budget deficit is a reasonable policy response. Some critics of these proposals argue that, even with the escape clauses, such a constitutional amendment would tie the hands of policymakers too severely. Others claim that a balanced-budget requirement can be evaded easily with accounting tricks. Despite these concerns, several Canadian provinces have introduced legislation that restricts the size of their deficits (New Brunswick in 1993, and Alberta, Saskatchewan, and Manitoba in 1995). The European Union also has such a rule. As this discussion makes clear, the debate over the desirability of a balanced-budget amendment is as much political as economic.

International Dimensions

Government debt may affect a nation's role in the world economy. As we first saw in Chapter 5, when a government budget deficit reduces national saving, it often leads to a trade deficit, which in turn is financed by borrowing from abroad. For instance, many observers have blamed U.S. fiscal policy for the recent switch of the United States from a major creditor in the world economy to a major debtor. This link between the budget deficit and the trade deficit leads to two further effects of government debt.

First, high levels of government debt may increase the risk that an economy will experience capital flight—an abrupt decline in the demand for a country's assets in world financial markets. International investors are aware that a government can always deal with its debt simply by defaulting. This approach was used as far back as 1335, when England's King Edward III defaulted on his debt to Italian bankers. More recently, several Latin American countries defaulted on their debts in the 1980s, and Russia did the same in 1998. The higher the level of the government debt, the greater the temptation of default. Thus, as government debt increases, international investors may come to fear default and curtail their lending. If this loss of confidence occurs suddenly, the result could be the classic symptoms of capital flight: a collapse in the value of the currency and an increase in interest rates. As we discussed in Chapter 12, this is precisely what happened to Mexico in the early 1990s when default appeared likely.

Second, high levels of government debt financed by foreign borrowing may reduce a nation's political clout in world affairs. This fear was emphasized by economist Ben Friedman in his 1988 book *Day of Reckoning.* He wrote, "World power and influence have historically accrued to creditor countries. It is not coincidental that America emerged as a world power simultaneously with our transition from a debtor nation . . . to a creditor supplying investment capital to the rest of the world." Friedman suggests that if the United States continues to run large trade deficits, it will eventually lose some of its international influence. So far, the record has not been kind to this hypothesis: the United States has run trade deficits throughout the 1980s, the 1990s, and the first decade of the 2000s, and it remains a leading superpower. But perhaps other events—such as the collapse of the Soviet Union—offset the fall in political clout that the United States would have experienced from its increased indebtedness. And Friedman's prediction was likely made with a somewhat longer time horizon in mind.

CASE STUDY

The Benefits of Indexed Bonds

Several years ago, the federal government started to issue bonds that pay a return based on the consumer price index. These bonds are long-term. They have a 20- to 25-year maturity period, and they pay a low interest rate (currently about 2 percent), so a $1,000 bond pays only $20 per year in interest. But that interest payment grows with the overall price level as measured by the CPI. In addition, when the $1,000 of principal is repaid, that amount is also adjusted for changes in the CPI. The 2 percent, therefore, is a real interest rate. No longer do professors of macroeconomics need to define the real interest rate as an abstract construct. They can open up the daily newspaper, point to the bond-yields table, and say, "Look here, this is a nominal interest rate, and this is a real interest rate." (Professors in the United Kingdom and several other countries have long enjoyed this luxury because indexed bonds have been trading in other countries for years.)

Of course, making macroeconomics easier to teach was not the reason that the government chose to index some of the government debt. That was just a positive externality. Its goal was to introduce a new type of government bond that should benefit bondholder and taxpayer alike. These bonds are a win–win proposition because they insulate both sides of the transaction from inflation risk. Bondholders should care about the real interest rate they earn, and taxpayers should care about the real interest rate they pay. When government bonds are specified in nominal terms, both sides take on risk that is neither productive nor necessary. The new indexed bonds eliminate this inflation risk.

In addition, the new bonds have three other benefits:

First, the bonds may encourage the private sector to begin issuing its own indexed securities. Financial innovation is, to some extent, a public good. Once an innovation has been introduced into the market, the idea is nonexcludable (people cannot be prevented from using it) and nonrival (one person's use of the idea does not diminish other people's use of it). Just as a free market will not adequately supply the public goods of national defense and basic research, it will not adequately supply financial innovation. The government's new bonds can be viewed as a remedy for that market failure.

Second, the bonds reduce the government's incentive to produce surprise inflation. After many years of large budget deficits, the government is now a substantial debtor, and its debts are specified almost entirely in dollar terms. What is unique about the federal government, in contrast to most debtors, is that it can just print the money it needs. The greater the government's nominal debts, the more incentive the government has to inflate away its debt. The government's small switch toward indexed debt reduces this potentially problematic incentive very slightly.

Third, if the bonds were issued for much shorter maturity periods, they could provide data that might be useful for monetary policy. Many macroeconomic theories point to expected inflation as a key variable to explain the relationship between inflation and unemployment. But what is expected inflation? One way to measure it is to survey private forecasters. Another way is to look at the difference between the yield on nominal bonds and the yield on real bonds. As this book goes to press, these yields differed by about 2 percentage points, so at the time, Canadians were expecting inflation of 2 percent per year over the coming 25 years.

In the past, economists have proposed a variety of rules that could be used to conduct monetary policy, as we discussed in the preceding chapter. Indexed bonds expand the number of possible rules. Here is one idea: The Bank of Canada announces a target for the inflation rate. Then, every day, the Bank measures expected inflation as the spread between the yield on nominal debt and the yield on indexed debt. If expected inflation is above the target, the Bank contracts the money supply. If expected inflation is below the target, the Bank expands the money supply. In this way, the Bank can use the bond market's inflation forecast to ensure that the money supply is growing at the rate needed to keep inflation close to its target.

Indexed bonds can, therefore, if made available for shorter terms, produce many benefits: less inflation risk, more financial innovation, better government incentives, more informed monetary policy, and easier lives for students and teachers of macroeconomics.[8] ∎

---

[8] To read more about indexed bonds, see John Y. Campbell and Robert J. Shiller, "A Scorecard for Indexed Government Debt," *NBER Macroeconomics Annual,* (1996): 155–197; and David W. Wilcox, "Policy Watch: The Introduction of Indexed Government Debt in the United States," *The Journal of Economic Perspectives* 12 (Winter 1998): 219–227.

16-6 Conclusion

Fiscal policy and government debt have been central in the Canadian political debate. When Paul Martin became Minister of Finance in 1993, he made reducing the budget deficit a high priority of the Liberal government. Some members of the Liberal party worried that they might lose popular support since deficit reduction was perceived as a priority more suited to the Reform and Conservative parties (separate political parties at the time).

This chapter has discussed the parallel debate among economists over government debt and budget deficits. Economists disagree about how fiscal policy is best measured and how fiscal policy affects the economy. To be sure, these are among the most important and controversial questions facing policymakers today. Given the growing fiscal dividend in the short term, and the aging of the baby boomers in the longer term, there seems little doubt that these debates will continue in the years to come.

Summary

1. Taken together, the current size of the federal and provincial government debts is fairly large by international standards. Nevertheless, after a 20-year rise in the federal debt–GDP ratio of 50 percentage points, this trend has ended and the debt ratio has been pulled back down by 35 of those 50 percentage points. Questions concerning the extent to which the government should gear current fiscal policy to reinforce this turnaround will dominate debate in the coming years.

2. Standard measures of the budget deficit are imperfect measures of fiscal policy because they do not correct for the effects of inflation, do not offset changes in government liabilities with changes in government assets, omit some liabilities altogether, and do not correct for the effects of the business cycle.

3. According to the traditional view of government debt, a debt-financed tax cut stimulates consumer spending and lowers national saving. This increase in consumer spending leads to greater aggregate demand and higher income in the short run, but it leads to a lower capital stock and higher foreign indebtedness, and so to lower income in the long run.

4. According to the Ricardian view of government debt, a debt-financed tax cut does not stimulate consumer spending because it does not raise consumers' overall resources—it merely reschedules taxes from the present to the future. The debate between the traditional and Ricardian views of government debt is ultimately a debate over how consumers behave. Are consumers rational or shortsighted? Do they face binding borrowing constraints? Are they economically linked to future generations through

altruistic bequests? Economists' views of government debt hinge on their answers to these questions.

5. Most economists oppose a strict rule requiring a balanced budget. A budget deficit can sometimes be justified on the basis of short-run stabilization, tax smoothing, or intergenerational redistribution of the tax burden.

6. Government debt can potentially have various additional effects. Large government debt or budget deficits may encourage excessively expansionary monetary policy and, therefore, lead to greater inflation. The possibility of running budget deficits may encourage politicians to unduly burden future generations when setting government spending and taxes. A high level of government debt may risk capital flight and diminish a nation's influence around the world. Economists differ in which of these effects they consider most important.

KEY CONCEPTS

Capital budgeting   Cyclically adjusted budget deficit   Ricardian equivalence

QUESTIONS FOR REVIEW

1. What was unusual about Canadian fiscal policy between the mid-1970s and the mid-1990s?

2. Why do many economists project falling, and then increasing, budget deficits and government debt over the next several decades?

3. Describe four problems affecting measurement of the government budget deficit.

4. According to the traditional view of government debt, how does a debt-financed tax cut affect public saving, private saving, and national saving?

5. According to the Ricardian view of government debt, how does a debt-financed tax cut affect public saving, private saving, and national saving?

6. Do you believe the traditional or the Ricardian view of government debt? Why?

7. Give three reasons why requiring a balanced budget might be too restrictive a rule for fiscal policy.

8. Why might the level of government debt affect the government's incentives regarding money creation?

PROBLEMS AND APPLICATIONS

1. On April 1, 1996, Taco Bell, the fast-food chain, ran a full-page ad in the *New York Times* with this news: "In an effort to help the national debt, Taco Bell is pleased to announce that we have agreed to purchase the Liberty Bell, one of our country's most historic treasures. It will now be called the *Taco Liberty Bell* and will still be accessible to the American public for viewing. We hope our move

will prompt other corporations to take similar action to do their part to reduce the country's debt." Would such actions by corporations actually reduce the national debt as it is now measured? How would your answer change if the government adopted capital budgeting? Do you think these actions represent a true reduction in the government's indebtedness? Do you think Taco Bell was serious about this plan? (*Hint:* Note the date.)

2. Draft a letter to the member of Parliament described in Section 15-3, explaining and evaluating the Ricardian view of government debt.

3. The Canada and Quebec pension system levies a tax on workers and pays benefits to the elderly. Suppose that government increases both the tax and the benefits. For simplicity, assume that the government announces that the increases will last for one year only.

   a. How do you suppose this change would affect the economy? (*Hint:* Think about the marginal propensities to consume of the young and the old.)

   b. Does your answer depend on whether generations are altruistically linked?

4. Some economists have proposed the rule that the cyclically adjusted budget deficit always be balanced. Compare this proposal to a strict balanced-budget rule. Which is preferable? What problems do you see with the rule requiring a balanced cyclically adjusted budget?

Estimating the Benefits of Deficit and Debt Reduction

As noted in this chapter, deficit and debt reduction is motivated by a desire to increase living standards for future generations. No specific answer can be given, concerning how much to pursue this policy, because many people have different views concerning what amount of redistribution across generations is appropriate. But debate on this topic can be more constructive if all persons involved have some feel for the *magnitude* of the effect on future living standards.

We can provide an answer to this question by recalling a key relationship from our analysis of a small open economy in Chapter 5. We learned there that a country's net exports equal the excess of the country's output over total spending. That is,

$$\left(\begin{array}{c}\text{Net} \\ \text{Exports}\end{array}\right) = NX = Y - C - I - G.$$

Now let us note how each of the terms in this equation is determined. First, long-run equilibrium implies that the level of a country's international indebtedness be a constant proportion of its GDP. If we define Z as the quantity of bonds sold to foreigners, then the foreign debt–GDP ratio is Z/Y. If this ratio is constant, $\Delta Z/Z = \Delta Y/Y$. Denoting the output growth rate by n, this constant-ratio requirement is satisfied when

$$\Delta Z = nZ.$$

The country's debt increases each period by ΔZ and this debt must rise whenever the trade surplus, NX, earns less foreign exchange than is necessary to cover the existing interest obligations to foreigners, rZ. That is,

$$\Delta Z = rZ - NX.$$

Combining this definition of debt growth with long-run equilibrium requirement that the debt–GDP ratio be constant yields

$$NX = (r - n)Z.$$

This expression for net exports can be substituted into the left side of the GDP identity above. Now we present expressions for the terms on the right side of that identity.

We take consumption to be proportional to disposable income:

$$C = a(Y + rB - T - rZ),$$

where B is the outstanding stock of government bonds. Disposable income is pre-tax factor earnings plus interest payment receipts from the domestic government debt minus taxes and interest payment obligations to foreigners.

The government budget deficit, D, is

$$D = G + rB - T.$$

Using this equation to replace the transfer payments less taxes term, $rB - T$, in the consumption function, we have

$$C = a(Y + D - G - rZ).$$

Finally, investment is a function of the interest rate:

$$\text{Investment} = I(r).$$

All these relationships can be combined to yield

$$(r - n)Z = Y - a(Y + D - G - rZ) - I(r) - G$$

or

$$Z = \left(\frac{1}{r(1 - a) - n} \right) \left(Y - a(Y + D - G) - I(r) - G \right).$$

This expression for foreign debt obligations can be used to estimate the effects of deficit reduction on domestic living standards. For simplicity, and to ensure that our calculation underestimates the full benefits of deficit reduction, we assume that lower debt does not decrease the risk premium demanded by foreign lenders.[9] With no change in the interest rate premium, the interest rate is exogenous for a small open economy. This fact means that investment spending is not affected by deficit reduction. Also, since the marginal product of capital equals the interest rate in long-run equilibrium, the quantity of capital and overall real GDP must be independent of deficit reduction as well.

But even though GDP for a small open economy is unaffected by deficit reduction in the long run, GNP *is* affected. GNP equals GDP minus interest payments to foreigners, so we can estimate the benefits of deficit reduction by calculating how much a lower deficit reduces our debt to foreigners.

As just noted, GNP represents the level of domestic income, $Y - rZ$. We substitute the expression for Z into this definition. We divide the resulting equation and the consumption function through by Y and use lowercase letters to denote ratios to GDP: $d = D/Y$, $g = G/Y$, $v = I/Y$, and $c = C/Y$. The result is

$$c = a \left[1 - \left(\frac{r}{r(1 - a) - n} \right) \left(1 - a(1 + d - g) - v - g \right) + d - g \right]$$

We assume that deficit reduction is accomplished through variations in taxes and transfer payments, so that, as a proportion of the economy, the size of government is constant ($\Delta g = 0$). Given this assumption, and the fact that the interest

---

[9] For an estimate of the benefits of lower interest rates, see the first case study in Chapter 18.

rate is exogenous for a small open economy (so that $\Delta v = 0$), this equation implies the following relationship when written in change form:

$$\Delta c = a\left(1 + \frac{r}{r(1-a) - n}\right)\Delta d.$$

Representative parameter values for the marginal propensity to consume, the average growth rate, and the yield earned by foreigners on stocks and bonds in Canada at the time when the deficit reduction program was initiated were $a = 0.9$, $n = 0.05$, and $r = 0.08$. Given recent fiscal policy, an interesting reduction in the deficit ratio is 5 percentage points so $\Delta d = -.05$ is representative. Substituting these values into the last equation indicates that consumption can be expected to rise by 3.2 percentage points of GDP. The fact that this is such a large increase in living standards is the reason why some individuals have been so passionate about deficit and debt reduction.[10] But while this estimated benefit is large, it is not quite as big as the estimated reduction in the growth of average living standards that will accompany the aging of the baby boom generation (as discussed in the first case study in this chapter). This is why our government has made a formal commitment to achieve significant debt reduction by 2015—before the aging problem is fully upon us.

---

[10] Estimates of this same order of magnitude emerge when a more sophisticated consumption function involving only a slight departure from pure Ricardian equivalence is involved in the calculations. See W.M. Scarth, *Deficit Reduction: Costs and Benefits,* Commentary No. 61 (Toronto: C.D. Howe Institute, 1994).

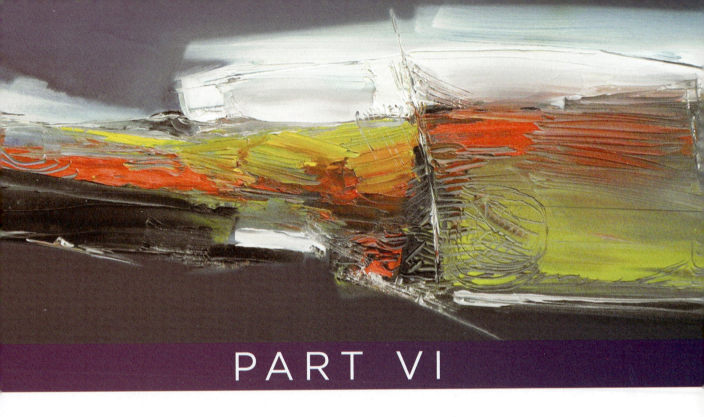

PART VI

More on the Microeconomics Behind Macroeconomics

Consumption

Consumption is the sole end and purpose of all production.

— *Adam Smith*

How do households decide how much of their income to consume today and how much to save for the future? This is a microeconomic question because it addresses the behaviour of individual decisionmakers. Yet its answer has important macroeconomic consequences. As we have seen in previous chapters, households' consumption decisions affect the way the economy as a whole behaves both in the long run and in the short run.

The consumption decision is crucial for long-run analysis because of its role in economic growth. The Solow growth model of Chapters 7 and 8 shows that the saving rate is a key determinant of the steady-state capital stock and thus of the level of economic well-being. The saving rate measures how much of its income the present generation is not consuming but is instead putting aside for its own future and for future generations.

The consumption decision is crucial for short-run analysis because of its role in determining aggregate demand. Consumption is almost six-tenths of GDP, so fluctuations in consumption are a key element of booms and recessions. The *IS–LM* model of Chapters 10 and 11 shows that changes in consumers' spending plans can be a source of shocks to the economy, and that the marginal propensity to consume is a determinant of the fiscal-policy multipliers.

In previous chapters we explained consumption with a function that relates consumption to disposable income: $C = C(Y - T)$. This approximation allowed us to develop simple models for long-run and short-run analysis. But it is too simple to provide a complete explanation of consumer behaviour. In this chapter we examine the consumption function in greater detail and develop a more thorough explanation of what determines aggregate consumption.

Since macroeconomics began as a field of study, many economists have written about the theory of consumer behaviour and suggested alternative ways of interpreting the data on consumption and income. This chapter presents the views of six prominent economists to show the diverse approaches to explaining consumption.

17-1 John Maynard Keynes and the Consumption Function

We begin our study of consumption with John Maynard Keynes's *General Theory,* which was published in 1936. Keynes made the consumption function central to his theory of economic fluctuations, and it has played a key role in macroeconomic analysis ever since. Let's consider what Keynes thought about the consumption function, and then see what puzzles arose when his ideas were confronted with the data.

Keynes's Conjectures

Today, economists who study consumption rely on sophisticated techniques of data analysis. With the help of computers, they analyze aggregate data on the behaviour of the overall economy from the national accounts and detailed data on the behaviour of individual households from surveys. Because Keynes wrote in the 1930s, however, he had neither the advantage of these data nor the computers necessary to analyze such large data sets. Instead of relying on statistical analysis, Keynes made conjectures about the consumption function based on introspection and casual observation.

First and most important, Keynes conjectured that the **marginal propensity to consume**—the amount consumed out of an additional dollar of income—is between zero and one. He wrote that the "fundamental psychological law, upon which we are entitled to depend with great confidence, . . . is that men are disposed, as a rule and on the average, to increase their consumption as their income increases, but not by as much as the increase in their income." That is, when a person earns an extra dollar, he typically spends some of it and saves some of it. As we saw in Chapter 10 when we developed the Keynesian cross, the marginal propensity to consume was crucial to Keynes's policy recommendations for how to reduce widespread unemployment. The power of fiscal policy to influence the economy—as expressed by the fiscal-policy multipliers—arises from the feedback between income and consumption.

Second, Keynes posited that the ratio of consumption to income, called the **average propensity to consume,** falls as income rises. He believed that saving was a luxury, so he expected the rich to save a higher proportion of their income than the poor. Although not essential for Keynes's own analysis, the postulate that the average propensity to consume falls as income rises became a central part of early Keynesian economics.

Third, Keynes thought that income is the primary determinant of consumption and that the interest rate does not have an important role. This conjecture stood in stark contrast to the beliefs of the classical economists who preceded him. The classical economists held that a higher interest rate encourages saving and discourages consumption. Keynes admitted that the interest rate could influence consumption as a matter of theory. Yet he wrote that "the main conclusion suggested by experience, I think, is that the short-period influence of the rate of interest on individual spending out of a given income is secondary and relatively unimportant."

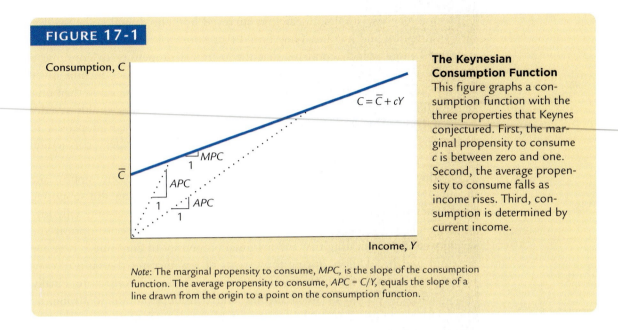

FIGURE 17-1

Consumption, C

$C = \overline{C} + cY$

$\overline{C}$

MPC
1

APC

1

APC
1

Income, Y

The Keynesian Consumption Function This figure graphs a consumption function with the three properties that Keynes conjectured. First, the marginal propensity to consume c is between zero and one. Second, the average propensity to consume falls as income rises. Third, consumption is determined by current income.

Note: The marginal propensity to consume, *MPC,* is the slope of the consumption function. The average propensity to consume, *APC* = C/Y, equals the slope of a line drawn from the origin to a point on the consumption function.

On the basis of these three conjectures, the Keynesian consumption function is often written as

$$C = \overline{C} + cY, \qquad \overline{C} > 0, \quad 0 < c < 1,$$

where C is consumption, Y is disposable income, $\overline{C}$ is a constant, and c is the marginal propensity to consume. This consumption function, shown in Figure 17-1, is graphed as a straight line.

Notice that this consumption function exhibits the three properties that Keynes posited. It satisfies Keynes's first property because the marginal propensity to consume c is between zero and one, so that higher income leads to higher consumption and also to higher saving. This consumption function satisfies Keynes's second property because the average propensity to consume *APC* is

$$APC = C/Y = \overline{C}/Y + c.$$

As Y rises, $\overline{C}/Y$ falls, and so the average propensity to consume C/Y falls. And finally, this consumption function satisfies Keynes's third property because the interest rate is not included in this equation as a determinant of consumption.

The Early Empirical Successes

Soon after Keynes proposed the consumption function, economists began collecting and examining data to test his conjectures. The earliest studies indicated that the Keynesian consumption function was a good approximation of how consumers behave.

In some of these studies, researchers surveyed households and collected data on consumption and income. They found that households with higher income consumed more, which confirms that the marginal propensity to consume is greater than zero. They also found that households with higher income saved more, which confirms that the marginal propensity to consume is less than one. In addition, these researchers found that higher-income households saved a larger fraction of their income, which confirms that the average propensity to consume falls as income rises. Thus, these data verified Keynes's conjectures about the marginal and average propensities to consume.

In other studies, researchers examined aggregate data on consumption and income for the period between the two world wars. These data also supported the Keynesian consumption function. In years when income was unusually low, such as during the depths of the Great Depression, both consumption and saving were low, indicating that the marginal propensity to consume is between zero and one. In addition, during those years of low income, the ratio of consumption to income was high, confirming Keynes's second conjecture. Finally, because the correlation between income and consumption was so strong, no other variable appeared to be important for explaining consumption. Thus, the data also confirmed Keynes's third conjecture that income is the primary determinant of how much people choose to consume.

Secular Stagnation, Simon Kuznets, and the Consumption Puzzle

Although the Keynesian consumption function met with early successes, two anomalies soon arose. Both concern Keynes's conjecture that the average propensity to consume falls as income rises.

The first anomaly became apparent after some economists made a dire—and, it turned out, erroneous—prediction during World War II. On the basis of the Keynesian consumption function, these economists reasoned that as incomes in the economy grew over time, households would consume a smaller and smaller fraction of their incomes. They feared that there might not be enough profitable investment projects to absorb all this saving. If so, the low consumption would lead to an inadequate demand for goods and services, resulting in a depression once the wartime demand from the government ceased. In other words, on the basis of the Keynesian consumption function, these economists predicted that the economy would experience what they called *secular stagnation*—a long depression of indefinite duration—unless the government used fiscal policy to expand aggregate demand.

Fortunately for the economy, but unfortunately for the Keynesian consumption function, the end of World War II did not throw Western economies into another depression. Although incomes were much higher after the war than before, these higher incomes did not lead to large increases in the rate of saving. Keynes's conjecture that the average propensity to consume would fall as income rose appeared not to hold.

The second anomaly arose when economist Simon Kuznets constructed new aggregate data on consumption and income for the United States dating back to

1869. Kuznets assembled these data in the 1940s and would later receive the Nobel Prize for this work. He discovered that the ratio of consumption to income was remarkably stable from decade to decade, despite large increases in income over the period he studied. Again, Keynes's conjecture that the average propensity to consume would fall as income rose appeared not to hold.

The failure of the secular-stagnation hypothesis and the findings of Kuznets both indicated that the average propensity to consume is fairly constant over long periods of time. This fact presented a puzzle that motivated much of the subsequent research on consumption. Economists wanted to know why some studies confirmed Keynes's conjectures and others refuted them. That is, why did Keynes's conjectures hold up well in the studies of household data and in the studies of short time-series, but fail when long time-series were examined?

Figure 17-2 illustrates the puzzle. The evidence suggested that there were two consumption functions. For the household data and for the short time-series, the Keynesian consumption function appeared to work well. Yet for the long time-series, the consumption function appeared to have a constant average propensity to consume. In Figure 17-2, these two relationships between consumption and income are called the short-run and long-run consumption functions. Economists needed to explain how these two consumption functions could be consistent with each other.

FIGURE 17-2

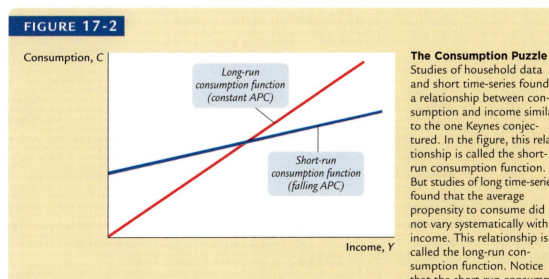

The Consumption Puzzle Studies of household data and short time-series found a relationship between consumption and income similar to the one Keynes conjectured. In the figure, this relationship is called the short-run consumption function. But studies of long time-series found that the average propensity to consume did not vary systematically with income. This relationship is called the long-run consumption function. Notice that the short-run consumption function has a falling average propensity to consume, whereas the long-run consumption function has a constant average propensity to consume.

In the 1950s, Franco Modigliani and Milton Friedman each proposed explanations of these seemingly contradictory findings. Both economists later won Nobel Prizes, in part because of their work on consumption. But before we see how Modigliani and Friedman tried to solve the consumption puzzle, we must discuss Irving Fisher's contribution to consumption theory. Both Modigliani's life-cycle hypothesis and Friedman's permanent-income hypothesis rely on the theory of consumer behaviour proposed much earlier by Irving Fisher.

17-2 Irving Fisher and Intertemporal Choice

The consumption function introduced by Keynes relates current consumption to current income. This relationship, however, is incomplete at best. When people decide how much to consume and how much to save, they consider both the present and the future. The more consumption they enjoy today, the less they will be able to enjoy tomorrow. In making this tradeoff, households must look ahead to the income they expect to receive in the future and to the consumption of goods and services they hope to be able to afford.

The economist Irving Fisher developed the model with which economists analyze how rational, forward-looking consumers make intertemporal choices—that is, choices involving different periods of time. Fisher's model illuminates the constraints consumers face, the preferences they have, and how these constraints and preferences together determine their choices about consumption and saving.

The Intertemporal Budget Constraint

Most people would prefer to increase the quantity or quality of the goods and services they consume—to wear nicer clothes, eat at better restaurants, or see more movies. The reason people consume less than they desire is that their consumption is constrained by their income. In other words, consumers face a limit on how much they can spend, called a *budget constraint*. When they are deciding how much to consume today versus how much to save for the future, they face an **intertemporal budget constraint,** which measures the total resources available for consumption today and in the future. Our first step in developing Fisher's model is to examine this constraint in some detail.

To keep things simple, we examine the decision facing a consumer who lives for two periods. Period one represents the consumer's youth, and period two represents the consumer's old age. The consumer earns income Y_1 and consumes C_1 in period one, and earns income Y_2 and consumes C_2 in period two. (All variables are real—that is, adjusted for inflation.) Because the consumer has the opportunity to borrow and save, consumption in any single period can be either greater or less than income in that period.

Consider how the consumer's income in the two periods constrains consumption in the two periods. In the first period, saving equals income minus consumption. That is,

$$S = Y_1 - C_1,$$

where S is saving. In the second period, consumption equals the accumulated saving, including the interest earned on that saving, plus second-period income. That is,

$$C_2 = (1 + r)S + Y_2,$$

where r is the real interest rate. For example, if the real interest rate is 5 percent, then for every $1 of saving in period one, the consumer enjoys an extra $1.05 of consumption in period two. Because there is no third period, the consumer does not save in the second period.

Note that the variable S can represent either saving or borrowing and that these equations hold in both cases. If first-period consumption is less than first-period income, the consumer is saving, and S is greater than zero. If first-period consumption exceeds first-period income, the consumer is borrowing, and S is less than zero. For simplicity, we assume that the interest rate for borrowing is the same as the interest rate for saving.

To derive the consumer's budget constraint, combine the two equations above. Substitute the first equation for S into the second equation to obtain

$$C_2 = (1 + r)(Y_1 - C_1) + Y_2.$$

To make the equation easier to interpret, we must rearrange terms. To place all the consumption terms together, bring $(1 + r)C_1$ from the right-hand side to the left-hand side of the equation to obtain

$$(1 + r)C_1 + C_2 = (1 + r)Y_1 + Y_2.$$

Now divide both sides by $(1 + r)$ to obtain

$$C_1 + \frac{C_2}{1 + r} = Y_1 + \frac{Y_2}{1 + r}.$$

This equation relates consumption in the two periods to income in the two periods. It is the standard way of expressing the consumer's intertemporal budget constraint.

The consumer's budget constraint is easily interpreted. If the interest rate is zero, the budget constraint shows that total consumption in the two periods equals total income in the two periods. In the usual case in which the interest rate is greater than zero, future consumption and future income are discounted by a factor $1 + r$. This **discounting** arises from the interest earned on savings. In essence, because the consumer earns interest on current income that is saved, future income is worth less than current income. Similarly, because future consumption is paid for out of savings that have earned interest, future consumption costs less than current consumption. The factor $1/(1 + r)$ is the price of second-period consumption measured in terms of first-period consumption: it is the

FIGURE 17-3

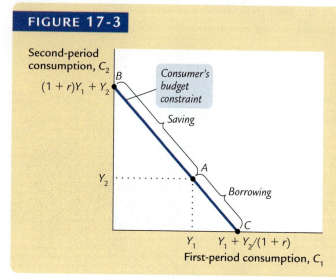

Second-period consumption, C_2

$(1 + r)Y_1 + Y_2$

B

Consumer's budget constraint

Saving

Y_2 ....

A

Borrowing

C

Y_1 $Y_1 + Y_2/(1 + r)$

First-period consumption, C_1

The Consumer's Budget Constraint
This figure shows the combinations of first-period and second-period consumption the consumer can choose. If the consumer chooses points between A and B, he consumes less than his income in the first period and saves the rest for the second period. If the consumer chooses points between A and C, she consumes more than her income in the first period and borrows to make up the difference.

amount of first-period consumption that the consumer must forgo to obtain 1 unit of second-period consumption.

Figure 17-3 graphs the consumer's budget constraint. Three points are marked on this figure. At point A, the consumer consumes exactly his income in each period ($C_1 = Y_1$ and $C_2 = Y_2$), so there is neither saving nor borrowing between the two periods. At point B, the consumer consumes nothing in the first period ($C_1 = 0$) and saves all income, so second-period consumption C_2 is $(1 + r)Y_1 + Y_2$. At point C, the consumer plans to consume nothing in the second period ($C_2 = 0$) and borrows as much as possible against second-period income, so first-period consumption C_1 is $Y_1 + Y_2/(1 + r)$. These are only three of the many combinations of first- and second-period consumption that the consumer can afford: all the points on the line from B to C are available to the consumer.

Consumer Preferences

The consumer's preferences regarding consumption in the two periods can be represented by **indifference curves.** An indifference curve shows the combinations of first-period and second-period consumption that make the consumer equally happy.

Figure 17-4 shows two of the consumer's many indifference curves. The consumer is indifferent among combinations $W, X,$ and $Y,$ because they are all on the same curve. Not surprisingly, if the consumer's first-period consumption is reduced, say from point W to point X, second-period consumption must increase to keep him equally happy. If first-period consumption is reduced again, from point X to point Y, the amount of extra second-period consumption he requires for compensation is greater.

The slope at any point on the indifference curve shows how much second-period consumption the consumer requires in order to be compensated for a 1-unit reduction in first-period consumption. This slope is the **marginal rate of**

FIGURE 17-4

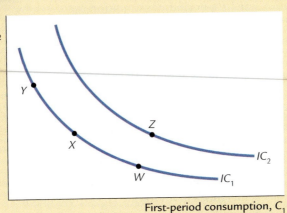

The Consumer's Preferences Indifference curves represent the consumer's preferences over first-period and second-period consumption. An indifference curve gives the combinations of consumption in the two periods that make the consumer equally happy. This figure shows two of many indifference curves. Higher indifference curves such as IC_2 are preferred to lower curves such as IC_1. The consumer is equally happy at points W, X, and Y, but prefers point Z to points W, X, or Y.

Present Value, or Why a $1,000,000 Prize Is Worth Only $623,000

The use of discounting in the consumer's budget constraint illustrates an important fact of economic life: a dollar in the future is less valuable than a dollar today. This is true because a dollar today can be deposited in an interest-bearing bank account and produce more than one dollar in the future. If the interest rate is 5 percent, for instance, then a dollar today can be turned into $1.05 dollars next year, $1.1025 in two years, $1.1576 in three years, . . . , or $2.65 in 20 years.

Economists use a concept called *present value* to compare dollar amounts from different times. The present value of any amount in the future is the amount that would be needed today, given available interest rates, to produce that future amount. Thus, if you are going to be paid X dollars in T years and the interest rate is r, then the present value of that payment is

$$\text{Present Value} = X/(1+r)^T.$$

In light of this definition, we can see a new interpretation of the consumer's budget constraint in our two-period consumption problem. The intertemporal budget constraint states that the present value of consumption must equal the present value of income.

The concept of present value has many applications. Suppose, for instance, that you won a million-dollar lottery. Such prizes are usually paid out over time—say, $50,000 a year for 20 years. What is the present value of such a delayed prize? By applying the above formula for each of the 20 payments and adding up the result, we learn that the million-dollar prize, discounted at an interest rate of 5 percent, has a present value of only $623,000. (If the prize were paid out as a dollar a year for a million years, the present value would be a mere $20!) Sometimes a million dollars isn't all it's cracked up to be.

FYI

substitution between first-period consumption and second-period consumption. It tells us the rate at which the consumer is willing to substitute second-period consumption for first-period consumption.

Notice that the indifference curves in Figure 17-4 are not straight lines and, as a result, the marginal rate of substitution depends on the levels of consumption in the two periods. When first-period consumption is high and second-period consumption is low, as at point *W*, the marginal rate of substitution is low: the consumer requires only a little extra second-period consumption to give up 1 unit of first-period consumption. When first-period consumption is low and second-period consumption is high, as at point *Y*, the marginal rate of substitution is high: the consumer requires much additional second-period consumption to give up 1 unit of first-period consumption.

The consumer is equally happy at all points on a given indifference curve, but he prefers some indifference curves to others. Because he prefers more consumption to less, he prefers higher indifference curves to lower ones. In Figure 17-4, the consumer prefers any of the points on curve IC_2 to any of the points on curve IC_1.

The set of indifference curves gives a complete ranking of the consumer's preferences. It tells us that the consumer prefers point *Z* to point *W*, but that should be obvious because point *Z* has more consumption in both periods. Yet compare point *Z* and point *Y*: point *Z* has more consumption in period one and less in period two. Which is preferred, *Z* or *Y*? Because *Z* is on a higher indifference curve than *Y*, we know that the consumer prefers point *Z* to point *Y*. Hence, we can use the set of indifference curves to rank any combinations of first-period and second-period consumption.

Optimization

Having discussed the consumer's budget constraint and preferences, we can consider the decision about how much to consume in each period of time. The consumer would like to end up with the best possible combination of consumption in the two periods—that is, on the highest possible indifference curve. But the budget constraint requires that the consumer also end up on or below the budget line, because the budget line measures the total resources available to him.

Figure 17-5 shows that many indifference curves cross the budget line. The highest indifference curve that the consumer can obtain without violating the budget constraint is the indifference curve that just barely touches the budget line, which is curve IC_3 in the figure. The point at which the curve and line touch—point O for "optimum"—is the best combination of consumption in the two periods that the consumer can afford.

Notice that, at the optimum, the slope of the indifference curve equals the slope of the budget line. The indifference curve is *tangent* to the budget line. The slope of the indifference curve is the marginal rate of substitution *MRS*, and the slope of the budget line is 1 plus the real interest rate. We conclude that at point O,

$$MRS = 1 + r.$$

The consumer chooses consumption in the two periods so that the marginal rate of substitution equals 1 plus the real interest rate.

FIGURE 17-5

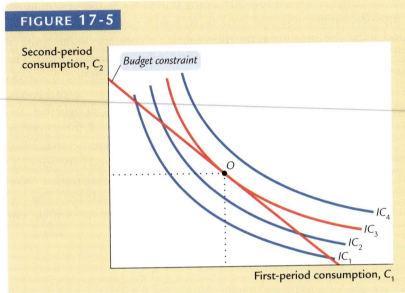

Second-period consumption, C_2

Budget constraint

O

IC_4

IC_3

IC_2

IC_1

First-period consumption, C_1

The Consumer's Optimum
The consumer achieves his highest level of satisfaction by choosing the point on the budget constraint that is on the highest indifference curve. At the optimum, the indifference curve is tangent to the budget constraint.

How Changes in Income Affect Consumption

Now that we have seen how the consumer makes the consumption decision, let's examine how consumption responds to an increase in income. An increase in either Y_1 or Y_2 shifts the budget constraint outward, as in Figure 17-6. The higher budget constraint allows the consumer to choose a better combination of first- and second-period consumption—that is, the consumer can now reach a higher indifference curve.

FIGURE 17-6

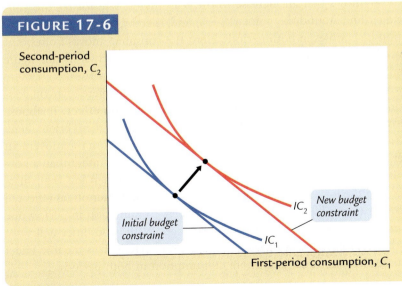

Second-period consumption, C_2

IC_2 New budget constraint

Initial budget constraint

IC_1

First-period consumption, C_1

An Increase in Income An increase in either first-period income or second-period income shifts the budget constraint outward. If consumption in period one and consumption in period two are both normal goods, this increase in income raises consumption in both periods.

In Figure 17-6, the consumer responds to the shift in his budget constraint by choosing more consumption in both periods. Although not implied by the logic of the model alone, this situation is the most usual. If a consumer wants more of a good when his or her income rises, economists call it a **normal good.** The indifference curves in Figure 17-6 are drawn under the assumption that consumption in period one and consumption in period two are both normal goods.

The key conclusion from Figure 17-6 is that regardless of whether the increase in income occurs in the first period or the second period, the consumer spreads it over consumption in both periods. This behaviour is sometimes called *consumption smoothing.* Because the consumer can borrow and lend between periods, the timing of the income is irrelevant to how much is consumed today (except, of course, that future income is discounted by the interest rate). The lesson of this analysis is that consumption depends on the present value of current and future income, which can be written as

$$\text{Present Value of Income} = Y_1 + \frac{Y_2}{1 + r}.$$

Notice that this conclusion is quite different from that reached by Keynes. *Keynes posited that a person's current consumption depends largely on his or her current income. Fisher's model says, instead, that consumption is based on the income the consumer expects over his or her entire lifetime.*

How Changes in the Real Interest Rate Affect Consumption

Let's now use Fisher's model to consider how a change in the real interest rate alters the consumer's choices. There are two cases to consider: the case in which the consumer is initially saving and the case in which he is initially borrowing. Here we discuss the saving case, and Problem 1 at the end of the chapter asks you to analyze the borrowing case.

Figure 17-7 shows that an increase in the real interest rate rotates the consumer's budget line around the point (Y_1, Y_2) and, thereby, alters the amount of consumption he chooses in both periods. Here, the consumer moves from point A to point B. You can see that for the indifference curves drawn in this figure first-period consumption falls and second-period consumption rises.

Economists decompose the impact of an increase in the real interest rate on consumption into two effects: an **income effect** and a **substitution effect.** Textbooks in microeconomics discuss these effects in detail. We summarize them briefly here.

The *income effect* is the change in consumption that results from the movement to a higher indifference curve. Because the consumer is a saver rather than a borrower (as indicated by the fact that first-period consumption is less than first-period income), the increase in the interest rate makes him better off (as reflected by the movement to a higher indifference curve). If consumption in period one and consumption in period two are both normal goods, the consumer will want to spread this improvement in his welfare over both periods. This income effect tends to make the consumer want more consumption in both periods.

FIGURE 17-7

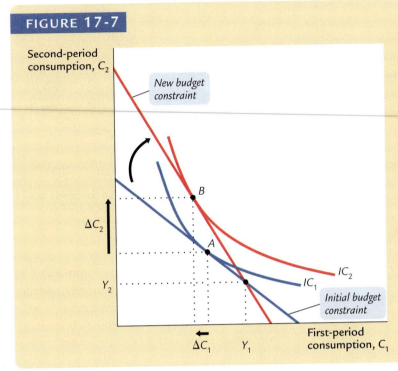

An Increase in the Interest Rate An increase in the interest rate rotates the budget constraint around the point (Y_1, Y_2). In this figure, the higher interest rate reduces first-period consumption by ΔC_1 and raises second-period consumption by ΔC_2.

The *substitution effect* is the change in consumption that results from the change in the relative price of consumption in the two periods. In particular, consumption in period two becomes less expensive relative to consumption in period one when the interest rate rises. That is, because the real interest rate earned on saving is higher, the consumer must now give up less first-period consumption to obtain an extra unit of second-period consumption. This substitution effect tends to make the consumer choose more consumption in period two and less consumption in period one.

The consumer's choice depends on both the income effect and the substitution effect. Because both effects act to increase the amount of second-period consumption; we can conclude that an increase in the real interest rate raises second-period consumption. But the two effects have opposite impacts on first-period consumption so the increase in the interest rate could either lower or raise it. *Hence, depending on the relative size of income and substitution effects, an increase in the interest rate could either stimulate or depress saving.*

Constraints on Borrowing

Fisher's model assumes that the consumer can borrow as well as save. The ability to borrow allows current consumption to exceed current income. In essence, when the consumer borrows, he consumes some of his future income today. Yet for many people such borrowing is impossible. For example, an unemployed individual wishing to go skiing at Whistler or to relax in Florida would probably be unable to finance these vacations with a bank loan. Let's examine how Fisher's analysis changes if the consumer cannot borrow.

The inability to borrow prevents current consumption from exceeding current income. A constraint on borrowing can therefore be expressed as

$$C_1 \leq Y_1.$$

This inequality states that consumption in period one must be less than or equal to income in period one. This additional constraint on the consumer is called a **borrowing constraint** or, sometimes, a *liquidity constraint*.

"What I'd like, basically, is a temporary line of credit just to tide me over the rest of my life."

Figure 17-8 shows how this borrowing constraint restricts the consumer's set of choices. The consumer's choice must satisfy both the intertemporal budget constraint and the borrowing constraint. The shaded area represents the combinations of first-period consumption and second-period consumption that satisfy both constraints.

Figure 17-9 shows how this borrowing constraint affects the consumption decision. There are two possibilities. In panel (a), the consumer wishes to consume less in period one than he earns. The borrowing constraint is not binding in this case and, therefore, does not affect consumption. In panel (b), the consumer would like to consume more in period one than he earns, but the borrowing constraint prevents him from consuming more. The best the consumer can do is to consume all of his first-period income, represented by point E.

FIGURE 17-8

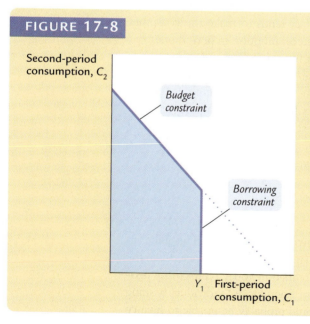

Second-period consumption, C_2

Budget constraint

Borrowing constraint

Y_1 First-period consumption, C_1

A Borrowing Constraint If the consumer cannot borrow, he faces the additional constraint that first-period consumption cannot exceed first-period income. The shaded area represents the combinations of first-period and second-period consumption the consumer can choose.

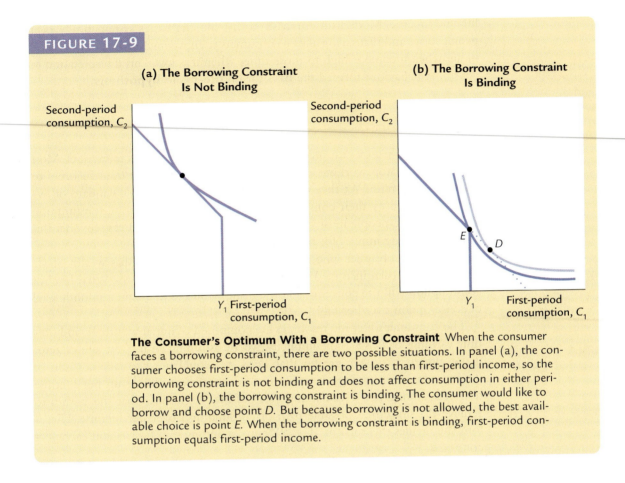

FIGURE 17-9

(a) The Borrowing Constraint Is Not Binding

(b) The Borrowing Constraint Is Binding

Second-period consumption, C_2

Second-period consumption, C_2

Y_1 First-period consumption, C_1

Y_1 First-period consumption, C_1

The Consumer's Optimum With a Borrowing Constraint When the consumer faces a borrowing constraint, there are two possible situations. In panel (a), the consumer chooses first-period consumption to be less than first-period income, so the borrowing constraint is not binding and does not affect consumption in either period. In panel (b), the borrowing constraint is binding. The consumer would like to borrow and choose point D. But because borrowing is not allowed, the best available choice is point E. When the borrowing constraint is binding, first-period consumption equals first-period income.

The analysis of borrowing constraints leads us to conclude that there are two consumption functions. For some consumers, the borrowing constraint is not binding, and consumption in both periods depends on the present value of lifetime income, $Y_1 + [Y_2/(1 + r)]$. For other consumers, the borrowing constraint binds, and the consumption function is $C_1 = Y_1$ and $C_2 = Y_2$. *Hence, for those consumers who would like to borrow but cannot, consumption depends only on current income.*

17-3 Franco Modigliani and the Life-Cycle Hypothesis

In a series of papers written in the 1950s, Franco Modigliani and his collaborators Albert Ando and Richard Brumberg used Fisher's model of consumer behaviour to study the consumption function. One of their goals was to solve the consumption puzzle—that is, to explain the apparently conflicting pieces of evidence that came to light when Keynes's consumption function was confronted with data. According to Fisher's model, consumption depends on a person's lifetime income. Modigliani emphasized that income varies systematically over people's lives and that saving allows consumers to move income from those times in life when income is high to those times when it is low. This interpretation of consumer behaviour formed the basis for his **life-cycle hypothesis.**[1]

The Hypothesis

One important reason that income varies over a person's life is retirement. Most people plan to stop working at about age 65, and they expect their incomes to fall when they retire. Yet they do not want a large drop in their standard of living, as measured by their consumption. To maintain their level of consumption after retirement, people must save during their working years. Let's see what this motive for saving implies for the consumption function.

Consider a consumer who expects to live another T years, has wealth of W, and expects to earn income Y until she retires R years from now. What level of consumption will the consumer choose if she wishes to maintain a smooth level of consumption over her life?

The consumer's lifetime resources are composed of initial wealth W and lifetime earnings of $R \times Y$. (For simplicity, we are assuming an interest rate of zero; if the interest rate were greater than zero, we would need to take account of interest earned on savings as well.) The consumer can divide up her lifetime resources among her T remaining years of life. We assume that she wishes to achieve the smoothest possible path of consumption over her lifetime. Therefore, she divides this total of $W + RY$ equally among the T years and each year consumes

$$C = \frac{W + RY}{T}.$$

We can write this person's consumption function as

$$C = \frac{1}{T}W + \frac{R}{T}Y.$$

For example, if the consumer expects to live for 50 more years and work for 30 of them, then $T = 50$ and $R = 30$, so her consumption function is

$$C = 0.02W + 0.6Y.$$

This equation says that consumption depends on both income and wealth. An extra \$1 of income per year raises consumption by \$0.60 per year, and an extra \$1 of wealth raises consumption by \$0.02 per year.

---

[1] For references to the large body of work on the life-cycle hypothesis, a good place to start is the lecture Modigliani gave when he won the Nobel Prize. Franco Modigliani, "Life Cycle, Individual Thrift, and the Wealth of Nations," *American Economic Review* 76 (June 1986): 297–313. For an example of more recent research in this tradition, see Pierre-Olivier Gourinchas and Jonathan A. Parker, "Consumption over the Life Cycle," *Econometrica 70* (January 2002): 47–89.

If every individual in the economy plans consumption like this, then the aggregate consumption function is much the same as the individual one. In particular, aggregate consumption depends on both wealth and income. That is, the economy's consumption function is

$$C = \alpha W + \beta Y,$$

where the parameter α is the marginal propensity to consume out of wealth, and the parameter β is the marginal propensity to consume out of income.

Implications

Figure 17-10 graphs the relationship between consumption and income predicted by the life-cycle model. For any given level of wealth W, the model yields a conventional consumption function similar to the one shown in Figure 17-1. Notice, however, that the intercept of the consumption function, which shows what would happen to consumption if income ever fell to zero, is not a fixed value, as it is in Figure 17-1. Instead, the intercept here is αW and, thus, depends on the level of wealth.

This life-cycle model of consumer behaviour can solve the consumption puzzle. According to the life-cycle consumption function, the average propensity to consume is

$$C/Y = \alpha \frac{W}{Y} + \beta.$$

Because wealth does not vary proportionately with income from person to person or from year to year, we should find that high income corresponds to a low average propensity to consume when looking at data across individuals or over short

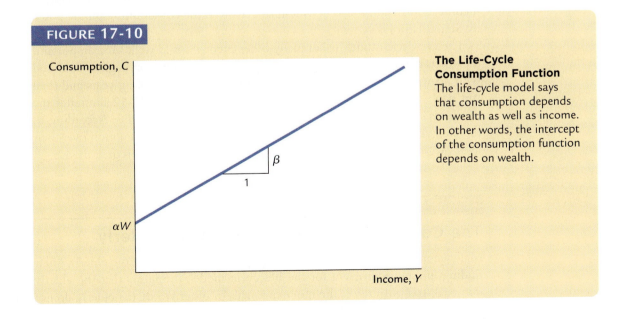

FIGURE 17-10

The Life-Cycle Consumption Function
The life-cycle model says that consumption depends on wealth as well as income. In other words, the intercept of the consumption function depends on wealth.

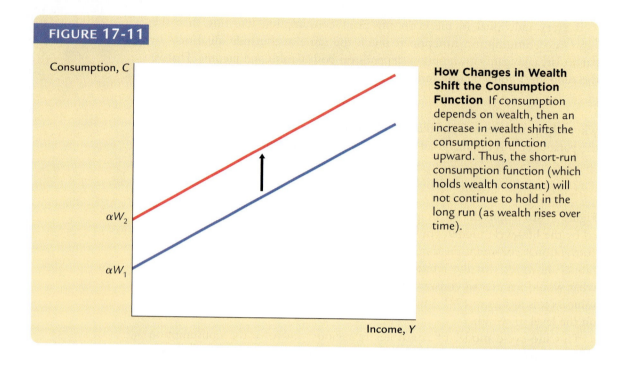

FIGURE 17-11

Consumption, C

αW_2

αW_1

Income, Y

How Changes in Wealth Shift the Consumption Function If consumption depends on wealth, then an increase in wealth shifts the consumption function upward. Thus, the short-run consumption function (which holds wealth constant) will not continue to hold in the long run (as wealth rises over time).

periods of time. But, over long periods of time, wealth and income grow together, resulting in a constant ratio W/Y and thus a constant average propensity to consume.

To make the same point somewhat differently, consider how the consumption function changes over time. As Figure 17-10 shows, for any given level of wealth, the life-cycle consumption function looks like the one Keynes suggested. But this function holds only in the short run when wealth is constant. In the long run, as wealth increases, the consumption function shifts upward, as in Figure 17-11. This upward shift prevents the average propensity to consume from falling as income increases. In this way, Modigliani resolved the consumption puzzle posed by Simon Kuznets's data.

The life-cycle model makes many other predictions as well. Most important, it predicts that saving varies over a person's lifetime. If a person begins adulthood with no wealth, she will accumulate wealth during her working years and then run down her wealth during her retirement years. Figure 17-12 illustrates the consumer's income, consumption, and wealth over her adult life. According to the life-cycle hypothesis, because people want to smooth consumption over their lives, the young who are working save, while the old who are retired dissave.

CASE STUDY

The Consumption and Saving of the Elderly

Many economists have studied the consumption and saving of the elderly. Their findings present a problem for the life-cycle model. It appears that the elderly do not dissave as much as the model predicts. In other words, the elderly do not

FIGURE 17-12

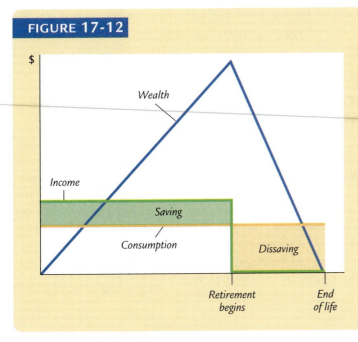

Consumption, Income, and Wealth Over the Life Cycle If the consumer smooths consumption over her life (as indicated by the horizontal consumption line), she will save and accumulate wealth during her working years and then dissave and run down her wealth during retirement.

run down their wealth as quickly as one would expect if they were trying to smooth their consumption over their remaining years of life.

There are two chief explanations for why the elderly do not dissave to the extent that the model predicts. Each suggests a direction for further research on consumption.

The first explanation is that the elderly are concerned about unpredictable expenses. Additional saving that arises from uncertainty is called **precautionary saving.** One reason for precautionary saving by the elderly is the possibility of living longer than expected and thus having to provide for a longer than average span of retirement. Another reason is the possibility of illness and large medical bills. The elderly may respond to this uncertainty by saving more in order to be better prepared for these contingencies.

The precautionary-saving explanation is not completely persuasive, because the elderly can largely insure against these risks. To protect against uncertainty regarding life span, they can buy *annuities* from insurance companies. For a fixed fee, annuities offer a stream of income that lasts as long as the recipient lives. Uncertainty about medical expenses should be largely eliminated by both public and private insurance plans.

The second explanation for the failure of the elderly to dissave is that they may want to leave bequests to their children. Economists have proposed various theories of the parent–child relationship and the bequest motive. In Chapter 16 we discussed some of these theories and their implications for consumption and fiscal policy.

Overall, research on the elderly suggests that the simplest life-cycle model cannot fully explain consumer behaviour. There is no doubt that providing for retirement is an important motive for saving, but other motives, such as precautionary saving and bequests, appear important as well.[2] ∎

17-4 Milton Friedman and the Permanent-Income Hypothesis

In a book published in 1957, Milton Friedman proposed the **permanent-income hypothesis** to explain consumer behaviour. Friedman's permanent-income hypothesis complements Modigliani's life-cycle hypothesis: both use Irving Fisher's theory of the consumer to argue that consumption should not depend on current income alone. But unlike the life-cycle hypothesis, which emphasizes that income follows a regular pattern over a person's lifetime, the permanent-income hypothesis emphasizes that people experience random and temporary changes in their incomes from year to year.[3]

The Hypothesis

Friedman suggested that we view current income Y as the sum of two components, **permanent income** Y^P and **transitory income** Y^T. That is,

$$Y = Y^P + Y^T.$$

Permanent income is the part of income that people expect to persist into the future. Transitory income is the part of income that people do not expect to persist. Put differently, permanent income is average income, and transitory income is the random deviation from that average.

To see how we might separate income into these two parts, consider these examples:

- Maria, who has a law degree, earned more this year than John, who is a high-school dropout. Maria's higher income resulted from higher permanent income, because her education will continue to provide her a higher salary.

- Sue, a strawberry grower in the Niagara peninsula area in Ontario, earned less than usual this year because dry weather reduced her crop. Bill, a strawberry grower in British Columbia, earned more than usual because

---

[2] To read more about the consumption and saving of the elderly, see Albert Ando and Arthur Kennickell, "How Much (or Little) Life Cycle Saving Is There in Micro Data?" in Rudiger Dornbusch, Stanley Fischer, and John Bossons, eds., *Macroeconomics and Finance: Essays in Honor of Franco Modigliani* (Cambridge, MA: MIT Press, 1986); Michael Hurd, "Research on the Elderly: Economic Status, Retirement, and Consumption and Saving," *Journal of Economic Literature* 28 (June 1990): 565–589; and Xiaofen Lin, "Income, Consumption and Saving Before and After Retirement," in Frank T. Denton, Deb Fretz, and Byron G. Spencer, eds., *Independence and Economic Security in Old Age* (Vancouver: UBC Press, 2000).

[3] Milton Friedman, *A Theory of the Consumption Function* (Princeton, NJ: Princeton University Press, 1957).

the scarcity of strawberries in Ontario drove up selling prices. Bill's higher income resulted from higher transitory income, because he is no more likely than Sue to have good weather next year.

These examples show that different forms of income have different degrees of persistence. A good education provides a permanently higher income, whereas good weather provides only transitorily higher income. Although one can imagine intermediate cases, it is useful to keep things simple by supposing that there are only two kinds of income: permanent and transitory.

Friedman reasoned that consumption should depend primarily on permanent income, because consumers use saving and borrowing to smooth consumption in response to transitory changes in income. For example, if a person received a permanent raise of $10,000 per year, his consumption would rise by about as much. Yet if a person won $10,000 in a lottery, he would not consume it all in one year. Instead, he would spread the extra consumption over the rest of his life. Assuming an interest rate of zero and a remaining life span of 50 years, consumption would rise by only $200 per year in response to the $10,000 prize. Thus, consumers spend their permanent income, but they save rather than spend most of their transitory income.

Friedman concluded that we should view the consumption function as approximately

$$C = \alpha Y^{\mathrm{P}},$$

where α is a constant that measures the fraction of permanent income consumed. The permanent-income hypothesis, as expressed by this equation, states that consumption is proportional to permanent income.

Implications

The permanent-income hypothesis solves the consumption puzzle by suggesting that the standard Keynesian consumption function uses the wrong variable. According to the permanent-income hypothesis, consumption depends on permanent income Y^{P}; yet many studies of the consumption function try to relate consumption to current income Y. Friedman argued that this *errors-in-variables problem* explains the seemingly contradictory findings.

Let's see what Friedman's hypothesis implies for the average propensity to consume. Divide both sides of his consumption function by Y to obtain

$$APC = \frac{C}{Y} = \frac{\alpha Y^{\mathrm{P}}}{Y}.$$

According to the permanent-income hypothesis, the average propensity to consume depends on the ratio of permanent income to current income. When current income temporarily rises above permanent income, the average propensity to consume temporarily falls; when current income temporarily falls below permanent income, the average propensity to consume temporarily rises.

Now consider the studies of household data. Friedman reasoned that these data reflect a combination of permanent and transitory income. Households with high permanent income have proportionately higher consumption. If all variation in current income came from the permanent component, the average propensity to consume would be the same in all households. But some of the variation in income comes from the transitory component, and households with high transitory income do not have higher consumption. Therefore, researchers find that high-income households have, on average, lower average propensities to consume.

Similarly, consider the studies of time-series data. Friedman reasoned that year-to-year fluctuations in income are dominated by transitory income. Therefore, years of high income should be years of low average propensities to consume. But over long periods of time—say, from decade to decade—the variation in income comes from the permanent component. Hence, in long time-series, one should observe a constant average propensity to consume, as in fact Kuznets found.

CASE STUDY

Income Taxes versus Sales Taxes as an Instrument for Stabilization Policy

The permanent-income hypothesis can help us to interpret how the economy responds to changes in fiscal policy. According to the *IS–LM* model of Chapters 10 and 11, income-tax cuts stimulate consumption and raise aggregate demand, and income-tax increases depress consumption and reduce aggregate demand. The permanent-income hypothesis, however, states that consumption responds only to changes in permanent income. Therefore, transitory changes in income taxes will have only a negligible effect on consumption and aggregate demand. If a change in personal income taxes is to have a large effect on aggregate demand, it must be permanent.

Several income-tax changes in the United States illustrate the relevance of this reasoning. The first example occurred in 1964 when personal income-tax rates were cut by about 18 percent. At the time, the public was told that the growth in U.S. GDP since World War II had been sufficient to permit the government's revenue needs to be met with lower tax rates. Thus, the tax cut was viewed as permanent, and consumer spending rose markedly. Then, in 1968, the U.S. government wanted to dampen private spending temporarily (while government spending was very high because of the war in Vietnam). The U.S. government introduced a temporary personal income-tax "surcharge" of about 10 percent. Consumption, however, was reduced by only a small amount, just as the permanent-income theory predicts.

The U.S. government tried another temporary tax change in 1975. Because of the recession that followed the Oil Petroleum Exporting Countries (OPEC) crisis, the U.S. government returned to taxpayers some of the taxes already paid in 1974 and reduced income-tax rates for the balance of 1975. Once again, the public realized that this tax break was temporary, and so it had little effect on households' expectations about their long-run average income. Not surprisingly, households saved a large part of their tax rebates instead of spending them.

In the next episode, President Ronald Reagan introduced a series of tax cuts in the 1981–1984 period, reducing personal income-tax rates by about 23 percent. Households knew that Reagan had campaigned on a promise of smaller government, so the tax cuts were interpreted as likely to be permanent. As a result, these tax cuts did stimulate consumption spending significantly. Finally, in 2008, President George W. Bush enacted a tax rebate which was explicitly designed to be a temporary response to the recession. The estimates showed that 80 percent of these tax rebates were saved—an outcome very close to the predictions of the permanent income hypothesis.

Another American initiative during the 2009 recession was the Car Allowance Rebate System (CARS), the official name for the cash-for-clunkers program. If households traded in their old car and bought one of a specified list of new environmentally friendly cars—within a relatively short period of time—they received a significant government subsidy toward the new purchase. This program was essentially a temporary sales tax cut for new car purchases. As explained below, this initiative does receive support from the permanent income hypothesis, and the evidence showed that households significantly changed the timing of their car-replacement purchases—bringing them forward in time so that these purchases lessened the magnitude of the recession. But because the program only changed the timing of spending that was likely to take place anyway, it was not a successful initiative for saving the automobile industry or for fundamentally affecting the environment. However, despite contributing very little to these long-term objectives, the program was a success with respect to its short-term objective of providing a stabilization policy during a recession.

How have Canadian authorities responded to these U.S. policy experiments? In the 1978 federal budget, the Canadian government tried to stimulate spending with a general sales-tax cut instead of an income-tax cut. A sales tax does not affect consumption only by raising or lowering households' estimates of their permanent income. Instead, a temporary sales-tax cut lowers the price of buying goods now, compared to the price in the future. Indeed, the *more* temporary a sales-tax change is, the more effective it is in changing the timing of people's spending.[4] Thus, sales taxes represent a much more reliable intrument for accomplishing stabilization policy. After all, the whole point of stabilization is to introduce a series of temporary stimuli to aggregate demand.

Unfortunately, until the GST was introduced in 1991, the federal government did not have a retail sales tax with which to implement stabilization policy. The 1978 budget tried to overcome this problem by having the federal government transfer some of its share of the personal income-tax revenue to the provinces in exchange for the provinces agreeing to lower provincial sales-tax rates for a specified time period. Even though an agreement was reached "behind closed doors," the Quebec government refused to cooperate after the federal budget was made public. Quebec officials claimed that they must resist Ottawa's meddling in provincial affairs. Unfortunately, the political wrangling that ensued left the federal government uninterested in pursuing agreements of this sort again.

By 1991 the federal government had the GST, which gave the government a more predictable and powerful lever to use in attempts to adjust consumer expenditures for stabilization policy purposes. However, the GST has been very

---

[4] Solid evidence is provided in Peter Gusson, "The Role of Provincial Governments in Economic Stabilization: The Case of Ontario's Auto Sales Tax Rebate" (Ottawa: Conference Board of Canada, 1978).

unpopular, and the government has tried to avoid drawing any attention to it by not using it as an instrument for short-run stabilization policy.

The Conservative government of Stephen Harper—a leader who has an MA degree in economics—has conducted sales-tax policy in a way that is inconsistent with the permanent income hypothesis. In their first two years in office, the Conservatives cut the GST from 7 percent to 5 percent on a permanent basis, and (as we learned in Chapters 7 and 8) this is likely to lower economic growth compared to what would have emerged had they cut personal income taxes permanently instead. Then, in their 2009 budget, when they needed a timely stimulus package, the Conservatives thought that they had no room left to offer a temporary GST cut. This is unfortunate, since this is just what would have been most helpful during the recession. The government chose to focus on the GST when such an initiative was not supported by the permanent income hypothesis, and to ignore the GST when changing it was recommended.

The fact that personal income-tax changes have significant effects on consumer spending only when those changes are expected to be permanent is a dramatic illustration of the importance of the Lucas critique (which we discussed in Chapter 15). As explained there, the prominent economist Robert Lucas has emphasized that predictions of policy impact are quite inaccurate if economists do not focus on how policy affects expectations. The permanent-income hypothesis is a convenient way of organizing our analysis so that the Lucas critique is respected.

The permanent-income hypothesis has received support from numerous episodes other than government fiscal policies. For example, the dramatic stock market crash of 1987 was widely viewed as transitory, and (as the theory predicts) that event had little effect on consumer spending. ∎

17-5 Robert Hall and the Random-Walk Hypothesis

The permanent-income hypothesis is founded on Fisher's model of intertemporal choice. It builds on the idea that forward-looking consumers base their consumption decisions not only on their current income but also on the income they expect to receive in the future. Thus, the permanent-income hypothesis highlights that consumption depends on people's expectations.

Recent research on consumption has combined this view of the consumer with the assumption of rational expectations. The rational-expectations assumption states that people use all available information to make optimal forecasts about the future. You might recall from Chapter 13 that this assumption has potentially profound implications for the costs of stopping inflation. It can also have profound implications for consumption.

The Hypothesis

The economist Robert Hall was the first to derive the implications of rational expectations for consumption. He showed that if the permanent-income hypothesis is correct, and if consumers have rational expectations, then changes in consumption over time should be unpredictable. When changes in a variable are unpredictable, the variable is said to follow a **random walk.** According to Hall, the combination of the permanent-income hypothesis and rational expectations implies that consumption follows a random walk.

Hall reasoned as follows. According to the permanent-income hypothesis, consumers face fluctuating income and try their best to smooth their consumption over time. At any moment, consumers choose consumption based on their current expectations of their lifetime incomes. Over time, they change their consumption because they receive news that causes them to revise their expectations. For example, a person getting an unexpected promotion increases consumption, whereas a person getting an unexpected demotion decreases consumption. In other words, changes in consumption reflect "surprises" about lifetime income. If consumers are optimally using all available information, then they should be surprised only by events that were entirely unpredictable. Therefore, changes in their consumption should be unpredictable as well.[5]

Implications

The rational-expectations approach to consumption has implications not only for forecasting but also for the analysis of economic policies. *If consumers obey the permanent-income hypothesis and have rational expectations, then only unexpected policy changes influence consumption. These policy changes take effect when they change expectations.* For example, suppose that today the federal government passes a tax increase to be effective next year. In this case, consumers receive the news about their lifetime incomes when the government passes the law (or even earlier if the law's passage was predictable). The arrival of this news causes consumers to revise their expectations and reduce their consumption. The following year, when the tax hike goes into effect, consumption is unchanged because no news has arrived.

Hence, if consumers have rational expectations, policymakers influence the economy not only through their actions but also through the public's expectations of their actions. Expectations, however, cannot be observed directly. Therefore, it is often hard to know how and when changes in fiscal policy alter aggregate demand.

CASE STUDY

Do Predictable Changes in Income Lead to Predictable Changes in Consumption?

Of the many facts about consumer behaviour, one is impossible to dispute: income and consumption fluctuate together over the business cycle. When the economy goes into a recession, both income and consumption fall, and when the economy booms, both income and consumption rise rapidly.

---

[5] Robert E. Hall, "Stochastic Implications of the Life Cycle–Permanent Income Hypothesis: Theory and Evidence," *Journal of Political Economy* 86, no. 6 (December 1978): 971–987.

By itself, this fact doesn't say much about the rational-expectations version of the permanent-income hypothesis. Most short-run fluctuations are unpredictable. Thus, when the economy goes into a recession, the typical consumer is receiving bad news about his lifetime income, so consumption naturally falls. And when the economy booms, the typical consumer is receiving good news, so consumption rises. This behaviour does not necessarily violate the random-walk theory that changes in consumption are impossible to forecast.

Yet suppose we could identify some *predictable* changes in income. According to the random-walk theory, these changes in income should not cause consumers to revise their spending plans. If consumers had reason to expect income to rise or fall, they should have adjusted their consumption already in response to that information. Thus, predictable changes in income should not lead to predictable changes in consumption.

Data on consumption and income, however, appear not to satisfy this implication of the random-walk theory. When income is expected to fall by $1, consumption will typically fall at the same time by about $0.50. In other words, predictable changes in income lead to predictable changes in consumption that are roughly half as large.

Why is this so? One possible explanation of this behaviour is that some consumers may fail to have rational expectations. Instead, they may base their expectations of future income excessively on current income. Thus, when income rises or falls (even predictably), they act as if they received news about their lifetime resources and change their consumption accordingly. Another possible explanation is that some consumers are borrowing-constrained and, therefore, base their consumption on current income alone. Regardless of which explanation is correct, Keynes's original consumption function starts to look more attractive. That is, current income appears to have a larger role in determining consumer spending than the random-walk theory suggests.[6] ■

17-6 David Laibson and the Pull of Instant Gratification

Keynes called the consumption function a "fundamental psychological law." Yet, as we have seen, psychology has played a small role in the subsequent study of consumption. Most economists assume that consumers are rational maximizers of utility who are always evaluating their opportunities and plans to obtain the

---

[6] John Y. Campbell and N. Gregory Mankiw, "Consumption, Income, and Interest Rates: Reinterpreting the Time-Series Evidence," *NBER Macroeconomics Annual* (1989): 185–216; Jonathan A. Parker, "The Response of Household Consumption to Predictable Changes in Social Security Taxes," *American Economic Review* 89, no. 4 (September 1999): 959–973; and Nicholas S. Souleles, "The Response of Household Consumption to Income Tax Refunds," *American Economic Review* 89, no. 4 (September 1999): 947–958.

highest lifetime satisfaction. This model of human behaviour was the basis for all the work on consumption theory from Irving Fisher to Robert Hall.

More recently, economists have started to return to psychology. They have suggested that consumption decisions are not made by the ultrarational *homo economicus* but by real human beings whose behaviour can be far from rational. This new subfield infusing psychology into economics is called *behavioural economics.* The most prominent behavioural economist studying consumption is Harvard professor David Laibson.

The Hypothesis

Laibson notes that many consumers judge themselves to be imperfect decisionmakers. In one survey of the American public, 76 percent said they were not saving enough for retirement. In another survey of the baby boom generation, respondents were asked the percentage of income that they save and the percentage that they thought they should save. The saving shortfall averaged 11 percentage points.

According to Laibson, the insufficiency of saving is related to another phenomenon: the pull of instant gratification. Consider the following two questions:

1. Would you prefer (A) a candy today or (B) two candies tomorrow?

2. Would you prefer (A) a candy in 100 days or (B) two candies in 101 days?

Many people confronted with such choices answer A to the first question and B to the second. In a sense, they are more patient in the long run than they are in the short run.

Implications

This raises the possibility that consumers' preferences may be *time-inconsistent:* they may alter their decisions simply because time passes. A person confronting question 2 may choose B and wait the extra day for the extra candy. But after 100 days pass, he finds himself in a new short run, confronting question 1. The pull of instant gratification may induce him to change his mind.

We see this kind of behaviour in many situations in life. A person on a diet may have a second helping at dinner, while promising himself that he will eat less tomorrow. A person may smoke one more cigarette, while promising herself that this is the last one. And a consumer may splurge at the shopping center, while promising himself that tomorrow he will cut back his spending and start saving more for retirement. But when tomorrow arrives, the promises are in the past, and a new self takes control of the decisionmaking, with its own desire for instant gratification.

These observations raise as many questions as they answer. Will the renewed focus on psychology among economists offer a better understanding of consumer behaviour? Will it offer new and better prescriptions regarding, for instance, tax policy toward saving? It is too early to give a full evaluation, but without doubt, these questions are on the forefront of the research agenda.[7]

CASE STUDY

How to Get People to Save More

Many economists believe that it would be desirable for Canadians to increase the fraction of their income they saved. There are several reasons for this conclusion. From a microeconomic perspective, greater saving would mean that people would be better prepared for retirement; this goal is especially important as the baby boom generation moves into retirement over the next 20 years. From a macroeconomic perspective, greater saving would increase the supply of loanable funds available to finance investment; the Solow growth model shows that increased capital accumulation leads to higher income. From an open-economy perspective, greater saving would mean that less domestic investment would be financed by capital flows from abroad, so GNP would rise relative to GDP. Finally, the fact that many individuals say that they are not saving enough may be sufficient reason to think that increased saving should be a national goal.

The difficult issue is how to get people to save more. The burgeoning field of behavioural economics offers some answers.

One approach is to make saving the path of least resistance. For example, consider registered retirement savings plans (RRSPs). The similar arrangement in the United States is called the 401(k) plans. These are tax-advantaged retirement savings accounts available to many workers through their employers. In most firms, participation in the plan is an option that workers can choose by filling out a simple form. In some firms, however, workers are automatically enrolled in the plan but can opt out by filling out a simple form. Studies have shown that workers are far more likely to participate in the second case than in the first. If workers were rational maximizers, as is so often assumed in economic theory, they would choose the optimal amount of retirement saving, regardless of whether they had to choose to enroll or were enrolled automatically. In fact, workers' behaviour appears to exhibit substantial inertia. As a result, policymakers who want to increase saving can take advantage of this inertia by making automatic enrollment in these savings plans more common. In 2009, U.S. President Obama attempted to do just that. According to legislation suggested in his first budget proposal, employers without retirement plans would be required to automatically enroll workers in direct-deposit retirement accounts. Employees would then be able to opt out of the system if they wished. Whether this proposal would become law was still unclear as this book was going to press.

---

[7] For more on this topic, see David Laibson, "Golden Eggs and Hyperbolic Discounting," *Quarterly Journal of Economics* 62 (May 1997): 443–477; George-Marios Angeletos, David Laibson, Andrea Repetto, Jeremy Tobacman, and Stephen Weinberg, "The Hyperbolic Buffer Stock Model: Calibration, Simulation, and Empirical Evidence," *Journal of Economic Perspectives* 15 (Summer 2001): 47–68.

A second approach to increase saving is to give people the opportunity to control their desires for instant gratification. One intriguing possibility is the "Save More Tomorrow" program proposed by economist Richard Thaler. The essence of this program is that people commit in advance to putting a portion of their future salary increases into a retirement savings account. When signing up, a worker makes no sacrifice of lower consumption today but instead commits to reducing consumption growth in the future. When this plan was implemented in several firms, it had a large impact. A high proportion (78 percent) of those offered the plan joined. In addition, of those enrolled, the vast majority (80 percent) stayed with the program through at least the fourth annual pay raise. The average saving rates for those in the program increased from 3.5 percent to 13.6 percent over the course of 40 months.

How successful would more widespread applications of these ideas be in increasing the national saving rate? It is impossible to say for sure. But given the importance of saving to both personal and national economic prosperity, many economists believe these proposals are worth a try.[8]

One straightforward way of stimulating saving is to shift from an income-based tax system to an expenditure-based tax system. This approach is supported by both traditional economic analysis (the intertemporal theory of Irving Fisher) and by psychological considerations. We now have about 55 years of survey data from a number of countries in which people are asked to rank how happy they feel. The startling conclusion is that people's subjective happiness has not increased over this period, despite the fact that per-capita consumption has risen quite dramatically. Why isn't this increase in material welfare registering in self-reported subjective happiness? Cornell economist Robert Frank rekindled the profession's interest in James Duesenberry's[9] relative income hypothesis as an answer to this question. Frank focuses on what he calls positional goods. He argues that much of the satisfaction that individuals derive from these possessions stems from the fact that they allow the individual to demonstrate that they are relatively well-off—compared to others. In other words, people get higher utility from their own consumption (just as traditional analysis assumes), but, other things equal, they get lower utility when the consumption level of others rises (as psychological studies suggest). If everyone is consuming more positional goods as economic growth proceeds, the benefits—in terms of generating more happiness—can largely cancel out (since no one is doing relatively better than others). If consumption does generate negative externalities of this sort, standard microeconomic analysis gives us a clear policy prescription. Negative externalities need to be internalized with a tax. Hence, consumption taxes are supported by both Irving Fisher's traditional analysis and by the positional-goods analysis. ∎

---

[8] James J. Choi, David I. Laibson, Brigitte Madrian, and Andrew Metrick, "Defined Contribution Pensions: Plan Rules, Participant Decisions, and the Path of Least Resistance," in James Poterba, ed., *Tax Policy and the Economy,* 16 (2002): 67–113; Richard H. Thaler and Shlomo Benartzi, "Save More Tomorrow: Using Behavioral Economics to Increase Employee Saving," *Journal of Political Economy,* 112 (2004): S164–S187.

[9] See James Duesenberry, *Income, Saving and the Theory of Consumer Behavior* (Cambridge, Mass.: Harvard University Press) 1949, and Robert H. Frank, "Positional Externalities Cause Large and Preventable Welfare Losses," *American Economic Review Papers and Proceedings* 95, (2005): 137–141.

17-7 Conclusion

In the work of six prominent economists, we have seen a progression of views on consumer behaviour. Keynes proposed that consumption depends largely on current income. Since then, economists have argued that consumers understand that they face an intertemporal decision. Consumers look ahead to their future resources and needs, implying a more complex consumption function than the one that Keynes proposed. Keynes suggested a consumption function of the form

$$\text{Consumption} = f(\text{Current Income}).$$

Recent work suggests instead that

$$\text{Consumption} = f(\text{Current Income, Wealth, Expected Future Income, Interest Rates}).$$

In other words, current income is only one determinant of aggregate consumption.

Economists continue to debate the relative importance of these determinants of consumption. There remains disagreement about, for example, the influence of interest rates on consumer spending, the prevalence of borrowing constraints, and the importance of psychological effects. Economists sometimes disagree about economic policy because they assume different consumption functions. For instance, as we saw in the previous chapter, the debate over the effects of government debt is partly a debate over the determinants of consumer spending. The key role of consumption in policy evaluation is sure to maintain economists' interest in studying consumer behaviour for many years to come.

Summary

1. Keynes conjectured that the marginal propensity to consume is between zero and one, that the average propensity to consume falls as income rises, and that current income is the primary determinant of consumption. Studies of household data and short time-series confirmed Keynes's conjectures. Yet studies of long time-series found no tendency for the average propensity to consume to fall as income rises over time.

2. Recent work on consumption builds on Irving Fisher's model of the consumer. In this model, the consumer faces an intertemporal budget constraint and chooses consumption for the present and the future to achieve the highest level of lifetime satisfaction. As long as the consumer can save and borrow, consumption depends on the consumer's lifetime resources.

3. Modigliani's life-cycle hypothesis emphasizes that income varies somewhat predictably over a person's life and that consumers use saving and borrowing to smooth their consumption over their lifetimes. According to this hypothesis, consumption depends on both income and wealth.

4. Friedman's permanent-income hypothesis emphasizes that individuals experience both permanent and transitory fluctuations in their income. Because consumers can save and borrow, and because they want to smooth their consumption, consumption does not respond much to transitory income. Instead, consumption depends primarily on permanent income.

5. Hall's random-walk hypothesis combines the permanent-income hypothesis with the assumption that consumers have rational expectations about future income. It implies that changes in consumption are unpredictable, because consumers change their consumption only when they receive news about their lifetime resources.

6. Laibson has suggested that psychological effects are important for understanding consumer behaviour. In particular, because people have a strong desire for instant gratification, they may exhibit time-inconsistent behaviour and end up saving less than they would like.

KEY CONCEPTS

Marginal propensity to consume

Average propensity to consume

Intertemporal budget constraint

Discounting

Indifference curves

Marginal rate of substitution

Normal good

Income effect

Substitution effect

Borrowing constraint

Life-cycle hypothesis

Precautionary saving

Permanent-income hypothesis

Permanent income

Transitory income

Random walk

QUESTIONS FOR REVIEW

1. What were Keynes's three conjectures about the consumption function?

2. Describe the evidence that was consistent with Keynes's conjectures and the evidence that was inconsistent with them.

3. How do the life-cycle and permanent-income hypotheses resolve the seemingly contradictory pieces of evidence regarding consumption behaviour?

4. Use Fisher's model of consumption to analyze an increase in second-period income. Compare the case in which the consumer faces a binding borrowing constraint and the case in which he does not.

5. Explain why changes in consumption are unpredictable if consumers obey the permanent-income hypothesis and have rational expectations.

6. Give an example in which someone might exhibit time-inconsistent preferences.

PROBLEMS AND APPLICATIONS

1. The chapter uses the Fisher model to discuss a change in the interest rate for a consumer who saves some of his first-period income. Suppose, instead, that the consumer is a borrower. How does that alter the analysis? Discuss the income and substitution effects on consumption in both periods.

2. Jack and Jill both obey the two-period Fisher model of consumption. Jack earns $100 in the first period and $100 in the second period. Jill earns nothing in the first period and $210 in the second period. Both of them can borrow or lend at the interest rate r.

   a. You observe both Jack and Jill consuming $100 in the first period and $100 in the second period. What is the interest rate r?

   b. Suppose the interest rate increases. What will happen to Jack's consumption in the first period? Is Jack better off or worse off than before the interest-rate rise?

   c. What will happen to Jill's consumption in the first period when the interest rate increases? Is Jill better off or worse off than before the interest-rate increase?

3. The chapter analyzes Fisher's model for the case in which the consumer can save or borrow at an interest rate of r and for the case in which the consumer can save at this rate but cannot borrow at all. Consider now the intermediate case in which the consumer can save at rate r_s and borrow at rate r_b, where $r_s < r_b$.

   a. What is the consumer's budget constraint in the case in which he consumes less than his income in period one?

   b. What is the consumer's budget constraint in the case in which he consumes more than his income in period one?

   c. Graph the two budget constraints and shade the area that represents the combination of first-period and second-period consumption the consumer can choose.

   d. Now add to your graph the consumer's indifference curves. Show three possible outcomes: one in which the consumer saves, one in which he borrows, and one in which he neither saves nor borrows.

   e. What determines first-period consumption in each of the three cases?

4. Explain whether borrowing constraints increase or decrease the potency of fiscal policy to influence aggregate demand in each of the following two cases:

   a. A temporary personal income-tax cut.

   b. An announced future personal income-tax cut.

5. In the discussion of the life-cycle hypothesis in the text, income is assumed to be constant during the period before retirement. For most people, however, income grows over their lifetimes. How does this growth in income influence the lifetime pattern of consumption and wealth accumulation shown in Figure 17–12 under the following conditions?

   a. Consumers can borrow, so their wealth can be negative.

   b. Consumers face borrowing constraints that prevent their wealth from falling below zero.

   Do you consider case (a) or case (b) to be more realistic? Why?

6. Demographers predict that the fraction of the population that is elderly will increase over the next 20 years. What does the life-cycle model predict for the influence of this demographic change on the national saving rate?

7. One study found that the elderly who do not have children dissave at about the same rate as the elderly who do have children. What might this finding imply about the reason the elderly do not dissave as much as the life-cycle model predicts?

8. Consider two savings accounts that pay the same interest rate. One account lets you take your money out on demand. The second requires that you give 30-day advance notification before withdrawals. Which account would you prefer? Why? Can you imagine a person who might make the opposite choice? What do these choices say about the theory of the consumption function?

CHAPTER 18

Investment

The social object of skilled investment should be to defeat the dark forces of time and ignorance which envelope our future.

— *John Maynard Keynes*

While spending on consumption goods provides utility to households today, spending on investment goods is aimed at providing a higher standard of living at a later date. Investment is the component of GDP that links the present and the future.

Investment spending plays a key role not only in long-run growth but also in the short-run business cycle because it is the most volatile component of GDP. When expenditure on goods and services falls during a recession, much of the decline is usually due to a drop in investment spending. In the severe recession of 1982, for example, real GDP fell $14 billion whereas investment spending fell $11 billion, accounting for more than three-quarters of the fall in spending.

Economists study investment to better understand fluctuations in the economy's output of goods and services. The models of GDP we saw in previous chapters, such as the *IS–LM* model in Chapters 10 and 11, were based on a simple investment function relating investment to the real interest rate: $I = I(r)$. That function states that an increase in the real interest rate reduces investment. In this chapter we look more closely at the theory behind this investment function.

There are three types of investment spending. **Business fixed investment** includes the machinery, equipment, and structures that businesses buy to use in production. **Residential investment** includes the new housing that people buy to live in and that landlords buy to rent out. **Inventory investment** includes those goods that businesses put aside in storage, including materials and supplies, work in process, and finished goods. Figure 18-1 plots total investment and its three components in Canada from 1970 to 2008. You can see that all types of investment fall substantially during recessions, which are shown as shaded areas in the figure.

In this chapter we build models of each type of investment to explain these fluctuations. The models will shed light on the following questions:

- Why is investment negatively related to the interest rate?
- What causes the investment function to shift?
- Why does investment rise during booms and fall during recessions?

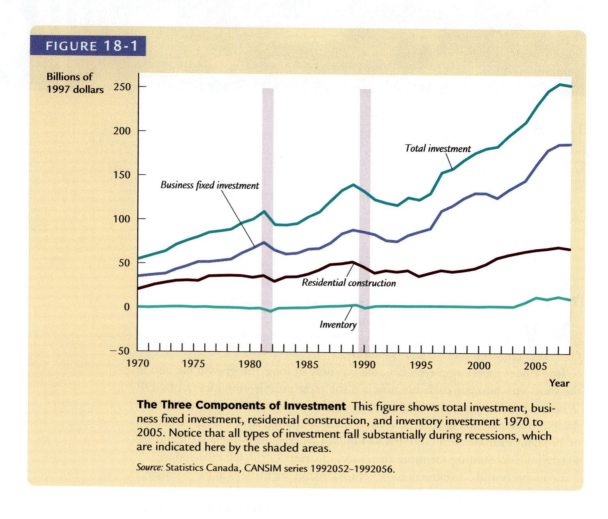

FIGURE 18-1

Billions of 1997 dollars

The Three Components of Investment This figure shows total investment, business fixed investment, residential construction, and inventory investment 1970 to 2005. Notice that all types of investment fall substantially during recessions, which are indicated here by the shaded areas.

Source: Statistics Canada, CANSIM series 1992052–1992056.

At the end of the chapter, we return to these questions and summarize the answers that the models offer.

18-1 Business Fixed Investment

The largest piece of investment spending, is business fixed capital investment. The term "business" means that these investment goods are bought by firms for use in future production. The term "fixed capital" means that this spending is for capital that will stay put for a while, as opposed to inventory investment, which will be used or sold within a short time. Business fixed investment includes everything from office furniture to factories, computers to company cars.

The standard model of business fixed investment is called the **neoclassical model of investment.** The neoclassical model examines the benefits and costs to firms of owning capital goods. The model shows how the level of investment—the addition to the stock of capital—is related to the marginal product of capital, the interest rate, and the tax rules affecting firms.

To develop the model, imagine that there are two kinds of firms in the economy. *Production firms* produce goods and services using capital that they rent. *Rental firms* make all the investments in the economy; they buy capital and rent it out to the production firms. Of course, most firms in the actual economy perform both functions: they produce goods and services, and they invest in capital for future production. We can simplify our analysis and clarify our thinking, however, if we separate these two activities by imagining that they take place in different firms.

The Rental Price of Capital

Let's first consider the typical production firm. As we discussed in Chapter 3, this firm decides how much capital to rent by comparing the cost and benefit of each unit of capital. The firm rents capital at a rental rate R and sells its output at a price P; the real cost of a unit of capital to the production firm is R/P. The real benefit of a unit of capital is the marginal product of capital MPK—the extra output produced with one more unit of capital. The marginal product of capital declines as the amount of capital rises: the more capital the firm has, the less an additional unit of capital will add to its output. Chapter 3 concluded that, to maximize profit, the firm rents capital until the marginal product of capital falls to equal the real rental price.

Figure 18-2 shows the equilibrium in the rental market for capital. For the reasons just discussed, the marginal product of capital determines the demand curve. The demand curve slopes downward because the marginal product of capital is low when the level of capital is high. At any point in time, the amount of capital in the economy is fixed, so the supply curve is vertical. The real rental price of capital adjusts to equilibrate supply and demand.

FIGURE 18-2

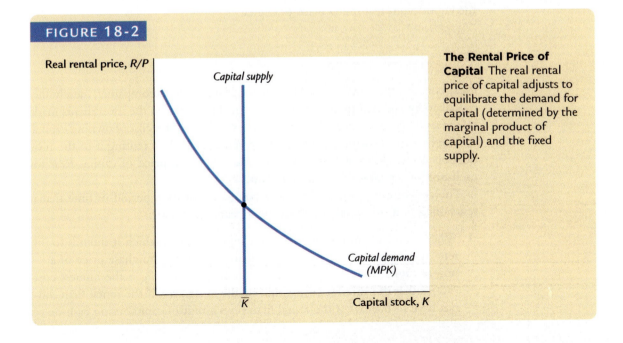

The Rental Price of Capital The real rental price of capital adjusts to equilibrate the demand for capital (determined by the marginal product of capital) and the fixed supply.

To see what variables influence the equilibrium rental price, let's consider a particular production function. As we saw in Chapter 3, many economists consider the Cobb–Douglas production function a good approximation of how the actual economy turns capital and labour into goods and services. The Cobb–Douglas production function is

$$Y = AK^{\alpha}L^{1-\alpha},$$

where Y is output, K capital, L labour, A a parameter measuring the level of technology, and α a parameter between zero and one that measures capital's share of output. The marginal product of capital for the Cobb–Douglas production function is

$$MPK = \alpha A(L/K)^{1-\alpha}.$$

Because the real rental price equals the marginal product of capital in equilibrium, we can write

$$\frac{R}{P} = \alpha A \left(\frac{L}{K}\right)^{1-\alpha}.$$

This expression identifies the variables that determine the real rental price. It shows the following:

- The lower the stock of capital, the higher the real rental price of capital
- The greater the amount of labour employed, the higher the real rental price of capital
- The better the technology, the higher the real rental price of capital

Events that reduce the capital stock (an earthquake), or raise employment (an expansion in aggregate demand), or improve the technology (a scientific discovery) raise the equilibrium real rental price of capital.

The Cost of Capital

Next consider the rental firms. These firms, like car-rental companies, merely buy capital goods and rent them out. Since our goal is to explain the investments made by the rental firms, we begin by considering the benefit and cost of owning capital.

The benefit of owning capital is the revenue earned by renting it to the production firms. The rental firm receives the real rental price of capital R/P for each unit of capital it owns and rents out.

The cost of owning capital is more complex. For each period of time that it rents out a unit of capital, the rental firm bears three costs:

1. When a rental firm borrows to buy a unit of capital, which it intends to rent out, it must pay interest on the loan. If P_K is the purchase price of a unit of capital and i is the nominal interest rate, then iP_K is the interest cost. Notice that this interest cost would be the same even if the rental firm did not have to borrow: if the rental firm buys a unit of capital using cash on

hand, it loses out on the interest it could have earned by depositing this cash in the bank. In either case, the interest cost equals iP_K.

2. While the rental firm is renting out the capital, the price of capital can change. If the price of capital falls, the firm loses, because the firm's asset has fallen in value. If the price of capital rises, the firm gains, because the firm's asset has risen in value. The cost of this loss or gain is $-\Delta P_K$. (The minus sign is here because we are measuring costs, not benefits.)

3. While the capital is rented out, it suffers wear and tear, called **depreciation.** If δ is the rate of depreciation—the fraction of value lost per period because of wear and tear—then the dollar cost of depreciation is δP_K.

The total cost of renting out a unit of capital for one period is therefore

$$\text{Cost of Capital} = iP_K - \Delta P_K + \delta P_K$$
$$= P_K(i - \Delta P_K/P_K + \delta).$$

The cost of capital depends on the price of capital, the interest rate, the rate at which capital prices are changing, and the depreciation rate.

For example, consider the cost of capital to a car-rental company. The company buys cars for $10,000 each and rents them out to other businesses. The company faces an interest rate i of 10 percent per year, so the interest cost iP_K is $1,000 per year for each car the company owns. Car prices are rising at 6 percent per year, so, excluding wear and tear, the firm gets a capital gain ΔP_K of $600 per year. Cars depreciate at 20 percent per year, so the loss due to wear and tear δP_K is $2,000 per year. Therefore, the company's cost of capital is

$$\text{Cost of Capital} = \$1,000 - \$600 + \$2,000$$
$$= \$2,400.$$

The cost to the car-rental company of keeping a car in its capital stock is $2,400 per year.

To make the expression for the cost of capital simpler and easier to interpret, we assume that the price of capital goods rises with the prices of other goods. In this case, $\Delta P_K/P_K$ equals the overall rate of inflation π. Because $i - \pi$ equals the real interest rate r, we can write the cost of capital as

$$\text{Cost of Capital} = P_K(r + \delta).$$

This equation states that the cost of capital depends on the price of capital, the real interest rate, and the depreciation rate.

Finally, we want to express the cost of capital relative to other goods in the economy. The **real cost of capital**—the cost of buying and renting out a unit of capital measured in units of the economy's output—is

$$\text{Real Cost of Capital} = \left(\frac{P_K}{P}\right)(r + \delta).$$

This equation states that the real cost of capital depends on the relative price of a capital good P_K/P, the real interest rate r, and the depreciation rate δ.

The Determinants of Investment

Now consider a rental firm's decision about whether to increase or decrease its capital stock. For each unit of capital, the firm earns real revenue R/P and bears the real cost $(P_K/P)(r + \delta)$. The real profit per unit of capital is

$$\text{Profit Rate} = \text{Revenue} - \quad \text{Cost}$$

$$= \quad R/P \quad - \left(\frac{P_K}{P}\right)(r + \delta).$$

Because the real rental price in equilibrium equals the marginal product of capital, we can write the profit rate as

$$\text{Profit Rate} = MPK - \left(\frac{P_K}{P}\right)(r + \delta).$$

The rental firm makes a profit if the marginal product of capital is greater than the cost of capital. It incurs a loss if the marginal product is less than the cost of capital.

We can now see the economic incentives that lie behind the rental firm's investment decision. The firm's decision regarding its capital stock—that is, whether to add to it or to let it depreciate—depends on whether owning and renting out capital is profitable. The change in the capital stock, called **net investment**, depends on the difference between the marginal product of capital and the cost of capital. *If the marginal product of capital exceeds the cost of capital, firms find it profitable to add to their capital stock. If the marginal product of capital falls short of the cost of capital, they let their capital stock shrink.*

We can also now see that the separation of economic activity between production and rental firms, although useful for clarifying our thinking, is not necessary for our conclusion regarding how firms choose how much to invest. For a firm that both uses and owns capital, the benefit of an extra unit of capital is the marginal product of capital, and the cost is the cost of capital. Like a firm that owns and rents out capital, this firm adds to its capital stock if the marginal product exceeds the cost of capital. Thus, we can write

$$\Delta K = I_n \left[MPK - \left(\frac{P_K}{P}\right)(r + \delta) \right],$$

where $I_n(\ )$ is the function showing how much net investment responds to the incentive to invest.

We can now derive the investment function. Total spending on business fixed investment is the sum of net investment and the replacement of depreciated capital. The investment function is

$$I = I_n \left[MPK - \left(\frac{P_K}{P}\right)(r + \delta) \right] + \delta K.$$

Business fixed investment depends on the marginal product of capital, the cost of capital, and the amount of depreciation.

This model shows why investment depends on the interest rate. A decrease in the real interest rate lowers the cost of capital. It therefore raises the amount of

FIGURE 18-3

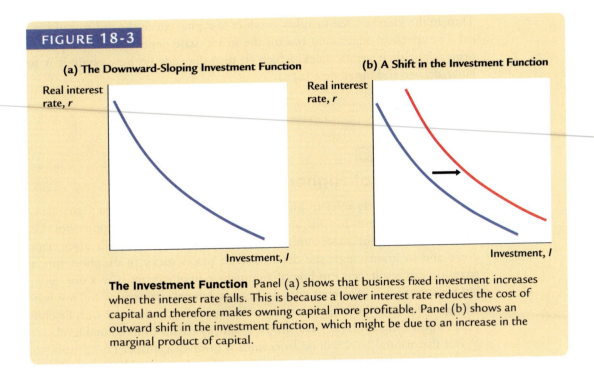

(a) The Downward-Sloping Investment Function

Real interest rate, r

Investment, I

(b) A Shift in the Investment Function

Real interest rate, r

Investment, I

The Investment Function Panel (a) shows that business fixed investment increases when the interest rate falls. This is because a lower interest rate reduces the cost of capital and therefore makes owning capital more profitable. Panel (b) shows an outward shift in the investment function, which might be due to an increase in the marginal product of capital.

profit from owning capital and increases the incentive to accumulate more capital. Similarly, an increase in the real interest rate raises the cost of capital and leads firms to reduce their investment. For this reason, the investment schedule relating investment to the interest rate slopes downward, as in panel (a) of Figure 18-3.

The model also shows what causes the investment schedule to shift. Any event that raises what business managers expect the marginal product of capital to be, increases the profitability of investment and causes the investment schedule to shift outward, as in panel (b) of Figure 18-3. For example, a technological innovation that increases the production function parameter A raises the marginal product of capital and, for any given interest rate, increases the amount of capital goods that rental firms wish to buy. Similarly, a drop on consumer confidence will lead managers to fear that their sales will be low. In revenue terms, then capital's marginal product is expected to be low, so the investment schedule shifts inward.

Finally, consider what happens as this adjustment of the capital stock continues over time. If the marginal product begins above the cost of capital, the capital stock will rise and the marginal product will fall. If the marginal product of capital begins below the cost of capital, the capital stock will fall and the marginal product will rise. Eventually, as the capital stock adjusts, the marginal product of capital approaches the cost of capital. When the capital stock reaches a steady-state level, we can write

$$MPK = \left(\frac{P_K}{P}\right)(r + \delta).$$

Thus, in the long run, the marginal product of capital equals the real cost of capital. The speed of adjustment toward the steady state depends on how quickly firms adjust their capital stock, which in turn depends on how costly it is to build, deliver, and install new capital.[1]

CASE STUDY

The Burden of Higher Interest Rates

Journalists frequently refer to high interest rates as a "burden" for Canadians. There are two reasons for this, and we are now in a position to appreciate this concern. First, in the short run, an increase in interest rates pulls investment down and so lowers aggregate demand. With prices sticky in the short run, a recession can result. But this line of argument cannot explain why a one-time, but permanent, rise in interest rates is a burden. After all, investment will not *keep* falling—long after the one-time increase in borrowing costs—and with flexible prices in the long run, real GDP should gradually return to its natural level.

But that natural level will be *lower* since it involves a smaller capital stock; as we have learned, firms arrange their affairs so that the marginal product of capital equals the real (rental) cost of capital:

$$MPK = r + \delta.$$

(Units have been chosen so that the purchase price of capital, P_K, equals the purchase price of other goods, P.) In Chapter 3, we learned that the Cobb–Douglas production function is a good approximation of production processes in Canada, and that for this production function, the marginal product of capital is given by

$$MPK = \frac{\alpha Y}{K} = \frac{\alpha y}{k}.$$

where α is capital's share of output. Substituting this expression for MPK into the steady-state capital-demand relationship yields

$$\alpha y = (r + \delta)k.$$

Rewriting this equilibrium condition in change form (holding α and δ constant) results in

$$\alpha \Delta y = (r + \delta)\Delta k + k\Delta r.$$

---

[1] Economists often measure capital goods in units such that the price of 1 unit of capital equals the price of 1 unit of other goods and services ($P_K = P$). This was the approach taken implicitly in Chapters 7 and 8, for example. In this case, the steady-state condition says that the marginal product of capital net of depreciation, $MPK - \delta$, equals the real interest rate r.

Since we also know that $\Delta y = MPK\Delta k = (r + \delta)\Delta k$, we can use this relationship to eliminate Δk by substitution. The result, after dividing by y, is

$$\Delta y/y = \frac{-k/y}{1 - \alpha}\Delta r.$$

We can use this equation to illustrate the steady-state "burden" of higher interest rates. Suppose the real interest rate increases permanently by one-half of one percentage point. To see the implications, we substitute $\Delta r = 0.005$ into the equation, along with representative values for the other parameters, $(k/y) = 3$ and $\alpha = 0.33$. The result is

$$\Delta y/y = -2.2 \text{ percent.}$$

This result implies that Canadians lose an amount of material welfare equal to 2.2 percent of GDP *every* year if the interest rate is permanently higher by just one half of one percentage point. As this book goes to press, this loss amounts to $35 billion every year. This *annual* loss represents *a lot* of valuable items, such as hospitals and day-care facilities. It appears that standard macroeconomic analysis supports journalists who refer to even "small" increases in interest rates as a major "burden." ■

Taxes and Investment

Tax laws influence firms' incentives to accumulate capital in many ways. Sometimes policymakers change the tax laws in order to shift the investment function and influence aggregate demand. Here we consider three of the most important provisions of corporate taxation: the corporate profit tax rate itself, depreciation allowances, and the investment tax credit.

The effect of a **corporate profit tax** on investment depends on how the law defines "profit" for the purpose of taxation. Suppose, first, that the law defined profit as we did above—the rental price of capital minus the cost of capital. In this case, even though firms would be sharing a fraction of their profits with the government, it would still be rational for them to invest if the rental price of capital exceeded the cost of capital, and to disinvest if the rental price fell short of the cost of capital. A tax on profit, measured in this way, would not alter investment incentives.

Yet, because of the tax law's definition of profit, the corporate profit tax does affect investment decisions. There are many differences between the law's definition of profit and ours. One major difference is the treatment of depreciation. Our definition of profit deducts the *current* value of depreciation as a cost. That is, it bases depreciation on how much it would cost today to replace worn-out capital. By contrast, under the corporate tax laws, firms deduct depreciation using *historical* cost. That is, the **depreciation allowance** is based on the price of the capital when it was originally purchased. In periods of inflation, true replacement cost is greater than historical cost, so the corporate tax tends to understate the cost of depreciation and overstate profit. As a result, the tax law sees a profit and levies a tax even when economic profit is zero, which makes owning capital less attractive. For this and other reasons, many economists believe that the corporate profit tax discourages investment.

The **investment tax credit** is a tax provision that encourages the accumulation of capital. The investment tax credit reduces a firm's taxes by a certain amount for each dollar spent on capital goods. Because a firm recoups part of its expenditure on new capital in lower taxes, the credit reduces the effective purchase price of a unit of capital P_K. Thus, the investment tax credit reduces the cost of capital and raises investment.

Tax incentives for investment are one tool policymakers can use to control aggregate demand. For example, an increase in the investment tax credit reduces the cost of capital, shifts the investment function outward, and raises aggregate demand. Similarly, a reduction in the tax credit reduces aggregate demand by making investment more costly.

From the mid-1950s to the mid-1970s, the government of Sweden attempted to control aggregate demand by encouraging or discouraging investment. A system called the *investment fund* subsidized investment, much like an investment tax credit, during periods of recession. When government officials decided that economic growth had slowed, they authorized a temporary investment subsidy. When the officials concluded that the economy had recovered sufficiently, they revoked the subsidy. Eventually, however, Sweden abandoned the use of temporary investment subsidies to control the business cycle, and the subsidy became a permanent feature of Swedish tax policy.

Should investment subsidies be used to combat economic fluctuations? Some economists believe that for the two decades it was in effect the Swedish policy reduced the magnitude of the business cycle. Others believe that such a policy could have had unintended and perverse effects: for example, if the economy begins to slow down, firms may anticipate a future subsidy and delay investment, making the slowdown worse. Because the use of countercyclical investment subsidies could either reduce or amplify the size of economic fluctuations, their overall impact on economic performance is hard to evaluate.[2]

CASE STUDY

Canada's Experience With Corporate Tax Concessions

Capital goods typically wear out at a slower rate than that assumed by the tax laws. Firms would like governments to think that all capital goods completely wear out during the purchase year, so that they can claim the entire cost of the machine as a *current* expense. By reducing *reported* profits that first year, tax obligations are less.

---

[2] John B. Taylor, "The Swedish Investment Funds System as a Stabilization Rule," *Brookings Papers on Economic Activity* (1982:1): 57–106.

Of course in later years, because firms have already claimed the full expense for the machine, *reported* profits (and therefore tax obligations) are then larger. But a tax saving today is worth more than one in the future, and firms are happy to accept an interest-free loan from governments whenever they can.

The corporate tax laws define how rapidly machinery wears out for tax purposes. For example, in the manufacturing and processing sector, depreciation allowances have allowed one-half the machinery expense to be claimed in each of the first two years following its purchase. As far as generating a tax deduction, the present value of each dollar spent on investment is

$$v = 0.5 + \frac{0.5}{1 + r},$$

where r is the rate of interest. With an interest rate of 8 percent, for example, this formula implies that v is 0.963.

The Canadian legislation is almost as generous as the tax law can be. The maximum possible value for v is 1, and this occurs if firms are allowed to claim the entire cost of the machinery in the first year. A less generous depreciation allowance makes v lower. For example, if, for tax purposes, machinery is deemed to wear out over five years, the formula for v is

$$v = 0.2 + \frac{0.2}{1 + r} + \frac{0.2}{(1 + r)^2} + \frac{0.2}{(1 + r)^3} + \frac{0.2}{(1 + r)^4},$$

and, for the assumed 8 percent interest rate, v is 0.86. The federal government has opted for generous depreciation allowances in an attempt to stimulate investment expenditures.

Another initiative of the government is to reduce the corporate income tax rate itself. But this policy has often proven to be a very inefficient way to stimulate investment spending. We can understand why by noting that a lower tax rate brings both a benefit *and* a cost to firms. If it were not for the allowed deductions for depreciation, a 10-percent cut in the corporate tax rate would lower tax obligations by 10 percent. But a lower tax rate means that smaller deductions can be claimed. The loss in deduction equals v times 10 percent.

With v *almost* unity in Canada, it makes *almost* no sense to cut the corporate tax rate. The benefit and the cost to firms change by almost the same amount, so the incentive for firms to invest is hardly increased at all—despite a major revenue loss for the government. Thus introducing accelerated depreciation allowances (raising v) can stimulate investment spending, but once this has been done, the rationale for cutting the tax rate itself is reduced.

This discussion pertains to Canadian-owned firms. The case against using corporate tax concessions as a means of stimulating investment spending is even stronger in the case of foreign-owned firms. Firms that are subsidiaries of multinationals based in other countries get to deduct all taxes paid in Canada when calculating corporate taxes in their home countries (up to an amount equal to what they would have paid in their home country). In this case, the corporate tax concession in Canada does not lower the rental cost of capital. These tax concessions simply transfer revenue to foreign governments, and so they have no effect on investment. ■

The Stock Market and Tobin's *q*

Many economists see a link between fluctuations in investment and fluctuations in the stock market. The term **stock** refers to the shares in the ownership of corporations, and the **stock market** is the market in which these shares are traded. Stock prices tend to be high when firms have many opportunities for profitable investment, since these profit opportunities mean higher future income for the shareholders. Thus, stock prices reflect the incentives to invest.

The Nobel-Prize-winning economist James Tobin proposed that firms base their investment decisions on the following ratio, which is now called **Tobin's *q*:**

$$q = \frac{\text{Market Value of Installed Capital}}{\text{Replacement Cost of Installed Capital}}.$$

The numerator of Tobin's *q* is the value of the economy's capital as determined by the stock market. The denominator is the price of the capital if it were purchased today.

Tobin reasoned that net investment should depend on whether *q* is greater or less than 1. If *q* is greater than 1, then the stock market values installed capital at more than its replacement cost. In this case, managers can raise the market value of their firms' stock by buying more capital. Conversely, if *q* is less than 1, the stock market values capital at less than its replacement cost. In this case, managers will not replace capital as it wears out.

Although at first the *q* theory of investment may appear quite different from the neoclassical model developed above, in fact the two theories are closely related. To see the relationship, note that Tobin's *q* depends on current and future expected profits from installed capital. If the marginal product of capital exceeds the cost of capital, then firms are earning profit on their installed capital. These profits make the rental firms desirable to own, which raises the market value of these firms' stock, implying a high value of *q*. Similarly, if the marginal product of capital falls short of the cost of capital, then firms are incurring losses on their installed capital, implying a low market value and a low value of *q*.

Formally, the *q* theory and the neoclassical model can be related as follows. The owners of capital receive the *MPK* for each unit of capital every year forever. Assuming, for simplicity, that capital's marginal product is expected to stay constant in the future, the present value of that stream of receipts in nominal terms is

$$P(MPK)(x + x^2 + \cdots),$$

where

$$x = \frac{1}{1 + r + \delta}.$$

Since $(x + x^2 + \cdots)$ equals $[(1 + x + x^2 + \cdots) - 1]$, and since we learned in Chapter 10 that the geometric series $(1 + x + x^2 + \cdots)$ equals $[(1/1 - x)]$, we can simplify the present value of receipts expression to

$$\frac{P(MPK)}{r + \delta}$$

for each unit of capital. The discount factor, $(r + \delta)$, involves the rate at which interest is forgone by tying up funds in the ownership of capital, r, and the rate at which capital is wearing out, δ. Buyers and sellers in the stock market should recognize that this present value is what an owner of the stock receives. Thus, this present value, when multiplied by the total quantity of capital, is the market value of the existing capital stock. q is the ratio of this market value to the purchase cost of capital $P_K K$. Thus, q is

$$\frac{MPK}{(P_K/P)\,(r + \delta)},$$

and $q > 1$ implies that capital's marginal product exceeds its rental cost, so investment is profitable.

Finally, the investment function can be derived more formally by specifying that firms minimize the following cost function:

$$(K_t - K_t^*)^2 + \theta(K_t - K_{t-1})^2,$$

where K and K^* denote the actual and desired levels of the capital stock and the subscripts indicate time periods. Firms incur costs when the capital stock is not at its desired value (when K differs from K^*), and they incur disruption costs whenever they adjust their holdings of capital (when the current value of K differs from its value in the previous time period). The two terms in the cost function capture these two considerations. The quadratic form is the simplest function that does so, and parameter θ represents the relative importance of the adjustment costs.

With both the long-run desired level of capital and the preexisting level of capital given at each point in time, firms minimize costs by differentiating the cost function with respect to K_t and setting the result equal to zero. The result is

$$(K_t - K_{t-1}) = \gamma(K_t^* - K_{t-1})$$

where $\gamma = 1/(1 + \theta)$, or more simply,

$$\Delta K = \gamma(K^* - K)$$

or

$$\Delta K/K = \gamma[(K^*/K) - 1].$$

Since γ is a fraction, this investment function involves net investment closing a fraction of the gap between the desired and the actual capital stock each period. And we have just learned that the (K^*/K) ratio exceeds unity whenever the rental price of capital exceeds the cost of capital—that is, when Tobin's q exceeds one.

The advantage of Tobin's q as a measure of the incentive to invest is that it reflects the *expected future* profitability of capital as well as the current profitability. For example, suppose that the federal government legislates a reduction in the corporate profit tax beginning next year. This expected fall in the corporate tax means greater profits for the owners of capital. These higher expected profits raise the value of stock today, raise Tobin's q, and therefore encourage investment today. Thus, Tobin's q theory of investment emphasizes that investment decisions depend not only on current economic policies, but also on policies expected to prevail in the future.[3]

Keynes argued that firm managers and households that buy the firm's stocks have quite volatile expectations. This fact is reflected in Tobin's q rising and falling fairly dramatically over time. According to the theory, investment spending should be a very volatile component of aggregate demand—and it is. Keynes emphasized this fact by arguing that investment is as much a function of people's waves of optimism and pessimism (what he called their "animal spirits") as it is a function of the interest rate. It is reassuring that, according to the q theory, both are important influences on investment.

CASE STUDY

The Stock Market as an Economic Indicator

"The stock market has predicted nine out of the last five recessions." So goes Paul Samuelson's famous quip about the stock market's reliability as an economic indicator. The stock market is in fact quite volatile, and it can give false signals about the future of the economy. Yet one should not ignore the link between the stock market and the economy. Figure 18-4 shows that changes in the stock market often reflect changes in real GDP.

Why do stock prices and economic activity tend to fluctuate together? One reason is given by Tobin's q theory, together with the model of aggregate demand and aggregate supply. Suppose, for instance, that you observe a fall in stock prices. Because the replacement cost of capital is fairly stable, a fall in the stock market is usually associated with a fall in Tobin's q. A fall in q reflects investors' pessimism about the current or future profitability of capital. This means that the investment function has shifted inward: investment is lower at any given interest rate. As a result, the aggregate demand for goods and services contracts, leading to lower output and employment.

There are two additional reasons why stock prices are associated with economic activity. First, because stock is part of household wealth, a fall in stock prices makes people poorer and thus depresses consumer spending, which also reduces aggregate demand. Second, a fall in stock prices might reflect bad news about technological progress and long-run economic growth. If so, this means that the natural level of output—and thus aggregate supply—will be growing more slowly in the future than was previously expected.

---

[3] To read more about the relationship between the neoclassical model of investment and q theory, see Fumio Hayashi, "Tobin's Marginal q and Average q: A Neoclassical Approach," *Econometrica* 50 (January 1982): 213–224; and Lawrence H. Summers, "Taxation and Corporate Investment: A q-theory Approach," *Brookings Papers on Economic Activity* (1981:1): 67–140.

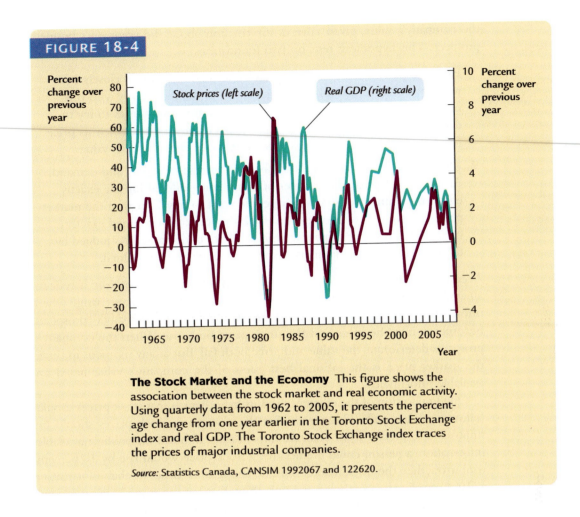

FIGURE 18-4

The Stock Market and the Economy This figure shows the association between the stock market and real economic activity. Using quarterly data from 1962 to 2005, it presents the percentage change from one year earlier in the Toronto Stock Exchange index and real GDP. The Toronto Stock Exchange index traces the prices of major industrial companies.

Source: Statistics Canada, CANSIM 1992067 and 122620.

These links between the stock market and the economy are not lost on policy-makers, such as those at the Bank of Canada. Indeed, because the stock market often anticipates changes in real GDP, and because data on the stock market are available more quickly than data on GDP, the stock market is a closely watched economic indicator. A case in point is the deep economic downturn in 2008 and 2009: the substantial declines in production and employment were preceded by a steep decline in stock prices. ■

Alternative Views of the Stock Market: The Efficient Markets Hypothesis Versus Keynes's Beauty Contest

One continuing source of debate among economists is whether stock market fluctuations are rational.

Some economists subscribe to the **efficient markets hypothesis,** according to which the market price of a company's stock is the fully rational valuation of the company's value, given current information about the company's business prospects. This hypothesis rests on two foundations:

1. Each company listed on a major stock exchange is followed closely by many professional portfolio managers, such as the individuals who run mutual funds. Every day, these managers monitor news stories to try to determine the company's value. Their job is to buy a stock when its price falls below its value and to sell it when its price rises above its value.

2. The price of each stock is set by the equilibrium of supply and demand. At the market price, the number of shares being offered for sale exactly equals the number of shares that people want to buy. That is, at the market price, the number of people who think the stock is overvalued exactly balances the number of people who think it's undervalued. As judged by the typical person in the market, the stock must be fairly valued.

According to this theory, the stock market is *informationally efficient*: it reflects all available information about the value of the asset. Stock prices change when information changes. When good news about the company's prospects becomes public, the value and the stock price both rise. When the company's prospects deteriorate, the value and price both fall. But at any moment in time, the market price is the rational best guess of the company's value based on available information.

One implication of the efficient markets hypothesis is that stock prices should follow a *random walk*. This means that the changes in stock prices should be impossible to predict from available information. If, based on publicly available information, a person could predict that a stock price would rise by 10 percent tomorrow, then the stock market must be failing to incorporate that information today. According to this theory, the only thing that can move stock prices is news that changes the market's perception of the company's value. But such news must be unpredictable—otherwise, it wouldn't really be news. For the same reason, changes in stock prices should be unpredictable as well.

What is the evidence for the efficient markets hypothesis? Its proponents point out that it is hard to beat the market by buying allegedly undervalued stocks and selling allegedly overvalued stocks. Statistical tests show that stock prices are random walks, or at least approximately so. Moreover, index funds, which buy stocks from all companies in a stock market index, outperform most actively managed mutual funds run by professional money managers.

Although the efficient markets hypothesis has many proponents, some economists are less convinced that the stock market is so rational. These economists point out that many movements in stock prices are hard to attribute to news. They suggest that, when buying and selling, stock investors are less focused on companies' fundamental values than on what they expect other investors will later pay.

John Maynard Keynes proposed a famous analogy to explain stock market speculation. In his day, some newspapers held beauty contests in which the paper printed the picture of 100 women and readers were invited to submit a list of the five most beautiful. A prize went to the reader whose choices most closely matched those of the consensus of the other entrants. A naïve entrant would have simply picked the five most beautiful women. But a slightly more sophisticated strategy would have been to guess the five women that other people considered the most beautiful. Other people, however, were likely thinking along the same lines. So an even more sophisticated strategy would have been to try to guess what other people thought other people thought were the most beautiful women. And so on. In the end of the process, judging true beauty would be less important to winning the contest than guessing other people's opinions of other people's opinions.

Similarly, Keynes reasoned that, because stock market investors will eventually sell their shares to others, they were more concerned about other people's valuation of a company than the company's true worth. The best stock investors, in his view, were those who were good at outguessing mass psychology. He believed that movements in stock prices often reflect irrational waves of optimism and pessimism (the "animal spirits") of investors.

The two views of the stock market persist to this day. Some economists see the stock market through the lens of the efficient markets hypothesis. They believe fluctuations in stock prices are a rational reflection of changes in underlying economic fundamentals. Other economists, however, take Keynes's beauty contest as a metaphor for stock speculation. In their view, the stock market often fluctuates for no good reason, and because it influences the aggregate demand for goods and services, these fluctuations are a source of short-run economic fluctuations.[4]

Financing Constraints

When a firm wants to invest in new capital, say by building a new factory, it often raises the necessary funds in financial markets. This financing may take several forms: obtaining loans from banks, selling bonds to the public, or selling shares in future profits on the stock market. The neoclassical model assumes that if a firm is willing to pay the cost of capital, the financial markets will make the funds available.

Yet sometimes firms face **financing constraints**—limits on the amount they can raise in financial markets. Financing constraints can prevent firms from undertaking profitable investments. When a firm is unable to raise funds in financial markets, the amount it can spend on new capital goods is limited to the amount it is currently earning. Financing constraints influence the investment behaviour of firms just as borrowing constraints influence the consumption behaviour of households. Borrowing constraints cause households to determine their consumption on the basis of current rather than permanent

---

[4] A classic reference on the efficient markets hypothesis is Eugene Fama, "Efficient Capital Markets: A Review of Theory and Empirical Work," *Journal of Finance* 25 (1970): 383–417. For the alternative view, see Robert J. Shiller, "From Efficient Markets Theory to Behavioral Finance," *Journal of Economic Perspectives* 17 (Winter 2003): 83–104.

income; financing constraints cause firms to determine their investment on the basis of their current cash flow rather than expected profitability.

To see the impact of financing constraints, consider the effect of a short recession on investment spending. A recession reduces employment, the rental price of capital, and profits. If firms expect the recession to be short-lived, however, they will want to continue investing, knowing that their investments will be profitable in the future. That is, a short recession will have only a small effect on Tobin's q. For firms that can raise funds in financial markets, the recession should have only a small effect on investment.

Quite the opposite is true for firms that face financing constraints. The fall in current profits restricts the amount that these firms can spend on new capital goods and may prevent them from making profitable investments. Thus, financing constraints make investment more sensitive to current economic conditions.[5]

Banking Crises and Credit Crunches

Throughout economic history, problems in the banking system have often coincided with downturns in economic activity. This was true, for instance, during the Great Depression of the 1930s (which we discussed in Chapter 11). Soon after the Depression's onset, many banks in the United States found themselves insolvent, as the value of their assets fell below the value of their liabilities. These banks were, therefore, forced to suspend operations. Many economists believe the widespread bank failures in the United States during this period help explain the Depression's depth and persistence.

Similar patterns, although less severe, can be observed more recently. Problems in the banking system were also part of a slump in Japan and of the financial crises in Indonesia and other Asian economies (as we saw in Chapter 12). More recently, in the United States, the recession of 2008–2009 came on the heels of a widespread financial crisis that began with a downturn in the housing market (as we discussed in Chapter 11).

Why are banking crises so often at the center of economic downturns? Banks have an important role in the economy because they allocate financial resources to their most productive uses: they serve as *intermediaries* between those people who have income they want to save and those people who have profitable investment projects but need to borrow the funds to invest. When banks become insolvent or nearly so, they are less able to serve this function. Financing constraints become more prevalent, and some investors are forced to forgo some potentially profitable investment projects. Such an increase in financing constraints is sometimes called a *credit crunch*.

---

[5] For empirical work supporting the importance of these financing constraints, see Steven M. Fazzari, R. Glenn Hubbard, and Bruce C. Petersen, "Financing Constraints and Corporate Investment," *Brookings Papers on Economic Activity* (1988:1): 141–195.

We can use the *IS–LM* model to interpret the short-run effects of a credit crunch. When some would-be investors are denied credit, the demand for investment goods falls at every interest rate. The result is a contractionary shift in the *IS* curve, which in turn leads to a fall in aggregate demand and reduced production and employment. The long-run effects of a credit crunch are best understood from the perspective of growth theory, with its emphasis on capital accumulation as a source of growth. When a credit crunch prevents some firms from investing, the financial markets fail to allocate national saving to its best use. Less productive investment projects may take the place of more productive projects, reducing the economy's potential for producing goods and services.

Because of these effects, central bankers are always trying to monitor the health of the nation's banking system. Their goal is to avert banking crises and credit crunches and, when they do occur, to respond as quickly as possible to minimize the resulting disruption to the economy. That job is not easy, as the financial crisis and economic downturn of 2008–2009 illustrates. In this case, as we discussed in Chapter 11, many banks had made large bets on the housing markets through their purchases of mortgage-backed securities. When those bets turned bad, many banks found themselves insolvent or nearly so, and bank loans became hard to come by. Bank regulators at the Federal Reserve and other U.S. government agencies, like many of the bankers themselves, were caught off guard by the magnitude of the losses and the resulting precariousness of the banking system. What kind of regulatory changes will be needed to try to reduce of likelihood of future banking crises remains a topic of active debate.

18-2 Residential Investment

In this section we consider the determinants of residential investment. We begin by presenting a simple model of the housing market. Residential investment includes the purchase of new housing both by people who plan to live in it themselves and by landlords who plan to rent it to others. To keep things simple, however, it is useful to imagine that all housing is owner-occupied.

The Stock Equilibrium and the Flow Supply

There are two parts to the model. First, the market for the existing stock of houses determines the equilibrium housing price. Second, the housing price determines the flow of residential investment.

Panel (a) of Figure 18-5 shows how the relative price of housing P_H/P is determined by the supply and demand for the existing stock of houses. At any point in time, the supply of houses is fixed. We represent this stock with a vertical supply curve. The demand curve for houses slopes downward, because high prices cause people to live in smaller houses, to share residences, or sometimes even to become homeless. The price of housing adjusts to equilibrate supply and demand.

FIGURE 18-5

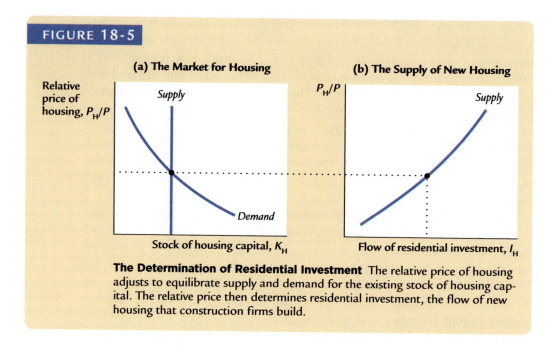

(a) The Market for Housing

Relative price of housing, P_H/P

Supply

Demand

Stock of housing capital, K_H

(b) The Supply of New Housing

P_H/P

Supply

Flow of residential investment, I_H

The Determination of Residential Investment The relative price of housing adjusts to equilibrate supply and demand for the existing stock of housing capital. The relative price then determines residential investment, the flow of new housing that construction firms build.

Panel (b) of Figure 18-5 shows how the relative price of housing determines the supply of new houses. Construction firms buy materials and hire labour to build houses, and then sell the houses at the market price. Their costs depend on the overall price level P (which reflects the cost of wood, bricks, plaster, etc.), and their revenue depends on the price of houses P_H. The higher the relative price of housing, the greater the incentive to build houses, and the more houses are built. The flow of new houses—residential investment—therefore depends on the equilibrium price set in the market for existing houses.

This model of residential investment is similar to the q theory of business fixed investment. According to q theory, business fixed investment depends on the market price of installed capital relative to its replacement cost; this relative price, in turn, depends on the expected profits from owning installed capital. According to this model of the housing market, residential investment depends on the relative price of housing. The relative price of housing, in turn, depends on the demand for housing, which depends on the imputed rent that individuals expect to receive from their housing. Hence, the relative price of housing plays much the same role for residential investment as Tobin's q does for business fixed investment.

Changes in Housing Demand

When the demand for housing shifts, the equilibrium price of housing changes, and this change in turn affects residential investment. The demand curve for housing can shift for various reasons. An economic boom raises national income and therefore the demand for housing. A large increase in the population, perhaps because of immigration, also raises the demand for housing. Panel (a) of Figure 18-6 shows

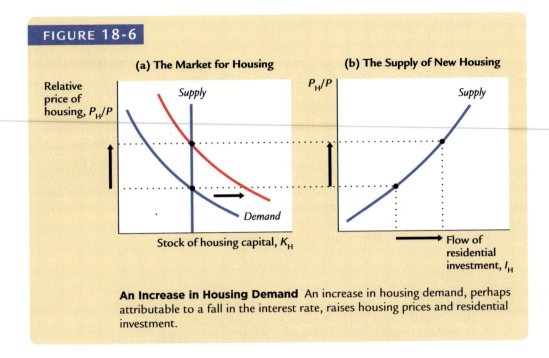

FIGURE 18-6

(a) The Market for Housing

Relative
price of
housing, P_H/P

Supply

Demand

Stock of housing capital, K_H

(b) The Supply of New Housing

P_H/P

Supply

Flow of
residential
investment, I_H

An Increase in Housing Demand An increase in housing demand, perhaps attributable to a fall in the interest rate, raises housing prices and residential investment.

that an expansionary shift in demand raises the equilibrium price. Panel (b) shows that the increase in the housing price increases residential investment.

One important determinant of housing demand is the real interest rate. Many people take out loans—mortgages—to buy their homes; the interest rate is the cost of the loan. Even the few people who do not have to borrow to purchase a home will respond to the interest rate, because the interest rate is the opportunity cost of holding their wealth in housing rather than putting it in a bank. A reduction in the interest rate therefore raises housing demand, housing prices, and residential investment.

Another important determinant of housing demand is credit availability. When it is easy to get a loan, more households buy their own homes, and they buy larger ones than they otherwise might, thus increasing the demand for housing. When credit conditions become tight, fewer people buy their own homes or trade up to larger ones, and the demand for housing falls.

An example of this phenomenon occurred during the first decade of the 2000s in the United States. Early in this decade, interest rates were low, and mortgages were easy to obtain. Many households with questionable credit histories—called *subprime* borrowers—were able to get mortgages with small down payments. Not surprisingly, the housing market boomed. Housing prices rose, and residential investment was strong. A few years later, however, it became clear that the situation had gotten out of hand, because many of these subprime borrowers could not keep making their mortgage payments. When interest rates rose and credit conditions tightened, housing demand and housing prices fell dramatically. When the housing market turned down in 2007 and 2008, the result was a significant downturn in the overall economy, which was discussed in a Case Study in Chapter 11.

What Price House Can You Afford?

When someone takes out a mortgage to buy a house in Canada, the bank often places a ceiling on the size of the loan. That ceiling depends on the person's income and the market interest rate. A typical bank requirement is that the monthly mortgage payment—including both interest and repayment of principal—not exceed 30 percent of the borrower's monthly income.

Table 18-1 shows how the interest rate affects monthly payments on a $100,000 25-year mortgage, and how the interest rate affects the minimum annual income that is required before banks will grant a mortgage.

As you can see, small changes in the interest rate can have a large influence on who can buy a home. For example, an increase in the interest rate from 5 percent to 7 percent raises the monthly payment on a typical mortgage by 20 percent. It also cuts out of the mortgage market all families in the $23,280–$28,000 income range. An increase in the interest rate therefore reduces housing demand, which in turn depresses housing prices and residential investment.

TABLE 18-1

How High Interest Rates Reduce Mortgage Eligibility and Housing Demand for a 25-year $100,000 Mortgage

Interest Rate	Monthly Payment	Annual Income Required
5%	$582	$23,280
6	640	25,600
7	700	28,000
8	763	30,520
9	828	33,120
10	894	35,760
11	963	38,520
12	1,032	41,280

The Tax Treatment of Housing

Just as the tax laws affect the accumulation of business fixed investment, they also affect the accumulation of residential investment. In this case, however, their effects are nearly the opposite. Rather than discouraging investment, as the corporate profit tax does for businesses, the personal income tax encourages households to invest in housing.

One can view a homeowner as a landlord with himself as a tenant. But he is a landlord with a special tax treatment. The Canadian personal income-tax system does not require him to pay tax on the imputed rental income (the rent he "pays" himself). Nor does he have to pay any capital gains tax when the value of his home increases. Many economists have criticized the tax treatment of home-ownership. They believe that, because of this subsidy, Canada invests too much in housing compared to other forms of capital.

18-3 Inventory Investment

Inventory investment—the goods that businesses put aside in storage—is at the same time negligible and of great significance. It is one of the smallest components of spending, averaging about 1 percent of GDP. Yet its remarkable volatility makes it central to the study of economic fluctuations. In recessions, firms stop replenishing their inventory as goods are sold, and inventory investment becomes negative. In a typical recession, more than half the fall in spending can come from a decline in inventory investment.

Reasons for Holding Inventories

Inventories serve many purposes. Before presenting a model to explain fluctuations in inventory investment, let's discuss some of the motives firms have for holding inventories.

One use of inventories is to smooth the level of production over time. Consider a firm that experiences temporary booms and busts in sales. Rather than adjusting production to match the fluctuations in sales, the firm may find it cheaper to produce goods at a steady rate. When sales are low, the firm produces more than it sells and puts the extra goods into inventory. When sales are high, the firm produces less than it sells and takes goods out of inventory. This motive for holding inventories is called **production smoothing.**

A second reason for holding inventories is that they may allow a firm to operate more efficiently. Retail stores, for example, can sell merchandise more effectively if they have goods on hand to show to customers. Manufacturing firms keep inventories of spare parts to reduce the time that the assembly line is shut down when a machine breaks. In some ways, we can view **inventories as a factor of production:** the larger the stock of inventories a firm holds, the more output it can produce.

A third reason for holding inventories is to avoid running out of goods when sales are unexpectedly high. Firms often have to make production decisions before knowing the level of customer demand. For example, a publisher must decide how many copies of a new book to print before knowing whether the book will be popular. If demand exceeds production and there are no inventories, the good will be out of stock for a period, and the firm will lose sales and profit. Inventories can prevent this from happening. This motive for holding inventories is called **stock-out avoidance.**

A fourth explanation of inventories is dictated by the production process. Many goods require a number of steps in production and, therefore, take time to produce. When a product is only partly completed, its components are counted as part of a firm's inventory. These inventories are called **work in process.**

The Accelerator Model of Inventories

Because there are many motives for holding inventories, there are many models of inventory investment. One simple model that explains the data well, without endorsing a particular motive, is the **accelerator model.** This model was developed about sixty years ago, and it is sometimes applied to all types of investment. Here we apply it to the type for which it works best—inventory investment.

The accelerator model of inventories assumes that firms hold a stock of inventories that is proportional to the firms' level of output. There are various reasons for this assumption. When output is high, manufacturing firms need more materials and supplies on hand, and they have more goods in the process of being completed. When the economy is booming, retail firms want to have more merchandise on the shelves to show customers. Thus, if N is the economy's stock of inventories and Y is output, then

$$N = \beta Y,$$

where β is a parameter reflecting how much inventory firms wish to hold as a proportion of output.

Inventory investment I is the change in the stock of inventories ΔN. Therefore,

$$I = \Delta N = \beta \Delta Y.$$

The accelerator model predicts that inventory investment is proportional to the change in output. When output rises, firms want to hold a larger stock of inventory, so inventory investment is high. When output falls, firms want to hold a smaller stock of inventory, so they allow their inventory to run down, and inventory investment is negative.

We can now see how the model earned its name. Because the variable Y is the rate at which firms are producing goods, ΔY is the "acceleration" of production. The model says that inventory investment depends on whether the economy is speeding up or slowing down.

The accelerator mechanism is one of the reasons that business cycles develop momentum and are therefore so difficult to control. We can appreciate this fact by considering the following scenario and applying the accelerator to all components of investment. Suppose that the economy is at its natural level and that a loss in export sales then reduces GDP and causes a recession. The fact that output has fallen (ΔY is negative) means that investment falls. This makes the recession more severe. Then, when the economy is recovering (ΔY is positive), investment rises. This fact forces the economy to overshoot the natural level (since ΔY is positive at that point, and that keeps investment high). As time proceeds, the (positive) changes in output get smaller, and this pushes investment lower. The fall-off in investment is what causes the next recession. Thus, it is quite likely that a *onetime* shock like a drop in export sales can set in motion a whole series of overshoots—an *ongoing* business cycle—because of the accelerator mechanism.

How the Real Interest Rate and Credit Conditions Affect Inventory Investment

Like other components of investment, inventory investment depends on the real interest rate. When a firm holds a good in inventory and sells it tomorrow rather than selling it today, it gives up the interest it could have earned between today and tomorrow. Thus, the real interest rate measures the opportunity cost of holding inventories.

When the real interest rate rises, holding inventories becomes more costly, so rational firms try to reduce their stock. Therefore, an increase in the real interest rate depresses inventory investment. For example, in the 1980s many firms adopted "just-in-time" production plans, which were designed to reduce the amount of inventory by producing goods just before sale. The high real interest rates that prevailed during most of this decade are one possible explanation for this change in business strategy.

Inventory investment also depends on credit conditions. Because many firms rely on bank loans to finance their purchases of inventories, they cut back when these loans are hard to come by. During the credit crisis of 2008, for example, firms reduced their inventory holdings substantially. As in many economic downturns, the decline in inventory investment was a key part of the overall decline in aggregate demand.

18-4 Conclusion

The purpose of this chapter has been to examine the determinants of investment in more detail. Looking back on the various models of investment, we can see three themes.

First, all types of investment spending are inversely related to the real interest rate. A higher interest rate raises the cost of capital to firms that invest in plant and equipment, raises the cost of borrowing to home buyers, and raises the cost of holding inventories. Thus, the models of investment developed here justify the investment function we have used throughout this book.

Second, there are various causes of shifts in the investment function. An improvement in the available technology raises the marginal product of capital and raises business fixed investment. An increase in the population raises the demand for housing and raises residential investment. Finally, various economic policies, such as changes in the investment tax credit and the corporate profit tax, alter the incentives to invest and thus shift the investment function.

Third, it is natural to expect investment to be volatile over the business cycle, because investment spending depends on the output of the economy as well as on the interest rate. In the neoclassical model of business fixed investment, higher employment raises the marginal product of capital and the incentive to invest. Higher output also raises firms' profits and, thereby, relaxes the financing constraints that some firms face. In addition, higher income raises the demand for houses, in turn raising housing prices and residential investment. Higher output raises the stock of inventories firms wish to hold, stimulating inventory investment. Our models predict that an economic boom should stimulate investment and a recession should depress it. This is exactly what we observe.

Summary

1. The marginal product of capital determines the real rental price of capital. The real interest rate, the depreciation rate, and the relative price of capital goods determine the cost of capital. According to the neoclassical model, firms invest if the rental price is greater than the cost of capital, and they disinvest if the rental price is less than the cost of capital.

2. Various parts of the corporate profit tax system influence the incentive to invest. The tax itself discourages investment, while generous depreciation allowances and the investment tax credits encourage it.

3. An alternative way of expressing the neoclassical model is to state that investment depends on Tobin's q, the ratio of the market value of installed capital to its replacement cost. This ratio reflects the current and expected future profitability of capital. The higher is q, the greater is the market value of installed capital relative to its replacement cost, and the greater is the incentive to invest.

4. Economists debate whether fluctuations in the stock market are a rational reflection of companies' true value or are driven by irrational waves of optimism and pessimism.

5. In contrast to the assumption of the neoclassical model, firms cannot always raise funds to finance investment. Financing constraints make investment sensitive to firms' current cash flow.

6. Residential investment depends on the relative price of housing. Housing prices in turn depend on the demand for housing and the current fixed supply. An increase in housing demand, perhaps attributable to a fall in the interest rate, raises housing prices and residential investment.

7. Firms have various motives for holding inventories of goods: smoothing production, using them as a factor of production, avoiding stock-outs, and storing work in process. How much inventories firms hold depends on the real interest rate and on credit conditions. One model of inventory investment that works well without endorsing a particular motive is the accelerator model. According to this model, the stock of inventories depends on the level of GDP, and inventory investment depends on the change in GDP.

KEY CONCEPTS

Business fixed investment	Depreciation	Depreciation allowance
Residential investment	Real cost of capital	Investment tax credit
Inventory investment	Net investment	Stock
Neoclassical model of investment	Corporate profit tax	Stock market

Tobin's q

Efficient markets hypothesis

Financing constraints

Production smoothing

Inventories as a factor of production

Stock-out avoidance

Work in process

Accelerator model

QUESTIONS FOR REVIEW

1. In the neoclassical model of business fixed investment, under what conditions will firms find it profitable to add to their capital stock?

2. What is Tobin's q, and what does it have to do with investment?

3. Explain why an increase in the interest rate reduces the amount of residential investment.

4. List four reasons firms might hold inventories.

PROBLEMS AND APPLICATIONS

1. Use the neoclassical model of investment to explain the impact of each of the following on the rental price of capital, the cost of capital, and investment:

   a. Anti-inflationary monetary policy raises the real interest rate.

   b. An earthquake destroys part of the capital stock.

   c. Immigration of foreign workers increases the size of the labour force.

2. Suppose that the government levies a tax on oil companies equal to a proportion of the value of the company's oil reserves. (The government assures the firms that the tax is for one time only.) According to the neoclassical model, what effect will the tax have on business fixed investment by these firms? What if these firms face financing constraints?

3. The *IS–LM* model developed in Chapters 10 and 11 assumes that investment depends only on the interest rate. Yet our theories of investment suggest that investment might also depend on national income: higher income might induce firms to invest more.

   a. Explain why investment might depend on national income.

   b. Suppose that investment is determined by

   $$I = \bar{I} + aY,$$

   where a is a constant between zero and one, which measures the influence of national income on investment. With investment set this way, what are the fiscal-policy multipliers in the Keynesian-cross model? Explain.

   c. Suppose that investment depends on both income and the interest rate. That is, the investment function is

   $$I = \bar{I} + aY - br,$$

   where a is a constant between zero and one, which measures the influence of national income on investment, and b is a constant greater than zero, which measures the influence of the interest rate on investment. Use the *IS–LM* model to consider the short-run impact of an increase in government purchases on national income Y, the interest rate r, consumption C, and investment I. How might this investment function alter the conclusions implied by the basic *IS–LM* model?

4. When the stock market crashes, as it did in October 1929 and October 1987, what influence does it have on investment, consumption, and aggregate demand? Why? How should the Bank of Canada respond? Why?

5. It is an election year, and the economy is in a recession. The opposition candidate campaigns on a platform of passing an investment tax

credit, which would be effective next year after she takes office. What impact does this campaign promise have on economic conditions during the current year?

6. Canada experienced a large increase in the number of births in the 1950s. People in this baby-boom generation reached adulthood and started forming their own households in the 1970s.

a. Use the model of residential investment to predict the impact of this event on housing prices and residential investment.

b. For the years 1970 and 1980, compute the real price of housing, measured as the residential investment deflator divided by the GDP deflator. What do you find? Is this finding consistent with the model? (Hint: A good source of data is the Canadian Economic Observer, published monthly by Statistics Canada and available in the Government Documents section of your university library. Alternatively, you can consult Statistics Canada via the internet, as explained in the preface of this book.)

7. Canadian tax laws encourage investment in housing and discourage investment in business capital. What are the long-run effects of this policy? (*Hint:* Think about the labour market.)

CHAPTER **19**

Money Supply and Money Demand

There have been three great inventions since the beginning of time: fire, the wheel, and central banking.

— *Will Rogers*

The supply and demand for money are crucial to many issues in macro-economics. In Chapter 4, we discussed how economists use the term "money," how the central bank controls the quantity of money, and how monetary policy affects prices and interest rates in the long run when prices are flexible. In Chapters 10 and 11, we saw that the money market is a key element of the *IS–LM* model, which describes the economy in the short run when prices are sticky.

This chapter examines money supply and money demand more closely. In Section 19-1 we see that the banking system plays a key role in determining the money supply, and we discuss various policy instruments that the Bank of Canada can use to influence the banking system and alter the money supply. We also discuss some of the regulatory problems that central banks confront— an issue that rose in prominence during the financial crisis and economic downturn of 2008 and 2009. In Section 19-2 we consider the motives behind money demand, and we analyze the household's decision about how much money to hold. We also discuss how recent changes in the financial system have blurred the distinction between money and other assets and how this development complicates the conduct of monetary policy.

19-1 Money Supply

Chapter 4 introduced the concept of "money supply" in a highly simplified manner. In that chapter we defined the quantity of money as the number of dollars held by the public, and we assumed that the Bank of Canada controls the supply of money by increasing or decreasing the number of dollars in circulation through open-market operations. Although this explanation is a good first

633

approximation, it is incomplete, for it omits the role of the banking system in determining the money supply. We now present a more complete explanation.

In this section we see that the money supply is determined not only by Bank of Canada policy, but also by the behaviour of households that hold money and of banks in which money is held. We begin by recalling that the money supply includes both currency in the hands of the public and deposits at banks that households can use on demand for transactions. That is, letting M denote the money supply, C currency, and D deposits, we can write

$$\text{Money Supply} = \text{Currency} + \text{Deposits}$$
$$M = C + D.$$

To understand the money supply, we must understand the interaction between currency and deposits and how Bank of Canada policy influences these two components of the money supply.

100-Percent-Reserve Banking

We begin by imagining a world without banks. In such a world, all money takes the form of currency, and the quantity of money is simply the amount of currency that the public holds. For this discussion, suppose that there is $1,000 of currency in the economy.

Now introduce banks. At first, suppose that banks accept deposits but do not make loans. The only purpose of the banks is to provide a safe place for depositors to keep their money.

The deposits that banks have received but have not lent out are called **reserves.** Some reserves are held in the vaults of local banks throughout the country, but most are held at a central bank, such as the Bank of Canada. In our hypothetical economy, all deposits are held as reserves: banks simply accept deposits, place the money in reserve, and leave the money there until the depositor makes a withdrawal or writes a cheque against the balance. This system is called **100-percent-reserve banking.**

Suppose that households deposit the economy's entire $1,000 in Firstbank. Firstbank's **balance sheet**—its accounting statement of assets and liabilities—looks like this:

Firstbank's Balance Sheet

Assets		Liabilities	
Reserves	1,000	Deposits	1,000

The bank's assets are the $1,000 it holds as reserves; the bank's liabilities are the $1,000 it owes to depositors. Unlike banks in our economy, this bank is not making loans, so it will not earn profit from its assets. The bank presumably charges depositors a small fee to cover its costs.

What is the money supply in this economy? Before the creation of Firstbank, the money supply was the $1,000 of currency. After the creation of Firstbank, the money supply is the $1,000 of deposits. A dollar deposited in a bank reduces currency by $1 and raises deposits by $1, so the money supply remains the same. *If banks hold 100 percent of deposits in reserve, the banking system does not affect the supply of money.*

Fractional-Reserve Banking

Now imagine that banks start to use some of their deposits to make loans— for example, to families who are buying houses or to firms that are investing in new plants and equipment. The advantage to banks is that they can charge interest on the loans. The banks must keep some reserves on hand so that reserves are available whenever depositors want to make withdrawals. But as long as the amount of new deposits approximately equals the amount of withdrawals, a bank need not keep all its deposits in reserve. Thus, bankers have an incentive to make loans. When they do so, we have **fractional-reserve banking,** a system under which banks keep only a fraction of their deposits in reserve.

Here is Firstbank's balance sheet after it makes a loan:

Firstbank's Balance Sheet

Assets		Liabilities	
Reserves	$200	Deposits	$1,000
Loans	$800		

This balance sheet assumes that the *reserve–deposit ratio*—the fraction of deposits kept in reserve—is 20 percent. Firstbank keeps $200 of the $1,000 in deposits in reserve and lends out the remaining $800.

Notice that Firstbank increases the supply of money by $800 when it makes this loan. Before the loan is made, the money supply is $1,000, equaling the deposits in Firstbank. After the loan is made, the money supply is $1,800: the depositor still has a deposit of $1,000, but now the borrower holds $800 in currency. *Thus, in a system of fractional-reserve banking, banks create money.*

The creation of money does not stop with Firstbank. If the borrower deposits the $800 in another bank (or if the borrower uses the $800 to pay someone who then deposits it), the process of money creation continues. Here is the balance sheet of Secondbank:

Secondbank's Balance Sheet

Assets		Liabilities	
Reserves	$160	Deposits	$800
Loans	$640		

Secondbank receives the $800 in deposits, keeps 20 percent, or $160, in reserve, and then loans out $640. Thus, Secondbank creates $640 of money. If this $640 is eventually deposited in Thirdbank, this bank keeps 20 percent, or $128, in reserve and loans out $512, resulting in this balance sheet:

Thirdbank's Balance Sheet

Assets		Liabilities	
Reserves	$128	Deposits	$640
Loans	$512		

The process goes on and on. With each deposit and loan, more money is created.

Although this process of money creation can continue forever, it does not create an infinite amount of money. Letting rr denote the reserve–deposit ratio, the amount of money that the original $1,000 creates is

$$\text{Original Deposit} = \$1,000$$
$$\text{Firstbank Lending} = (1 - rr) \times \$1,000$$
$$\text{Secondbank Lending} = (1 - rr)^2 \times \$1,000$$
$$\text{Thirdbank Lending} = (1 - rr)^3 \times \$1,000$$
$$\vdots$$

$$\text{Total Money Supply} = [1 + (1 - rr) + (1 - rr)^2$$
$$+ (1 - rr)^3 + \cdots] \times \$1,000$$
$$= (1/rr) \times \$1,000$$

Each $1 of reserves generates $(1/rr)$ of money. In our example, $rr = 0.2$, so the original $1,000 generates $5,000 of money.[1]

The banking system's ability to create money is the primary difference between banks and other financial institutions. As we first discussed in Chapter 3, financial markets have the important function of transferring the economy's resources from those households that wish to save some of their income for the future to those households and firms that wish to borrow to buy investment goods to be used in future production. The process of transferring funds from savers to borrowers is called **financial intermediation.** Many institutions in the economy act as financial intermediaries: the most prominent examples are the stock market, the bond market, mortgage loan companies, credit unions, trust companies, and the banking system. For simplicity, we focus in this chapter on just the chartered banks.

Note that although the system of fractional-reserve banking creates money, it does not create wealth. When a bank loans out some of its reserves, it gives borrowers the ability to make transactions and therefore increases the supply of money. The borrowers are also undertaking a debt obligation to the bank,

---

[1] *Mathematical note:* The last step in the derivation of the total money supply uses the algebraic result for the sum of an infinite geometric series (which we used previously in computing the multiplier in Chapter 10). According to this result, if x is a number between -1 and 1, then

$$1 + x + x^2 + x^3 + \cdots = 1/(1 - x).$$

In this application, $x = (1 - rr)$.

however, so the loan does not make them wealthier. In other words, the creation of money by the banking system increases the economy's liquidity, not its wealth.

A Model of the Money Supply

Now that we have seen how banks create money, let's examine in more detail what determines the money supply. Here we present a model of the money supply under fractional-reserve banking. The model has three exogenous variables:

- The **monetary base** B is the total number of dollars held by the public as currency C and by the banks as reserves R. It can be directly controlled by the Bank of Canada.

- The **reserve–deposit ratio** rr is the fraction of deposits that banks hold in reserve. It is determined by the business policies of banks and, for many years, by the laws regulating banks. By mid-1994 the phasing out of reserve requirement laws was complete, and Canadian banks were no longer subject to any minimum reserve requirement.

- The **currency–deposit ratio** cr is the amount of currency C people hold as a fraction of their holdings of deposits D. It reflects the preferences of households about the form of money they wish to hold.

Our model shows how the money supply depends on the monetary base, the reserve–deposit ratio, and the currency–deposit ratio. It allows us to examine how Bank of Canada policy and the choices of banks and households influence the money supply.

We begin with the definitions of the money supply and the monetary base:

$$M = C + D,$$

$$B = C + R.$$

The first equation states that the money supply is the sum of currency and deposits. The second equation states that the monetary base is the sum of currency and bank reserves. To solve for the money supply as a function of the three exogenous variables (B, rr, and cr), we begin by dividing the first equation by the second to obtain

$$\frac{M}{B} = \frac{C + D}{C + R}.$$

Then divide both the top and bottom of the expression on the right by D.

$$\frac{M}{B} = \frac{C/D + 1}{C/D + R/D}.$$

Note that C/D is the currency–deposit ratio cr, and that R/D is the reserve–deposit ratio rr. Making these substitutions, and bringing the B from the left to the right side of the equation, we obtain

$$M = \frac{cr + 1}{cr + rr} \times B.$$

This equation shows how the money supply depends on the three exogenous variables.

We can now see that the money supply is proportional to the monetary base. The factor of proportionality, $(cr + 1)/(cr + rr)$, is denoted m and is called the **money multiplier.** We can write

$$M = m \times B.$$

Each dollar of the monetary base produces m dollars of money. Because the monetary base has a multiplied effect on the money supply, the monetary base is sometimes called **high-powered money.**

Here's a numerical example that approximately describes the Canadian economy in 2008 if M2 is taken as the measure of the money supply. Suppose that the monetary base B is \$50 billion, the reserve–deposit ratio rr is 0.005, and the currency–deposit ratio cr is 0.07. In this case, the money multiplier is

$$m = \frac{0.07 + 1}{0.07 + 0.005} = 14.3,$$

and the money supply is

$$M = 14.3 \times \$50 \text{ billion} = \$715 \text{ billion}.$$

Each dollar of the monetary base generates 14.3 dollars of money, so the total M2 money supply is \$715 billion.

We can now see how changes in the three exogenous variables—B, rr, and cr—cause the money supply to change.

1. The money supply is proportional to the monetary base. Thus, an increase in the monetary base increases the money supply by the same percentage.

2. The lower the reserve–deposit ratio, the more loans banks make, and the more money banks create from every dollar of reserves. Thus, a decrease in the reserve–deposit ratio raises the money multiplier and the money supply.

3. The lower the currency–deposit ratio, the fewer dollars of the monetary base the public holds as currency, the more base dollars banks hold as reserves, and the more money banks can create. Thus, a decrease in the currency–deposit ratio raises the money multiplier and the money supply.

This stark summary of the model makes it sound as if central bankers can control the value of the money supply rather precisely. In fact, they cannot, for two reasons. First, officials at the Bank of Canada do not know what reserve–deposit ratio will be chosen by the chartered banks. Years ago, chartered banks were forced by law to hold enough reserves to satisfy the reserve-requirement laws. Banks cannot make large profits if they hold too many low-yielding reserves, however; so they tended to satisfy the reserve-requirement laws by holding the very minimum possible. As a result, the reserve–deposit ratio was predictable after all. For many years now, there have been no minimum reserve-requirement laws. These regulations were removed when the chartered banks argued that it was unfair to have them subject to such regulations when their competitors (for example, trust companies) were not so constrained. The net result is that the reserve–deposit ratio is now less predictable. Given the formula that we have just developed, the money supply is somewhat unpredictable as well—even though the Bank of Canada can set the monetary base quite accurately to a specifically chosen value. The second reason the money supply is hard to set is that the other component of the multiplier—the public's currency—deposit ratio—is a matter of choice (and therefore beyond the direct control of Bank of Canada officials).

Despite the imprecision in our ability to apply the money-supply model, we can use it as a guide to discuss the ways in which the Bank of Canada influences the money supply.

The Instruments of Monetary Policy

In previous chapters we made the simplifying assumption that the Bank of Canada controls the money supply directly. In fact, the Bank of Canada controls the money supply indirectly by altering the monetary base. To do this, the Bank of Canada has at its disposal two instruments of monetary policy: open-market operations and deposit-switching.

Open-market operations are the purchases and sales of federal government bonds by the Bank of Canada. When the Bank of Canada buys bonds from the public, the dollars it pays for the bonds increase the monetary base and thereby increase the money supply. When the Bank of Canada sells bonds to the public, the dollars it receives reduce the monetary base and thus decrease the money supply.

Open-market operations are also carried out in the foreign exchange market. To fix the exchange rate, and even just to limit what exchange-rate changes are occurring, the Bank of Canada can enter the foreign exchange market. To keep the Canadian dollar high when the market pressure is pushing it down, the Bank buys lots of Canadian dollars. This is done by selling some of Canada's foreign exchange reserves, which are held by the Bank of Canada. Since the Canadian dollars bought by the Bank are no longer in private use, the monetary base is reduced. Similarly, to keep the Canadian dollar from rising in value, the Bank sells lots of Canadian dollars. The Bank does this by using the currency to purchase foreign exchange (thus building up the country's foreign exchange reserves). The new currency that is used to pay for the foreign exchange forms part of the domestic monetary base. As a result, buying foreign exchange causes a multiple expansion in the money supply, just like an open-market purchase of bonds does.

Understanding the mechanics behind these open-market operations is fundamental to having an informed opinion about the plausibility of a small country like Canada having a monetary policy that is independent from that of the United States. If a completely floating exchange-rate policy is chosen, the Bank of Canada is under no obligation to make any trades in the foreign exchange market. Thus, open-market operations can be confined to the domestic bond market, and they can be initiated only when domestic monetary policy objectives call for action. If a fixed-exchange-rate policy is chosen, however, the Bank of Canada gets to decide neither the timing nor the magnitude of its open-market operations. These decisions are made by the private participants in the foreign exchange market, and the Bank's role is a residual one—just issuing or withdrawing whatever quantity of domestic monetary base necessary to keep the exchange rate constant.

The moral of the story is this: We *cannot* fix *both* the quantity and the price of our currency. A fixed exchange rate is inconsistent with independent monetary policy. A floating exchange rate is what permits independent monetary policy.

Deposit-switching is the other method used by the Bank of Canada to alter the monetary base. The government of Canada holds large bank deposits because it receives tax payments on a daily basis. These deposits are held both at the Bank of Canada and at the various chartered banks. In terms of the security of its funds, the government does not care where these deposits are held. But from the perspective of monetary policy, the government *does* have a preference. To understand why, consider a switch of government deposits from the Bank of Canada to any one of the chartered banks. (This operation or its reverse is performed daily by the Bank of Canada, on behalf of the government.) The deposit switch increases chartered bank reserves and deposits on a one-for-one basis. With a fractional reserve system, we know that the chartered bank will use a good part of this increase in reserves to extend new loans. Thus, the deposit switch toward chartered banks sets in motion a multiple expansion of the money supply. Similarly, a switch of government deposits away from chartered banks depletes their reserves—inducing a contraction of loans and so a decrease in the money supply.

The **Bank Rate** is the interest rate that the Bank of Canada uses to determine how much it charges if it ever has to lend reserves to chartered banks. Because an increase in the Bank Rate can be interpreted as an increase in chartered bank costs, it is taken as a signal that banks will be cutting back loans and that the money supply is shrinking. Similarly, a decrease in the Bank Rate is a signal that banks can afford to expand loans and that the monetary policy is expansionary.

Although the broad outline of this interpretation is perfectly correct, it is misleading in its detail. Because Canada has only a few major banks, with branch offices all over the country, they rarely have to borrow reserves from the Bank of Canada. If one branch runs a bit short to meet its customers' needs, reserves are just passed on from another branch, or from the "head office." Also, chartered banks can borrow from each other on the "overnight" market. Given these facts, an increase in the Bank Rate has no direct effect on chartered bank costs.

Individuals and firms write a great many cheques every day to finance their purchases. When these cheques are cleared at the end of the day, they represent instructions for banks to transfer funds to each other (for honouring each other's cheques). Banks make these transfers on a net basis by writing cheques to each other against their own deposit accounts at the Bank of Canada. The total of these accounts is known as the quantity of settlement balances. Banks are not allowed to end the day with a negative balance in their settlement account. The Bank of Canada uses deposit-switching to alter the overall quantity of settlement balances, and so affect the ability of charter banks to make loans.

It is convenient to pay attention to the changes in the Bank Rate because it represents a summary indicator of what the Bank of Canada has been doing. By following the Bank Rate, individuals can be aware of the stance of monetary policy without having to know the details of the fundamental instruments of policy—open-market operations and deposit-switching. To appreciate why, we must understand how the Bank Rate is set and how the overnight loan market operates.

The overnight lending rate is the rate at which chartered banks and other participants in the money market borrow from and lend to each other one-day funds. The Bank of Canada establishes a range—called the *operating band*—in which the overnight lending rate can move up or down. The Bank Rate is set at the upper limit of this band, which is half a percentage point wide. The Bank of Canada commits to lend out reserves at a rate given by the upper limit of the band, and to pay interest on the deposits of private financial institutions at the Bank at the lower limit of the band. These commitments ensure that the overnight rate stays within the band.

By changing the operating band and thus the overnight lending rate, the Bank of Canada sends a clear signal about the direction in which interest rates will be moving. On the one hand, Bank Rate changes are "trend-setting," since it is the Bank that has announced any change in the operating band. But in another sense, Bank Rate changes follow the market. The Bank only changes the operating band (at one of the eight prespecified press-conference announcement dates each year) when it has been conducting behind-the-scenes transactions—deposit-switching and open-market operations—and these initiatives are what determine the change in both market yields and the overnight lending rate.

Although the two instruments—open-market operations and deposit-switching—and the summary indicator of these operations—the overnight lending rate—give the Bank of Canada substantial power to influence the money supply, the Bank cannot control the money supply perfectly. Chartered bank discretion in conducting business can cause the money supply to change. For example, banks may decide to hold more reserves than usual, and households may choose to hold more cash. Such increases in rr and cr reduce the money supply, even though the Bank of Canada might have thought the initial size of the money supply was the appropriate level for maintaining aggregate demand in the economy.

There is a frustrating irony in this sort of development. When banks and their customers get nervous about the future and rearrange their assets to have a higher proportion of cash, they raise the chances that there will actually be a recession. One of the reasons that the Bank of Canada constantly monitors financial market developments is to try to counteract events like this. The Bank tries to use open-market and deposit-switching operations in such a way that the monetary base moves in the opposite direction to the change in the money multiplier (which is caused by the changes in household and banking preferences and practices). By promising in advance to keep the overall money supply from shrinking—even when a crisis of confidence occurs and the consequent move toward cash lowers the money multiplier—the Bank of Canada makes it very unlikely that such panics will occur in the first place.

There is a second method of dealing with crises of confidence in financial institutions: the government can insure individuals' deposits in banks and trust companies, a system called **deposit insurance.** Canada has the Canada Deposit Insurance Corporation (CDIC), which insures all deposits up to a maximum of $100,000 per customer. The idea is quite simple. If a bank or trust company extends too many risky loans and goes bankrupt as a result, customers do not lose their deposits. The general taxpayer, through the CDIC, will pay customers up to $100,000 to protect them from the company's failure. Armed with this insurance, depositors do not have to move more into cash when they get nervous, and, as a result, the Bank of Canada has an easier job trying to keep the money supply on course.

Bank Failures and Deposit Insurance

As noted earlier, given Canada's branch banking system, banks almost never go bankrupt. Some smaller trust companies, however, have failed. Indeed, there were several such failures in the late 1980s and early 1990s, and since the CDIC went beyond what was then the $60,000 limit and covered all deposits, the CDIC has run up quite a bill for taxpayers to cover. This development has sparked some controversy concerning possible reforms to the deposit insurance system. Before evaluating this controversy, however, it is instructive to consider the situation in the United States. U.S. banking is regulated at the state level, which means that there is much less branch banking. Many banks operate in only one state. This unit banking system is far more prone to bank failures. Indeed, whereas Canada had no bank failures during the Great Depression of the 1930s, there were a great many in the United States. And these failures help explain the severity of the Great Depression.

Between August 1929 and March 1933, the U.S. money supply fell 28 percent. As we discussed in Chapter 11, many economists believe that this large decline in the money supply was a primary cause of the Great Depression. But we did not discuss why the money supply fell so dramatically.

The three variables that determine the money supply—the monetary base, the reserve–deposit ratio, and the currency–deposit ratio—are shown in Table 19-1 for 1929 and 1933. You can see that the fall in the money supply cannot be attributed to a fall in the monetary base: in fact, the monetary base rose 18 percent over this period. Instead, the money supply fell because the money multiplier fell 38 percent. The money multiplier fell because the currency–deposit and reserve–deposit ratios both rose substantially.

TABLE 19-1

The Money Supply and Its Determinants: 1929 and 1933

	August 1929	March 1933
Money Supply	26.5	19.0
Currency	3.9	5.5
Deposits	22.6	13.5
Monetary Base	7.1	8.4
Currency	3.9	5.5
Reserves	3.2	2.9
Money Multiplier	3.7	2.3
Reserve–deposit ratio	0.14	0.21
Currency–deposit ratio	0.17	0.41

Source: Adapted from Milton Friedman and Anna Schwartz, *A Monetary History of the United States, 1867–1960* (Princeton, N.J.: Princeton University Press, 1963), Appendix A.

Most economists attribute the fall in the money multiplier to the large number of bank failures in the early 1930s. From 1930 to 1933, more than 9,000 banks suspended operations, often defaulting on their depositors. The bank failures caused the money supply to fall by altering the behaviour of both depositors and bankers.

Bank failures raised the currency–deposit ratio by reducing public confidence in the banking system. People feared that bank failures would continue, and they began to view currency as a more desirable form of money than deposits. When they withdrew their deposits, they drained the banks of reserves. The process of money creation reversed itself, as banks responded to lower reserves by reducing their outstanding balance of loans.

In addition, the bank failures raised the reserve–deposit ratio by making bankers more cautious. Having just observed many bank runs, bankers became apprehensive about operating with a small amount of reserves. They therefore increased their holdings of reserves to well above the legal minimum. Just as households responded to the banking crisis by holding more currency relative to deposits, bankers responded by holding more reserves relative to loans. Together these changes caused a large fall in the money multiplier.

Although it is easy to explain why the money supply fell, it is more difficult to decide whether to blame the U.S. central bank, the Federal Reserve. One might argue that the monetary base did not fall, so the Fed should not be blamed. Critics of Fed policy during this period make two arguments. First, they claim that the Fed should have taken a more vigorous role in preventing bank failures by acting as a *lender of last resort* when banks needed cash during bank runs. This would have helped maintain confidence in the banking system and prevented the large fall in the money multiplier. Second, they point out that the

Fed could have responded to the fall in the money multiplier by increasing the monetary base even more than it did. Either of these actions would likely have prevented such a large fall in the money supply, which in turn might have reduced the severity of the Great Depression.

Like Canada, the United States now has deposit insurance, so a sudden fall in the money multiplier is much less likely today. But also like Canada, U.S. taxpayers are frustrated with how the deposit insurance system requires the general taxpayer to subsidize depositors that do not exercise care concerning where they deposit their funds. This is a classic problem that is involved with any form of insurance. In this case, insurance lowers the cost to depositors of failures, but it also raises the probability that those very failures will occur. This is because the insurance eliminates the need for depositors to assess and monitor the riskiness of financial institutions. Recent discussions in Canada have raised suggestions like following the "co-insurance" system of Great Britain. The essential feature of this reform is that there is a deductible, so that individuals lose 2 percent or 3 percent of their deposits when the institution fails. With this feature, depositors remain well protected, but they still have some incentive to avoid institutions that are obviously shaky. During the panic of the financial crisis of 2008–2009 in the United States, the authorities were not concerned about this moral hazard issue. The only change in legislation in that case was that the Federal Deposit Insurance Corporation raised the amount guaranteed from $100,000 to $250,000 per depositor. ■

Bank Capital, Leverage, and Capital Requirements

The model of the banking system presented in this chapter is simplified. That is not necessarily a problem; after all, all models are simplified. But it is worth drawing attention to one particular simplifying assumption.

In the bank balance sheets presented so far, a bank takes in deposits and uses those deposits to make loans or to hold reserves. Based on this discussion, you might think that it does not take any resources to open a bank, but that is not true. Starting a bank requires some capital. That is, the bank owners must start with some financial resources to get the business going. Those resources are called **bank capital** or, equivalently, the equity of the bank's owners.

Here is what a more realistic balance sheet for a bank would look like:

A Bank's Balance Sheet

Assets		Liabilities and Owners' Equity	
Reserves	$200	Deposits	$750
Loans	$500	Debt	$200
Securities	$300	Capital (owners' equity)	$50

The bank obtains resources from its owners, who provide capital, and also by taking in deposits and issuing debt. It uses these resources in three ways. Some funds are held as reserves; some are used to make bank loans; and some are used to buy financial securities, such as government or corporate bonds. The bank allocates its resources among these asset classes, taking into account the risk and return that each offers and any regulations that restrict its choices. The reserves, loans, and securities on the left side of the balance sheet must equal, in total, the deposits, debt, and capital on the right side of the balance sheet.

This business strategy relies on a phenomenon called **leverage,** which is the use of borrowed money to supplement existing funds for purposes of investment. The *leverage ratio* is the ratio of the bank's total assets (the left side of the balance sheet) to bank capital (the one item on the right side of the balance sheet that represents the owners' equity). In this example, the leverage ratio is $1000/$50, or 20. This means that for every dollar of capital that the bank owners have contributed, the bank has $20 of assets and, thus, $19 of deposits and debts.

One implication of leverage is that, in bad times, a bank can lose much of its capital very quickly. To see how, let's continue with this numerical example. If the bank's assets fall in value by a mere 5 percent, then the $1,000 of assets are now worth only $950. Because the depositors and debt holders have the legal right to be paid first, the value of the owners' equity falls to zero. That is, when the leverage ratio is 20, a 5-percent fall in the value of the bank assets leads to a 100-percent fall in bank capital. The fear that bank capital may be running out, and thus that depositors may not be fully repaid, is typically what generates bank runs when there is no deposit insurance.

One of the restrictions that bank regulators put on banks is that the banks must hold sufficient capital. The goal of such a **capital requirement** is to ensure that banks will be able to pay off their depositors. The amount of capital required depends on the kind of assets a bank holds. If the bank holds safe assets such as government bonds, regulators require less capital than if the bank holds risky assets such as loans to borrowers whose credit is of dubious quality.

In 2008 and 2009, many U.S. banks found themselves with too little capital after they had incurred losses on mortgage loans and mortgage-backed securities. The shortage of bank capital reduced bank lending, contributing to a severe economic downturn. (This event was discussed in a Case Study in Chapter 11.) In response to this problem, the U.S. Treasury, working together with the Federal Reserve, started putting public funds into the banking system, increasing the amount of bank capital and making the U.S. taxpayer a part owner of many banks. The goal of this unusual policy was to recapitalize the banking system so bank lending could return to a more normal level.

19-2 Money Demand

We now turn to the other side of the money market and examine what determines money demand. In previous chapters, we used simple money demand functions. We started with the quantity theory, which assumes that the demand for real balances is proportional to income. That is, the quantity theory assumes

$$(M/P)^d = kY,$$

where k is a constant measuring how much money people want to hold for every dollar of income. We then considered a more general and realistic money demand function that assumes the demand for real money balances depends on both the interest rate and income:

$$\left(\frac{M}{P}\right)^{\text{d}} = L(i, Y).$$

We used this money demand function when we discussed the link between money and prices in Chapter 4 and when we developed the *IS–LM* model in Chapters 10 and 11.

There is, of course, much more to say about what determines how much money people choose to hold. Just as studies of the consumption function rely on microeconomic models of the consumption decision, studies of the money demand function rely on microeconomic models of the money demand decision. In this section we first discuss in broad terms the different ways to model money demand. We then develop one prominent model.

Recall that money serves three functions: it is a unit of account, a store of value, and a medium of exchange. The first function—money as a unit of account—does not by itself generate any demand for money, because one can quote prices in dollars without holding any. By contrast, money can serve its other two functions only if people hold it. Theories of money demand emphasize the role of money either as a store of value or as a medium of exchange.

Portfolio Theories of Money Demand

Theories of money demand that emphasize the role of money as a store of value are called **portfolio theories.** According to these theories, people hold money as part of their portfolio of assets. The key insight is that money offers a different combination of risk and return than other assets. In particular, money offers a safe (nominal) return, whereas the prices of stocks and bonds may rise or fall. Thus, some economists have suggested that households choose to hold money as part of their optimal portfolio.[2]

Portfolio theories predict that the demand for money should depend on the risk and return offered by money and by the various assets households can hold instead of money. In addition, money demand should depend on total wealth, because wealth measures the size of the portfolio to be allocated among money and the alternative assets. For example, we might write the money demand function as

$$\left(\frac{M}{P}\right)^{\text{d}} = L(r_{\text{s}}, r_{\text{b}}, E\pi, W),$$

---

[2] James Tobin, "Liquidity Preference as Behavior Toward Risk," *Review of Economic Studies* 25 (February 1958): 65–86.

where r_s is the expected real return on stock, r_b is the expected real return on bonds, $E\pi$ is the expected inflation rate, and W is real wealth. An increase in r_s or r_b reduces money demand, because other assets become more attractive. An increase in $E\pi$ also reduces money demand, because money becomes less attractive. (Recall that $-E\pi$ is the expected real return to holding money.) An increase in W raises money demand, because higher wealth means a larger portfolio.

From the standpoint of portfolio theories, we can view our money demand function, $L(i, Y)$, as a useful simplification. First, it uses real income Y as a proxy for real wealth W. If we think of wealth very broadly defined to include human capital, income is the yield on wealth. Second, the only return variable it includes is the nominal interest rate, which is the sum of the real return on bonds and expected inflation (that is, $i = r_b + E\pi$). According to portfolio theories, however, the money demand function should include the expected returns on other assets as well.

Are portfolio theories useful for studying money demand? The answer depends on which measure of money we are considering. The most narrow measures of money, such as $M1$, include only currency and deposits in chequing accounts. These forms of money earn zero or very low rates of interest. There are other assets—such as savings accounts, treasury bills, and guaranteed investment certificates—that earn higher rates of interest and have the same risk characteristics as currency and chequing accounts. Economists say that money ($M1$) is a **dominated asset:** as a store of value, it exists alongside other assets that are always better. Thus, it is not optimal for people to hold money as part of their portfolio, and portfolio theories cannot explain the demand for these dominated forms of money.

Portfolio theories are more plausible as theories of money demand if we adopt a broad measure of money. The broad measures include many of those assets that dominate currency and chequing accounts. $M2$, for example, includes savings and other notice accounts. When we examine why people hold assets in the form of $M2$, rather than bonds or stock, the portfolio considerations of risk and return may be paramount. Hence, although the portfolio approach to money demand may not be plausible when applied to $M1$, it may be a good theory to explain the demand for $M2$ or $M3$.

CASE STUDY

Currency and the Underground Economy

How much currency are you holding right now in your wallet? How many $100 bills?

In Canada today, the amount of currency per person is about $1,000 and about half of that is in large-denomination notes. Most people find this fact surprising, because they hold much smaller amounts and in smaller denominations.

Some of this currency is used by people in the underground economy—that is, by those engaged in illegal activity such as the drug trade and by those trying to hide income to evade taxes. People whose wealth was earned illegally may have fewer options for investing their portfolio, because by holding wealth in banks, bonds, or stock, they assume a greater risk of detection. For criminals, currency may not be a dominated asset: it may be the best store of value available.

Some economists point to the large amount of currency in the underground economy as one reason that some inflation may be desirable. Recall that inflation is a tax on the holders of money, because inflation erodes the real value of money. A drug dealer holding $20,000 in cash pays an inflation tax of $2,000 per year when the inflation rate is 10 percent. The inflation tax is one of the few taxes those in the underground economy cannot evade. Estimates of the underground economy are hard to come by, but the government studied the issue in 1994 and estimated its size to be 4.5 percent of GDP. ■

Transactions Theories of Money Demand

Theories of money demand that emphasize the role of money as a medium of exchange are called **transactions theories.** These theories acknowledge that money is a dominated asset and stress that people hold money, unlike other assets, to make purchases. These theories best explain why people hold narrow measures of money, such as currency and chequing accounts, as opposed to holding assets that dominate them, such as savings accounts or treasury bills.

Transactions theories of money demand take many forms, depending on how one models the process of obtaining money and making transactions. All these theories assume that money has the cost of earning a low rate of return and the benefit of making transactions more convenient. People decide how much money to hold by trading off these costs and benefits.

To see how transactions theories explain the money demand function, let's develop one prominent model of this type. The **Baumol–Tobin model** was developed in the 1950s by economists William Baumol and James Tobin, and it remains a leading theory of money demand.[3]

The Baumol–Tobin Model of Cash Management

The Baumol–Tobin model analyzes the costs and benefits of holding money. The benefit of holding money is convenience: people hold money to avoid making a trip to the bank every time they wish to buy something. The cost of this convenience is the forgone interest they would have received had they left the money deposited in a savings account that paid interest.

To see how people trade off these benefits and costs, consider a person who plans to spend Y dollars gradually over the course of a year. (For simplicity, assume that the price level is constant, so real spending is constant over the year.)

[3] William Baumol, "The Transactions Demand for Cash: An Inventory Theoretic Approach," *Quarterly Journal of Economics* 66 (November 1952): 545–556; James Tobin, "The Interest Elasticity of the Transactions Demand for Cash," *Review of Economics and Statistics* (August 1956): 241–247.

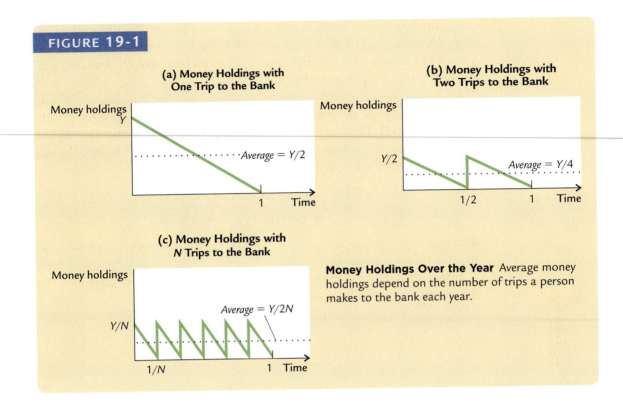

FIGURE 19-1

(a) Money Holdings with One Trip to the Bank

Money holdings

Average = Y/2

1   Time

(b) Money Holdings with Two Trips to the Bank

Money holdings

Y/2

Average = Y/4

1/2   1   Time

(c) Money Holdings with N Trips to the Bank

Money holdings

Average = Y/2N

Y/N

1/N   1   Time

Money Holdings Over the Year Average money holdings depend on the number of trips a person makes to the bank each year.

How much money should he hold in the process of spending this amount? That is, what is the optimal size of average cash balances?

Consider the possibilities. He could withdraw the Y dollars at the beginning of the year and gradually spend the money. Panel (a) of Figure 19-1 shows his money holdings over the course of the year under this plan. His money holdings begin the year at Y and end the year at zero, averaging $Y/2$ over the year.

A second possible plan is to make two trips to the bank. In this case, he withdraws $Y/2$ dollars at the beginning of the year, gradually spends this amount over the first half of the year, and then makes another trip to withdraw $Y/2$ for the second half of the year. Panel (b) of Figure 19-1 shows that money holdings over the year vary between $Y/2$ and zero, averaging $Y/4$. This plan has the advantage that less money is held on average, so the individual forgoes less interest, but it has the disadvantage of requiring two trips to the bank rather than one.

More generally, suppose the individual makes N trips to the bank over the course of the year. On each trip, he withdraws Y/N dollars; he then spends the money gradually over the following $1/N$th of the year. Panel (c) of Figure 19-1 shows that money holdings vary between Y/N and zero, averaging $Y/(2N)$.

The question is, what is the optimal choice of N? The greater N is, the less money the individual holds on average and the less interest he forgoes. But as N increases, so does the inconvenience of making frequent trips to the bank.

Suppose that the cost of going to the bank is some fixed amount F. We can view F as representing the value of the time spent traveling to and from the bank and waiting in line to make the withdrawal. For example, if a trip to the bank takes 15 minutes and a person's wage is $12 per hour, then F is $3. Also, let i denote the interest rate; because money does not bear interest, i measures the opportunity cost of holding money.

Now we can analyze the optimal choice of N, which determines money demand. For any N, the average amount of money held is $Y/(2N)$, so the forgone interest is $iY/(2N)$. Because F is the cost per trip to the bank, the total cost of making trips to the bank is FN. The total cost the individual bears is the sum of the forgone interest and the cost of trips to the bank:

$$\text{Total Cost} = \text{Forgone Interest} + \text{Cost of Trips}$$
$$= iY/(2N) + FN.$$

The larger the number of trips N, the smaller the forgone interest, and the larger the cost of going to the bank.

Figure 19-2 shows how total cost depends on N. There is one value of N that minimizes total cost. The optimal value of N, denoted N^*, is[4]

$$N^* = \sqrt{iY/2F}.$$

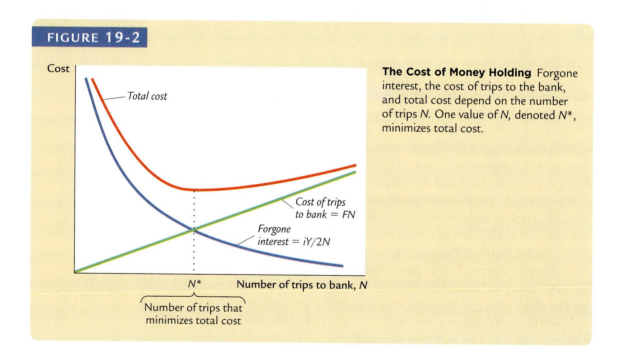

FIGURE 19-2

Cost

Total cost

Cost of trips to bank = FN

Forgone interest = iY/2N

N^* Number of trips to bank, N

Number of trips that minimizes total cost

The Cost of Money Holding Forgone interest, the cost of trips to the bank, and total cost depend on the number of trips N. One value of N, denoted N^*, minimizes total cost.

---

[4] *Mathematical note:* Deriving this expression for the optimal choice of N requires simple calculus. Differentiate total cost C with respect to N to obtain

$$dC/dN = -iYN^{-2}/2 + F.$$

At the optimum, $dC/dN = 0$, which yields the formula for N^*.

Average money holding is

$$\text{Average Money Holding} = Y/(2N^*)$$
$$= \sqrt{YF/2i}.$$

This expression shows that the individual holds more money if the fixed cost of going to the bank F is higher, if expenditure Y is higher, or if the interest rate i is lower.

So far, we have been interpreting the Baumol–Tobin model as a model of the demand for currency. That is, we have used it to explain the amount of money held outside of banks. Yet one can interpret the model more broadly. Imagine a person who holds a portfolio of monetary assets (currency and chequing accounts) and nonmonetary assets (stocks and bonds). Monetary assets are used for transactions but offer a low rate of return. Let i be the difference in the return between monetary and nonmonetary assets, and let F be the cost of transferring nonmonetary assets into monetary assets, such as a brokerage fee. The decision about how often to pay the brokerage fee is analogous to the decision about how often to make a trip to the bank. Therefore, the Baumol–Tobin model describes this person's demand for monetary assets. By showing that money demand depends positively on expenditure Y and negatively on the interest rate i, the model provides a microeconomic justification for the money demand function, $L(i, Y)$, that we have used throughout this book.

One implication of the Baumol–Tobin model is that any change in the fixed cost of going to the bank F alters the money demand function—that is, it changes the quantity of money demanded for any given interest rate and income. It is easy to imagine events that might influence this fixed cost. The spread of automatic teller machines, for instance, reduces F by reducing the time it takes to withdraw money. Similarly, the introduction of internet banking reduces F by makes it easier to transfer funds among accounts. On the other hand, an increase in real wages increases F by increasing the value of time. And an increase in banking fees increases F directly. Thus, although the Baumol–Tobin model gives us a very specific money demand function, it does not give us reason to believe that this function will necessarily be stable over time.

CASE STUDY

Empirical Studies of Money Demand

Many economists have studied the data on money, income, and interest rates to learn more about the money demand function. One purpose of these studies is to estimate how money demand responds to changes in income and the interest rate. The sensitivity of money demand to these two variables determines the slope of the LM curve; it thus influences how monetary and fiscal policy affect the economy.

Another purpose of the empirical studies is to test the theories of money demand. The Baumol–Tobin model, for example, makes precise predictions for how income and interest rates influence money demand. The model's square-root formula implies that the income elasticity of money demand is 1/2: a 10-percent increase in income should lead to a 5-percent increase in the demand for real balances. It also says that the interest elasticity of money demand is 1/2: a 10-percent increase in the interest rate (say, from 10 percent to 11 percent) should lead to a 5-percent decrease in the demand for real balances.

Most empirical studies of money demand do not confirm these predictions. They find that the income elasticity of money demand is larger than 1/2 and that the interest elasticity is smaller than 1/2. Thus, although the Baumol–Tobin model may capture part of the story behind the money demand function, it is not completely correct.

One possible explanation for the failure of the Baumol–Tobin model is that some people may have less discretion over their money holdings than the model assumes. For example, consider a person who must go to the bank once a week to deposit her paycheque; while at the bank, she takes advantage of her visit to withdraw the currency needed for the coming week. For this person, the number of trips to the bank, N, does not respond to changes in expenditure or the interest rate. Because N is fixed, average money holdings ($Y/2N$) are proportional to expenditure and insensitive to the interest rate.

Now imagine that the world is populated with two sorts of people. Some obey the Baumol–Tobin model, so they have income and interest elasticities of 1/2. The others have a fixed N, so they have an income elasticity of 1 and an interest elasticity of zero. In this case, the overall demand for money looks like a weighted average of the demands of the two groups. The income elasticity will be between 1/2 and 1, and the interest elasticity will be between 1/2 and zero, as the empirical studies find.[5] ■

Financial Innovation and the Rise of Near Money

Traditional macroeconomic analysis groups assets into two categories: those used as a medium of exchange as well as a store of value (currency, chequing accounts) and those used only as a store of value (stocks, bonds, savings accounts). The first category of assets is called "money." In this chapter we discussed its supply and demand.

Although the distinction between monetary and nonmonetary assets remains a useful theoretical tool, in recent years it has become more difficult to use in practice. In part because of deregulation of banks and other financial institutions, and in part because of improved computer technology, the past decade has seen rapid financial innovation. Monetary assets such as chequing accounts once paid

---

[5] To learn more about the empirical studies of money demand, see Stephen M. Goldfeld and Daniel E. Sichel, "The Demand for Money," *Handbook of Monetary Economics,* volume 1 (Amsterdam: North-Holland, 1990): 299–356; and David Laidler, *The Demand for Money: Theories and Evidence,* 3d ed. (New York: Harper & Row, 1985).

no interest; today they can earn market interest rates and are comparable to non-monetary assets as stores of value. Nonmonetary assets such as stocks and bonds were once inconvenient to buy and sell; today mutual funds allow depositors to hold stocks and bonds and to make withdrawals simply by writing cheques from their accounts. These nonmonetary assets that have acquired some of the liquidity of money are called **near money.**

The existence of near money complicates monetary policy by making the demand for money unstable. Since money and near money are close substitutes, households can easily switch their assets from one form to the other. Such changes can occur for minor reasons and do not necessarily reflect changes in spending. Thus, the velocity of money becomes less predictable, and the quantity of money gives faulty signals about aggregate demand.

One response to this problem is to use a broad definition of money that includes near money. Yet, since there is a continuum of assets in the world with varying characteristics, it is not clear how to choose a subset to label "money." Moreover, if we adopt a broad definition of money, the Bank of Canada's ability to control this quantity may be limited.

The potential instability in money demand caused by near money has been an important practical problem for the Bank of Canada. Sometimes different measures of the money supply have given rather conflicting signals. For example, in 1990, $M2$ grew by almost 11 percent while $M1$ shrank by 1 percent. Then, in 1993, $M2$ growth had fallen to 3.2 percent while $M1$ growth had shot up to 10.4 percent. It is partly because of these problems that the Bank of Canada shifted away from attempting to target any particular monetary aggregate in the 1980s. Since then, the Bank has been adjusting the monetary base by whatever it takes to set the overnight lending rate at whatever level is estimated to be required for the Bank to hit the inflation rate target. This practice has proved to be a remarkably effective operating procedure.

19-3 Conclusion

Money is at the heart of much macroeconomic analysis. Models of money supply and money demand can help shed light on the long-run determinants of the price level and the short-run causes of economic fluctuations. The rise of near money in recent years has shown that there is still much to be learned. Building reliable microeconomic models of money and near money remains a central challenge for macroeconomists.

Summary

1. The system of fractional-reserve banking creates money, because each dollar of reserves generates many dollars of deposits.

2. The supply of money depends on the monetary base, the reserve–deposit ratio, and the currency–deposit ratio. An increase in the monetary base leads to a proportionate increase in the money supply. A decrease in the reserve–deposit ratio or in the currency–deposit ratio increases the money multiplier and thus the money supply.

3. The Bank of Canada changes the money supply using two policy instruments. It can increase the monetary base by making an open-market purchase of bonds or foreign exchange, or by switching government deposits out of the Bank of Canada and into the chartered banks. Both of these operations cause a reduction of interest rates, and so they can be monitored by observing a drop in the Bank Rate.

4. To start a bank, the owners must contribute some of their own financial resources, which become the bank's capital. Because banks are highly leveraged, however, a small decline in the value of their assets can potentially have a major impact on the value of bank capital. Bank regulators require that banks hold sufficient capital to ensure that depositors can be repaid.

5. Portfolio theories of money demand stress the role of money as a store of value. They predict that the demand for money depends on the risk and return on money and alternative assets.

6. Transactions theories of money demand, such as the Baumol–Tobin model, stress the role of money as a medium of exchange. They predict that the demand for money depends positively on expenditure and negatively on the interest rate.

7. Financial innovation has led to the creation of assets with many of the attributes of money. These near monies make the demand for money less stable, which complicates the conduct of monetary policy.

KEY CONCEPTS

Reserves	Money multiplier	Capital requirement
100-percent-reserve banking	High-powered money	Portfolio theories
Balance sheet	Open-market operations	Dominated asset
Fractional-reserve banking	Deposit-switching	Transactions theories
Financial intermediation	Bank Rate	Baumol–Tobin model
Monetary base	Deposit insurance	Near money
Reserve–deposit ratio	Bank capital	
Currency–deposit ratio	Leverage	

QUESTIONS FOR REVIEW

1. Explain how banks create money.

2. What are the two ways in which the Bank of Canada can influence the money supply?

3. Why might a banking crisis lead to a fall in the money supply?

4. Explain the difference between portfolio and transactions theories of money demand.

5. According to the Baumol–Tobin model, what determines how often people go to the bank? What does this decision have to do with money demand?

6. In what way does the existence of near money complicate the conduct of monetary policy?

PROBLEMS AND APPLICATIONS

1. The U.S. money supply fell during the years 1929 to 1933 because both the currency–deposit ratio and the reserve–deposit ratio increased. Use the model of the money supply and the data in Table 19-1 to answer the following hypothetical questions about this episode.

   a. What would have happened to the money supply if the currency–deposit ratio had risen but the reserve–deposit ratio had remained the same?

   b. What would have happened to the money supply if the reserve–deposit ratio had risen but the currency–deposit ratio had remained the same?

   c. Which of the two changes was more responsible for the fall in the money supply?

2. To increase tax revenue, the U.S. government in 1932 imposed a 2-cent tax on cheques written on deposits in bank accounts. (In today's dollars, this tax was about 25 cents per cheque.)

   a. How do you think the cheque tax affected the currency–deposit ratio? Explain.

   b. Use the model of the money supply under fractional-reserve banking to discuss how this tax affected the money supply.

   c. Now use the *IS–LM* model to discuss the impact of this tax on the economy. Was the cheque tax a good policy to implement in the middle of the Great Depression?

3. Give an example of a bank balance sheet with a leverage ratio of 10. If the value of the bank's assets rises by 5 percent, what happens to the value of the owners' equity in this bank? How large a decline in the value of bank assets would it take to reduce this bank's capital to zero?

4. Suppose that an epidemic of street crime sweeps the country, making it more likely that your wallet will be stolen. Using the Baumol–Tobin model, explain (in words, not equations) how this crime wave will affect the optimal frequency of trips to the bank and the demand for money.

5. Let's see what the Baumol–Tobin model says about how often you should go to the bank to withdraw cash.

   a. How much do you buy per year with currency (as opposed to cheques or credit cards)? This is your value of *Y*.

   b. How long does it take you to go to the bank? What is your hourly wage? Use these two figures to compute your value of *F*.

   c. What interest rate do you earn on the money you leave in your bank account? This is your value of *i*. (Be sure to write *i* in decimal form—that is, 6 percent should be expressed 0.06.)

   d. According to the Baumol–Tobin model, how many times should you go to the bank each year, and how much should you withdraw each time?

   e. In practice, how often do you go to the bank, and how much do you withdraw?

f. Compare the predictions of the Baumol–Tobin model to your behaviour. Does the model describe how you actually behave? If not, why not? How would you change the model to make it a better description of your behaviour?

6. In Chapter 4, we defined the velocity of money as the ratio of nominal expenditure to the quantity of money. Let's now use the Baumol–Tobin model to examine what determines velocity.

a. Recalling that average money holdings equal $Y/(2N)$, write velocity as a function of the number of trips to the bank N. Explain your result.

b. Use the formula for the optimal number of trips to express velocity as a function of expenditure Y, the interest rate i, and the cost of a trip to the bank F.

c. What happens to velocity when the interest rate rises? Explain.

d. What happens to velocity when the price level rises? Explain.

e. As the economy grows, what should happen to the velocity of money? (*Hint:* Think about how economic growth will influence Y and F.)

f. Suppose now that the number of trips to the bank is fixed rather than discretionary. What does this assumption imply about velocity?

What We Know, What We Don't

If all economists were laid end to end, they would not reach a conclusion.

— *George Bernard Shaw*

The theory of economics does not furnish a body of settled conclusions immediately applicable to policy. It is a method rather than a doctrine, an apparatus of the mind, which helps its possessor to draw correct conclusions.

— *John Maynard Keynes*

The first chapter of this book states that the purpose of macroeconomics is to understand economic events and to improve economic policy. Now that we have developed and used many of the most important models in the macroeconomist's toolbox, we can assess whether macroeconomists have achieved these goals.

Any fair assessment of macroeconomics today must admit that the science is incomplete. There are some principles that almost all macroeconomists accept and on which we can rely when trying to analyze events or formulate policies. Yet there are also many questions about the economy that remain open to debate. In this last chapter we briefly review the central lessons of macroeconomics, and we discuss the most pressing unresolved questions.

The Four Most Important Lessons of Macroeconomics

We begin with four lessons that have recurred throughout this book and that most economists today would endorse. Each lesson tells us how policy can influence a key economic variable—output, inflation, or unemployment— either in the long run or in the short run.

Lesson No. 1: In the long run, a country's capacity to produce goods and services determines the standard of living of its citizens.

Of all the measures of economic performance introduced in Chapter 2 and used throughout this book, the one that best measures economic well-being is GDP. Real GDP measures the economy's total output of goods and services and, therefore, a country's ability to satisfy the needs and desires of its citizens. Nations with higher GDP per person have more of almost everything—bigger homes, more cars, higher literacy, better health care, longer life expectancy, and more Internet connections. Perhaps the most important question in macroeconomics is what determines the level and the growth of GDP.

The models in Chapters 3, 7, and 8 identify the long-run determinants of GDP. In the long run, GDP depends on the factors of production—capital and labour—and on the technology for turning capital and labour into output. GDP grows when the factors of production increase or when individuals become better at turning the inputs into an output of goods and services.

This lesson has an obvious but important corollary: public policy can raise GDP in the long run only by improving the productive capability of the economy. There are many ways in which policymakers can attempt to do this. Policies that raise national saving—either through higher public saving or higher private saving—eventually lead to a larger capital stock. Policies that raise the efficiency of labour—such as those that improve education or increase technological progress—lead to a more productive use of capital and labour. All these policies increase the economy's output of goods and services and, thereby, improve the standard of living. It is less clear, however, which of these policies is the best way to raise an economy's productive capability.

Lesson No. 2: In the short run, aggregate demand influences the amount of goods and services that a country produces.

Although the economy's ability to *supply* goods and services is the sole determinant of GDP in the long run, in the short run GDP depends also on the aggregate *demand* for goods and services. Aggregate demand is of key importance because prices are sticky in the short run. The *IS–LM* model developed in Chapters 10, 11, and 12 (along with the no-LM-curve version given in the appendix of Chapter 11) shows what causes changes in aggregate demand and, therefore, short-run fluctuations in GDP.

Because aggregate demand influences output in the short run, all the variables that affect aggregate demand can influence economic fluctuations. Monetary policy, fiscal policy, and shocks to the money and goods markets are often responsible for year-to-year changes in output and employment. Because changes in aggregate demand are central to short-run fluctuations, policymakers monitor the economy closely. Before making any change in monetary or fiscal policy, they want to know whether the economy is booming or heading into a recession.

Lesson No. 3: In the long run, the rate of money growth determines the rate of inflation, but it does not affect the rate of unemployment.

In addition to GDP, inflation and unemployment are among the most closely watched measures of economic performance. Chapter 2 discussed how these two variables are measured, and subsequent chapters developed models to explain how they are determined.

The long-run analysis of Chapter 4 stresses that growth in the money supply is the ultimate determinant of inflation. That is, in the long run, a currency loses real value over time if and only if the central bank prints more and more of it. This lesson can explain the decade-to-decade variation in the inflation rate that we have observed in Canada, as well as the far more dramatic hyperinflations that various countries have experienced from time to time.

We have also seen many of the long-run effects of high money growth and high inflation. In Chapter 4 we saw that, according to the Fisher effect, high inflation raises the nominal interest rate (so that the real interest rate would remain unaffected if it were not for the fact that the Canadian income-tax system taxes *nominal* interest income and capital gains). In Chapter 5 we saw that high inflation leads to a depreciation of the currency in the market for foreign exchange.

The long-run determinants of unemployment are very different. According to the classical dichotomy—the irrelevance of nominal variables in the determination of real variables—growth in the money supply does not affect unemployment in the long run. As we saw in Chapter 6, the natural rate of unemployment is determined by the rates of job separation and job finding, which in turn are determined by the process of job search and by the rigidity of the real wage. In our study of efficiency wages, we saw that real wages can be rigid, even without minimum wage laws or unions, if firms find it profitable to use high wages as a mechanism to induce higher productivity from their workforce. Thus, we concluded that persistent inflation and persistent unemployment are unrelated problems. To combat inflation in the long run, policymakers must reduce the growth in the money supply. To combat unemployment, they must alter the structure of labour markets. In the long run, there is no tradeoff between inflation and unemployment.

Lesson No. 4: In the short run, policymakers who control monetary and fiscal policy face a tradeoff between inflation and unemployment.

Although inflation and unemployment are not related in the long run, in the short run there is a tradeoff between these two variables, which is illustrated by the short-run Phillips curve. As we discussed in Chapter 13, policymakers can use monetary and fiscal policies to expand aggregate demand, which lowers unemployment and raises inflation. Or they can use these policies to contract aggregate demand, which raises unemployment and lowers inflation.

Policymakers face a fixed tradeoff between inflation and unemployment only in the short run. Over time, the short-run Phillips curve shifts for two reasons. First, supply shocks, such as changes in the price of oil, change the short-run tradeoff; an adverse supply shock offers policymakers the difficult choice between higher inflation or higher unemployment. Second, when people change their expectations of inflation, the short-run tradeoff between inflation and unemployment changes. The adjustment of expectations ensures that the tradeoff exists only in the short run. That is, only in the short run does unemployment deviate from its natural rate, and only in the short run does monetary policy have real effects. In the long run, the classical model of Chapters 3 through 8 describes the world.

The Four Most Important Unresolved Questions of Macroeconomics

So far, we have been discussing some of the broad lessons about which most economists would agree. We now turn to four questions about which there is continuing debate. Some of the disagreements concern the validity of alternative economic theories; others concern how economic theory should be applied to economic policy.

Question No. 1: How should policymakers try to promote growth in the economy's natural level of output?

The economy's natural level of output depends on the amount of capital, the amount of labour, and the level of technology. Any policy designed to raise output in the long run must aim to increase the amount of capital, improve the use of labour, or enhance the available technology. There is, however, no simple and costless way to achieve these goals.

The Solow growth model of Chapters 7 and 8 shows that increasing the amount of capital requires raising the economy's rate of saving and investment. Therefore, many economists advocate policies that are designed to increase national saving. Yet the Solow model also shows that raising the capital stock requires a period of reduced consumption for current generations. Some argue that policymakers should not encourage current generations to make this sacrifice, because technological progress will ensure that future generations are better off than current generations. (One waggish economist asked, "What has posterity ever done for me?") Even those who advocate increased saving and investment disagree about how to encourage additional saving and whether the investment should be in privately owned plants and equipment or in public infrastructure, such as roads and schools. Finally, when trying to decide how much current consumption should be discouraged, we must take a position on the importance of positional goods (a recent research topic we discussed in Chapter 16). We know that the bigger is the negative externality generated by consumption, the more we should use the tax system to stimulate saving. But there is no definitive evidence on the size of this consumption externality.

To improve the economy's use of its labour force, most policymakers would like to lower the natural rate of unemployment. As we discussed in Chapter 6, the large differences in unemployment that we observe across countries, as well as the large changes in unemployment we observe over time within countries, suggest that the natural rate is not an immutable constant but depends on a nation's policies and institutions. Yet reducing unemployment is a task fraught with perils. The natural rate of unemployment could likely be reduced by decreasing employment-insurance benefits (and thus increasing the search effort of the unemployed) or by decreasing the minimum wage (and thus bringing wages closer to equilibrium levels). Yet these policies would also hurt some of those members of society most in need and, therefore, do not command a consensus among economists.

In many countries, the natural level of output is depressed by a lack of institutions that people in developed nations take for granted. Canadian citizens today do not worry about revolutions, coups, or civil wars. For the most part, they trust the police and the court system to respect the laws, maintain order, protect property rights, and enforce private contracts. In nations without such institutions, however, people face the wrong incentives: if creating something of economic value is a less reliable path to riches than is stealing from a neighbour, an economy is unlikely to prosper. All economists agree that setting up the right institutions is a prerequisite for increasing growth in the world's poor nations, but changing a nation's institutions requires overcoming difficult political hurdles.

Raising the rate of technological progress is, according to some economists, the most important objective for public policy. The Solow growth model shows that persistent growth in living standards ultimately requires continuing technological progress. Despite much work on the new theories of endogenous growth, which highlight some of the societal decisions that determine technologicial progress, economists cannot offer a reliable recipe to ensure rapid advances in technology. The good news is that around 1995, in the United States at least, productivity growth accelerated. Perhaps this means the end of the productivity slowdown that began in the mid-1970s. Yet it remains unclear how long this propitious development will last and whether it will spread to the rest of the world.

Question No. 2: Should policymakers try to stabilize the economy?

The model of aggregate supply and aggregate demand developed in Chapters 9 through 13 shows how various shocks to the economy cause economic fluctuations and how monetary and fiscal policy can influence these fluctuations. Some economists believe that policymakers should use this analysis in an attempt to stabilize the economy. They believe that monetary and fiscal policy should try to offset shocks in order to keep output and employment close to their natural levels.

Yet, as we discussed in Chapter 15, others are skeptical about our ability to stabilize the economy. These economists cite the long and variable lags inherent in economic policymaking, the poor record of economic forecasting, and our still-limited understanding of the economy. They conclude that the best policy is a passive one. In addition, many economists believe that policymakers are all too often opportunistic or follow time-inconsistent policies. They conclude that policymakers should not have discretion over monetary and fiscal policy but should be committed to following a fixed policy rule. Or, at the very least, their discretion should be somewhat constrained, as is the case when central banks adopt a policy of inflation targeting.

There is also debate among economists about which macroeconomic tools are best suited for purposes of economic stabilization. Typically, monetary policy is the front line of defense against the business cycle. In the deep downturn of 2008–2009, however, western central banks cut interest rates to their lower bound of zero, and with the ability of central banks to provide further stimulus in doubt, the focus of many macroeconomic discussions turned to fiscal policy. Among economists, there was widespread disagreement about the extent to which fiscal policy should be used to stimulate the economy in downturns and whether tax cuts or spending increases are the preferred policy tool.

A related question is whether the benefits of economic stabilization—assuming stabilization could be achieved—would be large or small. Without any change in the natural rate of unemployment, stabilization policy can only reduce the magnitude of fluctuations around the natural rate. Thus, successful stabilization policy would eliminate booms as well as recessions. Some economists have suggested that the average gain from stabilization would be small.

Finally, not all economists endorse the model of economic fluctuations developed in Chapters 9 through 14, which assumes sticky prices and monetary non-neutrality. According to real business cycle theory, discussed in the appendices to Chapters 8 and 14, economic fluctuations are the optimal response of the economy to changing technology. This theory suggests that policymakers should not stabilize the economy, even if this were possible.

Question No. 3: How costly is inflation, and how costly is reducing inflation?

Whenever prices are rising, policymakers confront the question of whether to pursue policies to reduce the rate of inflation. To make this decision, they must compare the cost of allowing inflation to continue at its current rate to the cost of reducing inflation. Yet economists cannot offer accurate estimates of either of these two costs.

The cost of inflation is a topic on which economists and laymen often disagree. When inflation reached 10 percent per year in the late 1970s, opinion polls showed that the public viewed inflation as a major economic problem. Yet, as we discussed in Chapter 4, when economists try to identify the social costs of inflation, they can point only to shoeleather costs, menu costs, the costs of a nonindexed tax system, and so on. These costs become large when countries experience hyperinflation, but they seem relatively minor at the moderate rates of inflation experienced in most major economies. Some economists believe that the public confuses inflation with other economic problems that coincide with inflation. For example, growth in productivity and real wages slowed in the 1970s; some laymen might have viewed inflation as the cause of the slowdown in real wages. Yet it is also possible that economists are mistaken: perhaps inflation is in fact very costly, and we have yet to figure out why.

The cost of reducing inflation is a topic on which economists often disagree among themselves. As we discussed in Chapter 13, the standard view—as described by the short-run Phillips curve—is that reducing inflation requires a period of low output and high unemployment. According to this view, the cost of reducing inflation is measured by the sacrifice ratio, which is the number of percentage points of a year's GDP that must be forgone to reduce inflation by 1 percentage point.

But some economists think that the cost of reducing inflation can be much smaller than standard estimates of the sacrifice ratio indicate. According to the rational-expectations approach discussed in Chapter 13, if a disinflationary policy is announced in advance and is credible, people will adjust their expectations quickly, so the disinflation need not cause a recession.

Other economists believe that the cost of reducing inflation is much larger than standard estimates of the sacrifice ratio indicate. The theories of hysteresis discussed in Chapter 13 suggest that a recession caused by disinflationary policy could raise the natural rate of unemployment. If so, the cost of reducing inflation is not merely a temporary recession but a persistently higher level of unemployment.

Because the costs of inflation and disinflation remain open to debate, economists sometimes offer conflicting advice to policymakers. Perhaps with further research, we can reach a consensus on the benefits of low inflation and the best way to achieve that goal.

Question No. 4: How big a problem are government budget deficits?

In the 1980s and 1990s, large budget deficits were a primary topic of debate among policymakers in many countries. In Canada, the ratio of federal government debt to GDP tripled from 1973 to 1994—an event unprecedented in peacetime. Although the federal government's budget has been in surplus for the decade up to 2009, the issue resurfaced with the deep recession of that year, and it will again as the large baby-boom generation reaches retirement age and starts drawing on government benefits for the elderly. As we discussed in Chapter 16, the effect of government budget deficits is a topic about which economists often disagree.

Most of the models in this book, and most economists, take the traditional view of government debt. According to this view, a budget deficit leads to lower national saving, lower investment, and a trade deficit. In the long run, it leads to a smaller steady-state capital stock and a larger foreign debt. Those who hold the traditional view conclude that budget deficits place a burden on future generations.

Yet not all economists agree with this assessment. Advocates of the Ricardian view of government debt are skeptical. They stress that a budget deficit merely represents a substitution of future taxes for current taxes. As long as consumers are forward-looking, as the theories of consumption presented in Chapter 17 assume, they will save today to meet their or their children's future tax liability. These economists believe that budget deficits have only a minor effect on the economy.

Still other economists believe that the budget deficit is an imperfect measure of fiscal policy. Although the government's choices regarding taxes and spending have great influence on the welfare of different generations, many of these choices are not reflected in the size of the government debt. The level of public pension benefits and contributions, for instance, determines the welfare of the elder beneficiaries versus the working-age taxpayers, but measures of the budget deficit do not reflect this policy choice. According to some economists, we should stop focusing on the government's current budget deficit and the associated level of debt, and concentrate instead on the longer-term generational impacts of fiscal policy.

Conclusion

Economists and policymakers must deal with ambiguity. The current state of macroeconomics offers many insights, but it also leaves many questions open. The challenge for economists is to find answers to these questions and to expand our knowledge. The challenge for policymakers is to use the knowledge we now have to improve economic performance. Both challenges are formidable, but neither is insuperable.

glossary

Accelerator model: The model according to which investment depends on the change in output.

Accommodating policy: A policy that yields to the effect of a shock and thereby prevents the shock from being disruptive; for example, a policy that raises aggregate demand in response to an adverse supply shock, sustaining the effect of the shock on prices and keeping output at the natural level.

Accounting profit: The amount of revenue remaining for the owners of a firm after all the factors of production except capital have been compensated. (Cf. economic profit, profit.)

Acyclical: Moving in no consistent direction over the business cycle. (Cf. countercyclical, procyclical.)

Adaptive expectations: An approach that assumes that people form their expectation of a variable based on recently observed values of the variable. (Cf. rational expectations.)

Adverse selection: An unfavourable sorting of individuals by their own choices; for example, in efficiency-wage theory, when a wage cut induces good workers to quit and bad workers to remain with the firm.

Aggregate: Total for the whole economy.

Aggregate demand curve: The negative relationship between the price level and the aggregate quantity of output demanded that arises from the interaction between the goods market and the money market.

Aggregate-demand externality: The macroeconomic impact of one firm's price adjustment on the demand for all other firms' products.

Aggregate supply curve: The relationship between the price level and the aggregate quantity of output firms produce.

Animal spirits: Exogenous and perhaps self-fulfilling waves of optimism and pessimism about the state of the economy that, according to some economists, influence the level of investment.

Appreciation: A rise in the value of a currency relative to other currencies in the market for foreign exchange. (Cf. depreciation.)

Arbitrage: The act of buying an item in one market and selling it at a higher price in another market in order to profit from the price differential in the two markets.

Automatic stabilizer: A policy that reduces the amplitude of economic fluctuations without regular and deliberate changes in economic policy; for example, an income tax system that automatically reduces taxes when income falls.

Average propensity to consume (APC): The ratio of consumption to income (C/Y).

Balance sheet: An accounting statement that shows assets and liabilities.

Balanced budget: A budget in which receipts equal expenditures.

Balanced trade: A situation in which the value of imports equals the value of exports, so net exports equal zero.

Bank capital: The resources the bank owners have put into the institution.

Bank of Canada: The central bank of Canada.

Bank Rate: The interest rate that the Bank of Canada charges if it makes loans to chartered banks.

Baumol–Tobin model: A model of money demand positing that people choose optimal money holdings by comparing the opportunity cost of the forgone interest from holding money and the benefit of making less frequent trips to the bank.

Bond: A document representing an interest-bearing debt of the issuer, usually a corporation or the government.

Borrowing constraint: A restriction on the amount a person can borrow from financial institutions, limiting that person's ability to spend his or her future income today; also called a liquidity constraint.

Budget constraint: The limit that income places on expenditure. (Cf. intertemporal budget constraint.)

Budget deficit: A shortfall of receipts from expenditure.

Budget surplus: An excess of receipts over expenditure.

Business cycle: Economy-wide fluctuations in output, incomes, and employment.

Business fixed investment: Equipment and structures that businesses buy for use in future production.

Capital: 1. The stock of equipment and structures used in production. 2. The funds to finance the accumulation of equipment and structures.

Capital budgeting: An accounting procedure that measures both assets and liabilities.

Capital requirement: A minimum amount of bank capital mandated by regulators.

Central bank: The institution responsible for the conduct of monetary policy, such as the Bank of Canada in Canada.

Classical dichotomy: The theoretical separation of real and nominal variables in the classical model, which implies that nominal variables do not influence real variables. (Cf. neutrality of money.)

Classical model: A model of the economy derived from the ideas of the classical, or pre-Keynesian, economists; a model based on the assumptions that wages and prices adjust to clear markets and that monetary policy does not influence real variables. (Cf. Keynesian model.)

Closed economy: An economy that does not engage in international trade. (Cf. open economy.)

Cobb–Douglas production function: A production function of the form $F(K, L) = AK^{\alpha}L^{1-\alpha}$, where K is capital, L is labour, and A and α are parameters.

Commodity money: Money that is intrinsically useful and would be valued even if it did not serve as money. (Cf. fiat money, money.)

Competition: A situation in which there are many individuals or firms so that the actions of any one of them do not influence market prices.

Constant returns to scale: A property of a production function whereby a proportionate increase in all factors of production leads to an increase in output of the same proportion.

Consumer price index (CPI): A measure of the overall level of prices that shows the cost of a fixed basket of consumer goods relative to the cost of the same basket in a base year.

Consumption: Goods and services purchased by consumers.

Consumption function: A relationship showing the determinants of consumption; for example, a relationship between consumption and disposable income, $C = C(Y - T)$.

Contractionary policy: Policy that reduces aggregate demand, real income, and employment. (Cf. expansionary policy.)

Coordination failure: A situation in which decisionmakers reach an outcome that is inferior for all of them because of their inability to jointly choose strategies that would result in a preferred outcome.

Corporate profit tax: The tax levied on the accounting profit of corporations.

Cost of capital: The amount forgone by holding a unit of capital for one period, including interest, depreciation, and the gain or loss from the change in the price of capital.

Cost-push inflation: Inflation resulting from shocks to aggregate supply. (Cf. demand-pull inflation.)

CPI: *See* consumer price index.

Crowding out: The reduction in investment that results when expansionary fiscal policy raises the interest rate.

Currency: The sum of outstanding paper money and coins.

Cyclical unemployment: The unemployment associated with short-run economic fluctuations; the deviation of the unemployment rate from the natural rate.

Cyclically adjusted budget deficit: The budget deficit adjusted for the influence of the business cycle on government spending and tax revenue; the budget deficit that would occur if the economy's production and employment were at their natural rates.

Debt-deflation theory: A theory according to which an unexpected fall in the price level redistributes real wealth from debtors to creditors and, therefore, reduces total spending in the economy.

Deflation: A decrease in the overall level of prices. (Cf. disinflation, inflation.)

Deflator: *See* GDP deflator.

Demand deposits: Assets that are held in banks and can be used on demand to make transactions, such as chequing accounts.

Demand-pull inflation: Inflation resulting from shocks to aggregate demand. (Cf. cost-push inflation.)

Demand shocks: Exogenous events that shift the aggregate demand curve.

Deposit insurance: Insurance provided by the Canada Deposit Insurance Corporation (CDIC) to individuals and firms that deposited funds in a bank or trust company that has gone bankrupt.

Deposit switching: The switching of federal government deposits between the Bank of Canada and the chartered banks for the purposes of regulating the money supply.

Depreciation: 1. The reduction in the capital stock that occurs over time because of aging and use. 2. A fall in the value of a currency relative to other currencies in the market for foreign exchange. (Cf. appreciation.)

Depreciation allowances: Deductions permitted in the calculation of corporate taxes to allow for the wearing out of capital equipment.

Depression: A very severe recession.

Devaluation: An action by the central bank to decrease the value of a currency under a system of fixed exchange rates. (Cf. revaluation.)

Diminishing marginal product: A characteristic of a production function whereby the marginal product of a factor falls as the amount of the factor increases while all other factors are held constant.

Discounting: The reduction in value of future expenditure and receipts, compared to current expenditure and receipts, resulting from the presence of a positive interest rate.

Discouraged workers: Individuals who have left the labour force because they believe that there is little hope of finding a job.

Disinflation: A reduction in the rate at which prices are rising. (Cf. deflation, inflation.)

Disposable income: Income remaining after the payment of taxes.

Dominated asset: An asset that offers an inferior return compared to another asset in all possible realizations of future uncertainty.

Double coincidence of wants: A situation in which each of two individuals has precisely the good that the other wants.

Economic profit: The amount of revenue remaining for the owners of a firm after all the factors of production have been compensated. (Cf. accounting profit, profit.)

Efficient markets hypothesis: The theory that asset prices reflect all publicly available information about the value of an asset.

Efficiency of labour: A variable in the Solow growth model that measures the health, education, skills, and knowledge of the labour force.

Efficiency units of labour: A measure of the labour force that incorporates both the number of workers and the efficiency of each worker.

Efficiency-wage theories: Theories of real-wage rigidity and unemployment according to which firms raise labour productivity and profits by keeping real wages above the equilibrium level.

Elasticity: The percentage change in a variable caused by a 1 percent change in another variable.

Employment insurance (EI): A government program under which unemployed workers can collect benefits for a certain period after losing their jobs.

Endogenous growth theory: Models of economic growth that try to explain the rate of technological change.

Endogenous variable: A variable that is explained by a particular model; a variable whose value is determined by the model's solution. (Cf. exogenous variable.)

Equilibrium: A state of balance between opposing forces, such as the balance of supply and demand in a market.

Euler's theorem: The mathematical result economists use to show that economic profit must be zero if the production function has constant returns to scale and if factors are paid their marginal products.

***Ex ante* real interest rate:** The real interest rate anticipated when a loan is made; the nominal interest rate minus expected inflation. (Cf. *ex post* real interest rate.)

***Ex post* real interest rate:** The real interest rate actually realized; the nominal interest rate minus actual inflation. (Cf. *ex ante* real interest rate.)

Exchange rate: The rate at which a country makes exchanges in world markets. (Cf. nominal exchange rate, real exchange rate.)

Exogenous variable: A variable that a particular model takes as given; a variable whose value is independent of the model's solution. (Cf. endogenous variable.)

Expansionary policy: Policy that raises aggregate demand, real income, and employment. (Cf. contractionary policy.)

Exports: Goods and services sold to other countries.

Factor of production: An input used to produce goods and services; for example, capital or labour.

Factor price: The amount paid for one unit of a factor of production.

Factor share: The proportion of total income being paid to a factor of production.

Federal Reserve (the Fed): The central bank of the United States.

Fiat money: Money that is not intrinsically useful and is valued only because it is used as money. (Cf. commodity money, money.)

Financial intermediation: The process by which resources are allocated from those individuals who wish to save some of their income for future consumption to those individuals and firms who wish to borrow to buy investment goods for future production.

Fiscal dividend: The new room in the budget that is created by decreased interest payment obligations on the national debt.

Financing constraint: A limit on the quantity of funds a firm can raise—such as through borrowing—in order to buy capital.

Fiscal policy: The government's choice regarding levels of spending and taxation.

Fisher effect: The one-for-one influence of expected inflation on the nominal interest rate.

Fisher equation: The equation stating that the nominal interest rate is the sum of the real interest rate and expected inflation ($i = r + \pi^e$).

Fixed exchange rate: An exchange rate that is set by the central bank's willingness to buy and sell the domestic currency for foreign currencies at a predetermined price. (Cf. floating exchange rate.)

Flexible prices: Prices that adjust quickly to equilibrate supply and demand. (Cf. sticky prices.)

Floating exchange rate: An exchange rate that the central bank allows to change in response to changing economic conditions and economic policies. (Cf. fixed exchange rate.)

Flow: A variable measured as a quantity per unit of time. (Cf. stock.)

Foreign debt: The debt accumulated by domestic households, firms, and governments that must be financed by sending interest payments to foreigners each year.

Fractional-reserve banking: A system in which banks keep only some of their deposits on reserve. (Cf. 100-percent-reserve banking.)

Frictional unemployment: The unemployment that results because it takes time for workers to search for the jobs that best suit their skills and tastes. (Cf. wait unemployment.)

Full-employment budget deficit: *See* cyclically adjusted budget deficit.

GDP: *See* gross domestic product.

GDP deflator: The ratio of nominal GDP to real GDP; a measure of the overall level of prices that shows the cost of the currently produced basket of goods relative to the cost of that basket in a base year.

General equilibrium: The simultaneous equilibrium of all the markets in the economy.

GNP: *See* gross national product.

Gold standard: A monetary system in which gold serves as money or in which all money is convertible into gold.

Golden rule level of capital: The saving rate in the Solow growth model that leads to the steady state in which consumption per worker (or consumption per efficiency unit of labour) is maximized.

Government purchases: Goods and services bought by the government. (Cf. transfer payments.)

Government-purchases multiplier: The change in aggregate income resulting from a one-dollar change in government purchases.

Gross domestic product (GDP): The total income earned domestically, including the income earned by foreign-owned factors of production; the total expenditure on domestically produced goods and services.

Gross national product (GNP): The total income of all residents of a nation, including the income from factors of production used abroad; the total expenditure on the nation's output of goods and services.

High-powered money: The sum of currency and bank reserves; also called the monetary base.

Hyperinflation: Extremely high inflation.

Hysteresis: The long-lasting influence of history, such as on the natural rate of unemployment.

Identification problem: The difficulty of isolating a particular relationship in data when two or more variables are related in more than one way.

Imperfect-information model: The model of aggregate supply emphasizing that individuals do not always know the overall price level because they cannot observe the prices of all goods and services in the economy.

Import quota: A legal limit on the amount of a good that can be imported.

Imports: Goods and services bought from other countries.

Imputed value: An estimate of the value of a good or service that is not sold in the marketplace and therefore does not have a market price.

Income effect: The change in consumption of a good resulting from a movement to a higher or lower indifference curve, holding the relative price constant. (Cf. substitution effect.)

Index of leading indicators: *See* leading indicators.

Indexed bonds and taxes: Bonds with interest each year equal to a specified real return plus whatever the previous year's inflation had been; a tax system in which all exemptions and tax-bracket boundaries are adjusted each year by the rate of inflation.

Indifference curves: A graphical representation of preferences that shows different combinations of goods producing the same level of satisfaction.

Inflation: An increase in the overall level of prices. (Cf. deflation, disinflation.)

Inflation–Real Output Volatility Trade-off: The proposition that a central bank—when responding to supply shocks—must choose between minimizing the effect of the shocks on how much real output varies around its natural value and the effect of the shocks on how much inflation varies around its target value.

Inflation targeting: A monetary policy under which the central bank announces a specific target, or target range, for the inflation rate.

Inflation tax: The revenue raised by the government through the creation of money; also called seigniorage.

Inside lag: The time between a shock hitting the economy and the policy action taken to respond to the shock. (Cf. outside lag.)

Insiders: Workers who are already employed and therefore have an influence on wage bargaining. (Cf. outsiders.)

Interest rate: The market price at which resources are transferred between the present and the future; the return to saving and the cost of borrowing.

Intermediation: *See* financial intermediation.

Intertemporal budget constraint: The budget constraint applying to expenditure and income in more than one period of time. (Cf. budget constraint.)

Intertemporal substitution of labour: The willingness of people to trade off working in one period for working in future periods.

Inventory investment: The change in the quantity of goods that firms hold in storage, including materials and supplies, work in process, and finished goods.

Investment: Goods purchased by individuals and firms to add to their stock of capital.

Investment tax credit: A provision of the corporate income tax that reduces a firm's tax when it buys new capital goods.

IS curve: The negative relationship between the interest rate and the level of income that arises in the market for goods and services. (Cf. *IS–LM* model, *LM* curve.)

IS–LM model: A model of aggregate demand that shows what determines aggregate income for a given price level by analyzing the interaction between the goods market and the money market. (Cf. *IS* curve, *LM* curve.)

Keynesian cross: A simple model of income determination, based on the ideas in Keynes's *General Theory,* which shows how changes in spending can have a multiplied effect on aggregate income.

Keynesian model: A model derived from the ideas of Keynes's *General Theory*; a model based on the assumptions that wages and prices do not adjust to clear markets and that aggregate demand determines the economy's output and employment. (Cf. classical model.)

Labour-augmenting technological progress: Advances in productive capability that raise the efficiency of labour.

Labour force: Those in the population who have a job or are looking for a job.

Labour-force participation rate: The percentage of the adult population in the labour force.

Large open economy: An open economy that can influence its domestic interest rate; an economy that, by virtue of its size, can have a substantial impact on world markets and, in particular, on the world interest rate. (Cf. small open economy.)

Laspeyres price index: A measure of the level of prices based on a fixed basket of goods. (Cf. Paasche price index.)

Leading indicators: Economic variables that fluctuate in advance of the economy's output and thus signal the direction of economic fluctuations.

Leverage: The use of borrowed money to supplement existing funds for purposes of investment.

Life-cycle hypothesis: The theory of consumption that emphasizes the role of saving and borrowing as transferring resources from those times in life when income is high to those times in life when income is low, such as from working years to retirement.

Liquid: Readily convertible into the medium of exchange; easily used to make transactions.

Liquidity constraint: A restriction on the amount a person can borrow from a financial institution, which limits the person's ability to spend his future income today; also called a borrowing constraint.

Liquidity-preference theory: A simple model of the interest rate, based on the ideas in Keynes's *General Theory*, which says that the interest rate adjusts to equilibrate the supply and demand for real money balances.

LM curve: The positive relationship between the interest rate and the level of income (while holding the price level fixed) that arises in the market for real money balances. (Cf. *IS–LM* model, *IS* curve.)

Loanable funds: The flow of resources available to finance capital accumulation.

Lucas critique: The argument that traditional policy analysis does not adequately take into account the impact of policy changes on people's expectations.

M1, M2, M2$^+$, M3: Various measures of the stock of money, where larger numbers signify a broader definition of money.

Macroeconometric model: A model that uses data and statistical techniques to describe the economy quantitatively, rather than just qualitatively.

Macroeconomics: The study of the economy as a whole. (Cf. microeconomics.)

Marginal product of capital (MPK): The amount of extra output produced when the capital input is increased by one unit.

Marginal product of labour (MPL): The amount of extra output produced when the labour input is increased by one unit.

Marginal propensity to consume (MPC): The increase in consumption resulting from a one-dollar increase in disposable income.

Marginal rate of substitution (MRS): The rate at which a consumer is willing to give up some of one good in exchange for more of another; the slope of the indifference curve.

Market-clearing model: A model that assumes that prices freely adjust to equilibrate supply and demand.

Medium of exchange: The item widely accepted in transactions for goods and services; one of the functions of money. (Cf. store of value, unit of account.)

Menu cost: The cost of changing a price.

Microeconomics: The study of individual markets and decisionmakers. (Cf. macroeconomics.)

Model: A simplified representation of reality, often using diagrams or equations, that shows how variables interact.

Monetarism: The doctrine according to which changes in the money supply are the primary cause of economic fluctuations, implying that a stable money supply would lead to a stable economy.

Monetary base: The sum of currency and bank reserves; also called high-powered money.

Monetary neutrality: *See* neutrality of money.

Monetary policy: The central bank's choice regarding the supply of money.

Monetary transmission mechanism: The process by which changes in the money supply influence the amount that households and firms wish to spend on goods and services.

Monetary union: A group of economies that have decided to share a common currency and thus a common monetary policy.

Money: The stock of assets used for transactions. (Cf. commodity money, fiat money.)

Money demand function: A function showing the determinants of the demand for real money balances; for example, $(M/P)^{\mathrm{d}} = L(i, Y)$.

Money multiplier: The increase in the money supply resulting from a one-dollar increase in the monetary base.

Moral hazard: The possibility of dishonest behaviour in situations in which behaviour is imperfectly monitored; for example, in efficiency-wage theory, the possibility that low-wage workers may shirk their responsibilities and risk getting caught and fired.

Multiplier: *See* government-purchases multiplier, money multiplier, or tax multiplier.

Mundell-Fleming model: The *IS-LM* model for a small open economy.

Mundell-Tobin effect: The fall in the real interest rate that results when an increase in expected inflation raises the nominal interest rate, lowers real money balances and real wealth, and thereby reduces consumption and raises saving.

National income accounting: The accounting system that measures GDP and many other related statistics.

National income accounts identity: The equation showing that GDP is the sum of consumption, investment, government purchases, and net exports.

National saving: A nation's income minus consumption and government purchases; the sum of private and public saving.

Natural rate of unemployment: The steady-state rate of unemployment; the rate of unemployment toward which the economy gravitates in the long run.

Natural-rate hypothesis: The premise that fluctuations in aggregate demand influence output, employment, and unemployment only in the short run, and that in the long run these variables return to the levels implied by the classical model.

Near money: Assets that are almost as useful as money for engaging in transactions and, therefore, are close substitutes for money.

Neoclassical model of investment: The theory according to which investment depends on the deviation of the marginal product of capital from the cost of capital.

Net capital outflow: The net flow of funds being invested abroad; domestic saving minus domestic investment; also called net foreign investment.

Net exports: Exports minus imports.

Net foreign investment: *See* net capital inflow.

Net investment: The amount of investment after the replacement of depreciated capital; the change in the capital stock.

Neutrality of money: The property that a change in the money supply does not influence real variables. (Cf. classical dichotomy.)

New classical theory: The theory according to which economic fluctuations can be explained by real changes in the economy (such as changes in technology) and without any role for nominal variables (such as the money supply). (Cf. real business cycle theory.)

New Keynesian theory: The school of thought according to which economic fluctuations can be explained only by admitting a role for some microeconomic imperfection, such as sticky wages or prices. (Cf. new classical theory.)

Nominal: Measured in current dollars; not adjusted for inflation. (Cf. real.)

Nominal exchange rate: The rate at which one country's currency trades for another country's currency. (Cf. exchange rate, real exchange rate.)

Nominal interest rate: The return to saving and the cost of borrowing without adjustment for inflation. (Cf. real interest rate.)

Normal good: A good that a consumer demands in greater quantity when his or her income rises.

Okun's law: The negative relationship between unemployment and real GDP, according to which a decrease in unemployment of 1 percentage point is associated with additional growth in real GDP of approximately 2 percent.

100-percent-reserve banking: A system in which banks keep all deposits on reserve. (Cf. fractional-reserve banking.)

Open economy: An economy in which people can freely engage in international trade in goods and capital. (Cf. closed economy.)

Open-market operations: The purchase or sale of government bonds by the central bank for the purpose of increasing or decreasing the money supply.

Outside lag: The time between a policy action and its influence on the economy. (Cf. inside lag.)

Outsiders: Workers who are not employed and therefore have no influence on wage bargaining. (Cf. insiders.)

Paasche price index: A measure of the level of prices based on a changing basket of goods. (Cf. Laspeyres price index.)

Payroll taxes: Taxes levied on employees and employers that, up to a specified maximum, are proportional to the worker's wage income.

Permanent income: Income that people expect to persist into the future; normal income. (Cf. transitory income.)

Permanent-income hypothesis: The theory of consumption according to which people choose consumption based on their permanent income, and use saving and borrowing to smooth consumption in response to transitory variations in income.

Phillips curve: A negative relationship between inflation and unemployment; in its modern form, a relationship among inflation, cyclical unemployment, expected inflation, and supply shocks, derived from the short-run aggregate supply curve.

Pigou effect: The increase in consumer spending that results when a fall in the price level raises real money balances and, thereby, consumers' wealth.

Political business cycle: The fluctuations in output and employment resulting from the manipulation of the economy for electoral gain.

Portfolio theories of money demand: Theories that explain how much money people choose to hold and that stress the role of money as a store of value. (Cf. transactions theories of money demand.)

Precautionary saving: The extra saving that results from uncertainty regarding, for example, longevity or future income.

Present value: The amount today that is equivalent to an amount to be received in the future, taking into account the interest that could be earned over the interval of time.

Private saving: Disposable income minus consumption.

Production function: The mathematical relationship showing how the quantities of the factors of production determine the quantity of goods and services produced; for example, $Y = F(K, L)$.

Production smoothing: The motive for holding inventories according to which a firm can reduce its costs by keeping the amount of output it produces steady and allowing its stock of inventories to respond to fluctuating sales.

Profit: The income of firm owners; firm revenue minus firm costs. (Cf. accounting profit, economic profit.)

Public saving: Government receipts minus government spending; the budget surplus.

Purchasing-power parity: The doctrine according to which goods must sell for the same price in every country, implying that the nominal exchange rate reflects differences in price levels.

q **theory of investment:** The theory according to which expenditure on capital goods depends on the ratio of the market value of installed capital to its replacement cost.

Quantity equation: The identity stating that the product of the money supply and the velocity of money equals nominal expenditure ($MV = PY$);

coupled with the assumption of stable velocity, an explanation of nominal expenditure called the quantity theory of money.

Quantity theory of money: The doctrine emphasizing that changes in the quantity of money lead to changes in nominal expenditure.

Quota: *See* import quota.

Random walk: The path of a variable whose changes over time are unpredictable.

Rational expectations: An approach that assumes that people optimally use all available information—including information about current and prospective policies—to forecast the future. (Cf. adaptive expectations.)

Real: Measured in constant dollars; adjusted for inflation. (Cf. nominal.)

Real business cycle theory: The theory according to which economic fluctuations can be explained by real changes in the economy (such as changes in technology) and without any role for nominal variables (such as the money supply). (Cf. new classical theory.)

Real exchange rate: The rate at which one country's goods trade for another country's goods. (Cf. exchange rate, nominal exchange rate.)

Real interest rate: The return to saving and the cost of borrowing after adjustment for inflation. (Cf. nominal interest rate.)

Real money balances: The quantity of money expressed in terms of the quantity of goods and services it can buy; the quantity of money divided by the price level (M/P).

Real rental price of capital: The amount paid to rent one unit of capital.

Recession: A sustained period of falling real income.

Reserves: The money that banks have received from depositors but have not used to make loans.

Residential investment: New housing bought by people to live in and by landlords to rent out.

Revaluation: An action undertaken by the central bank to raise the value of a currency under a system of fixed exchange rates. (Cf. devaluation.)

Ricardian equivalence: The theory according to which forward-looking consumers fully anticipate the future taxes implied by government debt, so that government borrowing today coupled with a tax increase in the future to repay the debt has the same effect on the economy as a tax increase today.

Sacrifice ratio: The number of percentage points of a year's real GDP that must be forgone to reduce inflation by 1 percentage point.

Saving: *See* national saving, private saving, and public saving.

Seasonal adjustment: The removal of the regular fluctuations in an economic variable that occur as a function of the time of year.

Sectoral shift: A change in the composition of demand among industries or regions.

Seigniorage: The revenue raised by the government through the creation of money; also called the inflation tax.

Shock: An exogenous change in an economic relationship, such as the aggregate demand or aggregate supply curve.

Shoeleather cost: The cost of inflation from reducing real money balances, such as the inconvenience of needing to make more frequent trips to the bank.

Small open economy: An open economy that takes its interest rate as given by world financial markets; an economy that, by virtue of its size, has a negligible impact on world markets and, in particular, on the world interest rate. (Cf. large open economy.)

Solow growth model: A model showing how saving, population growth, and technological progress determine the level of and growth in the standard of living.

Solow residual: The growth in total factor productivity, measured as the percentage change in output minus the percentage change in inputs, where the inputs are weighted by their factor shares. (Cf. total factor productivity.)

Stabilization policy: Public policy aimed at reducing the severity of short-run economic fluctuations.

Stagflation: A situation of falling output and rising prices; combination of stagnation and inflation.

Steady state: A condition in which key variables are not changing.

Sticky prices: Prices that adjust sluggishly and, therefore, do not always equilibrate supply and demand. (Cf. flexible prices.)

Sticky-price model: The model of aggregate supply emphasizing the slow adjustment of the prices of goods and services.

Stock: 1. A variable measured as a quantity at a point in time. (Cf. flow.) 2. Shares of ownership in a corporation.

Stock market: A market in which shares of ownership in corporations are bought and sold.

Stock-out avoidance: The motive for holding inventories according to which firms keep extra goods on hand to prevent running out if sales are unexpectedly high.

Store of value: A way of transferring purchasing power from the present to the future; one of the functions of money. (Cf. medium of exchange, unit of account.)

Structural unemployment: The unemployment resulting from wage rigidity and job rationing. (Cf. frictional unemployment.)

Substitution effect: The change in consumption of a good resulting from a movement along an indifference curve because of a change in the relative price. (Cf. income effect.)

Supply shocks: Exogenous events that shift the aggregate supply curve.

Tariff: A tax on imported goods.

Taylor Rule: A summary of central bank behaviour which involves the bank raising (lowering) the nominal interest rate above (below) its long-run average value whenever inflation is above (below) its target value and whenever real GDP is above (below) its natural-rate value.

Taylor Principle: The proposition that the central bank should increase (decrease) the nominal interest rate by more than one percentage point when the inflation rate is one percentage point above (below) its target value.

Tax multiplier: The change in aggregate income resulting from a one-dollar change in taxes.

Technology shocks: Variations in the level of technological ability that result in more or less output being produced from any given combination of labour and capital.

Time inconsistency: The tendency of policymakers to announce policies in advance in order to influence the expectations of private decisionmakers, and then to follow different policies after those expectations have been formed and acted upon.

Tobin's *q*: The ratio of the market value of installed capital to its replacement cost.

Total factor productivity: A measure of the level of technology; the amount of output per unit of input, where different inputs are combined on the basis of their factor shares. (Cf. Solow residual.)

Trade balance: The receipts from exports minus the payments for imports.

Transactions theories of money demand: Theories that explain how much money people choose to hold and that stress the role of money as a medium of exchange. (Cf. portfolio theories of money demand.)

Transfer payments: Payments from the government to individuals that are not in exchange for goods and services, such as public pension and employment insurance receipts. (Cf. government purchases.)

Transitory income: Income that people do not expect to persist into the future; current income minus normal income. (Cf. permanent income.)

Trickle-down economics: The school of thought according to which tax breaks for the rich indirectly provide benefits for those further down the income scale. The opposite approach, which emphasizes the indirect benefits for the rich that accompany policies aimed at those on lower incomes, is known as percolate-up economics.

Underground economy: Economic transactions that are hidden in order to evade taxes or conceal illegal activity.

Unemployment rate: The percentage of those in the labour force who do not have jobs.

Unit of account: The measure in which prices and other accounting records are recorded; one of the functions of money. (Cf. medium of exchange, store of value.)

Value added: The value of a firm's output minus the value of the intermediate goods the firm purchased.

Velocity of money: The ratio of nominal expenditure to the money supply; the rate at which money changes hands.

Wage: The amount paid for one unit of labour.

Wage rigidity: The failure of wages to adjust to equilibrate labour supply and labour demand.

Work in process: Goods in inventory that are in the process of being completed.

Worker-misperception model: The model of aggregate supply emphasizing that workers sometimes perceive incorrectly the overall level of prices.

World interest rate: The interest rate prevailing in world financial markets.

index

Federal Government Deficit–GDP Ratio

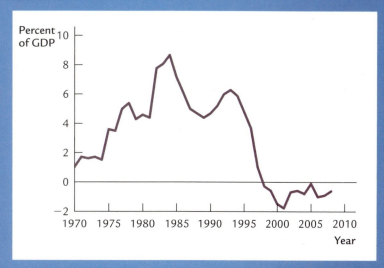

Money Growth (*M*1)

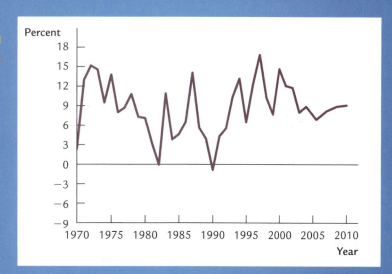